McCORMICK ON EVIDENCE

Fifth Edition

By

John W. Strong

General Editor
Rosenstiel Professor of Law, Emeritus
University of Arizona College of Law

Contributing Authors

Kenneth S. Broun

Henry Brandis Professor of Law, University of North Carolina

George E. Dix

A.W. Walker Centennial Professor of Law, The University of Texas

Edward J. Imwinkelried

Professor of Law, University of California at Davis School of Law

D. H. Kaye

Regents' Professor of Law, Arizona State University

Robert P. Mosteller

Professor of Law, Duke University

E. F. Roberts

Edwin H. Woodruff Professor of Law, Emeritus, The Cornell Law School

This book is an abridgement of "McCormick on Evidence, Fifth Edition,
Volumes 1 & 2. Practitioner Treatise Series".

HORNBOOK SERIES®

**WEST
GROUP**

A THOMSON COMPANY

ST. PAUL, MINN., 1999

Hornbook Series, *WESTLAW*, and the West Group symbol
are registered trademarks used herein under license.

COPYRIGHT © 1954, 1972, 1984, 1987, 1992 WEST PUBLISHING CO.

COPYRIGHT © 1999 By WEST GROUP
                    610 Opperman Drive
                    P.O. Box 64526
                    St. Paul, MN 55164–0526
                    1–800–328–9352

All rights reserved
Printed in the United States of America

ISBN 0–314–23238–9

*TEXT IS PRINTED ON 10% POST
CONSUMER RECYCLED PAPER*

1st Reprint—2001

Preface

The first edition of this treatise, and the only one personally authored by Professor McCormick, was clearly intended principally as a resource for students of Evidence. It provided a trenchant, concise, and readily accessible statement of the basic principles of the subject, largely unencumbered by exhaustive citations of authority. For those users in need of supporting authorities, plentiful citation to the treasure trove of Wigmore's 3rd edition were provided.

The continuing popularity of the treatise has led to a series of editions, with the recently published 5th edition being the latest. By the time of publication of the 4th edition in 1992, however, the basic volume had by natural accretion grown to such a size as to be both overly expensive and unwieldy for student use. The resulting pleas of those wishing to use the book as a conventional study aid or as the text supporting a problem method approach to the study of Evidence led to the preparation of a student edition, offering the identical text but with the bulk of the supporting citations omitted. The popularity of this alternative has justified offering the present volume embodying the same approach. And as in the 4th edition, no excissions of either text or chapters have been made. The section numbers of this volume are thus identical with those in the parent work, which should facilitate the work of those in need of authoritative support of the principles stated.

Some additional reduction in the size of the present edition has been accomplished by limiting the scope of Chapters 13, 14, and 15, to a discussion of the specific evidentiary consequences of doctrines of constitutional law. This curtailment, justifiable even in the principal work, is further warranted in the student edition by the now generally accepted curricular transfer of much of this material out of the Evidence course and into courses on Criminal Procedure. Finally, the chapter on evidence in administrative proceedings has been omitted from the present edition. Professor McCormick's original work contained no treatment of this subject, and in today's curriculum it is covered, if at all, in the course on Administrative Law.

The list of contributing authors to the 5th edition remains the same as that of the 4th edition, with the exception of Professor Michael H. Graham, who was forced to withdraw from participation for personal reasons. Professor Graham's contribution to the 4th edition was substantial, and his absence from the present edition is regretted. At the same time, however, the editor and remaining authors feel exceptionally fortunate in being joined in this edition by Professor Edward J. Imwinkelried of the University of California at Davis, a widely known authority in the field.

Black Butte, Or.
September, 1999

*

WESTLAW® Overview

McCormick on Evidence offers a detailed and comprehensive treatment of basic rules, principles and issues relating to evidence. To supplement the information contained in this book, you can access Westlaw, a computer-assisted legal research service of West Group. Westlaw contains a broad array of legal resources, including case law, statutes, rules, expert commentary, current developments and various other types of information.

Learning how to use these materials effectively will enhance your legal research abilities. To help you coordinate the information in the book with your Westlaw research, this volume contains an appendix listing Westlaw databases, search techniques and sample problems.

THE PUBLISHER

*

Summary of Contents

Table of Contents

McCORMICK ON EVIDENCE

*

Title 1

INTRODUCTION

Chapter 1

PREPARING AND PRESENTING
THE EVIDENCE

Table of Sections

---

§ 1. Planning and Preparation of Proof as Important as the Rules of Evidence

The law of evidence is the system of rules and standards regulating the admission of proof at the trial of a lawsuit. The last section in this chapter presents an overview of the procedural regulations governing the sequence in which proof is admitted at trial. But it should be emphasized that this trial stage, when proof is offered and the rules of evidence come into play, is a late phase in a long process. Thus, in every case dealing with a dispute over a rule of evidence or its application, the lawyers have earlier shouldered many other tasks in the planning and production of testimony. They perform these pretrial tasks in anticipation of problems of proof at the trial under the law of evidence, long before any evidentiary question is presented to the court. As a reminder, some of these earlier stages in the problem of proof will be mentioned in this chapter. The next to last section discusses the use of formal discovery devices to prepare to present evidence at trial while the section immediately following this one reviews the informal methods of readying for trial.

§ 2. Preparation for Trial on the Facts Without Resort to the Court's Aid

In many cases, the lawyers collect evidence for trial without resorting to formal discovery devices. Informal discovery techniques tend to be faster and less expensive than formal discovery. Moreover, the use of informal discovery methods can preserve the element of surprise. There is no element of surprise if the lawyer deposes a witness to an accident; the opponent can attend the deposition and is entitled to a transcript of the deposition hearing. In contrast, the opponent may gain little or no advance notice if the lawyer is content to informally interview the witness.

As a starting point in informal discovery, the client must be interviewed to ascertain the facts. These interviews should include a tactful but searching mock cross-examination to overcome the client's natural tendency to confine the story to the facts favorable to himself. The lawyer should contact not only the client but also other witnesses with personal knowledge of the relevant facts. The witnesses who have firsthand knowledge of the transaction in controversy must likewise be interviewed, and where possible, their written statements taken.[1] The statement might become evidence at trial, or the lawyer could need the statement to refresh the witness's memory at trial if the witness has difficulty recalling the pertinent facts.

Apart from the ordinary eyewitnesses, it is increasingly necessary to arrange for technical experts, such as physicians in personal injury cases, epidemiologists in toxic tort actions, chemists and physicists in patent litigation, engineers and architects in controversies over construction contracts, genetic marker analysts and psychiatrists in criminal cases, and handwriting experts in disputes over the genuineness of documents.

In addition to contacting the potential witnesses, it will often be necessary to assemble documentary evidence, such as contracts, letters, receipts, loose-leaf records, deeds, certified copies of conveyances, judgments, and decrees. Other physical evidence, such as the assailant's revolver, the victim's perforated coat in a murder case, or a sample of the goods in an action for breach of warranty, should be tracked down and preserved for use at the trial. The lawyer must be creative in planning aids to the senses such as computer generated animations, photographs, motion picture films, X-rays, plats, diagrams, and models. Visual aids not only help the lawyer grab the jurors' short-term attention; more importantly, they increase the jurors' long-term memory of the data depicted by the aid. The use of visual aids is especially important when the lawyer contemplates offering scientific evidence. Jurors sometimes find scientific testimony confusingly abstract, and a visual aid can simplify the testimony for the jury's benefit.

Where practicable, the task of proof at trial should be lightened by securing the opponent's pretrial written stipulations to facts not in controversy, such as the execution of documents or the ownership of a vehicle involved in the suit. If the terms of a document in the adversary's possession will need to be proved by use of a copy, written notice to produce the

original at the trial must be given to opposing counsel.

All of this preparation must be carefully planned. The plan will evolve as new information is disclosed; but as the trial approaches, a definite program must be formulated. Each fact involved in the claim or defense should be listed, with the witnesses and documents by which it will be proved. This can be supplemented by both a list of the witnesses in the order in which they will be called, including the subjects upon which they will be examined, and a separate list of exhibits, including the witnesses to authenticate each exhibit. Finally, at the last minute before the witnesses take the stand, the counsel who calls them must reinterview each witness to confirm what he is prepared to swear to, to refresh his memory, if necessary, and to warn him of the probable cross-examination. The counsel must keep evidence law in mind as he takes these preparatory pretrial steps; every task must be performed with a view of the ultimate objective of ensuring that there will be ample, admissible evidence at trial.

§ 3. Invoking the Court's Aid in Preparing for Trial: Right to Interview Witnesses: Discovery and Depositions: Requests for Admission: Pretrial Conferences

As the preceding section pointed out, one of the essential steps in informal trial preparation is interviewing the potential witnesses with firsthand knowledge of the relevant facts. From time to time the question arises whether counsel has a right to an opportunity to interview a witness. Resort to the court may be required to settle the matter. The question usually arises when opposing counsel has instructed a witness not to "talk" at all or only on conditions. The right is enforceable against the prosecution in the sense that prosecutors may not pressure a potential witness into refusing to cooperate with the defense. Generally, a criminal defendant has the right to an opportunity to interview witnesses privately.

§ 2

1. See § 3 infra concerning the right to interview witnesses.

Apparently the prosecution in a criminal case has a similar right. There is an emerging parallel right for both parties in civil cases. Nevertheless, there are a few situations in which a court may refuse to interfere even when witnesses are advised by counsel to limit or refuse interviews. Absent a subpoena, on his own motion, the witness is generally free to refuse an interview. As § 2 explained, despite the existence of formal discovery devices, the opportunity to informally interview is important in trial preparation. However, when the witness refuses to submit to an interview, the lawyer may need to resort to court to secure an interview.

Adequate preparation often requires the use of the official fact-gathering procedures available once a lawsuit commences. The official discovery procedures in the various jurisdictions are treated at length in treatises and one-volume works concerning civil and criminal procedure. Consequently, only a very short, summary review of these procedures is included here. Since the pleadings in civil cases may be fairly general and need not specify the facts in any detail in many jurisdictions, the civil rules provide for fairly thorough post-pleading discovery processes by which each party can learn the possible evidence in the case, and ascertain what specific fact issues may arise for trial.

In many states and federal judicial districts, the official procedures include a statute or court rule requiring mandatory pre-discovery disclosures. For example, under a 1993 amendment to Federal Rule of Civil Procedure 26(a), even absent a request by the opposing attorney, the litigant must reveal specified information about potential witnesses, relevant documents, and experts. If those disclosures do not satisfy the opposing attorney, the attorney can resort to formal discovery devices.

One of the most important discovery devices in civil cases is the deposition procedure by which each party can orally examine the other under oath and likewise question other persons who have knowledge of the subject matter of the lawsuit. Over half the states have substantially copied the federal rules for this procedure.[1] Although an order for a commission authorizing an officer to preside at an oral examination is still necessary in some states, the procedure for taking oral depositions ordinarily requires only a notice to the person to be examined, a subpoena ordering him to appear at a certain time and place for the examination before a notary public, and notice of the examination to the opposing party if he is not the person to be examined. In many jurisdictions, following the lead of the federal civil discovery process, at an oral deposition the examiner may seek any information "reasonably calculated to lead to the discovery of admissible evidence" even if the information will not be admissible at the trial. Thus, at a deposition a lawyer can demand that the deponent disclose hearsay statements that would be inadmissible at trial. Effective employment of depositions will enable a party to discover the evidence both for and against his position. Moreover, the deposition of an opposing witness allows the attorney to evaluate the witness's demeanor: Will the deponent probably be an effective witness at trial? The witnesses' performance during their depositions can have a major impact on the settlement value of the case.

Depositions are not the only formal discovery devises. In civil cases, written interrogatories may also be directed to the opponent in many states, and he must answer them. Usually these interrogatories are used hand in hand with oral depositions. For instance, if the opponent is a corporation, the lawyer might use interrogatories about the corporation's structure to identify potential deponents. Further, a party is often permitted to secure a production order requiring the adversary to permit him to examine papers and things—even real property—relating to the subject matter of the suit. Next, in personal injury actions, and sometimes other suits in which a party's physical or mental condition is in issue, an order for the physical or mental examination of a party may be secured in over half the states. Lastly,

§ 3

1. Rules 26–37, Rules of Civil Procedure for the District Courts of the United States.

although not strictly speaking a discovery device, in many states a party can send requests for admissions to his opponent who must either admit or deny the request. By way of example, a lawyer might ask that the opponent admit the facts necessary to lay the evidentiary foundation for introducing an exhibit at trial.

After the close of discovery, a pretrial hearing or conference is authorized for civil cases in many jurisdictions, although it is rarely used in some states. When the case approaches the time for trial, usually two or three weeks before the date set, the judge summons counsel for both sides and sometimes the parties. At the conference, the judge seeks to settle questions of pleading, to define the scope of the dispute, and to secure stipulations as to the facts not really at issue. The original federal rule authorizing conferences[2] mentions, as among the objectives of the hearing:

"(1) The simplification of the issues;

"(3) The possibility of obtaining admissions of fact and of documents which will avoid unnecessary proof;

"(4) The limitation of the number of expert witnesses; [and]

"(5) The advisability of a preliminary reference of issues to a master for findings to be used as evidence when the trial is to be by jury".

The pretrial conference can serve as a vehicle for reaching agreement on various factual issues, although it does not necessarily yield that result.

One other procedure should be mentioned before concluding this summary of ways in which the court's aid is invoked to prepare for trial: the procurement of the issuance and service of writs of subpoena for the witnesses who are to be called at trial. In the case of a document or other physical evidence held by a third party, the party who desires its production at the trial may secure a subpoena duces

tecum addressed to the third party commanding him to attend the trial and to bring with him the document or other object.

The use of some of these discovery devices may result in creating testimony and other evidence which can be introduced at trial. One of the risks of resorting to formal discovery is that the lawyer might inadvertently preserve unfavorable evidence for trial. (That risk explains why experienced litigators routinely conduct informal discovery before using formal discovery devices; a deposition is less risky if the lawyer knows beforehand what the deponent is likely to testify to.) The deposition testimony may be introduced under varying circumstances. Under the federal rules, an opposing party's deposition may be admitted virtually without any conditions. The most common conditions for the introduction of deposition testimony of non-party witnesses are the requirements set out in the Federal Rules of Civil Procedure. There are also provisions in the Federal Rules of Evidence regulating the admissibility of depositions at trial.[3] For example, in most jurisdictions, a non-party deponent's deposition is admissible if the deponent is unavailable to testify in person at trial.

Discovery procedures available to a criminal defendant also deserve mention. Only in recent times have rules or statutes been enacted to guarantee true discovery for criminal defendants,[4] and even these procedures are limited. The 1970 Crime Control Act authorizes witness depositions primarily for the preservation of the evidence (for future use as evidence) and not merely for the purpose of discovery; the defendant must make a preliminary showing that the prospective deponent will probably be unavailable at trial. For the first time depositions were authorized on motion of the government.[5] Federal Rule of Criminal Procedure 16 is a broad discovery provision concerning defense discovery of reports, tests, grand jury testimony, books, papers, documents, tangible objects, and places. There is a

2. Fed.R.Civ.P. 16.
3. See § 254 infra.
4. See § 97 infra.

5. 18 U.S.C.A. § 3503. See Wright, Federal Practice and Procedure: Criminal § 241.

more limited provision for discovery of matters of this kind by the government. Rule 16 has been amended several times, most recently in 1997. The 1993 amendment is particularly noteworthy, since it expands the discovery of expert testimony which either the government or the defense contemplates offering at trial.

The preceding paragraphs survey the most frequently used formal discovery devices. In various states, there are miscellaneous official discovery procedures, but no detailed review is attempted here.

Whether the lawyer relies primarily on formal or informal discovery techniques to prepare for trial, the objective is the same: gathering a large quantity of believable, admissible evidence for trial. If the lawyer achieves that pretrial objective, the lawyer's client should gain either an advantageous settlement or a favorable trial verdict. In the vast majority of instances, the case settles without going to trial; but the settlement is largely driven by the quantity and quality of the admissible evidence unearthed during formal and informal pretrial discovery.

§ 4. The Order of Presenting Evidence at the Trial

If the case does not settle, the litigant proceeds to trial. Evidence law figures even more prominently at this stage than it does during the pretrial phase.

If the hearing will be a jury trial, the jury must be selected before the lawyers begin to present their evidence. Depending on the jurisdiction, during the voir dire examination of the panelists the judge might permit the attorney to question the them about potential items of evidence in the case. A panelist could conceivably have such a negative reaction to the evidence that he would be challengeable for cause, or the attorney might want to employ a peremptory strike to remove him from the jury.

After the jury has been selected, the attorneys present opening statements. During the statements, the attorneys preview their evidence for the jury. According to American Bar Association Rule of Professional Conduct

3.4(e), in opening a lawyer may not "allude to any matter that the lawyer does not reasonably believe ... will ... be supported by admissible evidence ..." at trial. The most common objection during opening statement is that a particular statement is argumentative. In this context, "argumentative" means that the statement is a conclusion which would be inadmissible under the evidence rules governing opinion testimony. As a rule of thumb, an attorney may not make a statement during opening unless, under the governing opinion rules, it would be permissible for one of the attorney's witnesses to make the statement on the stand.

After the opening statements, testimony begins. Under the usual order of proceeding at the trial, including a trial under the Federal Rules of Evidence, the plaintiff, with the burden of establishing his claim, first introduces the evidence to prove the facts necessary to enable him to recover, such as the formation of the contract, his fulfillment of the conditions to the defendant's duty, the defendant's breach, and the amount of damages. At this stage the plaintiff brings forward all the witnesses on whom he relies to establish these facts, together with the pertinent documents, which will be offered when they have been authenticated by the witness's testimony. During this stage, each witness will first be questioned by the plaintiff's counsel on direct examination and then cross-examined by opposing counsel. These examinations may be followed by re-direct and re-cross examinations. When all the plaintiff's witnesses to his main case have been subjected to this process of questioning and cross-questioning, the plaintiff signifies the completion of his case in chief by announcing that he rests. In most jurisdictions, the judge presiding at trial has a discretionary power to permit testimony be presented out of normal order. Thus, if it is impossible for a key defense witness to appear later in the hearing, the judge could allow the witness to testify as one of the initial witnesses during the hearing.

Assume that in the normal order, the plaintiff rests. If the defense counsel believes that at this point the plaintiff has not presented a legally sufficient case, the counsel moves for a nonsuit or directed verdict. For purposes of this motion, the judge assumes that all the evidence introduced by the plaintiff is admissible. The motion poses this question: If the trier of fact decides to believe all the plaintiff's testimony, does the testimony have sufficient cumulative probative value to rationally sustain a plaintiff's verdict? If the testimony lacks adequate probative worth, the judge makes a peremptory ruling against the plaintiff. Otherwise, the trial continues.

Then the defendant presents the witnesses and the tangible evidence supporting his case. At this stage the defendant produces evidence in denial of the plaintiff's claim, such as testimony that the alleged contract was never actually agreed on, or in a negligence case that some bodily injury was not permanent as claimed by the plaintiff. The defense can also support any affirmative defenses which the defendant has pleaded, such as fraud in the procurement of a contract sued on or the execution of a release of a personal injury claim. Here again each witness's story on direct examination is subject to being tested by cross-examination and supplemented on re-direct. When the defendant has completed the presentation of his proof of affirmative defenses, if any, and his evidence in denial of the plaintiff's claims, the defendant announces that he rests.

At the conclusion of the defense case-in-chief, the defense could once again move for a directed verdict or nonsuit. At this point, the defense can argue alternatively that it has so weakened the plaintiff's case that no rational juror could find for the plaintiff or that the evidence of an affirmative defense is so strong that no rational juror could reject the defense.

The plaintiff now has another turn at bat; he may present a case in rebuttal. At this stage, the plaintiff is not entitled to present witnesses who merely support the allegations of the complaint, but is confined to testimony refuting the defense evidence, unless the court in its discretion permits him to depart from the regular scope of proof. The plaintiff's rebuttal witnesses may be new ones, but he can recall witnesses who testified for him on the case in chief to answer some point first raised by the defendant's witnesses. In this, as in the other stages, the witness may not only be examined on direct, but also cross-examined and re-examined. When the plaintiff's case in rebuttal is finished, he closes his case. If new points are brought out in the plaintiff's rebuttal, the defendant may meet them by evidence in rejoinder or surrebuttal. Otherwise, he closes his case at once.

When both parties have announced that they have closed, the evidentiary hearing comes to an end; and the trial proceeds with the closing argument of counsel and the court's instructions to the jury. The instructions often include jury charges about the evidence in the case. For example, the judge might give the jury a limiting instruction that they may use a certain item of evidence only for a particular purpose. Or the judge could read the jurors a cautionary instruction informing them that they should be especially careful in evaluating a certain type of evidence such as eyewitness testimony.

To sum up, the stages of the hearing of the facts are:

(1) the plaintiff's main case or evidence in chief;

(2) the defendant's case in chief or evidence in defense;

(3) the plaintiff's evidence in rebuttal; and

(4) the defendant's evidence in rejoinder or surrebuttal.

In each stage, all the witnesses to the facts appropriate at that stage will be called, and each witness's examination may pass through these steps:

(1) the direct examination, conducted by the party who calls the witness;

(2) the cross-examination by the adversary;

(3) re-direct; and

(4) re-cross.

The Federal Rules of Evidence do not prescribe an order for the presentation of evidence at trial. However, under Rule 611(a), the common law trial order is ordinarily followed. According to Rule 611(a), the court "shall exercise reasonable control over the . . . order of interrogating witnesses and presenting evidence so as to (1) make the interrogation and presentation effective for the ascertainment of the truth, (2) avoid needless consumption of time, and (3) protect witnesses from harassment or undue embarrassment." As a practical matter, judges rarely find a sufficient reason to depart from the normal sequence of the major stages of the hearing described above. The primary focus of Rule 611 is the control of the steps examining individual witnesses. Hence, even trials conducted under the Federal Rules follow the normal order developed at common law.

Title 2

EXAMINATION OF WITNESSES

Chapter 2

THE FORM OF QUESTIONS ON DIRECT:
THE JUDGE'S WITNESSES:
REFRESHING MEMORY

Table of Sections

§ 5. The Form of Questions: (a) Questions Calling for a Free Narrative Versus Specific Questions

Any experienced litigator knows that at trial, the vast majority of objections relate to the issue of the form of the question rather than substantive evidence doctrines such as hearsay. Form objections can arise on either direct or cross-examination. The art of direct examination of your own witness, telling a composite story from the mouths of your own witnesses, is far more important, though perhaps less difficult, than that of cross-examination.

One of the premier tactical decisions on direct is whether a particular witness's testimony will better be elicited by several questions about specific facts or brought out more effectively by a general question. In the latter case, the witness's attention is directed to the relevant incident by asking him whether he was on the scene at the time and then requesting him to recount what he saw and heard on that occasion. This latter method, narrative testimony, is often more persuasive. The narrative does not seem to come from the counsel,

as it might when specific interrogation is employed. If the witness has a good memory, a pleasant personality, and some effectiveness in speaking, his spontaneous statement of his own story may be more interesting and impressive. Narrative testimony allows the witness to put his honesty and intelligence on display for the jury. Scientific experiments indicate that spontaneous narrative is more accurate (because less influenced by suggestion) while the fully interrogated testimony tends to be more complete. Specific interrogation may be desirable to ensure the presentation of complicated testimony in proper order; to help a nervous witness; to supplement the testimony by visual aids; and to prevent dull testimony.

When a witness is to be examined by the narrative method, counsel must be ready to interrupt with specific questions if the testimony becomes confusing, or to supplement the narrative by questions to bring out omitted facts. For example, if an expert uses a technical term of art, counsel should invite the expert to define the term for the jury.

In their courtrooms, some trial judges enforce a general prohibition of questions calling for a narrative. These judges are concerned about the risk that the witness will narrate in a jumbled, confusing fashion. Under the prevailing view, though, there is no general rule of law requiring or even preferring either form of questioning. Some courts have voiced concern about the danger that when asked to tell his story, the witness will mention hearsay or other incompetent testimony; but a proper caution by court or counsel, on the adversary's request, will usually prevent this.

It is true that if the witness blurts out an improper statement, the only remedy is striking that part of the evidence and giving the jury a curative instruction to disregard the stricken testimony. There is also a danger that counsel may waive an objection if he does not interrupt promptly and move to strike. However, the need for eliciting the witness's knowledge in the most vivid, accurate way is a legitimate interest to be balanced against these dangers. The guiding principle is that the trial judge has a discretion, not reviewable except for abuse, to control the form of examination, to the end that the facts are clearly and expeditiously presented. Hence he may permit either method discussed. Whenever circumstances make narrative testimony feasible, its use is likely to be in the interest of both the examining party and the accurate disclosure of the truth. Its use is seldom curbed by enlightened judges, except, perhaps, in criminal trials when it entails the risk that it will expose the jury to constitutionally inadmissible testimony. As a practical matter, in civil cases many judges begin with the presumption that the lawyer may elicit the witness's testimony in narrative form. The presumption will be rebutted—and the judge will insist on more specific questions—only if the witness's narrative becomes confused or the witness makes repeated references to inadmissible matter.

These principles are consistent with Federal and Revised Uniform Rule (1974) 611(a),[1] which provides:

> The court shall exercise reasonable control over the mode and order of interrogating witnesses and presenting evidence so as to (1) make the interrogation and presentation effective for the ascertainment of the truth, (2) avoid needless consumption of time, and (3) protect witnesses from harassment or undue embarrassment.

§ 6. The Form of Questions: (b) Leading Questions

The preceding section compared the technique of soliciting the witness's free narrative on direct examination with that of drawing out testimony by specific questions. A danger of the latter method is that the witness may acquiesce in a false suggestion. That danger gives rise to another major form problem on direct examination, namely, leading or suggestive phrasing. The suggestion itself can plant the belief in its truth. Some empirical studies confirm many judges' belief that this danger is greater than the average layperson would suppose. A friendly or pliant witness may follow suggestions on direct examination. On the other hand, it can be urged that there is little reason for barring suggestive questions. To be frank, before trial the witness is exposed to numerous, more powerful suggestive influences. In many instances, by the time of trial the objection is trivial.

Nevertheless, subject to the conditions and limitations discussed in the remainder of this section, objections to leading questions have been preserved by the modern common law and Rule 611(c) of the Federal and Revised Uniform Rules of Evidence. The first sentence of Rule 611(c) announces a general norm that [l]eading questions should not be used on the direct examination. . . ." The Advisory Committee Note emphasizes that the sentence is "phrased in words of suggestion rather than command."

A leading question is one that suggests to the witness the answer desired by the examiner. A question may be leading because of its form, but often the mere form of a question does not indicate whether it is leading. Some types of phrasing such as "Did he not?" are obviously leading, but almost any other type of

§ 5

1. See § 4 supra.

question can be leading, depending on its content and context. It is sometimes supposed that any question which can be answered yes or no is ipso facto leading but that the neophyte attorney can always take refuge in neutral, alternative wording ("State whether or not * * * ") to escape the charge of leading. However, quite frequently the former kind of question is not leading, and equally often the latter kind will be. The real issue is whether an ordinary witness would get the impression that the questioner desired one answer rather than another. The form of a question, or previous questioning, may indicate the desire, but the most important circumstance for consideration can be the extent of the particularity of the question itself. When the question describes an incident in detail and asks if the incident happened, the natural inference is that the questioner expects an affirmative answer. Or if one alternative branch of a question is concrete and detailed but the other vague ("Was the sound like the loud scream of a woman in fear or was it otherwise?"), the wording conveys the impression that the first alternative is suggested. In contrast, when a question is neutral ("At what time did this occur?") or balanced ("Was the water hot or cold?"), it is not leading.

After we have defined the expression, "leading question," the next issue that arises is when it is permissible to employ leading phrasing. The courts have developed different norms for direct and cross-examination. As we have seen, the normal practice is for the careful lawyer to informally interview in advance all witnesses whom he expects to call for direct examination. This practice is ethical, but it does create a probability that by the time of trial, the lawyer and the witness will have reached an *entente* making the witness especially susceptible to the lawyer's suggestions. However, when counsel cross-examines a witness called by the adversary, he may have had no prior opportunity to talk to the witness, and there is less likelihood of an understanding between them about the facts. Hence the practice: upon objection, the judge ordinarily forbids leading questions on direct examination but usually permits them on cross-exami-

nation. The matter of the allowability of leading questions is discretionary, and the judge's action will not be reviewed unless it is charged that it contributed to an unfair trial.

When the normal assumption about the relation between the witness and the examining counsel or his client is unfounded, the usual practice is reversed. If the witness on direct is legally identified with the opponent, appears hostile to the examiner, or is reluctant or uncooperative, the danger of suggestion disappears; and the judge therefore will permit leading questions. Conversely, when on cross-examination the witness appears biased in the cross-examining party's favor, counsel may be prohibited from leading.

In many other situations, leading questions are permitted on direct examination. For instance, they may be used to bring out preliminary matters such as the witness's name and occupation, or to elicit matters not substantially in dispute. They may be employed to suggest a subject or topic, as distinguished from an answer. Additional relaxations are grounded in necessity. Thus, when need appears, the judge will ordinarily allow leading questions to children or adult witnesses so ignorant, timid, weak-minded, or deficient in the English language that they cannot otherwise understand what information is sought. Admittedly, in these cases, especially as to children, there is a danger of false suggestion; but it is better to face that danger than to abandon altogether the effort to bring out the witness's knowledge. Similarly, when a witness has been directed to the subject by nonleading questions without securing a complete account of what he is believed to know, his memory is said to be "exhausted"; and in that event the judge will permit the examiner to ask questions which by their particularity may revive his memory but which can suggest the answer desired. Likewise, many courts liberally allow specific, leading questions during the direct examination of experts. These courts reason that if the expert were allowed free rein, his testimony could easily become "complicated" and confusing to the jury.

In some jurisdictions, there is a longstanding practice permitting leading questions to a witness who, for impeachment purposes, is to testify to a previous witness's statement that is inconsistent with the previous witness's testimony. Necessity is said to be the justification. It might otherwise be impossible to quickly get to the point and call the second witness's attention to the subject of the testimony. It has been argued, however, that the practice should not be followed. But most courts have rejected the argument and continue to uphold the practice.

§ 7. The Form of Questions: (c) Argumentative, Misleading, and Indefinite Questions

We turn now to form problems of primary importance on cross-examination. The examiner may not ask a question that merely invokes the witness's assent to the questioner's inferences from or interpretations of the facts proved or assumed. Rather than attempting to elicit new testimony, a cross-examiner might in reality challenge a witness about an inference from the testimony already in the record. For instance, evincing disbelief in his demeanor, the cross-examiner might ask, "Do you really expect the jury to believe that?" or "How can you reconcile those statements?" This kind of question is objectionable as "argumentative." The trial judge has a wide range of discretion in enforcing the rule, particularly on cross-examination where such questions are more frequent. There is no unfairness in the judges' enforcement of the rule during cross-examination, since the cross-examiner will later have an opportunity to argue the inference during his summation to the jury.

Another common vice is for the examiner to couch the question so that it assumes as true matters to which the witness has not testified, and which are disputed between the parties. The danger is two-fold. First, when the examiner puts the question to a friendly witness, the recitation of the assumed fact may be leading, suggesting the desired answer. Second, whether the witness is friendly or hostile, the answer can be misleading. If the witness answers the question without separating out the assumption, it is impossible to determine whether the assumption was ignored or affirmed. When the question suffers from this vice, the opposing counsel usually objects that the question "is misleading" or "assumes facts not in evidence."

Occasionally questions are considered objectionable because they are too broad or indefinite. Often this objection is in reality an objection of lack of relevancy. Indefinite or ambiguous questions can be especially dangerous an cross-examination. For instance, if the cross-examiner asks a witness whether he has had any "trouble," "problems," or "run-ins with the law," in response the witness might mention both convictions admissible for impeachment and other misconduct that was both inadmissible and prejudicial.

The principles mentioned in this section are not specifically codified in the Federal or Revised Uniform Rules (1974), but they may be enforced in the trial judge's discretion under Rules 403 and 611(a). As to Rule 403 see § 185 infra.

§ 8. The Judge May Examine and Call Witnesses

Sections 5–7 deal with some of the form questions which arise when attorneys call and question witnesses. Problems can also materialize when judges call or question witnesses. Under the Anglo–American adversary trial system, the parties' counsel have the primary responsibility for finding, selecting, and presenting the evidence. However, our system of party-investigation and party-presentation has limitations. The system is a means to the end of disclosing truth and administering justice; and in order to reach that very end, the judge may exercise various powers to intervene to supplement the parties' evidence.

Notably, the judge has the powers to call and question witnesses. Under the case law and the Federal Rule of Evidence 614(b), the judge has discretion to examine any witness to clarify testimony or to bring out needed facts which have not been elicited by the parties. The trial judge is not a mere umpire or passive moderator. Some appellate courts have even gone to the length of stating that the trial judge may have a duty to question witnesses, but the supposed duty does not appear to have been enforced by any appellate decision.

In those states—the great majority—in which the judge does not retain the common law power to comment on the weight of the evidence, the judge's questioning in jury cases must be cautiously guarded to avoid implied comment. If the judge uses leading questions suggesting the desired answer, the questions may strongly imply that the desired answer is the truth, and thus amount to comment. Subject to the limitation that a leading question may constitute prohibited comment, it has been held that the policy against leading questions by counsel, namely, avoiding false testimony prompted by partisan suggestion,[1] has no application to judges. After all, the judge's office is impartial. However, this reasoning is questionable. Since the judge is an authority figure, there is a grave risk that the witness will adopt any suggestion implicit in the judge's question. Again, leading judicial questions aimed at discrediting or impeaching the witness, though allowable for counsel, can intimate the judge's belief that the witness has been lying, and thus be a verboten implied comment.

In the federal courts and the few states retaining the common law power to comment, and in judge-tried cases in all jurisdictions, these restrictions on judicial questions are relaxed. Nevertheless, even then, the judge must avoid extreme exercises of the power to question. He must not assume the role of an advocate or a prosecutor. If his questions are too partisan or extensive, he runs the risk that the appellate court will find that he has crossed the line between judging and advocacy. However, the mere number of judicial questions is not dispositive. The nature of the questions is the most important consideration.

Not only may the judge examine witnesses called by the parties, but in his discretion he may also, again for the purpose of bringing out needed facts, call witnesses whom the parties have chosen not to call. The power to call

witnesses has most often been exercised when the prosecution expects that a necessary witness will be hostile and desires to escape the necessity of calling him and being cumbered by the traditional rule against impeaching one's own witness. Concededly, under the Federal Rules of Evidence, a party may impeach the party's own witness. Yet, as a practical matter the prosecutor may not wish to call the witness and thereby be identified with the witness in the jurors' minds. If the witness has a long criminal record, his "affiliation" with the government might taint the prosecution case in the jurors' minds. The prosecutor could then invoke the judge's discretion under Rule 614(a) to call the witness. If the judge calls the witness, either party may cross-examine and impeach him.

Another use of the power, implemented by statute in some jurisdictions, is to mediate the battle of partisan expert witnesses employed by the parties. In effect, the judge resurrects the ancient power to call an expert of his own choosing or one agreed upon by the parties, to give impartial testimony to aid him or the jury in resolving a scientific issue. In 1993, the Supreme Court decided that in order to determine the admissibility of purportedly scientific testimony, federal trial judges must evaluate the extent and quality of the empirical validation of the underlying theory or technique.[2] That decision has prompted trial judges to appoint experts with greater frequency. However, the scope of the judge's power of calling witnesses in aid of justice is broader and is not limited to expert testimony cases.

§ 9. Refreshing Recollection

Whether the questioner is a counsel or the judge, an anxious witness may forget a relevant fact. It is clear from everyday experience that the latent memory of an experience may be revived by an image seen or a statement heard. In the words of one court, the inspiration for the revival "may be a line from Kipling or the dolorous strain of 'The Tennessee Waltz'; a whiff of hickory smoke; the running

§ 8
1. See § 6 supra.

2. Daubert v. Merrell Dow Pharmaceuticals, Inc., 509 U.S. 579 (1993).

of the fingers across a swatch of corduroy; the sweet carbonation of a chocolate soda; [or] the sight of a faded snapshot in a long-neglected album."[1] This is one of the phenomena which the classical psychologists called the law of association. The retrieval of any part of a past experience helps to recall the other parts in the same field of awareness, and a new experience tends to stimulate the recall of prior like experiences. The effect is a reminder, which creates the sensation of recognizing as familiar a forgotten happening and which prompts our memory to retrieve associated experiences.[2]

As we have seen,[3] the interviewing of witnesses by counsel who will examine them in court is a necessary step in preparing for trial. At this stage the witness's memory can best be refreshed about the facts of the case, by giving her the opportunity to read her own previous written statements, letters, maps, or other documents. However, on occasion, even if the attorney properly prepared the witness before trial, the witness forgets on the stand. In that event, the attorney must attempt to refresh or revive the witness's memory in order to elicit the witness's testimony about the forgotten fact.

At trials, the practice has long been established that in interrogating a witness, counsel may hand her a memorandum to inspect for the purpose of "refreshing her recollection." When she speaks from a memory thus revived, her testimony is the evidence, not the writing. This is the process of *refreshing recollection at trial* in the original, strict sense.

But after this simple practice become established, it was natural for counsel to seek to carry it a step further. Suppose that the witness, even after being shown the writing, states that her memory is not revived and that she cannot testify from a refreshed recollection. She may nevertheless vouch that she recognizes the writing as a memorandum she made when the facts were fresh in her mind, and add that though she has no present mem-

ory of the facts, she is willing to testify that the facts were correctly recited in the memorandum. Here the writing itself becomes the evidence. This latter situation is quite different than the process of *refreshing recollection*. In the practice of refreshing recollection, the witness testifies orally on the basis of her present refreshed memory. In contrast, when her memory is not jogged, the counsel relies on the witness's voucher for the recital of things remembered in the past as a basis for introducing the writing.

The procedure of tendering a memorandum to the witness is followed in both cases, but the underlying justification in the second situation is fundamentally different. The justification rests on the reliability of a writing which the witness swears is a *record of her past recollection*. The writing itself is introduced into evidence. Safeguarding, foundational rules have been developed for this kind of memorandum. The rules require that the memo must have been written by the witness or examined and found correct by her, and that it must have been prepared so promptly after the events recorded that the events were fresh in the witness's mind when the record was made, or examined and verified by her. In this treatise these latter memoranda are considered separately as the past recollection recorded exception to the hearsay rule.[4]

Apparently, the earlier English cases on genuine refreshment of recollection imposed no restrictions on *the use of memoranda at the trial to refresh*. The memoranda were not required to have been written by the witness or under her direction, or to have been made near in time to the event. However, in the case of the practice of introducing records of *past recollection*, restrictions of this kind were prescribed with good reason. Since, however, the old name of "refreshing recollection" was often applied to both practices, it was natural that the two practices would be confused and the restrictions developed for one kind of memoranda would spill over to the other.

---

§ 9

1. Baker v. State, 371 A.2d 699 (Md. App. 1977).
2. See § 49 infra.
3. See § 2 supra.

4. See Ch. 28 infra. But if the memorandum was prepared by the witness, it may be admissible as a non-hearsay statement. See § 251 infra.

Which is the wiser practice, the older rule, championed Wigmore and most modern courts, that any memorandum, without restriction of authorship, time, or correctness, may be used to revive memory; or the doctrine requiring that the memorandum to refresh meet the same tests as the record of past recollection? Even if the latter doctrine is an historical blunder, by happenstance it could be a desirable safeguard in the search for truth.

Any kind of stimulus, a song, a face, or a newspaper item, can produce the "flash" of recognition, the feeling that "it all comes back to me now." But the sincerity of the feeling is no guarantee of the correctness of the image recalled. The danger that the mind will "remember" something that never happened is at least as great here as in the case of leading questions. "Imagination and suggestion are twin artists ever ready to retouch the fading daguerrotype of memory."[5] Thus, there is a plausible policy argument in favor of importing into the realm of refreshing memory the safeguards developed for memoranda of past recollection recorded, to be specific, the requirements that the witness must have made the writing or recognized it as correct, and that the making or recognition must have occurred while the event was still fresh in memory.

Nevertheless, most courts today adhere to the "classical" view that any memorandum or other object may be used as a stimulus to present memory without restriction as to authorship, guarantee of correctness, or time of making. On balance, this liberal practice seems wiser because there are sufficient other safeguards to protect against abuse. The first safeguard is the trial judge's power of control. It is a preliminary question for her decision under Rule 104(a) whether the memorandum actually does refresh. From the nature of the memorandum and the witness's testimony, she may find that it does not. She had additional statutory control under Rule 403. In the exercise of her discretion to control the manner of the examination, she may decline to permit the use of the aid to memory when, under 403,

she regards the danger of undue suggestion as substantially outweighing the probative value.

When the witness seeks to resort to the memorandum, a second safeguard is the rule entitling the adverse party to inspect the memorandum so that she may object to its use if ground appears, and to use the memorandum in cross-examining the witness. With the memorandum before her, the cross-examiner has a good opportunity to test the credibility of the witness's claim that her memory has been revived, and to search out any discrepancies between the writing and the testimony. For instance, if there is no evident nexus between the contents of the writing and the nature of the fact purportedly remembered, the cross-examiner can attack the plausibility of the witness's testimony that viewing the writing helped the witness remember that fact. In the past, this inspection right was usually limited to writings used by the witness on the stand, but the reasons seem equally applicable to writings used by the witness to refresh her memory before she testifies. The subject of inspection and use of writings to which the witness referred before testifying at trial is discussed at the end of the instant section.

Not only may the adversary inspect the memoranda used to refresh memory during the witness's examination, but she may also submit them to the jury for their examination. The party offering the witness may not do so unless the memoranda constitute independent evidence not barred by the hearsay rule. The consensus is that unless they may be introduced under the hearsay rule or one of its exceptions, memoranda used to refresh are not evidence, but only memory joggers or aids. Consequently, the best evidence rule is inapplicable; and a copy may be used without accounting for the original.

The line between using the writing merely as a memory jogger and treating it as a correct record of past memory can be shadowy. Must it be shown that the witness has no present recollection whatsoever of the matters embodied in the memorandum before she can resort to it as an aid to memory? It is sometimes said,

5. Gardner, The Perception and Memory of Witnesses, 18 Corn.L.Q. 390, 401 (1933).

even in opinions issued under the Federal Rules of Evidence, that this must appear, but that requirement is unsound. The witness may believe that she remembers completely but, on looking at the memorandum, she would recall additional facts. As the ancient proverb has it, "The palest ink is clearer than the best memory." To be sure, there is a danger that a suggestible witness may mistakenly think that she remembers a fact merely because she reads it. It seems eminently a matter for discretion, rather than rule. Similarly, a witness may recognize from present memory the correctness of successive facts set out in a memorandum; but, despite this recognition, she may be unable to detail those facts from memory without continuing to consult the writing. Accordingly, the statement that a witness once refreshed must speak independently of the writing is too inflexible. Again, the matter is discretionary. The trial judge may permit the witness to consult the memorandum as she speaks, especially where it is so lengthy and detailed that even a witness with a fresh memory would realistically be unable to recite all the items unaided.

As mentioned previously in the instant section, many older cases refused to enforce a demand for production at trial of matter reviewed by a witness to refresh memory before testifying. However, there have been many decisions to the contrary. The most important factor in this trend has been the adoption of Federal Rule of Evidence 612. Rule 612 announces that if a witness uses a writing to refresh her memory even before testifying, an adverse party is entitled to have the writing produced at the hearing, to inspect it, to cross-examine the witness about the writing, and to introduce into evidence the portions relating to the witness's testimony, although only if the court in its discretion determines production is necessary in the interests of justice.

Consider the significance of the sweeping wording of Rule 612. A writing consulted to refresh memory could be a privileged one, such as a letter written by the client-witness to her attorney about the case. In this event, the possibility of conflict arises between Rule 612's disclosure requirement and the privilege for confidential communications between attorney and client. Should the pretrial act of consulting the writing effect a waiver of the privilege? Finding a waiver when the writing is consulted by the witness while testifying is obviously warranted; for a witness in effect to say that she can consult the writing while testifying in open court but refuse to allow the opposing counsel to see the writing, would be patently unfair. The proper result is more debatable when a privileged writing is consulted in advance of trial. Ordinarily the privilege involved will be either attorney-client[6] or the qualified privilege for "work product".[7] The problem of waiver is discussed further in connection with those privileges.[8] At this point, it suffices to say that the clear trend in the federal cases has been to hold that Rule 612 overrides all privileges claims, at least when the witness consulted the writing pretrial for the specific purpose of freshening his memory in order to testify.

A further matter which must be considered in connection with Federal Rule of Evidence 612 is the relationship between that rule and Federal Rule of Criminal Procedure 26.2. Rule 26.2 is the successor to the so-called Jencks Act, 18 U.S.C.A. § 3500. That relationship is explored in a later section.[9]

Lastly, the use of hypnosis as a technique for refreshing a witness's recollection is treated in the chapter on scientific and experimental evidence.[10]

---

6. See generally Ch. 10 infra.

7. See § 96 infra.

8. See § 93 infra.

9. See § 97 infra.

10. See § 206 infra.

Chapter 3

THE REQUIREMENT OF FIRSTHAND KNOWLEDGE: THE OPINION RULE: EXPERT TESTIMONY

Table of Sections

§ 10. The Requirement of Knowledge From Observation

The common law system of proof is exacting in its insistence on the most reliable sources of information. This insistence is reflected in the opinion rule, the hearsay doctrine, and the documentary originals rule. One of the earliest and most pervasive manifestations of this attitude is the rule requiring that a witness to a fact which can be perceived by the senses must have had an opportunity to observe, and must have actually observed the fact. The same general requirement applies to declarations coming in under exceptions to the hearsay rule; as a general proposition, the declarant must have had an opportunity to observe the fact declared.

This requirement may easily be confused with the hearsay rule barring the repetition of out-of-court statements considered hearsay under that rule.[1] Technically, if the witness's testimony on its face purports to be a description of observed facts, but the testimony rests on statements of others, the objection is that the witness lacks firsthand knowledge. In contrast, when the form of the testimony indicates the witness is repeating out-of-court statements, a hearsay objection is appropriate. Often courts disregard this distinction.

The burden of laying a foundation showing that the witness had an adequate opportunity to observe is upon the party offering the testimony. By failing to object the adversary waives the preliminary proof, but not the substance of the requirement. Hence, if it later appears that the witness lacked opportunity or did not actually observe the fact, his testimony will be stricken; and the jury will be given a curative instruction to disregard the stricken testimony. When under the circumstances, reasonable persons could differ as to whether the witness had an adequate opportunity to

§ 10

1. See § 247 infra.

18

observe, under Federal Rule 104(b) the witness's testimony should come in, and the jury will appraise his opportunity to know in evaluating the weight of the testimony.

In laying the foundation, the examiner may elicit from the witness the particular circumstances which led him to notice, observe, or remember the fact. Why was the fact so important and memorable for the witness? If the witness had a special reason to be attentive, the jury is likely to attach more weight to the witness's purported recollection.

While the law is exacting in demanding firsthand observation, it is not so impractical as to insist upon either precision of attention by the witness, or certainty of recollection in recounting the facts. Accordingly, even when a witness uses such expressions as "I think," "My impression is," or "In my opinion," this is no ground of objection if he merely speaks from an inattentive observation or an unsure memory. However, an objection will be sustained if the expressions are found to mean that he speaks from conjecture or hearsay. When the state of the record is unclear, the judge may exercise his power under Rule 614 to question the witness before making a final ruling on the objection.

A person who has no knowledge of a fact except what another has told him does not, of course, satisfy the requirement of knowledge from observation. When the witness, however, bases his testimony partly upon firsthand knowledge and partly upon the accounts of others, the problem calls for a practical compromise. As a case in point, when a witness speaks of his own age or his kinship with a relative, the courts allow the testimony. Strictly speaking, it is impossible for the witness to have personal knowledge of such facts; no matter how precocious a child might be, she will not recall her own birth. Hence, there is an element of necessity in this situation. Moreover, the witness's knowledge of this type of fact is likely to have a trustworthy basis, namely, reports from close relatives who do possess firsthand knowledge. In short, when the witness testifies to facts that he knows partly at first hand and partly from reports, the judge should admit or exclude according to the overall reliability of the evidence.

THE OPINION RULE

§ 11   The Evolution of the Rule Against Opinions: Opinions of Laymen

Though it originated from practices and expressions of the English courts, the opinion rule was enforced more widely and far more inflexibly here than in the mother country. The original rule against "opinions" had a different meaning for the English judge. In English usage of the 1700's and earlier, "opinion" had the primary meaning of "notion" or "persuasion of the mind without proof or certain knowledge." The expression carried an implication of lack of grounds, which is absent from the contemporary meaning of the term "opinion" in this country. Today we use the word as denoting an inference, belief, or conclusion without necessarily suggesting that the inference is completely unfounded.

The requirement that witnesses have personal knowledge, discussed in the preceding section, is a very old rule with roots in medieval law. The early courts demanded that witnesses speak only "what they see and hear." Coke's classic dictum in 1622, that "It is no satisfaction for a witness to say that he 'thinketh' or 'persuadeth himself' "[1] and Mansfield's statement in 1766, "It is mere opinion, which is not evidence"[2] ought to be understood as condemning only testimony not based upon personal knowledge. Statements founded purely on hearsay or conjecture would fall under this ban. But as Wigmore interprets the historical evidence, until the 1800's there was no judicial support for an opinion rule excluding even inferences by witnesses possessing personal knowledge.[3]

By the middle of the 1800's the disparagement of "mere opinion" in the limited sense of

---

§ 11

1. Adams v. Canon, Dyer 53b, quoted 7 Wigmore, Evidence § 1917, p. 2 (Chadbourn rev.1979).

2. Carter v. Boehm, 3 Burr. 1905, 1918 (1766) quoted 7 Wigmore, Evidence § 1917, p. 7 (Chadbourn rev.1978).

3. 7 Wigmore, Evidence § 1917 (Chadbourn rev.1979).

a notion or conjecture not rooted in observation had evolved into a much more questionable canon of exclusion. This canon was the doctrine that witnesses generally must give the "facts" and not their "inferences, conclusions, or opinions."

That doctrine is based on the simplistic assumption that "fact" and "opinion" differ in kind and are readily distinguishable. The formula proved to be one of the clumsiest tools for regulating the examination of witnesses. It is clumsy because its basic assumption is an illusion. As the Supreme Court has remarked, "the distinction between statements of fact and opinion is, at best, one of degree."[4] The witness's words cannot "give" or recreate the "facts," that is, the objective situations or happenings about which the witness is testifying. Drawings, maps, photographs, and even motion pictures are only remote, partial portrayals of those "facts". How much more distant approximations of reality are the word pictures of oral or written testimony. Any conceivable statement, no matter however specific, detailed, and "factual," is in some measure the product of inference as well as observation and memory. The distinction between the statement, "He was driving on the left-hand side of the road" (which would be categorized as "fact" under the rule), and "He was driving carelessly" (which would be called "opinion") is merely a difference between a more concrete, specific form of descriptive statement and a less specific form. The distinction between so-called "fact" and "opinion" is not a difference between opposites or contrasting absolutes, but instead a mere difference in degree with no bright line boundary.

If trial judges are given the task of distinguishing on the spur of the moment between "fact" and "opinion", no two judges, acting independently, can be expected to consistently reach the same results on the questions. Of course, many questions have recurred and have customarily been classified as calling for either "fact" or "opinion". But in a changing world there will constantly be a myriad of new statements to which the judge must apply the distinction. Thus, good sense demands that the

trial judge be accorded a wide range of discretion at least in classifying evidence as "fact" or "opinion," and probably in admitting evidence even where found to constitute opinion. Various courts have expressed this viewpoint. It is incorporated in Federal Rule of Evidence and Revised Uniform Rule of Evidence (1974) 701.

The recognition of the impossibility of administering the opinion standard as a mandatory rule, however, came slowly. The relaxation of the strictness of the standard was initially limited to cases of strict necessity. A norm excluding opinion except in instances of strict necessity survives as the "orthodox" view in a few state courts. Even in states which have not adopted the Federal Rules of Evidence or a similar statutory reform, the actual practice is becoming, if indeed it has not always been, far more liberal than the older formulas. The practice is more accurately reflected in a formula expressed by some courts sanctioning the admission of opinions on grounds of "expediency" or "convenience" rather than "necessity." The so-called "collective fact" or "short-hand rendition" rule, permitting opinions on such subjects as a person's age, a car's speed, or a person's intoxication, incorporates this more liberal notion. The same notion underlies "skilled lay observer" opinion on such topics as the identification of a person's handwriting style. "Convenience" is the standard codified in Federal Rule of Evidence 701. Rather than restricting lay opinion to cases of strict necessity, by its terms Rule 701 authorizes the receipt of any lay opinion "helpful" to the trier of fact.

The standard actually applied by many contemporary trial judges includes the principle espoused by Wigmore, namely, that lay opinions should be rejected only when they are superfluous in the sense that they will be of no value to the jury. The value of opinions to the jury is the principal test of Federal Rule of Evidence and Revised Uniform Rule of Evidence (1974) 701. In light of Rule 701, the prevailing practice in respect to the admission of lay opinions should be described not as a

---

4. Beech Aircraft Corp. v. Rainey, 488 U.S. 153, 168 (1988).

rigid rule excluding opinions, but as a rule of preference. The more concrete description is preferred to the more abstract. To be sure, to the extent reasonably feasible, the witness should attempt to articulate the concrete primary facts. However, when it is impractical for the witness to verbalize all the data supporting an inference, the preference yields; and the witness's inferential testimony is admissible. Moreover, the principal impact of the rule is upon the form of examination. The questions, while they cannot suggest the particular details desired else they will be leading, should call for the most specific account that the witness can give. For example, he ought not be asked, "Did they reach an agreement?" but rather "What did they say?" When conceived as a matter of the form of the examination rather than the substance of the testimony— again, a difference of degree—the opinion rule, like other form regulations such as the control over leading questions and questions calling for a free narrative, falls naturally in the realm of discretion. The habit of Anglo–American lawyers to examine about specific details is a valuable heritage. The challenge is to preserve this habit but yet curb time-wasting quibbles over trivial "opinion" objections which can still be voiced in jurisdictions wedded to a literal application of the older formulas.

One solution is simply to eliminate the matter of lay opinion from the category of matters governed by "rules". Supporters of that solution find a sufficient substitute in lawyers' natural desire to present a detailed, convincing case and the cross-examiner's ability to expose the non-existence or inconsistency of details not developed on direct. Federal Rule of Evidence and Revised Uniform Rule of Evidence 701 does not go that far, but it does embrace a viable alternative solution short of altogether jettisoning the opinion doctrine. Under Rule 701 and Rule 602, the witness must have personal knowledge of matter forming the basis of testimony of opinion; the testimony must be based rationally on the witness's perception; and the opinion must be helpful to the jury (the principal test). Under these statutory rules, many courts have be-

come more receptive to lay opinions about the state of mind of third parties. Modernly, the courts tend to accept such opinions so long as the witness makes it clear that she is expressing an inference about the third party's apparent state of mind based on factors such as the third party's demeanor and behavior. Contrary to some early decisions, provided personal knowledge is adequately established the witness need not recite the observed matters that are the basis of opinion, although the judge has discretion to require preliminary testimony about the facts observed. Finally, Rule 403 permits exclusion of inferences that are prejudicial, confusing, misleading, or time-wasting.

§ 12. The Relativity of the Opinion Rule: Opinions on the Ultimate Issue

As pointed out in the preceding section, the terms "fact" and "opinion" denote merely a difference of degree of concreteness of description or a distinction in nearness or remoteness of inference. The opinion rule prefers the more concrete description to the less concrete, and the direct form of statement to the inferential. But there is still another variable in the equation. The purpose of the testimony has an impact on the required degree of concreteness. In the outer circle of collateral fact near the rim of relevancy, evidence will be received with relative freedom; but as we come closer to the hub of the issue, the courts are more careful to call for details instead of inferences.

The trial judge may well be more liberal in exercising discretion to admit opinions and inferences about collateral matters and less indulgent when testimony is adduced as to more crucial matters. Is it expedient to go further and to tie his hands by a categorical rule forbidding opinion-evidence as to these "ultimate" matters?

Undoubtedly there is a kind of statement by the witness which amounts to no more than an expression of his general belief as to how the case should be decided or as to the amount of damages which would be just. All courts exclude such extreme, conclusory expressions. There is no necessity for this kind of evidence; to receive it tends to suggest that the judge and jury may shift responsibility for the decision to the witnesses. In any event, it is worthless to the trier of fact.

But until about a half century ago, a very substantial number of courts went far beyond this commonsense reluctance to listen to the witness's views as to how the judge and jury should perform their functions; these courts had announced the general doctrine that witnesses would not be permitted to give their opinions or conclusions on an ultimate fact in issue.

The stated justification was sometimes that such testimony "usurps the function" or "invades the province" of the jury. Obviously these expressions were not intended to be taken literally, but merely to suggest the danger that the jury might forego independent analysis of the facts and bow too readily to the opinion of an expert or other influential witness.

Although the rule had been followed in many states prior to 1942, a trend emerged to abandon it. In a majority of state courts, an expert may now state his opinion on an ultimate fact, provided that all other requirements for admission of expert opinion are met. The trend culminated in the adoption of Federal Rule of Evidence 704, now subdivision 704(a):

> Except as provided in subdivision (b), testimony in the form of an opinion or inference otherwise admissible is not objectionable because it embraces an ultimate issue to be decided by the trier of fact.

On its face, 704(a) is not limited to expert opinions. Some courts had already adopted the rule that laypersons' opinions on ultimate facts were not precluded. However, such opinions may run afoul of other restrictions in particular instances, e.g., opinions as to how the case should be decided and what amount of money damages would be appropriate. Even under the most liberal rules, those opinions may be excludable on the ground that their value is outweighed by "the danger of unfair

prejudice, confusion of issues, or misleading the jury, or by considerations of undue delay, waste of time, or needless presentation of cumulative evidence." However, there is no categorical ban on opinions, either lay or expert, addressing ultimate facts.

This change in viewpoint concerning "ultimate fact" opinion resulted from the realization that the rule excluding opinion on ultimate facts is unduly restrictive, and can pose many close questions of application. The rule can unfairly obstruct the presentation of a party's case, to say nothing of the illogic of the notion that opinions on ultimate facts usurp the jury's function. In jurisdictions in which the traditional prohibition survives, there can be difficult questions whether an opinion concerns an ultimate fact.

Regardless of the rule concerning admissibility of opinion upon ultimate facts, at common law courts do not allow opinion on a question of law, unless the issue concerns foreign law.[1] Nor do the Federal Rules of Evidence permit opinion on law except questions of foreign law. One federal court voiced the typical judicial attitude when it wrote that "in a trial there is only one legal expert—the judge."[2]

Even a court which does not automatically ban opinion on the ultimate issue may nevertheless condemn a question phrased in terms of a legal criterion not adequately defined by the questioner so as to be correctly understood by laymen. Some jurisdictions still adhere to a general rule that a witness may never opine on a question of law or a mixed question of law and fact. But it is often convenient or desirable to use questions phrased in terms of some legal standard familiar to lawyers. There is thus a problem of interpretation of the questions. How do we ensure that the jury properly interprets the part of the question alluding to the legal standard?

The problem frequently arises in relation to testimony on the issue of capacity to make a will. Thus, a court taking the view that there

§ 12

1. See § 335 infra.

2. Pivot Point Intern., Inc. v. Charlene Products, Inc., 932 F.Supp. 220, 225 (N.D.Ill. 1996).

may be opinion on an ultimate issue would approve a question, "Did X have mental capacity sufficient to understand the nature and effect of his will?". That phrasing incorporates the substantive standard for testamentary capacity. However, even such a court would frown on the question, "Did X have sufficient mental capacity to make a will?" because the latter question may be misunderstood by the witness and the jury if they do not know the law's definition of "capacity to make a will." But a court prohibiting opinions on the ultimate issue might condemn both forms of questions, and perhaps even one where the questioner breaks down "testamentary capacity" into its factual elements as legally defined. Similar problems may arise in respect to such issues as undue influence, total and permanent disability, and negligence.

On the whole, the danger posed by these questions is slight, since they will seldom be asked except when the popular meaning is roughly the same as the legal meaning. In a jurisdiction where there is no general rule against opinions on the ultimate issue, a request by the adversary that the questioner define his terms should be the only recourse. If the questioner makes the definition clear to the jury, many jurisdictions accept opinions couched as conclusions on mixed questions of law and fact.

Although the statutory provision which is now Rule 704(a) appears to abolish any ultimate fact prohibition, to a degree subdivision 704(b) resurrects the prohibition. 704(b) was enacted in part as a backlash against the acquittal of John Hinckley on insanity grounds after his attempted assassination of President Reagan. Federal Rule of Evidence 704(b) provides that when an accused's mental state or condition is in issue (such as premeditation in homicide, lack of predisposition in entrapment, or the true affirmative defense of insanity), an expert witness may not testify that the defendant did or did not have the mental state or condition constituting an element of the crime charged or of the defense. Rule 704(b) seeks to eliminate the confusing spectacle of competing medical experts testifying to directly contradictory conclusions on the ultimate legal issue to be found by the trier of fact. Even under Rule 704(b), presumably the medical expert may answer the questions, "Was the accused suffering from a mental disease or defect?"; "Explain the characteristics of the mental disease and defect."; and "Was his act the product of that disease or defect?" However, the expert may not answer the question "Was the accused able to appreciate the nature and quality of his acts", or "Was the accused able to appreciate the wrongfulness of his acts?" Whether Rule 704(b) will have the intended effect of substantially moderating battles of experts over mental condition remains to be seen.

§ 13. Expert Witnesses: Subjects of Expert Testimony: Qualifications: Cross–Examination

In the past two decades, the use of expert witnesses has skyrocketed. In a Rand study of California Superior Court trials in the late 1980s, experts appeared in 86% of the trials; and on average, there were 3.3 experts per trial.[1] Some commentators claim that the American judicial hearing is becoming trial by expert. A lay observer is qualified to testify because he has firsthand knowledge of the situation or transaction at issue. The expert has something different to contribute. This is the power–the knowledge or skill–to draw inferences from the facts which a jury could not draw at all or as reliably.

Proper subject for expert inference. To warrant the use of expert testimony, the proponent must establish at least two general elements. First, traditionally the subject of the inference must be so distinctively related to a science, profession, business, or occupation as to be beyond the ken of lay persons. Some cases say that the judge has discretion in administering this rule. Other cases admit expert opinion concerning matters about which the jurors may have general knowledge if the expert opinion would still aid their understand-

§ 13

1. Gross, Expert Evidence, 1991 Wis.L.Rev. 1113, 1118–19.

ing of the issue. The latter standard is codified in Federal Rule of Evidence and Revised Uniform Rule of Evidence 702. In fact, Rule 702 seems to permit expert opinion even when the matter is within the jurors' competence if specialized knowledge will be helpful, as it may be in particular situations. Under this liberal reading of Rule 702, a psychologist may testify about the supposed unreliability of eyewitness testimony; and human factors engineers may opine about the behavior of an average person.

The witness's qualification as an expert. Second, the witness must have sufficient skill or knowledge related to the pertinent field or calling that his inference will probably aid the trier in the search for truth. The knowledge may be derived from reading alone in fields (education), from practice alone in other fields (experience), or as is more commonly the case from both. While the court may rule that a certain subject of inquiry requires that a member of a particular profession, such as a doctor, engineer, or chemist be called, usually a specialist in a particular branch of a profession is not required. The question is not whether this witness is more qualified than other experts in the field; rather, the issue is whether the witness is more competent to draw the inference than the lay jurors and judge. The practice in respect to experts' qualifications has not for the most part crystallized in specific rules, but is entrusted to the trial judge's discretion reviewable only for abuse. Reversals for abuse are rare.

The validity of the expert's underlying theory or technique. In addition to the issues of the propriety of the topic for an expert opinion and the qualifications of the alleged expert, there is the question of whether opinion evidence is admissible if the court does not believe that the state of the art or scientific knowledge permits a reliable opinion to be formed even by an expert. Is the expert's major premise trustworthy? As § 203 notes, prior to 1993 most jurisdictions held that purportedly scientific testimony has to be based on a generally accepted theory or technique. In its 1993 *Daubert* decision, the Supreme Court announced that when the proponent proffers the

witness as a scientific expert, the proponent must establish that the witness's underlying theory or technique qualifies as reliable "scientific ... knowledge" within the meaning of that expression in Federal Rule 702.[2] The Court explained that to qualify, the expert's hypothesis must be empirically validated. The Court stated that in evaluating the validation of the expert's hypothesis, trial judges should consider the following factors, inter alia: whether the proposition is testable and has been tested; whether the proposition has been subjected to peer review and publication; whether the methodology has a known error rate; whether there are standards for using the methodology; and whether the methodology is generally accepted.

The question has arisen as to whether *Daubert*'s empirical validation test applies to other types of expert testimony. On its face, Rule 702 refers in the alternative to "scientific, technical, or other specialized knowledge." Thus, the wording of the statute suggests that there can be nonscientific "technical" and nonscientific, nontechnical "specialized" experts in addition to scientific experts. Do *Daubert*'s test and list of relevant factors apply to nonscientific experts? In a copyright infringement case, the plaintiff might call an expert musician to testify about the degree of similarity between two songs. The musician is arguably testifying about "technical ... knowledge," and there are widespread conventions as to technique and methodology within the music field; but in most cases the musician's methodology cannot be validated in an empirical, scientific manner. Likewise, a prosecutor might call an experienced police officer to testify about the typical modus operandi for a crime. Again, the officer's testimony may represent "specialized knowledge," but the officer will not be opining on the basis of systematic, controlled scientific research. Does the court nevertheless have to subject the underlying assumptions of the musician and officer to scrutiny under *Daubert*?

The courts have divided into three camps. On the one hand, some courts have ruled that

---

2. Daubert v. Merrell Dow Pharmaceuticals, Inc., 509 U.S. 579 (1993).

"technical" and "specialized" expertise are exempt from the *Daubert* test. In footnote 8 of its opinion, the *Daubert* Court disclaimed any intention to prescribe admissibility standards for nonscientific expert testimony. Under *Frye*, *Daubert's* predecessor, most courts took a laissez-faire attitude toward the reliability of the premises underlying nonscientific expert testimony; any doubts about the reliability of the expert's theory went "largely unregarded."[3] At the polar extreme, other courts have taken the position that the *Daubert* test extends to other types of expert testimony. Some not only apply the general *Daubert* test but also attempt to evaluate the reliability of nonscientific expertise in terms of the factors enumerated in *Daubert*.

The second camp, insisting that nonscientific testimony satisfy the *Daubert* factors is wrong-minded. In effect, these cases endeavor to fit round pegs in square holes. It is meaningful to talk about error rates for scientific techniques, but that factor is hardly appropriate in the analysis of nonscientific expert testimony by musicians, police officers, lawyers, and farmers. A third position is the most sensible: while the proponent of nonscientific testimony must demonstrate the reliability of the expert's underlying assumptions, the trial judge need not use the *Daubert* factors to gauge reliability. Rather, the judge should engage in a more flexible analysis; the judge ought to pose such questions as whether in the real world members of the public routinely turn to this profession for services other than testimony and whether the expert's assumption rests on a large body of experience in situations quite similar to the fact situation before the court. The Judicial Conference has proposed an amendment to Rule 702 which in effect would extend a foundational reliability requirement to major premises used by all types of experts, nonscientific as well as scientific.

In 1999, the issue reached the Supreme Court in *Kumho Tire Co. v. Carmichael*.[4] In a majority opinion authored by Justice Breyer, the Court cited the proposed amendment to Rule 702 and essentially endorsed the third position. On the one hand, the Court stated that "a *Daubert*-style scrutiny" is appropriate for all types of expert testimony. As a matter of statutory construction, the Court argued that all kinds of expert testimony must amount to "knowledge" to qualify for admission under Rule 702. The Court added that "the evidentiary rationale" underlying *Daubert* is a concern about reliability, and in the Court's judgment that rationale is equally applicable to non-scientific expertise. Finally, the Court asserted that "it would prove difficult, if not impossible, for judges to administer evidentiary rules under which a gatekeeping obligation depended upon a distinction between 'scientific' knowledge and 'technical' or 'other specialized' knowledge."

On the other hand, the *Kumho* majority made it clear that non-scientific testimony need not satisfy each of the *Daubert* factors in order to qualify for admission. The trial judge "may" consider the factors which he or she finds pertinent, but in a given case some or most of those factors might be inapposite. The Court commented that "we can neither rule out, nor rule in, for all cases ... the applicability of the factors mentioned in *Daubert*...." In 1997 in *General Electric Co. v. Joiner*,[5] the Court had ruled that abuse of discretion is the appropriate standard for appellate review of trial judge rulings under *Daubert*. In *Kumho*, the Court analogized to *Joiner*. The *Kumho* Court declared that "[t]he trial court must have the same kind of latitude in deciding how to test a [non-scientific] expert's reliability...." The Court stressed that "whether *Daubert's* specific factors are, or are not, reasonable measures of reliability in a particular case is a matter that the law grants the trial judge broad latitude to determine."

The trustworthiness of the expert's minor premise. Expert opinion need not be admitted if the court believes that an opinion is premised on particular facts and it is unreasonable to assume the truth of those facts. If the expert proposes opining about an evaluation of the specific facts in the pending case, there must be a proper basis for the assumptions about those facts. Sections 14–16 discuss the potential sources for that information.

Cross-examination of experts. There are not only special rules for an expert's direct examination; peculiar problems can also arise

---

3. Strong, Language and Logic in Expert Testimony: Limiting Expert Testimony by Restrictions on Function, Reliability, and Form, 71 Or.L.Rev. 349, 361 (1992).

4. 119 S.Ct. 1167 (1999).

5. 522 U.S. 136 (1997).

during cross. On cross-examination, opposing counsel may require the expert to reveal facts and data underlying the expert's opinion not previously disclosed. With respect to the facts and data forming the basis of the expert's opinion, the cross-examiner may explore whether, and if so how, the non-existence of any fact or the existence of a contrary fact, would or might affect the opinion. Counsel is permitted to test the expert's reasoning process and fairness by inquiring as to what changes of conditions would affect his opinion. In conducting that inquiry, the cross-examiner is not limited to facts supported by the record.

However, there are limitations on the cross-examiner's ability to use passages in published treatises and articles to attack the theory or technique underlying the expert's opinion. An expert witness may, of course, be impeached with a learned treatise, admissible as substantive evidence under the hearsay exception set out in Fed.R.Evid. 803(18). Many jurisdictions go farther and allow the cross-examiner to use texts and articles even when they do not fall within the scope of the hearsay exception. Some jurisdictions do so by statute. Others allow the practice by case law. Depending on the jurisdiction, the cross-examiner may confront the expert with a contrary passage in a publication which is judicially noticeable as a standard authority in the field or which the cross-examiner has shown to be authoritative. When the publication is used for the limited purpose of impeachment, it is admitted only to attack the quality of the expert's reasoning, not as substantive evidence.

Cross-examination of an expert directed at establishing bias through financial interest is proper. The cross-examiner may seek to establish (1) financial interest in the case at hand by reason of compensation for services, including services performed which enabled him to testify, (2) continued employment by a party, or (3) the fact of prior testimony for the same party or the same attorney. When it comes to questions about (1) the amount of previous compensation from the same party, (2) the relationship between the expert's income from testifying on behalf of a party or a category of party and the expert's total income, or (3) the mere fact of prior testimony on behalf of other similarly situated persons or entities, the com-

mon law authorities are in disagreement. The better view is that such inquiries should be permitted.

While the precise scope of cross-examination of expert witnesses rests within the trial judge's discretion, this discretion should not be applied in a narrow manner, especially with respect to experts voicing opinions as to matters exceeding the common knowledge and experience of laymen.

§ 14. Grounds for Expert Opinion: Hypothetical Questions

The traditional view has been that an expert may state an opinion based on his firsthand knowledge of the facts, resting on facts in the record at the time he states his opinion, or based partly on firsthand knowledge and partly on the facts of record. If the opinion is to be based on the facts of record, the facts can be in the expert's possession by virtue of the expert's presence at the taking of the testimony about those facts, or they may be furnished to the expert by including them in a hypothetical question asking the expert to assume their truth and then state a requested opinion based upon them. However, these methods of eliciting expert opinion have been subject to sharp criticism; and in response to the criticisms, they are permitted but have been liberalized in a growing number of jurisdictions, including those that have adopted the Federal and Revised Uniform Rules of Evidence. Two major general changes have been made. First, on direct examination an expert may state an opinion and the theoretical "reasons" for the opinion without prior disclosure of the underlying data or facts, leaving the disclosure of the data to the opponent on cross-examination, if the opponent desires disclosure. This change eliminates the need for a lengthy statement of the underlying facts on direct examination. Second, the expert need not base her opinion on either firsthand knowledge or an hypothesis; specified types of facts and data such as certain types of hearsay reports are now considered proper grounds for the expert's opinion. This change brings the legal practice more in line with the practice of experts outside the courtroom, since in their own practice they often rely on trustworthy hearsay reports. At the same time, in these more liberal jurisdictions the traditional methods and procedures for eliciting expert opinion may still be employed. The traditional views mentioned above are considered in this section, and the more modern liberal rule, is discussed in Sections 15 and 16.

If an expert witness has firsthand knowledge of material facts, he may describe what he has observed and give his inferences under both traditional views and the Federal Rules of Evidence. When the expert has no personal knowledge of the situation at issue and has made no firsthand investigation of the facts, the orthodox common law method of securing the benefit of the expert's skill is by asking the expert to assume certain facts and then, on the basis of this hypothesis, to state opinions or inferences. These questions are known as hypothetical questions. Unfortunately, the rules regulating their form and content have developed more on the basis of theoretical logic than on the basis of practicalities. At the judge's discretion, hypothetical questions are permissible under the Federal Rules of Evidence and other liberal rules.

In most jurisdictions committed to the more traditional views, it is allowable to have an expert witness in court during the taking of testimony. Later when the expert is called as a witness, the counsel can simplify a hypothetical question by merely asking the witness to assume the truth of the previous testimony heard by the witness, or some specified part of it, and to state an opinion upon that assumption. This practice is permissible in the court's discretion under the Federal Rules of Evidence and other liberal rules. The practice has some advantages and some limitations. Two obvious requirements are that the assumed facts be clear to the jury and not conflicting. Otherwise the jury will not be given any aid. A question asking the witness to assume the truth of one previous witness's testimony will usually meet these requirements. However, as the range of assumption is widened to cover the testimony of several witnesses or all the testimony for one side, the risk of infraction of these requirements increases. When a hypothetical question covers all the testimony in the case, the question can be approved only when the testimony on the issue relating to the question is consistent and simple enough for the jury to recall its outlines without having them recited.

The type of questions just discussed, namely those based on other testimony in the case, satisfies the basic traditional requirement imposed on all hypothetical questions— that the facts assumed be supported by independent, admissible evidence in the record. However, this rule is not a requirement for hypothetical questions in jurisdictions following the Federal Rules of Evidence. The traditional requirement is based on the notion that if the opinion is premised on a fact which the jury, for lack of evidence, cannot find to be true, the jurors are equally disabled from using the opinion as the basis for a finding. There must be admissible evidence supporting each assumed fact, but direct testimony is not required. It is sufficient if the fact is fairly inferable from the circumstances proved. Moreover, at common law the supporting evidence need not have been already adduced if the interrogating counsel gives assurance that it will be forthcoming. Further, it is no objection that the supporting evidence is controverted. The proponent is entitled to put his side of the case to the witness for his opinion. However, there is a danger that by omitting some critical facts, the proponent may present an unfair, slanted picture to the expert and that the jury may give undue weight to the opinion without considering its faulty basis. For instance, the proponent might elicit an unreliable estimate of a car's speed from an accident reconstruction expert if the proponent's hypothesis omitted any mention of undisputed evidence about the length of the skidmarks left by the car. Are there any safeguards against this danger? Some decisions require that all facts material to the question be embraced in the hypothesis. However, this view seems undesirable because it is likely to multiply disputes as to the sufficiency of the hypothesis, and can cause counsel, out of excess of caution, to propound questions so lengthy as to be wearisome and almost meaningless to the jury. The more expedient, prevailing view is that there is no rule requiring that all material facts be included. Under the prevailing view, the safeguards are that the adversary may on cross-examination supply omitted facts and ask the expert if his opinion would be modified by them, and that if he deems the question unfair, the trial judge may require that the hypothesis be reframed to supply an adequate basis.

As indicated in Section 16, infra, however, none of these traditional rules governing the requirements for hypothetical questions has remedied the evils arising from the use of these questions.

§ 15. Expert's Opinion Based on Reports of Others and Inadmissible or Unadmitted Data and Facts[1]

As we have seen, at common law an expert could base an opinion either on personally known facts or facts stated in an hypothesis. However, those two bases do not exhaust the possibilities. The expert could also attempt to rest an opinion on third party hearsay reports. There formerly was a majority view, however, that a question is improper if it calls for the witness's opinion on the basis of reports that are inadmissible in evidence under the hearsay rule. The essential reason supporting this view was that as a matter of logic, the jury could not accept the opinion based on the facts if the only evidence of the facts is inadmissible. This view applies even when the witness was asked to give an opinion, not merely on the basis of reports of this kind, but on these matters supplemented by the witness's own observation. However, there has been a strong case law trend toward a contrary view. (There is also a suggested view that opinions based upon hearsay should be less objectionable if they concern subject matters that have an indirect relation to the fact issues in the case, rather than directly concerning the central facts in issue.)

The case law trend culminated in the new broader view in Federal Rule of Evidence 703, adopted in many state jurisdictions. Under Rules 703 and 705, an expert may give a direct opinion upon facts and data, including technically inadmissible reports, provided the reports or other data are "of a type reasonably relied upon by experts in the particular field in forming opinions or inferences upon the subject." The rationale for this view is that an expert in a science is competent to judge the reliability of statements made to him by other investigators or technicians. He is just as competent to do this as a judge and jury are to pass upon the credibility of an ordinary witness on the

stand. If the statements are attested by the expert as the basis for a judgment upon which he would ordinarily act in the practice of his profession, they should be a sufficient basis even standing alone for his professional opinion on the stand. This argument has special force when the opinion is founded not only on reports but also in part on the expert's first-hand observation. The data gained by observation puts the expert in an even better position to evaluate the reliability of the statement.

The substantive question under Rule 703. The principal substantive problem presented by Rule 703 is the interpretation of the language quoted above. The key language consists of the words, "reasonably relied upon". The liberal approach is that the judge must accept the experts' view in deciding whether the rule is met at least in matters in which the judge is not equipped to "second guess" the expert. The courts subscribing to this approach equate "reasonably" with "customarily." Under Rule 104(a) the judge makes a factual finding as to whether it is the customary practice of the expert's specialty to consider a certain type of report. If there is such a custom, the judge's hands are tied; the judge must allow the expert to rely on that type of report. There is a competing, restrictive approach that if the data would have been or was excluded from the record as hearsay and lacks any circumstantial guarantee of trustworthiness comparable to an exception to the hearsay rule, the standard of Rule 703 is not met. Neither approach is flawless. The difficulty with the liberal approach is that a party can employ an expert witness to place untrustworthy facts, data, or opinions before the jury–a sort of "backdoor" hearsay exception. Under the restrictive approach, a court may exclude material on which an expert may actually rely in the expert's practice. In the main, the restrictive approach is preferable both as a matter of policy and as a question of statutory construction. To be sure, the judge should typically defer to the speciality's customary practice. However, in an extreme case, the judge ought to have a residual power to second-guess the customary practice and rule that a particular type of hearsay source is too untrustworthy.

§ 15

1. See § 324.3, infra.

When the analogous Tort question arises as to whether an industrial practice is negligent, the courts consider evidence of the industry's customary practice; but the custom is not dispositive. The restrictive approach is also sounder as a matter of statutory interpretation. When the drafters wanted to make the application of an evidentiary rule dependent on the existence of a custom or routine practice, as they did in Rules 406 and 803(17), they found apt words to manifest their intention. In Rule 703, they opted to use the adverb "reasonably" rather than "customarily." "Reasonably" connotes an objective standard to be applied by the trial judge.

The judge and the attorneys may litigate this matter in a hearing under Rule 104. A problem under Rule 703 in criminal cases is whether the defendant should or must have the opportunity cross-examine the persons who originated the data upon which an expert relies under Rule 703. On balance, Rule 703 should probably be followed unless a government expert is in effect being used solely to bring before the jury otherwise inadmissible matter (particularly hearsay implicating the confrontation clause). A similar approach should be employed where the criminal defendant's mental health expert relies on the defendant's statements to support an opinion sanity.

The procedure for administering Rule 703. In addition to the substantive question of the meaning of "reasonably" in Rule 703, the rule presents a procedural issue. Assuming that it is substantively permissible for an expert to rely on a hearsay report as part of the basis of her opinion, how far may the expert go in describing the content of the report? The expert should certainly be allowed to generally indicate the type of report she is relying on. However, when the report is oral, may she quote the report in detail? When the report is in writing, may the proponent formally introduce the report, have the expert quote it, and even it submit to the jurors for their inspection? As § 324.3 points out, the courts have divided over this question. It has been argued that as a matter of logic, the jurors cannot thoroughly evaluate the expert's reasoning un-

less they have an in-depth understanding of all the bases of the opinion. Further, a case can be made that the wording of Rule 705 indicates that the drafters contemplated that the expert should be permitted to give the jurors a detailed description of the content of the report. However, the operative assumption here is that the report is not independently admissible; that is, it is not reliable enough to qualify for admission under any hearsay exception. With some support in the empirical studies, other commentators have cautioned that allowing the expert to detail the report's content creates a grave risk that the jurors will misuse the content as substantive evidence. Several jurisdictions have amended their version of Rule 703 to preclude the expert from elaborating on the content of the report; and a pending amendment to Federal Rule 703 would have the same effect.

Of course, in a broad sense almost all expert opinion about scientific propositions embodies hearsay indirectly. Whenever an expert testifies, she implicitly draws on such material as lectures she heard and textbooks she read during her education. It would be ridiculous to apply the hearsay rule to that material:

> Would we require a modern accident reconstruction expert to replicate Newton's seventeenth century experiments to derive the laws of motion? Suppose that a physicist is testifying about the safety of a nuclear power plant. If the physicist contemplates relying on the words of Fermi or Oppenheimer, would we require that the physicist duplicate their research?[2]

However, that problem is distinguishable from the issue analyzed in this section. That type of material relates to the expert's major premise, that is, the literature and research underpinning the expert's theory or technique. In this section, the question is quite different; the focus is on the content of the expert's minor premise, namely, the case-specific information about how the traffic accident occurred or the accused's behavior just before he shot the decedent. There is less justification for lifting the bar of the hearsay rule when the expert rests her opinion on out-of-court reports about that kind of information.

2. Imwinkelried, The "Bases" of Expert Testimony: The Syllogistic Structure of Scientific Testimony, 67 N.C.L.Rev. 1, 9 (1988).

§ 16. Should the Hypothetical Question Be Retained?

In theory, the hypothetical question is an ingenious device for enabling the jury to apply the expert's scientific knowledge to the facts of the case. Nevertheless in practice, it has been largely a failure and an obstruction to the administration of justice. If we require that it recite all the relevant facts, it becomes intolerably wordy. If we allow, as most courts do, the interrogating counsel to select such facts as he sees fit,[1] we tempt him to shape a one-sided hypothesis. Many expert witnesses view this partisan slanting of the hypothesis as a fatal weakness of the practice. The legal writers who have studied the problem seem equally agreed in condemnation.

What is the remedy? It hardly seems practicable to require the trial judge to undertake the thorough study of the case necessary to enable him to personally select the significant facts to be included. It might be feasible for the questions to be framed by both counsel in conference with the judge, either at a pretrial hearing or during the trial in the jury's absence. But that conferral process could be time-consuming. The only remaining expedient is the one generally advocated, namely, dispensing with the requirement that the question be accompanied by a recital of a hypothesis, unless the proponent elects to use the hypothetical form or the trial judge requires it. This is the procedure authorized by Federal and Revised Uniform Rule of Evidence (1974) 705 and a few other statutes and rules. It is for the cross-examiner to bring out the basis for the expert's opinion if that is desired. This approach does not lessen the partisanship of the question or the answer, but it simplifies the examination and removes the occasion for imperiling the trial judgment by appellate disputes over mistakes in the form of hypothetical questions. Rule 705 does, however, give the judge discretion to require prior disclosure of basis facts, and it may be assumed that he will do so when there has not been adequate opportunity to discover them in advance, especially in criminal cases.

§ 17. Proposals for Improvement of the Practice Relating to Expert Testimony

Common law countries employ the contentious or adversary system of trial, in which the opposing parties, not the judge as in other systems, have the responsibility and initiative in finding and presenting proof. Advantageous as this system is in many respects, its present application to the procurement and presentation of expert testimony is widely considered a sore spot in judicial administration. The critics point to two chief weaknesses. The first is the choice of experts by the party, who are naturally interested in finding not the best scientist, but the "best witness." As an English judge has said:

> " * * * the mode in which expert evidence is obtained is such as not to give the fair result of scientific opinion to the Court. A man may go, and does sometimes, to half-a-dozen experts * * * He takes their honest opinions, he finds three in his favor and three against him; he says to the three in his favor, 'will you be kind enough to give evidence?' and he pays the three against him their fees and leaves them alone; the other side does the same * * * I am sorry to say the result is that the Court does not get that assistance from the experts which, if they were unbiased and fairly chosen, it would have a right to expect."[1]

The second weakness is that the adversary method of eliciting scientific testimony, frequently by hypothetical questions based on a partisan choice of data, is ill-suited to the dispassionate presentation of technical data. In many cases, the net result is overemphasizing conflicts in scientific opinions which a jury can have difficulty resolving.

A potential remedy for the first weakness lies in the use of trial judges' common law power to call experts. Cases are recorded as early as the 14th century—before witnesses were heard by juries—of judges summoning experts to aid them in determining scientific

§ 16

1. See § 14.

§ 17

1. Jessel, M.R., in Thorn v. Worthington Skating Rink Co., L.R. 6 Ch.D. 415, 416 (1876), note to Plimpton v. Spiller, 6 Ch.D. 412 (1877).

issues. The existence of the judge's power to call witnesses generally and expert witnesses particularly is well recognized in this country. The power has been declared by rules and statutes in a substantial number of states. Some provisions apply to scientific issues in any case, civil or criminal, others are limited to criminal cases, and still others refer narrowly to sanity issues in criminal cases. The principle is implemented in the Model Expert Testimony Act approved by the Commissioners on Uniform State Laws,[2] and embodied in Uniform Rule of Evidence and Federal Rule of Evidence 706. Unfortunately, in the past judges have rarely exercised their power under Rule 706. That reluctance is understandable, though. Before their appointment to the bench, most judges are schooled as litigators in the adversary tradition. That tradition is so ingrained that some commentators believe that to overcome the judicial reluctance to appoint court experts, court appointment should be made mandatory in certain types of cases.

Another mechanism, establishing panels of impartial experts designated by groups in the appropriate fields from which panel court appointed experts would be selected, should also be considered as a possible antidote for the first weakness. An American Bar Association committee has approved in principle this procedure for impartial medical expert witnesses.

The second weakness in the system may also be remediable. It would not only be helpful to reduce the partisan element in selecting experts, it is also important that the contentious manner of presenting the results of the expert's investigation be modified. In the current system, lay jurors are often called upon to arbitrate a "battle of experts". In some kinds of controversies, a well-devised plan of scientific investigation and report could reduce greatly the need for contested trials. The Uniform Act provides that the court may require a conference of the experts, whether chosen by the court or the parties. The conference gives the experts an opportunity to resolve their differences of view and disagreements in interpreting the data. The conference might lead to a complete agreement which practically settles the issue for the parties. If not, it at least may narrow the controversy. Two or more experts, the Act provides, may join in a single report. At the trial, the expert's individual report expert witness or a joint report can be read to the court and jury as a part of his testimony, and he may be cross-examined about the report. The Act dispenses with the requirement to use hypothetical questions. There was a striking, if bizarre, example of the utility of joint reports in a New York DNA case, *People v. Castro.*[3] In that case,

> [i]n an unusual move, four of the expert witnesses—representing both the prosecution and the defense—met to review the scientific evidence after they had already testified. The result of this meeting was a two-page consensus statement that addressed the inadequacy of the scientific evidence and the legal procedures for assessing [the] evidence. Although the statement itself was not accepted as evidence in the pretrial hearing, the substance of the consensus document was introduced by the defense's recall of two prosecution expert witnesses to testify on its substance.[4]

Although these proposals addressing the two weaknesses have merit, both have been targets of criticism. For example, the expanded use of court appointed experts is not without critics. It has been argued in opposition to the court appointment of experts that there is no such thing as a truly impartial expert and, even assuming such experts exist, courts lack the ability to identify and locate them. In addition, the procedure associated with the employment of the expert at trial could result in excessive emphasis by the trier of fact on that witness's opinion. Once the jury learns that one expert is the "court's" witness, the jurors might leap to the conclusion that they should accept her opinion.

The two weaknesses mentioned above are not the only features of common law procedure which hamper the effectiveness of expert testimony. Other problem areas include first, the unsuitability of the jury, a body of lay persons usually required to be unanimous, as a tribunal for assessing scientific evidence; second, the rules of privilege, especially the at-

---

2. The Act is set out in 1937 Handbook, Nat'l Conf. Com'rs on Unif.State Laws 339–48.

3. 545 N.Y.S.2d 985 (1989).

4. Office of Technology Assessment, U.S. Cong., Genetic Witness: Forensic Uses of DNA Tests 103 (1990).

torney-client privilege, the physician-patient privilege, and the privilege against self-crimination;[5] and third, the employment of legal standards of civil liability and criminal responsibility, which do not accord with the scientific standards which the experts are accustomed to, as in the case of the "understanding of right and wrong" test for legal sanity.

More broadly, it should be borne in mind that the courts' need for better employment of the technical resources goes beyond the use of expert witnesses. One judge has observed:

> "The methods of courts might well be supplemented by the use of well tested examples of administrative tribunals, of expert investigators acting for the court—engineers, scientists, physicians, economic and social investigators, as needed—in addition to, not in substitute for, similar experts acting for the parties * * *.

> "Why should not judge and jury in cases involving multitudinous scientific exhibits, or scientific questions, have the benefit of the assistance of those competent to organize such data and analyze such questions? Why should not courts have adequate fact finding facilities for all kinds of cases? Boards of directors do. Administrative tribunals do. The parties, and in a large sense the public, have an interest in the decision of cases on whole truth, not on partial understanding. The machinery and expert staffs developed by the interstate commerce commission, state public service commissions, and workmen's compensation boards have values for fact finding which may profitably be studied in reference to judicial reorganization * * * "[6]

The American legal tradition has created an abundance of procedures which might conceivably be adapted to utilizing experts' services. Perhaps pretrial conferences could be tailored specifically to deal with matters involving expert opinion. Most important is the authority,

often conferred by statute or rule but in any event an "inherent" judicial power, to refer a question to a master, referee, auditor or similar officer, standing or special. The reference may contemplate merely an investigation and report, or a hearing followed by a report or a preliminary decision. Even if the courts are reluctant to extend these procedures to expert testimony problems, the procedures could be prescribed by statute. It has also been suggested that the courts make wider use of the technical resources of the sister branch of the government, the administrative agencies and commissions.

There are encouraging signs of progress on this front. As previously stated, until recently most judges have been reluctant to resort to techniques such as court appointment under Rule 706. However, in its 1993 *Daubert* decision,[7] the Supreme Court announced a new, empirical validation test for the admissibility of purportedly scientific testimony. That test requires trial judges to directly assess the validity of scientific hypotheses; the judges may no longer rely on "surrogates" for validity such as the popularity or general acceptance of they hypothesis. The shift to the new validation test should encourage trial judges to appoint experts under 706. Indeed, in the course of its opinion, the *Daubert* Court mentioned the possibility that in applying the new test, judges would find it useful to appoint experts under the rule. There are signs that the incidence of court appointment is gradually increasing.

§ 18. Application of the Opinion Rule to Out-of-Court Statements

Does the opinion rule apply to out-of-court statements, offered in court under some exception to the hearsay rule? Positing the traditional view that the opinion rule is a categorical rule of exclusion, it is natural to assume that if this kind of evidence is excluded when elicited from a witness on the stand, it should be rejected when offered in hearsay form. Consequently, many older decisions simply discuss

---

5. See §§ 99 and 134 infra.

6. Justice Harold M. Stephens, What Courts Can Learn from Commissions, 21 A.B.A.J. 141, 142 (1933). Also see generally Ch. 37 infra.

7. Daubert v. Merrell Dow Pharmaceuticals, Inc., 509 U.S. 579 (1993).

the admissibility of opinions contained in hearsay declarations as if they had been given by a witness on the stand, and reject or admit them accordingly.

However, the emerging view that the opinion rule is not an absolute rule of exclusion, but rather a relative rule for the examination of witnesses, preferring when it is feasible the more concrete testimony to the more general and inferential.[1] On that premise, the opinion rule has little or no sensible application to out-of-court statements. Sustaining an objection to counsel's question to a witness as calling for an "opinion" is usually not a serious matter; in most cases counsel can easily reframe the question on the spot to elicit the more concrete statement. But to automatically reject the same statement by an out-of-court narrator in a dying declaration mistakes the

function of the opinion rule and may shut out altogether a valuable source of proof. When the source is an unavailable hearsay declarant, the stark choice facing the court is admitting the opinionated hearsay statement or denying the jury any information from that source. Many of the cases and Wigmore take this enlightened view as to admissions,[2] and it is spreading to the other classes of declarations coming in under exceptions to the hearsay rule.[3]

The superficially similar question of the declarant's want of personal knowledge must be distinguished. If the out-of-court declarant had not observed at first hand the fact declared, that deficiency goes not to form but to substance and is often fatal to admissibility when the declaration is offered as substantive evidence to prove the fact.[4]

---

§ 18

1. See §§ 11, 12 supra.
2. See treatment of the various exclusions and exceptions to the hearsay rule in Chapters 25–33 infra.
3. As to dying declarations, see § 313 infra.

4. See §§ 313 and 280 infra. But the state of law is to the contrary with respect to admissions, see § 255 infra and the entry of items in business records, see § 290 infra.

Chapter 4

CROSS–EXAMINATION AND SUBSEQUENT EXAMINATIONS

Table of Sections

§ 19. The Right of Cross–Examination: Effect of Deprivation of Opportunity to Cross–Examine

For two centuries, common law judges and lawyers have regarded the opportunity of cross-examination as an essential safeguard of the accuracy and completeness of testimony. They have insisted that the opportunity is a right, not a mere privilege. This right is available at the taking of depositions as well as during the examination of witnesses at trial. The premise that the opportunity of cross-examination is an essential safeguard has been the principal justification for the general exclusion of hearsay statements.[1] It also under-

pins the recognition of a hearsay exception for reported testimony taken at a former hearing when the present adversary was afforded the opportunity to cross-examine.[2] State constitutional provisions guaranteeing the accused's right of confrontation have been interpreted as codifying this right of cross-examination, and the right of confrontation secured by the Sixth Amendment of the federal constitution has likewise been construed as guaranteeing the accused's right to cross-examination in criminal proceedings. Indeed, a majority of the Supreme Court appears to have embraced the notion that the right to cross-examination is the primary interest secured by the confronta-

---

§ 19

1. See § 245 infra.

2. See § 302 infra.

tion clause. Moreover, the courts have granted the right a measure of constitutional protection in civil cases.

What are the consequences of a denial or failure of the right? There are several common, recurring situations. First, a party testifying on his own behalf might unjustifiably refuse to answer questions necessary to a complete cross-examination. Here it is generally agreed that the adversary is entitled to have the direct testimony stricken, a result that seems warranted.

Second, a non-party witness may similarly refuse to be cross-examined, or to answer proper cross-examination questions. Here the proper result is less clear, but many judges and writers seem to sanction the same remedy of excluding the direct. This remedy minimizes the party's temptation to procure the witness's refusal, a collusion which is often hard to prove; the remedy forcefully protects the right of cross-examination. However, there is also some authority for the view that the matter should be left to the judge's discretion. In particular, there is support for the notion that if the privilege against self-incrimination is invoked to cross-examination questions which are logically relevant only to the witness's credibility and otherwise immaterial, the direct testimony should not be stricken or that at the least the judge ought to have a measure of discretion in ruling on that matter.

Third, the witness may become, or purport to become, sick or otherwise physically or mentally incapacitated, before cross-examination is begun or completed. The facts in many of these cases arouse suspicion of simulation, particularly when the witness is a party. Consequently, the party's direct examination is often stricken. In the case of the non-party witness, the same result is usually reached. However, at least in civil cases, this result should arguably be qualified so that the judge is directed to exclude unless he is clearly convinced that the incapacity is genuine. In that event he ought to let the direct testimony stand. He should then be authorized to give the jury a cautionary instruction to explain the weakness of uncross-examined evidence. (Tem-

porary incapacity may change this result, as indicated below.)

The fourth situation is that of the witness's death before the cross-examination. Here again it is usually said that the party denied cross-examination is entitled to have the direct testimony stricken, unless, presumably, the death occurred during a postponement of the cross-examination consented to or procured by that party. In case of death, there is no adequate reason for striking the direct testimony, except that exclusion may well be constitutionally compelled if the witness was a state's witness in a criminal case. It has been suggested that striking the direct should be discretionary. That suggestion has merit. No matter how valuable cross-examination may be, common sense tells us that the half-loaf of direct testimony is better than no bread at all. To let the direct testimony stand was the accepted practice in equity. It is submitted that except for the testimony of prosecution's witnesses, the judge should let the direct testimony stand but be required on request to instruct the jury to consider the lack of opportunity to cross-examine in weighing the direct testimony.

The above results may be modified in certain situations. For instance, it has been held that where the incapacity is temporary, the cross-examiner may not insist upon immediate exclusion of the direct testimony; he must be content with the offer of a later opportunity to cross-examine even when this makes it necessary for him to submit to a mistrial.

For simplicity's sake, it was assumed in the preceding paragraphs that, though some cross-questions may have been answered, a failure to secure a complete cross-examination would be treated as if cross-examination had been wholly denied. That assumption is an oversimplification. A cross-examination, though cut off before it is finished, may yet under the circumstances have been so substantially complete as to satisfy the requirement for an opportunity to cross-examine. In a given case, cross-examination may be regarded as sufficient as to part of the direct testimony to allow at least that part to stand though the rest must be stricken.

Finally, the infringement of the right of cross-examination may result, not from the witness's refusal or inability, but from the judge's action. The judge has wide discretionary control over the *extent* of cross-examination upon particular topics. However, the denial of cross-examination altogether or its arbitrary curtailment upon a proper, important subject of cross-examination is ground for reversal.

§ 20. Form of Interrogation

Assuming that a litigant has the right to cross-examine, questions can arise as to the scope and form of the cross. In contrast to direct examination, cross-examination may usually be conducted by questions which are leading in form. When the cross-examiner uses leading, narrowly-phrased questions, under the guise of asking questions the cross-examiner makes factual assertions on the record and forces the witness to assent. The cross-examiner's purpose is often to weaken the effect of the direct testimony, and the witness is commonly assumed to be more or less uncooperative. Consequently the danger of acquiescence in the examiner's suggestions is ordinarily absent. However, when it appears that the witness is biased in the cross-examiner's favor and likely to yield to the suggestions of leading questions, the judge in many jurisdictions may restrain the asking of them. In jurisdictions where the scope of cross-examination is limited, if the examiner goes beyond the proper field of cross-examination he may be required to refrain from leading the witness as to the new subject. The cross-examiner "adopts" the witness with respect to the new topic. There are, however, a number of somewhat illogical decisions permitting leading questions on cross-examination even though the witness seems biased in the cross-examiner's favor.

§ 21. Scope of Cross–Examination: Restriction to Matters Opened Up on Direct: The Various Rules

The practice varies widely in the different jurisdictions on the question of whether the cross-examiner is confined to the subjects testified about in the direct examination and, if

so, to what extent. Although this section reviews those varying practices, it is important for the reader to realize that there is a good deal of consensus over the proper scope of cross-examination. As § 22 notes, all the courts agree that the proper scope includes matters relevant to the witness's credibility. In addition, as we shall see later in this section and again in § 24, most jurisdictions accord the trial judge a measure of discretionary power over the scope of cross-examination on the merits. The point of disagreement is the normal scope of cross-examination on the historical merits of the case.

The traditional rule of wide-open cross-examination. In England and a few states, the simplest and freest practice prevails. In these jurisdictions, the cross-examiner is not limited to the topics which the direct examiner has chosen to open. The cross-examiner is free to question about any subject relevant to any issue on the merits in the entire case, including facts relating solely to the cross-examiner's own case or affirmative defense.

The "restrictive" rule, in various forms, limiting cross-examination to the scope of the direct. The majority of the states agree that the cross-examination must be limited to the matters testified to on the direct examination. This general rule was adopted by the Federal Rules of Evidence. While all these jurisdictions purport to embrace the restrictive rule, they differ markedly in the rigor with which they enforce the rule. To begin with, the doctrine can be employed narrowly to strictly confine the cross-questions to those relating only to the same acts or facts, and, perhaps, those occurring or appearing at the same time and place. The narrow version of the doctrine is sometimes called the factual or historical test. Thus, the cross-examination has been said to be limited to "the same points" brought out on direct, the "matters testified to," or the "subjects mentioned." Slightly more expansive is the extension to "facts and circumstances connected with" the matters stated on direct, but this phrasing still suggests a requirement of basic identity of transaction and proximity in time and space. Seemingly a wider expansion is accomplished by another variation of the formula. That variation is the statement that the cross-examination is limited to the matters opened in direct and to facts tending to explain, contradict, or discredit the direct testimony. The broadest formula includes facts tending to "rebut" any inference or deduction from the matters testified on direct. There is little consistency in the phrasing and use of formulas, even in the same jurisdiction. All these express criteria are too vague to be employed with precision. Even assuming that cross-examination is to be limited to the subject matter of the direct examination, the subject matter of questions on direct examination can always be defined with greater or lesser generality regardless of the express formula.

In defining the subject matter of the direct examination, Federal Rule of Evidence 611(b) should be interpreted to endorse the broader, more liberal views described above. That interpretation is consistent with the provision in 611(b) that the court may permit inquiry into additional matters as if on direct. As a practical matter, many federal trial judges apply the so-called legal test. This test equates "the subject matter of the direct" with the essential elements of the cause of action, crime, or defense mentioned on direct. At the end of the trial, the judge gives the jury substantive law instructions on the pertinent causes of action, crimes, and defenses. These instructions list the essential legal elements which the burdened party must prove to prevail on that theory. One of the essential elements of a true crime is a mens rea element. Suppose that on direct examination, a defense witness testified about the accused's mens rea at the time of the actus reus. Under the legal test, on cross-examination the prosecutor could inquire about distinct acts by the accused so long as the other acts were logically relevant to the element of mens rea; the prosecution would not be limited to the historical events mentioned during the witness's direct examination.

All these limiting formulas share an escape valve, namely, the notion that where part of a transaction, contract, conversation, or event has been revealed on direct, the remainder may be brought out on cross-examination.

The fact that this notion is substantially a mere statement of the converse of the limiting rule itself does not detract from its usefulness as an added tool for argument. This particular aspect of the rule of completeness is unaffected by Federal Rule of Evidence 106. Another escape valve for appeal purposes is the proposition that the trial judge has a certain amount of discretion in regulating the scope of cross-examination on the historical merits.

The half-open door: cross-examination extends to any matters except cross-examiner's affirmative case. A third view as to the scope of cross-examination takes a middle course between the two extremes. Under this view, now mostly obsolete, the cross-examiner could question the witness about any matters relevant to any issue in the action, *except* facts relating only to the cross-examiner's own affirmative case such as defendant's affirmative defenses or cross-claims or, in case of a plaintiff, his new matter in reply. In some states, this compromise standard served as a temporary half-way house for courts which later turned to the "wide-open" practice. It has the merit, as compared with the restrictive practice, of lessening dispute by widening the scope of examination. Its chief drawback is that it can often be difficult to determine, particularly under modern liberal pleading rules, whether the matter inquired about relates solely to the examiner's "distinct grounds of defense or avoidance."

§ 22. Cross–Examination to Impeach Not Limited to the Scope of the Direct

One of the main functions of cross-examination is to afford an opportunity to elicit answers impeaching the witness's veracity, capacity to observe, impartiality, and consistency. Even in jurisdictions adopting the most restrictive practice, cross-examination to impeach is not limited to matters brought out in the direct examination. On direct examination, a witness's proponent ordinarily may not bolster the witness's credibility; during direct—before there has been any attack on the witness's credibility—the proponent generally may not elicit testimony which is logically relevant only to the witness's believability. Nevertheless, by the simple act of testifying, the witness places her credibility in issue. For that reason, the witness's credibility is fair game on cross-examination. This view is adopted in Federal Rule of Evidence 611(b).

§ 23. Practical Consequences of the Restrictive Rules: Effect on Order of Proof: Side–Effects

It is sometimes asserted that the only "essential" difference between the "wide-open" and the restrictive rules as to scope of cross-examination is in the time or stage at which the witness may be called upon to testify to the facts inquired about. The primary difference between the rules is assertedly their effect on the order of proof. Under the "wide-open" rule the witness may be questioned about the new matter on cross-examination, while under the restrictive rules the cross-examiner postpones the questions until his own next stage[1] of putting on proof and then calls the witness to prove the same facts. This assertion, though, understates the impact of the restrictive practice. At a given trial, timing can be critical; and even a "mere" postponement can be important. Moreover, in many instances a postponement of the questions will not be the only result of a ruling excluding a cross-question as outside the scope of the direct. Unless the question is vital and he is fairly confident of a favorable answer, the cross-examiner might be unwilling to run the risk of calling the adversary's witness at a later stage as his own and will abandon the inquiry. Getting concessions from the opponent's witness hot on the heels of the direct while his story is fresh is worth trying for. It is a much less attractive option to call an unfriendly witness later when his first testimony is stale. In addition, it might not serve orderly presentation of proof, supposedly promoted by restrictive rules, in particular cases in which a party has injected an issue by one witness but not by a second witness who may not be cross-

examined on the issue although he has knowledge relevant to that issue. In that situation, it might be more orderly to have both witnesses testify about the fact in the same phase of the case, but the scope of rules will require the opponent to recall the second witness much later.

A ruling excluding questions as exceeding scope of direct is not the only consequence of the restrictive rule. There are many incidental effects. By way of example, the courts adopting the restrictive practice frequently say that if the cross-examiner, perhaps without objection, questions on new matter, he makes the witness his own. The cross-examiner "adopts" the witness with respect to the new matter. This notion is stated in Federal Rule of Evidence 611(b).[2] He is normally forbidden to ask leading questions about the new matter, and under the traditional rule against impeaching one's own witness[3] may be precluded from impeaching the witness as to those facts. However, since one may impeach one's own witness under Federal Rule of Evidence 607, the cross-examiner would not be precluded from impeaching the witness concerning the new matter brought out pursuant to Rule 611(b).

Furthermore, the invocation of the restrictive rule to exclude unfavorable testimony from the plaintiff's witness which might otherwise be elicited on cross-examination, could have another critical effect, saving the plaintiff from a directed verdict at the close of his case in chief. This can be a significant advantage. The plaintiff both survives the directed motion and, during the defense case, gains an opportunity to strengthen his case by eliciting favorable facts from his opponent's witnesses.

Finally, in one situation, the restrictive rule operates as a rule of final exclusion, not a mere postponement. In this situation, the witness has a privilege not to be called as a witness by the cross-examiner. Thus, the privileges of the accused and the accused's spouse not to be called by the state may prevent the prosecutor from eliciting the new facts at a

---

§ 23

1. As to the order of proof, by stages, of the respective parties, see § 4 supra.

2. See § 21 supra.

3. This rule, however, has been greatly liberalized in many jurisdictions. See § 38 infra.

later stage, if he cannot draw them out on cross-examination.[4]

§ 24. The Scope of the Judge's Discretion Under the Wide–Open and Restrictive Rules

Gibson, C.J.[1] and Story, J.[2] introduced the innovation upon the orthodox "wide-open" cross-examination by suggesting that questioning about new matter was improper at the stage of cross-examination. When they did so, they thought of their innovation as relating solely to the order of proof. Traditionally the order of proof and the conduct and extent of cross-examination have been subject to the trial judge's discretionary control. In keeping with that tradition, Federal Rule 611(a) empowers the judge to "exercise reasonable control over the ... order of interrogating witnesses and presenting evidence.... ; and 611(b) allows the judge to a degree to "exercise ... discretion" over the scope of cross.

Accordingly, the earlier decisions and many contemporary cases adopting the restrictive rule emphasize the trial judge's discretionary power to allow deviations. Indeed, it has been said that both the courts following the wide-open and those adopting the restrictive practice "recognize the discretionary power of the trial court to allow variations from the customary order and decline ordinarily to consider as an error any variation sanctioned by the trial court."[3] If this statement were completely accurate, the hazards of injustice at the trial, or of reversals on appeal, would be insubstantial. But the statement paints too bright a picture.

In the states adopting "the scope of the direct" test, trial courts tend to find it easier to administer the test as a mechanistic rule rather than as a flexible standard of discretion. Appellate courts have reversed many cases for error in the application of the test, although

there is a trend to accord wider latitude to the trial judge.

In jurisdictions following the traditional wide-open view, there has been little tendency to apply the notion that the order of proof is discretionary. Their tradition has not been shaped in terms of order of proof, but rather in the language of a right to cross-examine upon the whole case. The situation putting the greatest strain on the wide-open rule is the one in which a party, usually the plaintiff, finds himself compelled at the outset to call either the opposing party himself or an ally of the opponent to prove a formal fact not substantially in dispute. Should the opponent be allowed to disrupt the proponent's case at this stage by cross-examining the willing witness about matters of defense unrelated to the direct examination? This is an appealing situation for the exercise of a discretion to vary from the wide-open practice and to require the cross-examiner to recall the witness for these new matters when he puts on his own case later. However, as the decisions reveal, even in this extreme case, the discretion is rarely exercised in "wide-open" jurisdictions.[4]

§ 25. Application of Wide–Open and Restrictive Rules to the Cross–Examination of Parties: (a) Civil Parties

In the cross-examination of party witnesses, two situations must be distinguished: (1) the hostile cross-examination by the adversary of a party who calls himself as a witness in his own behalf, and (2) the friendly cross-examination by the counsel of a party who has been called as an adverse witness by his opponent. In the first situation, in jurisdictions following the restrictive rules it is sometimes held that while the range of discretion to permit the relaxation of the restrictive practice is wider, the general limitation to the "scope of the direct" still applies. However, relaxation of the restrictive practice *only* for parties as mentioned above does not appear to be authorized

---

4. See §§ 25, 26 infra.

§ 24

1. In Ellmaker v. Buckley, 16 Sarg. & Rawles 72 (Pa. 1827).

2. In Philadelphia & Trenton Railroad Co. v. Stimpson, 39 U.S. (14 Pet.) 448 (1840).

3. St. Louis, Iron Mountain & Southern Railway Co. v. Raines, 119 S.W. 665, 668 (Ark. 1909).

4. See § 25 infra.

by Federal Rule of Evidence 611(b); on its face, 611(b) does not differentiate between the cross-examination of parties and non-parties. Yet, without much discussion, a few cases have announced that upon the hostile cross-examination of a party, the limitation to the scope of the direct will not be applied. In the "wide-open" states, the usual freedom from the restriction is routinely accorded.

Contrast the second situation. When a party calls the adverse party as a hostile witness, it is usually provided by statute or rule that he may question him "as upon cross-examination;" he may ask leading questions, and he is not "bound" by the adverse witness's answers, meaning chiefly that he may impeach the testimony by showing inconsistent statements. When this direct examination, savoring of cross, is concluded, one view gives the witness no right to be further examined immediately by his own counsel; rather the judge has discretion to permit immediate questioning or to require that his examination be deferred until the witness-party's own case is put on. Most jurisdictions, however, allow the witness's immediate further examination by his own counsel. Presumably upon request, the trial judge would forbid leading questions. In the restrictive jurisdictions, during this "cross-examination" of a friendly witness, there is no tendency to relax the usual restrictions limiting the questions to the scope of the direct.

§ 26. Application of Wide–Open and Restrictive Rules to the Cross–Examination of Parties: (b) The Accused in a Criminal Case

As a means of implementing the prescribed order of producing evidence, the restrictive rules limiting cross-examination to the scope of the witness's direct or to the proponent's case are burdensome, but understandable. The cross-examiner who has been temporarily halted has at least a theoretical remedy. He may recall the witness for questioning when he puts on his own next stage of evidence. However, when the restrictive practice is applied to the criminal accused, as it is in most jurisdictions following that practice, the accused can permanently preclude the prosecution from questioning the accused about facts outside the scope of the accused's direct. The accused may carefully limit his direct examination to a single aspect of the case such as age, sanity, or alibi[1] and then invoke the court's ruling that the cross-examination be limited to the matter thus opened. At the very outset of the direct examination, the defense counsel might expressly announce that she was going to question the accused "only" about a specified topic; counsel would do so to put herself in a better position to later urge scope objections. This application of the restrictive practice to the cross-examination of the accused has been criticized. Of course, there is no problem of the accused escaping searching inquiry on the whole case if the scope of cross-examination is "wide-open."

Regardless of whether the result under the restrictive rule is desirable as a matter of policy, the scope of the accused's cross-examination might not be controlled solely by evidence case law, statutes, or rules.[2] Federal Rule 611(b) is not intended to govern the extent to which a testifying accused waives the constitutional privilege against self-incrimination.[3] The outer limits of cross-examination may well be governed by constitutional doctrine concerning the degree to which the accused waives his privilege of self-incrimination by taking the stand and testifying. Some judicial language suggests that under the Fifth Amendment of the United States Constitution, the waiver extends only to questions concerning matters mentioned upon direct examination. If this position ultimately prevails, state practice would be governed by the constitutional limits of waiver, rendering "wide-open" cross-examination of criminal defendants, and

---

§ 26

1.　Except, of course, that cross-examination to impeach is not confined to the scope of the direct (see § 22 supra).

2.　See generally § 132 infra.

3.　The scope of waiver by a testifying defendant is discussed in § 134 infra.

perhaps even liberal variations of the restrictive rules, unconstitutional.

§ 27. Merits of the Systems of Wide–Open and Restricted Cross–Examination

The principal virtue claimed for the restrictive rules is that they pressure the parties to present their facts in logical order, first the facts on which the plaintiff has the burden, then those which the defendant must prove, and so on.[1] The restrictive rules minimize the danger that one party's plan of presenting his facts will be interrupted by the interjection on cross-examination of new and damaging matters constituting his adversary's case. This interjection, if permitted, lessens the impact and persuasiveness of the proponent's facts. The nice case which he planned to lay out fact by fact has been muddled during its very presentation by contrary facts drawn out in cross-examination of the proponent's own witnesses. The "case," formerly a single melody, becomes convertible to counterpoint. The contemporary litigator views himself as a storyteller—telling the jury a coherent, compelling version of the disputed events. The litigator understandably becomes resentful when the opposition attempts to disrupt the continuity and flow of the story. For that reason, most practitioners probably prefer the restrictive views of the scope of cross.

It must be remembered, however, that like all rules of order, the common law order of proof by "cases" or stages is to some extent arbitrary. Since two witnesses cannot be allowed to speak at once, some rules must be worked out as to who shall call the witnesses and in what order. A further rule, however, that a witness who knows many facts about the case shall be allowed to tell only certain ones at his first appearance, and as to others must be called later, seems artificial. There is a natural order to the freer, wide-open practice; on direct examination the regular order of proof of the respective parties' "cases" is maintained, but the adversary is free to draw out damaging facts on cross-examination. The procedure by which each witness successively tells all he knows about the case, is a system which would be followed spontaneously in any informal investigation untrammeled by rules. Jeremy Bentham, the great critic of "artificial" procedural rules, favored a "natural" system of evidence, that is, the practices which a family might turn to in order to resolve a factual question. It serves the witnesses' convenience and may appear to the jury as a more natural way of developing the facts. Furthermore, if it is objected that diversion into new paths on cross-examination lessens the persuasiveness of the direct examiner's presentation of his story, it is hardly self-evident that the direct examiner is entitled to the psychological advantage of presenting his facts in this oversimplified, one-sided way. Is he in justice entitled to make an favorable first impression on the jurors which, though answered later, can be hard to dislodge?

Another factor is the consideration of economy of time and energy. The wide-open rule creates little or no opportunity for wrangling over its application at either the trial or appellate level. In contrast, the restrictive practice can produce courtroom bickering over the choice of the numerous variations of the "scope of the direct" criterion, and their application to particular cross-questions. These controversies often resurface on appeal, and there is the possibility of reversal for error. Observance of these vague, ambiguous restrictions is a matter of constant concern to the cross-examiner. If these disputes and delays were necessary incidents to guarding substantive rights or the fundamentals of fair trial, they might be worth the cost. As the price of enforcing a debatable regulation of the order of evidence, the sacrifice is misguided. The American Bar Association's Committee for the Improvement of the Law of Evidence remarked:

'The rule limiting cross-examination to the precise subject of the direct examination is probably the most frequent rule (except the Opinion rule) leading in trial practice today to refined and technical quibbles which obstruct the progress of the trial, confuse the jury, and give rise to

§ 27

1. See § 4 supra.

appeal on technical grounds only. Some of the instances in which Supreme Courts have ordered new trials for the mere transgression of this rule about the order of evidence have been astounding.

'We recommend that the rule allowing questions upon any part of the issue known to the witness * * * be adopted * * *.'[2]

In short, there are strong policy reasons for the "wide-open" rule. Thus, while most practitioners favor the restrictive approach, the "wide-open" rule enjoys the support of many reformers, academics, and jurists.

§ 28. Cross–Examination About Witness's Inconsistent Past Writings: Must Examiner Show the Writing to the Witness Before Questioning About Its Contents?

A fatal weakness of many liars is letter writing. Betraying letters are often inspired by boastfulness or sometimes by stupidity. Properly used, letters have destroyed many a witness intent on perjury. An eminent trial lawyer observed:

> * * * There is an art in introducing the letter contradicting the witness' testimony. The novice will rush in. He will obtain the false statement and then quickly hurl the letter in the face of the witness. The witness, faced with it, very likely will seek to retrace his steps, and sometimes do it skillfully, and the effect is lost.
>
> The mature trial counsel will utilize the letter for all it is worth. Having obtained the denial which he wishes, he will, perhaps, pretend that he is disappointed. He will ask that same question a few moments later, and again and again get a denial. And he will then phrase—and this requires preparation—he will then phrase

a whole series of questions not directed at that particular point, but in which is incorporated the very fact which he is ready to contradict—each time getting closer and closer to the language in the written document which he possesses, until he has induced the witness to assert not once, but many times, the very fact from which ordinarily he might withdraw by saying it was a slip of the tongue. Each time he draws closer to the precise language which will contradict the witness, without making the witness aware of it, until finally, when the letter is sprung, the effect as compared with the other method is that, let us say, of atomic energy against a firecracker.[1]

However, in some courts there would be an obstacle to using this method. The obstacle is the rule in *Queen Caroline's Case,* pronounced by English judges in an 1820 advisory opinion.[2] The opinion announced that the cross-examiner cannot ask the witness about any written statements made by the witness, or ask whether the witness has ever written a letter of a given tenor, without *first* producing the writing or letter and exhibiting it to the witness. The cross-examiner must permit the witness to read the writing or the part of it the cross-examiner seeks to ask him about. In effect, the examiner is required to telegraph his punch. Thus, in vain is the potential trap laid before the eyes of the bird. While reading the letter, the witness will be forewarned not to deny it. Worse still, a clever witness may be able to quickly weave a new web of deception .

In *Queen Caroline's Case* the judges conceived of the rule that the writing must first be shown to the witness before he can be questioned about it as an application of the best evidence doctrine requiring the production of the original document *when its contents*

---

2. See 6 Wigmore, Evidence § 1888, p. 711 (Chadbourn rev. 1976) where the relevant part of the Committee's report is set out in full.

§ 28

1. Nizer, The Art of Jury Trial, 32 Corn.L.Q. 59, 68 (1946). An instructive, similar suggestion as to the tech-

nique of "exposure by document" is found in Love, Documentary Evidence, 38 Ill.Bar J. 426, 429–30 (1950). See also 4 Belli, Modern Trials § 63.30 (2d ed. 1982).

2. 2 B. & B. 284, 286–90, 129 Eng.Rep. 976, 11 Eng. Rul.C. 183 (1820).

are sought to be proved.[3] This notion was a misconception in at least two respects. First, the cross-examiner is not seeking to prove *at this stage* the contents of the writing. On the contrary, his hope is that the witness will deny the existence of the letter. Second, the original documents rule requires the production of the document as proof of its contents to the judge and jury, not to the witness. So obstructive did the Victorian barristers find the rule in the *Queen's Case* that they secured its abrogation by Parliament in 1854.[4]

However, when urged upon them, this practice requiring exhibition to the witness was unquestioningly accepted by many American courts and occasionally by American legislatures. The actual invocation of the rule at trial is relatively infrequent in most states in which the rule is still in effect, and even today many judges and practitioners in these jurisdictions are unaware of this hidden pitfall in the cross-examiner's path.

So far, the rule has been discussed as it operates in the context in which the cross-examiner seeks to uncover in a dramatic, devastating fashion a calculating witness's perjury. In this situation, the rule seems to blunt one of counsel's sharpest weapons. But the weapon may be misdirected in the typical case. Innocent and well-meaning witnesses write letters, forget their contents, and years later testify mistakenly to facts inconsistent with the assertions in the letters. Their forgetfulness may need to be revealed, and their present testimony discredited to that extent. Arguably, however, they should not be invited by subtle questioning to widen the gap between their present testimony and their past writings. Under this view, the judge should be vested with the discretion whether to permit the questioning about the writing without requiring its exhibition to the witness.

In recognition of the disadvantages of the rule of *Queen Caroline's Case,* the Federal Rules of Evidence abolish the rule by permitting cross-examination without a prior show-ing of the writing to the witness. Rule 613 substitutes a requirement that the writing be shown or disclosed to opposing counsel on request as an assurance of the cross-examiner's good faith.

§ 29. The Standard of Relevancy as Applied on Cross–Examination: Trial Judge's Discretion

There are three main functions of cross-examination: (1) to attack the credibility of the direct testimony of this witness and other opposing witnesses, (2) to elicit additional facts on the historical merits related to those mentioned on direct,[1] and (3) in states following the "wide-open" rule, to bring out additional facts which tend to elucidate any issue in the case. As to cross-examination designed to serve the second or third function, the usual standard of relevancy governing testimony offered on direct examination applies to facts to be elicited on cross-examination.

However, when she is performing the first function, that of attacking the credibility of the direct testimony, the cross-examiner's purpose is radically different than in the other two functions. In the first function, the cross-examiner is not directly targeting the historical merits of the case. Here the test of relevancy is not whether the answer sought will shed light on any issue on the merits, but whether it aids the court or jury in appraising the witness's credibility and assessing the probative value of the direct testimony. At common law there are many recognized lines of questioning for this purpose, none of which has any direct relevance to the historical merits. In general the common law principles stated in this section are pertinent under Federal Rule of Evidence and Revised Uniform Rule of Evidence 611(b), authorizing cross-examination concerning "matters affecting the credibility of the witness."

One familiar type of credibility inquiry is the preliminary series of cross questions, asking about residence and occupation, designed

---

3. This doctrine, called the best evidence rule, is analyzed in Ch. 23 infra.

4. St. 17 & 18 Vict. c. 125, § 24.

§ 29

1. See § 21 supra.

to place the witness in his setting. Either the witness's residence or occupation might give rise to an inference of bias. Another common question is, "Have you talked to anyone about this case?" Like a witness's residence or occupation, a witness's pretrial contacts could have a biasing influence. Still another is the testing, exploratory question. In this kind of question, the cross-examiner (who may not have the advantage of having previously interviewed the witness) asks disarming questions often remote from the main inquiry. The questions are designed to experimentally test the witness's ability to remember detailed facts of the same nature as those recited on direct, his capacity accurately to perceive facts, or his willingness to tell the truth without distortion or exaggeration. This is part of the tradition and art of cross-examination, and many of the most famous instances of cross-examinations are of this variety. The courts recognize that a rule limiting cross questions to those relevant to the issues on the historical merits would cripple this kind of examination. A final instance of credibility cross-examination is the direct attack by impeaching questions seeking to show such matters as inconsistent statements or conviction of crime.[2] Again, these facts have no necessary relevance to the historical merits.

As to all the lines of inquiry mentioned in the preceding paragraph, the criteria of relevancy are vague, since the purpose of the cross-examiner is frequently exploratory. Too tight a rein upon the cross-examiner may unduly curb the utility of the examination. However, dangers of undue prejudice to the party or the witness and of potential waste of time are apparent. Consequently, the trial judge has a discretionary power to control the extent of examination. This exercise of discretion will be reviewed only for abuse resulting in substantial harm to the complaining party. A survey of a large number of these cases leaves the distinct impression that in practice, abuse is more often found when complaint is that the judge has unduly limited the examination than when undue extension is charged.

§ 30. The Cross–Examiner's Art

An overview of the art of cross-examination, gleaned from the prolific writing on the subject, may help the beginning advocate appreciate some of the wisdom lawyers have learned from hard experience. It may also aid in considering the topic of the next section, evaluating the significance of cross-examination.

Preparation is the key. Some lawyers seem to have a natural talent for effective cross-examination. A great Victorian advocate, Montagu Williams, voiced this view when he said, "I am by trade a reader of faces and minds." Today, however, the stress is upon painstaking preparation, not upon sudden sallies of divine inspiration. Improvisation is often necessary, but its results are usually small compared to those yielded by planned questions based on facts methodically dug out before trial. The steps in planning are explained in many of the works concerning cross-examination. Not all steps need to be taken as to all adverse witnesses. Nor can every case bear the expense of thorough preparation. Nevertheless, preparation before trial is the soil from which, in the day-to-day run of cases, successful cross-examination grows. Some lawyers recommend that at trial, notes in preparation for later questions be made by an associate or the client, rather than the cross-examiner. Oral suggestions to the examiner in court should be avoided. During the direct examination, the cross-examiner cannot afford to spend a good deal of time preparing notes or conversing; the task at hand for the cross-examiner is to listen intently to every word coming out of the mouth of the direct examiner and witness. In sum, two of the keys are pretrial preparation and concentration at trial.

No cross-examination without a purpose. In the movies, aimless cross-examinations routinely yield startling revelations. In the real world, they are usually ineffective and often counter-productive; the cross-examiner typically succeeds only in having the witness repeat the damaging testimony, and during cross hostile witnesses frequently add damning facts

---

2. See Ch. 5 infra, dealing with impeachment of witnesses.

which were omitted on direct. As a general proposition, the attorney should not cross at all unless he is convinced that he can probably achieve one of the useful purposes of cross. As we have seen, these purposes may be, first, to elicit new facts on the merits, qualifying the direct or in some states bearing on any issue in the case; second, to test the witness's story by exploring its details and implications, in the hope of disclosing inconsistencies or impossibilities; and third, to elicit facts such as prior inconsistent statements, bias, and conviction of crime to impeach either this witness or another opposing witness. In considering pursuing any of these objectives, but particularly the latter two, the cross-examiner must be conscious that the odds are stacked against him. An unfavorable answer is more damaging when elicited on cross-examination. It is hard for a cross-examiner to win his case on cross-examination; but it is easy for him to lose it. Accordingly, if the witness has done no harm on direct examination, a cross-examination for the second or third purpose is usually ill-advised. In many cases, when the direct examiner tenders the witness to the cross-examiner, the cross-examiner should say only, "No questions, Your Honor. This witness may be excused."

There remains the witness whose direct testimony has been damaging, or even threatens to be destroy of the cross-examiner's case if the jury believes it. The cross-examiner must make an on-the-spot, situational judgment: Was the direct testimony so devastating that the jurors will probably regard a waiver of cross as an admission of the truth of the testimony, and, on that basis, find against the cross-examiner's client? In that situation cross-examination is usually necessary. Whether the object shall be a skirmish far from the crucial issues, or a frontal attack on the witness, will depend on the availability of impeaching material disclosed by preparation and a judgment of the risks. To be blunt, if the direct testimony was devastating and the cross-examiner has no real ammunition against the witness, the cross-examiner must contemplate either launching a fishing expedition or seeking a recess to renew settlement discussions.

A question about a pivotal fact should seldom be posed to an adverse witness unless the cross-examiner is reasonably confident the answer will be favorable. Similarly, broad questions which open the door for an eager witness to reinforce his direct testimony, e.g., "How do you explain that?" or "How did it happen?" are ordinarily ill-advised. If a discrepant fact has been drawn out on cross-examination, it is often better to wait and stress the inconsistency in argument than to continue to press the witness. If the cross-examiner presses with another question, the additional question may give the witness an opportunity to recover and explain away the concession.

In conducting a testing or exploratory examination, it is inadvisable to follow the order of the witness's direct testimony. One commentator suggests: "If the witness is falsifying, jump quickly with rapid-fire questions from one point of the narrative to the other, without time or opportunity for a connected narrative: backward, forward, forward, backward from the middle to the beginning, etc."

Cross-examine for the jury, not for your client. It is often a temptation for the cross-examiner to display his wit and skill before his client, or to feed the client's hostility toward opposing witnesses by humiliating them. Frequently small victories on collateral matters are easy to secure. However, the odds between the experienced advocate and the witness, nervous in new surroundings, are not even. The cross-examiner needs constantly to remind herself that the jury is keenly aware of this inequality of position and that most jurors are prone to imagine themselves in the witness's shoes. The cross-examiner must be especially polite in questioning sympathetic witnesses such as children, crime victims, and bereaved relatives. Better results with the witness, and a better impression upon the jury usually flow from tact and politeness than from bulldozing and ridicule. However, in the rare case when the cross-examiner is convinced that a crucial witness has committed perjury and that he can demonstrate it, the attack must be pressed home to the jugular. Once it is clear to the jury that the cross-examiner has "the goods" on the witness, the cross-examiner can adopt a more overtly aggressive attitude toward the witness. But the cross-examiner should always be conscious of his duty to use his skills fairly. He must so conduct himself that the jury, despite its sympathy for witnesses, will be impressed with his civility.

Make one or two big points; end on a high note. When the cross-examiner has secured an important admission, he should not dull the edge of the effect by continuing the questioning to obtain additional details or risk a recantation by calling for a repetition. He ought to move to another important point if he has one, and end the examination when his last big point is made. End on a high note: "When you have struck oil stop boring." The impact of a cross-examination depends on the overall impression left at the end of the cross rather the number of technical debating points which the cross-examiner scores against the witness.

While these generalities are worthwhile guidelines, the cross-examiner must adapt his techniques to the specific situation he faces. Different seasoned litigators might use different techniques in cross-examining the same witness. As on direct, during cross-examination the litigator needs to adopt a questioning style suited to her personality. Whatever else the litigator does during trial, she must project sincerity to the jury. If the litigator attempts to mimic another attorney's style and persona, her presentation may strike the jury as insincere.

§ 31. Cross–Examination Revalued

Early Victorian writers on advocacy exaggerated the strategic importance of cross-examination. One wrote, "There is never a cause contested, the result of which is not mainly dependent upon the skill with which the advocate conducts his cross-examination."[1] This romanticism contrasts with the realism of Scarlett, a great "leader" of a later day, who remarked, "I learned by much experience that the most useful duty of an advocate is the examination of witnesses, and that much more mischief than benefit generally results from cross-examination. I therefore rarely allowed that duty to be performed by my colleagues. I cross-examined in general very little, and more with a view to enforce the facts I meant to rely upon than to affect the witness's credit,—for the most part a vain attempt."[2] Reed, one of the most sensible early 20th century writers on trial tactics, observed, "Sometimes a great speech bears down the adversary, and sometimes a searching cross-examination turns a witness inside out and shows him up to be a perjured villain. But ordinarily cases are not won by either speaking or cross-examining."[3] Even today most lawyers who write concerning the art of cross-examination believe that failure to use this tool effectively can lose a case. However, to the contemporary advocate, cross-examination is more important as a means of gleaning additional facts on the merits to support the cross-examiner's theory of the case; in the real world—as opposed to movies—the cross-examiner rarely destroys the credibility of an opposing witness. It is true that cross-examination of experts is critical in many cases. Federal Rule of Evidence 705 makes the opportunity to cross-examine particularly important when, as the rule permits on direct examination, an expert states only her opinion and the theoretical reasons for the opinion; in that situation, Rule 705 places the burden on the cross-examiner to expose the facts or data about the specific case on which the opinion is based. However, even in this context, the focus is ordinarily on the validity of the expert's reasoning process rather than the expert witness's personal credibility. In summary, while realistically cross-examination does not loom large as a determinant of victory in most cases, it can still be an important ingredient at some trials.

An evaluation of cross-examination as an engine for discovering truth should factor into

1. Quoted from Cox, The Advocate 434, in Reed, Conduct of Lawsuits 277 (2d ed. 1912).

2. Memoir of Lord Abinger 75, quoted in Reed, supra note 1 at 278.

3. Reed, supra note 1 at 276.

any discussion of the reform of American evidence law. The traditional assumption is that if opportunity for cross-examination is not afforded, the statement of a declarant or witness is so fatally lacking in reliability that it is not even worth hearing at trial. The traditional mindset is that the opportunity for cross-examination is indispensable. Obviously, cross-examination is a useful device to ensure greater accuracy and completeness in the witness's testimony; and in the hands of a skillful advocate, it will sometimes expose fraud or honest error. But it has its own potential for producing errors. It may be the honest but timid witness, rather than the rogue, who most often goes down under the fire of cross-examination. Every witness in judicial proceedings should in fairness be made available for cross-examination wherever feasible. However, it is overstated to presume that where cross-examination is impossible, as in the case of an out-of-court statement or a witness who dies before cross-examination, the statement or testimony should normally be excluded for that reason alone. Cross-examination ought to be considered useful, but not indispensable, as a means of discovering truth; and absence of opportunity to cross-examine should be only one relevant factor in determining whether the statement or testimony should be received. This reformist approach to hearsay problems might lead us to conclude that when opportunity to cross-examine a witness is permanently cut off without either party's fault, the direct testimony should nevertheless be received.[4] It might also prompt us to conclude that hearsay statements ought to be admitted if (1) the statement was made by the declarant on personal knowledge and reported by the witness at first hand, and if the declarant is now dead or unavailable for cross-examination or, (2) the declarant is alive and still available for cross-examination.[5] Perhaps written statements ought to be admitted wherever production for cross-examination can fairly be dispensed with.

Although this reformist viewpoint is supportable, there are special constitutional problems concerning the criminal defendant's right of cross-examination under the Fifth, Sixth, and Fourteenth Amendments.[6] Those constitutional guarantees may constrain the liberalization of cross-examination practice and the hearsay rule.

§ 32. Redirect and Subsequent Examinations

One who calls a witness is normally required to elicit on the witness's first direct examination all that he wishes to prove by him. This norm of proving everything so far as feasible at the first opportunity is in the interest of fairness and expedition. Whether the cross-examiner is limited to answering the direct is, as we have seen, a matter on which jurisdictions divide, with a much greater number favoring the restrictive rule.[1] However, as to the redirect and all subsequent examinations, there is no such division; the uniform practice is that the party's examination is typically limited to answering any new matter drawn out in the adversary's immediately preceding examination. It is true that the judge under his general discretionary power to vary the normal order of proof may permit the party to bring out on redirect examination relevant matter which through oversight he failed to elicit on direct. Under Federal Rule of Evidence 611(a), the judge has discretion over the scope of redirect. However, reply to new matter drawn out on cross-examination is the customary function of the redirect. Examination for this purpose is often deemed a matter of right, but even then its extent is subject to the judge's discretionary control.

A skillful re-examiner can frequently remove the sting of a seemingly lethal cross-examination. The reply on redirect may take the form of explanation, avoidance, or qualification of the new substantive facts or impeachment matters elicited by the cross-examiner. Suppose, for example, that on cross-examination, the witness conceded that he made an

4. Compare § 19, supra.
5. Compare Ch. 34, infra.
6. See § 19 supra, and § 252, infra.

§ 32

1. See § 21 supra.

apparently inconsistent statement. On redirect, the examiner might invite the witness to explain away the apparent inconsistency by telling the jury that he used a key term in the statement in a peculiar sense. The straightforward approach, such as "What did you mean by" or "What was your reason for" a witness's statement on cross-examination, is frequently effective. However, a mere reiteration of assertions previously made on the direct or cross-examination is usually prohibited, although the judge has discretion in this matter.

The re-examiner often invokes the rule of completeness,[2] permitting proof of the remainder of a transaction, conversation, or writing when a part has been proven by the adversary so far as the remainder relates to the same subject-matter. This principle is not abrogated by Federal Rule of Evidence 106. Moreover, the principle of curative admissibility,[3] under which irrelevant or incompetent evidence may sometimes be answered, is likewise frequently resorted to by the examiner on redirect.

Recross-examination, following the rule of first opportunity mentioned above, is normally confined to questions directed to explaining or avoiding new matter brought out on redirect.

2. See § 56 infra.

3. See § 57 infra.

Chapter 5

IMPEACHMENT AND SUPPORT

Table of Sections

§ 33. Introductory: The Stages of Impeachment and the Modes of Attack

Assume that a witness on the stand gives some testimony or that a counsel introduces an out-of-court declarant's hearsay statement as substantive evidence. As soon as the testimony or hearsay statement is admitted, the credibility of the witness or declarant becomes a fact of consequence within the range of dispute at trial under Federal Rule 401.

There are three groups of credibility rules. The first relates to the attempts by a witness's proponent to bolster the witness's credibility even before it has been impeached. The second concerns the various techniques which the opponent may employ to attack or impeach the witness's credibility. Finally, a third set of rules addresses the methods which the witness's proponent may use to rehabilitate the witness's credibility after impeachment, in effect to undo the damage done by impeachment.

Both at common law and under the Federal Rules, the general norm is that the witness's proponent may not bolster the witness's credibility before any attempted impeachment. For example, on direct examination it would be improper for the witness's proponent to elicit the witness's testimony that the witness "always tells the truth." There are some exceptional situations in which the witness's proponent is permitted to bring out bolstering evidence on direct examination. However, as a general proposition, bolstering evidence is inadmissible. As of the direct examination, it is uncertain whether the cross-examiner will attack the witness's credibility; the counsel might waive cross-examination or cross-examine solely for the purpose of eliciting new facts on the merits which support the counsel's theory of the case. If the opposing counsel does so, all the time devoted to the bolstering evidence on direct examination will have been wasted. For that reason, the witness's proponent must ordinarily hold information favorable to the witness's credibility in reserve for rehabilitation.

Although the common law was hostile to bolstering evidence, the common law and the Federal Rules liberally admit impeaching evidence. There are five main modes of attack upon a witness's credibility. The first, and probably most frequently employed, is self contradiction, that is, proof that the witness on a previous occasion has made statements inconsistent with his present testimony. The second is an attack showing that the witness is partial on account of emotional influences such as kinship for one party or hostility to another, or motives of pecuniary interest, whether legitimate or corrupt. The third is an attack on the witness's character, but lack of religious belief is not available as a basis of attack on credibility. The fourth is an attack showing a defect of the witness's capacity to observe, remember, or recount the matters testified about. The fifth is specific contradiction, that is, proof by other witnesses that material facts are otherwise than as testified to by the witness under attack.[1] Some of these attacks are not specifically or completely treated by the Federal or Revised Uniform Rules of Evidence, but nevertheless they are authorized by those rules. Article VI of the Federal Rules contains several provisions expressly regulating impeachment techniques such as proof of prior inconsistent statements, and the proof of other facts logically relevant to witness credibility is governed by the general analytic framework set out in Federal Rules 401–03.

The process of impeachment may proceed in two different stages. First, the facts discrediting the witness or his testimony may be elicited from the witness himself on cross-examination. A good faith basis for the inquiry is required. Certain modes of attack are limited to this stage; the shorthand expression is, "You must take his answer." When the mode of attack is limited in this manner, the cross-examiner is sometimes said to be restricted to "intrinsic" impeachment. Second, in other situations, the facts discrediting the witness may be proved by extrinsic evidence; the assailant waits until the time for putting on his own case in rebuttal, and then proves by a second witness or documentary evidence, the facts discrediting the testimony of the witness attacked.[2]

There is a cardinal rule of impeachment. Never launch an attack implying that the witness has lied deliberately, unless the attack is justifiable and essential to your case. An assault which fails often produces in the jury's mind an indignant sympathy for the intended victim. Unless you can show the jury that you have "the goods" on the witness, an aggressive attack on the witness can easily backfire.

In general, there is less emphasis on impeachment of witnesses today than formerly. The elaborate system of rules regulating impeachment which developed in the past is now applied with less strictness. The system has been simplified by confiding the control less to rules and more to judicial discretion. Again, Article VI of the Federal Rules contains only a handful of provisions expressly regulating impeachment techniques. In the case of all other impeachment techniques, a federal judge applies the general relevancy principles codified in Federal Rules 401–03.

§ 34. Prior Inconsistent Statements: Degree of Inconsistency Required

As § 33 noted, the most widely used impeachment technique is proof that the witness made a pretrial statement inconsistent with

§ 33

1. See § 49 infra.

2. See §§ 45 and 49 infra.

her trial testimony. This generalization certainly holds true in civil actions where pretrial depositions are commonplace. Sections 34 and 35 address the threshold question of whether there is sufficient inconsistency between the witness's trial testimony and a pretrial statement to allow the opponent to resort to this impeachment technique. Section 36 discusses the question of when the proof of the inconsistent statement is restricted to intrinsic impeachment, that is, cross-examination. Finally, assuming that the opponent is not confined to cross-examination, § 37 addresses the other conditions which the opponent must satisfy before presenting extrinsic evidence of the inconsistent statement.

Before turning to this impeachment technique, though, we must distinguish the technique from the related issue of the substantive use of prior inconsistent statements. When a witness testifies to facts material in a case, the opponent may have available proof that the witness previously made statements inconsistent with his present testimony. Under a modern view of the hearsay rule, some or all such previous statements are exempt from the rule and admissible as substantive evidence of the facts stated. This view is discussed in the chapter concerning hearsay.[1] However, under the more traditional views these previous statements will often be inadmissible as evidence of what they assert because they constitute hearsay and are not within any exemption from or exception to the hearsay rule.[2] Even though inadmissible hearsay as evidence of the facts asserted, they are nevertheless admissible for the limited purpose of impeaching the witness.[3] They may be admitted for that purpose with a limiting instruction. Subject to the exception that some prior inconsistent statements are exempt from the hearsay rule if they were made under oath subject to the penalty of perjury at a trial, hearing, or deposi-

tion, the Federal and Revised Uniform Rules of Evidence preserve this traditional view.

The treatment of inconsistent statements in this chapter is confined to the situation in which the statements are introduced for impeachment purposes but may not be used as substantive evidence (over proper objection of the opponent).[4] For this purpose, the making of the previous statements may be drawn out in cross-examination of the witness himself; and at common law if on cross-examination the witness denied making the statement or failed to remember it,[5] the statement may be proved by another witness. In contrast, under the Federal and Revised Uniform Rules of Evidence the making of the statement may also be brought out by the second witness without prior inquiry during the cross-examination of the witness who made it.[6] This form of impeachment is sometimes called "self-contradiction". It is to be distinguished from "specific contradiction" impeachment, the mere production of other evidence as to material facts conflicting with the testimony of the assailed witness. The mere production of other evidence conflicting with a witness's testimony is discussed in a later section.[7]

The attack by prior inconsistent statement is not based on the theory that the present testimony is false and the former statement true but rather upon the notion that talking one way on the stand and another way previously is blowing hot and cold, raising a doubt as to the truthfulness of both statements. Suppose that although at trial the witness testified that a car was going 70 miles an hour, pretrial she told the police that the car was going 50 miles an hour. The pretrial statement is relevant to the witness's credibility even if both that statement and the trial testimony are wrong. The fact *of* the inconsistent statement is relevant to the witness's credibility even when the fact *in* the statement—the car's asserted speed—is false. Even if in truth

§ 34

1. See § 251 infra.

2. See generally Chapter 24 infra.

3. The use of unconstitutionally obtained evidence for purposes of impeachment is discussed in § 182 infra.

4. The use of prior inconsistent statements as substantive evidence is discussed in § 251 infra.

5. See § 37 infra.

6. See § 37 infra. This discussion assumes the matter is noncollateral, §§ 36 and 49 infra.

7. See § 45 infra.

the car was going 60 miles an hour, the fact of the inconsistency shows that the witness is either uncertain or untruthful. In either event, the inconsistency calls into question the witness's believability. More particularly the prior statement, assuming it is inadmissible as substantive evidence under the hearsay rule, may be used in this context only as an aid in judging the credibility of the testimony inconsistent with the previous statement.[8] On request, the trial judge will give the jury a limiting instruction about the evidentiary status of the statement.

To create a doubt about the witness's credibility, what degree of inconsistency between the witness's testimony and his previous statement is required? The language of some cases is overstrict, suggesting that a contradiction must be found. Under the more widely accepted view, any material variance between the testimony and the previous statement suffices. The pretrial statement need "only bend in a different direction" than the trial testimony. Accordingly, if the prior statement omits a material fact presently testified to, which it would have been natural to mention in the statement, the statement is sufficiently inconsistent. In the same vein, a witness's earlier statement that he had no knowledge of facts now testified to, should be provable. The test should be, could the jury reasonably find that a witness who believed the truth of the facts testified to would have been unlikely to make a prior statement of this tenor? The Federal and Revised Uniform Rules of Evidence do not expressly prescribe a test for inconsistency. The more liberal standards for inconsistency should govern under these statutory schemes. Thus, if the previous statement is ambiguous and according to one meaning inconsistent with the testimony, it ought to be admitted for the jury's consideration. In applying the criterion of material inconsistency reasonable judges can differ, and a fair range of discretion must be accorded the trial judge. Instead of restricting the use of prior statements by a mechanical test

of inconsistency, the courts should lean toward receiving such statements in case of doubt, to aid in evaluating the testimony. The pretrial statements, indeed, having been made when memory was more recent and when less time for the play of influence had elapsed, are often more trustworthy than the testimony. A logical extension of this reasoning justifies the admission of prior testimony about an independent, unrelated event so strikingly similar to the present testimony as to arouse suspicion of fabrication.

§ 35. Prior Inconsistent Statements: Opinion in Form

The question addressed in this section is a variation of the issue analyzed in § 34: What type of pretrial statement may be considered "inconsistent" with a witness's trial testimony? If a witness, such as an expert, testifies in terms of opinion, all courts permit impeachment by showing the witness's previous expression of an inconsistent opinion. More troublesome is the question which arises when the witness testifies to specific facts but then is sought to be impeached by prior inconsistent expressions of opinion. For example, in a collision case the plaintiff's witness testifies to particular facts inculpating the bus driver involved in the accident. The defense proposes to show that just after seeing the collision, the witness said "The bus was not to blame." The witness's pretrial, opinionated statement is inconsistent with the effect or impression created by the witness's trial testimony. Is that enough?

Should the opinion rule be applied to exclude such an impeaching statement? The early, strict rule against opinions has been substantially relaxed in recent years.[1] What was once supposed to be a difference in kind between fact and opinion is now conceived as a mere difference in degree.[2] Wigmore considers that the rule goes no farther than excluding opinion as superfluous when more concrete

---

8. See Chapter 24 infra.

§ 35
1. See §§ 11, 12, 17 supra.
2. See §§ 11, 12 supra.

statements can be resorted to.[3] Thus, the principal value of the opinion rule is at trial as a regulation requiring the examining counsel to bring out his facts by more specific questions if practicable, before using more general ones. It is often a mistake to apply the rule to out-of-court statements, since the out-of-court declarant might be unavailable and the proponent may not have the option to eliciting the testimony in a more concrete form.[4] Moreover, when the out-of-court statement is not offered as evidence of the fact asserted but only to show the asserter's inconsistency, the essential purpose of the opinion rule, to improve the objectivity and hence reliability of testimonial assertions, is inapplicable. It is true that many earlier American decisions, influenced perhaps by a statement in Greenleaf[5] and a casual English holding at *nisi prius,*[6] and some later opinions exclude impeaching statements in opinion form. However, the trend and the majority view are in accord with the common-sense notion that if there is a substantial inconsistency, the form of the impeaching statement is immaterial. Federal and Revised Uniform Evidence Rule 701 lends support to that view by codifying a broad version of the opinion rule.

§ 36. Prior Inconsistent Statements: Extrinsic Evidence: Previous Statements as Substantive Evidence of the Facts Stated

Assume that there is sufficient inconsistency between the witness's pretrial statement and trial testimony to permit the opposing attorney to resort to this impeachment technique. The next question which arises is when will the attorney be restricted to cross-examination or "intrinsic" impeachment. On cross-examination strict rules of relevancy are relaxed.[1] Generally the trial judge in his discretion may permit the cross-examiner to inquire about any previous statements inconsistent with assertions, which the witness has testi-

fied to on direct or cross. At this stage, there is no categorical requirement that the previous impeaching statements must not deal with "collateral" matters; even if the matter has no relevance to the historical merits of the case, it bears on the witness's credibility, and credibility is in issue on cross. But as appears in the next paragraph, when the cross-examination inquiry is as to inconsistent statements about "collateral" matters, the cross-examiner must "take the answer"—he cannot later call other witnesses to prove the making of the alleged statement. This restriction, the collateral fact rule, evolved as a creature of case law, but some courts continue to enforce it under the Federal and Revised Uniform Rules of Evidence.

Extrinsic evidence, that is, the production of other witnesses, for impeachment by inconsistent statements, is restricted for obvious reasons of economy of time. The tag, "You cannot contradict as to collateral matters," applies. Here the tag means that to impeach by extrinsic proof of prior inconsistent statements, the statements must have as their subject facts relevant to the issues on the historical merits in the case. Although the Federal and Revised Uniform Rules of Evidence do not codify a categorical prohibition on the use of extrinsic evidence to impeach on collateral matters, the judge may factor the same policy considerations (for example, balancing probative worth against time consumption) into her analysis under Rule 403.

A distinct but somewhat cognate notion is the view that if a party interrogates a witness about a fact which would be favorable to the examiner if true, but receives a reply which is merely negative in its effect on examiner's case, the examiner may not by extrinsic evidence prove that the witness earlier stated that the fact was true as desired by the inquirer. An affirmative answer would have been material and subject to impeachment by an

---

3.   7 Wigmore, Evidence § 1918 (Chadbourn rev. 1978).

4.   See § 18 supra.

5.   Greenleaf, Evidence § 449 (3d ed. 1846).

6.   Elton v. Larkins, 5 Car. & P. 385, 172 Eng.Rep. 1020 (1832).

§ 36

1.   See § 29 supra.

inconsistent statement, but a negative answer is not damaging to the examiner, merely disappointing. The disappointing answer may not be impeached by extrinsic evidence; when the witness's only response is a negative answer, the opponent is limited to intrinsic impeachment on cross. In this situation the policy involved is not the saving of time and confusion, as before, but the protection of the other party against the risk that the jury will misuse the statement as substantive proof in violation of the hearsay rule. With respect to the Federal and Revised Uniform Rules of Evidence view, see § 38.

As previously indicated,[2] a witness's inconsistent statements are primarily treated in this chapter on the assumption that they are inadmissible as substantive evidence under the traditional hearsay rule still administered in numerous states and under the limited exemption in the Federal and Revised Uniform Rules of Evidence (1974) 801(d)(1). Of course, under that exemption or special hearsay exceptions in various jurisdictions, particular inconsistent prior statements of a witness may be admissible as substantive evidence as well as for impeachment purposes. More broadly, under another view, all prior inconsistent statements of a person available as a witness at the trial may be considered substantive evidence, not barred by the hearsay rule, and consequently not restricted to the purpose of impeachment. This latter view is discussed in § 251.

§ 37.　Prior Inconsistent Statements: Requirement of Preliminary Questions on Cross–Examination as "Foundation" for Proof by Extrinsic Evidence

Assume both that there is sufficient inconsistency between the witness's pretrial statement and trial testimony and that the collateral fact rule does not confine the counsel to intrinsic impeachment on cross-examination. Even on those assumptions, there may be further conditions which the counsel must satisfy before the judge will permit the introduction of extrinsic evidence of the inconsistent state-

ment. To be specific, before presenting the extrinsic evidence, the counsel might have to: (1) lay a foundation during the witness's cross-examination; and (2) elicit the witness's denial of making the inconsistent statement. At common law, the genesis for these conditions was *Queen Caroline's Case.*

In 1820 in the judges' answers in *Queen Caroline's Case,* it was announced: "If it be intended to bring the credit of a witness into question by proof of anything he may have said or declared touching the cause, the witness is first asked, upon cross-examination, whether or not he has said or declared that which is intended to be proved."[1] The announcement crystallized a practice which had previously been occasional and discretionary. Later the practice was almost universally accepted in this country. It came to be applied to both written and oral inconsistent statements.[2] The purposes of this traditional requirement are: to avoid unfair surprise to the adversary; to save time, since an admission by the witness may make extrinsic proof unnecessary; and to give the witness a fair chance to explain the discrepancy.

To satisfy the initial condition of a foundational question, the cross-examiner will ask the witness whether the witness made the alleged statement, giving its substance, and naming the time, the place, and the person to whom made. The purpose of this particularity is, of course, to refresh the witness's memory as to the supposed statement by reminding the witness of the accompanying circumstances. As a second condition, the witness's answer to the foundational question must necessitate the cross-examiner's resort to extrinsic evidence. If the witness denies making the statement or fails to admit it, for example by saying "I don't know" or "I don't remember", the element of necessity is satisfied; and the cross-examiner, at the next stage of giving evidence, may prove the making of the alleged statement. When, however, the witness unequivocally admits making the statement, may the cross-examiner

---

2. See § 34 supra.

§ 37

1. 2 Brod. & Bing. 284, 313, 129 Eng.Rep. 976 (1820).

2. See § 28 supra.

still choose to prove it again by another witness? Wigmore, with some support, suggests that the cross-examiner may. However, the prevailing view is to the contrary, and in the usual situation this seems the more expedient practice.

Under Federal and Revised Uniform Rule 613, the only requirements for introducing a witness's prior inconsistent written or oral statements are that (1) while questioning the witness concerning written statements or the substance of the statements, they shall be shown or disclosed to the opposing counsel upon request, and (2) at some point in time— even after the introduction of the extrinsic evidence—the witness is afforded a chance to deny or explain the statement, and opposing counsel shall have the opportunity to question the witness about the statement. Even the witness's opportunity to explain or deny later and the opposing counsel's opportunity to question later can be dispensed with in the judge's discretion "in the interests of justice." For instance, if despite the exercise of reasonable diligence the counsel did not discover the witness's inconsistent statement until after the witness was permanently excused from further testimony, on balance it serves the interest of substantive justice to permit counsel to introduce extrinsic evidence of the statement.

Thus, on their face, the Federal and Revised Uniform Rules of Evidence adopt a liberal view, abolishing the rigid notion that the witness must on cross-examination be shown an inconsistent statement or be advised of its contents before being questioned about its substance. Rule 613 abandons the traditional requirement that the foundation questions be put to the witness on cross-examination before extrinsic evidence of the statement is introduced, i.e., before other witnesses testify to it or before an inconsistent writing is introduced. As the Advisory Committee's Note to Federal Rule 613 indicates, "[t]he traditional insistence that the attention of the witness be directed to the statement on cross-examination is relaxed in favor of simply providing the witness an opportunity to explain and the opposite party an opportunity to examine on the statement, with no specification of any particular time or sequence." The Note approvingly cites California Evidence Code § 770 expressly allowing the counsel attacking the witness's credibility to offer extrinsic evidence of an inconsistent statement so long as the witness is excused subject to recall; excusing the witness in that manner obviates the need for any foundation during the witness's cross-examination. The Advisory Committee's Note suggests that Rule 613 facilitates the questioning of collusive witnesses by permitting several such witnesses to be examined before disclosure of a joint prior inconsistent statement. Such joint inconsistent statements are rare. That rather infrequent benefit hardly explains Rule 613's general dispensation with the requirement that a foundation be laid on cross-examination. According to the Note, the rationale for Rule 613's general dispensation derives from two factors: (1) Rule 801(d)(1), as proposed by the Advisory Committee and the Supreme Court, gave substantive effect to all prior inconsistent statements, and (2) perceived lawyer incompetence.

To understand why the Advisory Committee originally proposed Rule 613, one must keep in mind that if prior inconsistent statements are admissible only for purposes of impeachment, the traditional foundation requirement serves the useful function of fostering the use of such statements as to credibility while discouraging the trier of fact from giving them substantive consideration. In practice, the foundation requirement placed a prior statement in immediate juxtaposition to the trial testimony of the witness sought to be impeached. In addition, by enabling the witness to admit a prior statement, the foundation requirement reduced the likelihood that extrinsic evidence of the prior inconsistent statement will be introduced—extrinsic evidence that is much harder for the jury not to treat substantively. Under the scheme of the proposed evidence rules, as initially drafted by the Advisory Committee however, all prior inconsistent statements were to be admissible as substantive evidence pursuant to Rule 801(d)(1). Positing the substantive admissibility of all such prior statements, the function served by the foundation requirement was obsolete, and a more practical consideration became paramount. Again according to the Note, the practicality was that trial lawyers often forget to lay or in some cases never learned how to lay a proper foundation for extrinsic evidence. The Advisory Committee politely referred to such forgetfulness or incompetence as "oversight." With substantive admissibility, these "oversight[s]" could be legitimized by permitting introduction of prior inconsistent statements at any time so long as the witness was eventually given an opportunity to deny or explain.

However, as finally enacted by Congress, Rule 801(d)(1) does not sanction the substantive admission of all prior inconsistent statements. Congress balked at embracing the Advisory Committee's position. Under the final versions of Rules 613 and 801 as at common law, some inconsistent statements are admissible only for the limited purpose of impeachment. Thus the traditional foundation requirements' utility in encouraging the jury to consider a prior inconsistent statement solely as an indication of credibility and not as substantive evidence remains relevant. Since all prior inconsistent statements are not substantively admissible, counsel should not have the unfettered right to introduce extrinsic evidence of the statement before the witness has an opportunity to admit, deny, or explain the declaration. Earlier introduction of extrinsic evidence places a prior statement before the trier of fact on multiple occasions under circumstances implicitly inviting the statement's treatment as substantive evidence. Accordingly, a strong case can be constructed that federal courts and state courts operating under an identical scheme should require under Rules 403 and 611 that the traditional foundation be laid on cross-examination before the introduction of extrinsic evidence of prior statements admissible solely to impeach unless the interests of justice otherwise require. Several courts have held that under the statutes, they possess the discretion to mandate that the cross-examiner follow the traditional practice. Indeed, some authorities assert that "most

(though not all) of the circuits" which have passed on the question still adhere to "the traditional common law requirement" for a foundation on cross.

If the witness attacked is not on the stand but the testimony introduced was given at a deposition or some other trial, at common law most prior decisions otherwise applying the traditional requirements exclude the inconsistent statement unless the foundation question was asked at the prior hearing. In this situation, at the judge's discretion, the Federal and Revised Uniform Rule 613 should not require the opportunity for any denial or explanation by the witness or questioning by the opposing counsel. Even when otherwise applicable, the traditional requirements ought to be abandoned in the case of depositions based upon written interrogatories (which must be prepared in advance) and inconsistent statements made after the prior testimony was taken.

If a party takes the stand as a witness, and the adversary desires to use the party's prior inconsistent statement, the statement is receivable in two aspects, first as the admission of the opposing party,[3] and second, as an inconsistent statement to impeach the witness. In the first aspect, it is relevant to the factual issues on the historical merits of the case; in the second aspect, it is not. Yet even in jurisdictions requiring traditional foundation questions for impeachment, the prevailing view is that the requirement is inapplicable. There is less danger of surprising a party than a witness, and the party will have ample opportunity to deny or explain after the inconsistent statement is proved; as a litigant, the party can simply call himself as a witness later. In these jurisdictions the courts on occasion inadvertently assume that the requirement applies to the party-witness. Sometimes courts have imposed the requirement if the proponent offers the statement only for impeachment, and one appellate court held the trial judge has discretion to impose the requirement for a foundation question as prerequisite to proof of a party-witness admission. These petty qualifications are hardly worth their salt. In jurisdic-

---

3. See Chapter 26 infra.

tions which otherwise require the foundation question, the more sensible practice is dispensing with the "foundation" entirely for parties' admissions.

Federal and Revised Uniform Rule 613 have nothing to do with the introduction into evidence of parties' admissions, even if the admissions have some effect on the party's credibility as a witness. Nor do the rules have any impact upon the introduction of a hearsay statement pursuant to a hearsay exception contained in Federal and Revised Uniform Rules 803 when the out of court declarant testifies. However, Federal and Revised Uniform Rule 613 applies when a prior inconsistent statement is admitted as substantive evidence solely by virtue of Federal and Revised Uniform Rule 801(d)(1)(A); the terms of Rule 801(d)(1)(A) render 613 applicable because they expressly refer to statements admitted as being "inconsistent with the declarant's [trial] testimony. . . . "

Again in jurisdictions in which a foundation question is required but the cross-examiner overlooks it, the judge should have discretion to consider such factors as the cross-examiner's ignorance of the inconsistent statement when the witness was cross-examined, the importance of the testimony under attack, and the practicability of recalling the witness. After weighing these factors, the judge ought to permit the impeachment without the foundation or allow departure from the traditional time sequence if it seems fairer to do so.

§ 38. Prior Inconsistent Statements: Rule Against Impeaching One's Own Witness

The case law voucher rule forbidding a party to impeach her own witness is of obscure origin. It is probably a late manifestation of the evolution of the common law trial procedure from an inquisitorial to a contentious or adversary system. The prohibition was general, applying to all forms of impeachment. It applied not only to attack by inconsistent statements but to attack on character or a showing of bias, interest, or corruption. It did not, however, forbid the party to introduce other evidence to specifically contradict the facts testified to by her witness.

Among the reasons (or rationalizations) advanced for the rule are, first, that the party by calling the witness vouches for the witness's trustworthiness, and second, that the power to impeach is the power to coerce the witness to testify as desired, under the implied threat of assassinating the witness's character if the witness does not. Both rationales are flawed. The answer to the first reason is that, except in a few instances such as character witnesses or experts, the party has little or no choice of witnesses. The party must call those who happen to have observed the particular facts in controversy. You take your witnesses as you find them. The answers to the second reason are that (a) it applies only to two kinds of impeachment, the attack on character and the showing of corruption, and (b) to forbid the attack by the calling party leaves the party at the mercy of the witness and the adversary. When the truth lies on the side of the calling party but the witness's character is bad, the witness may be attacked by the adversary if the witness tells the truth; but when the witness tells a lie, the adversary will not attack, and the calling party, under the rule, cannot. The voucher rule should not be carried to an absurd extreme; if the witness has been bribed to change the story, the calling party should certainly be allowed to disclose this fact to the court.

As previously stated, the most frequently used kind of impeachment is by inconsistent statements. Most voucher cases involve this type of impeachment. It is difficult to see any justification for prohibiting this sort of showing as to a witness who has testified contrary to a previous position. Perhaps there is a fear that the previous statement will be misused by the jury as substantive evidence of the facts asserted if, as in various jurisdictions, the use of the statement for that purpose would be inadmissible hearsay.[1] Except in those jurisdictions which have altogether abandoned it, the common law rule against impeaching one's

§ 38
1. See § 251 infra.

own witness persists for the most part with respect to proof of bias and attacks upon character. It has been relaxed in a number of jurisdictions by statute or decision insofar as it prohibits impeachment by inconsistent statements. A provision in the draft of the 1849 Field Code of Civil Procedure bore fruit in the 1854 English Common Law Procedure Act, as follows (St. 17 & 18 Vict. c. 125, § 22): "[1] A party producing a witness shall not be allowed to impeach his credit by general evidence of bad character; [2] but he may, in case the witness shall in the opinion of the judge prove adverse, [3] contradict him by other evidence, [4] or by leave of the judge prove that he has made at other times a statement inconsistent with his present testimony." This statute was copied in a few states. Other states, following the example of Massachusetts, adopted the English statute but omitted the statutory condition that the witness must have proved "adverse." Some courts reached a similar result by decision.

These statutes and decisions open the door to the most important type of impeachment of one's own witness, namely, prior inconsistent statements. But whether the reform is effected by statute or decision, two troublesome limitations have been imposed by some courts. The first is that the party seeking to impeach must show that she is surprised at the witness's testimony. The second is that she cannot impeach unless the witness's testimony is positively harmful or adverse to her cause, worse than a mere failure ("I do not remember," "I do not know") to give expected favorable testimony. A mere failure is simply disappointing, not positively damaging to her case.[2] These limitations are explicable only as attempts to safeguard the hearsay policy preventing the party from proving the witness's prior statement in situations where it appears that its only real value to the proponent will be as substantive evidence of the facts asserted. The rule against substantive use of the statements, and the debatable soundness of its policy, is the subject of a subsequent section.[3]

The voucher rule prohibiting the impeachment of one's own witness is being abandoned in more and more jurisdictions. Its repeal is accomplished by Federal and Revised Uniform Rule of Evidence (1974) 607. The standard methods of impeachment are permitted under these rules. There is some dispute whether and under what circumstances impeachment of one's own witness is impermissible because of prejudice to the opposing party, particularly in criminal cases. It has been widely held that a criminal prosecutor may not employ a prior inconsistent statement to impeach a witness as a "mere subterfuge" or for the "*primary*" purpose" of placing before the jury substantive evidence which is otherwise inadmissible. Application of the "mere subterfuge" or "*primary* purpose" doctrine focuses on the content of the witness's testimony as a whole. If the witness's testimony is useful to establish any fact of consequence significant in the context of the litigation, the witness may be impeached by means of a prior inconsistent statement as to any other matter testified to. In the words of one commentator, the pivotal question is whether the "party [is] calling a witness with the reasonable expectation that the witness will testify something helpful to the party's case aside from the prior inconsistent statement." While the power to attack the character of one's own witness may often be of little value to the attacker, subject to the foregoing limitation, a rule against showing prior inconsistent statements of one's own witness to aid in evaluating the witness's testimony is a serious obstruction to the ascertainment of truth, even in criminal cases. A criminal defendant could even urge that forbidding him from attacking a defense witness is unconstitutional in particular instances.[4]

§ 39. Partiality

Case law recognizes the slanting effect on human testimony of the witness's emotions or feelings toward the parties or the witness's self-interest in the outcome of the case. Partiality, or any acts, relationships, or motives reasonably likely to produce it, may be proved

---

2. See § 36, supra.

3. § 251 infra.

4. Chambers v. Mississippi, 410 U.S. 284 (1973).

to impeach credibility. While Article VI of the Federal Rules of Evidence does not explicitly refer to attacking the witness by showing bias, interest, corruption, or coercion, it authorizes the use of that ground of impeachment. The inclusion of Article VI in the Federal Rules reflects the fact that a witness's credibility is a fact of consequence under Rule 401; and Rule 402 states that evidence logically relevant to a fact of consequence is admissible unless there is a statutory basis for exclusion. Thus, Rule 402 is the only statutory authorization needed for the continued use of the bias impeachment technique in federal practice. In criminal cases the defendant has a qualified constitutional right to show the bias of government witnesses. In any event, a good faith basis in fact for the inquiry is required.[1]

The kinds and sources of partiality are too varied to be reviewed exhaustively, but a few of the common instances will be mentioned. *Favor* or friendly feeling toward a party may be evidenced by family or business relationship, employment by a party or the party's insurer, sexual relations, shared membership in an organization, or the witness's conduct or expressions evincing such feeling. It is commonly held in collision cases that when a witness appears for defendant, the fact that he made a claim against the defendant and has been paid a sum in settlement tends to show bias in defendant's favor.[2] Similarly, *hostility* toward a party may be evidenced by the fact that the witness has had a fight or quarrel with him, has a lawsuit pending against him, has contributed to the defense, or employed special counsel to aid in prosecuting the party. In criminal cases, the witness's attitude toward the victim sheds light on his feeling about the charge. The witness's *self-interest* is manifest when he is himself a party or a surety on the debt sued on. Similarly, it may be shown that he is being paid by a party to give evidence, even though payment in excess of regular witness fees may as in the case of an expert be entirely lawful. *Self-interest* may also be shown in a criminal case when the witness testifies for the state and an indictment is pending against him, the witness has not been charged with a crime, has been promised leniency, has been granted immunity, is awaiting sentence, is being held in protective custody, or is an accomplice or co-indictee in the crime on trial. Self-interest in an extreme form may be manifest in the witness's *corrupt* activity such as seeking to bribe another witness, taking or offering to take a bribe to testify falsely, or making similar baseless charges on other occasions. The trial court has a great deal of discretion in deciding whether particular evidence indicates partiality. A large majority of appellate decisions examined approve the trial judge's ruling on this score.

Foundational question on cross-examination. At common law, a majority of the courts impose the requirement of a foundation question as in the case of impeachment by prior inconsistent statements. Before the witness can be impeached by calling other witnesses to prove acts or declarations showing partiality, the witness under attack must first be asked about these facts during cross-examination. There is pre-Rules federal case authority to this effect. Fairness to the witness is most often given as the reason for the requirement, but the saving of time by making unnecessary the extrinsic evidence seems even more important. Some courts, analogizing to inconsistent statements, distinguish between declarations and conduct evidencing partiality and require the preliminary question for the former but not as to the latter. However, as suggested in a leading English case, words and conduct are usually intermingled in proof of partiality, and "nice and subtle distinctions" should be avoided in shaping this rule. It is better require a "foundation" as to both or neither. Jurisdictions imposing the requirement ought to recognize a discretion in the judge to dispense with it when matters of indisputable relationship, such as kinship, are concerned, where the foundation was overlooked and it is infeasible to recall the witness, or where other exceptional circumstances make it unfair to insist on the prerequisite.

§ 39

1. See § 49 infra.

2. See § 266 infra.

At common law a minority of holdings do not require any foundational question on cross-examination of the principal witness as a preliminary to the introduction of extrinsic evidence of partiality. The Federal and Revised Uniform Rules (1974) are silent on the subject. The discretion granted the judge in Rule 611(a) is adequate authority to follow the same pattern for partiality as that employed for prior inconsistent statements under Rule 613(b). Given Rule 402, the judge could not announce the practice as a categorical, invariable requirement; but she could requires a foundation if the specific facts of the instant case warranted. Following the preferred method for impeachment by a prior inconsistent statement,[3] on cross-examination the witness under attack would first be asked about the acts or statements showing partiality.

Cross-examination and extrinsic evidence; main circumstances. In many states the impeacher must inquire as to the facts of partiality on cross-examination as the first step in impeachment. If the witness fully admits the facts, the impeacher should not be allowed to prolong the attack by calling other witnesses to the admitted facts. At the very least, when the main circumstances from which the partiality proceeds have been proven, the trial judge has a discretion to determine how far the details may be probed, whether on cross-examination or by other witnesses. After all, impeachment is not relevant to the historical merits of the case; and the trial judge, though he may not deny a reasonable opportunity at either stage to prove the witness's partiality, has a discretion to control the extent to which the proof may go. He has the responsibility to see that the sideshow does not take over the circus. The existence of this discretion is confirmed by several cases under the Federal Rules of Evidence. It follows from the trial judge's power to "exercise reasonable control" under the terms of Rule 611(a). On the other hand, if the witness on cross-examination denies or does not fully admit the facts claimed

to show bias, the attacker has the need and right to prove those facts by extrinsic evidence. In courtroom parlance, facts showing bias are considered so highly probative of credibility that they are not deemed 'collateral'"; the cross-examiner is not required to "take the answer" of the witness,[4] but may call other witnesses to prove them. There are similar holdings under the Federal Rules of Evidence.

§ 40. Character: In General

The witness's character for truthfulness or mendacity is relevant circumstantial evidence on the question of the truthfulness of the witness's testimony. The fact that the witness previously engaged in deception tends to show the witness has a character trait for untruthfulness, and in turn the existence of that character trait at least slightly increases the probability that the witness lied during his testimony. The subject of character-impeachment raises several balancing questions, notably these: How far in any particular situation does the danger of unfair prejudice against the witness and the party calling her from this type of impeachment outweigh the probative value of the light shed on credibility? Should character-impeachment be limited to an attack on the particular trait of truthfulness, or should it extend to "general" character for its undoubted though more remote bearing upon truthfulness, on the notion that the greater includes the lesser?[1]

The growing tendency is to use this form of attack more sparingly. The empirical studies of untruthfulness indicate that a person's general character trait for truthfulness is a poor predictor of whether she is untruthful on a specific occasion. It was part of the melodrama of the pioneer trial to find "the villain of the piece." It fits less comfortably into the more businesslike atmosphere of the modern courtroom. Moreover, as a method of advocacy, the danger to the attacker is great if the attack fails of its mark or is pressed too far. Finally,

---

3. See § 37.

4. See references to "taking the answer" in § 36 supra and §§ 45 and 49 infra.

§ 40

1. See the general discussion of relevancy and its counterweights in Ch. 16 infra, and of the relevancy of character evidence in various other situations in Ch. 17 infra.

the legal ethics rules reinforce the trial advocacy lesson; lawyers must be conscious of their duty not to ask a question that the lawyer believes is relevant only to degrade a witness.

§ 41   Character: Misconduct, for Which There Has Been No Criminal Conviction

The methods of proving a witness's character trait for untruthfulness include prior convictions (discussed in § 42) and proof of untruthful acts which have not resulted in a conviction, the subject of this section. As we shall see, evidence of prior convictions is more liberally admissible than the latter type of proof of bad character for truthfulness. The differential treatment of the two types of evidence is justifiable. To begin with, when the witness has already been convicted of the act, there is strong evidence that the witness in fact committed the act calling his credibility into issue. Moreover, the availability of the written judgment of conviction reduces the risk that there will be a time-consuming, potentially distracting dispute over the question of whether the witness committed the act. In terms of the policy considerations recognized in Federal Rule of Evidence 403, there is a much stronger case for permitting conviction impeachment.

Yet, the English common law tradition of "cross-examination to credit" permits counsel to inquire into the witness's associations and personal history including any misconduct tending to discredit his character, though it has not been the basis of a conviction. (This is the kind of misconduct referred to in this section unless otherwise indicated.) Under the common law tradition the courts trusted the bar's disciplined discretion to avoid abuses. In this country, there is a confusing variety of decisions, occasionally even in the same jurisdiction. At present, however, the majority of courts limit the cross-examination attack on character to acts which have a significant relation to the witness's credibility. By its terms,

Federal Rule 608(b) permits the cross-examiner to inquire about acts which "refer only to [the witness's] character for ... untruthfulness...."[1] However, some courts permit a broader attack upon character by fairly wide-open cross-examination about acts of misconduct which show bad moral character and have only an attenuated relation to credibility. Finally, at the other extreme, several jurisdictions prohibit altogether cross-examination as to acts of misconduct for impeachment purposes; the cross-examiner must have a conviction. This latter view is arguably the fairest and most expedient because of the dangers of prejudice (particularly if the witness is a party), of distraction and confusion, of abuse by asking unfounded questions, and of the difficulties, as demonstrated in the appellate cases, of determining whether particular acts relate to character for truthfulness.

This impeachment technique should be distinguished from showing conduct which indicates partiality, conduct as an admission, and conduct for impeachment by contradiction.[2]

In this country, the danger of victimizing witnesses and of undue prejudice to the parties has led most courts permitting this impeachment technique to recognize that cross-examination concerning acts of misconduct is subject to the trial judge's discretionary control. To emphasize the existence of that control, Rule 608(b) expressly uses the phrase "in the discretion of the court." Some of the factors that sway discretion are (1) whether the witness's testimony is crucial or unimportant, (2) the relevancy of the act of misconduct to truthfulness, (3) the nearness or remoteness of the misconduct to the time of trial, (4) whether the matter inquired into is likely to lead to time-consuming, distracting explanations on cross-examination or re-examination, and (5) whether there will be unfair humiliation of the witness and undue prejudice. A good faith

<hr>

§ 41

1. See § 42 infra.

2. See § 39 supra re partiality, §§ 261–67 infra re admissions by conduct, and § 45 infra re impeachment by contradiction. Inconsistent conduct is yet another subject. See § 37 supra.

basis in fact for the inquiry is always required.[3]

In the formative period of evidence law, there came to be recognized, as a sort of vague corollary of the privilege against self-incrimination, a witness's privilege not to answer questions calling for answers which would degrade or disgrace him, provided such questions were immaterial to the historical merits in the case. Though sporadically recognized during the 1800s, today that privilege has been generally abandoned, except as it is preserved by the codes of a few states. Although the privilege affords the witness some protection, the protection is not as effective as that given by a rule altogether prohibiting such cross-examination; the privilege must be claimed by the witness, and a claim in open court is almost as degrading as an affirmative answer. Taking a somewhat intermediate position, Federal and Revised Uniform Rule of Evidence (1974) 611(a) gives the court discretion to prevent harassment or embarrassment of witnesses when they are cross-examined about acts of misconduct.

In jurisdictions permitting character-impeachment by proof of misconduct for which there has been no conviction, an important safeguard is the accepted rule limiting proof to intrinsic impeachment, that is, cross-examination. Thus, if the witness stands his ground and denies the alleged misconduct, the examiner must "take his answer." Not that he may not further cross-examine to extract an admission, for instance, by reminding the witness of the penalties for perjury; but in the sense that he may not call other witnesses to prove the discrediting acts.[4] This limitation is adopted by Federal Rule of Evidence 608(b). On the one hand, on cross-examination, the questioner should ask the witness directly and bluntly whether he committed the untruthful act. It is improper to inquire whether the witness was "fired," "disciplined," or "demoted" for the alleged act—those terms smuggle into the record implied hearsay statements by third parties who may lack personal knowledge. On the

other hand, if the witness himself authored a writing mentioning the act, by the better view it is permissible for the cross-examiner to confront the witness with the writing. The principal rationale for the collateral fact rule is that the presentation of extrinsic evidence on collateral matters entails an undue consumption of trial time. However, when the witness is competent to authenticate the writing in question during cross, there is little expenditure of additional time. Thus, it does not serve the purpose of the rule to apply it in this situation.

Another important curb is the privilege against self-incrimination. A witness who without objecting makes a partial disclosure of incriminating matter cannot later invoke the privilege when asked to complete the disclosure.[5] However, the mere act of testifying does not waive the privilege as to criminal activities relevant solely to attacking his credibility. While an accused, unlike an ordinary witness, has an option whether to testify at all, exacting a waiver as the price of taking the stand leaves little to the right to testify in one's own behalf. Therefore Federal Rule of Evidence and Revised Uniform Rule of Evidence 608(b) provide that the giving of testimony by any witness, including an accused, does not waive the privilege as to matters relating only to credibility.

§ 42. Character: Conviction of Crime

At common law a person's conviction of treason, any felony, or a misdemeanor involving dishonesty or false statement (crimen falsi) or the obstruction of justice, rendered the convict altogether incompetent as a witness. These were said to be "infamous" crimes. By statutes or rules virtually universal in the common law world, this primitive absolutism has been abandoned; the disqualification for conviction of crime has been abrogated, and by specific provision or decision it has been reduced to a mere ground for impeaching credibility. Unfortunately, just as the common law definition of disqualifying crimes was not very

---

3. See § 49 infra.

4. See also § 49 infra.

5. For more detailed discussion, see § 140 infra.

precise, the abrogating statutes and rules suffer from indefiniteness. In particular, the definitions of crimes for which a conviction shall be ground of impeachment vary widely among the states that have not adopted Federal Rule of Evidence 609.

This section initially discusses the types of convictions which may be used for purposes of impeachment and the related question of the judge's discretion to bar the use of an otherwise admissible conviction. The section then takes up the topic of the mechanics of this impeachment technique, including the use of written copies of convictions and the degree to which the cross-examiner may elicit the underlying details of the criminal act.

The types of convictions usable for impeachment. A rule strictly limiting impeachment to conviction of crimes involving dishonesty or false statement would be fairly definite and simple for administrative purposes. It would also have the virtue that it is not an entirely arbitrary criterion.

The federal statutory scheme is more complex. The Federal Rule governing impeachment by proof of conviction of crime is the product of compromise. Under Rule 609(a)(2), crimes of "dishonesty or false statement," regardless of the imposable punishment, may be used against any witness, including an accused. Other misdemeanor-grade crimes (punishable by less than imprisonment in excess of one year) are never usable. Under Rule 609(a)(1), against an accused who takes the stand, felony-grade crimes (punishable by death or imprisonment in excess of one year) may be used, if the court determines that the probative value of the conviction outweighs its prejudicial effect to the defendant. In civil cases or against all criminal witnesses other than the accused, 609(a)(1) crimes are usable unless under the normal Rule 403 standard the court determines that the probative value of the conviction is substantially outweighed by its prejudicial effect. Crimes involving "dishonesty or false statement," regardless of the punishment or against whom used, do not require balancing of probative value against prejudice; under 609(a)(2), they are automatically admissible.

The meaning of the phrase "dishonesty and false statement" in Rule 609(a)(2) has been subject to debate. The Report of the Conference Committee stated:

> By the phrase "dishonesty and false statement" the Conference means crimes such as perjury or subornation of perjury, false statement, criminal fraud, embezzlement, or false pretense, or any other offense in the nature of crimen falsi, the commission of which involves some element of deceit, untruthfulness, or falsification bearing on the accused's propensity to testify truthfully.

Arguably, given the language in the Report of the Conference Committee limiting the phrase "dishonesty or false statement" to offenses involving crimen falsi, the courts should ascribe little meaning to the term "dishonesty" with the possible exception of embezzlement. The controversy initially surfaced in reported decisions trying to determine whether the term "dishonesty or false statement" applied to convictions involving petty larceny, robbery, shoplifting and narcotics. Notwithstanding that controversy, it quickly became settled that crimes involving solely the use of force such as assault and battery, and crimes such as drunkenness and prostitution do not involve "dishonesty or false statement," while the crime of fraud does. In 1990, when Rule 609 was amended, the Advisory Committee issued a new Note to the rule. The Note expresses disapproval of the minority of cases which read Rule 609(a)(2) broadly as including theft offenses.

Especially after the 1990 amendment, the pattern that has emerged in the cases evidences a willingness to follow the Conference Committee Report. Hence, the trend is to restrict "dishonesty or false statement" to a crime "which involves some element of deceit, untruthfulness, or falsification bearing on the accused's propensity to testify truthfully." Several additional crimes have now been held on their face to meet this definition. However, federal courts and most state courts are unwilling to classify offenses such as petty larceny, shoplifting, robbery, possession of a weapon, and narcotic violations as per se crimes of "dishonesty or false statement." Without more, a post-offense attempt to remain unde- tected does not convert the offense into a crime involving dishonesty or false statement.

Suppose that the party wishing to employ a conviction not considered per se a crime of "dishonesty or false statement" can show by going behind the judgment that the particular offense was perpetrated by deceit, untruthful- ness or falsification, i.e., involved some ele- ment of active misrepresentation. On that sup- position, the prior conviction perhaps could be employed to impeach credibility. Many juris- dictions, though, do not permit the party to go beyond the judgment. As previously stated, the courts are receptive to this impeachment tech- nique in part because the use of the written judgment reduces the risk of undue time con- sumption. If the parties were allowed to go behind the judgment, the amount of time en- tailed by this technique could increase dramat- ically.

Convictions in any state or in federal court are usable to impeach. The trend is to hold that a conviction is sufficiently final as soon as the guilty verdict is entered even if sentence has not been imposed yet. The fact of the conviction establishes the witness's com- mission of the underlying act; and for that purpose, the verdict is sufficient. Though a judgment against a lawyer of suspension or disbarment for criminal misconduct is not technically a conviction, there is authority that it is provable to impeach. Statutes relating to juvenile court proceedings frequently provide that a finding of delinquency shall not be used in evidence against the child in any other court and is not deemed a "conviction." These statutes are usually construed as precluding the finding from being employed to impeach credibility. In various jurisdictions, as under the Federal Rules of Evidence, this matter is dealt with in detail by evidence rules or stat- utes. Sometimes juvenile adjudications are ad- missible under such provisions.

By case law, a pardon does not prevent the use of the conviction to impeach. The Federal Rules of Evidence adopt the same rule under stated conditions. The primary condi-

tion is that under Rule 609(c)(2), a pardon bars the use of the conviction if the pardon "or other equivalent procedure" was "based on a finding of innocence." By the predominant view, including the Federal Rules of Evidence, the pendency of an appeal does not preclude the use of the conviction. Most courts hold that lapse of time may prevent use of a convic- tion too remote in time from trial when the judge in his discretion finds that under the circumstances it lacks probative value. The Federal Rule of Evidence is more specific; un- der Rule 609(b), convictions are presumptively considered remote and inadmissible when more than 10 years have elapsed. Case author- ity is divided over the use of a judgment based upon a plea of *nolo contendere*. The Federal Rule of Evidence should be interpreted as per- mitting its use.

The mechanics of using the conviction for impeachment. Assume that the conviction in question is usable for impeachment purposes. What mechanical steps should the attorney follow to employ the conviction for that pur- pose? The general rule in other situations is that if feasible, proof of an official record must be made by a certified or examined copy in preference to oral testimony of its contents. That rule was applied in England to proof of records of conviction, precluding the cross-ex- aminer from asking about convictions. This practice still lingers in a few states. However, the inconvenience of the requirement, and the obvious reliability of the witness's answer ac- knowledging his own conviction, have led most jurisdictions, by statute, rule, or decision, to permit the proof by either production of the record or a copy, or the oral statement of the convicted witness himself. Here the cross-ex- aminer need not "lay a foundation" for proof by copy or record. Nor is he bound to "take the answer" if the witness denies the convic- tion, but may prove it by the record. It is a common tactic for the party who calls a wit- ness with a provable criminal record to bring out the prior conviction on direct examination. This practice was never viewed as true im- peachment of a party's own witness but rather as anticipatory disclosure designed to reduce the prejudicial effect of the evidence if revealed for the first time on cross-examination.[1] It is "a time-honored trial tactic" to attempt to beat the opposing attorney to the punch; when the witness's proponent discloses the impeaching fact on direct, the jury may have a higher regard to the proponent's candor, and the disclosure might take some of the sting out of the later cross-examination. Anticipatory disclosure is particularly common when the criminal defendant testifies on his own behalf.

How far may the cross-examiner go in his inquiries about convictions? There is consensus that he may ask about the name of the crime committed, i.e. murder or embezzlement. It would certainly add to the pungency of the impeachment where the crime was an aggravated one if he could also ask about any lurid circumstances, for example, whether the murder victim was both a baby and the witness's own niece. It has been suggested by a few courts that since proof by record is allowable, cross-examination should be permitted to touch all the facts that the record mentions. On the whole, however, the more reasonable position, minimizing prejudice and distraction from the issues, restricts the cross-examiner to the basic facts reflected on the very face of the judgment: the name of the crime, the time and place of conviction, and sometimes the punishment. Further details such as the victim's name and the aggravating circumstances may not be inquired into unless the specific circumstance in question is independently admissible under another theory of logical relevance such as Rule 404(b) or 608(b).

It could be argued that if the impeacher is foreclosed from showing details and circumstances of aggravation, even-handedness dictates that the witness similarly be precluded from explaining or extenuating the conviction or denying his guilt. It is unquestionably impractical and forbidden to retry the case on which the conviction was based. Many cases prohibit any explanation, extenuation, or denial of guilt even by the witness himself on redirect. This prohibition is a logical consequence of the premise of finality or conclusiveness of the judgment. It does not, however,

satisfy our feeling that some reasonable outlet for the instinct of self-defense by one attacked should be conceded, if it can be done without too much distraction from the business at hand. Accordingly a substantial number of courts, while not opening the door to retry the conviction, allow the witness himself to make a brief, general statement in explanation, mitigation, or denial of guilt, or recognize a discretion in the trial judge to permit it. Wigmore aptly terms it a "harmless charity to allow the witness to make such protestations on his own behalf as he may feel able to make with a due regard to the penalties of perjury."[2]

The most prejudicial impact of impeachment by conviction (as is true also of cross-examination as to misconduct, see § 42, above) is on one particular type of witness, namely, the criminal accused who elects to take the stand. When the accused is forced to admit that he has a "record" of past convictions, particularly if the convictions are for crimes similar to the one on trial, there is an obvious danger; despite instructions, the jury might misuse the evidence and give more heed to the past convictions as evidence that the accused is the kind of man who would commit the crime charged, or even that he ought to be imprisoned without too much concern for present guilt or innocence, than they will to the legitimate bearing of the past convictions on credibility. The accused, who has a "record" but who thinks he has a defense to the present charge, thus faces a harsh dilemma. One horn of the dilemma is that if he stays off the stand, his silence alone might prompt the jury to believe him guilty. However, if he elects to testify, his "record" becomes provable to impeach him, and this again is likely to doom his defense. Where does the balance lie? Most prosecutors argue with force that it is misleading to permit the accused to appear as a witness of blameless life, and this argument has prevailed widely. One intermediate view, between generally allowing convictions to be introduced and excluding all of an accused's convictions, is a proposal that the convictions

---

§ 42

1. As to impeaching one's own witness, see § 38 supra.

2. 4 Wigmore, Evidence § 1117, p. 251 (Chadbourn rev. 1972).

be restricted to those bearing directly upon character for truthfulness. Another intermediate view, but with the disadvantage of uncertainty, permits the introduction of the defendant's prior convictions in the discretion of the judge, who is to balance in each instance the possible prejudice against the probative value of the conviction as to credibility. As already noted, the Federal Rule of Evidence is a compromise. Federal Rule 609 essentially embraces the latter intermediate view. In Pennsylvania, the accused who takes the stand is shielded, under certain circumstances, from cross-examination as to misconduct or conviction of crime when offered to impeach but not from proof by the record of conviction. Finally, the former Uniform Rule provided that if the accused does not offer evidence supporting his own credibility, the prosecution shall not be allowed, on cross-examination or otherwise, to prove for impeachment purposes his conviction. The very variety of solutions, both actual and proposed, indicates the stubborn nature of the problem.

In view of the difficulties encountered in the balancing approach, the suggestion has been made that the "mere fact" method be substituted for convictions punishable by death or imprisonment in excess of one year. The method is described as follows:

> [T]he proper procedural approach is simply to ask the witness the straight-forward question as to whether he had ever been convicted of a crime. The inquiry must end at this point unless the witness denies that he has been convicted. In the event of such denial the adverse party may then in the presentation of his side of the case produce and file in evidence the record of any such conviction. If the witness admits prior conviction of a crime, the inquiry by his adversary may not be pursued to the point of naming the crime for which he was convicted. If the witness so desires he may of his own volition state the nature of the crime and offer any relevant testimony that would eliminate any adverse implications; for example, the fact that he

had in the meantime been fully pardoned or that the crime was a minor one and occurred many years before.[3]

Few courts have adopted this method.

The suggestion has also been made that impeachment of the accused by showing prior convictions is unconstitutional, but to date, no federal or state court has embraced the suggestion.

§ 43. Character: Impeachment by Proof of Opinion or Bad Reputation

In most jurisdictions the impeacher may attack a prior witness's character by putting the following formulaic questions to another witness:

> "Do you know the general reputation at the present time of William Witness in the community in which he lives, for truth and veracity?"
>
> "Yes."
>
> "What is that reputation?"
>
> "It is bad."

This routine is the distillation of traditions which became established in a majority of American courts. The common law tradition is the result of choices between alternative solutions. Some choices were wise, but others were misguided.

For instance, one misguided choice was the threshold decision that this attack on character for truth must take the abstract, debilitated form of proof of reputation. By what is apparently a misreading of legal history, at common law the American courts generally prohibited proof of character by having a witness describe his belief or opinion of the prior witness's character even when the belief or opinion is based upon extensive personal experience with the witness under attack and observation of his conduct. The limitation to reputation was defended on the ground that to let in opinion would provoke distracting side disputes about specific conduct of the witness attacked, since the impeaching witness may be cross-examined about the basis of his opinion. That danger undoubtedly exists, and the con-

---

3. McArthur v. Cook, 99 So.2d 565, 567 (Fla.1957).

troversies would need to be held to reasonable limits by the judge. However, the choice of reputation (instead of opinion based on observation) has eliminated much of the objectivity from the attempt to appraise character, and encouraged the parties to select character witnesses who, under the guise of reputation, voice prejudice and ill-will. The hand is that of Esau, but the voice is Jacob's. In addition, reputation in modern, impersonal urban centers is often evanescent or non-existent.

The Federal Rules of Evidence and the Revised Uniform Rules of Evidence break with tradition and permit attack by opinion, while at the same time retaining the traditional attack upon character by reputation. Indeed, the Federal Rules seem to authorize the admission of expert opinion on the topic. Although Article VII of the Federal Rules expressly distinguishes between lay and expert opinion, Rule 608(a) refers generally to "opinion." Various aspects of this rule are considered in the remainder of this section.

The courts faced a further choice—a recurrent one in various phases of character-impeachment—namely, should the inquiry extend to "general character" and other specific bad traits such as sexual immorality, or shall it be directed solely to the trait of veracity? Surely in this elusive realm of character, it is best to insist on the highest degree of relevancy attainable. Fortunately the great majority of courts take this view and limit the inquiry to "reputation for truth and veracity." Opinion, as well as reputation, pursuant to Federal and Revised Uniform Rule of Evidence 608(a) is likewise restricted; the rule mentions solely "character for truthfulness or untruthfulness." Only a few jurisdictions open the door to reputation for "general character" or "general moral character." Fewer still permit proof of reputation for specific traits other than veracity.

As we shall see in Chapter 17, the common law and the Federal Rules allow an accused to introduce character evidence on the historical merits of the case; when the accused does so, the evidence must relate to the accused's character at the time of the alleged actus reus. Here, however, the temporal focus

is different. The crucial time when the witness's character influences his truth-telling is the time he testifies. But obviously reputation takes time to form and is the result of earlier conduct and demeanor. Hence, the reputation does not reflect character exactly at the trial date. The practical solution is to do what most courts do, that is, (1) to permit the reputation-witness to testify about the impeachee's "present" reputation as of the time of the trial, if he knows it, and (2) to accept testimony about reputation as of any time before trial which the judge in his discretion finds is not too remote. This practice should be followed under Federal Rule of Evidence 608(a). A witness's opinion permitted by the federal rule ought to have a similar temporal relation to the trial.

As to the place of reputation, the traditional inquiry is as to general reputation for veracity "in the community where he lives." The object of this limitation of place is to restrict evidence of repute to reputation among the people who know the witness best. The residential limitation was appropriate for the situation in England (and less so in America) before the Industrial Revolution, when most people lived in small towns or rural villages. But as an exclusive limitation, it is inappropriate today. A person may be virtually anonymous in the suburb or city neighborhood where he lives, but well known in another locality where he spends his workdays or several localities where he regularly does business. Thus, it is now generally agreed that proof may be made not only of the reputation of the witness where he lives, but also of his repute, as long as it is established, in any substantial group of people among whom he is well known, such as the persons with whom he works, does business, or goes to school. Even a jail population can qualify as a community. These standards should apply under Federal Rule of Evidence 608(a). The trial judge has a measure of discretion to determine whether the group in question meets these standards.

Other problems arise when the attack on character is by opinion as authorized by Federal Rule of Evidence 608(a). A lay person's opinion should rest on some firsthand knowledge pursuant to Rule 602 so that the opinion can be based on rational perception and of aid to the jury as required by Rule 701. However, specific untruthful acts cannot be elicited during the witness's direct examination even for the limited purpose of showing the basis of the opinion. An adequate preliminary showing to meet the requirements of Rule 701 would be made by evidence of sufficient acquaintance with the witness to be attacked. Impeachment by experts rather than lay testimony is considered in the next section.

§ 44. Defects of Capacity: Sensory or Mental

Assume that the witness has a sensory deficiency but one which is not so extreme that it renders the person incompetent as a witness under the standards discussed in Chapter 7. Any deficiency of the senses, such as deafness or color blindness, which would substantially lessen the ability to perceive the facts which the witness purports to have observed, ought to be provable to attack the witness's credibility, either upon cross-examination or by producing other witnesses to prove the defect. The limits of human powers of perception should probably be studied more intensively in the interest of a more accurate, objective administration of justice.

As to the mental qualities of intelligence and memory, a distinction must be made between attacks on competency[1] and attacks on credibility, the subject of this section. Sanity in a general sense is no longer a test of competency, and a so-called insane person is generally permitted to testify if he is able to report correctly the matters to which he testifies and understands the duty to speak the truth. Federal Rule of Evidence 601, applicable at least in federal question cases in federal courts, precludes the trial judge from treating insane persons as automatically incompetent to testify, although a prospective witness could conceivably be treated as incompetent if he did not have the capacity to recall, understand the duty to tell the truth, or acquire personal knowledge. More commonly, however, the fact of mental "abnormality" at either the time of

observing the facts or testifying is provable to impeach, on cross or by extrinsic evidence, as under the federal rules, in the judge's discretion. The use of expert opinion as extrinsic evidence in this situation is discussed in the last part of this section.

What of defects of mind within the range of normality, such as a slower than average mind or a poorer than usual memory? These qualities are sometimes exposed in a testing cross-examination by a skilled questioner. May they be proved by other witnesses? The decisions are divided. It seems eminently a case for discretion. The trial judge would determine whether the crucial character of the testimony attacked and the insight gained into the witness's credibility outweigh the time and distraction involved in opening this side-dispute. The development of standardized tests for intelligence and their widespread use in business, government and the armed forces, suggest that they may eventually come to serve as useful aids in evaluating testimony.

Abnormality is a horse of a different color. It is a standard ground of impeachment. One form of abnormality comes into play when one is under the influence of drugs or alcohol. If the witness was under the influence at the time of the happenings which he reports in his testimony or at the time he testifies, this condition is provable, on cross or by extrinsic evidence, to impeach. Habitual addiction is treated differently. Standing alone, the mere fact of chronic alcoholism is ordinarily not provable on credibility. Apart from the minimal probative value of evidence of alcoholism, its admission arguably violates the general prohibition against using character as circumstantial proof of conduct; in the final analysis, the attorney is simply arguing that since the witness was intoxicated on previous occasions, it is more likely that the witness was intoxicated when he observed the relevant events. On the other hand, when the abnormality is a drug addiction carrying even more social odium, many decisions allow it to be shown to impeach, even without evidence that in the particular case it affected truth-telling. Howev-

§ 44

1.   See § 62 infra.

er, more courts exclude it, absent a showing of a specific effect on the witness's veracity. Most federal cases agree with the majority view. The excluding courts have the better of the argument. It can scarcely be contended that there is sufficient scientific consensus to warrant judicial notice that addiction in and of itself usually affects credibility. Worse still, the evidence is pregnant with prejudice.

In recent decades with the growth of psychiatry, psychiatrists' testimony about issues of sanity in cases of wills and crimes has become commonplace. The use of expert psychiatric testimony about mental disorders and defects is a potential aid in determining a witness's credibility in any kind of litigation. In one type of litigation, namely sex offenses prosecutions, Wigmore and other commentators characterized this kind of testimony as indispensable, and in the distant past it was routinely approved by the courts.[2] However, Wigmore's positions that women who testify they have been sexually attacked *often* report such matters falsely, and that a judge should *always* be sure that the female victim's mental history is scrutinized by a qualified physician, are both chauvinist and inaccurate. Most courts now hold that the admission of psychiatric testimony is in the judge's discretion, and more often than not the discretion is exercised in favor of excluding evidence of the witness's past psychiatric problems. Further, these courts hold that the discretion to order an examination and permit such testimony should be exercised only for compelling reasons in exceptional circumstances. The criteria for identifying such circumstances are not at all clear; if compelled examinations are to be permitted at all, strict limiting conditions should be announced. Indeed, there is respectable state authority that there is no power to order a psychiatric examination and admit the resulting testimony in rape trials.

Psychiatric testimony has been offered in cases other than sexual assault prosecutions. Various courts have taken the position that there may be impeachment of principal witnesses in other cases by expert psychiatric opinion. However, the federal courts have been disinclined to exercise their discretion to permit attacks by experts on mental capacity affecting credibility. When there is a solid ground for believing that a principal witness is subject to a severe mental abnormality affecting credibility, there may be a legitimate need to employ the resources of psychiatry. Many contemporary courts accept the principle that psychiatric evidence should be received, at least in the judge's discretion, when its value outweighs the cost in time, distraction, and expense.

The value depends, inter alia, upon the importance of the witness's testimony and the adequacy of the expert's opportunity to form a reliable opinion. This first factor, the importance of the testimony, is relevant to the justifiability of subjecting witnesses (even party-witnesses) to the ordeal of psychiatric attack. The second factor is the adequacy of the opportunity to form a trustworthy opinion. An opinion based solely upon a hypothetical question is almost valueless. Only slightly more reliable is an opinion resting on the subject's demeanor and testimony in the courtroom. The courtroom is not only a foreign environment for most witnesses; worse still, the prospect of testifying can create anxiety which distorts the witness's demeanor on the stand. Most psychiatrists say that a satisfactory opinion can be formed only after the witness has been subjected to a thorough clinical examination. A discretionary power has been recognized in a few instances to empower the judge to order an examination of a prosecuting witness, but the conditions for exercising that discretion are unclear. In principle, the discretionary power ought to exist in any type of case. The exercise of the discretion should be informed by such factors as whether undue expenditure of time or expense and undue distraction will result, whether the witness is a key witness, and whether there are solid indications that the witness is suffering from mental abnormality at the time of trial or the time of the happening about which he testifies. Only if there is no power to order an examination should expert opinion based on courtroom

2. See 3A Wigmore, Evidence §§ 934a, 924a, and 924b (Chadbourn rev. 1970).

observation and reading of the record be admitted. Even then, permitting opinion based on such material seems dubious.

Expert opinion on character for truthfulness or untruthfulness authorized by Federal and Revised Uniform Rule 608(a) must be distinguished from the subject discussed above, opinion about the witness's mental capacity to tell the truth. Rule 608(a) should not be considered direct authority for the type of opinion testimony discussed in this section.

§ 45. Impeachment by "Specific Contradiction"[1]

"Specific contradiction" may be explained as follows. In the course of testifying about an accident or crime, Witness One mentions that at the time he witnessed these matters, the day was snowy and he was wearing a green sweater. Suppose that the statements about the snow and the sweater can be "disproved." This can happen in several ways. Witness One on direct or cross-examination may later acknowledge that he was in error. Or judicial notice may be taken that at the time and place—Tucson in July—it could not have been snowing. But commonly disproof or "contradiction" is attempted by calling Witness Two to testify to the contrary that the day was warm and Witness One was in his shirt-sleeves. This is the sense in which the term "contradiction" is meant in this section.

What impeaching value does the contradiction have in the above situation? If Witness One is wrong and Witness Two right, it tends to show that Witness One has erred about or falsified certain facts, and therefore is capable of error or lying. That showing should be considered negatively in weighing other statements by Witness One. But all human beings are fallible, and all testimony ought to be discounted to some extent for this weakness. It is true that the trial judge in his discretion may permit the cross-examiner to test the power of Witness One to observe, remember

and recount facts unrelated to the case to "explore" these capacities.[2] However, to allow a prolonged dispute about such extraneous, "collateral" facts as the weather and the witness's clothing by allowing the attacker to call other witnesses to disprove them, is impractical. Dangers of surprise, confusion of the jury's attention, and waste of time are apparent.

To combat these dangers, at common law many courts enforced the restriction that a witness may not be impeached by producing extrinsic evidence of "collateral" facts "contradicting" the first witness's assertions about those facts. A matter is "collateral" if the matter itself is irrelevant in the litigation to establish a fact of consequence,[3] i.e., irrelevant for a purpose other than mere contradiction of the prior witness's in-court testimony. When the collateral fact sought to be contradicted is elicited on cross-examination, this restriction is often expressed by saying that the answer is conclusive or that the cross-examiner must "take the answer." By the better view, if the "collateral" fact happens to have been drawn out on direct, the rule against extrinsic contradiction still applies. The danger of surprise is lessened, but waste of time and confusion of issues persist as objections.

Article VI of the Federal Rules does not expressly mention specific contradiction as a permissible method of impeachment. However, the federal courts continue to permit resort to this technique. They are correct in doing so. The Supreme Court's reasoning in *United States v. Abel*[4] is apposite. As in the case of specific contradiction, Article VI is silent on the bias impeachment technique. However, the *Abel* Court noted that bias is certainly logically relevant to a witness's credibility; and consequently, even without more, Rule 402 is sufficient statutory authorization for the continuation of the practice of bias impeachment. Like bias, specific contradiction is relevant to impeach a prior witness's credibility. The judge may exercise her discretion under Rule 403 to

---

1. The extent to which evidence obtained in violation of a constitutional right may be used to impeach is treated in § 182 infra. The use of treatises to impeach experts is dealt with in § 321 infra.

2. See § 29 supra.

3. See generally § 49 infra.

4. 469 U.S. 45 (1984).

limit specific contradiction impeachment; but when it is logically relevant, specific contradiction evidence is presumptively admissible under Rule 402.

§ 46. Beliefs Concerning Religion

As indicated in a subsequent section,[1] the common law required as a qualification for taking the witness's oath the belief in a God who would punish untruth. This requirement grew up in a religious climate which has weakened with the passage of time. It has been abandoned in most common law jurisdictions. General provisions like that in the Illinois constitution to the effect that "no person shall be denied any civil or political rights, privilege or capacity on account of his religious opinions" have been construed as abrogating the rule of incompetency to take the oath. Nor is belief in God required by the Federal Rules of Evidence.

The overall tendency, as indicated in Sections 43 and 65, has been to convert the old grounds of incompetency to testify, such as interest and infamy, into bases for impeaching credibility. This principle of conversion has sometimes been expressly enacted in constitutional provisions and statutes. Should the principle be applied to permit a witness's credibility to be attacked by showing that she is an atheist or agnostic and does not believe in Divine punishment for perjury? The greater number of courts that addressed the question have said no by interpreting either general provisions such as that in the Illinois constitution, or specific constitutional, statutory, or rule language. Thus many states recognize a witness's privilege not to be examined about her own religious faith or beliefs, except so far as the judge in her discretion finds that the relevance of the inquiry to some fact of consequence in the case outweighs the interest of privacy and the danger of prejudice. A few old cases, either reasoning from the conversion of grounds of incompetency into bases for impeachment or following the peculiar language of specific statutory provisions, seemingly allowed this ground of impeachment; but those cases are badly dated and have little modern precedential value. Even under the old cases, courts would not permit inquiry about particular creeds, faiths, or affiliations except as they shed light on the witness's belief in a God who will punish untruth.

There is a strong argument that legislatures and courts should, in addition to recognizing a witness's privilege not to answer questions about her own religious beliefs, forbid the party to impeach by bringing other witnesses to attack the first witness's faith. Today, there is no basis for believing that the lack of faith in God's avenging wrath is an indication of greater than average untruthfulness. Without that basis, the evidence of atheism is irrelevant to the question of credibility.

Federal Rule of Evidence 610 provides:

> Evidence of the beliefs or opinions of a witness on matters of religion is not admissible for the purpose of showing that by reason of their nature the witness' credibility is impaired or enhanced.

A juror might wrongfully discount the credibility of the member of an unconventional or unusual religion, and Rule 610 guards against that type of prejudice. However, the prohibition is not complete. In some cases, evidence of the witness's religion will be admissible on an alternative theory of logical relevance. For example, the Advisory Committee Note to Rule 610 adds that "disclosure of affiliation with a church which is a party to the litigation would be allowable under the rule," since it could bear on the witness's bias.

§ 47. Supporting the Witness

As § 33 noted, there are three stages in credibility analysis: bolstering before attempted impeachment, impeachment, and rehabilitation after attempted impeachment. Impeachment is not a dispassionate study of the witness's capacities and character, but rather is regarded in our tradition as an *attack* upon his credibility. Under our adversary system of trials, the witness's proponent must be given an opportunity to meet this attack by evidence rehabilitating the witness. As we

1. See § 63 infra.

have seen, one general principle, operative under both case law and the Federal Rules of Evidence, is that absent an attack upon credibility, no bolstering evidence is allowed. Conversely, when there has been evidence of impeaching facts the witness's proponent may present contradictory evidence disproving the alleged impeaching facts. Such disproof is relevant and generally allowable.

As just stated, absent the introduction of impeaching facts, the witness's proponent ordinarily may not bolster the witness's credibility. The rationale is that we do not want to devote court time to the witness's credibility and run the risk of distracting the jury from the historical merits unless and until the opposing attorney attacks the witness's credibility. Admittedly, there are exceptions to this general norm. The fact of a complaint of rape and in some instances the details of the complaint have been held admissible. Both the fact of complaint and, where allowed, the details of the complaint may be admissible on the theory of rehabilitating or bolstering the complaining witness; but since this evidence may also come in as substantive evidence under some theories, the matter is dealt with later. Likewise, prior consistent statements of identification can be admissible substantively or to bolster; but precisely because prior identifications may be introduced as substantive evidence and trigger constitutional requirements, the subject is discussed elsewhere. With the exception of fresh complaints and prior identifications, the witness's proponent may proffer evidence of the witness's truthfulness only as rehabilitation after attempted impeachment.

A discussion of rehabilitation and support of witnesses is best organized around the techniques employed, as was the case with impeachment. The two most common rehabilitative methods are (1) introduction of supportive evidence of good character of the witness attacked, and (2) proof of the witness's consistent statements. The basic question is whether these two types of rehabilitation evidence represent a proper response in kind to the specific methods of impeachment that have been attempted. The general test of admissibility is whether evidence of the witness's good charac-

ter or consistent statements is logically relevant to explain the impeaching fact. The rehabilitating facts must meet the impeachment with relative directness. The wall, attacked at one point, may not be fortified at another, distinct point. Credibility is a side issue, and the circle of relevancy in this context should be drawn narrowly. When we reach the stage of rehabilitation after impeachment, we are rather far afield from the historical merits of the case; and the courts justifiably insist on a stronger showing of relevance to minimize the risk that the jury will lose sight of the merits. As a rule of thumb, the courts demand that the rehabilitation be a response in kind to the impeachment. How responsive is a question of degree as to which reasonable courts differ.

Proof of the witness's character trait for truthfulness. When may the party supporting the impeached witness offer evidence of the witness's good character for truth? Certainly attacks by evidence of bad reputation, bad opinion of character for truthfulness, conviction of crime, or misconduct which has not resulted in conviction, all open the door to character support. The evidence of good character for truth is a logically relevant response in kind to these modes of impeachment. Moreover, a slashing cross-examination may carry strong accusations of misconduct and bad character, which even the witness's denial will not remove from the jury's mind. If the judge considers that fairness requires it, he may permit evidence of good character, a mild palliative for the insinuation of a combative cross-examination.

A witness's corrupt conduct showing bias should also be regarded as an attack on veracity-character and thus warrant character support. However, impeachment for bias or interest by facts not involving corruption, such as proof of family relationship, may not be met by proof of good character for truthfulness.

Attempts to support the witness by showing his good character for truthfulness have resulted in contradictory conclusions when the witness has been impeached only by evidence of an inconsistent statement or the opponent's evidence specifically contradicting the facts to which the witness testified. If the witness has been impeached by an inconsistent statement, perhaps the numerical majority of courts permit a showing of his good character for truthfulness. However, if the adversary has merely introduced evidence denying the facts to which the witness testified, the greater number of cases forbid a showing of the witness's good character for truthfulness. Convenient as hard-and-fast answers to these seemingly minor trial questions may be, it is unsound to resolve them in a mechanical fashion. A more sensible view is that in each case the judge should consider whether a particular impeachment for inconsistency or a conflict in testimony amounts in effect to an attack on character for truthfulness and accordingly exercise discretion to admit or exclude the character-support. An important consideration is whether the inconsistency or contradiction relates to a matter on which the witness could be innocently mistaken. If the inconsistency or contradiction is so flat that the common sense inference is a lie rather than an innocent mistake, the judge can treat the impeachment as an attack on the witness's truthfulness. This view is arguably codified in the Federal Rules of Evidence.

Proof of the witness's prior consistent statements. Turning to attempts to rehabilitate an attacked witness by introducing a prior statement consistent present testimony, a similar question arises. What kind of attack upon the witness opens the door to evidence of the witness's prior statements consistent with his present story on the stand? When the attack takes the form of character impeachment by showing misconduct, convictions, or bad reputation, there is no justification for rehabilitating by consistent statements. The rehabilitation does not meet the assault and fails the response-in-kind rule of thumb. Further, at common law under the prevailing temporal priority doctrine, if the attacker has charged bias, interest, corrupt influence, contrivance to falsify, or want of capacity to observe or remember, the prior consistent statement is deemed irrelevant to refute the charge unless the consistent statement was made *before the* source of the bias, interest, influence or inca-

pacity originated. If the statement was made later, proof of the statement does not assist the jury to evaluate the witness's testimony because the reliability of the statement is subject to the same doubt as the trial testimony. Many courts continue to enforce the temporal priority doctrine under the Federal Rules; but there is a large body of contra authority. In *United States v. Tome,*[1] the Supreme Court held that Rule 801(d)(1)(B), governing the admission of consistent statements as substantive evidence, incorporates the temporal priority doctrine. Although the Court disclaimed ruling on the question of whether the doctrine applies when the consistent statement under "any other evidentiary principle" such as rehabilitation, some commentators read the opinion as a signal that the Court will eventually extend the same limitation to consistent statements proffered for the limited purpose of rehabilitation.

There is a division of opinion on the question whether impeachment by inconsistent statements opens the door to support by proving consistent statements. A few courts hold generally that the support is permissible. This holding has the merit of easy application. At the opposite extreme, some courts, since the inconsistency remains despite all consistent statements, hold generally that it does not. That holding seems preferable, but certain qualifications to that holding should be recognized. By the way of example, when the attacked witness denies making the inconsistent statement, evidence of consistent statements very near the time of the alleged inconsistent one is relevant to corroborate his denial. Again, if in the particular situation, the attack by inconsistent statement is accompanied by or interpretable as a charge of a recent plan or contrivance to give false testimony, proof of a consistent statement antedating the plan or contrivance tends strongly to disprove that the testimony was the result of contrivance; the testimony could not be the product of the alleged contrivance because the witness said the same thing before the supposed contrivance. Here all courts agree. It is for the judge

§ 47

1.   513 U.S. 150 (1990).

to decide whether the impeachment at least implies a charge of contrivance. The implication is evident when the cross-examiner asks the witness to admit that he "didn't come up with this story" until the witness spoke with an attorney or party. If there is no such implication, the attack often amounts to a mere imputation of inaccurate memory. If so, only consistent statements made when the event was recent and memory fresh should be received in support. Recognition of these qualifications still leaves it open for the courts to exclude statements procured after the inconsistent statement, and thus to discourage pressure on witnesses to furnish counter-statements.

These qualifications can be recognized consistently with the text of the Federal Rules of Evidence. Under a broader viewpoint, common law temporal priority doctrine does not apply to consistent statements offered for the limited purpose of rehabilitation in federal practice; and the judge has discretion under Rules 401 and 403 to determine whether the particular circumstances justify admission of consistent statements to rehabilitate the witness. Suppose, for example, that the cross-examiner forced the witness to concede that the witness had made a seemingly inconsistent statement. To rehabilitate the witness, it would be logically relevant to elicit the witness's description of other out-of-statements in which he used a key term in a peculiar sense which eliminated the seeming inconsistency. The other statements would be relevant on that theory even if they were made after the apparently inconsistent statement. Of course, this result would obtain only when the proponent offers the evidence for the limited purpose of rehabilitation and not as substantive evidence under Rule 801.

§ 48. Attacking the Supporting Character Witness

As § 41 explained, Rule 608(b)(1) permits the cross-examiner to impeach a witness by forcing the witness to admit that she had committed an untruthful act, even if the act has not resulted in a conviction. Rule 608(b)(2) also deals with impeachment, but the target of the impeachment is different.

Under Federal and Revised Uniform Rule of Evidence (1974) 608(b)(2) and at common law, a character witness who has testified to his favorable opinion or the good reputation of another witness ("principal witness") for truth and veracity[1] can be cross-examined about the principal witness's specific prior acts, if probative of untruthfulness. Specific instances of conduct sufficiently probative of untruthfulness not having resulted in a conviction[2] normally involve dishonesty or false statement.[3] Extrinsic evidence with respect to specific instances of the principal witness's conduct not resulting in a conviction is inadmissible; the cross-examiner must take the character witness's answer.[4]

To be sure, a character witness testifying to the principal witness's reputation for truthfulness may be cross-examined concerning with whom, where, and when the witness discussed the principal witness's reputation. Opinion testimony must be based on the character witness's personal knowledge of the principal witness; and consequently, the extent of the relationship with the principal witness is a proper subject of inquiry on cross-examination. Moreover, as the next paragraph explains, the cross-examiner may go farther and ask about specific acts by the principal witness.

When a character witness testifies on direct as to the principal witness's reputation for truthfulness, the correct phasing of the cross-examination question about specific instances of the principal witness's conduct is "Have you heard?". Where the direct testimony of the character witness is in the form of an opinion, the proper form of the question is either "Do you know?" or "Are you aware?". The distinction, while correct in theory, is of such slight practical importance that it could easily be

---

1. For a discussion of when good character testimony is admissible to support a witness's character for truth and veracity, see § 47.

2. See § 42 supra with respect to the admissibility of prior convictions to impeach.

3. See § 41 supra.

4. See also § 49 infra.

eliminated at common law if the Federal Rules had not already abandoned the distinction.[5] The character witness may be asked directly not only about the principal witness's specific acts probative of untruthfulness, but also about familiarity with the principal witness's convictions, arrests, and indictments. All these matters have a natural bearing upon the principal witness's reputation and character witness's opinion of the principal witness. These events are disreputable and inconsistent with the good reputation which the character witness has vouched for. Lack of familiarity with such matters is relevant to an assessment of the basis for the character witness's testimony. If the witness answers that he is unfamiliar with these matters, the witness's answer impeaches the extent of the witness's knowledge of the principal witness's character. Familiarity with the matters impeaches the character witness' standard of "truthfulness" or "untruthfulness"; if the witness answers that he is familiar with the unfavorable fact and yet vouches for the principal witness's good character, the character witness is either lying or using a rather strange standard for evaluating good character. Whatever the form of the question, the cross-examiner must have a good faith basis supporting the inquiry.

Inquiry on cross-examination of the character witness about principal witness's acts probative of untruthfulness not resulting in a conviction may be precluded if the court determines that the probative value of such cross-examination is substantially outweighed by the danger of unfair prejudice. The rather tenuous relevance of character testimony to veracity, coupled with the risk of unfair prejudice when the principal witness is also a party, militate in favor of the court exercising discretion to prohibit inquiry into specific acts. In principle, a strong case can be made for a blanket prohibition of cross-examination about specific acts allegedly committed by the principal witness.

§ 49. Contradiction: Collateral and Non–Collateral Matters; Good Faith Basis

On cross-examination, every permissible type of impeachment has as one of its purposes testing the witness's credibility. The use of extrinsic evidence to contradict is more restricted due to considerations of confusion of the issues, misleading the jury, undue consumption of time, and unfair prejudice. If a matter is considered collateral, the counsel may be limited to intrinsic impeachment; the witness's testimony on direct or cross-examination stands—the cross-examiner must take the witness's answer; and contradictory extrinsic evidence, evidence offered other than through the witness himself, is not permitted. When the matter is not collateral, extrinsic evidence may be introduced disputing the witness's testimony on direct examination or cross.

The topic of the collateral fact rule can be confusing. It is helpful to approach the topic in the following sequence. First, we shall explore the limited procedural significance of a determination that the rule bars extrinsic evidence to impeach a witness. Second, we will identify the impeachment techniques exempt from the rule and, by process of elimination, the techniques subject to the rule. Finally, we shall explore how the courts determine whether a particular matter is "collateral" for purposes of the rule.

The procedural significance of a determination that the rule bars extrinsic evidence. The rule does not limit cross-examination. During cross-examination, the questioner may attempt to challenge virtually any aspect of the witness's direct testimony. An error in any facet of the direct examination can reflect adversely on the witness's perceptual ability, memory, narrative ability, or sincerity; and all those factors are relevant to the jury's assessment of the witness's credibility. Subject to the trial judge's discretionary control under Rule 403, the cross-examiner can question about these factors to his or her heart's content. Moreover, even if the witness initially gives the cross-examiner an unfavorable answer, the questioner may apply pressure during cross by, for example, reminding the wit-

---

5. See § 191 infra.

ness of the penalties for perjury. The courts sometimes say that when the collateral fact rule applies, the cross-examiner must "take the witness's answer," but that expression does not mean that the cross-examiner is obliged to accept the initial answer out of the witness's mouth. Lastly, although there is a split of judicial sentiment on the issue, there is modern authority that to apply further pressure for a truthful answer, the cross-examiner may confront the witness with any contrary writing which the witness would be competent to authenticate. One of the principal justifications for the rule is the courts' desire to minimize the amount of court time devoted to matters relevant only to a witness's credibility. There might be a considerable time expenditure if, after the witness leaves the stand, the attorney calls a second witness to impeach the prior witness. However, little additional time will be consumed if the cross-examiner presents the witness with a writing he or she can authenticate. What is then the procedural significance of the rule? The core prohibition applies when the witness to be impeached has already left the stand and the former cross-examiner later calls a second witness or proffers an exhibit to impeach the earlier witness's credibility. At common law if the collateral fact rule applies at this juncture, the second witness's testimony or the exhibit is automatically inadmissible.

Which impeachment techniques are exempt from, and which subject to, the collateral fact rule? Most impeachment techniques are exempt from the collateral fact rule. In some cases, the exemption arises from the very nature of the impeachment technique. Suppose, for instance, that as a matter of policy, a jurisdiction has decided to permit impeachment by polygraphists or the testimony of other persons about a prior witness's character trait for untruthfulness. Those impeachment techniques necessarily involve extrinsic evidence: After the witness to be impeached leaves the stand, the former cross-examiner calls the polygraphist or the bad character witness. If the policy decision has been made to countenance these impeachment tech-

niques, the techniques must be exempted from the collateral fact rule.

Moreover, other techniques are exempted because the impeaching facts are deemed highly probative on credibility. For example, proof of (1) bias, interest, corruption, or coercion, (2) alcohol or drug use, (3) deficient mental capacity, (4) want of physical capacity or lack of exercise of the capacity to acquire personal knowledge and (5) a prior conviction[1] are exempt. These matters can possess such great probative worth on the issue of the witness's credibility that the courts tolerate the expenditure of the additional time entailed in the subsequent presentation of extrinsic evidence.

Which techniques are then subject to the collateral fact rule? By process of elimination, we conclude that there are only three: proof the witness has committed untruthful act which has not resulted in a conviction, proof that the witness made an inconsistent pretrial statement, and specific contradiction.

When is a particular topic deemed collateral? Assume both that the former cross-examiner is proffering extrinsic evidence to impeach the prior witness and that the counsel is using one of the impeachment techniques subject to the collateral fact rule. When is the specific impeaching evidence deemed collateral and inadmissible?

In the case of proof of the witness's untruthful acts which have not resulted in a conviction, the answer is relatively simple. With one exception, extrinsic evidence of such acts is always deemed collateral. On the one hand, if the witness initially denies perpetrating the act, the cross-examiner may pressure the witness for an honest answer by reminding the witness of the penalties of perjury and perhaps by confronting the witness with his or her writing mentioning the act. On the other hand, when the witness sticks to his or her guns and adamantly refuses to concede the act, the cross-examiner must "take the answer" even when it would be relatively easy for the cross-examiner to expose the perjury. Even if a person with personal knowledge of

§ 49

1. See § 42 supra.

the witness's act were sitting in the court-room, the cross-examiner could not later call that person to the stand to prove the prior witness's commission of the deceitful act.

The solitary exception to this general rule applies when the witness's testimony triggers the curative admissibility or "door opening" doctrine. Extrinsic evidence concerning a collateral matter may be admitted under the doctrine of "door opening." Admission of evidence under this doctrine tends to occur where the government seeks to introduce evidence on rebuttal to contradict specific factual assertions raised during an accused's direct examination.[2] Suppose, for example, that on direct examination, an accused witness made a sweeping, superlative assertion that he had "never" committed a deceitful act. That assertion is such a serious violation of the rules limiting bolstering evidence that on a curative admissibility theory, many courts allow the opposing counsel to both cross-examine about the assertion and later introduce extrinsic evidence rebutting the assertion. However, with this single exception, impeaching evidence of a witness's other untruthful acts which have not resulted in a conviction is always subject to the collateral fact rule.

The determination of whether the extrinsic impeachment evidence relates to a collateral matter is more complex when the former cross-examiner resorts to extrinsic evidence to prove a prior inconsistent or specifically contradict the earlier witness's testimony. Although extrinsic evidence of untruthful acts is almost always considered collateral, extrinsic evidence offered for these purposes is sometimes collateral and sometimes non-collateral.

In these situations, there are two ways in which the extrinsic impeaching evidence can qualify as non-collateral. To begin with, the matter is non-collateral and extrinsic evidence consequently admissible if the matter is itself relevant to a fact of consequence on the historical merits of the case.[3] When the fact is logically relevant to the merits of the case as well as the witness's credibility, it is worth the

additional court time entailed in hearing extrinsic evidence. Moreover the extrinsic evidence is non-collateral and again admissible when it relates to a so-called "linchpin" fact. Under this prong of the test, for purposes of impeachment a part of the witness's story may be attacked where as a matter of human experience, he could not be mistaken about that fact if the thrust of his testimony on the historical merits was true.

Consider the following illustration. Bob is called to testify that the color of the traffic light facing Apple Street was red at the time of an automobile accident he witnessed at the corner of Apple and Main. On direct examination, Bob testifies that he was driving east on Apple Street heading toward the Piagano's Pizza Restaurant located on the corner of Apple and Peach. On cross-examination counsel asks, "Isn't it true that Piagano's Pizza Restaurant is located on Apple three blocks east of Peach at Maple?" Although this cross-examination question is permissible as potentially affecting the jury's assessment of Bob's power of recollection and concern for detail, if Bob continues to maintain that the restaurant is on Peach Street, extrinsic evidence may not be offered during the cross-examiner's case in chief as to the location of the restaurant. The matter is collateral because the location of the restaurant is not relevant in the litigation other than to contradict the witness's testimony. Even if Bob denied on cross-examination making a prior statement in which he allegedly said that the restaurant was on Apple and Maple, extrinsic evidence of the prior statement would be inadmissible because the matter remains collateral. On the other hand, the color of the traffic light is non-collateral; the color of the traffic light is itself relevant in the case. Thus specific contradiction evidence that the light facing Apple Street was green is admissible. Similarly, if Bob denies on cross-examination having previously stated that the traffic light was green, extrinsic evidence of Bob's prior inconsistent statement is admissible.

---

2. See § 57 infra.

3. With respect to prior inconsistent statements, see also § 36 supra.

Assuming Bob is then asked on cross-examination if he was wearing his glasses while driving, a yes answer may be contradicted by extrinsic evidence that his only pair of glasses was being repaired at the time of the accident. Evidence disputing the witness's acquisition of personal knowledge of facts relevant in the case is non-collateral. Likewise, if Bob denied on cross-examination that his wife was related to the plaintiff, extrinsic evidence of that fact would be admissible. Evidence of the witness's partiality is non-collateral. Extrinsic evidence offered to establish the witness's bias, interest, corruption, or coercion may be admitted following a witness's denial of a fact giving rise to such an inference of bias. Finally, restructuring the initial illustration, if Piagano's Pizza Restaurant is located on Birch Street and its location on Birch in relation to Bob's location prior to leaving for the restaurant would naturally place Bob on Main, not Apple, as he approached the intersection, extrinsic evidence of the location of the restaurant would be admissible. In this variation of the illustration, any error as to the location of the restaurant brings into question the trustworthiness of Bob's testimony on the historical merits of the case. Bob may have seen the light facing Main, not the light facing Apple. The location of the restaurant would be considered a "linchpin" fact, and extrinsic evidence would therefore be admissible to impeach Bob. A fact negating the assumption that the witness was in the right place at the right time to observe what he testified to is a "linchpin" fact.

What is the status of the common law collateral fact rule under the Federal Rules? The continued application of the standard theory of collateral contradiction in federal practice has been criticized on the ground that it is a mechanistic doctrine which ignores pertinent policy considerations. It has been urged that the discretionary approach of Rule 403 should be substituted. That approach is the better construction of the federal statutes. Although Rule 608(b) expressly prohibits extrinsic evidence of a witness's untruthful acts, the Federal Rules do not expressly codify a categorical collateral fact restriction. For example, there is

no mention of that restriction in Rule 613 governing prior inconsistent statement impeachment. Given Rule 402, there is a powerful argument that the collateral fact rule was impliedly repealed by the enactment of the Federal Rules. Under this reading of the Federal Rules, there is no rigid prohibition of introducing extrinsic evidence to impeach a witness on a collateral matter; rather, under Rule 403, the judge would make a practical judgment as to whether the importance of the witness's testimony and the impeachment warrant the expenditure of the additional trial time. However, the collateral fact rule was so ingrained at common law that many federal opinions continue to mention "collateral" evidence.

The abolition of the collateral fact doctrine by the Federal Rules is a two-edged sword. The preceding paragraph noted that under Rule 403, the witness's testimony and the impeaching evidence could have such practical importance that the judge might permit extrinsic evidence which would have been barred at common law. However, it is equally true that the judge could conceivably bar evidence which would technically have been considered non-collateral and admissible at common law. Thus, standing alone, compliance with the common law rule does not guarantee the admissibility of extrinsic evidence under the federal statutes.

§ 50. Exclusion and Separation of Witnesses

The immediately preceding paragraphs discuss the techniques which the counsel may use to either attack or support a witness's credibility. However, there are also steps which the judge can take to help ensure credible testimony. Judicial exclusion and separation orders are illustrative. If a witness hears the testimony of others before he or she takes the stand, it will be much easier for the witness to deliberately tailor her own story to that of other witnesses. Witnesses may also be influenced subconsciously. In either event, the cross-examiner will find it more difficult to expose fabrication, collusion, inconsistencies, or inaccuracies in the testimony of witnesses who have heard others testify. Separation prevents improper influence during the trial by prohibiting witness-to-witness communication both inside and outside the courtroom.

At common law the court in its discretion may exclude witnesses in the interests of the ascertainment of truth. Rather than adopting a discretionary approach, Federal and Revised Uniform Rule of Evidence (1974) 615 treat the exclusion of witnesses as a matter of right: "At the request of a party, the court shall order witnesses excluded." The court is also empowered to order exclusion on its own motion. A request to exclude witnesses is often referred to as "invoking the rule on witnesses." No time period is specified in which to make the request. Several standards have been applied in determining whether a trial judge's failure to order a witness's exclusion requires a reversal of the judgment.

Not all witnesses may be excluded and separated. Neither case law nor Rule 615 authorizes exclusion of (1) a party who is a natural person, (2) an officer or employee of a party which is not a natural person designated as its representative by its attorney which includes a government's investigative agent, (3) a person whose presence is shown by the party to be essential to the presentation of the cause, or (4) as of 1997, the victim of the offense an accused is charged with when the prosecution contemplates calling the victim as a witness during a subsequent sentencing hearing. In criminal cases, judges routinely invoke (2) to permit the attendance of the investigating case agent at trial. An example of a witness whose presence may be essential under (3) is an expert witness. It is sometimes vital to give counsel the benefit of an expert's assistance while an opposing expert is testifying. In particular, assistance may be necessary in connection with technical matters as to which counsel lacks sufficient familiarity to try the case effectively on his own. When the counsel lacks that familiarity, she may need an expert "at her elbow" during the opposing expert witnesses' testimony; without the expert's assistance, the counsel would be handicapped in preparing to conduct an immediate cross-examination. A strong argument can also be made for permitting the presence of an expert witness who intends to give an opinion at trial based in part on evidence presented at trial. Exclusion and separation do not extend to rebuttal witnesses or witnesses called to impeach credibility. Congress added exception (4) to Rule 615 in the 1997 Victim Rights Clarification Act.

While Rule 615 does not explicitly provide for the separation of witnesses, courts have inherent authority to take further measures designed to prevent communication between witnesses such as ordering them to remain physically apart, not to discuss the case with one another, and not to read a transcript of another witness's trial testimony.

If a witness violates an order of exclusion or sequestration, the appropriate remedy is committed to the trial judge's sound discretion. The court may refuse to permit a witness to testify, declare a mistrial, or give the jury a cautionary instruction to weigh the witness's credibility in light of the witness's presence in court or discussions with another witness. The court can also hold the witness in contempt. The courts are markedly reluctant to resort to the drastic remedy of disqualifying the witness. The strongest case for altogether barring the witness's testimony is a fact situation in which the witness heard testimony which could influence his or her own testimony and the party or counsel calling the witness colluded in the violation of the sequestration order. Unfortunately once it is decided to permit the witness to testify, the alternatives of comment or contempt are not without their drawbacks. The best approach is to avoid the problem beforehand as much as possible by the court impressing upon both the witness and counsel the importance of obeying the court's ruling excluding and separating the witness.

*

Title 3

ADMISSION AND EXCLUSION

Chapter 6

THE PROCEDURE OF ADMITTING
AND EXCLUDING EVIDENCE

Table of Sections

§ 51. Presentation of Evidence: Offer of Proof

To gain a working knowledge of evidence law, you must appreciate the procedural framework within which evidence doctrine operates. Our adversary system requires the parties to present trial evidence pursuant to rules that make it clear when proof has been presented before it is officially introduced and then may be considered by the trier of fact in resolving fact issues. The rules of practice concerning presentation of evidence, offers of proof, and objections all are designed to secure this result.

The presentation of things such as writings, photographs, knives, guns, and other tangible objects often proves troublesome to neophytes. There are variations in local procedures, but the general process may be briefly described here. The party wishing to introduce evidence of this type should first have the thing marked by the clerk for identification as an exhibit. After the proponent has the thing marked by the clerk for identification as an exhibit, the proposed exhibit ought to be submitted to the opposing attorney for his inspection, at least upon his request. After showing the exhibit to the opponent, the proponent approaches the witness. At this point, the proponent "lays the foundation" for its introduction as an exhibit by having it appropriately identified or authenticated by the witness's testimony. Although the courts often speak of laying "the foundation" in the singular, in truth the proponent may have to lay multiple foundations. Thus, a single exhibit such as a letter might require authentication, best evidence, and hearsay foundations.

After laying all the required foundations or predicates, the proponent tenders the exhibit to the judge by stating, "Plaintiff offers this (document or object, describing it), marked, 'Plaintiff's Exhibit No. 2' for identification, as Plaintiff's Exhibit No. 2." At this juncture, the opponent can object to its receipt in evidence, and the judge will rule on the objection. Assuming the judge rules that the exhibit will be accepted in evidence, if it is a writing, it may be read to the jury by the counsel offering it or by the witness. When it is a gun or knife, it may be shown or passed to the jurors, in the judge's discretion or in accordance with local custom or rules, for their inspection.

Of course, the usual way of presenting oral testimony is to call the witness to the stand and ask him questions. Normally, (but not always) the opponent must object to testimony by voicing objections to the questions before the witness answers the questions.[1] Ordinarily, the admissibility of testimony is decided by the judge's sustaining or overruling objections to questions. If the court sustains an objection to a question, the witness is prevented from answering the question and from testifying to that extent.

When the judge sustains an objection, for two reasons the proponent of the question should usually make "an offer of proof." The usual practice is for the proponent to explain to the judge what the witness would say if he were permitted to answer the question and what the expected answer is logically relevant to prove. One reason for an offer of proof is that it permits the trial judge to reconsider the claim for admissibility. Prior to the offer of proof, the judge might not have appreciated the relevance of the line of inquiry. However, the primary, formal reason is to preserve the issue for appeal by including the proposed answer and expected proof in the official record of trial. In case of appeal from the judge's ruling, the appellate court can better understand the scope and effect of the question and proposed answer to decide whether the judge's ruling sustaining an objection was error, whether the error was prejudicial, and what final disposition to make on appeal. The trial judge usually requires this offer of proof to be made outside the jury's hearing. The judge has already ruled the evidence inadmissible; and if the offer were made in the jury's hearing, the jury would be exposed to inadmissible testimony which could improperly influence their deliberation. Federal Rule of Evidence 103(c) im-

poses the requirement for an offer of proof. Significantly, on cross-examination, the requirement can be relaxed; some jurisdictions eliminate the need for an offer of proof on cross-examination while most courts accept less specific offers on cross than they demand on direct.

For the purpose of appeal, a question, in the context of the record, may itself so clearly indicate the tenor of the expected answer that the appellate court will consider the propriety of the ruling on the question without an offer of proof. But when, as is more usual, an offer of proof is required before the appellate court will consider a ruling sustaining an objection to a question, the statement constituting the offer of proof must be reasonably specific identifying the purpose of the proof offered unless the purpose is apparent. Thus, the proponent must tell the judge what the tenor of the evidence would be and why the evidence is logically relevant. Where the sustained objection challenges the materiality or competency of the testimony, the offer of proof should indicate the facts on which relevancy depends or why the objection is unsound. These general guidelines apply under Federal Rule of Evidence 103 as well as at common law.

If counsel specifies a purpose for which the proposed evidence is inadmissible and the judge excludes, counsel cannot complain of the ruling on appeal though it could have been admitted for another purpose.

Likewise, if part of the evidence offered, as in the case of a deposition, letter, or conversation, is admissible but a part is not, it is incumbent on the offeror, not the judge, to single out the admissible part. When counsel offers both good and bad together and the judge rejects the entire offer, the offeror may not complain on appeal.

The offer of proof methodology described above assumes there is a witness upon the stand who is being questioned. Suppose that there are several available witnesses, but not in court, to prove a line of facts. However, the judge's rulings indicate that he will probably exclude this entire line of testimony, or the

§ 51

1. See § 52 infra.

judge rules in advance that the line of testimony is inadmissible. Must the party produce each witness, question him, and on exclusion, state the purport of each expected answer? A few decisions have said that this procedure must be followed. Obviously that procedure entails a waste of time which witnesses, counsel, and trial judge would like to avoid. The better view is that it is not invariably essential; under this view, an adequate offer of proof can be made without producing all the witnesses, if it is sufficiently specific and there is nothing in the record to indicate a want of good faith or inability to produce the proof.

§ 52. Objections

If the administration of the exclusionary rules of evidence is to be fair and workable, the judge must be informed promptly of contentions that evidence should be rejected, and the reasons supporting the contentions. The burden is placed on the party opponent, not the judge. The general approach, accordingly, is that a failure to object assigning the ground to a proffer of evidence at the time the offer is made, is a waiver upon appeal of any ground of complaint against its admission. However, this usual approach is modified by the doctrine of plain error, discussed at the end of this section.

Time of Making: Motions to Strike. Consistently with the above approach, the opponent is not allowed to gamble on the possibility of a favorable answer. Rather, the opponent must object to the admission of evidence as soon as the ground for objection becomes apparent. Usually, in taking a witness's testimony, an objection is apparent as soon as the question is asked, since the wording of the question is likely to indicate that it calls for inadmissible evidence. Then counsel must, if there is an opportunity, state her objection before the witness answers. But sometimes an objection before an answer is infeasible. An eager witness may answer so quickly that counsel does not have a fair chance to object. In that event, the counsel may move to strike the answer for the purpose of interposing an objection to the question; if the judge thinks that the witness "jumped the gun" and grants

the motion, the counsel then states her objection to the question. Or a question which is unobjectionable may be followed by a partially or completely nonresponsive answer. In this situation, the questioner has the right to have the nonresponsive material stricken. Or after the evidence is received, a ground of objection to the evidence may later be disclosed for the first time. For example, although on direct examination the witness purported to testify from personal knowledge, it might become evident for the first time on cross that in reality, the witness is relying on inadmissible hearsay. In all these cases, an "after-objection" may be stated as soon as the ground appears. The proper technique is to move to strike the objectionable evidence and request a curative instruction to the jury to disregard the evidence. Ideally, counsel should use the term of art "motion to strike," but any phraseology directing the judge's attention to the grounds as soon as they appear ought to suffice.

Suppose that the evidence is a transcript of a previously taken deposition. The time when objections must be made to deposition questions is variously regulated by rules and statutes in the different jurisdictions. Usually objections going to the "manner and form" of the questions or answers, such as objections to leading questions or nonresponsive answers— sometimes opinions and secondary evidence are put in this class—must be made during taking the deposition (and disposed of by pretrial motion). The rationale is that in all these cases, if the opponent had objected on the spot, the proponent could have cured the problem by, for instance, rephrasing the question or establishing an excuse for the non-production of the original writing. In contrast, objections going to the "substance," such as relevancy and hearsay, may ordinarily be urged for the first time when the deposition is offered at trial.

Assume that there was a prior trial rather than a prior deposition hearing. If evidence was introduced at the earlier trial of the case, and an available objection was not made then, may the same evidence when tendered at a second trial of the same case be objected to for the first time? See § 259 infra.

Motions in Limine. A motion for an advance ruling on the admissibility of evidence is a relatively modern device for obtaining rulings on evidence even before the evidence is sought to be introduced. The purpose of such motions may be to shield the jury from exposure to prejudicial inadmissible evidence or to afford a basis for strategic decisions. For instance, an advance ruling might help the counsel decide whether to mention an item of evidence during opening statement or advise her client whether to take the stand. Advance rulings upon objections can be sought before trial or during trial before the presentation of the evidence. The usual rule is that the judge has a wide discretion to make or refuse to make advance rulings, although there is some old authority forbidding advance rulings. Unless the decision on a motion requires a factual background of the evidence as it develops at the trial, and as long as the matter is left primarily within the trial judge's discretion, the use of motions in limine for these purposes should be encouraged. In view of some disagreement in the published opinions, it has been recommended both that objections which have been overruled at a hearing on a motion in limine be repeated at trial and that where an objection has been sustained, an offer of proof be made at trial. If she loses the motion, the prevailing view requires the opponent to renew the objection at trial in order to preserve the issue for appeal. However, some appellate courts dispense with a requirement for renewal when the trial judge's ruling is explicit and purportedly definitive. If motions in limine are to be permitted as a means of advance objection by the opponent, in fairness the future proponent of evidence should be allowed to seek an advance ruling. Like the opponent, the proponent would like to know whether it is safe or even necessary to mention a particular item of evidence during voir dire examination and opening statement.

The instant type of motion should be distinguished from motions for suppression.[1] Suppression motions typically rest on constitutional grounds rather than statutory and common law evidence rules. Moreover, in most jurisdictions, the party must make suppression motions before trial under pain of waiver.[2]

General and Specific Objections. It is a commonplace assertion that objections must be accompanied by a definite statement of the grounds; in other words, objections must reasonably indicate the appropriate rules of evidence relied on as reasons for the objections. These objections are labeled "specific" objections in contrast to so-called general objections assigning no such grounds for the objection. The specificity requirement serves important purposes at the trial level; the requirement helps to ensure that the trial judge understands the objection raised and that the adversary has an opportunity to remedy the defect, if possible. This precept does not *per se* ban the use of general objections (objections which state no grounds) at trial. When the evidence is objectionable on some ground, the judge has discretion to sustain a general objection. However, as we shall see, the requirement is enforced to a certain extent on appeal. The second purpose of the requirement is to make a proper record for the reviewing court in the event of an appeal.

If the judge *overrules* a general objection, the objecting party may not ordinarily complain of the ruling on appeal by urging a ground not mentioned when the objection was made at trial. Yet, there are three exceptional situations in which the appellate court will disregard this requirement and consider a meritorious objection that was not voiced to the trial judge. First, if the ground for exclusion should have been obvious to judge and opposing counsel, the want of specification of the ground is immaterial for purposes of appealing the judge's action overruling the general objection. This exception is simple good sense. Second, it has been held that if the evidence is inadmissible for any purpose, a general objection may suffice to secure appellate review of the judge's overruling the objection. This exception makes little sense if the ground is not apparent; when the ground is

---

1. See § 180 infra.

2. See § 53 infra.

not evident, there is still a need for specification for appeal. Third, it has been suggested that if the omitted ground could not have been obviated, a general objection can secure appellate consideration of an unstated, specific objection. The case for this exception overlooks an important consideration: Although the objection to the particular evidence could not have been obviated, if the objection had been stated and the proponent realized the validity of the objection, the proponent might have withdrawn the inadmissible evidence and substituted other evidence to fill the gap. This third exception is not codified under Federal Rule Evid. 103(a)(1).

As a result of the above-mentioned rules, a trial judge's action in overruling a general objection will usually be upheld on appeal. If the trial judge *sustains* a general objection, the appellate court is again charitable toward the trial judge's ruling. "When evidence is *excluded* upon a mere general objection, the ruling will be upheld, if any ground in fact existed for the exclusion. It will be assumed, in the absence of any request by the opposing party or the court to make the objection definite, that it was understood, and that the ruling was placed upon the right ground."[3]

Examples of general objections are "I object;" objections on the ground that the evidence is "inadmissible," "illegal," "incompetent," "foundation," is not "proper" testimony, or an objection "on all the grounds ever known or heard of". One of the most overworked forms is an objection that the evidence is "incompetent, irrelevant and immaterial." Its rhythm and alliteration have seduced some lawyers to employ it as a routine ritual. Courts frequently treat this form as equivalent merely to the general objection, "I object." The word "incompetent" as applied to evidence means no more than inadmissible, and thus does not state a ground of objection. However, "irrelevant and immaterial," though somewhat general in wording, do state a distinct, substantial ground for exclusion. A requirement that the objector state specifically the reason why the evidence

is irrelevant or immaterial, as some courts demand, can be unduly burdensome; it requires the opponent to prove a negative. It would be more practical to consider the irrelevancy objection in this form as a specific objection with the qualification that if the judge has any doubt of relevancy, she may ask the proponent to explain the purpose of the proof.

To make a sufficiently specific objection, the opponent should name the generic evidentiary rule being violated: "calls for information protected by the attorney-client privilege," "lack of authentication," "not the best evidence," or "hearsay"—the level of specificity found in the phrasing of the titles of the various articles in the Federal Rules of Evidence. Under the prevailing view, it is unnecessary to be any more specific. From a tactical perspective, it is usually undesirable to be more specific; if the opponent names the specific deficiency in the foundation, the opponent has in effect educated the proponent, and the proponent now knows exactly how to cure the defect in the foundation. However, there is a minority view requiring the opponent to specify the missing foundational element. This view has the advantage of forcing the opponent to get right to the point and thereby saving trial time.

While an "irrelevancy" objection has on occasion been held sufficient to preserve a claim of prejudice in the sense of arousing personal animus against the party, that phrasing does not explicitly raise the policy concerns listed in Federal Rule 403. These concerns can readily be raised specifically and do not entail the burden of establishing a negative. The judge should demand that the opponent cite Rule 403 or identify probative dangers mentioned in Rule 403.

Objections ought to be specific not only with regard to the ground, but also with respect to the particular part of an offer. Suppose that evidence sought to be introduced consists of several statements or items tendered as a unit in a deposition, letter, conversation, or transcript of testimony. The objec-

---

3. Tooley v. Bacon, 70 N.Y. 34, 37 (1877).

tion is to the whole of the evidence when parts are subject to the objection made but parts are not. In this situation, the judge will not be held to have erred in overruling the objection. It is not the judge's responsibility to sever the bad parts if some are good. That is the opponent's task. Obviously this rule should not be administered rigidly by the appellate courts but with due concession to the realities of the particular trial situation.

Now assume that evidence offered is properly admissible on a particular issue but not upon some other issue, or is admissible against one party but not against another. Here, though she assigns grounds, an objector who asks that this evidence be excluded altogether cannot complain on appeal if her objection is overruled. She should ask that the admission of the evidence be limited to the particular purpose or party. When the counsel represents only one party at trial, she is obviously claiming that the evidence is inadmissible against her client. However, when counsel appears on behalf of multiple clients at the same trial, the evidence might be admissible as against one but inadmissible as against the other. In this situation, counsel runs the risk of waiving the objection if she does not identify the client whom the evidence is inadmissible against.

On appeal, the *overruling* of an untenable specific objection will not be reversed because there was a tenable ground for exclusion which was not urged in the trial court.

When an untenable specific objection is *sustained*, there is authority that the appellate court will uphold the ruling if there is any other ground for doing so, even though not urged below. There is no point in ordering a retrial if the evidence would then be excluded on the proper ground. However, some qualifications must be made. When the correct objection, had it been made, could have been obviated, or admissible evidence could have been substituted, a retrial is appropriate. If a ruling upon the proper objection at the second trial would involve the judge's discretion, again a new trial is appropriate unless the judge determines that on remand her discretion would be

exercised in favor of exclusion. A similar result should follow where findings of fact are required as a preliminary to determining admissibility.

Repetition of Objections. A offers one witness's testimony which his adversary, B, thinks is inadmissible. B objects, and the objection is *sustained*. In that event, when A offers similar testimony by the same or another witness, B must repeat her objection if she is to complain of the later evidence. Suppose, however, the first objection is *overruled*. Must B then repeat her objection when other similarly objectionable evidence is offered? A few decisions intimate that she must—a requirement which places B in the unenviable posture of a contentious obstructor, and conduces to wasting time and fraying patience. Most courts, however, hold that B is entitled to assume that the judge will continue to make the same ruling and she need not repeat the objection. The logical consequences of this view are that the first objection is not waived and that in addition, the reach of this objection extends to all subsequent, similar evidence vulnerable to the same objection. In any jurisdiction where the practice in this respect is at all doubtful, it is a wise precaution for objecting counsel to ask the judge to have the record reflect that the objection is "continuing," going to all other like evidence, and when later evidence is offered, to have it noted that the earlier objection applies.

The Exception. Closely associated with the objection but distinct from it was the classic common law exception. The federal rules and the practice in most states dispense with exceptions, and provide that for all purposes, "it is sufficient that a party, at the time the ruling or order of the court is made or sought, makes known to the court the action which the party desires the court to take or his objection * * * and the party's grounds therefor."[4] Nevertheless, for reasons such as an attempt to impress a jury, some attorneys persist in announcing that they except to a ruling at jury trials even in jurisdictions where exceptions are unnecessary.

4. Fed.R.Civ.P. 46; Fed.R.Crim.P. 51.

The Tactics of Objecting. Jurors want to know the facts. They may resent objections as attempts to hide the facts, and view successful objections as the suppression of the truth. If this description of the jury's attitude is accurate, certain conclusions as to desirable tactics follow.

No objections should be made unless there is reason to believe that making the objection will do more good than harm. Conduct a cost/benefit analysis. In some situations, an objection can be counterproductive. Objections to leading questions or opinion evidence frequently result in strengthening the examiner's case by requiring her to elicit the testimony in more concrete, convincing form. In a given case, an authentication, best evidence, or hearsay objection can have the same result and backfire. Further, if an objection has little chance of being sustained at trial or on appeal, it should usually not be made. An unsuccessful objection may succeed only in magnifying the importance of unfavorable evidence; the jurors might reason that the opponent must have thought that the evidence was damning because he went to the length of trying to exclude it. Objections ought to be few in number, they should target only evidence which will be substantially harmful, and even then only when the objector believes she can probably obtain a favorable ruling at trial or on appeal.

Finally, when objections are made in the jury's presence, the objector's demeanor and the phrasing of the objection are important. An objection ought to be phrased so that it does not sound as if it rests merely on some technical rule. Thus, an objection to a copy under the best evidence rule should not be stated solely in terms of "secondary evidence" but should also cite the unreliability of the incomplete copy. Likewise, the objection "hearsay" ought to be expanded to mention the need to produce the declarant so that the jury can see him, and his sources of knowledge may be tested. The art of making effective objections at a jury trial consists in adding an adjective, adverb, or brief phrase which signals the jury that the ground of the objection relates to substantive justice. However, most judges do not tolerate lengthy "speaking" ob-

jections. If a counsel is foolish enough to attempt such an objection, the judge might admonish counsel in the jury's hearing.

Withdrawal of Evidence. The Federal and revised Uniform Rules of Evidence (1974) do not deal explicitly with the subject of withdrawal of evidence. A reasonable interpretation of Rule 611(a), however, would include permitting withdrawal as an aspect of the court's discretionary control over the presentation of evidence. The discretion could be exercised in accordance with the following case law principles. If a party has introduced evidence which is not objected to and which turns out to be favorable to the adversary, it has sometimes been intimated that the offering party may withdraw the evidence as of right. The accepted rule, however, is that withdrawal is not of right. Rather, the adversary is entitled to have the benefit of the testimony, unless the special situation makes it fair for the judge in her discretion to allow withdrawal. On the other hand, if the evidence is admitted over the adversary's objection, and the proponent later decides to yield to the objection and asks to withdraw the evidence, the court may revoke its ruling and permit the withdrawal.

Plain Error Rule. Many of the criteria for the so-called "harmless error" rule and the "plain error" rule are similar, but the two concepts should be distinguished. Federal and Revised Uniform Rule of Evidence (1974) 103(a) codify the "harmless error" concept with the statement, "Error may not be predicated upon a ruling which admits or excludes evidence unless a substantial right of a party is affected * * *." Thus, only harmful errors warrant relief. Plain error is defined in Rule 103(d), "Nothing in this rule precludes taking notice of plain errors affecting substantial rights although they were not brought to the attention of the court." In contrast to harmful error, harmless error denotes a ruling which is incorrect but which is not cause for reversal. Plain error denotes a harmful error that is sufficiently serious to justify considering it on appeal despite a failure to observe the usual procedural requirements for saving error for review. This section is confined to plain error.

There are several key distinctions between plain and harmful error. To begin with, there is a difference in degree between harmful and plain error. For error not to be harmless, the courts speak as though the error must be prejudicial to the appellant; but for plain error, the error must have *very* prejudicial effects. To qualify as plain error, the error must be a "blockbuster." Harmful error is the genus, and plain error is the species. Moreover, to trigger the plain error doctrine, the error must create a risk of a miscarriage of substantive justice. Many exclusionary rules of evidence bar the admission of relevant, reliable evidence in order to promote an extrinsic social policy. While those rules are certainly legitimate, it may be difficult to persuade an appellate court that a ruling admitting relevant, trustworthy evidence was likely to cause justice to miscarry. Despite the fundamental theoretical distinctions between the two concepts, surprisingly little difference can be found in the way the harmful and plain error concepts are applied in actual cases.

For many reasons, including the appellate courts' hesitancy to interfere with lower court trial responsibilities[5] and lack of details in the appellate record relating to the question of whether there was prejudicial error, there is a marked judicial tendency to avoid finding error even in criminal cases. A holding of plain error is far more likely in cases involving the constitutional rights of criminal defendants. Reversals on the basis of plain error are much less common in civil suits than in criminal cases, in part because liberty and life are not at stake in a civil lawsuit.

The application of the plain error doctrine depends upon a fact intensive, case specific analysis. Findings of plain error are not only rarities; they also have limited precedential value.

§ 53. Preliminary Questions of Fact Arising on Objections

The great body of evidence law consists of rules that operate to exclude relevant evidence. Examples are the hearsay doctrine, the rule preferring original writings, and the privileges for confidential communications. All these exclusionary rules are "technical" in the sense that they were developed by a special professional group, judges and lawyers, and in the further sense that for long-term ends they sometimes obstruct the ascertainment of truth in the particular case. Most of these technical exclusionary rules and their exceptions are conditioned upon the existence of certain facts. These are not the facts on the historical merits of the case under Federal Rule of Evidence 401. Rather, these are foundational or preliminary facts falling under Rule 104. For example, a copy of a writing will not be received unless the original is lost, destroyed, or otherwise unavailable.[1] Suppose a copy is offered and there is conflicting evidence as to whether the original is destroyed or intact. The judge, of course, announces the rule of evidence law setting up the criterion of admission or exclusion. However, who is to decide whether the original is lost, destroyed or unavailable—the preliminary question of fact upon which hinges the *application* of the rule of evidence law?

Issues of fact are usually left to the jury, but there are strong reasons for not doing so here. If the special question of fact were submitted to the jury when objection was made, cumbersome problems about unanimity would be raised. If the judge submitted the evidence (such as the copy in the hypothetical) to the jury and directed them to disregard it unless they found that the disputed fact existed, the aim of the exclusionary rule might be frustrated for two reasons. First, the jury would often be unable to erase the evidence from their minds even after they found that the conditioning fact did not exist. For instance, even if the jury found that an accused's statement to his attorney was technically privileged and inadmissible, common sense suggests that they would have a difficult time forgetting that they had learned that the accused admitted committing the charged offense. Second, some jurors might be unwilling to perform the intel-

---

5. See § 55 infra.

1. See § 230 infra.

lectual gymnastic of "disregarding" the evidence. They are intent mainly on reaching a verdict in accord with what they believe to be true, rather than in promoting the long-term policies of evidence law. The policy of protecting privacy interests justifies enforcing privileges, but the jurors might view a privilege as an impediment to their task of doing justice in the case before them.

Foundational facts conditioning the application of technical exclusionary rules. Accordingly, under the traditional and still generally accepted view, the trial judge finally decides the preliminary questions of fact conditioning the admissibility of evidence objected to under exclusionary rules such as the hearsay doctrine.[2] This principle is incorporated in Federal and Revised Uniform Rule of Evidence (1974) 104(a). The same practice extends to the determination of preliminary facts conditioning the application of the rules as to witnesses' competency and privileges. On all these preliminary questions the judge, on request, will hold a hearing at which each side may produce evidence. When the opponent objects, she can request the opportunity to conduct voir dire in support of the objection. In effect, the voir dire is a mini cross-examination. During the voir dire, the opponent questions the witness solely about the foundational fact which the proponent attempted to establish. Between the proponent's foundation and the opponent's voir dire, the judge hears all the evidence both pro and con on the foundational issue. The judge acts as a factfinder in determining the existence of the foundational fact. The judge may consider the credibility of the foundational testimony. Thus, the judge can decide to disbelieve the proponent's testimony even if it is facially sufficient.

Foundational facts conditioning the logical relevance of the evidence. The foregoing discussion involves situations where the evidence is sought to be excluded under a "technical" exclusionary rule. Those situations must be distinguished from another type of situation, namely one in which the logical relevancy—the fundamental probative value—of

the evidence depends on the existence of a preliminary fact. As the Advisory Committee's Note to Federal Rule of Evidence 104(b) observes:

> Thus when a spoken statement is relied upon to prove notice to X, it is without probative value unless X heard it. Or if a letter purporting to be from Y is relied upon to establish an admission by him, it has no probative value unless Y wrote ... it. Relevance in this sense has been labelled "conditional relevancy." Morgan, Basic Problems of Evidence 45–56 (1962).[3]

These factual questions of conditional relevancy under Rule 104(b) not only differ from questions falling under Rule 104(a); they also differ from questions whether particular evidence is relevant as a matter of law under Rule 401, such as the issue of whether evidence that on the day before a murder the accused purchased a weapon of the type used in the killing is relevant. Questions of the latter nature are, of course, for the judge. Distinguish that Rule 401 question of law from the Rule 104(b) question of fact whether the gun marked as prosecution exhibit #3 for identification is the very gun the accused purchased.

Conditional relevancy questions under 104(b) are well within the jurors' competency; they involve the kind of questions which jurors are accustomed to decide. Did A say such-and-such? Did B hear him? Did C sign the letter offered in evidence? The jury's role would be greatly curtailed if judges made the final decisions on these questions. The judge is not, however, entirely eliminated from the picture but divides responsibility with the jury in the following manner. The judge requires the proponent to bring forward evidence from which a rational jury could find the existence of the preliminary fact. At this point, the judge plays a limited, screening role. The judge cannot pass on the credibility of the foundational testimony. Rather, the judge must accept the testimony at face value and ask only this question: If the jury decides to believe the testimony, is there a rational, permissive inference of

2. See § 162 infra, for rules concerning the admission of a criminal defendant's confession.

3. See the general treatment of authentication as an aspect of conditional relevancy, Ch. 22 infra.

the existence of the preliminary fact? When the judge determines that the jury could not find the existence of the preliminary fact, he excludes the evidence. Otherwise, the question is for the jury. Although in fact many trial judges permit the opponent to conduct voir dire on conditional relevance issues, strictly speaking the opponent has no right to voir dire on this type of issue. When the opponent has contrary evidence, the opponent submits it to the jury rather than the judge. On request, in the final instructions the judge directs the jury to determine the existence of the foundational fact and to disregard the evidence if they find that the foundational fact has not been proven.

This procedure is followed at modern common law and prescribed by Federal and Revised Uniform Rule of Evidence (1974) 104(b), reading:

> When the relevancy of evidence depends on the fulfillment of a condition of fact, the court shall admit it upon, or subject to, the introduction of evidence sufficient to support a finding of the fulfillment of the condition.

Federal Rule 602 expressly applies this procedure to the preliminary issue of a lay witness's personal knowledge, and Rule 901(a) extends the procedure to the foundational issue of the authenticity of exhibits. The drafters reasoned that the jurors could be trusted to decide these preliminary issues; if the jurors find that a lay witness did not see the accident he testified about or that a letter allegedly written by the accused is a forgery, common sense should lead them to disregard the witness's testimony or the letter during their deliberations. In short, the jurors can be trusted to make these determinations.

Some situations have not readily lent themselves to classification as falling in either of the two categories of facts and accordingly require further discussion.[4]

First, confessions are subject to their own special rules, which are treated elsewhere.[5]

Second, in cases involving dying declarations some courts give the jury a role in deciding the preliminary question whether declarant had the settled, hopeless expectation of death required for that hearsay exception.[6] This practice is not followed under Federal and Revised Uniform Rule of Evidence (1974) 104.

Third, in a troublesome group of cases, the preliminary fact question coincides with one of the ultimate disputed fact-issues that the jury normally decides. There are several examples. (1) In a bigamy prosecution, the first marriage is disputed, the second wife is called as a state's witness, and defendant objects under a statute disqualifying the wife to testify against her husband. (2) Plaintiff sues on a lost writing, and defendant raises a best evidence objection and contends that it was not lost because it never existed. (3) In a prosecution, the state offers an alleged coconspirator's declaration made during the course of and in furtherance of the conspiracy. Defendants deny that the conspiracy ever existed. The published common law opinions on these three issues are split.

In Example (1) the preliminary question involves the witness's competency, a question for the judge at common law or under Rule 104(a) if it were not for the overlap with the jury issue on the merits of whether she was validly married to the accused. Allowing the judge to decide her competency does not interfere with the jury's function in any way; his decision need not be communicated to the jury, and additional relevant evidence may be made available to the jury. Accordingly the cases tend to leave the decision to the judge. Even if the judge decides to overrule the competency objection and permit the spouse's testimony, the accused can litigate the question

---

4. In Huddleston v. United States, 485 U.S. 681 (1988), the Court held that Rule 104(b) governs the foundational question of whether the accused committed an act of uncharged misconduct proffered under Rule 404(b), for example, another murder allegedly committed with the

same distinctive modus operandi. A number of courts have refused to follow Huddleston.

5. Infra § 162.

6. The nature of the requirement is discussed in § 310 infra.

of the validity of the second marriage to the jury during the trial on the merits.

In Example (2) the preliminary question whether a writing was lost is ordinarily for the judge at common law or under Rule 104(a), but the writing obviously cannot have been lost if it never existed. Aside from the question of loss, the execution of the document would be a jury question; the preliminary question of authentication under Rule 901 is allocated to the jury at common law and under Rule 104(b). The basic issue in the case is whether the original writing ever existed; the question whether it has been lost is subsidiary. Sound judgment calls for the assignment of the decision of the basic question to the jury, rather than having it subsumed into the judge's authority to determine the application of the best evidence rule. This is the result both by decision and under Rule 1008. If the judge decided that the writing never existed and excluded the secondary evidence, the case would end without ever going to the jury on the central issue.

In Example (3), at common law the cases divide as to whether the judge should make the preliminary determination whether a conspiracy existed and defendant and declarant were members of it, or whether the judge ought to admit the evidence upon a prima facie showing, instructing the jury to disregard it if they find these matters not proved. Supporting the first position is the argument that the judge is dealing with the applicability of a hearsay doctrine, the exemption for co-conspirator declarations. This reasoning points to the application of Rule 104(a) under the Federal and Revised Uniform Rules. In contrast, under one view of the hearsay definition, virtually all co-conspirator declarations qualify as "verbal acts,"[7] and hence nonhearsay in the first place. This reasoning would lead to the jury making the determination, after screening by the judge, as a question of conditional relevancy. Whatever the relative merits of these positions, the United States Supreme Court in

Bourjaily v. United States[8] declared authoritatively that determining the admissibility of a co-conspirator's statement is solely a matter for the judge under Rule 104(a) and that the judge must apply the more probably true than not (preponderance) standard of proof. This result probably reflects two considerations: the difficulty, and to some extent unreality, of submitting the preliminary question to the jury, and the courts' understandable wish to limit the use of conspiracy charges by prosecutors.

A closely related question is whether Rule 104(a) or 104(b) governs the foundational facts conditioning the hearsay exemption for authorized admissions in civil cases. One would think that the same procedure should govern the foundations for both hearsay exemptions; after all, a conspiracy is a criminal agency. However, even after the Supreme Court rendered its decision in *Bourjaily*, there was a strong statutory construction argument that Rule 104(b) controlled the foundational facts for the civil exemption. The Advisory Committee Note to Rule 104 approvingly quotes Professor Morgan as indicating that it is a conditional relevance question whether a principal "authorized" an admission made by an alleged agent. Some jurisdictions are firmly committed to the view that these are conditional relevance questions. However, the December 1, 1997 amendment to Federal Rule 801 makes it clear that the courts are to apply the same procedure to both sets of foundational facts. Since *Bourjaily* squarely holds that Rule 104(a) governs the facts conditioning the co-conspirator exemption, a fortiori 104(a) now controls the preliminary facts for authorized admissions.

§ 54. Availability as Proof of Evidence Admitted Without Objection

As indicated in section 52, a failure to make a sufficient objection to incompetent evidence waives any ground of complaint as to the admission of the evidence.[1] But it has

---

7. Infra § 259.

8. 483 U.S. 171 (1987).

§ 54

1. This statement is subject to the "plain error" rule. See § 52 supra.

another equally important effect. If the evidence is received without objection, it becomes part of the evidence in the case and is usable as proof to the extent of its rational persuasive power. The fact that it was inadmissible does not prevent its use as proof so far as it has probative value. The incompetent evidence, unobjected to, may be relied on in argument, and alone or in part it can support a verdict or finding. This principle is almost universally accepted. The Federal and Revised Uniform Rules of Evidence are silent on this subject but raise no doubt as to the continued viability of the common law rule. The principle applies to any ground of incompetency under the exclusionary rules. It is most often invoked in respect to hearsay, but it has been applied to secondary evidence of writings, opinions, evidence elicited from incompetent witnesses, privileged information, and evidence subject to objection because of the lack of authentication of a writing, of firsthand knowledge, or of expert qualification.

Relevancy and probative worth, however, stand on a different footing. If the evidence has no probative force or insufficient probative value to sustain the proposition for which it is offered, the want of objection adds nothing to its worth; and it will not support a finding. It is still irrelevant or insufficient. However, the failure to object to evidence related to the controversy but not covered by the pleadings, can amount to the informal framing of new issues and an implied amendment of the pleadings. When this is held to have occurred, the failure to object on the ground that the evidence is irrelevant to any issue raised by the pleadings is waived, and the evidence can support the proponent's position on the new informal issue.

§ 55.   Waiver of Objection

A failure to assert an objection promptly and specifically is a waiver.[1] What other conduct constitutes a waiver?

Demand for inspection of a writing. Federal Rule of Civil Procedure 34 authorizes a litigant to demand that the opponent produce writings and objects for pretrial inspection. One party, D, gives notice to his opponent, O, to produce a document, and O produces it at the trial. Then in open court D asks to inspect it and is allowed to do so. Assume that under some evidentiary doctrine the document, if offered by O, would be inadmissible except for the notice, production, and inspection. Do these facts preclude D from objecting when the document is offered by O? Old precedents in England, Massachusetts, and a few other states said yes, D is precluded from objecting. This result was originally rationalized on the notion that it would be unconscionable to permit the demanding party to examine the producing party's private papers without being subjected to some corresponding risk. A later case, however, attempted to justify the result on the ground that the party who is called on in open court before a jury to produce a writing for inspection may be suspected of evasion or concealment unless he is allowed to introduce the writing.

The modern cases recognize that the old policy against compelled disclosure of relevant writings in a party's possession is outmoded. The prevailing policy is just the opposite, namely, that of pressuring full disclosure except for privileged matter. Accordingly, today the overwhelming majority of states reject the old rule and permit D to assert any pertinent objection if O offers the writing. This rule is consistent with Federal and Revised Uniform Rule of Evidence (1974) 103(a)(1). The older view is at odds with the pretrial discovery policy of the federal civil rules, which have been adopted widely in the states. The matter today is in fact largely, if not totally, historical. In this fact situation, it is silly to infer that the party requesting production has waived all evidentiary objections to the introduction of the writing; the party cannot forecast the potential objections until he or she has had an opportunity to review the contents of the writing.

Failure to object to earlier like evidence. A party has introduced evidence of particular facts without objection. Later he offers additional evidence, perhaps by other witnesses or

1. See § 52 supra.

writings, of the same facts. May the adversary now object, or has he waived his right by his earlier quiescence? It is often summarily stated in the opinions that he is precluded from objecting. But in opinions where the question is carefully analyzed, it is usually concluded that the mere earlier failure to object to other like evidence is not a waiver of objection to the new inadmissible evidence. This conclusion should be reached under the Federal and Revised Uniform Rules of Evidence. Of course, overruling the new objection will frequently not be harmful error, since the earlier evidence could render the error harmless; but that is a different question. The best trial attorneys withhold objection unless the evidence would clearly be damaging. Their practice is in the interest of judicial economy and encouraged by the nonwaiver rule. The conventional wisdom is that an attorney should not assert every technically available objection; to avoid alienating the jury, the attorney ought to object only when the objection is both tactically and legally sound—as when the evidence in question would do major damage to the attorney's theory of the case. It might have been tactically inadvisable to object to the earlier evidence; although the testimony could have been technically objectionable under evidence law, its contents might have been innocuous or positively helpful. It would be wrong-minded to infer a waiver from the earlier failure to object. On the other hand, when the evidence of the fact, admitted without objection, is extensive, and the evidence though inadmissible has some probative value, the trial judge should be conceded a discretion to find that the objector's conduct amounted to a waiver. Again, this approach can be followed under the Federal and Revised Uniform Rules of Evidence.

The Offering of Like Evidence by the Objector. If a party who has objected to evidence of a certain fact himself produces evidence from his own witness of the same fact, he has waived his objection. This result should obtain under the Federal and Revised Uniform Rules of Evidence. However, when his objection is made and overruled, he is entitled to treat this

ruling as the "law of the trial" and to explain or rebut, if he can, the evidence admitted over his protest. Consequently, there is no waiver if he cross-examines the adversary's witness about the matter, even though the cross-examination entails a repetition of the fact, or if he meets the testimony with other evidence which, under the theory of his objection, would be inadmissible. The Federal and Revised Uniform Rules of Evidence should not be construed as changing these results.

Exclusion by Judge in Absence of Objection. A party's failure to object usually waives the objection and forecloses the party from complaining if the evidence is admitted.[2] But the party's failure does not preclude the trial judge from excluding the evidence on his own motion if the witness is disqualified for want of capacity or the evidence is inadmissible, and the judge believes the interests of justice require the exclusion of the testimony. The Federal and Revised Uniform Rules of Evidence grant the judge sufficiently broad power to intervene *sua sponte* in such circumstances. However, much evidence such as reliable affidavits or copies of writings, though inadmissible under the technical exclusionary rules, is reliable and valuable. In that case, absent an objection, the trial judge would be unjustified in excluding the evidence. The judge should exercise his discretionary power to intervene only when the evidence is irrelevant, unreliable, misleading, or prejudicial, as well as inadmissible.

However, privileged evidence, such as confidential communications between husband and wife, ought to be treated differently. The privileges protect the holder's outside interests, not the parties' interest in securing justice in the present litigation. Accordingly, when privileged matter is called for and the holder is present, the judge may, if necessary, explain the privilege to the holder; but the judge should not assert it of his own motion if the holder decides against claiming the privilege. In contrast, when the holder is absent, the judge in some jurisdictions has a discre-

---

2. See § 52 supra.

tionary power to assert it on the holder's behalf.

§ 56. The Effect of the Introduction of Part of a Writing or Conversation

The immediately preceding sections discuss the procedures which apply when the opposing attorney negatively attempts to exclude the evidence proffered by the proponent. In some cases, though, the opponent endeavors to turn the proponent's proffer to an affirmative advantage; the opponent argues that the proponent's proffer allows the opponent to introduce evidence that might otherwise be inadmissible. Sections 56 and 57 discuss these cases. This section addresses the rule of completeness, and § 57 describes the curative admissibility doctrine.

Two competing considerations come into play when a party offers in evidence only a portion of a writing, oral statement, or conversation. The first is the danger of admitting only the portion, wresting that part of the expression out of its context. "The fool hath said in his heart, there is no God,"[1] where the only last phrase is quoted, is a classic example of the possibilities of distortion. You could quote the Bible as saying "there is no God;" but to do so would be a misleading half-truth because it divorces the quotation from its context. This danger, moreover, is not completely averted by a later, separate reading of the omitted parts. The distorted impression may sometimes linger, and work its influence at the subconscious level. Second is the opposing danger of requiring that the whole be offered, thereby wasting time and attention by cluttering the trial record with passages which have no bearing on the present controversy.

What is the proper balance between these two dangers? In the light of the dangers, is a party who seeks to introduce part of a writing or statement required to offer it in entirety, or at least all that is relevant to the facts sought to be proved? Under the common law version of the rule of completeness, the prevailing practice permits the proponent to prove only such part as he desires. At common law, the opponent cannot force the proponent to broaden the scope of his questioning of the witness. However, when the proponent turns the witness over to the opponent for questioning, the opponent can then elicit the other parts relevant to the same topic. Although the Federal Rules of Evidence do not expressly codify this aspect of the rule of completeness, the opponent can still invoke this doctrine in modern federal practice.[2]

However, there is a strong policy argument that to guard against the danger of an ineradicable, false first impression, the adversary should have an additional right; the adversary ought to be permitted to require the proponent to prove both the part which the proponent desires to introduce and other passages which are an essential part of its context. Federal and Revised Uniform Rule of Evidence (1974) 106 go beyond the common law completeness rule and give the opponent the right to demand that the proponent expand the scope of his questioning of the witness to avoid creating a misleading initial impression. The statute prescribes this rule for writings or recorded statements. It is sometimes stated that the additional material may be introduced only if it is otherwise admissible. However, as a categorical rule, that statement is unsound. In particular, the statement is inaccurate as applied to hearsay law. At least when the other passage of the writing or statement is so closely connected to the part the proponent contemplates introducing that it furnishes integral context for that part, the passage is admissible on a nonhearsay theory. Moreover, since the complex of admissibility doctrines includes the concept of waiver of objection through "door opening"[3], otherwise inadmissible part often becomes admissible. Ultimately, whether an otherwise inadmissible part offered to explain, modify, or qualify the

§ 56

1.　The oft-repeated classic illustration, see 7 Wigmore, Evidence § 2094 (Chadbourn rev. 1978).

2.　In Beech Aircraft Corp. v. Rainey, 488 U.S. 153 (1988), the Court indicated that Rule 106 "partially codified" the completeness doctrine.

3.　For further discussion of "opening the door," see § 57 infra.

part already received is admitted should depend upon whether its probative value for that purpose is substantially outweighed by dangers of unfair prejudice, confusion of the issues, misleading the jury, or waste of time.

As to the adversary's other alternative, namely, later invoking the more limited, common law completeness rule, the state of the case law is clearer and more consistent. She may wait until her own next stage of presenting proof. Then merely by reason of the fact that the first party has introduced a part, she has the right to introduce the remainder of the writing, recording, statement, correspondence, former testimony, or conversation relating to the same subject matter. The more drastic doctrine, Rule 106, does not come into play unless the other passage is so closely related to the part the proponent offers that presenting only that part to the jury would mislead the jury. In contrast, the common law right applies so long as the other passage is logically relevant to the same topic as the part the proponent offers. This right is subject to the qualification set forth above where the remainder is inadmissible.

§ 57. Fighting Fire With Fire: Inadmissible Evidence as Opening the Door

One party offers evidence which is inadmissible. Because the adversary fails to object, he has no opportunity to do so, or the judge erroneously overrules an objection, the inadmissible evidence comes in. Is the adversary entitled to answer this evidence, by testimony in denial or explanation of the facts so proved? The question has prompted a sharp split of authority. It has been asserted that in some jurisdictions the adversary is not entitled to meet the evidence, in others he may do so, and finally in still others he may do so if he would be prejudiced by denying him an opportunity to meet the evidence. However, in reaching these results, many decisions seem merely to affirm the trial judge's action. Most courts seem to subscribe to the general proposition that "one who induces a trial court to let down the bars to a field of inquiry that is not competent or relevant to the issues cannot complain if his adversary is also allowed to avail himself of the opening."[1] Federal cases have on occasion applied this general notion.

Appellate pronouncements afford little guidance on the question as to how the trial judge should deal with the problem. Because of the many variable factors affecting the solution in a particular case, the diverse situations do not lend themselves easily to neat generalizations. However, the published decisions do identify two key factors, the prejudicial nature of the evidence and whether the opponent made a timely objection to block the admission of the evidence. The following generalizations, having some support in the decisions, are submitted as reasonable:

(1) If the inadmissible evidence sought to be answered is irrelevant and not prejudice-arousing, the judge, to save time and to avoid distraction from the issues, should refuse to hear answering evidence; but if he does hear it, under the prevailing view the party opening the door has no standing to complain. Consider, for example, a case in which one party improperly injects evidence of the good character of one of his distant relatives who played a minor role in the litigated event. That type of evidence is unlikely to change the outcome of the trial; and it would hardly be an abuse of discretion for the judge to exclude the opponent's evidence attacking the relative's character.

(2) Suppose alternatively that the evidence, though inadmissible, is relevant to the issues and hence presumably damaging to the adversary's case, or though irrelevant is materially prejudicial and the adversary seasonably objected or moved to strike. Here the adversary should be entitled to give answering evidence as of right. By objecting he did his best to save the court from mistake. His remedy of assigning appellate error to the ruling is inadequate. He needs a fair opportunity to win his case at the trial level by refuting the damaging evidence. In many cases, the adversary simply

§ 57

1. Warren Live Stock Co. v. Farr, 142 F. 116, 117 (C.C.A.Colo.1905).

cannot afford the expense of a second trial after an appeal. Assume that a litigant succeeds in introducing inadmissible evidence of his own good character. That evidence is much more likely to impact the verdict than testimony about a distant relative's character. This situation should be distinguished from the question, considered in section 55, whether the prior objection is waived if the answering evidence is permitted.

(3) If the first inadmissible evidence is relevant, or though irrelevant is prejudicial, but the adversary has failed to object or to move to strike out where an objection might have avoided the harm, the allowance of answering evidence should rest in the judge's discretion. The judge ought to weigh the probable impact of the first evidence, the time and distraction incident to answering it, and the likely effectiveness of a curative instruction to the jury to disregard it. However, here several courts have indicated that introduction of the answering evidence is a matter of right and not allowed merely in the judge's discretion.

(4) In any event, if the inadmissible evidence or even the inquiry eliciting it is so prejudice-arousing that an objection or motion to strike would not have erased the harm, the adversary should be entitled to answer it as of right.

The question discussed in this section as to rebutting inadmissible evidence differs from the issue of whether a party's introduction of evidence inadmissible under some exclusionary rule (such as hearsay) gives the adversary license to introduce other evidence which (1) is inadmissible under the same exclusionary rule but (2) bears on a different issue or is irrelevant to the original inadmissible evidence. The doctrine has not been extended that far; the door does not swing open that widely.

§ 58. Admissibility of Evidence Dependent on Proof of Other Facts: "Connecting Up"

The relevancy or admissibility of evidence of a particular fact frequently hinges upon the proof of other facts. Thus, proof that a swaying automobile passed a given spot at a certain time, or that there was a conversation between the witness and an unidentified stranger at a given time and place, will become relevant only when the automobile is identified as the defendant's or the stranger is shown to be the plaintiff. In the same manner, evidence of acts and declarations might not become material until they are shown to be those of the defendant's agent, and a copy of a writing may not become competent evidence until the original is proven to be lost or destroyed. In terms of logic, some of these missing facts may be thought of as preliminary to the fact offered, and others as co-ordinate with it. It matters not. In either event, often only one fact can be proven at a time or by a witness. In a given case, the sequence of convenience in calling witnesses may not be the order of strict logic. Logic might dictate that a doctor testify first, but logic might have to yield to an emergency surgery.

Who decides the order of facts? In the first instance, the offering counsel does so by making the offer. However, in his general discretionary supervision over the order of proof, the judge may, to avoid a danger of prejudice or confusion, require that the missing fact be proved first. But the trial judge seldom does so. The everyday common law method of handling the situation when the adversary objects to the relevancy or the competency of the offered fact is to admit it conditionally, on the proponent's express or implied assurance that she will "connect up" the tendered evidence by proving the missing facts later. Federal and Revised Uniform Rules of Evidence 104(b) and 611(a) grant the court this same authority.

However, in a long trial with many witnesses and complex facts, it is easy for the offering counsel to later forget the need to present the required "connecting" proof, and for the judge and the adversary to overlook this gap in the evidence. Who invokes the condition subsequent on its failure? The burden is placed on the objecting party to renew the objection and invoke the condition. By the majority view this is to be done by a motion to strike the evidence conditionally received, when the failure of condition becomes apparent. The failure becomes apparent when the offering party completes the particular stage of the case in which the evidence was offered. When the proponent "rests" without introducing the missing proof, the adversary should then move to strike; if the opponent fails to do, she cannot later as of right invoke the condition. Some weight ought to be given, however, to the responsibility the proponent assumed by promising to furnish the connecting proof. That responsibility can best be recognized by according the trial judge a discretion to allow the adversary to invoke the condition later, if the continuing availability of the missing proof makes it fair to do so, at any time before the case is submitted to the jury or before final judgment in a bench case. It is especially appropriate for the judge to exercise discretion in the adversary's favor when the offering party's case-in-chief was a lengthy one; in that circumstance, the adversary's failure is relatively excusable. Though some courts have considered the difference in form dispositive, a motion to strike, a motion to withdraw the fact from the jury, or a request that the jury be instructed to disregard the evidence all should be regarded as a sufficient invocation of the condition. The discussion in this paragraph is compatible with Federal and Revised Uniform Rules of Evidence 104(b) and 611(a).

To be distinguished from the practice of conditional receipt pending further proof, is the provisional admission of evidence where objection is made, taking the objection under advisement subject to a later ruling when the record has been more amply developed. Here again the objecting counsel, to preserve the objection, must renew the objection before the case is concluded. The practice seems appropriate enough in a judge-tried case. However, in a jury trial there is danger that letting the evidence in, even provisionally, may make an impression on the jury that a later ruling of exclusion cannot erase—a risk that seems unnecessary to incur. Accordingly this practice, though doubtless in the realm of discretion, has been criticized. It should be avoided.

§ 59.   Evidence Admissible for One Purpose, Inadmissible for Another: "Limited Admissibility"

An item of evidence may be logically relevant in several aspects, leading to distinct in-ferences or bearing upon different issues. For one of these purposes it may be admissible but for another inadmissible. In this common situation, subject to the limitations outlined below, the normal practice in case law and under the Federal and Revised Uniform Rules of Evidence (1974) is to admit the evidence. The opponent's legitimate interest is protected, not by an objection to its admission, but by a request at the time of the offer for an instruction that the jury is to consider the evidence only for the allowable purpose. Realistically, the instruction may not always be effective, but admission of the evidence with the limiting instruction is normally the best reconciliation of the competing interests. However, in situations where the danger of the jury's misuse of the evidence for the inadmissible purpose is acute, and its value for the legitimate purpose is slight or the point for which it is admissible can readily be proved by other evidence, the judge's power to exclude the evidence altogether is clear in case law and under the Federal and Revised Uniform Rule of Evidence 403. Some hearsay problems cry out for the invocation of Rule 403. When the proponent offers an out-of-court statement for a nonhearsay purpose but on its face the declaration asserts facts directly relevant to a critical issue in the case and the declarant would presumably have personal knowledge of the facts, common sense suggests that there is a grave risk that the jurors will misuse the testimony as substantive evidence.

Similarly, subject to the restrictions stated in the above and following paragraphs, evidence is frequently admissible as against one party, but not as against another. In that event, the accepted practice is to admit the evidence with an instruction, if requested, that the jurors are to consider it only as to the party against whom it is properly admissible.

However, even limiting instructions are insufficient to insure against jury misuse of the confessions or admissions of a codefendant who does not take the stand when the confession implicates the defendant. In this situation, the confession is admissible against the non-testifying codefendant as a personal admission; but it may be inadmissible against the defendant, as when codefendant made the statement after he had been arrested and ceased being an active member of the conspiracy with the defendant. In similar situations, at a joint trial the traditional solution is to admit the evidence with a limiting instruction barring its use against the defendant. However, when the other evidence in the record indicates that there is a close relationship between the two and that the codefendant had personal knowledge of the facts asserted in his confession, there is an intolerable risk that the jury will disregard any limiting instruction and misuse the confession as proof of the defendant's guilt. A violation of the Sixth Amendment right to confront witnesses results.[1] This rule is enforceable in state courts. However if the case against the defendant was so overwhelming, apart from the codefendant's confession, that its admission was harmless beyond a reasonable doubt, the appellate court will not reverse. It cannot be generalized that if one purpose of two or more uses of evidence against a criminal defendant violates the defendant's constitutional rights, the evidence is completely inadmissible.[2] In a number of cases, the Supreme Court has ruled that although a constitutional exclusionary rule precluded the use of an item of evidence as substantive proof, the evidence was admissible for impeachment purposes subject to a limiting instruction.

§ 60. Admission and Exclusion of Evidence in Trials Without a Jury

The rules of evidence at common law and pursuant to the Federal and Revised Uniform Rules of Evidence (1974) apply in trials without a jury. Nevertheless as Thayer states, our law of evidence is to a great extent a "product of the jury system * * * where ordinary untrained citizens are acting as judges of fact." The Advisory Committee Note to Federal Rule of Evidence 104 reiterates the conventional wisdom that the common law courts developed

the exclusionary rules in large part due to their doubts about the capacity of lay jurors. For their part, judges possess professional experience in valuing evidence, greatly lessening the need for exclusionary rules. At common law, there was a sense that it was inexpedient to apply these restrictions to judges; that sense caused appellate courts to say that the same strictness need not be observed in applying the rules of evidence in bench trials as in jury trials. A court should arguably reach the same result under the Federal and Revised Uniform Rule of Evidence (1974).

The most important influence encouraging trial judges to take a relaxed attitude toward evidence rules in nonjury cases is a doctrine obtaining in most appellate courts. These appellate courts are of the mind that in reviewing a case tried without a jury, the receipt of inadmissible evidence over objection will not ordinarily be a ground of reversal if there was other, admissible evidence sufficient to support the findings. The judge is presumed to have disregarded the inadmissible and relied on the admissible evidence. However, when the judge errs in the opposite direction by excluding evidence which ought to have been received, the judge's ruling is subject to reversal if it is substantially harmful to the losing party. On the other hand, some appellate decisions decline to apply the presumption when the evidence was objected to and the objection overruled. Moreover, the presumption may be rebutted by a contrary showing. The rebuttal showing could take the form of statements from the bench, or express reliance on improperly admitted evidence in specific findings of fact either prepared separately or as part of an opinion or memorandum of decision.

In practice, considerations of waste of time, predictability and consistency lead most trial judges to apply the rules of evidence in a nonjury trial to exclude evidence that "is *clearly* inadmissible, privileged, or too time consuming in order to guard against reversal." However, where the admissibility of evi-

§ 59
1. Bruton v. United States, 391 U.S. 123 (1968). See § 279 infra.

2. See, e.g., United States v. Havens, 446 U.S. 620 (1980); Harris v. New York, 401 U.S. 222 (1971).

dence is debatable, the appellate courts' contrasting attitudes toward errors in receiving and excluding evidence account for the emergence of the practice adopted by many experienced trial judges in nonjury cases; that practice is to provisionally admit all arguably admissible evidence, even if objected to with the announcement that all admissibility questions are reserved until all the evidence is in. In considering any objections renewed by motion to strike at the end of the case, the judge leans toward admission rather than exclusion but seeks to find clearly admissible testimony on which to base his findings of fact. The practice lessens the time spent in arguing objections and helps ensure that appellate courts have in the record the evidence that was rejected as well as that which was received. A more complete trial record sometimes enables the appellate court to dispose of the case by entering a final judgment rather than merely remanding to the trial court for further proceedings.[1]

§ 60

1. See also the discussion of offers of proof, supra § 51.

Title 4

COMPETENCY

Chapter 7

THE COMPETENCY OF WITNESSES

Table of Sections

§ 61. In General

Most evidentiary rules regulate the content of proposed testimony. However, competency rules address the threshold question of whether a prospective witness is qualified to give any testimony at all in the case. For the most part, the competency standards relate to the prospective witness's status and personal capacities rather than the content of the testimony the witness is prepared to give. The early common law rules of incompetency were harsh, but they have been undergoing a process of piecemeal statutory revision for over a century. Today most of the former grounds for barring a witness altogether have been converted into mere grounds of impeaching his credibility.

Since the disqualification of witnesses for incompetency is thus dwindling in importance, and since the statutory reforms of the common law competency rules vary from state to state, this text does not assay a detailed review of the law in the different jurisdictions. Instead, the common law grounds of incompetency and the general lines of statutory and rule reform are summarized in the following sections.

§ 62. Mental Incapacity and Immaturity: Oath or Affirmation

At modern common law, there is no rule automatically excluding an insane person as such, or a child of any specified age, from testifying. In each case, the test is whether the witness has enough intelligence to make it worthwhile to hear him at all and whether he recognizes a duty to tell the truth. Is his capacity to perceive, record, recollect, and narrate, such that he can probably add valuable knowledge of the facts to the record? At common law, following the procedure for foundational facts conditioning the competency of evidence,[1] the trial judge determines as a matter of fact whether the prospective witness possesses the requisite testimonial qualities,

---

§ 62

1. See § 53 supra.

notably the capacities to perceive, remember, narrate, and understand the duty to tell the truth under oath. Children as young as three years old have been ruled competent as witnesses. Likewise, persons suffering from mental disorders often satisfy the competency standards. The person is ruled incompetent only in extreme cases such as when he experiences insane delusions directly relevant to the subject-matter of his testimony or suffers from a psychosis likely to grossly distort his testimony.

The major reason for the severe, early common law disqualification standards was the judges' distrust of a jury's ability to assess the words of a small child or a deranged person. Conceding the jury's deficiencies, the remedy of excluding such a witness, who may be the only person knowing the facts, seems inept and primitive. Though the tribunal may be unskilled and the testimony difficult to weigh, on balance it is still better to let the evidence come in for what it is worth with cautionary instructions.

Although the more contemporary common law rules are relatively lax, the statutory reforms go even farther. Many states have enacted statutes specifically providing that the alleged victim is per se a competent witness in a child abuse prosecution. Furthermore, most modern evidence codes contain general provisions liberalizing the competency standards. Revised Uniform Rule of Evidence 601 and the first sentence of Federal Rule of Evidence 601 typify such codes by announcing every person is competent to be a witness unless "otherwise provided" in the rules. The only general competency requirements "otherwise provided" by the Federal and Revised Uniform Rules of Evidence are contained in Rule 603 (prescribing that every witness declare that he will testify truthfully by oath or affirmation) and Rule 602 (mandating that the witness possess personal knowledge). A plain meaning interpretation of Rule 601 would be that there are no remaining competency standards and that all the prospective witness need do is to take the oath. The very first sentence of the Advisory Committee Note to Rule 601 states that

"[n]o mental or moral qualifications for testifying as a witness are specified."

However, that sweeping interpretation of Rule 601 has evidently struck many courts as too revolutionary. Rather than construing Rule 601 literally, they have taken the position that the rule has a more limited impact and merely creates a presumption of competency. However, at most, the Federal Rules can be construed as requiring that: (1) the witness have the capacity to accurately perceive, record and recollect impressions of fact (physical and mental capacity), (2) the witness did perceive, record and can recollect impressions having any tendency to establish a fact of consequence in the litigation (personal knowledge), (3) the witness declare that he will tell the truth, understands the duty to tell the truth (oath or affirmation), and appreciates the difference between the truth and a lie or fantasy, and (4) the witness possesses the capacity to comprehend questions and express himself intelligibly, where necessary with an interpreter's aid (narration). Rule 602 requires personal knowledge, and Rule 603 mandates an oath. In light of the text of Rules 601–03, an argument can be made that on an appropriate objection, the witness's proponent must make this four-fold showing to satisfy both the letter and spirit of those rules. The statutes expressly require the proponent to show that the witness acquired firsthand knowledge, and the argument runs that as a matter of logic, the witness could not have gained that unless she possessed the capacities listed in this foundation. However, given the wording of Rule 601, it does not seem supportable to require anything more than this foundation. It would certainly be indefensible to announce any hard-and-fast rules concerning the incompetency of children of a particular age or adults suffering from a particular mental disorder.

Even the more conservative interpretation of the Federal Rules, though, leads to a substantial relaxation of the competency standards. As previously stated, at common law the trial judge decided as a question of fact whether the prospective witness possessed all the requisite capacities—the preliminary fact-finding procedure now employed under Federal Rule 104(a). However, Rule 602 expressly indicates that the judge is to apply the conditional relevance procedure set out in Rule 104(b). Before a witness will be permitted to testify, the proponent need only introduce evidence sufficient to support a permissive inference of personal knowledge, i.e., that the witness had the capacity to and actually did observe, receive, record, and can now recollect and narrate impressions obtained through any of his senses, and the witness must declare by oath or affirmation that he will testify truthfully. That minimalist approach is consistent with the Advisory Committee's Note to Rule 601. The Note asserts that the common law standards of mental capacity had proved elusive, few witnesses were actually disqualified, and a witness wholly without mental capacity is difficult to imagine.

Despite this analysis of Rule 601, the testimony of a witness whose mental capacity has been seriously impaired could still conceivably be excluded on the ground that no reasonable juror could possibly believe that the witness possesses personal knowledge, or understands the difference between the truth and a lie or fantasy. The proponent's foundation could be so weak that it does not satisfy even the lax Rule 104(b) standard. Alternatively, the opponent's evidence of the prospective witness's deficiencies could be so strong that as a matter of law, the trial judge could justifiably bar the witness under Rule 403.

In sum, a witness's competency to testify at most requires only a minimal ability to observe, recollect, and recount as well as an understanding of the duty to tell the truth. Where a witness's capacity has been brought into question, the ultimate question is whether a reasonable juror must believe that the witness is so bereft of powers of perception, recollection, or narration that it is not worth the time to listen to his testimony. This test of competency requires only minimum credibility. The trend is to resolve doubts as to the witness's credibility in favor of permitting the jury to hear the testimony and evaluate the witness's credibility for itself. Thus proof of mental deficiency ordinarily has the effect of reducing the weight to be given to testimony

rather than keeping the witness off the stand. Nevertheless, as previously stated, under Rule 403 in an extreme case testimony of a witness passing the test of minimum credibility might be excluded on the basis of perceived trial dangers such as misleading or confusing the jury and unfair prejudice.

§ 63. Religious Belief

Belief in a divine being who, in this life or hereafter, will punish false swearing was a prerequisite at common law to the capacity to take the oath. Members of many major religions met the test, but followers of other religions, as well as atheists and agnostics, could not. That early approach is obviously inconsistent with the democratic principle of freedom of conscience. This ground of incapacity has fortunately been abandoned in state jurisdictions by: explicit state constitutional or statutory provisions, expansive interpretation of state provisions forbidding deprivation of rights for religious beliefs, changing the common law "in the light of reason and experience" because such a requirement is inconsistent with the spirit of our institutions, or adoption of Federal Rules of Evidence or Revised Uniform Rules of Evidence 601 and 603. In any event, the enforcement of this former rule of incapacity appears prohibited in any state or federal court by the first and fourteenth amendments of the national constitution.

The witness himself can object to an oath directly or inferentially requiring him to avow a belief in God. If the witness has a scruple against oaths, the witness may "affirm" under penalty of perjury rather than "swear". No particular form of oath or affirmation is necessary. However, it has been held that routinely swearing witnesses to tell the truth using the phrase, "so help me God," does not vitiate a trial, when the witnesses themselves have not objected. The losing party probably has no standing to object on appeal. However, in some circumstances, as perhaps when it became evident to the jury that the party shared the beliefs which prevented the witness from swearing, the party could make a strained argument that he has an interest and was prejudiced. Inquiry into the witness's religious opinions for impeachment purposes is discussed in another section.[1]

§ 64. Conviction of Crime

The common law disqualified altogether a prospective witness who had been convicted of treason, felony, or a crime involving fraud or deceit. In England and most states during the last hundred years, this disqualification has been swept away by legislation. In 1917, the United States Supreme Court determined that "the dead hand of the common law rule" of disqualification should no longer be applied in federal criminal cases.[1] The disqualification is not recognized in Federal Rule of Evidence and Revised Uniform Rule of Evidence (1974) 601. In a few states, however, it has been retained for conviction of perjury and subornation. Even these statutes are now of questionable validity under a Supreme Court ruling declaring unconstitutional Texas statutes barring persons charged or convicted as co-participants in the same crime from testifying for each other.[2]

§ 65. Parties and Persons Interested: The Dead Man Statutes

By far the most drastic common law incompetency rule was the doctrine excluding testimony by parties to the lawsuit and all persons having a direct pecuniary or proprietary interest in the outcome. In effect, this rule both imposed a disability on the party to testify in his own behalf and granted him a privilege not to be called as a witness against himself by the adversary. The disability had the specious justification of preventing self-interested perjury; the privilege lacked even that specious rationale. It is almost unbelievable that the rule continued in force in England until the middle of the 19th century, and in this country for a few decades longer. In England, the reform was sweeping, and no shred of disqualification in civil cases remains.

In this country, however, a compromise was forced upon the reformers. The objection was raised that in controversies over consensual transactions, such as contracts, or other events such as traffic accidents where one party died but the other survived, fraud could result if the surviving parties or interested persons were permitted to testify about the transaction or the event. The survivor could testify though the adverse party's lips had been sealed in death. This is a seductive argument. It was accepted in nearly all the early statutes, at a time when the real dispute was whether the general disqualification should be abolished or retained. At that time, the concession for survivors' cases undoubtedly seemed a minor one. But the concession survives in many states; and where it still exists, it has become so ingrained in legal habits of thinking that it is hard to dislodge by argument.

Accordingly, statutes in numerous states still provide that the common law disqualification of parties and interested persons is abolished, with the single exception that they remain disqualified to testify concerning a transaction or communication with a person since deceased in a suit prosecuted or defended by the decedent's executor or administrator. However, it is often a proviso by statute or case law that the surviving party or interested person may testify if called by the adversary, that is, the decedent's executor or administrator; the proviso abrogates the privilege feature of the common law rule. The practical consequence of these statutes is that when a survivor has rendered services, furnished goods, or lent money to a person whom he trusted without an outside witness or admissible written evidence, he is helpless if the other dies and the representative of his estate declines to pay. The survivor's mouth may even be closed in an action arising from a fatal automobile collision, or a suit on a note or account which the survivor paid in cash without obtaining a receipt.

---

§ 63

1. See § 46 supra.

§ 64

1. Rosen v. United States, 245 U.S. 467 (1917).
2. Washington v. Texas, 388 U.S. 14 (1967).

These restrictions are purely creatures of statute. Consequently, when a case raises a dead man's issue, the primary task is statutory construction. As Felix Frankfurter said, "Read the statute." To dissect the statute, keep the following questions in mind:

— What types of proceedings does the statute apply to? Must the decedent's personal representative be formally joined as a party? Does the statute apply only to causes of action derived from the decedent such as suits for the decedent's pain and suffering prior to death, or does it also extend to causes of action for wrongful death which are conferred by statute directly on the heirs?

— Who is disqualified? All statutes disqualify the surviving party. Some statutes also disqualify the surviving party's spouse. Many similarly bar testimony by "interested persons." The courts tend to limit the scope of the latter expression to persons such as a surviving party's business partner who would benefit by the direct legal operation of the judgment in the case.

— What is the nature of the competence? Is the statute's bar limited to "communications" with the decedent? Or does the statute use broader language, typically "transactions"? How expansively should the term "transaction" be interpreted? Since the decedent's death has deprived the estate of the decedent's testimony based on personal knowledge, there is a strong argument that the "transaction" should be construed purposively to include any fact or event which the decedent had firsthand knowledge of.

— Are there any special exceptions to the scope of the prohibition? Many statutes lift the bar of the statute when the survivor and the decedent stood in the relationship of employer and employee or partners. If the statute applied to such relations, it would be difficult to enforce routine agreements between the parties.

— What acts constitute a waiver of the statute? The estate certainly loses the protection of the statute when it calls an otherwise disqualified person as a witness at trial. Is there also a waiver if the estate merely deposes the person before trial? In some states, there is deep-seated judicial hostility to the continued existence of the statutes; and that hostility translates into the courts' willingness to strain to find a waiver.

More fundamentally, most commentators agree that the expedient of refusing to listen to the survivor is, in Bentham's words, "blind and brainless". In seeking to avoid injustice to one side, the statutory drafters ignored the equal possibility of creating injustice to the other. The survivor's temptation to fabricate a claim or defense is evident enough—so obvious indeed that any jury should realize that his story must be cautiously heard. A searching cross-examination will often, in case of fraud, reveal discrepancies in the "tangled web" of deception. In any event, the survivor's disqualification is more likely to disadvantage the honest than the dishonest survivor. One who would resort to perjury will hardly hesitate at suborning a third person, who would not be disqualified, to swear to the false story.

The lawmakers and courts are gradually being brought to see the stupidity of the traditional survivors' evidence acts, and liberalizing changes are being adopted. A few states provide that the survivor may testify, but his testimony will not support a judgment unless corroborated by other evidence. Others authorize the trial judge to permit the survivor to testify when it appears that his testimony is necessary to prevent injustice. Both of these solutions have reasonably apparent drawbacks which are avoided by a third type of statute. The third statutory scheme sweeps away the disqualification entirely and allows the survivor to testify without restriction, but seeks to minimize the danger of injustice to the decedent's estate by admitting any relevant writings or oral statements by the decedent, both of which would ordinarily be excluded as hearsay.

Federal Rule of Evidence (except in diversity cases) and Revised Uniform Rule of Evidence (1974) 601 abandon the instant disqualification altogether. However, not all states which have copied the Federal Rules have done so.

Interest, then, as a disqualification in civil cases has been discarded, except for the fragmentary relic of the survivors' evidence statutes. The common law disqualification of parties defendant in criminal cases which prevented the accused from being called as a witness by either side has been abrogated in England and this country to the extent it disabled the defendant to testify in his own behalf. However, it survives to the extent that the prosecution cannot call him. In this form, it is a rule of privilege and constitutes one aspect of the privilege against self-incrimination, treated in a later section.[1]

While the disqualification of parties and persons interested in the result of the lawsuit has thus been almost entirely swept away, the fact of a witness's interest is by no means disregarded. It may still be proved to impeach credibility,[2] and in most jurisdictions the court will instruct that a party's testimony may be weighed in the light of his interest.

§ 66. Husbands and Wives of Parties

Closely allied to the parties' disqualification and even more arbitrary and misguided, was the early common law disqualification of the party's husband or wife. This disqualification prevented the party's husband or wife from testifying either for or against the party in any case, civil or criminal. The disability of the husband or wife as a witness to testify *for* the party-spouse was a disqualification, based upon the supposed infirmity of interest, while the rule enabling the party-spouse to prevent the husband or wife from testifying *against* the party functioned as a privilege.

Of course, the common law rule has been modified. In the majority of jurisdictions, statutes have made the husband or wife fully competent to testify for or against the party-spouse in civil cases. In criminal cases, the disqualification of the husband or wife to testi-

fy for the accused spouse has been removed; but it is sometimes provided that the prosecution may not call the spouse, without the accused spouse's consent, thus preserving the accused's privilege to keep the spouse off the stand altogether. In some jurisdictions either spouse may assert the privilege. The Supreme Court has announced that in federal criminal cases, only the spouse who is to be called by the prosecution as a witness may claim the privilege.[1] The privilege has occasionally been defended on the ground that it protects family harmony. However, family harmony is almost always past saving when the witness spouse is willing to aid the prosecution. In declaring the existence of the witness spouse's privilege, the Supreme Court looked to Rule 501 rather than Rule 601; at first blush, Rule 601 would seem to govern, but the Court noted that its original draft of Article V of the Federal Rules touched on the privilege and that Congress had not objected to the treatment of the issue as an Article V problem. In other states spouses may be called to the stand to testify in criminal cases just as any other witness.

Even at common law the instant privilege was denied an accused husband in criminal prosecutions for wrongs directly against the wife's person. The application of the privilege in such prosecutions would frustrate the enforcement of the criminal statutes in question, since the victim spouse is typically a vital source of prosecution evidence. The statutes retaining the instant privilege usually broaden this injured spouse exception to include prosecution of any "crime committed by one against the other" and various other offenses, including crimes against the marital relation such as adultery. There is some disagreement concerning the duration of the privilege, but most courts regard the initial time at which it comes into being as the date of the creation of the marriage and the terminus as the date of termination of marriage, as by divorce.

Several procedural questions may arise. Of course, the holder of the privilege must be

§ 65

1. See §§ 116, 131, infra.
2. See § 39 supra.

§ 66

1. Trammel v. United States, 445 U.S. 40 (1980).

ascertained. As previously stated, there is a division of authority over the identity of the holder. There is a further disagreement whether it is error for the prosecution to call the spouse to the stand, thereby forcing the accused spouse or the witness's spouse to object in the jury's presence. Most courts reinforce the privilege by precluding comment on its exercise.

The privilege is sometimes applied to the spouse's extra-judicial statements. However, the Supreme Court has indicated that the federal version of the privilege is limited to in-court testimony.[2]

Limiting the scope of the privilege is a step in the right direction. The privilege is an archaic survival of a mystical religious dogma and reflects an outmoded social attitude toward marriage. The Supreme Court's draft of Federal Rule of Evidence 504 would have abolished the privilege; and on the balance, the abolition of the privilege would probably be desirable.

Both the instant privilege and the ancient disqualification must be distinguished from another privilege—the privilege against disclosure of confidential communications between husband and wife. The spousal communications privilege is discussed in another section.[3] The disqualification and the instant privilege can have the effect of keeping the spouse altogether off the witness stand. In contrast, while the spouse is on the stand, the communications privilege merely bars the spouse from disclosing certain information acquired from the other spouse.

§ 67. Incompetency of Husband and Wife to Give Testimony on Non-access

In 1777, in an ejectment case involving the issue of the claimant's legitimacy, Lord Mansfield delivered a pronouncement which apparently was new-minted doctrine. He declared "that the declarations of a father or mother cannot be admitted to bastardize the

issue born after marriage * * * it is a rule founded in decency, morality and policy, that they shall not be permitted to say after marriage that they have had no connection and therefore that the offspring is spurious * * *."[1] Mansfield's invention was justly criticized by Wigmore as inconsistent and obstructive.[2] Yet, it was followed by later English decisions until overruled by statute, and has been accepted by some American courts. A few courts have wisely rejected it by construing the general statutes abolishing the incompetency of parties and of spouses as overturning this eccentric incompetency, but other courts have not yielded to this argument.

Even the jurisdictions which recognize the rule differ over the scope of the rule. The points of controversy about the rule are: (a) whether it is limited strictly to evidence of non-access, or whether it reaches other types of evidence showing that someone other than the husband is the father, (b) whether the rule applies only in proceedings where legitimacy is in issue or extends to divorce suits where the question is adultery rather than the child's legitimacy, and (c) whether it is confined to prohibiting the testimony of husband and wife on the stand, or also excludes evidence of the spouses's previous out-of-court declarations. In view of the unsoundness of the rule, in all these instances the more restrictive position is preferable.

§ 68. Judges, Jurors and Lawyers

A judicial officer called to the stand in a case in which she is not sitting as a judge is not disqualified by his office from testifying. But when a judge is called as a witness in a trial before her, her appearance as witness is obviously inconsistent with her impartial role in the adversary system of trial. Nevertheless, under the older common law view she was generally regarded as a competent witness, though she had a discretion to decline to testify. Shockingly, this view is preserved in some

---

2. Trammel v. United States, 445 U.S. 40, 52 n. 12 (1990).

3. See Ch. 9 infra.

§ 67

1. Goodright v. Moss, 2 Cowp. 291, 98 Eng.Rep. 1257 (1777).

2. 7 Wigmore, Evidence § 2064 (Chadbourn rev. 1978).

state statutes. The view is obviously subject to criticism. The criticism led to a shift toward a second view that the judge is disqualified from testifying to material, disputed facts, but may testify to matters merely formal and undisputed. This distinction is not easy to draw. Moreover, there seems little need for the judge's testimony on these topics, since formal matters nearly always can be proved by other witnesses. Accordingly, there is growing support for a third view that a judge is incompetent to testify in a case which she is trying. The view is as sensible as it is simple. This view is embodied in Federal and Revised Uniform Rule of Evidence 605. The rule provides for an "automatic" objection.

A similar threat to the tribunal's impartiality arises when a juror sitting in a case is called as a witness. To meet that danger, Federal and Revised Uniform Rule of Evidence (1974) 606(a) provides that the juror is incompetent as a witness. By adoption of this rule in state jurisdictions, substantial inroads have been made on the traditional common law and the contrary statutes. These problems rarely arise, since in the vast majority of cases panelists with pre-knowledge of the facts of the case are stricken during jury selection.

There is a separate traditional doctrine that a juror is incompetent to testify in impeachment of the juror's verdict. By virtue of this doctrine, the juror is barred from testifying about matters that "inhere" in the deliberation process. While once criticized, this doctrine is now firmly entrenched. The traditional version of the doctrine, often called the Mansfield rule, broadly prohibits jurors from testifying about both their mental processes and events which transpired during deliberations. Barring juror impeachment of the verdict promotes the finality of verdicts and encourages frank jury deliberation, while discouraging later harassment of jurors by losing parties. A few courts have abandoned the Mansfield rule, and permit jurors to testify to misconduct and irregularities which are ground for new trial. Under this so-called Iowa view, jurors may testify about "objective" facts and events occurring during deliberation—occurrences which are objective in the sense that other

jurors could observe them and corroborate the juror's testimony about the fact or event. For protection of finality, these courts trust to a narrower doctrine excluding evidence of the jurors' expressions and arguments in their deliberations and evidence as to their own subjective motives, beliefs, mistakes, and mental operations. Federal and Revised Uniform Rule of Evidence (1974) 606(b) are in accord with prior federal case law and adopt the traditional, Mansfield doctrine.

It is important to appreciate the limits to the scope of statutory provisions such as Rule 606(b). First, these rules do not equate with, or specify, the substantive grounds for a new trial, but merely govern the jurors' competency to testify to establish such grounds. Second, in addition to jurors' subjective thought processes, discussions, motives, beliefs, and mistakes, the rules exclude irregular juror conduct in the jury room. Again, Rule 606(b) is a version of the Mansfield approach. Thus, the federal courts have held that the rule bars testimony about racist remarks during deliberations and jurors' consumption of alcohol at lunch. Third, in one respect, Federal Rule 606 appears to broaden the scope of the common law rule. While that rule barred juror testimony and affidavit only when it was offered to impeach a verdict, the wording of 606(b) is so expansive that it seems to apply whether the evidence is offered to impeach or support the verdict. Fourth, the rules do not exclude juror testimony of extraneous prejudicial influences. Thus, a criminal juror could testify that he had received a threatening phone call; and in a civil case involving accident reconstruction testimony, one juror could supply an affidavit indicating that another juror had brought a text on accident reconstruction into the deliberation room and read aloud passages to the other jurors. Finally, the rules do not preclude testimony of others about their knowledge of jury misconduct. The bar applies only to jurors. Hence, if the door to the jury deliberation room was ajar and a passing bailiff heard one juror threaten another, the bailiff would be competent to testify about the threat.

To be distinguished from these rules of incompetency and exclusion, is the doctrine supported by Wigmore[1] and a few judicial opinions, that each juror has a privilege against the disclosure in court of her communications to the other jurors during their retirement.

At common law and under Federal and Revised Uniform Rule of Evidence 601, a lawyer for a party is not per se incompetent to testify. Nevertheless, the court has wide discretion to refuse to permit a lawyer to testify in his client's favor. Discretion is routinely exercised to prevent such testimony where other sources of evidence about the fact of consequence are available or where the necessity for the lawyer's testimony could have been avoided. Even where no other witness is available and the lawyer is willing to withdraw, discretion is frequently exercised to preclude the lawyer from testifying. If the lawyer both testified and continued to try the case, there is a risk that the jury would confuse the lawyer's testimony as a witness with the lawyer's arguments as an advocate—a risk that brings Federal Rule of Evidence 403 into play.

ABA Model Rule of Professional Conduct, 3.7, Lawyer as Witness, promulgated in 1983, reads:

> (a) A lawyer shall not act as advocate at a trial in which the lawyer is likely to be a necessary witness except where:
>
> (1) the testimony relates to an uncontested issue
>
> (2) the testimony relates to the nature and value of legal services rendered in the case; or
>
> (3) disqualification of the lawyer would work substantial hardship on the client.
>
> (b) A lawyer may act as advocate in a trial in which another lawyer in the lawyer's firm is likely to be called as a witness unless precluded from doing so by [conflict of interest] Rule 1.7 or Rule 1.9.

Subdivision (a) generally bars the attorney's testimony when the attorney is personally in-volved in the trial of the case, but subdivision (b) rejects vicarious disqualification—the attorney may testify at a trial being conducted by another member of the attorney's firm.

California has gone even farther in liberalizing the advocate-witness prohibition. California Rule of Professional Conduct 5–210 lifts even the personal disqualification by providing that a lawyer-advocate may testify before a jury if the lawyer "has the informed, written consent of the client." As previously stated, the courts which routinely bar such testimony reason that there is a danger that the jury will confuse the lawyer's testimony and lawyer's arguments. However, the proponents of the California rule counter that the courts often permit the same witness to testify about facts and opinions. By way of example, the cases are legion allowing an experienced police officer to both describe an accused's conduct and voice an opinion that the conduct fits the modus operandi for a particular type of crime. If anything, such testimony presents the risk to a greater degree than a lawyer-advocate's testimony. When a police officer testifies in that manner, during the same testimony the officer states opinions as well as facts. In contrast, if the lawyer's testimony is restricted to facts, at least there is a gap between the factual testimony and the opinionated summation. That gap should reduce the risk of confusion.

§ 69. Firsthand Knowledge and Expertness

Two other rules, already considered, relate to the subject of witnesses' competency. These rules are the requirement that a witness testifying to objective facts must have had means of knowing them from observation,[1] and the doctrine that one testifying to his inference or opinion in matters requiring special knowledge or skill must qualify as an expert in the field.[2] Unlike most other competency doctrines, going to the capacity to testify at all, these two rules are directed at his capacity to speak to a particular matter.

---

§ 68

1. 8 Evidence § 2346 (McNaughton rev. 1961).

§ 69

1. See § 10 supra.
2. See § 13 supra.

§ 70. The Procedure of Disqualification

Under the common law practice, the witness is not sworn until she is placed on the stand to begin her testimony. At early common law before the oath was administered, the adversary had an opportunity to object to her competency; and the judge or counsel would then examine the witness about her qualifications, before she was sworn as a witness. This was known as a voir dire examination. Traditionally when the witness was first called to the stand to testify, the opponent was required to immediately challenge her competency, if grounds of challenge were then known to her. If the opponent did not voice a competency objection before the witness took the oath, the objection was waived.

Except possibly for diversity cases, the procedure described above is quite different from that obtaining under Federal Rule of Evidence 601 in federal court, because of the reduced scope of the limitations on witnesses' competency. The situation is also different under Revised Uniform Rule of Evidence 601. Under those statutes, the common law incompetency standards have largely been supplanted by specific provisions such as Rules 602 and 603. Rule 602 requires that a witness possess firsthand knowledge, and an objection squarely premised on 602 would have to be urged after the witness took the oath but before he answered a question relating to a fact which he lacked personal knowledge of. Rule 603 mandates that the prospective witness take an oath, but again the opponent could not object before the person took the oath; quite to the contrary, an objection would usually be appropriate only after the person refused to take the oath. The procedure for challenging judges and jurors as witnesses is prescribed by Rules 605 and 606.[1] The upshot is that under the new statutes, there appears to be only one case in which the opponent must routinely follow the common law procedure; in federal criminal cases, objections based on the spouse witness's privilege not to be called by the prosecution must still probably be asserted before the spouse witness takes the stand. In contrast, in jurisdictions giving Rule 601 a literal, plain meaning interpretation, there are no competency objections to be raised independently of Rules 602 and 603; and there would be no challenge to interpose before the witness begins to testify.[2] Even in federal diversity cases the judge is not bound by the exact procedures followed in any particular state for disposing of competency objections.

Finally, under both expert opinion case law and the Federal and Revised Uniform Rules of Evidence, the offering party must first show knowledge or skill, usually by questioning the witness herself to establish the witness is qualified.[3] However, those requirements come into play after the witness has begun to testify. Although the opponent could raise the issue in advance of the witness's testimony by filing an in limine motion, the opponent is not required to do so; and the opponent would not waive the objection by neglecting to raise the issue before the witness takes her oath.

If a foundational question of fact is disputed or doubtful on the evidence, the trial judge sitting with a jury does not submit this question of fact to the jury, except questions whether the witness has firsthand knowledge.[4] Hence, if a spousal disqualification objection raises the preliminary question of whether the party and witness spouse are validly married, the judge follows the procedure prescribed by Rule 104(a). In contrast, the judge would apply Rule 104(b)'s conditional relevance procedure to the preliminary question of whether the witness had personal knowledge. In federal court the procedure for determining the competency of a child witness is governed by statute, 18 U.S.C. § 3509(c).

§ 71. Probable Future of the Rules of Competency

The rules disqualifying witnesses with knowledge of relevant facts and mental capaci-

---

§ 70

1. See § 68 supra.
2. See § 62.

3. See §§ 10, 13 supra.
4. See § 69.

ty to convey that knowledge are serious obstructions to the ascertainment of truth. In the first edition of this treatise, Dean McCormick remarked, "The manifest destiny of evidence law is a progressive lowering of the barriers to truth."[1] For a century, the steady course of legal evolution has been in the direction of sweeping away these obstructions. To that end Federal Rules of Evidence 601 through 606 or the similar provisions of the Revised Uniform Rules of Evidence should be adopted by all states. For its part, Congress ought to exercise the power to mandate these rules without qualification for diversity cases.

1. C. McCormick. Handbook of the Law of Evidence § 81 (1954).

Title 5

PRIVILEGE: COMMON LAW
AND STATUTORY

Chapter 8

THE SCOPE AND EFFECT OF THE EVIDENTIARY PRIVILEGES

Table of Sections

§ 72. The Purposes of Rules of Privilege: (a) Other Rules of Evidence Distinguished

The overwhelming majority of all rules of evidence have as their ultimate justification some tendency to promote the objectives set forward by the conventional witness' oath, the presentation of "the truth, the whole truth, and nothing but the truth." Thus such prominent exclusionary rules as the hearsay rule, the opinion rule, the rule excluding bad character as evidence of crime, and the original documents (or "Best Evidence") rule, have as their common purpose the elucidation of the truth, a purpose which these rules seek to effect by operating to exclude evidence which is unreliable or which is calculated to prejudice or mislead.

By contrast the rules of privilege, of which the most familiar are the rule protecting against self-incrimination and those shielding the confidentiality of communications between husband and wife, attorney and client, and physician and patient, are not designed or intended to facilitate the fact-finding process or to safeguard its integrity. Their effect instead is clearly inhibitive; rather than facilitating the illumination of truth, they shut out the light.

Rules which serve to render accurate ascertainment of the truth more difficult, or in some instances impossible, may seem anomalous in a rational system of fact-finding. Nevertheless, rules of privilege are not without a rationale. Their warrant is the protection of interests and relationships which, rightly or wrongly, are regarded as of sufficient social importance to justify some sacrifice of availability of evidence relevant to the administration of justice.

The interests allegedly served by privileges, as might be expected, are varied. The great constitutional protections which have evolved around self-incrimination, confessions, and unlawfully obtained evidence are considered elsewhere.[1] They are commonly classed as privileges.

Of the rules treated here, a substantial number operate to protect communications made within the context of various professional relationships, e.g., attorney and client, physician and patient, clergyman and penitent. The rationale traditionally advanced for these privileges is that public policy requires the encouragement of the communications without which these relationships cannot be effective. This rationale, today sometimes referred to as the utilitarian justification for privilege, found perhaps its strongest supporter in Dean Wigmore who seems to have viewed it as the chief, if not the exclusive, basis for privilege. Wigmore's views have been widely accepted by the courts, and have largely conditioned the development of thinking about privilege.

More recently another, and analytically distinct, rationale for privilege has been advanced. According to this theory certain privacy interests in the society are deserving of protection by privilege irrespective of whether the existence of such privileges actually operates substantially to affect conduct within the protected relationships. Thus, while it has been suggested that communications between husband and wife and physician and patient are not primarily induced by the privileges accorded them, some form of these privileges is nevertheless seen as justified on the alternative basis that they serve to protect the essential privacy of certain significant human relationships. Given its comparatively recent origin, this latter rationale probably has not operated as a conscious basis for either the judicial or legislative creation of existing privileges. Today's judicial tendency to pour new wine into old bottles, however, may serve to make the nonutilitarian theory a factor in the subsequent development of thinking about privilege.

It is open to doubt whether all of the interests and relationships which have sometimes been urged as sufficiently important to justify the creation of privileges really merit this sort of protection bought at such a price. Moreover, even if the importance of given interests and relationships be conceded, there remain questions as to whether evidentiary privileges are appropriate, much less sufficient, mechanisms for accomplishing the desired objectives. In any event, it is clear that in drawing their justifications from considerations unrelated to the integrity of the adjudication process, rules of privilege are of a different order than the great bulk of evidentiary rules.

§ 72.1 The Purposes of Rules of Privilege: (b) Certain Rules Distinguished

As developed in a subsequent section,[1] true rules of privilege may be enforced to prevent the introduction of evidence even though the privilege is that of a person who is not a party to the proceeding in which the privilege is involved. This characteristic serves to distinguish certain other rules which, like privileges, are intended to encourage or discourage certain kinds of conduct. Among these latter rules may be included those excluding offers of compromise[2] and subsequent remedial measures following an injury.[3]

Functionally, the policies toward which these latter rules are directed may be fully realized by implementing the rules only in litigation to which the person sought to be actuated by the rule is a party. For example, the rule excluding evidence of offers of compromise is designed to encourage compromise; admitting the evidence in a case to which the offeror is not a party will in no wise operate to discourage compromises. Accordingly, such rules may be asserted only by a party. This

§ 72

1.　See Chs. 13, 14, and 15 infra.

§ 72.1

1.　§ 73 infra.
2.　See § 266 infra.
3.　See § 267 infra.

consideration, in addition to the fact that these rules are also justified in part by considerations relating to relevancy, makes their classification as rules of privilege analytically imprecise.

Again, true rules of privilege operate generally to prevent revelation of confidential matter within the context of a judicial proceeding. Thus, rules of privilege do not speak directly to the question of unauthorized revelations of confidential matter outside the judicial setting, and redress for such breaches of confidence must be sought in the law of torts or professional responsibility.

§ 73. Procedural Recognition of Rules of Privilege

In one important procedural respect, rules of privilege are similar to other evidentiary rules. The fact that most exclusionary rules are intended to protect the integrity of the fact-finding process while rules of privilege look toward the preservation of confidences might lead the casual reflector to conclude that the former will operate inexorably to exclude untrustworthy evidence while the latter will only be enforced at the option of the holder of the privilege. Such, we know, is not the case. Neither set of rules is self-executing: rules of exclusion, no less than rules of privilege, must be asserted to be effective, and if not asserted promptly will ordinarily be waived. Instead, the distinction in purpose between the two types of rules is reflected by a difference in the persons who may claim their benefit and, perhaps today, in what forum.

§ 73.1 Procedural Recognition of Rules of Privilege: (a) Who May Assert?

This difference in foundation between the two groups of rules manifests itself in another line of cleavage. The rule of exclusion or preference, being designed to make the trial more efficient as a vehicle of fact disclosure, may be invoked as of right only by the person whose interest in having the verdict follow the facts is at stake in the trial. Thus, when evidence condemned by one of these rules is offered, only the adverse party may object, unless the judge elects to interpose. But by contrast, if the evidence is privileged, the right to object does not attach to the opposing party as such, but to the person vested with the outside interest or relationship fostered by the particular privilege. True, other persons present at the trial, including the adverse party, may call to the court's attention the existence of the privilege, or the judge may choose to intervene of his own accord to protect it, but this is regarded as having been done on behalf of the owner of the privilege.

The right to complain on appeal is a more crucial test. If the court erroneously recognizes an asserted privilege and excludes proffered testimony on this ground, clearly the tendering party has been injured in his capacity as litigant and may complain on appeal. But if a claim of privilege is wrongly denied, and the privileged testimony erroneously let in, the distinction which we have suggested between privilege and a rule of exclusion would seem to be material. If the adverse party to the suit is likewise the owner of the privilege, then, while it may be argued that the party's interest *as a litigant* has not been infringed, most courts decline to draw so sharp a line, and permit him to complain of the error.

Where, however, the owner of the privilege is not a party to the suit, it is somewhat difficult to see why this invasion of a third person's interest should be ground of complaint for the objecting party, whose only grievance can be that the overriding of the outsider's rights has resulted in a fuller fact-disclosure than the party desires. It has not been thought necessary to afford this extreme sanction in order to prevent a break-down in the protection of privilege. In at least two classes of privileges, the privileges against self-incrimination[1] and against the use of evidence secured by unlawful search or seizure,[2] this distinction has been clearly perceived and the party is quite consistently denied any ground for reversal, despite the constitutional bases of the two privileges. The results in cases of

§ 73.1

1. See § 120 infra.

2. See § 179 infra.

erroneous denials of other privileges are more checkered; a considerable number of the older cases seem to allow the party to take advantage of the error on appeal.

The California Code of Evidence, one of the few modern codifications to address the question, is clear-cut. It provides: "A party may predicate error on a ruling disallowing a claim of privilege only if he is the holder of the privilege, except that a party may predicate error on a ruling disallowing a claim of privilege by his spouse * * *."[3]

§ 73.2 Procedural Recognition of Rules of Privilege: (b) Where May Privilege Be Asserted?—Rules of Privilege in Conflict of Laws.

Under traditional choice of law doctrine all rules of evidence, including those of privilege, were viewed as procedural and thus appropriately supplied by the law of the forum. This approach naturally tended to suppress any consideration of the differences in purpose clearly existing between rules of exclusion and preference on the one hand, and rules of privilege on the other.

Modern conflict of laws analysis, by contrast, inclines toward resolution of choice of law questions through evaluation of the policy interests of the respective jurisdictions which have some connection with the transaction in litigation. Under this approach, the forum will almost invariably possess a strong interest in a correct determination of the facts in dispute before its courts, and therefore a strong interest in the application of its rules of exclusion and preference. By contrast, the forum may have virtually no interest in applying its rules of privilege in a case where the relationship or interest sought to be promoted or protected by the privilege had its contacts exclusively with another jurisdiction.

Thus, for example, if a given professional relationship is carried out exclusively in State X which itself does not extend a privilege to protect that relationship, there would seem to be no compelling reason for the forum, State Y, to apply its own rules of privilege, thus

denying its court the benefit of helpful evidence. No interest either of the forum or of State X argues for recognition of the forum's privilege in such a case.

On the other hand, if the relationship is carried out exclusively in State X, which does extend a privilege to the communication in question, circumstances may exist in which in which the forum, State Y, may want to recognize that privilege even though there would be no comparable privilege under its law.

§ 74. Limitations on the Effectiveness of Privileges: (a) Risk of Eavesdropping and Interception of Letters

Since privileges operate to deny litigants access to every person's evidence, the courts have generally construed them no more broadly than necessary to accomplish their basic purposes. One manifestation of this tendency is to be seen in the general rule that a privilege operates only to preclude testimony by parties to the confidential relationship. Accordingly, a number of older decisions held that an eavesdropper may testify to confidential communications, and that a letter, otherwise confidential and privileged, is not protected if it is purloined or otherwise intercepted by a third person. This principle, however, has only infrequently been carried to the extent of allowing a privilege to be breached if the interception is made possible by the connivance of a party to the confidential relationship.

Though the same general rule is still sometimes applied, most modern decisions do no more than hold that a privilege will not protect communications made under circumstances in which interception was reasonably to be anticipated. Certainly, a qualification of the traditional rule in terms of the reasonable expectations of the privileged communicator may provide a desirable common law readjustment to cope with the alarming potential of the modern eavesdropper. While in earlier times the confidentiality of privileged communications could generally be preserved by a modest attention to security, homespun mea-

3.   West's Ann.Cal.Evid.Code § 918.

sures will hardly suffice against the modern panoply of electronic paraphernalia.

The vastly enhanced technology of eavesdropping has drawn a variety of legislative reactions more directly responsive to the problem. These have included state statutes prohibiting wiretapping and electronic surveillance and denying admissibility to evidence obtained in violation. Such provisions are of course in addition to that protection which may rest on constitutional grounds. Moreover, statutes and rules defining the privileges have begun to include provisions entitling the holder to prevent anyone from disclosing a privileged communication.

§ 74.1   Limitations on the Effectiveness of Privileges: (b) Adverse Arguments and Inferences From Claims of Privilege

The underlying conflict comes most clearly in view in the decisions relating to the allowability of an adverse inference from the assertion of privilege. Plainly, the inference may not ordinarily be made against a party when a witness for that party claims a privilege personal to the witness, for this is not a matter under the party's control.[1] But where the party himself suppresses evidence by invoking a privilege given to him by the law, should an adverse inference be sanctioned? The question may arise in various forms, for example, whether an inquiry of the witness, or of the party, calling for information obviously privileged, may be pressed for the pointed purpose of forcing the party to make an explicit claim of the privilege in the jury's hearing, or again, whether the inference may be drawn in argument, and finally, whether the judge in the instructions may mention the inference as a permissible one.

Under familiar principles an unfavorable inference may be drawn against a party not only for destroying evidence, but for the mere failure to produce witnesses or documents within his control.[2] No showing of wrong or fraud seems to be required as a foundation for the inference that the evidence if produced would have been unfavorable. Why should not this same conclusion be drawn from the party's active interposing of a privilege to keep out the evidence? A leading case for the affirmative is Phillips v. Chase,[3] where the court said:

> "It is a rule of law that the objection of a party to evidence as incompetent and immaterial, and insistence upon his right to have his case tried according to the rules of law, cannot be made a subject of comment in argument. * * * On the other hand, if evidence is material and competent except for a personal privilege of one of the parties to have it excluded under the law, his claim of the privilege may be referred to in argument and considered by the jury, as indicating his opinion that the evidence, if received, would be prejudicial to him."

An oft-quoted statement by Lord Chelmsford gives the contrary view:

> "The exclusion of such evidence is for the general interest of the community, and therefore to say that when a party refuses to permit professional confidence to be broken, everything must be taken most strongly against him, what is it but to deny him the protection which, for public purposes, the law affords him, and utterly to take away a privilege which can thus only be asserted to his prejudice?"[4]

The first of these arguments is based upon an unfounded distinction between incompetent and privileged evidence, namely, a supposition that the privilege can be waived and the incompetency cannot.[5] As we have seen, both may be waived with equal facility. As to the second, it may be an overstatement to say that permitting the inference "utterly takes away" the privilege. A privilege has its most substantial practical benefit when it enables a party to exclude from the record a witness, document,

---

§ 74.1

1. See § 73 supra, and more particularly as to self-incrimination § 120 infra.

2. See § 264 infra.

3. 87 N.E. 755, 758 (Mass.1909).

4. Wentworth v. Lloyd, 10 H.L.Cas. 589, 591 (1864).

5. See § 73 supra.

or line of proof which is essential to the adversary's case, lacking which he cannot get to the jury at all on a vital issue. The inference does not supply the lack of proof.[6] In other situations, the benefit accruing from a successful claim of privilege will depend upon circumstances. It is evident, however, that in a case which does survive a motion for a directed verdict or its equivalent, allowing comment upon the exercise of a privilege or requiring it to be claimed in the presence of the jury tends greatly to diminish its value. In Griffin v. California[7] the Supreme Court held that allowing comment upon the failure of an accused to take the stand violated his privilege against self-incrimination "by making its assertion costly." Whether one is prepared to extend this protection to all privileges probably depends upon his attitude towards privileges in general and towards the particular privilege involved. The cases, rather naturally, are in dispute. It is submitted that the best solution is to recognize only privileges which are soundly based in policy and to accord those privileges the fullest protection. Thus comment, whether by judge or by counsel, or its equivalent of requiring the claim to be made in the presence of the jury, and the drawing of inferences from the claim, all would be foreclosed.

§ 74.2 Limitations on the Effectiveness of Privileges: (c) Constitutional Limitations on Privilege

A hitherto unrecognized source of limitations on privilege in criminal cases has in recent years emerged as a result of decisions of the Supreme Court dealing with the Compulsory Process and Confrontation Clauses of the Constitution of the United States.

The three cases which have figured in this development are Washington v. Texas,[1] Davis v. Alaska,[2] and United States v. Nixon.[3] In Washington v. Texas, the Court held the provisions of the Compulsory Process Clause binding upon states as a component of due process,

and struck down a Texas statute which rendered persons charged or convicted as co-participants in the same crime incompetent to testify for one another. The Court's decision stressed the "absurdity" of the statute and specifically held only that the constitutional provision is violated by "arbitrary rules that prevent whole categories of defense witnesses from testifying * * * ."[4] The Court expressly disclaimed any implied disapproval of testimonial privileges which it noted are based upon quite different considerations.

In Davis v. Alaska, the Court held that the Confrontation Clause was violated by application of a state statute privileging juvenile records where the result was to deny the defendant the opportunity to elicit on cross-examination the probationary status of a critical witness against him. Recognizing the strength of the state policy in favor of preserving the confidentiality of juveniles' records, the Court nevertheless held that this policy must yield to the superior interest of the defendant in effective confrontation. Significantly, the Court's decision did not compel disclosure of the juvenile record, but only remanded the case for further proceedings not inconsistent with the Court's opinion.

Finally, in United States v. Nixon, the Court held that a claim of absolute privilege of confidentiality for general presidential communications in the performance of the office would not prevail "over the fundamental demands of due process of law in the fair administration of criminal justice. The generalized assertion of privilege must yield to the demonstrated, specific need for evidence in a pending criminal trial."[5]

Taken together, and despite the somewhat distinctive fact situations involved, these cases fairly raise the question as to the viability of a claim of privilege when a criminal defendant asserts: (1) a need to introduce the privileged matter as exculpatory, or (2) a need to use the

---

6. See § 264 infra.

7. 380 U.S. 609 (1965).

§ 74.2

1. 388 U.S. 14 (1967).

2. 415 U.S. 308 (1974).

3. 418 U.S. 683 (1974).

4. Washington v. Texas, 388 U.S. 14, 22 (1967).

5. 418 U.S. 683, 713 (1974).

privileged matter to impeach testimony introduced by the state. The question is of course not altogether a novel one. Privileges running in favor of the government, such as the informer's privilege, have long been qualified to accommodate the defendant's rights of confrontation.[6] Similarly, the state has frequently been precluded from relying upon the testimony of a witness whose claim of privilege on self-incrimination grounds prevents effective cross-examination.[7]

A number of state decisions, purporting to give effect to the constitutional holdings of *Davis* and *Nixon,* have resolved conflicts between the rights of a defendant on the one hand and claims of private privilege on the other by overriding the latter and forcing (or attempting to force) the testimony of the privilege holder.

Despite such decisions, the extent to which protection of the interests of a criminal defendant constitutionally requires invasion of private privilege was never clear, and has been placed even further in doubt in the decision of the Supreme Court in Pennsylvania v. Ritchie.[8] In *Ritchie,* the defendant, charged with rape and other related crimes, sought pretrial access to files of a state child protective agency. The defendant's chief interest in the files, which were protected by a qualified privilege under state statute, was to discover material of possible use in the cross-examination of his daughter, the complaining witness. The state supreme court, relying on *Davis,* held that the defendant had the right to inspect the files in question by virtue of the Confrontation and Compulsory Process clauses. The Supreme Court reversed this portion of the state judgment, a majority of the court concurring that the defendant was entitled only to have the file inspected in camera by the trial court. Only four justices, however, joined in the plurality opinion which based this result on due process grounds and stated that the Pennsylvania court's reliance on *Davis* was "mis-

placed" and that the Confrontation Clause creates only a "trial" right.

Not surprisingly, the *Ritchie* decision has been accorded a variety of interpretations. One approach adopted by several courts is to require that the defendant make a showing that there is reasonable ground to believe that failure to produce material which has been found privileged will be likely to impair defendant's right of confrontation. Once such a showing is made, the state must then obtain the privilege holder's waiver for purposes of an in camera inspection and, if the matter is found relevant, for trial presentation; otherwise the privilege-holder's testimony will be inadmissible. However, many decisions have failed to find that the defendant's constitutional rights require even so limited an intrusion on private privilege.

Even more dubious today is any right of the criminal defendant to obtain and present matter protected by private privilege which is relevant to the issues of the case but has no direct bearing upon the credibility of a witness for the prosecution.

§ 75. The Sources of Privilege

The earliest recognized privileges were judicially created, the origin of both the husband-wife and attorney-client privileges being traceable to the received common law.[1] The development of judge-made privileges, however, virtually halted over a century ago. Though it is impossible definitely to ascribe a reason for this cessation, a contributing factor was undoubtedly a judicial tendency to view privileges from the standpoint of their hindrance to litigation. Certainly the vantage point of the legal profession in general, and of the judiciary in particular, is such as to force into prominence the more deleterious aspects of privilege as impediments to the fact-finding process. By contrast, many of the beneficial consequences claimed for privilege can be expected to be observable only outside the courtroom, and

---

6. Roviaro v. United States, 353 U.S. 53 (1957).

7. See § 19 supra.

8. 480 U.S. 39 (1987).

§ 75

1. See §§ 78 and 87 infra.

even then are often difficult of empirical demonstration.

Perhaps as a consequence, during the 19th century the source of newly created privileges shifted decisively from the courts to the legislatures. New York enacted the first physician-patient privilege in 1828, and the vast majority of new privileges created since that time have been of legislative origin. The trend extended to codification even of the preexisting common law privileges, and today the husband-wife and attorney-client privileges are statutorily controlled in most states.

It may be argued that legitimate claims to confidentiality are more equitably received by a branch of government not preeminently concerned with the factual results obtained in litigation, and that the legislatures provide an appropriate forum for the balancing of the competing social values necessary to sound decisions concerning privilege. At the same time, while there is no doubt that some of the statutorily created privileges are soundly based, legislatures have on occasion been unduly influenced by powerful groups seeking the prestige and convenience of a professionally based privilege. One result of the process has been that the various states differ substantially in the numbers and varieties of privilege which they recognize.

Until very recently, the heavy consensus among commentators has favored narrowing the field of privilege, and attempts have been made, largely without success, to incorporate this view into the several 20th century efforts to codify the law of evidence. The draftsmen of both the Model Code of Evidence and the 1953 Uniform Rules of Evidence favored limitations on the number and scope of privileges. The final versions of both of these codifications, however, contained the generally recognized common law and statutory privileges substantially unimpaired.

The Federal Rules of Evidence as proposed by the Advisory Committee and approved by the Supreme Court contained provisions recognizing and defining nine nonconstitutional privileges: required reports, attorney-client, psychotherapist-patient, husband-wife, clergyman-communicant, political vote, trade secrets, secrets of state and other official information, and identity of informer. In addition, proposed Rule 501 specifically limited the privileges to be recognized in the federal courts to those provided for by the Rules or enacted by the Congress.[2] When the Rules were submitted to the Congress the privilege provisions excited particular controversy, with the result that all of the specific rules of privilege were excised from the finally enacted version of the Rules.[3]

The failure of Congress to enact specific rules of privilege left the Federal Rules of Evidence with a large gap when viewed as a potential model code for possible adoption by the states. Therefore, in promulgating the Revised Uniform Rules of Evidence (1974), based almost entirely on the Federal Rules, the National Conference of Commissioners on Uniform State Laws included specific rules of privilege. These are substantially the version of the Federal Rules submitted to Congress, but contain some notable changes. Some states adopting rules or codes based upon the Federal Rules have adopted the proposed Federal Rules concerning privilege, others have adopted the Uniform Rules on this subject, and some have retained their antecedent rules of privilege.

§ 76.　The Current Pattern of Privilege

The failure of Congress to enact specific rules of privilege for the federal courts effectively precluded any immediate prospect of substantial national uniformity in this area. It is arguable that, in light of the strength and

---

2. Deleted Federal Rule 501, 56 F.R.D. 230, reads:

Except as provided in these rules or in other rules adopted by the Supreme Court, no person has a privilege to:

(1) Refuse to be a witness; or

(2) Refuse to disclose any matter; or

(3) Refuse to produce any object or writing; or

(4) Prevent another from being a witness or disclosing any matter or producing any object or writing.

3. For the text of Fed.R.Evid. 501 as adopted by the Congress, see § 76 infra.

contrariety of views which the subject generates, hope for such a consensus was never realistic. In any event, the present form of Federal Rule of Evidence 501 perpetuates a fluid situation in the federal law of privilege and affords the states little inducement to adopt identical or similar schemes of privilege. The variegated pattern of privilege in both federal and state courts, described below, thus seems likely to remain the case for the foreseeable future.

§ 76.1 The Current Pattern of Privilege: (a) Privilege in Federal Courts

The Proposed Federal Rules of Evidence recognized only privileges emanating from federal sources and their enactment would have created a unitary scheme of privilege applicable to all cases regardless of jurisdictional ground. The congressionally enacted rules, however, establish a bifurcated system of privilege rules. Federal Rule of Evidence 501 provides:

> Except as otherwise required by the Constitution of the United States or provided by Act of Congress or in rules prescribed by the Supreme Court pursuant to statutory authority, the privilege of a witness, person, government, State, or political subdivision thereof shall be governed by the principles of the common law as they may be interpreted by the courts of the United States in the light of reason and experience. However, in civil actions and proceedings, with respect to an element of a claim or defense as to which State law supplies the rule of decision, the privilege of a witness, person, government, State, or political subdivision thereof shall be determined in accordance with State law.

Under Rule 501, then, common law, "as interpreted * * * in the light of reason and experience," will determine the privileges applicable in federal question and criminal cases, while privileges in diversity actions will derive from state law. In the former types of cases, it seems likely that the rules promulgated by the

Supreme Court will prove influential as indicators of "reason and experience." But it is also apparent that the intent of Rule 501 is not to limit the number and type of privileges recognized to those included in the proposed rules. A significant question exists whether this freedom should be used to recognize and apply state privileges in cases where Rule 501 does not require such to be done.

The situation with respect to cases in which state law provides the rule of decision, primarily diversity cases, is somewhat clearer. Presumably a federal court today would not, as was sometimes done prior to the enactment of Rule 501, enforce a privilege in a diversity case which is not recognized by applicable state law. A major question remains, however, as to the process by which the existence or absence of an "applicable" state privilege will be determined in conflict of law situations.

It has been argued that, given the status of Rule 501 as an Act of Congress, the federal courts, in determining the applicable state law of privilege, are not constrained to accept state conflict of laws principles. Though this position has been supported by a number of commentators, a majority of the cases decided since enactment of the Federal Rules have continued to follow the doctrine of Klaxon Co. v. Stentor Electric Manufacturing Co.[1] and thus to look to state choice of law rules in determining what state's privilege should be applied.

Issues of the application of state or federal privilege law also arise in cases in which there are both federal and state claims. In such instances, the better practice would seem to be to consider the predominant nature of the claims and the issues to which the arguably privileged information would be relevant.

§ 76.2 The Current Pattern of Privilege: (b) State Patterns of Privilege

State patterns in the recognition of privileges vary greatly. As developed in succeeding chapters, all states possess some form of hus-

1. 313 U.S. 487 (1941).

band-wife,[1] and attorney-client privilege.[2] All afford some protection to certain government information.[3] Most, though not all, allow at least a limited privilege to communications between physician and patient.[4] In addition several other privileges are worthy of specific mention.

Though probably not recognized at common law, a privilege protecting confidential communications between clergymen and penitents has now been adopted in all 50 states. Wigmore's seemingly grudging acceptance of the privilege perhaps reflects the difficulty of justifying its existence on exclusively utilitarian grounds, since at least where penitential communications are required or encouraged by religious tenets, they are likely to continue to be made irrespective of the presence or absence of evidentiary privilege. A firmer ground appears available in the inherent offensiveness of the secular power attempting to coerce an act violative of religious conscience. Implementing a decent regard for religious convictions while at the same time avoiding making individual conscience the ultimate measure of testimonial obligation has proved to be attended by some difficulties. Early statutory forms of the privilege undertook to privilege only penitential communications "in the course of discipline enjoined by the church" to which the communicant belongs. This limitation, however, has been urged to be unduly, perhaps unconstitutionally, preferential to the Roman Catholic and a few other churches. The statutes have, accordingly, generally been broadened. Revised Uniform Rule of Evidence (1974) 505 is typical in extending the privilege generally to "confidential communication[s] by a person to a clergyman in his professional character as spiritual advisor."

The states are split on the question of who can waive the clergyman-penitent privilege. Some provide that the privilege belongs only to the communicant, others provide that it belongs to the clergy member and still others hold that it belongs to both.

One of the most persistently advocated privileges for many years, but particularly during the past decade, has been one shielding journalists from being testimonially required to divulge the identities of news sources. The rationale asserted for this privilege is analogous to that underlying the long-standing governmental informers privilege and is exclusively utilitarian in character. Thus, it is contended that the news sources essential to supply the public's need for information will be "dried up" if their identities are subject to compelled disclosure. Numerous attempts to have the privilege enacted by federal statute have failed, and it is not one of those privileges incorporated into the Revised Uniform Rules of Evidence (1974). Moreover, the argument that a journalist's privilege is constitutionally to be implied from the First Amendment guarantee of a free press was rejected by the Supreme Court in Branzburg v. Hayes.[5] However, taking note that this rejection did not command an absolute majority of the Court, a substantial number of lower federal courts have undertaken to recognize a qualified journalist's privilege which may be penetrated by appropriate showings on the part of the party desiring the privileged information. Though occasionally referred to as a common law creation, the privilege has generally been said to derive from the First Amendment. Some form of privilege for journalists has been created by statute, or in a few cases by judicial decision, in a substantial number of states. A few state courts have also found the privilege to be implied by state constitutional provision. Unlike other professional privileges, it is generally conceived as belonging to the journalist, to be claimed or waived irrespective of the wishes of the news source.

Communications to accountants are privileged in perhaps a third of the states. This privilege is most closely analogous to that for attorney-client, though the social objective to

§ 76.2

1. See Ch. 9 infra.
2. See Ch. 10 infra.
3. See Ch. 12 infra.

4. See Ch. 11 infra.
5. 408 U.S. 665 (1972).

be furthered is arguably a distinguishable and lesser one.

In recent years much attention has been bestowed upon the plight of the rape victim, and some sort of sexual assault victim-counselor privilege has been created by statute or court decision in a substantial number of states. Such a privilege can claim a substantial basis in public policy, but inevitably comes into conflict with the constitutional rights of the criminal defendant.[6]

Even broader acceptance has been achieved by the principle that protection by evidentiary privilege is necessary for the deliberations of medical review committees.

There is occasional recognition of privilege for communications to confidential clerks, stenographers and other "employees" generally, school teachers, school counselors, participants in group psychotherapy, nurses, marriage counselors, private detectives, and social workers. A privilege for parent-minor child communications has been recommended but has received little judicial approval. Privileges for scientific researcher-subject and self-critical analysis have fared only somewhat better.

An attempt to obtain recognition of a federal privilege protecting against disclosure of confidential peer review materials of academic institutions has been rejected by the Supreme Court.[7]

§ 77. The Future of Privilege

Despite the rejection by the Congress of the Proposed Federal Rules of Evidence relating to privilege and the resultant failure to effect substantive changes in this area, several concurrent developments may portend certain new directions in the development of the law of privilege.

The vehemence of the attacks leveled at certain of the proposed Federal Rules on privilege suggests that the basic concept of evidentiary privilege, despite its deleterious consequences for the administration of justice, will not be abandoned in the foreseeable future. Many of these attacks, predictably, came from groups specifically interested in the preservation or creation of particular privileges. Much more significantly, the cause of privilege was also espoused by an unprecedentedly large segment of the academic community. The latter response was in large part precipitated by a generalized concern over the increasing intrusiveness of modern society into human privacy, a concern reflected in several Supreme Court decisions conferring constitutional status upon certain aspects of privacy.

While the ultimate strategic significance of evidentiary privilege as a bastion for defending privacy values may be doubted, the focus on privacy as an operative basis for the recognition of some privileges is believed to be a healthy and overdue development. At the optimum, it may offer a theoretical basis for a more satisfactory accommodation than has heretofore been achieved between the legitimate demands for freedom against unwarranted intrusion on the one hand and the basic requirements of the judicial system on the other.

The traditionally felt need, stemming largely from Wigmore's dictum, to justify all privileges in terms of their utilitarian value leads not only to the assertion of highly questionable sociological premises but also affords little prospect for meaningful reconciliation of values in this area. Traditional evidentiary privilege necessarily paints with a broad brush since the achievement of utilitarian objectives requires privileges which are essentially absolute in character. But if it is recognized that not all privileges are based on identical considerations or will have identical effects if allowed in litigation, it will be seen that not all privileges need make such large demands. If the object aimed at is not the inducement of conduct in certain relationships but the protection of individual privacy from unnecessary or trivial intrusions, the implementation of the privilege is amenable to the finer touch of the specific solution. Thus, a decision in the particular case that sufficiently grave considerations demand disclosure will, to be sure, impact

---

6. See § 74.2 supra.

7. University of Pennsylvania v. E.E.O.C., 493 U.S. 182 (1990).

adversely on the privilege holder, but no more extended societal interest will be impaired.

Another factor may also contribute to a greater use of qualified or conditional privileges which are subject to suspension on ad hoc determination of particular need for evidence in a given case. It is already clear that the law of privilege must to some extent accommodate to the developing rights of criminal defendants under the Confrontation and Compulsory Process Clauses.[1] At the same time it is desirable, whenever possible, to avoid a choice between the automatic and total override of privilege whenever a criminal defendant asserts a need for privileged matter, and the dismissal of the charges if the privilege is to be sustained. At least in those instances where accomplishment of the privilege objective does not necessitate absolute protection, an in camera weighing of the potential significance of the matter sought as against the considerations of privacy underlying the privilege may represent a desirable compromise.

Though necessarily entailing a certain amount of procedural inconvenience and a considerable amount of judicial discretion, this solution has recommended itself to a number of commentators and courts. It is perhaps reasonable to predict that an increased involvement of judges in the general area of privacy and confidentiality may be in the making.

§ 77

1. See § 74.2.

Chapter 9

THE PRIVILEGE FOR MARITAL COMMUNICATIONS

Table of Sections

§ 78. History and Background and Kindred Rules

We are dealing here with a late offshoot of an ancient tree. The older branches are discussed in another chapter.[1] Those earlier rules, to be sharply distinguished from the present doctrine, are first, the rule that the spouse of a party or person interested is disqualified from testifying in favor of the other spouse, and second, the privilege of a party against having the party's husband or wife called as an adverse witness. These two earlier rules forbid the calling of the spouse as a witness at all, for or against the party, regardless of the actual testimony to be elicited, whereas the privilege presently discussed is limited to a certain class of testimony, namely communications between the spouses or more broadly in some states, information gained on account of the marital relation.

The movement for procedural reform in England in the first half of the 1800s found expression in the evidence field in agitation for the break up of the system of disqualification of parties and spouses. One of the auxiliary reasons which had been given to justify the disqualification of spouses was that of preserving marital confidences. As to the disqualification of spouses the reform was largely accomplished by the Evidence Amendment Act, 1853. On the eve of this legislation, Greenleaf, writing in this country in 1842, clearly announced the existence of a distinct privilege for marital communications, and this pronouncement was echoed in England by Best in 1849, though seemingly there was little or no support for such a view in the English decisions. Moreover, the Second Report of 1853 of the Commissioners on Common Law Procedure, after rejecting the arguments for the outmoded rules of disqualification, calls attention to the special danger of "alarm and unhappiness occasioned to society by * * * com-

§ 78

1. See § 66 supra.

pelling the public disclosure of confidential communications between husband and wife * * * '' and declares that ''[a]ll communications between them should be held to be privileged.''

However, though the policy supporting a privilege for marital communications had thus been distinctly pointed out, there had been little occasion for its judicial recognition, since the wider disqualifications of the spouses of parties left small possibility for the question of the existence of such a privilege to arise.

Nevertheless, the English Act of 1853, mentioned above, after it abolished the disqualification of husbands and wives of the parties, enacted that ''no husband shall be compellable to disclose any communication made to him by his wife during the marriage, and no wife shall be compellable to disclose any communication made to her by her husband during the marriage.''[2] Moreover, nearly all the states in this country, while making spouses competent to testify, have included provisions disabling them from testifying to communications between them.

In the light of this history the Court of Appeal in England has denied that there was any common law privilege for marital communications. In this country, however, the courts have frequently said that the statutes protecting marital communications from disclosure are declaratory of the common law. Moreover, some courts have even held the ''common law'' rule to be in effect without benefit of statute, at least until legislatively abrogated.

In addition to the vitality which it has displayed in the courts, the rule discussed here has been viewed by some legal commentators as the most defensible of the various forms of marital privilege. However, Federal Rule of Evid. 505 as approved by the Supreme Court but deleted by the Congress, recognized no privilege for confidential communications between spouses, limiting the privilege to that of an accused in a criminal proceeding to prevent his or her spouse from testifying for the prose-

cution. The marital privilege under the Revised Uniform Rules, limited under the 1974 version of those rules to a privilege of the accused to prevent disclosure of confidential communications, was subsequently broadened by amendment of Uniform Rule of Evidence 504. The revised rule recognizes a privilege for adverse spousal testimony[3] as well as one for confidential communications in criminal and civil cases. Under Federal Rule of Evidence 501, as adopted by Congress, the federal courts have continued to recognize a marital communications privilege as effective by common law.

§ 79. What Is Privileged: Communications Only, or Acts and Facts?

Greenleaf, arguing in 1842 for a privilege distinct from marital incompetency, and furnishing the inspiration for the later statutes by which the privilege was formally enacted, spoke only of ''communications'' and ''conversations.''[1] Those later statutes themselves (except one or two) sanctioned the privilege for ''communications'' and for nothing beyond. Accordingly it would seem that the privilege should be limited to *expressions* intended by one spouse to convey a meaning or message to the other. These expressions may be by words, oral, written or in sign-language, or by expressive acts, as where the husband opens a trunk before his wife and points out objects therein to her. Moreover, the protection of the privilege will shield against indirect disclosure of the communication, as where a husband is asked for his wife's whereabouts which he learned only from her secret communication. It seems, nevertheless, that logic and policy should cause the courts to halt with communications as the furthest boundary of the privilege, and a substantial number have held steadfast at this line.

An equal or greater number of courts, however, have construed their statutes which say ''communications'' to extend the privilege to acts, facts, conditions, and transactions not amounting to communications at all. One

---

2. St. 16 & 17 Vict. c. 83, § 3.

3. The cognate privilege for adverse spousal testimony is treated in § 66 supra.

1. See § 78 supra.

group seems to announce the principle that acts done privately in the wife's presence amount to "communications." Another would go even further and say that any information secured by the wife as a result of the marital relation and which would not have been known in the absence of such relation is protected. Some at least of this latter group would hold that information secured by one spouse through observation during the marriage as to the health, or intoxication, habitual or at a particular time, or the mental condition of the other spouse, would be protected by the privilege.

All extensions beyond communications seem unjustified by the theory of this privilege. The attitude of the courts in these cases seems to reflect a confusion with the quite distinguishable purpose of preserving family harmony by disqualifying one spouse from giving any testimony whatsoever against the other.[2] Whatever the merits of the latter principle, its attempted implementation under the guise of a communications privilege can only lead to anomalous results, for the bulk of the cases involve factual situations in which the marriage has already been destroyed. It is believed a different attitude would be wiser, namely that of accepting the view that privileges in general, and this privilege for marital confidences in particular, are inept and clumsy devices for promoting the policies they profess to serve, but are extremely effective as stumbling blocks to obstruct the attainment of justice. Accordingly, at the very least, the movement should be toward restriction of these devices rather than their expansion through theoretically dubious applications.

A specific instance of development in the proper direction has recently been evident in statutes and cases which exclude from the protection of the privilege communications in furtherance of crime or fraud. This exception, long recognized to restrict the cognate privilege for attorney-client communications, seems amply justified in the present context as well.

§ 80. The Communication Must Be Confidential

Most statutes expressly limit the privilege to "confidential communications."[1] However, even where the words used are "any communication" or simply "communications," the notion that the privilege is born of the "common law" and the fact that the pre-statutory descriptions of the privilege had clearly based it upon the policy of protecting confidences, have actuated most courts to read into such statutes the requirement of confidentiality. Communications in private between husband and wife are assumed to be confidential, though of course this assumption will be strengthened if confidentiality is expressly affirmed, or if the subject is such that the communicating spouse would probably desire that the matter be kept secret, either because its disclosure would be embarrassing or for some other reason. However, a variety of factors, including the nature of the message or the circumstances under which it was delivered, may serve to rebut a claim that confidentiality was intended. In particular, if a third person (other than a child of the family) is present to the knowledge of the communicating spouse, this stretches the web of confidence beyond the marital pair, and the communication is unprivileged. If children of the family are present this likewise deprives the conversation of protection unless the children are too young to understand what is said. The fact that the communication relates to business transactions may show that it was not intended as confidential. Examples are statements about business agreements between the spouses, or about business matters transacted by one spouse as agent for the other, or about property or conveyances. Usually such statements relate to facts which are intended later to become publicly known. To cloak them with privilege when the transactions come into litigation would be productive of special inconvenience and injustice.

§ 81. The Time of Making the Communication: Marital Status

The privilege is created to encourage marital confidences and is limited to them. Conse-

2. See § 66, supra.

§ 80
1. See § 78 supra.

quently, communications between the husband and wife before they were married, or after their divorce, are not privileged. And attempts to assert the privilege by participants in "modern" living arrangements argued to be the functional equivalents of marriage have to date uniformly been rejected by the courts. The requirement of a valid marriage may be satisfied by a valid common law marriage, if it can be proved, but a bigamous marriage will not suffice. Although this latter holding should probably, by analogy to other privileges, be relaxed where the party seeking the benefit of the privilege was ignorant of the status of the other purported spouse, the courts have not consistently done so.

What of a husband and wife living apart? It has been urged that communication in this context is far more likely to be related to preservation of the marriage than are the vast bulk of admittedly privileged communications. This fact, coupled with the pragmatic difficulty involved in determining when hostility between the spouses has become implacable, argues for the more easily administered approach of terminating the privilege only upon a decree of divorce. Some courts have adopted such a view. However, other courts, especially the federal circuits, have refused to apply the privilege where the parties are separated at the time of the communication.

§ 82. Hazards of Disclosure to Third Persons Against the Will of the Communicating Spouse

The weight of decision seems to support the view that the privilege does not protect against the testimony of third persons who have overheard (either accidentally or by eavesdropping) an oral communication between husband and wife, or who have secured possession or learned the contents of a letter from one spouse to another by interception, or through loss or misdelivery by the custodian.

In addition, several courts, especially more recently, have held that particular statutes provide only that a spouse may not be examined about confidential statements. Under such statutes, the privilege does not prevent another person from testifying to the statements or the introduction of documents containing references to such communications.

Such rulings are perhaps best sustained on the view that, since the privilege has as its only effect the suppression of relevant evidence, its scope should be confined as narrowly as is consistent with reasonable protection of marital communications. In this view, it seems, since the communicating spouse can ordinarily take effective precautions against overhearing, he should bear the risk of a failure to use such precautions. Moreover, if he sends a messenger with a letter, he should ordinarily assume the risk that the chosen emissary may lose or misdeliver the message. The rationale that the spouses may ordinarily take effective measures to communicate confidentially tends to break down where one or both are incarcerated. However, communications in the jailhouse are frequently held not privileged, often on the theory that no confidentiality was or could have been expected.

As has been observed elsewhere, the development of sophisticated eavesdropping techniques has led to curbs upon their use and upon the admissibility of evidence obtained thereby.[1] It has also led to inclusion in rules governing privileged communications provisions against disclosure by third persons.

Except in those jurisdictions where the privilege is held only to prevent the spouse from testifying and not the introduction of other testimony or documents, most of the cases have held that the privilege will not be lost if the eavesdropping, or the delivery or disclosure of the letter is due to the betrayal or connivance of the spouse to whom the message is directed. Just as that spouse would not be permitted, against the will of the communicating spouse, to betray the confidence by testifying in court to the message, so he or she may not effectively destroy the privilege by out-of-court betrayal.

If the spouse to whom a letter is addressed dies and it is found among the effects of the deceased, may the personal representative be

§ 82
1. See § 74 supra, and §§ 169, 176 infra.

required or permitted to produce it in court? Here there is no connivance or betrayal by the deceased spouse, and on the other hand this is not a disclosure against which the sender could effectively guard. If the privilege is to be held, as most courts do,[2] to survive the death of one of the spouses, it seems that only a court which strictly limits the effect of the statute to restraining the spouses themselves from testifying, could justify a denial of the privilege in this situation.

§ 83. Who Is the Holder of the Privilege? Enforcement and Waiver

Greenleaf in 1842, in foreshadowing the protection of marital communications, wrote of the projected rule as a "privilege" based on "public policy." Many legislatures, however, when they came to write the privilege into law phrased the rule simply as a survival in this special case of the ancient incompetency of the spouses, which the same statutes undertook to abolish or restrict. So it is often provided that the spouses are "incompetent" to testify to marital communications. Consequently, the courts frequently overlook this "common law" background[1] of privilege, and permit any party to the action to claim the benefit of the rule by objection. Doubtless counsel often fail to point out that privilege, not incompetency, is the proper classification, and that the distinctive feature of privilege is that it can only be claimed by the holder or beneficiary of the privilege, not by a party as such.[2] The latter principle is clearly correct.

Who is the holder? Wigmore's argument, that the policy of encouraging freedom of communication points to the communicating spouse as the holder, seems convincing. Under this view, in the case of a unilateral oral message or statement, of a husband to his wife, only the husband could assert the privilege, where the sole purpose is to show the expressions and attitude of the husband. If the object, however, were to show the wife's adoption of the husband's statement by her silence,

then the husband's statement and her conduct both become her communication and she can claim the privilege. Similarly, if a conversation or an exchange of correspondence between them is offered to show the collective expressions of them both, either it seems could claim privilege as to the entire exchange.

A failure by the holder to assert the privilege by objection, or a voluntary revelation by the holder of the communication, or of a material part, is a waiver. The judge, however, may in some jurisdictions in his discretion protect the privilege if the holder is not present to assert it, and objection by a party not the holder may serve the purpose of invoking this discretion, though the party may not complain if the judge fails to protect this privilege belonging to the absent spouse.

§ 84. Controversies in Which the Privilege Is Inapplicable

The common law privilege against adverse testimony of a spouse was subject to an exception in cases of prosecution of the husband for offenses against the wife, at least those of violence.[1] When nineteenth century statutes in this country limited and regulated this privilege and the incompetency of spouses as witnesses and defined the new statutory privilege for confidential communications the common law exception above mentioned was usually incorporated and extended, and frequently other exceptions were added. Under these statutes it is not always clear whether the exceptions are intended to apply only to the provisions limiting the competency of the spouses as witnesses, or whether they apply also to the privilege for confidential communications. Frequently, however, in the absence of a contrary decision, it is at least arguable that the exception does have this latter application, and in some instances this intent is clearly expressed. Any other result would, in principle, indeed be difficult to justify.

2. See § 85 infra.

§ 83
1. See § 78, supra.
2. See § 73, supra.

§ 84
1. See § 66.

The types of controversies in which the marital communication privilege is made inapplicable vary, of course, from state to state. They may be derived from express provision, from statutory implication, or from decisions based upon common law doctrine. They may be grouped as follows:

1. Prosecutions for crimes committed by one spouse against the other or against the children of either. Besides statutes in general terms, particular crimes, most frequently family desertion and pandering, are often specified, and as to these latter the withdrawal of the privilege for communications is usually explicit.

2. Actions by one of the spouses against an outsider for an intentional injury to the marital relation. Thus far this exception has been applied, sometimes under statutes, sometimes as a continuation of common law tradition, chiefly in actions for alienation of affection or for criminal conversation. It is usually applied to admit declarations expressive of the state of affection of the alienated spouse.

3. Actions by one spouse against the other. Some of the statutes are in this broader form. Some apply only to particular kinds of actions between them, of which divorce suits are most often specified. This exception for controversies between the spouses, which should extend to controversies between the representatives of the spouses, seems worthy of universal acceptance. In the analogous case of clients who jointly consult an attorney, the clients are held to have no privilege for such consultation in controversies between themselves.[2] So here it seems that husband and wife, while they would desire that their confidences be shielded from the outside world, would ordinarily anticipate that if a controversy between themselves should arise in which their mutual conversations would shed light on the merits, the interests of both would be served by full disclosure.

4. A criminal prosecution against one of the spouses in which a declaration of the other spouse made confidentially to the accused

would tend to justify or reduce the grade of the offense.

§ 85. If the Communication Was Made During the Marriage, Does Death or Divorce End the Privilege?

The incompetency of husband or wife to testify for the other, and the privilege of each spouse against adverse testimony are terminated when the marriage ends by death or divorce.[1] The privilege for confidential communications of the spouses, however, was based, in the mind of its chief sponsor, Greenleaf, upon the policy of encouraging confidences, who thought that encouragement required not merely temporary but permanent secrecy. The courts in this country have accepted this need for permanent protection—though it may be an unrealistic assumption—and about one-half of the statutes codifying the privilege explicitly provide that it continues after death or divorce. In fact, this characteristic accounts for a large proportion of the attempted invocations of the communications privilege, since if the marriage has not been terminated one of the other, more embrasive marital privileges will frequently apply. But it is probably in these cases where the marital tie has been severed that the supposed policy of the privilege has the most remote and tenuous relevance, and the possibilities of injustice in its application are most apparent. Wigmore points out that in this area, "there must arise occasional instances of hardship where ample flexibility should be allowed in the relaxation of the rule."

In the famous English case of Shenton v. Tyler, the court was faced with one of those instances of hardship. The plaintiff sued a widow and alleged that her deceased husband had made an oral secret trust, known to the widow, for the benefit of plaintiff, and sought to interrogate the widow. The widow relied on section 3 of the Evidence Amendment Act, 1853, as follows: " * * * no wife shall be compellable to disclose any communication made to her during the marriage." The court rejected the Greenleaf theory of a common law

2. See § 91 infra.

1. See § 66, supra.

privilege for communications surviving the end of the marriage, and was "unable to find any warrant for extending the words of the section by construction so as to include widowers and widows and divorced persons." However debatable may be the court's position that there was no common law privilege for marital communications,[2] it seems clear that the actual holding that the privilege for communications ends when the marriage ends is preferable in policy to the contrary result reached under American statutes and decisions.

§ 86. Policy and Future of the Privilege

The argument traditionally advanced in support of the marital communications privilege is that the privilege is needed to encourage marital confidences, which confidences in turn promote harmony between husband and wife. This argument, now reiterated for almost a century and a half, obviously rests upon certain assumptions concerning the knowledge and psychology of married persons. Thus it must be assumed that spouses will know of the privilege and take its protection into account in determining to make marital confidences, or at least, which is not the same thing, that they would come to know of the absence of the privilege if it were withdrawn and be, as a result, less confiding than at present.

In the absence of any empirical validation, these propositions have appeared highly suspect to many, though not all, commentators. Thus the most convincing answer to the argument of policy appears to be that the contingency of courtroom disclosure would almost never (even if the privilege did not exist) be in the minds of the parties in considering how far they should go in their secret conversations. What encourages them to fullest frankness is not the assurance of courtroom privilege, but the trust they place in the loyalty and discretion of each other. If the secrets are not told outside the courtroom there will be little danger of their being elicited in court. In the lives

of most people appearance in court as a party or a witness is an exceedingly rare and unusual event, and the anticipation of it is not one of those factors which materially influence in daily life the degree of fullness of marital disclosures. Accordingly, we must conclude that, while the danger of injustice from suppression of relevant proof is clear and certain, the probable benefits of the rule of privilege in encouraging marital confidences and wedded harmony is at best doubtful and marginal.

Probably the policy of encouraging confidences is not the prime influence in creating and maintaining the privilege. It is really a much more natural and less devious matter. It is a matter of emotion and sentiment. All of us have a feeling of indelicacy and want of decorum in prying into the secrets of husband and wife.

As pointed out in an earlier section,[1] this "privacy" rationale, particularly in the case of marital privilege, has been widely advanced in recent years. It may be hoped that increasing recognition of the true operative basis for affording privilege to the marital partners will in turn draw with it acceptance of the logical implications of that rationale, and that the privilege can accordingly be reshaped into a less anomalous form.

A desirable first step is to recognize that delicacy and decorum, while worthy and deserving of protection, will not stand in the balance where there is a need for otherwise unobtainable evidence critical to the ascertainment of significant legal rights. This disproportion, together with the consideration that maintenance of privacy as a general objective is not critically impaired by its sacrifice in cases of particular need, argues for treating this privilege as a qualified one.[2] This view, in turn, would remove much of the felt need to hedge the privilege narrowly about with not completely logical exceptions and qualifications, perhaps largely out of the fear that a more liberal ambit of the privilege will inexor-

2. See § 78, supra.

§ 86

1. See § 72, supra.

2. See § 78, supra, concerning the expanded use of qualified or conditional privilege.

ably lead to loss of critical evidence in future cases.

Again, a particularly anomalous characteristic of the present privilege, if protection of marital privacy be accepted as its justification, is its extension to testimony sought after the termination of the marriage by death or divorce. This extension, which accounts for the majority of seriously deleterious consequences of the privilege, arguably serves, at most, the quite inferior privacy interest in the confidences of past marriages. The practical consequences of eliminating this feature would differ little from those occasioned by placing the privilege, as is sometimes done today,[3] in the hands of the testifying spouse or former spouse. However, the expedient suggested here is thought more compatible with the evolving theory of the privilege.

Finally, though the time is yet far removed, it may someday be recognized that a communications privilege, however appropriate to professional relationships, is highly unsuited to the marital context, being at some points too broad and at others too narrow appropriately to protect the essential private aspects of marriage.

---

3. See § 83, supra at note 4. See also Note, 86 Dick. L.Rev. 491 (1982) (advocating this modification).

Chapter 10

THE CLIENT'S PRIVILEGE: COMMUNICATIONS BETWEEN CLIENT & LAWYER

Table of Sections

---

§ 87. Background and Policy of the Privilege: (a) Theoretical Considerations

The notion that the loyalty owed by the lawyer to his client disables him from being a witness in his client's case is deep-rooted in Roman law. This Roman tradition may or may not have been influential in shaping the early English doctrine of which we find the first traces in Elizabeth's time, that the oath and honor of the barrister and the attorney protect them from being required to disclose, upon examination in court, the secrets of the client. But by the eighteenth century in England the emphasis upon the code of honor had lessened and the need of the ascertainment of truth for the ends of justice loomed larger than the pledge of secrecy. So a new justification for the lawyer's exemption from disclosing his client's secrets was found. This theory, which continues as the principal rationale of the privilege today, rests upon three propositions. First, the law is complex and in order for members of the society to comply with it in the management of their affairs and the settlement of their disputes they require the assistance of expert lawyers. Second, lawyers are unable to discharge this function without the fullest possible knowledge of the facts of the client's situation. And last, the client cannot be expected to place the lawyer in full possession of the facts without the assurance that the lawyer cannot be compelled, over the client's objection, to reveal the confidences in court. The consequent loss to justice of the power to bring

134

all pertinent facts before the court is, according to the theory, outweighed by the benefits to justice (not to the individual client) of a franker disclosure in the lawyer's office.

This clearly utilitarian justification, premised on the power of the privilege to elicit certain behavior on the part of clients, has a compelling common-sense appeal. The tendency of the client in giving his story to his counsel to omit all that he suspects will work against him is a matter of every day professional observation. It makes it necessary for the prudent lawyer to cross-examine his client searchingly about possible unfavorable facts. In criminal cases the difficulty of obtaining full disclosure from the accused is well known, and would certainly become an absolute impossibility if the defendant knew that the lawyer could be compelled to repeat what he had been told.

These justifications, however, have never been convincing to all. Jeremy Bentham, perhaps the most famous of the privilege's critics to date, argued that the privilege is not needed by the innocent party with a righteous cause or defense, and that the guilty should not be given its aid in concerting a false one. Bentham's apocalyptic division of the client world into righteous and guilty seems somewhat naive in a time when even the best-intended may doubt their compliance with an ever more overwhelming body of law. Nevertheless, none can deny the privilege's unfortunate tendency to suppress the truth, and it has commonly been urged that it is only the greater benefit of increased candor which justifies the continuation of the privilege. Wigmore, the great champion and architect of the privilege, subscribed to this view, though he acknowledged that "Its benefits are all indirect and speculative; its obstruction is plain and concrete."[1]

The trend of recent years toward attempted empirical verification of the intuitive judgments of the past has lent a special cogency to Wigmore's assessment. For the degree of efficacy of the privilege in achieving its avowed aims, speculated to be quite low by critics, is ironically likely to prove undemonstrable by reason of the privilege itself. Despite these difficulties, it is of course possible to proceed from the Cartesian postulate that the privilege effects some unknown and unknowable marginal alteration in client behavior. But such minimal claims, even when combined with efforts to structure the privilege so as to confine its operation to contexts in which it will most probably have an effect, seem to fall short of an adequate justification.

As a possible ancillary justification, it is today suggested with increasing frequency that considerations of privacy should play a role in supporting and ultimately defining the privilege. To date, this rationale has achieved only very little recognition in the courts as a supporting, much less a sufficient, justification for the attorney-client privilege. It is probable that the ultimate fate of this theory will depend upon the success of its advocates in suggesting what implications for the parameters for the privilege are implied by such a rationale.

At the present time it seems most realistic to portray the attorney-client privilege as supported in part by its traditional utilitarian justification, and in part by the integral role it is perceived to play in the adversary system itself. Our system of litigation casts the lawyer in the role of fighter for the party whom he represents. A strong tradition of loyalty attaches to the relationship of attorney and client, and this tradition would be outraged by routine examination of the lawyer as to the client's confidential disclosures regarding professional business. To the extent that the evidentiary privilege, then, is integrally related to an entire code of professional conduct, it is futile to envision drastic curtailment of the privilege without substantial modification of the underlying ethical system to which the privilege is merely ancillary.

The foregoing state of affairs is clearly less than optimum from the standpoint that predictability in the application of the privilege, logically indispensable for any utilitarian effect, is largely lacking in many areas. Advo-

§ 87
1. 8 Wigmore, Evidence § 2291, p. 554 (McNaughton rev. 1961).

cates of the supposedly inviolate privilege of yesteryear perceive even greater uncertainties interjected by the increasing uses of in camera inspection to determine the legitimacy of claims of privilege, and even in some jurisdictions the use of a balancing test to determine whether the privilege will be honored. While a balancing approach to the privilege is not totally consistent with the privilege's current rationales, it is suggested that increased use of these expedients will ultimately result in a fairer, surer, and more rational administration of the privilege than could be achieved through the traditional methodology of controlling its scope through the liberal extension of exceptions and application of waiver doctrine.

§ 87.1 Background and Policy of the Privilege: (b) Modern Applications

The application of the privilege for the benefit of a corporate client, as distinguished from a natural person, was never questioned until a federal district court in 1962 held that a corporation is not entitled to claim the privilege.[1] The decision attracted wide attention and much comment, most of which was adverse, until reversed on appeal.[2] There seems to be little reason to believe that the issue will arise soon again.

The scope of the privilege in the corporate context, however, has presented an exceptionally troublesome question which is even yet not fully resolved. The difficulty is basically one of extrapolating the essential operating conditions of the privilege from the paradigm case of the traditional individual client who both supplies information to, and receives counsel from, the attorney. Are both of these aspects of the relationship to be protected in the corporate setting, in which the corporate agents in a position to furnish the pertinent facts are not necessarily those empowered to take action responsive to legal advice based upon those facts? Early decisions focused upon the first half of this dichotomy, and extended

the privilege expansively to communications from any "officer or employee" of the client corporation. This emphasis was dramatically reversed by the case of City of Philadelphia v. Westinghouse Electric Corp.,[3] which propounded a "control group" test under which the privilege was restricted to communications made by those corporate functionaries "in a position to control or even to take a substantial part in a decision about any action which the corporation may take upon the advice of the attorney."

The "control group" theory was widely, though not universally, followed by the courts until the 1981 decision of the Supreme Court in Upjohn Co. v. United States.[4] While the Court specifically declined in Upjohn to attempt the formulation of a definitive rule, it did specifically reject the control group principle as one which "cannot * * * govern the development of the law in this area." The principal deficiency which the Court noted as inherent in the control group test is its failure to recognize the function of the privilege as protecting the flow of information to the advising attorney. The opinion does suggest limitations however, in that such information will be privileged only if: (1) it is communicated for the express purpose of securing legal advice for the corporation; (2) it relates to the specific corporate duties of the communicating employee; and (3) it is treated as confidential within the corporation itself.

The Upjohn decision evoked a large amount of commentary, much of which has been critical. In addition to the decision's failure to articulate the scope of the privilege of corporations more clearly, another frequent criticism has been Upjohn's reliance upon a utilitarian rationale without at the same time limiting the privilege to instances where it is likely to be effective for its stated purpose. Thus a lower level corporate employee sufficiently sophisticated to factor an evidentiary

---

§ 87.1

1. Radiant Burners, Inc. v. American Gas Association, 207 F.Supp. 771 (N.D.Ill.1962).

2. Radiant Burners, Inc. v. American Gas Association, 320 F.2d 314, 98 A.L.R.2d 228, and note, (7th Cir.1963).

3. 210 F.Supp. 483, 485 (E.D.Pa.1962), mandamus and prohibition denied sub nom. General Electric Co. v. Kirkpatrick, 312 F.2d 742 (3d Cir.1962).

4. 449 U.S. 383 (1981).

privilege into his decision to communicate with a corporate attorney is unlikely to be reassured by a privilege which is waivable in the exclusive discretion of the corporation. At a minimum, the privilege should apply only to corporate employees who either have, or are expressly conferred, the power to assert the privilege.

Though the *Upjohn* decision is not rested upon constitutional grounds, and is thus not binding upon the states, it has had considerable influence outside the federal system. At the same time, some states continue to subscribe to the control group test, thus adding the identity of the forum in which the privilege will ultimately be asserted to other sources of uncertainty as to its scope.

An *Upjohn* extension of the corporate attorney-client privilege almost necessitates extension of the privilege in other organizational structures. While under the control group test the scope of the corporate privilege might be roughly likened to that available to a proprietorship, extension to lower level employees without a corresponding extension to employees of various other entities is probably politically as well as theoretically indefensible.

Where the entity in question is governmental, however, significantly different considerations appear, which have led a number of states substantially to limit the privilege for such entities. On the federal level, cases arising from the investigation of President Clinton have held that any privilege applicable to communications between government attorneys and government officials will not apply to prevent disclosure in the face of a grand jury subpoena.

As noted above, there are situations which draw into question the application of the conventional rule that a corporation's privilege may be asserted or waived by the management of the corporation. One such situation is the derivative stockholder's action, in which both parties claim to be acting in the corporate interest. In the leading case of Garner v. Wolfinbarger,[5] the court addressed the problem thus raised by recognizing a qualified privilege

on the part of the corporate management, but one which may be pierced by a showing of good cause by the shareholders. Subsequent decisions, however, have found the "mutuality of interest" between management and shareholders relied upon in *Garner* to be lacking in a variety of similar situations.

§ 88. The Professional Relationship

The privilege for communications of a client with his lawyer hinges upon the client's belief that he is consulting a lawyer in that capacity and his manifested intention to seek professional legal advice. It is sufficient if he reasonably believes that the person consulted is a lawyer, though in fact he is not. Communications in the course of preliminary discussion with a view to employing the lawyer are privileged though the employment is in the upshot not accepted. The burden of proof rests on the person asserting the privilege to show that the consultation was a professional one. Payment or agreement to pay a fee, however, is not essential. But where one consults an attorney not as a lawyer but as a friend or as a business adviser or banker, or negotiator, or as an accountant, or where the communication is to the attorney acting as a "mere scrivener" or as an attesting witness to a will or deed, or as an executor or as agent, the consultation is not professional nor the statement privileged. There is some conflict in the decisions as to whether the privilege is available for communications to an administrative practitioner who is not a lawyer. However, the privilege will generally be applicable even where the services performed by a lawyer are not necessarily available only from members of the legal profession.

Ordinarily an attorney can lawfully hold himself out as qualified to practice only in the state in which he is licensed, and consultation elsewhere on a continuing basis would traditionally not be privileged, but exceptionally by custom he might lawfully be consulted elsewhere in respect to isolated transactions, and Revised Uniform Evidence Rule (1986 amendment) 502(a)(3) requires only that he be au-

---

5. 430 F.2d 1093 (5th Cir.1970).

thorized or reasonably be believed to be authorized "in any state or nation."

Traditionally, the relationship sought to
be fostered by the privilege has been that
between the lawyer and a private client, but
more recently the privilege has been held to
extend to communications to an attorney representing the state. However, disclosures to
the public prosecuting attorney by an informer
are not within the attorney-client privilege,
but an analogous policy of protecting the giving of such information has led to the recognition of a privilege against the disclosure of the
identity of the informer, unless the trial judge
finds that such disclosure is necessary in the
interests of justice. Communications to an attorney appointed by the court to serve the
interest of a party are of course within the
privilege. A communication by a lawyer to a
member of the Board of Governors of the state
bar association, revealing a fraudulent conspiracy in which he had been engaged and expressing his desire to resign from the practice of
law was held not privileged.

Wigmore argued for a privilege analogous
to the lawyer-client privilege for "confessions
or similar confidences" made privately by persons implicated in a wrong or crime to the
judge of a court. As to judges generally there
seems little justification for such a privilege if
the policy-motive is the furtherance of the
administration of justice by encouraging a full
disclosure. Unlike the lawyer the judge needs
no private disclosures in advance of trial to
enable him to perform his functions. In fact
such revelations would ordinarily embarrass
rather than aid him in carrying out his duties
as a trial judge. The famous case of Lindsey v.
People,[1] however, raised the question whether
the judge of a juvenile court does not stand in
a special position with regard to confidential
disclosures by children who come before him.
The majority of the court held that when a boy
under promise of secrecy confessed to the
judge that he had fired the shot that killed his
father the judge was compellable, on the trial
of the boy's mother for murder, to divulge the

confession. The court pointed out that a parent who had received such a confidence would
be compellable to disclose. In the case of this
particular court the need for encouraging confidences is clear, but in most cases the most
effective encouragement will come from the
confidence-inspiring personality of the judge,
even without the aid of assurances of secrecy.
The court's conclusion that the need for secrecy for this type of disclosure does not outweigh
the sacrifice to the administration of justice
from the suppression of the evidence seems
justifiable.

§ 89. Subject–Matter of the Privi-lege: (a) Communications

The modern justification of the privilege,
namely, that of encouraging full disclosure by
the client for the furtherance of the administration of justice,[1] might suggest that the privilege is only a one-way one, operating to protect communications of the client or his agents
to the lawyer or his clerk but not vice versa.
However, it is generally held that the privilege
will protect at least those attorney to client
communications which would have a tendency
to reveal the confidences of the client. In fact,
only rarely will the attorney's words be relevant for any purpose other than to show the
client's communications circumstantially, or to
establish an admission by the client by his
failure to object. Accordingly, the simpler and
preferable rule, adopted by a number of statutes and the Revised Uniform Evidence Rules
(1974) and by the better reasoned cases, extends the protection of the privilege also to
communications by the lawyer to the client.

An even more embrasive view, adopted by
statute in a few states, would protect against
disclosure by the attorney of any knowledge he
has gained while acting as such, even information obtained from sources other than the
client. Such an extension finds no justification
in the modern utilitarian theory of the privilege. In any event, the more widely prevailing
rule does not bar divulgence by the attorney of
information communicated to him or his

---

§ 88

1. 181 P. 531 (Colo.1919) (three judges dissenting).

§ 89

1. See § 87 supra.

agents by third persons. Nor does information so obtained become privileged by being in turn related by the attorney to the client in the form of advice.

The commonly imposed limitation of protection to communications passing between client and attorney, while logically derived from the policy rationale of the privilege, does raise certain problems of construction where the information acquired by the attorney does not come in the conventional form of oral or written assertions by the client. Initially it is fairly easy to conclude, as most authority holds, that observations by the lawyer which might be made by anyone, and which involve no communicative intent by the client, are not protected. Conversely, testimony relating intentionally communicative acts of the client, as where he rolls up his sleeve to reveal a hidden scar or opens the drawer of his desk to display a revolver, would as clearly be precluded as would the recounting of statements conveying the same information. Much more problematic are cases in which the client delivers tangible evidence such as stolen property to the attorney, or confides facts enabling the attorney to come into the possession of such evidence. Here the decisions are somewhat conflicting, reflecting the virtual impossibility of separating the act of confidence which may legitimately be within the privilege from the preexisting evidentiary fact which may not. To resolve the dilemma, one carefully reasoned argument is that the privilege should not operate to bar the attorney's disclosure of the circumstances of acquisition, since to preclude the attorney's testimony would offer the client a uniquely safe opportunity to divest himself of incriminating evidence without leaving an evidentiary trail.

Difficulties also arise in applying the communications-only theory when one assisting the lawyer, e.g., an examining physician, learns and communicates to the lawyer matters not known to the client. The privilege seems to apply with respect to the communication itself. If the physician is considered as aligned with the client, his knowledge would be that of the client and not privileged; but if

aligned with the lawyer, the privilege seems to apply, as held in the leading case.

The application of the privilege to writings presents practical problems requiring discriminating analysis. A professional communication in writing, as a letter from client to lawyer for example, will of course be privileged. These written privileged communications are readily to be distinguished from preexisting documents or writings, such as deeds, wills, and warehouse receipts, not in themselves constituting communications between client and lawyer. As to these preexisting documents two notions come into play. First, the client may make communications about the document by words or by acts, such as sending the document to the lawyer for perusal or handing it to him and calling attention to its terms. These communications, and the knowledge of the terms and appearance of the documents which the lawyer gains thereby are privileged from disclosure by testimony in court. Second, on a different footing entirely, stands the question, shall a lawyer who has been entrusted with the possession of a document by his client be subject to an order of court requiring him to produce the document at the trial or in pretrial discovery proceedings whether for inspection or for use in evidence? The policy of encouraging full disclosure does of course apply to encouraging the client to apprise his lawyer of the terms of all relevant documents, and the disclosure itself and the lawyer's knowledge gained thereby as we have seen are privileged. It is true also that placing the documents in the lawyer's hands is the most convenient means of disclosure. But the next step, that of adding to the privilege for communications a privilege against production of the preexisting documents themselves, when they would be subject to production if still in the possession of the client, would be an intolerable obstruction to justice. To prevent the court's gaining access to a relevant document a party would only have to send it to his lawyer. So here this principle is controlling: if a document would be subject to an order for production if it were in the hands of the client it will be equally subject to such an order if it is in the hands of his attorney. An opposite conclusion would serve the policy of encouraging the client to make full disclosure to his lawyer right enough, but reasonable encouragement is given by the privilege for communications *about* documents, and the price of an additional privilege would be intolerably high. There are other doctrines which may impel a court to recognize a privilege against production of a preexisting document,[2] but not the doctrine of privilege for lawyer-client communications.

§ 90. Subject–Matter of the Privilege: (b) Fact of Employment and Identity of the Client

When a client consults an attorney for a legitimate purpose, he will seldom, but may occasionally, desire to keep secret the very fact of consultation or employment of the lawyer. Nevertheless, consultation and employment are something more than a mere private or personal engagement. They are the calling into play of the services of an officer licensed by the state to act in certain ways in furtherance of the administration of justice, and vested with powers of giving advice on the law, of drafting documents, and of filing pleadings and motions and appearing in court for his client, which are limited to this class of officers.

Does the privilege for confidential communications extend to the fact of consulting or employing such an officer, when intended to be confidential? The traditional and still generally applicable rule denies the privilege for the fact of consultation or employment, including the component facts of the identity of the client, such identifying facts about him as his address and occupation, the identity of the lawyer, and the payment and amount of fees. Similarly, factual communications by the lawyer to the client concerning logistical matters such as trial dates are not privileged.

Several reasons have been advanced as a basis for denying protection to the client's

identity, most notably that "the mere fact of the engagement of counsel is out of the rule [of privilege] because the privilege and duty of silence do not arise until the fact is ascertained."[1] Additionally, it is said that a party to legal proceedings is entitled to know the identity of the adversary who is putting in motion or staying the machinery of the court. Such propositions, however, shed little light on the real issue, i.e., whether client anonymity is in some cases essential to obtaining the proper objectives of the privilege.

The inadequacy of a purely simplistic rule excluding client identity from the coverage of the privilege was revealed by the facts of the leading case of Baird v. Koerner,[2] in which the court upheld a claim of privilege by an attorney who had mailed a check for back taxes to the IRS on behalf of an anonymous client. Any other result on the facts of *Baird* would seem inconceivable, and the decision has served a wholesome purpose by introducing an element of flexibility into the general rule. However, a number of decisions following *Baird* arguably vastly extended the exceptions to the rule. Thus it was variously stated that exception is made "when the disclosure of the client's identity by his attorney would have supplied the last link in a existing chain of incriminating evidence * * *,"[3] or "where * * * a strong probability exists that disclosure of such information would implicate the client in the very criminal activity for which legal advice was sought."[4] Such decisions may have blazed a false trail in making the exceptions to the rule turn too largely upon the question of the severity of potential harm to the client rather than upon considerations germane to the privilege.

Today there is a marked trend toward refocusing upon the essential purpose of the privilege by extending its protection to client identity and fee arrangements only if the net effect of the disclosure would be to reveal the

---

2. See § 96 infra.

§ 90

1. People ex rel Vogelstein v. Warden of County Jail, 270 N.Y.S. at 362, 369, affirmed without opinion 271 N.Y.S. 1059 (App. Div.)

2. 279 F.2d 623 (9th Cir.1960).

3. In re Grand Jury Proceedings (Pavlick), 680 F.2d 1026, 1027 (5th Cir.1982) (en banc).

4. United States v. Hodge and Zweig, 548 F.2d 1347, 1353 (9th Cir.1977).

nature of a client communication. Protection should certainly be denied where agencies performed by attorneys are no necessary part of the attorney's unique role nor appropriate for immunization from public disclosure and scrutiny. Arguably, general application of a rule of disclosure seems the approach most consonant with the preservation of the repute of the lawyer's high calling. At the same time, much should depend upon the client's objective in seeking preservation of anonymity, and cases will arise in which protection of the client's identity is both proper and in the public interest.

§ 91. The Confidential Character of the Communications: Presence of Third Persons and Agents: Joint Consultations and Employments: Controversies Between Client and Attorney

It is of the essence of the privilege that it is limited to those communications which the client either expressly made confidential or which he could reasonably assume under the circumstances would be understood by the attorney as so intended. This common law requirement seems to be read into those statutes which codify the privilege without mentioning the confidentiality requirement. A mere showing that the communication was from client to attorney does not suffice, but the circumstances indicating the intention of secrecy must appear. Wherever the matters communicated to the attorney are intended by the client to be made public or revealed to third persons, obviously the element of confidentiality is wanting. Similarly, if the same statements have been made by the client to third persons on other occasions this is persuasive that like communications to the lawyer were not intended as confidential.

Questions as to the effect of the presence of persons other than the client and the lawyer often arise. At the extremes answers would be clear. Presumably the presence of a casual disinterested third person within hearing to the client's knowledge would demonstrate that the communication was not intended to be confidential. On the other hand if the help of an interpreter is necessary to enable the client

to consult the lawyer his presence would not deprive the communication of its confidential and privileged character. Moreover, in cases where the client has one of his agents attend the conference, or the lawyer calls in his clerk or confidential secretary, the presence of these intermediaries will be assumed not to militate against the confidential nature of the consultation, and presumably this would not be made to depend upon whether the presence of the agent, clerk or secretary was in the particular instance reasonably necessary to the matter in hand. It is the way business is generally done and that is enough. As to relatives and friends of the client, the results of the cases are not consistent, but it seems that here not only might it be asked whether the client reasonably understood the conference to be confidential but also whether the presence of the relative or friend was reasonably necessary for the protection of the client's interests in the particular circumstances.

When two or more persons, each having an interest in some problem, or situation, jointly consult an attorney, their confidential communications with the attorney, though known to each other, will of course be privileged in a controversy of either or both of the clients with the outside world, that is, with parties claiming adversely to both or either of those within the original charmed circle. But it will often happen that the two original clients will fall out between themselves and become engaged in a controversy in which the communications at their joint consultation with the lawyer may be vitally material. In such a controversy it is clear that the privilege is inapplicable. In the first place the policy of encouraging disclosure by holding out the promise of protection seems inapposite, since as between themselves neither would know whether he would be more helped or handicapped, if in any dispute between them, both could invoke the shield of secrecy. And secondly, it is said that they had obviously no intention of keeping these secrets from each other, and hence as between themselves it was not intended to be confidential. In any event, it is a qualification of frequent application and of even wider potentiality, not always recognized. Thus, in the situation mentioned in the previous paragraph where a client calls into the conference with the attorney one of the client's agents, and matters are discussed which bear on the agent's rights against the client, it would seem that in a subsequent controversy between client and agent, the limitation on the privilege accepted in the joint consultation cases should furnish a controlling analogy.

One step beyond the joint consultation where communications by two clients are made directly in each other's hearing is the situation where two parties separately interested in some contract or undertaking, as in the case of borrower and lender or insurer and insured, engage the same attorney to represent their respective interests, and each communicates separately with the attorney about some phase of the common transaction. Here again it seems that the communicating client, knowing that the attorney represents the other party also, would not ordinarily intend that the facts communicated should be kept secret from him. Whether the doctrine of limited confidentiality should be applied to communications by an insured to an agent of the insurer bound by contract to provide the defense for both has provoked differing judicial reactions. Where the statement is made directly to the attorney hired by the insurer, there is no question that the privilege applies in an action brought by a third person, nor does it seem disputed that there is no privilege where the controversy is between the insured, or someone claiming under him, and the company itself over the company's liability under the policy.

The weight of authority seems to support the view that when client and attorney become embroiled in a controversy between themselves, as in an action by the attorney for compensation or by the client for damages for the attorney's negligence, the seal is removed from the attorney's lips. Though sometimes rested upon other grounds it seems that here again the notion that as between the participants in the conference the intention was to

disclose and not to withhold the matters communicated offers a plausible reason. As to what is a controversy between lawyer and client the decisions do not limit their holdings to litigations between them, but have said that whenever the client, even in litigation between third persons, makes an imputation against the good faith of his attorney in respect to his professional services, the curtain of privilege drops so far as necessary to enable the lawyer to defend his conduct. <u>Perhaps the whole doctrine, that in controversies between attorney and client the privilege is relaxed, may best be based upon the ground of practical necessity that if effective legal service is to be encouraged the privilege must not stand in the way of the lawyer's just enforcement of his rights to be paid a fee and to protect his reputation.</u> The only question about such a principle is whether in all cases the privilege ought not to be subject to the same qualification, that it should yield when the evidence sought is necessary to the attainment of justice.

§ 92. The Client as the Holder of the Privilege: Who May Assert, and Who Complain on Appeal of Its Denial?

A rule regulating the *competency* of evidence or of witnesses—a so-called "exclusionary" rule—is normally founded on the policy of safeguarding the fact-finding process against error, and it is assertable by the party against whom the evidence is offered. The earmarks of a *privilege,* as we have seen, are first, that it is not designed to protect the fact-finding process but is intended to protect some "outside" interest, other than the ascertainment of truth at the trial, and second, that it cannot be asserted by the adverse party as such, but only by the person whose interest the particular rule of privilege is intended to safeguard.[1] While once it was conceived that the privilege was set up to protect the lawyer's honor, we know that today it is agreed that the basic policy of the rule is that of encouraging clients to lay the facts fully before their counsel. They will be encouraged by a privilege

---

1. See the discussion in § 72, supra of the distinction between competency and privilege. Of course, a party may be the holder of a privilege.

which they themselves have the power to invoke. To extend any benefit or advantage to someone as attorney, or as party to a suit, or to people generally, will be to suppress relevant evidence without promoting the purpose of the privilege.

Accordingly it is now generally agreed that the privilege is the client's and his alone, and Revised Uniform Rule (1974) 502(b) vests the privilege in the client. It is thought that this would be recognized even in those states which, before modern notions of privilege and policy were adequately worked out, codified the rule in terms of inadmissibility of evidence of communications, or of incompetency of the attorney to testify thereto. These statutes are generally held not to be intended to modify the common law doctrines.

It is not surprising that the courts, often faced with statutes drafted in terms of obsolete theories, and reaching these points rarely and usually incidentally, have not worked out a consistent pattern of consequences of this accepted view that the rule is one of privilege and that the privilege is the client's. It is believed that the applications suggested below are well grounded in reason and are supported by some authority, whether of text or decision.

First, it is clear that the client may assert the privilege even though he is not a party to the cause wherein the privileged testimony is sought to be elicited. Second, if he is present at the hearing whether as party, witness, or bystander he must assert the privilege personally or by attorney, or it will be waived. Third, in some jurisdictions, if he is not present at the taking of testimony, nor a party to the proceedings, the privilege may be called to the court's attention by anyone present, such as the attorney for the absent client, or a party in the case, or the court of its own motion may protect the privilege. Fourth: While if an asserted privilege is erroneously sustained, the aggrieved party may of course complain on appeal of the exclusion of the testimony, the erroneous denial of the privilege can only be complained of by the client whose privilege has been infringed. This opens the door to appellate review by the client if he is also a party and suffers adverse judgment. If he is not a party, the losing party in the cause, by the better view is without recourse. Relevant, competent testimony has come in, and the privilege was not created for his benefit. But the witness, whether he is the client or his attorney, may refuse to answer and suffer an adjudication of contempt and may, in some jurisdictions at least, secure review on habeas corpus if the privilege was erroneously denied. This remedy, however, is calculated to interrupt and often disrupt progress of the cause on trial. Does a lawyer on the witness stand who is asked to make disclosures which he thinks may constitute an infringement of his client's privilege, owe a duty to refuse to answer and if necessary to test the judge's ruling on habeas corpus or appeal from a judgment of contempt? It seems clear that, unless in a case of flagrant disregard of the law by the judge, the lawyer's duty is merely to present his view that the testimony is privileged, and if the judge rules otherwise, to submit to his decision.

§ 93. Waiver

Since as we have seen, it is the client who is the holder of the privilege, the power to waive it is his, and he alone, or his attorney or agent acting with his authority, or his representative, may exercise this power. In the case of the corporation, the power to claim or waive the privilege generally rests with corporate management, i.e., ultimately with the board of directors.

Waiver may be found, as Wigmore points out, not merely from words or conduct expressing an intention to relinquish a known right, but also from conduct such as partial disclosure which would make it unfair for the client to invoke the privilege thereafter.[1] Finding waiver in situations in which forfeiture of the privilege was not subjectively intended by the holder is consistent with the view, expressed by some cases and authorities, that

§ 93

1. 8 Wigmore, Evidence § 2327 (McNaughton rev. 1961).

the essential function of the privilege is to protect a confidence which, once revealed by any means, leaves the privilege with no legitimate function to perform. Logic notwithstanding, it would appear poor policy to allow the privilege to be overthrown by theft or fraud, and in fact most authority requires that to effect a waiver a disclosure must at least be voluntary.

Given the scope of modern discovery and the realities of contemporary litigation, a question of great practical importance today is whether a voluntary but inadvertent disclosure should result in waiver. In earlier times, the burden of avoiding such a disclosure of privileged matter, and the consequent waiver of the privilege, was relatively slight compared to that encountered today where enormous quantities of documents may be sought by an opponent through discovery. Under current conditions, some privileged material is likely to pass through even the most tightly woven screen. Since the consequences of such an oversight are potentially staggering, the question is raised as to whether traditional waiver doctrine ought to be modified. Not surprisingly, the decisions in the area have been somewhat divergent. However, while some courts apparently still adhere to a rather strict approach to waiver, others have considered factors such as the excusability of the error, whether prompt attempt to remedy the error was made, and whether preservation of the privilege will occasion unfairness to the opponent. The costs of attempting to avoid waiver under a strict rule would argue strongly for modification along these lines, and it is believed that the decisions are tending in this direction.

Turning then to the specific contexts in which waiver may be argued to occur, it will be recalled that as noted in an earlier section the commencement of a malpractice action against the attorney by the client will constitute a waiver of the privilege by the latter.[2] There are, in addition, a variety of other types of actions in which the advice of an attorney will sometimes be relied upon in support of a

claim or defense. It has accordingly become established that if a party interjects the "advice of counsel" as an essential element of a claim or defense, then that party waives the privilege as to all advice received concerning the same subject matter. While there can be no doubt of the desirability of a rule preventing a party from relying upon the advice of counsel as the basis of a claim or defense while at the same time frustrating a full exploration of the character of that advice, the problem of defining when such an issue has been interjected is an extremely difficult one. The cases are generally agreed that filing or defending a lawsuit does not waive the privilege. By contrast, specific reliance upon the advice either in pleading or testimony will generally be seen as waiving the privilege. Some decisions have gone much further, and have extended the doctrine broadly to cases in which a mental state asserted by the client is sought to be shown inconsistent with the advice of counsel. Such extensions seem dubious lacking full acceptance of the Benthamite principle that the privilege ought to be overthrown to facilitate the search for truth.

By the prevailing view, which seems correct, the mere voluntary taking the stand by the client as a witness in a suit to which he is party and testifying to facts which were the subject of consultation with his counsel is no waiver of the privilege for secrecy of the communications to his lawyer. It is the communication which is privileged, not the facts. If on direct examination, however, he testifies to the privileged communications, in part, this is a waiver as to the remainder of the privileged consultation or consultations about the same subject.

What if the client is asked on cross-examination about the communications with his lawyer, and he responds without asserting his claim of privilege? Is this a waiver? Unless there are some circumstances which show that the client was surprised or misled, it seems that the usual rule that the client's failure to claim the privilege when to his knowledge testimony infringing it is offered, would apply

2.   Section 91, supra.

here, and that the decisions treating such testimony on cross-examination as being involuntary and not constituting a waiver are hardly supportable.

How far does the client waive by calling the attorney as a witness? If the client elicits testimony from the lawyer-witness as to privileged communications this obviously would waive as to all consultations relating to the same subject, just as the client's own testimony would. It would seem also that by calling the lawyer as a witness he opens the door for the adversary to impeach him by showing his interest. And it seems reasonable to contend as Wigmore does that if the client uses the lawyer to prove matter which he would only have learned in the course of his employment this again should be considered a waiver as to related privileged communications. But merely to call the lawyer to testify to facts known by him apart from his employment should not be deemed a waiver of the privilege. That would attach too harsh a condition on the exercise of the privilege. Unless the lawyer-witness is acting as counsel in the case on trial, there is no violation of the Model Rules of Professional Conduct, and if he is, it recognizes that his testifying may be essential to the ends of justice. Moreover, these are matters usually governed not by the client but by the lawyer, to whom the ethical mandate is addressed.

In an earlier section[3] discussing a witness' use of a writing to refresh his recollection for purposes of testifying, it was pointed out that, under both common law and Federal Evidence Rule 612, if a witness consulted a writing to refresh his recollection while testifying, opposing counsel is entitled to inspect it, to cross-examine the witness upon it, and to introduce in evidence portions that relate to the testimony of the witness. It was further pointed out that if the document were privileged, e.g. an attorney-client communication, such act of consultation would effect a waiver of the privilege.[4] And finally, the problem area was said to be when the privileged writing was consulted

by the witness prior to testifying. At common law, authority generally was against requiring disclosure of writings consulted prior to testifying, and under that view the problem of waiver of privilege does not arise. However, an increasing number of cases have allowed disclosure, and Federal Evidence Rule 612 gives the trial judge discretion to order disclosure. Should this discretionary power of the judge extend also to deciding whether a waiver of privilege has occurred? Or should it be said that on the one hand waiver never occurs, or on the other that it always occurs? The Report of the House Committee on the Judiciary took a strict no-waiver position,[5] but no language to that effect was incorporated in Rule 612. Nor was there included any specific provision that privilege should always be waived. The discretionary provision was inserted almost as a matter of necessity to limit disclosure of the potentially vast volume and variety of documents that might be consulted before testifying to those truly bearing on the testimony of the witness, and similar considerations are pertinent to the waiver question. While the cases are mixed, the preferred view seems to be that the judge's discretion extends not only to the threshold question whether connection with the testimony is sufficient to warrant disclosure but also to the question whether its importance is sufficient to override the privilege, given all the circumstances.

When at an earlier trial or stage of the case the privilege has been waived and testimony as to the privileged communications elicited without objection, the prevailing view is that this is a waiver also for any subsequent hearing of the same case.

This result has traditionally been justified on the ground that once the confidence protected by the privilege is breached the privilege has no valid continuing office to perform. It should be noted, however, that the same result may here be supported by the distinguishable consideration that to allow a subse-

---

3. See § 9 supra.

4. See § 9 supra.

5. "The Committee intends that nothing in the Rule be construed as barring the assertion of a privilege with respect to writings used by a witness to refresh his memory." House Comm. on Judiciary, Fed.Rules of Evidence, H.R.Rep. No. 650, 93d Cong., 1st Sess., p. 13 (1973).

quent claim of the privilege would unfairly disadvantage the opponent who has reasonably assumed that the evidence would be available. The same reasons seem to apply where the waiver was publicly made upon the trial of one case, and the privilege later sought to be asserted on the hearing of another case.

Should the same rule of once published, permanently waived, apply to out-of-court disclosures made by the client or with his consent? Authority is scanty, but it seems that if the client makes or authorizes public disclosure, this should clearly be a waiver. Even where the privileged matter is privately revealed, or authorized to be revealed, to a third person, waiver has generally resulted and this conclusion may be supported by analogy to the cases which deny privilege when a third person is present at the consultation.[6] At the same time, it has been pointed out that considerations of fairness to the opponent rarely enter in where the disclosure is neither public nor made in the context of the litigation.

§ 94. The Effect of the Death of the Client

The accepted theory is that the protection afforded by the privilege will in general survive the death of the client. This settled view was fixed more firmly by the United States Supreme Court in Swidler & Berlin v. United States.[1] In Swidler, the Court held that the government, which sought information about an interview between the late Deputy White House Counsel Vincent W. Foster and his attorney shortly before Foster's suicide, had failed to make a showing sufficient to justify an overturning of the common law rule. The government had urged that the survival of the privilege be balanced against the government's need for the information in a criminal investigation. The Court rejected the concept of a privilege so qualified, emphasizing that the knowledge that communications will remain confidential even after death "encourages the

client to communicate fully and frankly with counsel."

In reaching its decision in Swidler, the Court acknowledged the existence of exceptions to the privilege both in instances where the communications are in furtherance of crime or fraud[2] and in cases involving the validity or interpretation of a will or other dispute between parties claiming by succession from the testator at his death. This testamentary exception has been reached by different routes. Sometimes the testator will be found to have waived the privilege in his lifetime, as by directing the attorney to act as an attesting witness. Wigmore argues, as to the will contests, that communications of the client with his lawyer as to the making of a will are intended to be confidential in his lifetime but that this is a "temporary confidentiality" not intended to require secrecy after his death[3] and this view finds approval in some decisions. Other courts say simply that where all the parties claim under the client the privilege does not apply. The distinction is taken that when the contest is between a "stranger" and the heirs or personal representatives of the deceased client, the heirs or representatives can claim privilege, and they can waive it. Even if the privilege were assumed to be applicable in will contests, it could perhaps be argued that since those claiming under the will and those claiming by intestate succession both equally claim under the client, each should have the power to waive.

This doctrine that the privilege is ineffective, on whatever ground, when both litigants claim under the deceased client has been applied to suits by the heirs or representatives to set aside a conveyance by the deceased for mental incapacity and to suits for the enforcement of a contract made by the deceased to make a will in favor of plaintiff. The cases encountered where the party is held to be a "stranger" and hence not entitled to invoke this doctrine are cases where the party asserts against the estate a claim of a promise by the

---

6. See § 91 supra.

1. 524 U.S. 399 (1998)..

2. See § 95, infra.

3. 8 Wigmore, Evidence § 2314 (McNaughton rev. 1961).

deceased to pay, or make provision in his will for payment, for services rendered.

None of this authority would seem to be eroded by the *Swidler* case. But certainly the survival of the privilege in the ordinary situation is now entrenched. The *Swidler* case is, of course, binding in the federal courts, and likely to be persuasive to the states, especially those that have held that way in the past. The principal question remaining is whether there will be other inroads on the privilege in special situations. For example, in *Swidler*, the dissent raised the specter of a deceased client's confession to a crime with which another is now charged.[4] In apparent response, the majority suggested that constitutional considerations might compel disclosure in such a situation.[5] It is difficult to imagine that the privilege would survive such a set of facts. Whether other scenarios might result in further exceptions to the privilege—for example, a more specific need for information by a criminal prosecutor than established in *Swidler*—remains to be seen.

§ 95. Consultation in Furtherance of Crime or Fraud

Since the policy of the privilege is that of promoting the administration of justice, it would be a perversion of the privilege to extend it to the client who seeks advice to aid him in carrying out an illegal or fraudulent scheme. Advice given for those purposes would not be a professional service but participation in a conspiracy. Accordingly, it is settled under modern authority that the privilege does not extend to communications between attorney and client where the client's purpose is the furtherance of a future intended crime or fraud. Advice secured in aid of a legitimate defense by the client against a charge of past crimes or past misconduct, even though he is guilty, stands on a different footing and such consultations are privileged. If the privilege is to be denied on the ground of unlawful purpose, the client's guilty intention is controlling, though the attorney may have acted innocently and in good faith. As to when the client must be shown to have had the guilty purpose, the traditional and apparent majority rule is that the purpose must exist at the time the legal advice is sought.

Both the procedure and standard for determining the application of the crime-fraud exception have been troublesome for the courts. The question of whether and when the court can examine documents *in camera* in aid of its application of the exception was decided for the federal courts in United States v. Zolin.[1] The judge may inspect documents *in camera* when there is a "factual basis adequate to support a good faith belief by a reasonable person" that such an inspection "may reveal evidence to establish the claim that the crime-fraud exception applies." Although the Supreme Court has not addressed the quantum of proof necessary for the second stage of the inquiry—the determination of whether the exception in fact applies—the federal and state courts considering the issue have used a similar standard. Although variously expressed, what is required is a prima facie case that the communication was in furtherance of crime or fraud, or in other words, that the one who seeks to avoid the privilege bring forward evidence from which the existence of an unlawful purpose could reasonably be found. Although the trial judge may consider information offered by the party opposing review, there is no requirement that such consideration be given. On the other hand, the court must determine that the communication was itself in furtherance of the crime or fraud, not merely that it has the potential of being relevant evidence of criminal or fraudulent activity.

Questions arise fairly frequently under this limitation upon the privilege in the situation where a client has first consulted one attorney about a claim, and then employs other counsel and brings suit. At the trial the defense seeks to have the first attorney testify to disclosures by the client which reveal that

---

4. Swidler & Berlin v. United States, supra n. 3 at 2089 (dissent by O'Connor, J).

5. Id. at 2087, n. 3.

1. 491 U.S. 554 (1989).

the claim was fabricated or fraudulent. This of course may be done, but if the statements to the first attorney would merely reveal variances from the client's later statements or testimony, not sufficient to evidence fraud or perjury, the privilege would stand.

It has been questioned whether the traditional statement of the area of the limitation, that is in cases of communications in aid of crime or fraud, is not itself too limited. Wigmore argues that the privilege should not be accorded to communications in furtherance of any deliberate scheme to deprive another of his rights by tortious or unlawful conduct.Stricter requirements such as that the intended crime be *malum in se* or that it involve "moral turpitude," suggested in some of the older decisions, seem out of place here where the only sanction proposed is that of opening the door to evidence concededly relevant upon the issue on trial. There further seems no apparent reason why the exception should not be applied equally to the work product privilege.

§ 96. Protective Rules Relating to Materials Collected for Use of Counsel in Preparation for Trial: Reports of Employees, Witness–Statements, Experts' Reports, and the Like

A heavy emphasis on the responsibility of counsel for the management of the client's litigation is a characteristic feature of the adversary or contentious system of procedure of the Anglo–American tradition. The privilege against disclosure in court of confidential communications between lawyer and client, as we have seen, is largely supported in modern times by the policy of encouraging free disclosure by the client in the attorney's office to enable the lawyer to discharge that responsibility.[1] The need for this encouragement is understood by lawyers because the problem of the guarded half-truths of the reticent client is familiar to them in their day-to-day work.

Closely allied to this felt need of promoting a policy of free disclosure by the client to permit the managing of the lawyer's affairs

most effectively in the interests of justice, is a feeling by lawyers of a need for privacy in their work and for freedom from interference in the task of preparing the client's case for trial. Certainly if the adversary were free at any time to inspect all of the correspondence, memoranda, reports, exhibits, trial briefs, drafts of proposed pleadings, and plans for presentation of proofs, which constitute the lawyer's file in the case, the attorney's present freedom to collect for study all the data, favorable and unfavorable, and to record his tentative impressions before maturing his conclusions, would be cramped and hindered.

The natural jealousy of the lawyer for the privacy of his file, and the court's desire to protect the effectiveness of the lawyer's work as the manager of litigation, have found expression, not only as we have seen in the evidential privilege for confidential lawyer-client communications, but in rules and practices about the various forms of pretrial discovery. Thus, under the old chancery practice of discovery, the adversary was not required to disclose, apart from his own testimony, the evidence which he would use, or the names of the witnesses he would call in support of his own case. The same restriction has often been embodied in, or read into, the statutory discovery systems.

Counterbalancing this need for privacy in preparation, of course, is the very need from which the discovery devices spring, namely, the need to make available to each party the widest possible sources of proof as early as may be so as to avoid surprise and facilitate preparation. The trend has been in the direction of wider recognition of this latter need, and the taboo against the "fishing expedition" has yielded increasingly to the proposition that the ends of justice require a wider availability of discovery than in the past. Accordingly there has developed an impressive arsenal of instruments of discovery, including interrogatories to the adverse party, demands for admissions, oral and written depositions of parties and witnesses, production of documents or things, entry upon land, and physical and

§ 96
1. See § 87 supra.

mental examinations. In recent years some disenchantment with discovery has surfaced with claims that it was used as an instrument of harassment, was unduly time-consuming, and was excessively costly. In an effort to reduce the abuse of discovery and to attempt to insure the flow of information from party to party, the Federal Rules of Civil Procedure were amended in 1993, principally to provide for mandatory disclosure of information without the need for invocation of particular discovery devices.[2] These amendments have some impact on the application of the privileges discussed in this chapter.

Attorney–Client privilege. In the first place, of course, it is recognized that if the traditional privilege for attorney-client communications applies to a particular writing which may be found in a lawyer's file, the privilege exempts it from pretrial discovery proceedings, such as orders for production or questioning about its contents in the taking of depositions. On the other hand, if the writing has been in the possession of the client or his agents and was there subject to discovery, it seems axiomatic that the client cannot secure any exemption for the document by sending it to an attorney to be placed in his files.

How do these distinctions apply to a report made by an agent to the client of the results of investigation by himself or another agent of facts pertinent to some matter which later becomes the subject of litigation, such as a business dispute or a personal injury. It has usually been held that an agent's report to his principal though made in confidence is not privileged as such, and looked on as a mere preexisting document it would not become privileged when sent by the client-principal to his lawyer for his information when suit is brought or threatened.[3] The problem frequently arises in connection with proceedings for discovery of accident reports by employees, with lists of eyewitnesses, and in connection with signed statements of witnesses attached to such reports or secured separately by inves-

tigators employed in the client's claim department or by an insurance company with whom the client carries insurance against liability. Revised Uniform Evidence Rule (1986) 502(b) extends the privilege to confidential communications for the purpose of facilitating the rendition of legal services to the client to communications "(4) between representatives of the client or between the client and representatives of the client * * *." The import of this provision remains largely unexplored.

Whether a communication by the client's agent, on behalf of the client, to the latter's attorney would be privileged, has been discussed elsewhere. Under the Supreme Court decision in Upjohn Co. v. United States[4] the attorney-client privilege will protect intra-corporate communications made for the purpose of securing legal advice if, additionally, the communication relates to the communicating employee's[5] assigned duties and is treated as confidential by the corporation. The communications in question were made by the employees directly to General Counsel and other lawyers representing the corporation in the investigation. An analogous rule would seem appropriate for application to agency situations not involving corporations.

By contrast, routine reports of agents made in the regular course of business, before suit is brought or threatened, have usually, though not always, been treated as pre-existing documents which not being privileged in the client's hands do not become so when delivered into the possession of his attorney. It is clear, however, that these classifications are not quite mutually exclusive and that some cases will fall in a doubtful borderland. And the law is in the making on the question whether a report of accident or other casualty, by a policy-holder or his agents to a company insuring the policy-holder against liability, is to be treated as privileged when the insurance company passes it on to the attorney who will represent both the company and the insured. Reasonably the insurance company may be

---

2. Fed.R.Civ.P. 26(a). Rule 26(a) provides that individual districts may opt out of its provisions. Many districts have done so.

3. See § 89 supra.

4. 449 U.S. 383 (1981).

5. See § 87 supra.

treated as an intermediary to secure legal representation for the insured, by whom the confidential communications can be transmitted as through a trusted agent. A report to a liability insurer can have no purpose other than use in potential litigation.

Work product. The discussion thus far has centered upon the extent to which the attorney-client privilege, just as any other privilege, can be invoked as a bar to discovery. Another, and much more frequently encountered limitation upon discovery of materials contained in the files of counsel, is furnished by the so-called "work product" doctrine, exempting trial preparations, in varying degrees, from discovery.

On June 14, 1946, the Advisory Committee on Federal Rules of Civil Procedure recommended the following amendment to Federal Rule 30(b):

> The court shall not order the production or inspection of any writing obtained or prepared by the adverse party, his attorney, surety, indemnitor, or agent in anticipation of litigation or in preparation for trial unless satisfied that denial of production or inspection will unfairly prejudice the party seeking the production or inspection in preparing his claim or defense or will cause him undue hardship or injustice. The court shall not order the production or inspection of any part of the writing that reflects an attorney's mental impressions, conclusions, opinions, or legal theories, or, except as provided in Rule 35, the conclusions of an expert.

The Supreme Court took no action on the proposed amendment but on January 3, 1947, handed down the decision in Hickman v. Taylor,[6] which is summarized below.

A tugboat, while helping tow a B. & O. Railroad carfloat, sank in the Delaware river, drowning five of the crew. Three days later, the two partner-owners of the tug and their underwriters hired Fortenbaugh's law firm to defend them against potential litigation arising from the drownings and to sue the railroad for damage to the tug. After a public Steamboat Inspectors' hearing, at which the four survivors testified, Fortenbaugh obtained signed statements from them. He also interviewed other persons, in some instances making memoranda. One action for death under the Jones Act was filed, the other death claims being settled. Plaintiff's Interrogatory 38 asked whether statements of witnesses were obtained; if written, copies were to be furnished; if oral, the exact provisions were to be set forth in detail. Upon refusal to comply, the two owners and Fortenbaugh were adjudged in contempt. The Third Circuit Court of Appeals reversed, and the Supreme Court granted certiorari.

During oral argument, the following exchange occurred:

> *Mr. Justice Jackson:* What would be the practical effect in the daily functioning of our judicial system if we order counsel to produce as requested in Interrogatory 38?
>
> *Mr. Fortenbaugh:* In my judgment, interviews will go unrecorded, unpleasant sources will not be pursued, and counsel will be tempted to keep files under his bed at home.

The Supreme Court affirmed the judgment of the Court of Appeals. The problem, said the Court, was to balance the interest in privacy of a lawyer's work against the interest supporting reasonable and necessary inquiries. Proper preparation of a client's case demands that information be assembled and sifted, legal theories be prepared, and strategy be planned "without undue and needless interference."[7] If the product of this work (interviews, statements, memoranda, etc.) were available merely on demand, the effect on the legal profession would be demoralizing. Discovery may be had where relevant and non-privileged facts, necessary for preparation of the opposing party's case, remain hidden, or the witness unavailable. The burden is on the party seeking to invade the privacy of the lawyer to show justification; this is "implicit in the rules as now

---

6.   329 U.S. 495 (1947).

7.   329 U.S. at 511.

[in 1947] constituted."[8] Rule 34 requires a showing of good cause for an order to produce documents, and Rule 30(b) gives the judge authority to limit examination upon the taking of a deposition when it appears that the examination is being conducted in bad faith or so as to annoy, embarrass, or oppress. Here no attempt was made to show need for the written statements. And as for the oral statements, to require Fortenbaugh to reproduce them would have a highly adverse effect upon the legal profession, making the lawyer more an ordinary witness than an officer of the court. Under the circumstances of this case, no showing could be made that would justify requiring disclosure of the mental impressions of counsel as to what the witnesses told him.

Considerable disagreement in the lower courts as to the meaning of Hickman v. Taylor followed that decision, no doubt resulting at least in part from the labored path followed by the Court to the conclusion that the matter of a qualified work product privilege was in fact covered by its own rules as then written. Finally after more than 20 years, the Court in 1970 adopted an amended Rule 26(b), with subdivision (3) directed in specific terms to the scope of the qualified work product protection. Nonetheless, Hickman v. Taylor remains a "brooding omnipresence," much cited and quoted by the courts, and in fact still governs an important area of the qualified work product protection.

These salient provisions of Rule 26(b)(3) should be noted:

(1) In terms its work product immunity extends only to "documents and tangible things," yet discovery of documents constituted only one-half the subject of Hickman v. Taylor. The other half, i.e. mental impressions and the like, receives only pendant mention in the second sentence of Rule 26(b)(3), discussed in paragraph (5) below.

(2) The document or thing must have been "prepared in anticipation of litigation or for trial." If this scope seems unduly limited, it must be remembered that litigation is the frame of reference for work product. When the lawyer is engaged in rendering other services, e.g. the drafting of a contract, information which he needs will most likely be communicated by the client, falling within the attorney-client privilege. Information from outside sources is peculiarly a characteristic of the litigation situation.

(3) Hickman v. Taylor on its facts dealt only with work produced by an attorney, leaving open a troublesome question as to the status of the product of claim adjusters, investigators, and the like. The rule, however, is specific, speaking of documents prepared "by or for another party or by or for that other party's representative (including the other party's attorney, consultant, surety, indemnitor, insurer, or agent)."

(4) The requirement of need is spelled out "only upon a showing that the party seeking discovery has substantial need of the materials in the preparation of his case and that he is unable without undue hardship to obtain the substantial equivalent of the materials by other means."

(5) The judge in ordering discovery of covered materials is directed to "protect against disclosure of the mental impressions, conclusions, opinions, or legal theories of an attorney or other representative of a party concerning the litigation." Literally read, the rule appears to protect mental impressions and the like of the lawyer only against disclosure that would be incidental to disclosure of documents and tangible things, in this regard being absolute in terms. If, however, counsel had not reduced a witness' statement to writing and counsel's deposition were taken in an effort to discover what the witness had said, Rule 26(b)(3) literally would not apply. Under these circumstances, however, it seems inconceivable that courts would not fall back upon Hickman v. Taylor and require an extraordinarily strong showing of need, as has indeed been the case.

(6) A person, whether a party or a witness, is entitled to a copy of his own statement merely by requesting it; no showing of need is required.

---

8. 329 U.S. at 512.

The rule, it should be observed, does not immunize facts, or the identities of persons having knowledge of facts, or the existence of documents as contrasted with the documents themselves. Nor does the rule spell out the breadth of application or the duration of the qualified privilege that it recognizes. Case law is meager on such significant questions as whether the privilege applies at trial or whether it can be invoked in other proceedings.

The 1993 amendments to Rule 26 affect claims of privilege and work product protection, especially with regard to the preparation of experts to testify. Rule 26(a)(2) requires at least a description of all documents or other tangible things in the possession or control of a party that are relevant to the disputed facts. Although the Advisory Committee Note to the amendment stresses that the disclosing party does not, by describing documents, waive its right to object to production on the basis of privilege or work product protection, amended Rule 26(b)(5) requires that any claim of privilege or protection must be made "expressly and shall describe the nature of the documents, communications, or things not produced or disclosed in a manner that, without revealing information itself privileged or protected, will enable other parties to assess the applicability of the privilege or protection."

Amended Rule 26(a)(2) requires experts whose testimony may be used at trial to submit a report disclosing the expert's opinions and other related information, including all data or other information considered by the witness in forming opinions. The Advisory Committee Note emphasizes that the amendment means that litigants should not be able to argue that "materials" furnished to their experts used in forming their opinions are protected from disclosure. Courts considering the issue under the amended rule have differed as to whether "materials" includes mental-impressions communications between the attorney and the expert.

§ 97. Discovery in Criminal Cases: Statements by Witnesses

The development of discovery in criminal cases has, for a variety of reasons, lagged far behind that available in the civil area. The pros and cons of the continuing debate on the subject are outside the scope of the present treatment, though it is pertinent to observe that the trend seems clearly in the direction of more liberal discovery in the criminal area. This expansion of criminal discovery, like its earlier civil analogue, has raised the question whether "work product" should be afforded protection, and even the more advanced rules and proposals on the subject do undertake to provide such protection.

A distinguishable question which has drawn considerable attention is whether disclosure should be granted of material at, as opposed to before, trial. At a fairly early date, both federal and state decisions had espoused the view that when the statements of prosecution witnesses contradicting their trial testimony are shown to be in the hands of the government the defendant is entitled to demand their production at the trial. But despite this background, the famous *Jencks*[1] case was widely viewed as a startling incursion into new territory. The Supreme Court held in that case that the trial court had erroneously denied defense requests to inspect reports of two undercover agents who were government witnesses. It was not required, said the Court, that defendant show that the reports were inconsistent with the witnesses' testimony; if they related to the same subject, defendant was entitled to make the decision whether they were useful to the defense. The dissent condemned the holding as affording the criminal "a Roman holiday for rummaging through confidential information [in government files] as well as vital national secrets."[2] This view was echoed in widespread protests by the press, by the Department of Justice, and in the halls of Congress where the so-called Jencks

§ 97

1. Jencks v. United States, 353 U.S. 657 (1957) (prosecution of labor union official for filing false non-Communist affidavit with NLRB).

2. 353 U.S. at 681–682.

Act of 1959 was hastily enacted. Despite this background, the Act was for the most part a codification of the decision which had been so vehemently attacked. The Act has now been superseded by Rule 26.2 of the Federal Rules of Criminal Procedure. However, the terms of the Act must be considered in examining the effect of Rule 26.2, as will appear from the subsequent discussion.

Subsection (a) of the Act as amended provided that no statement by a government witness or prospective witness should be the subject of subpoena, discovery, or inspection until the witness has testified on direct examination in the trial. Subsection (b) provided that after a witness called by the government has testified on direct the court should, on motion of defendant, order the government to produce any statement (as later defined) relating to the subject matter of his testimony. Under subsection (c) the court will in case of question examine the statement and excise portions not related to the testimony. If, under subsection (d), the government elects not to comply with the order to produce, the testimony is to be stricken or, if justice requires, a mistrial is to be declared. In subsection (e), "statement" as used in subsections (b), (c), and (d) is defined; the definition is very precise and narrow, designed to include only statements that beyond any reasonable question represent with a very high precision the words used by the witness. It will be observed that subsection (a) was designed to bar disclosure of any statement of a witness, regardless of how precise or imprecise a rendition it might be, unless and until the witness had testified for the government. After that testimony had been given, then disclosure was allowed and required but only as to highly precise statements, as defined in (e). If a writing were not a statement at all, in the broad sense of (a), the Act did not affect it. Writings which were statements in the broad sense of (a), but not within the strict definition of (e), or within (e) but whose maker did not testify, remained locked away, except as they might be obtainable under Brady v. Maryland,[3] or under Evidence Rule 612 discussed below.

For the most part Rule 26.2 transposed the Act into the Federal Rules of Criminal Procedure. Some changes must, however, be noted. Rule 26.2 does not contain the prohibition of subsection (a) of the Act against compelling disclosure of a statement, in the broad sense, unless and until the witness has testified on direct. Thus Rule 26.2 deals only with compelling production of statements within the strict definition of subsection (e) of the Act, which is retained as subdivision (F) of the Rule. But as a companion to Rule 26.2, there was at the same time added to Rule 17 of the Criminal Rules, which deals with subpoenas, a new subdivision (h):

Statements made by witnesses or prospective witnesses may not be subpoenaed from the government or the defendant under this rule, but shall be subject to production only in accordance with the provisions of Rule 26.2.

While superficially this may appear to constitute no more than a relocation of subsection (a) of the Act, in fact the separation undermines the force of any argument that Rule 26.2 controls all statements of witnesses and prospective witnesses, in the broad sense, and leaves it effective only with regard to statements as narrowly defined in subdivision (F) of Rule 26.2. This is important in connection with the relationship between Rule 26.2 and Evidence Rule 612, discussed below.

A further highly significant change effected by Rule 26.2 was the expansion of coverage to include statements by defense witnesses and prospective witnesses as well as those for the government. This change was stimulated by the Supreme Court's decision in United States v. Nobles.[4] As under the Act, the penalty for refusal is striking of the testimony, with the further provision that if the refusing party is the government a mistrial may be declared if justice requires. A defendant cannot, of course, be allowed to abort a trial by refusing to deliver a statement.

And in 1983, a related amendment to Rule 12(i) had the effect of extending the provisions

---

3.   373 U.S. 83 (1963). See § 252, infra.

4.   422 U.S. 225 (1975).

of Rule 26.2 to pretrial hearings of motions to suppress evidence. In an earlier section[5] attention was directed to the need to examine the relationship between Criminal Rule 26.2 and Evidence Rule 612. That section pointed out that when a witness while testifying refers to a writing to refresh his memory, an opposing party is entitled to inspect it, to cross-examine upon it, and to introduce in evidence portions related to the testimony of the witness; if the reference for refreshing was prior to testifying, access to and use of the writing is subject to the court's discretion. If the writing consulted for refreshment is the statement of a witness or prospective witness, the potential for conflict between Criminal Rule 26.2 and Evidence Rule 612 is seen. If the writing is a statement within the strict definition of Rule 26.2(f), the conflict is in reality no more than an overlap, as under either rule disclosure is required once the witness has testified on direct. But when the statement is a statement in the broad sense, as under subsection (a) of the Act, but not within the strict definition of subsection (e) of the Act, the construction in *Palermo*[6] as previously observed, was that no disclosure

was available. The confusion is compounded by the fact that Rule 612 opens with the phrase, "Except as otherwise provided in criminal proceedings by section 3500 of title 18, United States Code * * * " and has not been amended. What is the effect of the exception? Does subsection (a) of the Act continue with its former effect? Did *Palermo* survive, pro tanto, the subsequent enactment of Rule 612? A satisfactory resolution probably lies only in the legislative sphere. Meanwhile a look at fundamentals may suggest a satisfactory construction. Both the Act (and Rule 26.2) and Rule 612 are directed to testing the credibility of witnesses. One pursues that end by giving access to statements which, if inconsistent, undoubtedly qualify for impeachment by that route. The other pursues the same end by giving access to materials generally, whether statements or not, which may have influenced the memory and narrative of the witness. Both can operate side by side without real conflict. The tangle is one of language, not of goals. This result is fairly reachable within the present language in view of the disappearance of subsection (a) of the Act, as noted above.

5. See § 9 supra.

6. Palermo v. United States, 360 U.S. 343 (1959).

Chapter 11

THE PRIVILEGE FOR
CONFIDENTIAL INFORMATION
SECURED IN THE COURSE
OF THE PHYSICIAN–PATIENT
RELATIONSHIP

Table of Sections

§ 98. The Statement of the Rule and Its Purpose

The common law knew no privilege for confidential information imparted to a physician. When a physician raised the question before Lord Mansfield whether he was required to disclose professional confidences, the great Chief Justice drew the line clear. "If a surgeon was voluntarily to reveal these secrets, to be sure, he would be guilty of a breach of honor and of great indiscretion; but to give that information in a court of justice, which by the law of the land he is bound to do, will never be imputed to him as any indiscretion whatever."[1]

The pioneer departure from the common law rule was the New York statute of 1828 which in its original form was as follows: "No person authorized to practice physic or surgery shall be allowed to disclose any information which he may have acquired in attending any patient, in a professional character, and which information was necessary to enable him to prescribe for such patient as a physician, or to do any act for him as a surgeon."

Another early act which has been widely copied is the provision of the California Code of Civil Procedure of 1872, § 1881, par. 4, "A licensed physician or surgeon cannot, without the consent of his patient, be examined in a

§ 98

1. The Duchess of Kingston's Trial, 20 How.St.Trials 573 (1776).

civil action as to any information acquired in attending the patient which was necessary to enable him to prescribe or act for the patient."

The rationale traditionally asserted to justify suppression in litigation of material facts learned by a physician is the encouragement thereby given to the patient freely to disclose all matter which may aid in the diagnosis and treatment of disease and injury. To obtain this end, so the argument runs, it is necessary to secure the patient from disclosure in court of potentially embarrassing private details concerning health and bodily condition. The validity of this utilitarian justification of the privilege has been questioned by many on the ground that the average patient, in consulting a physician, will have his thoughts centered upon his illness or injury and the prospects for betterment or cure, and will spare little thought for the remote possibility of some eventual disclosure of his condition in court. Accordingly, if an assurance of confidentiality has little importance in the play of forces upon the patient, it might well be concluded that the privilege is largely ineffective in attaining its avowed objective. Despite these arguments, however, the number of states adhering to the common law and refusing any general physician-patient privilege has slowly but steadily dwindled.

Over the same period, there has been a strong trend toward the recognition of two related but distinguishable privileges protecting, respectively, communications between psychiatrist and patient and psychologist and patient. Though the former profession, being medically trained, has always come within the ambit of the older physician-patient privilege where that privilege is recognized, it has been cogently argued that accepted practice in the treatment of mental illness involves considerations not encountered in other medical contexts. The following statement is frequently quoted in this regard.

> Among physicians, the psychiatrist has a special need to maintain confidentiality. His capacity to help his patients is

completely dependent upon their willingness and ability to talk freely. This makes it difficult if not impossible for him to function without being able to assure his patients of confidentiality and, indeed, privileged communication * * *. A threat to secrecy blocks successful treatment.[2]

The uniqueness of the psychiatrist-patient relationship led to the inclusion in the proposed Federal Rules of Evidence of a psychotherapist-patient privilege even though no general physician-patient privilege was suggested. The Revised Uniform Rules (1974) retained this privilege, but make the rule optionally one extending to confidential communication to a physician as well as to a psychotherapist. In the same vein, several of the states which continue to reject a general physician-patient privilege have enacted privileges applicable to the more limited psychotherapeutic context. And, recognizing that the treatment of mental illness is carried out by clinical psychologists as well as by psychiatrists, several states have enacted psychologist-patient privileges.

The action of the states was bolstered by the recognition of a psychotherapist-patient privilege by the United States Supreme Court in Jaffee v. Redmond.[3] Relying on a utilitarian rationale, the Court emphasized that "the mere possibility of disclosure may impede development of the confidential relationship necessary for successful treatment."[4] The Court also noted the appropriateness of the recognition of the privilege in the federal courts in light of the fact that all states and the District of Columbia have enacted it into law in some form. The holding extended the privilege not only to psychiatrists and psychologists but, over the dissent of two justices, to licensed social workers as well. The Court also held that the privilege it recognized was absolute, rejecting the balancing test applied by the Court of Appeals in the Jaffee case and by several states.

The Court, confined to the facts before it, could not detail all of the contours of the

---

2. Report No. 45, Group for the Advancement of Psychiatry 92 (1960).

3. 518 U.S. 1 (1996).

4. Id at 10.

privilege it announced. It explicitly left open the application of the privilege if a serious threat of harm to the patient or to others can be averted only by means of a disclosure by the therapist. The lower federal courts have just begun to flesh out the dimensions of the privilege.

One theory absent from the Court's analysis in Jaffee was any suggestion that the recognition of the privilege was constitutionally required. However, some privilege-like protection of certain aspects of the physician-patient relationship appears to be emerging as a function of federal constitutional guarantees of the right of privacy. In Whalen v. Roe,[5] the constitutionality of a New York statute creating a state data bank of the names and addresses of persons obtaining certain drugs by medical prescription was challenged, *inter alia,* on the ground that patients would be deterred from obtaining appropriate medication by the apprehension that disclosure of their names would stigmatize them as drug addicts. Though garbed in constitutional vestments as an impairment of the right to make personal decisions, this argument bears a striking resemblance to the traditional rationale of privilege. While upholding the statute in *Whalen,* the Supreme Court did so on the basis of reasoning which strongly suggests the existence of some constitutional right on the part of patients to preserve confidentiality with respect to medical treatment.

Subsequent decisions of lower federal and state courts evidence considerable disagreement concerning the nature and scope, and even the existence, of the constitutionally based right intimated to exist in *Whalen.* A majority of the cases considering the point have involved information conveyed during psychotherapeutic treatment, a context in which the traditional utilitarian justification has been urged to possess particular validity. Nevertheless, even cases of the latter sort have generally been resolved on the particular facts against the claimant of privilege, and it would appear clear that any constitutional right to privacy in medical information is a highly qualified one.

§ 99. Relation of Physician and Patient

The first requisite for the privilege is that the patient must have consulted the physician for treatment or for diagnosis looking toward treatment. If consulted for treatment it is immaterial by whom the doctor is employed. Usually, however, when the doctor is employed by one other than the patient, treatment will not be the purpose and the privilege will not attach. Thus, when a driver at the request of a public officer is subjected to a blood test for intoxication, or when a doctor is appointed by the court or the prosecutor to make a physical or mental examination, or is employed for this purpose by the opposing party, or is selected by a life insurance company to make an examination of an applicant for a policy or even when the doctor is employed by plaintiff's own lawyers in a personal injury case to examine plaintiff solely to aid in preparation for trial, the information secured is not within the present privilege. But when the patient's doctor calls in a consultant physician to aid in diagnosis or treatment, the disclosures are privileged.

If the patient's purpose in the consultation is an unlawful one, as to obtain narcotics in violation of law, or as, by some authority, a fugitive from justice to have his appearance disguised by plastic surgery, the law withholds the shield of privilege.

It has been held that where a doctor has attended a mother in her confinement and the newborn child, the child is a patient and can claim privilege against the doctor's disclosure of facts as to the apparent maturity of the child at birth.

After the death of the patient the relation is ended and the object of the privilege can no longer be furthered. Accordingly, it seems the better view that facts discovered in an autopsy examination are not privileged.

§ 100. Subject Matter of the Privilege: Information Acquired in Attending the Patient and Necessary for Prescribing

Statutes conferring a physician-patient privilege vary extensively, though probably a

---

5. 429 U.S. 589 (1977).

majority follow the pioneer New York and California statutes in extending the privilege to "any information acquired in attending the patient."[1] Understandably, these provisions have been held to protect not only information explicitly conveyed to the physician by the patient, but also data acquired by examination and testing. Other statutes appear facially to be more restrictive and to limit the privilege to communications by the patient. This appearance, however, may frequently be misleading, for statutes of this sort have been construed to provide a privilege fully as broad as that available elsewhere. The confusion is further compounded by a line of authority which holds that facts observable by anyone without professional knowledge or training are not within the privilege.

While the information secured by the physician may be privileged, the fact that he has been consulted by the patient and has treated him, and the number and dates of his visits, are not within the shelter of the privilege.

The extent to which the privilege attaches to the information embodied in hospital records is discussed in the chapter on Business Records.[2]

§ 101. The Confidential Character of the Disclosure: Presence of Third Persons and Members of Family: Information Revealed to Nurses and Attendants: Public Records

We have seen that the statutes existing in many states codifying the privileges for marital communications and those between attorney and client usually omitted the requirement that to be privileged such communications must have been made in confidence. Nevertheless, the courts have read this limitation into these statutes, assuming that the legislatures must have intended this common law requirement to continue.[1] The statutes giving the patient's privilege for information gained in professional consultations again omit the adjective "confidential."[2] Should it

nonetheless be read in, not as a continuation of a common law requirement, but as an interpretative gloss, spelled out from policy and analogy? Certainly the policy arguments are strong. First is the policy of holding all privileges within reasonable bounds since they cut off access to sources of truth. Second, the argument that the purpose of encouraging those who would otherwise be reluctant, to disclose necessary facts to their doctors, will be adequately served by extending a privilege for only such disclosures as the patient wishes to keep secret.

This principle of confidentiality is supported by those decisions which hold that if a casual third person is present with the acquiescence of the patient at the consultation, the disclosures made in his presence are not privileged, and thus the stranger, the patient and the doctor may be required to divulge them in court. Whether this principle is to be applied when the stranger is a police officer who has escorted the patient to the hospital or doctor's office should, it would seem, turn on whether meaningful acquiescence on the patient's part is to be found on the facts.

If, however, the third person is present as a needed and customary participant in the consultation, the circle of confidence may be reasonably extended to include him and the privilege will be maintained. Thus the presence of one sustaining a close family relationship to the patient should not curtail the privilege. And the nurse present as the doctor's assistant during the consultation or examination, or the technician who makes tests or X-ray photographs under the doctor's direction, will be looked on as the doctor's agent in whose keeping the information will remain privileged. But the application of strict agency principles in this context would seem inconsistent with the realities of modern medical practice, and the preferable view is that of the courts which have based their decisions upon

---

§ 100

1. See § 98 supra.

2. See § 293 infra.

§ 101

1. See §§ 80, 91 supra.

2. See § 98 supra.

whether the communication was functionally related to diagnosis and treatment.

Many courts on the other hand do not analyze the problems in terms of whether the communications or disclosures were confidential and professional, but rather in terms of what persons are intended to be silenced as witnesses. This seems to be sticking in the bark of the statute, rather than looking at its purpose. Thus these courts, if casual third persons were present at the consultation, will still close the mouth of the doctor but allow the visitor to speak. And if nurses or other attendants or technicians gain information necessary to treatment they will be allowed by these courts to speak (unless the privilege statute specifically names them) but the physician may not.

When the attending physician is required by law to make a certificate of death to the public authority, giving his opinion as to the cause, the certificate should be provable as a public record, despite the privilege. The duty to make a public report overrides the general duty of secrecy, and in view of the availability of the record to the public, the protection of the information from general knowledge, as contemplated by the privilege, cannot be attained. Accordingly, under the prevailing view, the privilege does not attach.

Today, state and local laws increasingly impose upon physicians requirements to report various types of patient information related to the public health and safety, e.g., the treatment of gunshot wounds, venereal disease, HIV and AIDS, mental illness, and the occurrence of fetal death. Generally, state schemes for the collection and preservation of such data and its use by appropriate authorities have been upheld as against challenges based either upon a constitutional right of privacy or the professional privilege. In some instances, e.g., the reporting of gunshot wounds, the privilege has been held to be qualified to the extent of the reporting requirement, with the result that the physician may testify to any fact included within the report. Conversely, where the physician's re-

port is not required the physician would remain precluded from testifying to the facts in the report, though there is some authority that the privilege, being testimonial, does not bar use of the report to generate other admissible evidence. Many of the reporting systems, however, obviously do not envision general disclosure of the data collected, and maintenance of some degree of confidentiality may in fact be indispensable to constitutionality.

§ 102. Rule of Privilege, Not Incompetency: Privilege Belongs to the Patient, Not to an Objecting Party as Such: Effect of the Patient's Death

As has been pointed out in the discussion of privileges generally,[1] the rule which excludes disclosures to physicians is not a rule of incompetency of evidence serving the end of protecting the adverse party against unreliable or prejudicial testimony. It is a rule of privilege protecting the extrinsic interest of the patient and designed to promote health, not truth. It encourages free disclosure in the sickroom by preventing disclosure in the courtroom. The patient is the person to be encouraged and he is the holder of the privilege.

Consequently, he alone during his lifetime has the right to claim or to waive the privilege. If he is in a position to claim it and does not, it is waived and no one else may assert it. If the patient is not present, is unaware of the situation, or for some other reason is unable to claim the privilege, it is generally held that the privilege may be asserted on his behalf by a guardian, personal representative, or the health care provider, the latter being frequently held to have an enforceable duty to invoke the privilege in the absence of waiver by the patient. This necessary rule has unfortunately demonstrated considerable potential for allowing health care providers to advance personal interests under the guise of vindicating the privilege. It is to be hoped that it will not ultimately prove beyond judicial ingenuity in cases of this sort to allow the patient the ultimate decision as to whether the privilege will be invoked.

§ 102

1. See § 72 supra.

The adverse party as such has no interest to protect if he is not the patient, and thus cannot object as of right.

In order to facilitate full disclosure as well as to protect the privacy of the decedent, most courts hold that the privilege continues after death. However, in contests of the survivors in interest with third parties, e.g., actions to recover property claimed to belong to the deceased, actions for the death of the deceased, or actions upon life insurance policies, the personal representative, heir or next of kin, or the beneficiary in the policy may waive the privilege, and, by the same token, the adverse party may not effectively assert the privilege. In contests over the validity of a will, where both sides—the executor on the one hand and the heirs or next of kin on the other—claim under and not adversely to the decedent, the assumption should prevail that the decedent would desire that the validity of his will should be determined in the fullest light of the facts. Accordingly in this situation either the executor or the contestants may effectively waive the privilege without the concurrence of the other.

§ 103. What Constitutes a Waiver of the Privilege?

The physician-patient statutes, though commonly phrased in terms of incompetency, are nevertheless held to create merely a privilege for the benefit of the patient, which he may waive.

Generally it is agreed that a contractual stipulation waiving the privilege, such as is frequently included in applications for life or health insurance, or in the policies themselves, is valid and effectual.

Another context in which the privilege is waived anticipatorily is that in which a testator procures an attending doctor to subscribe his will as an attesting witness. This action constitutes a waiver as to all facts affecting the validity of the will.

The physician-patient privilege, like most other privileges, may also be waived in advance of trial by a disclosure of the privileged information either made or acquiesced in by

the privilege holder. Obviously, the law has no reason to conceal in court what has been freely divulged on the public street, and the only question in such cases becomes the voluntariness of the revelation and the scope of the waiver.

Waiver in connection with litigation is an area in which substantial changes have occurred in recent years. A shrinking from the embarrassment which comes from exposure of bodily disease or abnormality is human and natural. It is arguable that legal protection from exposure is justified to encourage frankness in consulting physicians. But it is not human, natural, or understandable to claim protection from exposure by asserting a privilege for communications to doctors at the very same time when the patient is parading before the public the mental or physical condition as to which he consulted the doctor by bringing an action for damages arising from that same condition. This, in the oft-repeated phrase, is to make the privilege not a shield only, but a sword.

The conclusion mandated by these considerations clearly is that a patient voluntarily placing his or her physical or mental condition in issue in a judicial proceeding waives the privilege with respect to information relative to that condition. Failure to find a waiver from assertion of a claim or defense predicated upon a physical or mental condition has the awkward consequence of effectively frustrating discovery on a central issue of the case unless one of a variety of temporizing expedients is pressed into service to accommodate the outmoded rule.

Happily today the once prevalent rule that no waiver results from raising a claim or defense has been widely reversed by statute. Thus, at present, the crucial questions concern the types of issues which sufficiently implicate a party's physical or mental condition, and what actions by a party serve to raise these issues within the meaning of the modern statutes. A claim for damages for personal injuries is of course the paradigm example, and will clearly waive the privilege in all jurisdictions where such waiver by filing is possible at all. Claims for damages for mental suffering have been treated similarly, but here some discernment is called for lest the privilege be seen to evaporate upon the filing of any claim whatsoever. In addition, cases applying the psychotherapist-patient privilege established in Jaffee v. Redmond[1] have not agreed as to whether and when a plaintiff who asserts a claim involving distress waives that privilege. With respect to defenses, a distinction is clearly to be seen between the allegation of a physical or mental condition, which will effect the waiver, and the mere denial of such a condition asserted by the adversary, which will not.

A much litigated point since the conversion to more liberal rules of waiver has been whether a waiver effected by filing a claim or defense will permit the waiving party's adversary in litigation to contact physicians on an ex parte basis. Those decisions approving such contacts stress the economies of informal discovery and the anomaly of treating any witness as "belonging" to a party, considerations which suffice to make permissibility of ex parte contact the better rule. A contrary position, however, has been taken by a greater number of courts, and possesses a substantial rationale in the consideration that the waiver following upon the filing of a claim or defense extends only to information relevant to the condition relied upon.

In the criminal area, waiver under the modern statutes has been seen to flow from assertion of the defenses of insanity and diminished responsibility.

Because of the principles discussed above, there will today be fewer occasions in which a cause will come on for trial with the patient's privilege still intact. Since the possibility still exists, however, it should be briefly considered how the privilege may be waived in trial.

How far does the patient's testifying waive the privilege? Doubtless, if the patient on direct examination testifies to, or adduces other evidence of, the communications exchanged or the information furnished to the doctor consulted this would waive in respect to such consultations. When, however, the patient in his direct testimony does not reveal

any privileged matter respecting the consultation, but testifies only to his physical or mental condition, existing at the time of such consultation, then one view is that, "where the patient tenders to the jury the issue as to his physical condition, it must in fairness and justice be held that he has himself waived the obligation of secrecy." This view has the great merit of curtailing the scope of an obstructive privilege, but there are a number of courts which hold that the patient's testimony as to his condition without disclosure of privileged matter is not a waiver. If the patient reveals privileged matter on cross-examination, without claiming the privilege, this is usually held not to be a waiver of the privilege enabling the adversary to make further inquiry of the doctors, on the ground that such revelations were not "voluntary." The counter-argument, that the failure to assert the privilege should be a complete waiver, seems persuasive.

If the patient examines a physician as to matters disclosed in a consultation, or course of treatment, of course this is a waiver and opens the door to the opponent to examine him about any other matters then disclosed. And if several doctors participated jointly in the same consultation or course of treatment the calling of one to disclose part of the shared information waives objection to the adversary's calling any other of the joint consultants to testify about the consultation, treatment or the results thereof. Liberal courts go further and hold that calling by the patient of one doctor and eliciting privileged matter from him opens the door to the opponent's calling other doctors consulted by the patient at other times to bring out any facts relevant to the issue on which the privileged proof was adduced. It is not consonant with justice and fairness to permit the patient to reveal his secrets to several doctors and then when his condition comes in issue to limit the witnesses to the consultants favorable to his claims. But a substantial number of courts balk at this step.

Though the privilege continues after death of the patient, it may then be waived by the personal representative of the decedent.

§ 103

1. 518 U.S. 1 (1996). See discussion in § 98, supra.

And where the personal representative is involved in litigation over the decedents estate with other persons claiming through the decedent, or where heirs-at-law are in opposition to one another, any one of the parties may waive the privilege.

§ 104. Kinds of Proceedings Exempted From the Application of the Privilege

The wide variation among state statutes creating and defining the physician-patient privilege renders it difficult to generalize usefully concerning the types of proceedings exempted from the operation of the privilege. Even where the Uniform Rule has been adopted, one or more qualifications have commonly been engrafted upon it. And though the now widely-adopted patient-litigant exception has undoubtedly reduced somewhat the differential application of the privilege, there remain many instances in which the holder of the privilege will not come within that exception. In short, it is indispensable to consult local statutes on the present point.

Probably the most common pattern to be observed in the statutes is that of a broadly defined privilege, applicable to both civil and criminal proceedings, to which a variety of specific exceptions are then attached. But there are states which deny the privilege in criminal cases generally, or in felony cases, or in cases of homicide.

With respect to other exceptions, the privilege has long been viewed as unworkable in worker compensation cases, and in medical malpractice cases and will generally be unavailable in these contexts. In more recent years, proceedings involving child abuse have claimed the attention of the legislatures, and these proceedings are now the most commonly singled out as involving policy considerations more weighty than those underlying the privilege. Other types of proceedings found withdrawn from the operation of the privilege are commitment proceedings, prosecutions for some types of drug offenses, and will contests.

The privilege is also sometimes withdrawn in child custody proceedings.

§ 105. The Policy and Future of the Privilege

Some statements of Buller, J., in 1792 in a case involving the application of the attorney-client privilege seem to have furnished the inspiration for the pioneer New York statute of 1828 on the doctor-patient privilege. He said: "The privilege is confined to the cases of counsel, solicitor, and attorney. * * * It is indeed hard in many cases to compel a friend to disclose a confidential conversation; and I should be glad if by law such evidence could be excluded. It is a subject of just indignation where persons are anxious to reveal what has been communicated to them in a confidential manner. * * * There are cases to which it is much to be lamented that the law of privilege is not extended; those in which medical persons are obliged to disclose the information which they acquire by attending in their professional characters."[1]

These comments reveal attitudes which have been influential ever since in the spread of statutes enacting the doctor-patient privilege. One attitude is the shrinking from forcing anyone to tell in court what he has learned in confidence. It is well understood today, however, that no such sweeping curtain for disclosure of confidences in the courtroom could be justified. Another is the complete failure to consider the other side of the shield, namely, the loss which comes from depriving the courts of any reliable source of facts necessary for the right decision of cases.

Perhaps the main burden of Justice Buller's remarks, however, is the suggestion that since the client's disclosures to the lawyer are privileged, the patient's disclosures to the doctor should have the same protection. This analogy has probably been more potent than any other argument, particularly with the lawyers in the legislatures. They would be reluctant to deny to the medical profession a recognition which the courts have themselves

§ 105

1. Wilson v. Rastall, 4 Term, Rep. 753, 759, 100 Eng. Rep. 1287 (K.B.1792).

provided for the legal profession. Manifestly, however, the soundness of the privilege may not be judged as a matter of rivalry of professions, but by the criterion of the public interest.

Some of the analytical weaknesses of the utilitarian rationale of the privilege, except in the psychotherapeutic context, have been noted earlier.[2] To these must be added the perplexities and confusions arising from judicial and legislative attempts to render tolerable a rule which essentially runs against the grain of truth. The uncertainties of application of a privilege so extensively and variously qualified and restricted certainly undermine any effort to justify it on utilitarian grounds. One familiar with the vagaries of its operation may not be disposed to repose confidence in its protection. Those not so knowledgeable will often find it a snare and a delusion.

A more tenable argument, however, has been increasingly advanced in recent years. This view holds that the privilege should not be viewed as operating to inspire the making of medical confidences but rather as protecting such confidences once made. The legitimate interest in the privacy of the physician-patient relationship should not be subject to casual breach by every litigant in single-minded pursuit of the last scrap of evidence which may marginally contribute to victory in litigation. Arguably the privilege does, at least on occasion, operate to prevent such unwarranted intrusions. The issue is whether the value of such protection is sufficiently great to justify both the suppression of critical evidence in other cases and the costs of administering a highly complex rule.

Regardless of how such a debate might be resolved in one's own mind, complete abolition of the privilege is unlikely given current political realities. One alternative resolution is legislation such as that which exists in North Carolina, which qualifies its statutory privilege with the provision that "the court, either at trial or prior thereto * * * may compel such disclosure when, in his opinion, the same is necessary to a proper administration of justice." Such a balancing was expressly rejected by the Court in Jaffee v. Redmond,[3] in connection with the psychotherapist-patient privilege. However, the adoption of such a limitation by statute is certainly possible and may be effective in protecting privacy against trivial intrusion while permitting the use of critical evidence.

---

2. See § 98 supra.

3. 518 U.S. 1 (1996), see discussion supra § 98.

Chapter 12

PRIVILEGES FOR GOVERNMENTAL SECRETS

Table of Sections

§ 106. Other Principles Distinguished

In discussing the evidentiary privileges and rules of exclusion regarding the production and admission of writings and information in the possession of government officers, other principles should be noted, which may hinder the litigant seeking facts from the government but which are beyond our present inquiry. Among these are: (a) questions of substantive privilege of government officers from liability for their acts and words, (b) questions as to executive immunity from liability, and (c) issues regarding the irremovability of official records.

§ 107. The Common Law Privileges for Military or Diplomatic Secrets and Other Facts the Disclosure of Which Would Be Contrary to the Public Interest

As the activities of modern government have expanded, the need of litigants for the disclosure and proof of documents and other information in the possession of government officials has correspondingly increased. When this need is asserted and opposed, the public interest in the secrecy of "classified" information comes into direct conflict with the public interest in the protection of the claim of the individual to due process of law in the redress of grievances. The proper resolution of this conflict requires careful judicial scrutiny.

A privilege and a rule of exclusion has been recognized for writings and information constituting military or diplomatic secrets of state. The justification for secrecy is obviously extremely strong when the material is vital to national security. In addition to military matters, the privilege has been extended to intelligence-gathering methods or capabilities and sensitive information concerning diplomatic relations with foreign governments. The courts have declined, however, to extend the privilege to matters that are not related to the national defense or international relations.

The Supreme Court has ruled that the government as holder of the privilege must assert it. The government may assert the privilege in actions to which it is not a party. Generally, private parties cannot claim the privilege. When a claim of state secrets privilege would be appropriate but is not made due to oversight or lack of knowledge, the court should assure that notice is given to the appropriate government officer.

The Court has also held that the privilege cannot be waived by a private party. However, when the government is prosecuting a criminal case, it may be forced to forego the privilege for documents essential to the litigation. The fact that similar information has been disclosed earlier does not constitute waiver or prevent the government from claiming the privilege in a later case. However, if the prior disclosure of confidential information revealed the same specific information, then the privilege is waived.

Congress has enacted two statutes that interact with and mirror the state secrets privilege: the national security exemption in the Freedom of Information Act (FOIA)[1] and the Classified Information Procedures Act (CIPA).[2]

Although the national security exemption of FOIA is similar to the state secrets privilege, it neither expands nor contracts existing privileges, nor does it create any new privileges. Some other differences exist between the privilege and the FOIA exemptions.

Similarly, CIPA does not create a new evidentiary rule. It recognizes a power in the executive branch to determine that public disclosure of classified information shall not be made in a criminal trial and outlines procedures to protect against the threat of disclo-sure or the unnecessary disclosure of classified information. CIPA procedures are intended to address situations where a criminal defendant is already in possession of classified informa-tion; it does not provide for discovery of classi-fied information. CIPA applies to classified testimony as well as classified documents. It requires a criminal defendant to give particu-larized notice of an intention to reveal classi-fied information as part of the defense. Upon receiving such notice, the government can seek a ruling that some or all of the information is immaterial, move for substitution of a non-sensitive summary for the information, or ad-mit the facts sought to be proven and thereby eliminate the need for disclosure. Where a determination of privilege prevents the defen-dant from disclosing classified information, the court may dismiss charges or provide the de-fendant appropriate lesser relief.

Wigmore seems to regard it as doubtful whether the denial of disclosure should go further than this, but some state statutes occa-sionally describe the privilege in broader terms, and the English decisions seem to have accepted the wide generalization that official documents and facts will be privileged whenev-er their disclosure would be injurious to the public interest. Whether this wider principle is justified in point of policy is open to serious question.

§ 108. Qualified Privileges for Government Information: The Constitutional Presidential Privilege; Common Law Privileges for Agency Deliberations and Law Enforcement Files

The case of United States v. Nixon[1] brought into sharp focus both the limits of the long-standing executive privilege protecting diplomatic and military secrets and the distin-guishable question as to whether some broader privilege protects confidential communications

---

§ 107

1. 5 U.S.C. § 552(b)(1). See generally U.S. Dep't of Justice, Justice Dep't Guide to the Freedom of Informa-tion <http://www.usdoj.gov/oip/foi-act.htm>.

2. 18 U.S.C. App. 3.

§ 108

1. 418 U.S. 683 (1974).

between the President and his immediate advisors. In *Nixon*, the Supreme Court recognized a constitutionally based privilege of this nature but held it to be qualified and subject to invasion upon a showing of demonstrable need for evidence relevant to a criminal proceeding. The presidential privilege has occasioned considerable discussion by constitutional scholars, and although of great importance when invoked, it is only occasionally encountered.

Of much greater everyday significance is the enormous quantity of information produced, collected, and compiled by the governmental agencies. Only an extremely small percentage of this governmental information will fall within the previously discussed privilege protecting military and diplomatic secrets. What then of the vast remainder?

Although not within any well-defined evidentiary privilege, securing information from this great store of information was often extremely difficult or impossible. Before it was amended in 1958, the Federal Housekeeping Act was assumed by administrators to authorize the issuance of regulations requiring governmental personnel in the actual possession of governmental documents and records to decline to produce them even when served with a subpoena issued by a court. These regulations were consistently upheld by the Supreme Court, and although the cases never went so far as to hold that the Act created a statutory privilege, the practical effect was that private litigants were unable to obtain the information. The 1958 amendment to the Act included a provision removing any possible implication that it was intended to create a statutory privilege, and this intent has been followed in subsequent court decisions.

Access to governmental information was even more substantially increased with the enactment by Congress[2] and many state legislatures of freedom of information legislation. While these statutes are directed toward availability of information for the public in general and the news media in particular, they have importance in clearing the way for discovery in

litigation. To proceed under the federal Freedom of Information Act, no standing or particularized need for the desired information need be shown, and any person is eligible to proceed under the provisions of the statute. For present purposes, however, the important question is the extent to which FOIA affects the question of evidentiary privilege for governmental information.

At the time of the enactment of the original federal FOIA in 1966, there was clearly some protection extended by the courts to sensitive government information which did not constitute a military or diplomatic secret. Thus, a qualified common law privilege protected some aspects of government agency policy deliberations, and another, less clearly defined privilege shielded agency investigative files. In enacting FOIA, Congress recognized the desirability of maintaining some degree of confidentiality in these areas and included them within the exemption provisions of the act.

FOIA itself does not address the question of evidentiary admissibility, and thus cannot be said to be a statutory enactment of the privileges in question. At the same time, it is obvious that the two are critically interrelated and that the exemption provisions mark the outermost limits of the privileges. It would be anomalous in the extreme to deny evidentiary admission on grounds of confidentiality to material available on request to even the casually interested. A moment's reflection, however, will suggest that the converse does not hold, and that the evidentiary privileges might meaningfully and reasonably be viewed as protecting *less* than the total sum of information denied the general public under the FOIA exceptions. Such a differentiation is justifiable on the ground that the litigant's interest in access to evidence will sometimes be stronger than the ordinary citizen's interest in obtaining information. Accordingly, not all information exempt from disclosure under the FOIA exceptions will necessarily be protected by privilege if sought by discovery processes for purposes of litigation. As the foregoing synop-

---

2. 5 U.S.C.A. § 552.

sis suggests, the numerous decisions construing FOIA's exception provisions will be of varying precedential value concerning the scope of the privileges discussed below.

(a) The Deliberative Process Privilege.

This privilege protects communications made between governmental personnel, or between governmental personnel and outside consultants, which consist of advisory opinions and recommendations preliminary to the formulation of agency policy. Like other communications privileges, that protecting governmental agency deliberations seeks to encourage a free flow of communication in the interest of some larger end—here, establishing agency policy only after consideration of the full array of contrasting views on the subject. As with other privileges, the assumption is that total candor will be enhanced, and the quality of governmental decision-making correspondingly improved, by an assurance of at least qualified confidentiality. Also, this privilege is justified by its avoidance of premature and potentially misleading public disclosure of possible agency action and by helping to assure that governmental decision-makers will be judged solely upon the quality of their decisions without regard to the quality of other options considered and discarded.

To come within the rationale of the privilege, the matter sought to be kept confidential must have been communicated prior to finalization of the policy and must have constituted opinion or evaluation as opposed to the mere reporting of objective facts. However, factual information that reflects or reveals the deliberative processes of the agency is protected by the privilege. Whether the communication reflected the view that ultimately became embodied in agency policy, or even whether the communication was considered or totally ignored by the decision-maker is immaterial. Also, the government is not required to identify a particular decision to which the communication contributed as long as the deliberative process involved and the role played by the communication are identified. The privilege is that of the government and apparently may be claimed indefinitely. It is not terminated by

the adoption of the policy concerned and likely not by the death of the author of the privileged matter. As further discussed below, the privilege is not absolute and is therefore subject to invasion upon a sufficient showing of necessity. The privilege also does not protect communications which demonstrate government misconduct or which are themselves the subject of litigation.

The question of privilege for government agency deliberations has arisen relatively infrequently in the context of state government. Many of the states enacting FOIA statutes have included exemption provisions protecting policy development materials from mandatory disclosure. Where the question of a true evidentiary privilege has arisen, i.e., where the material is sought for introduction into evidence rather than simply as information, a majority of the cases have upheld the existence of a qualified privilege on the federal model. The root of the privilege on the state level has almost invariably been said to be the doctrine of separation of powers.

(b) The Privilege for Information and Files Relating to Law Enforcement.

Prior to the enactment of the federal FOIA and its state counterparts, a privilege protecting the investigative results of government agencies appears to have been sporadically recognized but ill-defined, frequently being treated as an aspect of a more comprehensive but amorphous privilege for "government information." Clearly, however, disclosure of the files of law enforcement agencies may seriously hamper enforcement efforts by discouraging or compromising confidential informants; disclosing the existence, targets, or methods of investigation; endangering witnesses or law enforcement personnel; or undermining a criminal prosecution or civil enforcement proceeding by revealing the nature of the case in preparation. Congress recognized the legitimacy of these concerns in the enactment of a highly specific exemption to FOIA, which in the most recent iteration of the statute expands its protection to "records or information compiled for law enforcement purposes."[3] Today the exemption and the privilege, at least in federal law, seem inextricably intertwined, leaving no practical reason for distinguishing between them.

To come within the ambit of the privilege, the materials must have been compiled for law enforcement purposes and the agency must demonstrate that disclosure would have one of the six specified results in FOIA Exemption 7. The privilege is a qualified one and, as with other qualified governmental privileges, may be overcome through a showing of sufficient need. Though it has been said that the privilege, unlike that for agency policy deliberations, expires with the governmental undertaking to which the privileged matter relates, this seems an overly broad generalization. However, the protection will not attach absent an initial government demonstration that production "could reasonably be expected to" bring about one or more of the harms specified by the statute.

With regard to state law in this area, some states expressly confer privilege upon law enforcement records. Others have "classical" official information statutes, which cover at least some of such records under the rubric of communications made by or to a public officer in official confidence when the public interest would suffer from disclosure. Where, however, a state FOIA is in effect, courts appear to accord it primacy in determining the maximum sweep of this privilege.

§ 109. Effect of the Presence of the Government as a Litigant

To the extent that the Freedom of Information Act is available as a means for obtaining government records and information for use in evidence, as discussed in the preceding section, no distinction is made between situations where the litigation is between parties other than the government and those where the government is a party. However, when procedures other than under the Act are used, the difference may be substantial.

When the government is not a party and successfully resists disclosure sought by a par-

ty, the result is generally that the evidence is unavailable, as though a witness had died, and the case will proceed accordingly, with no consequences save those resulting from the loss of the evidence. This approach to dealing with the impact of governmental privilege upon litigation between third parties causes no insuperable difficulties where the privilege is a conditional one and a balancing of interests has be made, or where an absolute privilege is involved and the privileged matter does not bear critically on the central issues of the case. The approach may be inappropriate, however, where the invocation of the absolute privilege, such as for military secrets, makes impossible any approximation of a full presentation of the issues. Whether dismissal of the case is warranted where the sovereign has rendered its courts incapable of fairly trying the issues, dismissal has been granted at the behest of the government where continued litigation by adversary means threatens partial or indirect exposure of the protected secret.

The presence of the government in court as a litigant, whether as the moving party in a civil or criminal proceeding or by virtue of consenting to be sued as a defendant, raises the possibility that an exercise of privilege may be handled by ordinary judicial enforcement measures. Accordingly, in a criminal prosecution, the court may give the government the choice of disclosing matters of significance to the defense or having the case dismissed.

As the plaintiff in a civil action, the government is subject to the ordinary rules of discovery, and may face dismissal of its action if through the invocation of privilege it deprives the defendant of evidence useful to the defense. There would, however, seem to be no reason why the government, as distinguished from other litigants, should necessarily face dismissal for failure to provide discovery under all circumstances. Only where the governmental claim of privilege shields evidence of such importance as to deny the defendant due process should dismissal automatically result.

Where the government is defendant, as under the Tort Claims Act, an adverse finding

---

3.   5 U.S.C.A. § 552(b)(7).

cannot be rendered against it as the price of asserting an evidentiary privilege. This is not one of the terms upon which Congress has consented that the United States be subjected to liability. Accordingly, where the plaintiff's action cannot be proved without disclosure of the privileged matter, the plaintiff will remain remediless, although in light of the extreme nature of this result some courts seek ways to avoid it.

§ 110. The Scope of the Judge's Function in Determining the Validity of the Claim of Privilege

When the head of department has made a claim of privilege for documents or information under his control as being military or diplomatic secrets is this claim conclusive upon the judge? United States v. Reynolds,[1] which remains the Supreme Court's most comprehensive ruling on the privilege, has been extensively mined for the answer to this question. The generally accepted conclusions are that, while the judiciary is not to defer totally to the "caprice" of the executive, the judicial role is a limited one, focused largely upon the process of claiming the privilege rather than upon the merits of its invocation. Thus, the privilege must be asserted through a formal claim by the head of the executive department having charge of the material, and the statement of this official must indicate personal consideration of the claim, the identity (so far as possible) of the privileged material, and the reasons supporting the claim. In some instances, no more will be necessary in order to enable the court to rule in favor of the claim, but it is not unusual for the government to further support its claim with an affidavit, and perhaps other matter, to be reviewed in the absence of opposing counsel.

Whatever material is considered by the court, the standard applied is whether there exists a reasonable danger that disclosure will damage national security. If this danger is found, the privilege is absolute and is not affected by the extent of the litigant's need for the confidential information. That need is con-

sidered only when determining how deeply the court will probe to satisfy itself that a privilege claim is justified. Any relevant non-confidential information should be disentangled from other classified information when possible. However, if the information forms a mosaic and disclosure of an apparently innocuous part could lead to the disclosure of classified information, disentangling is not required.

Once outside the restricted area of military and diplomatic secrets, however, a greater role for the judiciary in the determination of governmental claims of privilege becomes not only desirable but necessary. The head of an executive department can appraise the public interest of secrecy as well (or perhaps better) than the judge, but predictably the official's position will tend to minimize the individual's interest. Under the normal routine, the question will come to chief administrators with recommendations from cautious subordinates against disclosure, and in the press of business, they are likely to approve the recommendations about apparently minor matters without much independent consideration. The determination of questions of fact and the applications of legal standards in passing upon the admissibility of evidence and the validity of claims of privilege are traditionally the trial judge's responsibility. As a public official, the judge should have respect for the executive's concern about disclosure, but, at the same time, judicial duties require an appraisal of private interests that must be reconciled with conflicting public policies. A judge may thus be better qualified than the executive to weigh both interests and to strike a proper balance.

The foregoing considerations largely explain why privileges running in favor of government, other than that for military and diplomatic secrets, are uniformly held to be qualified. Thus, where these privileges are claimed, the judge must determine whether the interest in governmental secrecy is outweighed in the particular case by the litigant's interest in obtaining the evidence. Striking a satisfactory balance will, on the

§ 110
1. 345 U.S. 1 (1953).

one hand, require consideration of the interests giving rise to the privilege and an assessment of the extent to which disclosure will realistically impair those interests. On the other hand, factors which will affect the litigant's need include the significance of the evidence sought for the case, the availability of the desired information from other sources, and the nature of the right being asserted in the litigation. Here, as with other qualified privileges, in camera inspection by the court offers a practical way for testing the claim of privilege without destroying irretrievably the secrecy which the privilege is designed to preserve.

§ 111. The Privilege Against the Disclosure of the Identity of an Informer

For entirely understandable reasons, informers fear disclosure, and if their names were subject to being readily revealed, this important aid to law enforcement would be seriously compromised. On this ground of policy, a privilege is recognized for disclosure of the identity of an informer who has given information about suspected crimes to a prosecuting or investigating officer or to another person to be relayed to such an officer. The privilege runs to the government and may be invoked by its officers who, as witnesses or otherwise, are asked for the information. According to some authority, the privilege also may be asserted by the alleged informer. In some jurisdictions when neither the government nor the informer is represented at the trial, the judge may invoke it for the absent holder, as in other cases of privilege.[1] Whether the privilege is confined to disclosure of identity or extends also to the contents of the communication is in dispute. The policy of the privilege does not appear to require shielding the communication from disclosure, but shielding the contents is required if revealing those contents would likely identify the informer, which is often the case.

The privilege has two important qualifications. The first is that when the identity has already become known to "those who would have cause to resent the communication," the privilege ceases.[2] The second is that when the privilege is asserted by the state in a criminal prosecution, and the evidence of the identity of the informer becomes important to the establishment of the defense, the court will require the disclosure, and if it is still withheld, that the prosecution be dismissed. While the inherent fairness of this second exception is apparent, its implementation is challenging if the privilege is not to be rendered meaningless by automatic defense allegations of the informer's potential value as a witness. To avoid this result, an in camera hearing is widely used, and sometimes required, to determine the nature of the informer's probable testimony. With or without an in camera hearing, the trial court's task is to assess the balance between the value of that testimony to the defense and the significance of the considerations underlying the privilege in the particular case. A variant of the second situation occurs when a search or seizure is challenged under the Fourth Amendment and the statement of an informant is essential to probable cause. Although resting less clearly on constitutional grounds, courts frequently employ in camera hearings when they determine that in order to decide probable cause they must resolve questions concerning the informer's existence or nature of the information actually provided by the informer. In recent years, courts have recognized a privilege analogous to the informer's privilege that protects the confidentiality of police surveillance locations so that private citizens permitting the police to use their property will not be subject to retaliation.

§ 112. Statutory Privileges for Certain Reports of Individuals to Government Agencies: Accident Reports, Tax Returns, etc.

A somewhat similar policy to that supporting the privilege for the identity of informers applies to reports that individuals are required by law to make to government agencies for the

§ 111
1. See § 73.1 supra.

2. Roviaro v. United States, 353 U.S. 53, 60 (1957).

administration of their public functions. If such statements are admissible against those reporting the information, full and true reporting may be discouraged. On the other hand, these reports often deal with facts highly material in litigation, and an early report to government may be reliable and important to ascertain the facts. The latter interest has generally prevailed with the courts, and in the absence of statutory authority, such reports are not privileged. However, policy arguments that a privilege is needed to encourage frank and full reporting have frequently prevailed with legislatures, and statutory privileges for reports of highway and industrial accidents; tax returns; selective service reports; social security, health, unemployment compensation, and census data; and bank records are common. Whether such privileges are absolute or qualified depends largely on the individual statute, but courts have construed many statutes as granting only a qualified privilege that may be overcome in appropriate circumstances. The privilege is held either by the reporter, the government, or both.

The soundness of a policy extending greater protection to these reports than is required by constitutional guarantees is dubious, and in some instances seems to imply a greater need for accuracy in governmental statistic gathering than in judicial fact-finding. But where the policy has been adopted by statute, any lack of wisdom does not justify judicial incursions against the protection afforded. While federal courts are not obliged to honor privileges created by state statute or court rule, they have occasionally done so, applying a variety of balancing tests to determine whether to honor the privilege.

§ 113. The Secrecy of Grand Jury Proceedings—(a) Votes and Expressions of Grand Jurors; (b) Testimony of Witnesses

The taking of evidence by grand jurors and their deliberations have traditionally been shrouded in secrecy. The ancient oath administered to the grand jurors bound them to keep secret "the King's counsel, your fellows' and your own."

Several objectives are commonly suggested as being promoted by the policy of secrecy: to guard the independence of action and freedom of deliberation of the accusatory body, to protect the reputations of those investigated but not indicted, to prevent the forewarning and flight of those accused before publication of the indictment, and to encourage free disclosure by witnesses. The procedure for attaining them assumes two forms, somewhat loosely described as "privilege." The first is a privilege against disclosure of the grand jurors' communications to each other during their deliberations and of their individual votes. The propriety of such a measure as an assurance of free and independent deliberation can scarcely be doubted, though it may be of slight practical importance in view of the infrequency with which these communications and votes will be relevant to any material inquiry. The second of these privileges involves disclosure of the testimony given by witnesses before the grand jury, and as an area of substantial controversy, deserves thoughtful scrutiny.

While the grand jury in its origins may have been an instrument of, and subservient to, the crown, its position as an important bulwark of the rights of English citizens was established by the end of the 17th century. This latter aspect is evident in the provision of the Fifth Amendment of the Constitution of the United States requiring presentment or indictment as a precondition of prosecution for a capital or infamous crime. During this period, the grand jury's independence from incursion by both prosecution and defense appears to have been well recognized, and prosecutors were admitted only by sufferance. However, the decline in the perceived need for the grand jury as a protector of individual liberties, which caused its abolition in England, seems in this country to have led to predominant emphasis on aiding the prosecution in investigating crime and serving as a powerful instrument of discovery. Thus, we find statutes and rules providing for the presence of prosecuting attorneys and stenographers except when the grand jury is deliberating or voting.

The veil of secrecy surrounding grand jury proceedings does not preclude all subsequent disclosure and use of the testimony and other material presented there. In the federal system, prosecutors have long had the use of grand jury material in criminal prosecutions stemming from the grand jury's investigations. Such use is perfectly consistent both with the practical operation of the grand jury and with the central purpose of that body which justifies its broad investigatory powers. However, government use of grand jury material for purposes other than criminal prosecution, such as in a regulatory proceeding dealing with the same facts, would generally be an abuse of the grand jury system and the federal statutory provisions.

Several decisions of the Supreme Court have examined the statutory provisions and imposed limitations on access to grand jury materials by government agencies. In the first of these decisions, United States v. Sells Engineering, Inc.,[1] the Court held that government attorneys, other than those working on the criminal matters before the grand jury, are not automatically entitled to access to grand jury materials without a court order, and further that to obtain such an order, not only must the requirements of the statute be met, but also a "particularized need" for the material must be shown. In United States v. Baggot,[2] the Court held that the Internal Revenue Service was not entitled to court ordered access to grand jury materials in connection with a civil tax investigation because such an investigation is not "preliminary to or in connection with a judicial proceeding" as required by the rule. Finally, in United States v. John Doe, Inc. I,[3] the Court qualified somewhat the impact of *Sells*. First, it allowed the attorney who conducted the grand jury investigation to continue using of grand jury materials in civil proceedings related to the investigation. Second, although continuing to recognize that "particularized need" must be shown before disclosure to other government attorneys, the Court noted that the policy concerns supporting grand jury secrecy were "implicated to a much

lesser extent" when disclosure involved other government attorneys.

In the federal system, both government agencies and private parties must show a "particularized need" for grand jury material before it is to be released. This requirement, though sometimes criticized by commentators, has consistently been reasserted by the Supreme Court. Clearly, federal grand jury secrecy will enjoy substantial protection for the foreseeable future.

Among others having a potential need for access to transcripts of testimony before a grand jury, perhaps the strongest case may be made for the criminal defendant. The right of an accused to a copy of his or her own recorded grand jury testimony is today recognized by statute or rule in a number of states and in the federal courts. Considerations of basic fairness (and the inapplicability of the justifications for grand jury secrecy in this context) argue strongly for this access. The defense is guaranteed access to the testimony of other grand jury witnesses who testify at trial by the Jencks Act,[4] which requires production of such testimony once they have testified on direct. No infringement of the objectives of secrecy mentioned at the beginning of this section can result from such disclosure, which constitutes the least acceptable minimum.

Despite the stringent language of the federal rule imposing secrecy on grand jury proceedings, witnesses are pointedly omitted from the list of those bound by its provisions. Whether a federal judge has authority to order grand jury witnesses not to disclose their own testimony in order to protect the integrity of an investigation is unclear. Absent such atypical orders, witnesses are free to divulge their testimony as they see fit after testifying. Indeed, the Supreme Court held that a state statute prohibiting a grand jury witness from ever disclosing testimony before the grand jury violated the First Amendment as applied to a witness who wished to disclose information independently acquired by him to which he

1. 463 U.S. 418 (1983).

2. 463 U.S. 476 (1983).

3. 481 U.S. 102 (1987).

4. 18 U.S.C.A. § 3500; Fed.R.Crim.P. 26.2.

had testified.[5] On the other hand, some authorities suggest that witnesses may not be compelled to disclose what their testimony was before the grand jury.

5.   Butterworth v. Smith, 494 U.S. 624 (1990).

*

Title 6

PRIVILEGE: CONSTITUTIONAL

Chapter 13

THE PRIVILEGE AGAINST
SELF–INCRIMINATION

Table of Sections

§ 114. The History and Development of the Privilege

Because of considerable dispute as to the wisdom of the privilege against self-incrimination, the origin and development of the rule have been of special interest to legal scholars. Unfortunately important aspects of the matter are still clouded with doubt. What is known suggests that the privilege had its roots in opposition to the use of the *ex officio* oath by the English ecclesiastical courts and that its development was intimately intertwined with the political and religious disputes of early England. The most significant ambiguity is whether the privilege as finally applied in the common law courts after 1700 represented a logical extension of principle underlying earlier opposition to the procedures of ecclesiastical courts, or rather, whether it represented condemnation by association of a procedure not inherently inconsistent with prevailing values.

Prior to the early 1200s, trials in the ecclesiastical courts had been by ordeal or compurgation oath, the formal swearing by the party and his oath helpers. Under the "inquisitorial oath," there was active interrogation of the accused by the judge in addition to the accused's uncomfortable consciousness of his oath to reveal the entire truth of the matter under inquiry. There was some formal limitation upon the power of the ecclesiastical courts to use this device.

The oath procedure was subsequently adopted by two controversial courts and used for essentially political purposes. In 1487 the Court of the Star Chamber was authorized to pursue its broad political mandate by means of the oath. The Star Chamber was not even subjected to the requirement of presentation that theoretically provided protection from use of the oath to engage in broad "fishing inquisitions" by the ecclesiastical courts. About one hundred years later the same procedure was authorized for the Court of the High Commission in Causes Ecclesiastical, established to maintain conformity to the recently estab-lished church. The freewheeling methods of these politically-minded courts, including the use of torture, undoubtedly stimulated a great deal of additional opposition to the oath procedures.

Required self-incrimination and the use of the oath were not confined to the ecclesiastical courts and the courts of High Commission and Star Chamber. In criminal trials the accused was expected to take an active part in the proceedings, often to his own detriment. He was examined before trial by justices of the peace, and the results of this examination were preserved for use by the judge at trial. Only in limited classes of cases was the examination under oath. This was not out of tenderness for the accused, but rather because it was believed that administering an oath would unwisely permit the accused to place before the jury an influential denial of guilt made under oath.

After 1641, the common law courts began to apply to their own procedure some of the restrictions on use of the oath that had been urged for their ecclesiastical counterparts. By 1700, extraction of an answer in any procedure in matters of criminality or forfeiture was improper. This was the privilege against compelled self-incrimination.

It is difficult to draw many helpful conclusions from the historical origin of the privilege. Wigmore accepts Bentham's suggestion that the privilege as ultimately applied in the common law courts was essentially an overreaction to abusive use of the oath procedure without proper presentment of charges.[1] But perhaps this is too narrow a reading of the historical material. Even if the initial objection was only to the impropriety of putting individuals to their oath without presentation, this policy suggests at least limited objection to the use of information extracted from the mouth of the accused as the basis for a criminal prosecution. This early suspicion of compulsory self-incrim-

§ 114

1. 8 Wigmore, Evidence § 2250 (McNaughten rev. 1961), p. 292.

ination, even if it extended only to situations where compulsion was exerted before an accusation had been made by some other method, seems to be based upon a perception that compelling an individual to provide the basis for his own penal liability should be limited because the position in which it places the individual, making a choice between violating a solemn oath and incurring penal liability, weighs against important policies of individual freedom and dignity.

There is significant disagreement regarding the early development of the privilege in America. Some evidence of the privilege in early colonial America exists. In any case, it was inserted in the constitutions or bills of rights of seven American states before 1789, and has since spread to all state constitutions except those of Iowa and New Jersey. In both of the latter states, however, it was accepted as a matter of nonconstitutional law.

§ 115.　Policy　Foundations　of　the Modern Privilege

Inquiry into the policies that do or might support the privilege often seems a frustrating and perhaps fruitless task. Despite the privilege's rich history, vigorous arguments have been made that the dangers of the Court of Star Chamber no longer exist and that the privilege has outlived its rationale. Even proponents of the privilege acknowledge that its popularity and acceptance was not based upon a careful scrutiny of its rationale and that its incorporation into our legal tradition occurred without thorough examination. Modern discussion has tended to undertake largely de novo development of justifications.

Whether a conceptually adequate justification exists may have little significance to the basic questions under modern law. Stuntz notes that judicial and academic writings tend to be dominated by standard explanations for the privilege that fail to explain adequately even the basic aspects of Fifth Amendment privilege law, "leading to a widespread sense that many of [the Fifth Amendment privi-

lege's] rules and limitations are simply inexplicable."[1]

Critics of the privilege, of course, stress that the privilege may lack a satisfactory and principled basis. In addition, they urge that the privilege involves disruptive difficulties of application and excessive costs. First, the privilege deprives the state of access to a valuable source of reliable information, the subject of the investigation himself, and therefore purchases whatever values it attains at too great a cost to the inquiry for truth. The subject may be an especially valuable source of information when the alleged crime is one of the sophisticated "white collar" offenses, and in such situations the privilege may deny the prosecution access to the *only* available information. Moreover, the privilege may as a practical matter be impossible to implement effectively. Although the law may extend the theoretical right to remain silent at no or minimal cost, in fact it is inevitable that inferences will be drawn from silence and that the inferences will be acted upon. Since these inferences are drawn from inherently ambiguous silence, they are less reliable than inferences from other sources, including compelled self-incriminatory testimony. The result is that one who chooses to invoke the privilege is not protected, but rather is subjected to potential prejudice in a manner ill designed to promote even his own best interest.

Rationales for the privilege can usefully be divided into systemic ones, based on the role of the privilege in maintaining a valuable criminal justice system, and individual ones, resting on the value of the privilege in implementing the interests or values of those suspected or accused of crime. These rationales may overlap, as is demonstrated by the argument that the privilege serves as a valuable means of preventing the conviction of innocent criminal defendants.

One who is under the strain of actual or potential accusation, although innocent, may be unduly prejudiced by his own testimony for reasons unrelated to its accuracy. For example,

§ 115

1.　Stuntz, Self-Incrimination and Excuse, 88 Colum.L.Rev. 1227, 1228 (1998).

he may have physical traits or mannerisms that would cause an adverse reaction from the trier of fact. He might, under the strain of interrogation, become confused and thereby give an erroneous impression of guilt. Or, his act of testifying may permit the prosecution to introduce his prior criminal convictions, ostensibly for impeachment purposes, and the trier of fact may uncritically infer his guilt from these. The privilege affords such an individual the opportunity to avoid these dangers possibly flowing from discussing an incriminating situation and thereby creating an unreliable but prejudicial impression of guilt.

Whether these considerations support the privilege is at best problematic. Few defendants may give misleading impressions of guilt, and juries may be more skilled at evaluating evidence than is sometimes believed. Even when there is a significant risk that testifying will create an erroneous impression of guilt, practical considerations are likely to lead many defendants to testify nevertheless. To the extent that these risks are real ones, other reforms in criminal procedure might better protect against them; the admissibility of prior convictions to impeach, for example, might be limited.

The privilege may also protect the innocent in less direct ways. It constitutes one part, but an important part, of our accusatorial system which requires that no criminal punishment be imposed unless guilt is established by a large quantum of especially reliable evidence. By denying the prosecution access to what is regarded as an inherently suspect type of proof, the self-incriminating admissions of the accused, the privilege forces the prosecution to establish its case on the basis of more reliable evidence. This arguably creates an additional assurance that every person convicted is in fact guilty as charged. Others, however, argue that the privilege is an ineffective means of encouraging the making of the guilt-innocence decision on reliable evidence. In many situations, for example, it denies defendants the right to call witnesses whose testimony might well be reliable and exculpatory.

Other systemic arguments run that the privilege serves to deny governments powers that might otherwise be abused, particularly in especially sensitive areas. It may also serve to maintain public confidence in the legal system by preventing the degeneration of trials into spectacles that many would find offensive. Of course, the privilege may in fact do neither. Public confidence in the legal system, to the contrary, may even be reduced when courts are compelled to eschew what appears to be the most reliable sources of information. To the extent that the privilege does accomplish these purposes, it may do so inefficiently, as by failing to identify and restrain those governmental powers most offensive and likely to be abused or those aspects of criminal procedure most offensive to the population in general.

Recent defenses of the privilege have tended to rely less upon systemic rationales than upon individual ones. These arguments, which again somewhat overlap, suggest that the privilege prevents the treatment of suspects and defendants in ways that would be offensive to notions of "privacy" or "individual autonomy." As the privilege applies to out-of-court law enforcement interrogation, for example, it may serve to prohibit interrogation techniques that, given the public's increased sensitivities, may now be as offensive as physical torture was at an earlier time in the privilege's development.

As applied in either the in-court or out-of-court situations, the privilege may prevent the treatment of suspects and accuseds in ways that are unacceptably "cruel." Intolerable cruelty may arise simply from compelling the accused to participate in the process itself. Or, the privilege may prevent the treatment of such persons in ways unacceptable because such treatment is inconsistent with developed notions of human dignity. Even a guilty person, for example, may be regarded as retaining aspects of dignity that are violated when that person is compelled to actively participate in the process of bringing punitive sanctions down upon him.

Gerstein[2] has developed a somewhat similar argument based on privacy concerns: Most

---

2. Gerstein, Privacy and Self-Incrimination, 80 Ethics 87, 87 (1970).

persons apprehended for a crime which they have committed regard themselves as a part of the same moral community as those who are the victims of criminal offenses. They regard the commission of an offense as a moral as well as a legal matter. For such persons, a confession involves not simply submission to legal liability but the acknowledgement of moral wrongdoing and often the revelation of remorse. A person's judgment of his own moral blameworthiness is special and perhaps unique and thus peculiarly private. This sort of "information," self-acknowledgment of moral blameworthiness, is so "private" that the individual ought to have full control over it. Even if the courts are empowered to convict an accused of a crime, they should not be empowered to force him to publicly make the judgment by which he condemns himself in his own conscience. He ought to be able to decide whether to share this only with his God or those to whom he feels bound by trust and affection.

A related argument runs that compelling even a guilty person to choose among incriminating himself, committing perjury, or suffering penalties such as contempt citation requires such a difficult or offensive choice that the privilege is justified by the need to prevent that choice. Exactly why the choice presented by this "cruel trilemma" is so offensive is not entirely clear. Perhaps it is because a person's natural instincts and personal interests so strongly suggest that he should lie in an effort to avoid criminal liability that it is somehow unfair to punish him for following those instincts. If no reasonable person could be expected to do other than what the witness did, fairness seems offended by punishing him. Perhaps the choice is offensive simply because the state is forcing the person to act. In many cases, Judge Frank argued, "the state would be forcing him to commit a crime and then punishing him for it." Yet the law often puts witnesses and others to choices that seem no less difficult or "unfair," and to single out a group of persons for solicitude, most of whom find themselves in their position because of their own criminal acts, may be inappropriate.

Stuntz[3] argues that other efforts to explain the privilege unsatisfactorily assume that the activity protected is in some sense "justified." He suggests that a more satisfactory explanation rests on quite different excuse grounds. Were the privilege not recognized, our legal system would be compelled to make available an excuse defense to those defendants who, when called as prosecution witnesses, perjured themselves rather than admit guilt. But such a defense would invoke quite heavy systemic costs. By removing the deterrents to perjury, for example, the defense would lead to a flood of perjurious testimony impairing juries' ability to accurately resolve cases. Recognizing the privilege avoids the need to pay those costs.

The Fifth Amendment and other versions of the privilege can only be regarded as supported by varying combinations of the considerations discussed above. Particular requirements imposed by them often must rest upon combinations of some but less than all of the considerations. The core situation covered by all versions of the privilege, direct trial examination of the sworn defendant under threat of contempt citations as to whether he committed the crime charged, implicates all of these considerations to a singularly significant degree. Whether or not other situations come within the privilege, however, must depend upon what considerations are implicated, the comparative weight given those considerations, and the degree to which they are implicated. The variety of purposes and rationales that can be called into play and the absence of historical or other guidelines for applying those purposes and rationales, however, means that courts have extraordinary flexibility in constructing policy analyses with which to address particular issues presented by the privilege in its various forms.

§ 116. Current Status of the Privilege

The Fifth Amendment privilege is, of course, applicable to the states by virtue of the

---

3. Stuntz, supra note 1.

Fourteenth Amendment. So holding in Malloy v. Hogan,[1] decided in 1964, the Supreme Court relied heavily upon the basic proposition that "the American system of criminal prosecution is accusatorial, not inquisitorial." "[T]he Fifth Amendment privilege," the Court continued, "is its essential mainstay. * * * Governments, state and federal, are thus constitutionally compelled to establish guilt by evidence independently and freely secured, and may not by coercion prove a charge against an accused out of his own mouth."

Malloy also rejected as "incongruous" the contention that the availability of the federal privilege to a witness in a state proceeding should be determined according to a less stringent standard than is applicable in a federal proceeding. "[T]he same standards," it concluded, "must determine whether an accused's silence in either a federal or state proceeding is justified."

Much recent self-incrimination discussion has focused upon the Supreme Court's construction of the Fifth Amendment's privilege. In some senses, this is unfortunate. Similar privileges are recognized in all states as a matter of either or both state constitutional provision or case law, and versions of the privilege are sometimes embodied in statutory provisions or court rule. Commentators and courts have increasingly recognized state courts' right and perhaps duty to construe state constitutional and statutory provisions "independently" of the Supreme Court's construction of even identically-phrased federal constitutional provisions. This jurisprudence of "new federalism" emphasizes that there is no single privilege against compelled self-incrimination. Specifically, discussion of legal protection against compelled self-incrimination must recognize the possibility that state law provides citizens with greater protection than does the Fifth Amendment privilege.

State privileges sometimes differ in phraseology from the Fifth Amendment. Seldom, however, do these differences in termi-

nology strongly suggest how current questions of construction should be resolved. The Fifth Amendment provides that no person is to be "compelled in any criminal case to be a witness against himself." State constitutional provisions, in contrast, sometimes specify that no person may be "compelled to give evidence against himself." While this suggests the possibility that the protection afforded by the state provisions is broader, it is difficult to regard the difference in language as necessarily controlling.

§ 117. Policy Foundation of the Privilege under Federal Constitutional and State Law

In Murphy v. Waterfront Comm'n of N.Y. Harbor,[1] the Supreme Court's expansive discussion suggested that the Court regarded a broad and flexible array of policy considerations as both supporting the federal constitutional privilege and as relevant to its content:

[The privilege] reflects many of our fundamental values and most noble aspirations: our unwillingness to subject those suspected of crime to the cruel trilemma of self-accusation, perjury or contempt; our preference for an accusatorial rather than an inquisitorial system of criminal justice; our fear that self-incriminating statements will be elicited by inhumane treatment and abuses; our sense of fair play which dictates a fair state-individual balance by requiring the government to leave the individual alone until good cause is shown for disturbing him and by requiring the government in its contest with the individual to shoulder the entire load; our respect for the inviolability of the human personality and of the right of each individual to a private enclave where he may lead a private life, our distrust of self-deprecatory statements; and our realization that the privilege, while sometimes a shelter to the guilty, is often a protection to the innocent.[2]

---

§ 116

1. 378 U.S. 1 (1964).

§ 117

1. 378 U.S. 52 (1964).
2. Id., at 55.

In United States v. Balsys,[3] however, a majority deprecatingly characterized the *Murphy* discussion as at most a "catalog [of] aspirations furthered by the [Fifth Amendment Self–Incrimination] Clause." The values reflected in the decision, it continued, are not "reliable"—or, almost certainly in the Court's view, appropriate—"guides to the actual scope of protection under the Clause."

Most specifically, *Balsys* construed *Murphy's* discussion as asserting that the federal constitutional privilege is designed to protect, and should be construed as protecting, "personal inviolability and the privacy of a testimonial enclave." This "comparatively ambitious conceptualization of personal privacy underlying the Clause," it concluded, rested upon *Murphy's* incorrect conclusion that earlier and narrower views of the Clause as reflecting the Framers' intent to embody the English common-law privilege in the Constitution were mistaken. With regard to the specific issue raised by *Balsys* and addressed by the *Murphy* discussion,[4] *Balsys* concluded–contrary to the *Murphy* discussion–that the common-law rule, embodied in the English common-law privilege, was clear. Considerations of personal testimonial integrity or privacy, as stressed in the *Murphy* discussion, would not support "a significant change in the scope of traditional . . . [Fifth Amendment] protection" as is suggested by the common-law rule.

What, then, is the significance for Fifth Amendment purposes of the policies that support the privilege or, in *Balsys'* terms, the aspirations furthered by the federal constitutional privilege? The Supreme Court has acknowledged that "the privilege has never been given the full scope which the values it helps to protect suggest."[5] Moreover, "[t]he policies behind the privilege are varied, and not all are implicated in any given application of the privilege."[6] *Balyses* suggests that the Court regards the major consideration in defining the content of the Fifth Amendment as the Framers' apparent intent to embody in the Fifth Amendment the English common-law privilege as then understood. More "ambitious conceptualization[s]" of the policies that might be furthered by the privilege are unlikely to move the Court to particular interpretations of that privilege as broader than its English common-law predecessor. As *Balsys* itself acknowledged, the *Balyses'* discussion rejects a reading of *Murphy* that if accepted would "invest[] the Clause with a more expansive promise."

§ 118. Distinction Between The Privilege of an Accused in a Criminal Proceeding and the Privilege of a Witness

When the English common law courts began to apply the privilege in their own proceedings, it soon became clear that the privilege could be invoked not only by a defendant in a criminal prosecution but also by a witness whose conviction could not procedurally be a consequence of the proceeding. There is no historical indication that this was recognized as an important step in the growth of the privilege, and the written decisions offered no rationale.

Early state constitutional provisions as well as the Fifth Amendment language can be read as prohibiting only compulsion to cause an individual to give oral testimony in a criminal proceeding in which that person is the defendant. Several authorities have argued that this was their original meaning. Nevertheless, in 1924 the Supreme Court rejected the contention that the Fifth Amendment applied only in criminal cases:

> The privilege is not ordinarily dependent upon the nature of the proceeding in which the testimony is sought or is to be used. It applies alike to civil and criminal proceedings, wherever the answer might tend to subject to criminal responsibility him who gives it. The privilege protects a mere witness as fully as it does one who is also a party defendant.[1]

§ 118

1. McCarthy v. Arndstein, 266 U.S. 34, 40 (1924).

---

3. 524 U.S. 666, 118 S.Ct. 2218 (1998).

4. See § 122.

5. Schmerber v. California, 384 U.S. 757, 762 (1966).

6. McGautha v. California, 402 U.S. 183, 214 (1971).

Courts now universally accept that state constitutional provisions as well as the Fifth Amendment may be invoked by one whose testimony is sought in a proceeding other than a criminal prosecution in which he is the defendant.

Significantly different problems are raised when the privilege is invoked by one not a defendant in a criminal prosecution. There is, therefore, analytical value in considering separately the two aspects or "branches" of the privilege: the privilege of the accused in a criminal proceeding, and the privilege of one not an accused (usually referred to as the privilege of a witness).

A criminal accused ordinarily need not affirmatively "invoke" his privilege, as he is even entitled not to be called as a witness at all. A non-accused who appears as a witness, in contrast, will ordinarily invoke the privilege as a response to particular questions asked on direct or cross-examination.

It is, of course, important to know when a person who is the subject of an official investigation becomes an accused in a criminal proceeding and entitled to the protection that accompanies this status. The traditional view has been that an individual does not become an accused until the criminal process has been formally brought to bear upon him. Thus at such preliminary and investigatory proceedings as a grand jury investigation, a coroner's inquest, and perhaps a preliminary hearing, the suspect or subject of the proceedings has no right to refuse all cooperation in the matter.

The Supreme Court has shown no inclination to abandon this position as a matter of Fifth Amendment law. While it has not addressed the issue directly, for example, the Court has suggested that the target of a grand jury investigation has no Fifth Amendment right to refuse to appear and take the witness stand when subpoenaed. On the other hand, the essence of the Court's holding in Miranda v. Arizona[2] is that one subjected to custodial law enforcement interrogation is an accused who need not affirmatively assert the privilege

in order to have its protection. Whether a person has the protection of an accused or only that of a witness obviously depends not simply on the proximity of events to the in-court trial but upon the extent to which the situation creates a risk that affording the person only the privilege of a witness will not be effective.

The propriety of this approach depends in large part upon what functions of the privilege of an accused are emphasized. An accused is afforded extraordinary protection by the privilege partly to avoid emphasizing to the trier of fact that he is invoking the privilege. This minimizes the risk that an adverse inference will be drawn from his doing so. Of course, this rationale supports the traditional position, since until formal proceedings have been commenced and the accused is brought before the trier of fact, this risk is not presented.

On the other hand, the extraordinary protection afforded an accused probably also rests in part on a perception that the risks to the interests implicated increases as a case progresses towards a trial. The prosecution's increased focus exclusively upon the accused when formal charges have been made to some extent increases the risk of the sort of overzealous activity that endangers interests protected by the privilege. To the extent that this rationale supports distinguishing the accused from other witnesses, the traditional position appears too inflexible. The privilege, under this approach, would best require examination of procedures such as grand jury appearances to determine whether they pose sufficient risks of this sort to justify or require that suspects involved in them be treated as "accuseds" and given a right to refuse to have queries put to them.

State courts may, of course, regard these or other considerations as indicating that state privileges should confer the status of an accused in a criminal proceeding upon one who is the subject of such preliminary proceedings. The New York Court of Appeals, for example, has read that state's constitution as giving one who is the target of an investigation a right not to be examined before the investigating grand jury.

---

2.   384 U.S. 436 (1966), discussed in § 149 infra.

§ 119. Personal Nature of the Privilege

Courts frequently describe the privilege against compelled self-incrimination as being personal in nature. These often offhand comments are, however, somewhat misleading.

The privilege is clearly personal in the sense that only the person who is at risk of incrimination can invoke it. A witness, therefore, cannot refuse to provide information on the ground that it would incriminate someone else and thus intrude upon their interests. If a lawyer is called as a witness before a grand jury, for example, he cannot rely on the privilege as a basis for refusing to respond to questions on the ground that the answers would incriminate his client. A criminal defendant cannot invoke the privilege of witnesses, codefendants, or even co-conspirators or accomplices. Nor, generally speaking, can a criminal defendant successfully complain that the self-incrimination rights of such persons were violated in the litigation process.

There has been some suggestion that the personal nature of the privilege means that it can only be invoked by the personal act or statement of the holder and thus that a lawyer cannot invoke it on behalf of the holder. This is unnecessary and undesirable. When a lawyer, acting under authorization of the client and on behalf of the client, invokes the client's privilege, there is nothing to be gained by requiring the client to invoke the privilege himself. On the other hand, it is reasonable (and perhaps necessary) to require that the decision as to whether or not to invoke the privilege be made by the client and not the lawyer. If the lawyer's authorization is in reasonable doubt, the trial judges should have authority to require that the client's authorization be established.

§ 120. Limitation of the Privilege to Protection Against Criminal Liability: (a) In General

The privilege protects its holders only against the risk of *legal criminal liability*. It provides no protection against the disgrace and practical excommunication from society which might result from disclosure of matter which, under the circumstances, could not give rise to criminal liability.

If the risk of criminal liability is removed there is no privilege. It is clear, then, that the privilege does not apply when prosecution and conviction is precluded by passage of the period of limitations, pardon, prior acquittal, or a grant of immunity.[1] When prior conviction removes the risk of criminal liability, then the privilege is similarly rendered inapplicable. Whether that risk is actually removed by prior conviction, however, presents some special problems.

If direct appeal from a conviction is pending or remains available, a convicted defendant might, despite his conviction, harbor hope that his conviction will be reversed on appeal and that any disclosures he makes would be used to incriminate him upon any retrial that follows. Because of this possibility, the courts have generally held that a convicted defendant retains the protection of the privilege until appeal is exhausted or until the time for appeal expires. The risk of a reversal and retrial is not so remote as to constitute a negligible risk under the prevailing standard.

Whether the possibility that a conviction might be invalidated in collateral attack should render the privilege available is another matter. Collateral attack is generally available at any time, so regarding the risk of retrial after a successful attack of this sort as preserving protection would dramatically expand the protection of the privilege. The best solution is to treat the possibility of successful collateral attack and retrial as raising the question of whether the facts present a "real and appreciable" danger of incrimination.[2] In the absence of some specific showing that collateral attack is likely to be successful, a conviction should be regarded as removing the risk of incrimination and consequently the protection of the privilege.

---

§ 120

1. See § 142 infra.

2. See § 123 infra.

Whether the privilege protects against adverse determinations in criminal litigation other than a finding of guilt is somewhat uncertain. The Supreme Court assumed in Estelle v. Smith[3] that a finding of competency to stand trial would not be incrimination. Clearly removal of a procedural barrier to continuation of a prosecution is not incrimination.

Under the Fifth Amendment privilege, incrimination is a combination of conviction and punishment. Consequently, a defendant which is convicted but not yet sentenced is still protected against compulsion to engage in testimonial conduct that might increase the severity of the sentence. In part, the Supreme Court reasoned in Mitchell v. United States,[4] this result is compelled by those terms of the Fifth Amendment that prohibit a defendant from being compelled to be a witness against himself "in any criminal case." A sentencing proceeding is undoubtedly a part of a "criminal case," and therefore a court cannot compel a defendat to testify against his interests at this stage of the case.

The same result would almost certainly be reached under a more functional analysis. Whether the reasons for barring the government from compelling testimonial admissions tending to prove literal guilt of a crime, those reasons also apply should the government seek admissions that tend only to increase the severity of the punishment to be imposed after conviction. In many criminal cases, there is no doubt of the government's ability to prove the accused's guilt but whether the government can persuade the sentencer to impose a severe sentence is uncertain and of major importance to both accused and the government. This provides an incentive for the government to abuse the power to extract testimonial admissions likely to increase the severity of the punishment. Extractions of such admissions would violate the same privacy or dignitary interests as may be violated by extraction of admissions tending to prove guilt in the literal sense.

Apparently, however, increased severity of punishment does not constitute incrimination for purposes of the Fifth Amendment privilege if it develops after the criminal prosecution itself has been completed. In Minnesota v. Murphy,[5] the Court indicated—albeit in dictum—that revocation of probation would not be incrimination for Fifth Amendment privilege purposes. Mitchell did not discuss or even cite Murphy, but Mitchell's discussion of incrimination assumes that it involves both guilt and severity of the sentence imposed by the trial court but extends no further. Thus a defendant has no protection against compulsion to make admissions that would result in revocation of probation or revocation (or refusal) of parole.

There is obvious tension between Mitchell's discussion and the Murphy dictum. On principle, Mitchell's rationale suggests that the Murphy dictum is incorrect and the Fifth Amendment privilege should protect against compulsion to provide admissions that increase the severity of punishment whether that occurs in sentencing or later during the sentence.

§ 121. Limitation of the Privilege to Protection Against Criminal Liability: (b) Distinguishing Criminal and Noncriminal Legal Liability

It is clear that the privilege does protect against the risk of conviction for what are technically criminal offenses and equally clear that it does not protect against the imposition of liability for damages on the basis of traditionally civil causes of action. Whether it protects against types of liability that are between these two poles is less clear.

In 1886, the Supreme Court held that "proceedings instituted for the purpose of declaring the forfeiture of a man's property by reason of offenses committed by him, though they may be civil in form, are in their nature criminal."[1] Thus the Fifth Amendment privilege protects against forfeiture, at least where such action is based on conduct that could also serve as the basis for a criminal prosecution. In Application of Gault,[2] the Court held that

3. 451 U.S. 454 (1981).
4. 119 S.Ct. 1307 (1999).
5. 465 U.S. 420 (1984).

§ 121
1. Boyd v. United States, 116 U.S. 616, 634 (1886).
2. 387 U.S. 1 (1967).

the federal constitutional privilege protected against compelled disclosures that could lead to a finding that a child was delinquent. This determination apparently rested largely upon the fact that such a finding could result in a loss of liberty which the Court concluded was indistinguishable from the imprisonment that might follow criminal conviction.

But in Baxter v. Palmigiano,[3] the Court almost offhandedly held that disciplinary penalties imposed upon convicted prison inmates were not "incrimination" and did not themselves invoke the protection of the Fifth Amendment privilege. Two years later, the Court held that a civil penalty imposed under the Federal Water Pollution Control Act for discharge of harmful substances into navigable waters was not "incrimination" within the Fifth Amendment meaning.

This line of decisions came to a head in Allen v. Illinois,[4] in which the Court considered whether the Fifth Amendment protected against being found a sexually dangerous person under the nominally civil Illinois Sexually Dangerous Persons Act. Under the Act, a person may be found a sexually dangerous person only upon proof that he has engaged in criminal sexual misconduct. If such a finding is made, he can be committed for an indeterminate period to a maximum-security institution run by correctional authorities. Generally, the Court held, the legislature's designation of liability as civil in nature will be sufficient to take it out of Fifth Amendment coverage. A "civil" label must be disregarded and the Fifth Amendment applied, however, upon " 'the clearest proof' that 'the statutory scheme [is] so punitive either in purpose or effect as to negate [the State's] intention' that the proceeding be civil * * *." The Illinois courts had determined that the proceedings were essentially civil in nature. Allen failed to make the required showing that the scheme was punitive in purpose or effect. Contrary to indications in *Gault*, the fact that liability may result in involuntary incarceration is insufficient to require application of the privilege.

Under *Allen*, a litigant seeking to establish that the Fifth Amendment protects against a nominally civil form of liability has a difficult task and is unlikely to succeed. In

that case, the Court assumed that the Fifth Amendment privilege does not protect against compulsory hospitalization for mental illness. Lower courts have held that the privilege does not protect members of the bar against disciplinary proceedings or judges against judicial discipline. Nor is protection afforded against civil penalties for practicing dentistry without a license, termination of parental rights, or liability for civil contempt of court. Criminal contempt, however, is probably incrimination within the meaning of the privilege.

§ 122. Limitation of the Privilege to Protection Against Criminal Liability: (c) Incrimination Under the Laws of Another Jurisdiction

A witness may assert the privilege on the basis of concern regarding criminal liability in the courts of a jurisdiction other than the one in which the witness's testimony is being sought. These situations can be divided as follows: (a) a witness in either state or federal court claims danger of incrimination under the laws of a foreign country; (b) a witness in a state court claims danger of incrimination under the laws of another state; (c) a witness in a state court claims danger of incrimination under federal law; and (d) a witness in a federal court claims a danger of incrimination under state law.

Traditionally, most courts took the position that the privilege protected only against incrimination under the laws of the sovereign which was attempting to compel the incriminating information. In part, the basis for such holdings was the view that the risk of prosecution by another sovereign was so low as not to invoke protection under the privilege. It has also been argued, however, that this result follows from the rationale for the privilege. To the extent that the privilege is based upon concern regarding brutality and other such excesses that a sovereign might commit when attempting to compel a person's assistance in achieving his own conviction, that risk is seldom presented when the only potential criminal liability lies under the laws of another jurisdiction. In such cases, the compelling sovereign is unlikely to have sufficient interest in incriminating the person to perform acts that invoke the rationale for the privilege.

3. 425 U.S. 308 (1976).
4. 478 U.S. 364 (1986).

With regard to the Fifth Amendment privilege, this traditional position was rejected by the Supreme Court in Murphy v. Waterfront Commission.[1] Murphy and several others had been subpoenaed to testify before the Waterfront Commission of New York Harbor regarding a work stoppage at certain New Jersey piers. They were granted immunity from prosecution under New York and New Jersey law but invoked their Fifth Amendment privilege on the ground that their responses would tend to incriminate them under federal law. The Supreme Court agreed that the Fifth Amendment privilege protects state witnesses from liability under federal as well as state law. Noting the high degree of cooperation among jurisdictions, it reasoned without extended discussion that most and perhaps all of the policies and purposes of the Fifth Amendment privilege are defeated when a witness possessing protection against incrimination under both state and federal law can be "whipsawed" into incriminating himself under both bodies of law by simply being called as a witness in the courts of first one and then the other jurisdiction. The defense of the traditional view noted earlier was dismissed as based upon too narrow a view of those policies supporting the Fifth Amendment privilege.

The court recognized, however, that to expand Murphy's Fifth Amendment protection in state courts to include protection against incrimination under federal law without providing the states with a means of obtaining his testimony would ignore the interests that both levels of Government have in investigating and prosecuting crime. Consequently, it held that when a state compels testimony incriminating under federal law, as for example under a grant of immunity, the Federal Government is prohibited from making any incriminating use of that compelled testimony and its fruits. Since Murphy and his companions were thus adequately protected against the use of their compelled testimony in securing their federal convictions, they could be compelled to testify.

Murphy expressly resolved only situation (c) above. But it removed any conceptual basis for the traditional view that the privilege was inapplicable in situations (b) and (d). In both situations, witnesses have protection. But the jurisdiction seeking their testimony may nevertheless compel it if the witness can be assured that the compelled testimony and evidence derived from it cannot be used to incriminate him under the laws of the other jurisdiction. This assurance is provided by the federal constitutional prohibitions against the use of coerced "confessions" in either federal or state protections.

There is, then, general agreement that a federal witness is protected against incrimination under state law and that a state witness is protected against incrimination under the law of other states. Similarly, it is clear that in either situation the witness can be granted immunity by the forum jurisdiction and compelled to answer. Neither the testimony nor evidence derived from it, however, will be usable in the other jurisdiction.

Situation (a) above was addressed by the Supreme Court in United States v. Balsys.[2] *Murphy*, as construed in *Balsys*, did not reject either the reading of the common-law privilege as limited to incrimination under the law of the sovereign seeking to compel the testimony or the significance of the common-law rule in defining the content of the Fifth Amendment privilege. Rather, *Murphy* rested on the limited rationale that since the Fifth Amendment privilege is binding on the States as well as the federal government, for purposes of applying this aspect of the Fifth Amendment "the state and federal jurisdictions were as one." There is, however, no reason to similarly regard the federal government and a foreign sovereign "as one," and therefore the common-law derived "same sovereign principle" applies. Since the foreign sovereign is not the same as that seeking the testimony, incrimination under the law of that sovereign does not trigger the privilege.

If the matter turned instead on a comparison of the likely costs and benefits of expanding the Fifth Amendment privilege to cover incrimination under the laws of foreign sovereigns, *Balsys* reasoned alternatively, the result would be the same. Despite the relatively few cases in which claims of incrimination under the laws of a foreign sovereign might be

§ 122

1. 378 U.S. 52 (1964).
2. 118 S.Ct. 2218 (1998).

raised, expansion of the privilege would result in loss of some evidence that might cause serious adverse consequences for domestic law enforcement. Since the Court has no role in conducting foreign relations, it could not properly assume expansion of the privilege would stimulate legislation and international agreements that would minimize this cost. Expansion of the privilege might not benefit those who might invoke an expanded privilege. Their silence in reliance on an expanded privilege might be used to deport them to countries where they would face criminal prosecution.

Balsys left open the possibility that the Fifth Amendment privilege could be invoked on the basis of a showing that a potential foreign prosecution that would be in essence brought by the foreign sovereign on behalf of the American jurisdiction seeking the testimony. Merely showing that the American jurisdiction supports foreign prosecution by treaty agreement to provide that foreign jurisdiction with evidence of criminal guilt is not sufficient. Rather, *Balsys* suggests, the issue would be raised only by a showing that the two jurisdictions had enacted substantively similar criminal codes targeting "offenses of international character," and that the American jurisdiction was seeking the testimony "for the purpose of obtaining evidence to be delivered to other nations as prosecutors of a crime common to both nations."

§ 123. Requirement of a "Real and Appreciable" Risk of Incrimination

Early in the development of the federal constitutional privilege the courts established that the danger of incrimination must be "real and appreciable." A danger only "imaginary and unsubstantial" would not support invocation of the privilege.

In several early decisions, the United States Supreme Court invoked this formulation of the required risk as a basis for holding the privilege inapplicable, and "real and appreciable" risk language is sometimes repeated. As now applied, however, the requirement is probably of little if any significance. Courts, for example, sustain claims of the privilege where criminal liability would rest on prohibi-

tions against sexual activity seldom and perhaps never enforced.

Some courts have expressly embraced what is clearly the functional rule. The District of Columbia Court of Appeals, for example, held explicitly that a court considering a claim of the privilege is not to attempt an assessment of the likelihood of prosecution. "[I]f the trial judge concludes that the proposed testimony would be incriminating and thereby poses the risk of possible future prosecution," the court reasoned, "that ends the inquiry and a claim of the privilege should be sustained."[1] A theoretical risk of liability is, then, sufficient.

Application of the general requirement of a real and appreciable risk to some more specific problems in the administration of the privilege does present difficulties. These are considered elsewhere in this chapter in connection with the compulsory production of documents and tangible items[2] and the task of determining whether a witness's response to a question is sufficiently related to criminal liability to support invocation of the privilege.[3]

§ 124. Limitation of the Privilege to Compelled "Testimonial" Activity

The Fifth Amendment privilege and those of almost all states protect only against compulsion to engage in *testimonial* self-incriminating activity. Exploration of what the courts mean by testimonial activity is necessary to consideration of the basis and wisdom of this limitation.

As early as 1910, the United States Supreme Court held that the Fifth Amendment prohibits only the compelled extraction of "communications." This was reaffirmed in Schmerber v. California[1], which explained that the privilege "protects an accused only from being compelled to testify against himself, or otherwise provide the state with evidence of a testimonial or communicative nature." In Doe v. United States[2], the Court approved the approach urged by the Government: an act is "testimonial" within the meaning of the Fifth Amendment privilege if it "explicitly or implicitly, relate[s] a factual assertion or disclose[s]

§ 123

1. Carter v. United States, 684 A.2d 331, 336–38 (D.C.App.1996) (en banc).

2. See § 138 infra.

3. See § 133 infra.

§ 124

1. 384 U.S. 757 (1966).

2. 487 U.S. 201 (1988).

information." It then elaborated that this means that compelled action is "testimonial" only if the action is sought as an indication of the subject's intentional expression of his knowledge or belief concerning factual matters. This approach was reaffirmed in Pennsylvania v. Muniz.[3]

Therefore, the privilege is implicated when, but only when, the Government imposes compulsion to cause the subject to act in a manner that the subject intends as a disclosure of his perception of, or belief as to, factual matters. Consequently, the government is not prohibited from compelling actions because it does so to learn the subject's thoughts. The privilege prohibits only compulsion to require the subject to intentionally reveal his thoughts.

Physical as well as verbal activity may be testimonial under this definition. The "vast majority" of verbal statements will be testimonial, however, because "[t]here are very few instances in which a verbal statement, either oral or written, will not convey information or assert facts."

Thus the privilege does not bar compulsion upon a suspect to put on a blouse for purposes of determining whether it fits him, to cause a suspect to cooperate in the extraction of a blood sample which would suggest his guilt, to require a suspect to participate in a lineup, or to obtain a voice or handwriting sample from a suspect. When compelled production of documents or other items involves compelled testimonial activity is a specialized problem considered elsewhere.

Even during trial, a criminal defendant can be compelled to engage in incriminating conduct before the jury if that conduct is not testimonial. The defendant can, of course, be compelled to be in the courtroom. Courts have upheld trial judges' requirements that defendants display a tattoo to a witness on the stand, show the jury the defendant's teeth, and put on the jacket, mask and cap worn by the perpetrator of the charged crime and say the words spoken by the perpetrator–"Give me the money" and "Hurry up."

In *Muniz,* the Supreme Court addressed the testimonial nature of several aspects of a stationhouse sobriety test. The officer conducting the test first asked Muniz his name, ad-

dress, height, weight, eye color, date of birth, and current age. Next, in an apparent effort to test Muniz' ability to calculate, he asked, "Do you know what the date was of your sixth birthday?" Finally, the officer instructed him, as he performed several physical dexterity tests, to count.

The *Muniz* majority assumed that the first questions, as to Muniz' name, address, height, weight, eye color, date of birth, and current age, did call for testimonial responses. It made clear, however, that the Fifth Amendment did not bar the officers from compelling Muniz to speak in order to determine whether he would slur his words. Slurred speech and other evidence of lack of muscular coordination do not involve testimonial components and thus their compelled demonstration does not invoke the Fifth Amendment privilege.

Controversy focused upon the second question—concerning whether Muniz knew the date of his sixth birthday—to which Muniz had responded, "No, I don't." Justice Brennan, speaking for a bare majority of five justices, explained that this question did not require exploration of the "outer boundaries of what is 'testimonial,' " because the "core meaning" of that concept made clear that Muniz' response to the question was testimonial. That the police were seeking to ascertain the physical nature of Muniz' brain processes was not controlling, he continued, if that inquiry was pursued by means that called for testimonial responses from the suspect. The question posed to Muniz called for a testimonial response, because it demanded that he communicate his perception or belief concerning his mental processes and their result. Functionally, he was communicating that he believed or knew that he was unaware of the date of his sixth birthday.

Whether a suspect's refusal to participate in a breath test for blood alcohol level is testimonial remains uncertain. The Court has commented that there is "considerable force" in the argument that a suspect's refusal to participate in a breath test for blood alcohol is like flight and thus noncommunicative conduct rather than a testimonial communication. Best

3. 496 U.S. 582, 594–95 (1990).

analyzed, such conduct is not testimonial. Although it does reveal the suspect's perception that he is too intoxicated to pass the test, it does not do so by compelling the suspect's intentional communication of his perception that he is so intoxicated. He does not intend his response as an assertion of the factual matter inferred from it–that he is conscious of his state of intoxication.

Muniz left unresolved whether recitation of letters or numbers in a specified sequence–reciting the alphabet, for example–is testimonial. Arguably these recitations involve implied assertions of the suspects' beliefs. Such a recitation of the alphabet can be viewed as an implied–but testimonial–assertion, "I believe E follows C." Nevertheless, most lower courts have held that such action is not testimonial. This is best based on the proposition that such a recitation does not involve an intentional disclosure of the person's beliefs but are rather a rote recitation of "a set of generic symbols" or–in the words of the Massachusetts court– "the reflexive functioning of the [person's] mental processes."[4]

Muniz suggested that the testimonial requirement should be applied–at least in part— by using a functional analysis based on the rationale for the privilege. At its core, the privilege is designed to protect those suspected of crime from modern-day analogues of the historic trilemma of self-accusation, perjury or contempt. "Whatever else it may include * * *," Justice Brennan explained in *Muniz*, "the definition of 'testimonial' evidence * * * must encompass all responses to questions that, if asked of a sworn suspect during a criminal trial, could place the suspect in the 'cruel trilemma.'" Arguably neither suspects asked to consent to tests nor those commanded to recite numbers or letters are placed in this posture. Offering what the persons perceive as more favorable but false answers to the officers' demands are simply not options.

Precisely why the privilege is limited to compulsion to engage in "testimonial" activity has seldom been addressed. Certainly the language of most if not all constitutional provi-

sions does not require this result. To the contrary, a broader construction of the privilege is somewhat suggested by the terms of some formulations of it, as for example those providing that no person "shall be compelled to give evidence against himself." Such nuances in terminology have not, however, been regarded as of much significance.

In *Doe*, the Supreme Court noted that so limiting the privilege is consistent with the history of the Fifth Amendment privilege and its predecessors, which were historically intended to prevent the use of legal compulsion to extract sworn communications from accuseds of facts, which would incriminate them. The Court acknowledged that the policies supporting the privilege would be served to some extent by applying the privilege more broadly. It did not, however, develop precisely why that does not support a broader formulation of the privilege's protection. "[T]he scope of the privilege," the *Doe* majority "explained," "does not coincide with the complex of values it helps to protect." But this observation is of little help in explaining why the testimonial requirement is imposed to determine the extent to which the scope will coincide with those values.

Doe conceded that the privilege is based in part upon the need to limit the Government's ability to compel the accused to "assist in his prosecution" in a broader sense, and that this purpose would be served by expanding the privilege to nontestimonial situations. It then simply assumed that the protected interests in "privacy, fairness, and restraint of governmental power" are not impermissibly offended by compelling the accused to cooperate in the prosecution's use of his body to develop "highly incriminating testimony." Apparently this assumption was based in part at least on the conclusions that other federal Constitutional provisions also serve that same purpose, apparently so effectively that the Fifth Amendment need not be developed so as to provide additional limits.

States remain free, of course, to define the protection afforded by their constitution-

---

4. Vanhouton v. Commonwealth, 676 N.E.2d 460, 466 (Mass.1997).

al, statutory, or case law privileges more broadly and as not limited to compelled testimonial conduct. Traditionally, there was considerable authority that some state privileges prohibited any compelled activity, whether testimonial or not, giving rise to incriminating evidence or information implicating the person so compelled. After the Utah Supreme Court's rejection of this position in 1985, however, apparently only Georgia still adheres to this approach.

Under the approach of the Georgia court, the privilege prohibits only compulsion to engage in *affirmative actions* that are self-incriminating. It does, therefore, prohibit compelling a suspect to produce a handwriting exemplar. But it does not bar compelled but passive submission to a surgical procedure required for removal of a bullet from the suspect's body, the taking of blood samples for chemical analysis, or the removal of a suspect's shoes.

Perhaps the rationales of the privilege simply cannot support a broad construction of the privilege that rejects a requirement that the compelled activity be testimonial. To the extent that the privilege is designed to minimize cruelty, arguably that purpose might be best effectuated by prohibiting compulsion to engage in any volitional affirmative act, since such situations provide an incentive to engage in potentially abusive persuasion until the subject complies. As the Utah court noted in the leading recent rejection of this position, however, other constitutional provisions are available to condemn excessive coercion. Moreover, the incentive for extreme, and thus cruel, persuasive measures is greatest in situations where communicative cooperation is sought, because there the subjects retain the power to control the contents of the sought responses.

Any use of a suspect himself to develop evidence with which to bring about the suspect's own downfall might be regarded as offending privacy concerns underlying the privilege; the more "affirmative" the compelled participation by the suspect, the greater the privacy intrusion might be. It is doubtful, however, whether today privacy considerations are of sufficient significance in supporting the privilege to serve as a foundation for defining its scope.

Difficulties in determining what forms of cooperation are sufficiently affirmative to come within a prohibition against compelled affirmative cooperation argue against defining the scope of a privilege in those terms. Yet, as *Muniz* illustrated, defining the privilege as limited to testimonial activity itself presents serious difficulties.

§ 125. Requirement of Compulsion

The privilege applies only when self-incriminatory and testimonial activity is "compelled." What compulsion means varies with the context of the testimonial activity, although the recent history of the privilege has involved significant expansion of the concept of compulsion.

Traditionally, the privilege was limited to situations in which "legal" compulsion, compulsion imposed under authority of law, was exerted upon the witness. Consequently, the privilege was inapplicable to police questioning, since law enforcement officers have no authority to compel answers to their inquiries. In Miranda v. Arizona,[1] however, the Supreme Court rejected this approach as a matter of Fifth Amendment law and held the privilege implicated in out-of-court custodial interrogation by police. Reasoning that coverage of such activity was necessary to avoid rendering the privilege at trial a mere empty formality, the Court rejected the requirement that the compulsion be legal. The Fifth Amendment privilege applies to and protects citizens in situations in which their freedom to abstain from self-incrimination "is curtailed in any significant way."

On the other hand, the requirement of compulsion is the conceptual basis for many of the procedural requirements that must be met for successful reliance upon the privilege and consequently serves to limit its effect. Most important, as a general rule, compulsion is present only if a witness has asserted a right to refuse to disclose self-incriminating infor-

1. 384 U.S. 436 (1966).

mation and this refusal has been overridden. "The answers of such a witness to questions put to him are not compelled within the meaning of the Fifth Amendment," the Supreme Court has held, "unless the witness is required to answer over his valid claim of the privilege."[2]

In Minnesota v. Murphy, the Court explained that this rule is inapplicable in three "well-defined" situations where the circumstances so suggest that the person's ability to make a free choice is impaired as to render inappropriate a requirement that the person expressly articulate a desire not to incriminate himself. One is where a citizen is subjected to custodial law enforcement interrogation. There, *Miranda* recognizes that the Fifth Amendment applies and imposes certain requirements even if the person does not first affirmatively assert a desire to avoid self-incrimination.

Another situation is where a person is confronted with such significant potential penalties for invoking the privilege that his failure to do so cannot reasonably be regarded as a free choice. Finally, the requirement of an assertion of the desire to remain silent has not been required in cases in which federal tax requirements imposed on gamblers require potentially incriminating filings with the government. Given especially that claiming the privilege would itself be self-incriminating in this situation, no such affirmative action is required.

The need for compulsion also explains the recent holdings that the Fifth Amendment privilege does not protect the contents of self-incriminatory documents from compelled production.[3] Since the person's arguably "testimonial" act of putting incriminatory information in the papers occurred before and without any effect from the compulsion of a later subpoena for those papers, the testimonial and self-incriminating act of so disclosing that informa-

tion was not compelled within the meaning of the privilege.

In South Dakota v. Neville,[4] the Supreme Court made clear that the compulsion must be "impermissible." At issue in *Neville* was the admissibility of a driver's refusal to submit to a blood alcohol test, offered by the prosecution as evidence of the driver's intoxication. To the extent that the refusal was testimonial,[5] any compulsion exerted upon him to take the test did not render his refusal compelled within the meaning of the Fifth Amendment privilege. The criminal process often requires suspects and defendants to make choices, the Court explained, and the Fifth Amendment does not necessarily preclude this:

> [T]he values behind the Fifth Amendment are not hindered when the state offers a suspect the choice of submitting to the blood-alcohol test or having his refusal used against him. * * * [T]he state could legitimately compel the suspect, against his will, to accede to the test. Given, then, that the offer of taking a blood-alcohol test is clearly legitimate, the action becomes no *less* legitimate when the State offers a second option of refusing to take the test, with the attendant penalties for making that choice.[6]

The refusal, therefore, is not an act coerced by the officer and trial use of evidence of that refusal is not barred by the privilege.

§ 126. The Privilege of an Accused in a Criminal Proceeding: (a) Inferences From and Comment Upon the Accused's Reliance Upon the Privilege in the Trial

A defendant's failure to testify in a criminal trial, the most basic invocation of the privilege imaginable, cannot be penalized by use of that action as tending to prove the defendant's guilt in that trial. Implementing this, however, has proven somewhat troublesome.

In Griffin v. California,[1] the Supreme Court held that the Fifth Amendment privi-

---

2. 465 U.S. 420, 427 (1984).

3. See generally §§ 137–138 infra.

4. 459 U.S. 553 (1983).

5. See § 124 supra.

6. South Dakota v. Neville, supra note 4, 459 U.S. at 565 (emphasis in original).

§ 126

1. 380 U.S. 609 (1965).

lege was violated by a prosecutor's argument which urged the jury to draw an inference of guilt from a defendant's failure to testify when his testimony could reasonably have been expected to deny or explain matters proved by the prosecution and a jury instruction that authorized the jury to draw that suggested inference. So encouraging the jury to infer guilt from the defendant's reliance upon the privilege, the Court concluded, constituted an impermissible penalty for exercising the privilege, despite the risk that even without argument or instruction the jury might do it anyway. "What the jury may infer given no help from the court is one thing," noted the Court. "What they may infer when the court solemnizes the silence of the accused into evidence against him is quite another."

Under *Griffin*, any explicit—or "direct"— invitation to a jury—by the trial judge, the prosecutor, or even counsel for a codefendant—to consider the defendant's failure to testify as tending to prove guilt is prohibited. Arguments and instructions that have other primary functions are often held permissible, even though they may also serve to call juries' attention to defendants' failure to testify. For example, the Supreme Court upheld an instruction permitting the jury to infer knowledge that property was stolen from evidence of possession of recently-stolen property, if the possession was not satisfactorily explained. Without elaboration, it simply observed that the instruction could not fairly be understood as a comment on the defendant's failure to testify.

Courts have had most difficulty identifying those arguments by prosecutors that are "indirect"—that is, that do not explicitly urge the jury to infer guilt from the defendant's failure to testify—but nevertheless are prohibited by *Griffin*. Lower courts have generally held that arguments possibly referring to the defendant's failure to testify must be considered in context and are impermissible under *Griffin* only if the prosecutor "manifestly intended" to comment on the defendant's silence or if the character of the argument was such

that a jury would "naturally and necessarily" construe it as a comment on the defendant's failure to testify.

Thus prosecutors violated *Griffin* when they argued, "[T]he only witness in this case [other than the decedent was] the defendant, and you can't consider * * * him not testifying" and "I'm not talking about [the defendant] testifying, he didn't have to. * * * He could have cleared all this up, though." Generally, prosecutors may safely argue that the State's evidence, or particular parts of it, are "uncontradicted." If the state of the evidence is that the only possible contradictory testimony would be from the defendant, however, such argument constitutes an impermissible indirect comment on the defendant's failure to testify.

Otherwise proper comment on the defendant's silence at trial is permissible, if it is a fair response to evidence or argument made by the defendant. Thus when defense counsel argued to the jury that the prosecution had unfairly denied the defendant the opportunity to explain his actions, the prosecutor was permitted to respond in argument that the defendant had "every opportunity," if he chose to use it, "to explain this to the ladies and gentlemen of the jury."

§ 127. Privilege of an Accused in a Criminal Proceeding: (b) Impeachment With Prior Silence and Other Penalties Upon Invoking the Privilege Before Trial

A criminal defendant may have invoked the privilege prior to the present trial. This may have occurred during the pretrial events that led to the present trial, it may have occurred in a prior trial of the same case, or it may have happened in a different proceeding. May the prosecution use any of those prior invocations of the privilege against the defendant, perhaps only to impeach the defendant if he testifies or perhaps as affirmative proof of guilt?

Griffin v. California,[1]—discussed in the last section—prohibits use of a defendant's invocation of the privilege *in the present trial*

§ 127

1. 380 U.S. 609 (1965).

to prove guilt. It does not, however, address the prosecution's ability to use invocation of the privilege in other contexts. A defendant who testifies and thus waives the privilege is generally held to have waived it for–but only for–the trial in which this occurs.[2] Does this approach work *against* the accused as well as for him, so that an invocation of the privilege in an earlier context can be used by the prosecution in the present–and arguably different–proceeding?

In Raffel v. United States,[3] the Supreme Court held that a defendant who testified at trial had no federal constitutional protection against cross-examination concerning his failure to testify at a prior trial on the same charge. This seemed to rest largely on a waiver notion, as the Court stressed that a defendant who takes the witness stand subjects himself to such cross-examination as is generally permitted. But other language in the opinion suggested that the basis of decision was rather that such a defendant has no right that warrants protection. Any Fifth Amendment right to be free from penalties for invoking the privilege, the Court suggested, extends only to penalties imposed in the same trial or proceeding in which the defendant involved the privilege.

Whether a defendant's out-of-court pretrial silence is protected at all by the Fifth Amendment privilege remains unclear. To the extent that it is protected, however, Jenkins v. Anderson held that *Raffel's* waiver rationale permitted a testifying defendant to be cross-examined concerning that silence.

May either or both a defendant's failure to testify in a prior trial or silence in the pretrial portion of the present prosecution be used to prove the defendant's guilt? *Raffel's* reasoning that the right to be free from penalties for invoking the privilege applies only to penalties imposed in the same trial or proceeding suggests that *Griffin's* absolute bar to inferring guilt from invocation of the privilege might be limited to invocations of the privilege during

the same trial in which the inference of guilt is sought.

There is widespread agreement that *Jenkins* and *Raffel*—to the extent that *Raffel* remains authoritative—rest on a waiver analysis that is triggered and limited by the defendant's trial testimony. Thus if the defendant does not testify the prosecution cannot use the defendant's pretrial silence to prove guilt. Most likely, further, if the defendant testifies and previous-trial or pre-trial silence is available to the prosecution, that evidence can be used only on the defendant's credibility and not to prove guilt.

§ 128. Privilege of an Accused in a Criminal Proceeding: (c) Instructing the Jury Regarding the Privilege

Whether instructions directing jurors to give no weight to a defendant's failure to testify can in fact be effective, of course, is open to dispute. In Carter v. Kentucky,[1] the Supreme Court nevertheless held that the Fifth Amendment requires trial judges upon request to instruct juries that no inferences are to be drawn from defendants' failure to testify. "No judge can prevent jurors from speculating about why a defendant stands mute in the face of a criminal accusation," the Court reasoned, "but a judge can, and must if requested to do so, use the unique power of the jury instruction to reduce that speculation to a minimum."

It is widely recognized, however, that reasonable persons differ with regard to when, if ever, such an instruction is likely to do more good than harm. The instruction, of course, reminds jurors of the defendant's failure to testify and emphasizes it albeit by stressing the law's demand that the failure be given no significance. Some lawyers, in at least some situations, believe that the giving of such an instruction increases rather than decreases the likelihood that the jury will actually consider the defendant's failure to testify. In light of this, may or should such an instruction be

---

2. See § 129 infra.

3. 271 U.S. 494 (1926).

§ 128

1. 450 U.S. 288 (1981).

given if the defendant does not request it or if the defendant actively opposes it?

In Lakeside v. Oregon,[2] the Supreme Court found no Fifth Amendment defect in a trial judge's giving of such an instruction over the defendant's objection. *Griffin* was concerned only with adverse comment, the Court reasoned. It then rejected as "speculative" Lakeside's argument that the jury might, in the absence of instructions, take no notice of his failure to testify but if given cautionary instructions might totally disregard those directives and draw an inference from his failure to testify. Sound nonconstitutional policy may direct that a trial judge respect a defendant's desire that cautionary instructions not be given, the Court commented, and states remain free to prohibit cautionary instructions over defendants' objection as a matter of state law.

It is difficult to find any significant interests furthered by the giving of such an instruction over the defendant's objection. Moreover, in light of the uncertainty as to whether and when such an instruction is more favorable to an accused than the absence of any instruction, there is little reason to permit the instruction if the defendant affirmatively objects. As the Pennsylvania Supreme Court noted, permitting the trial judge to decide whether to give the instruction removes the judge from the role of impartial presider and inserts that judge into the role of advocate for the defendant. This is clearly undesirable.[3]

An increasing number of jurisdictions require trial judges to omit the instruction if the defendant objects. This is sometimes by statute, and sometimes by constitutional or nonconstitutional case law.

§ 129. Privilege of an Accused in a Criminal Proceeding: (d) "Waiver" of the Privilege by Voluntary Testimony

A criminal accused's extensive rights under the privilege are diminished by his act of testifying in his own behalf during the trial.

Unlike the situation of a witness, who loses the privilege only by testifying to incriminating facts, the accused suffers this reduction in his rights merely by testifying, regardless of the incriminatory content of his testimony. In Brown v. United States[1] the Supreme Court explained:

"[The accused] has the choice, after weighing the advantage of the privilege against self-incrimination against the advantage of putting forward his version of the facts and his reliability as a witness, not to testify at all. He cannot reasonably claim that the Fifth Amendment gives him not only this choice but, if he elects to testify, an immunity from cross-examination on the matters he has himself put in dispute. It would make of the Fifth Amendment not only a humane safeguard against judicially coerced self-disclosure but a positive invitation to mutilate the truth a party offers to tell."[2]

The major problem in applying this rule has been defining the extent to which an accused loses the protection of the privilege by testifying. Traditionally, many courts have taken the position that a defendant who testifies becomes subject to cross-examination under the jurisdiction's applicable rules and loses the right to invoke the privilege in response to any question proper under those rules. Under this approach, a testifying defendant may be questioned concerning all matters related to the case and his credibility, regardless of whether he addressed those matters on direct examination. He may not invoke his privilege on the ground that answers to such questions would incriminate him further regarding the offenses for which he is being tried. Nor can he invoke it on the ground that his answers would incriminate him for other offenses.

This last statement is subject to one exception. Courts generally enforce the position adopted by Federal Rule 608(b) that a criminal defendant, like other witnesses, does not by testifying lose the right to invoke the privilege

---

2. 435 U.S. 333 (1978).

3. Commonwealth v. Edwards, 637 A.2d 259, 261 (Pa. 1993).

1. 356 U.S. 148 (1958).

2. Id. at 155–56.

regarding criminal misconduct relevant to the case only because that conduct tends to show the accused's lack of credibility.[3] If such misconduct is relevant to some other issue, however, the privilege cannot be invoked by the defendant to avoid incriminating answers to questions about it.

A defendant's loss of protection by virtue of testifying in his own defense should not be tied to the jurisdiction's rules concerning permissible cross-examination. Some jurisdictions restrict cross-examination to matters testified to on direct examination, while others permit cross-examination on all phases of the case.[4] There is no reason why the scope of an important constitutional right should vary depending upon the jurisdiction's choice of a cross-examination rule. Determining the scope of cross-examination is essentially a matter of control over the order of production of evidence. The primary policy served by limiting cross-examination is the orderly conduct of the trial; ordinary witnesses usually have no legitimate interest that is affected by the scope of permitted cross-examination. Defining the protection of the privilege, on the other hand, involves the "fairness" of requiring defendants to forfeit the protection of the privilege in order to place their own versions of the facts before triers of fact. This affects defendants' interests which are, generally speaking, protected by the privilege. The scope of protection retained by a testifying defendant should not be tied to the scope of cross-examination of the ordinary witness.

Some courts hold that a testifying defendant is barred from invoking the privilege only when cross-examination is reasonably related to the subject matter of his direct examination. Courts taking this approach, however, tend to construe this criterion broadly and to find no right to refuse to respond to questions with relatively attenuated relation to the matters inquired into on direct examination. This formulation of the testifying defendant's remaining protection seldom leads to results different

from those that would be reached under the traditional approach.

Testifying defendants are required to submit to cross-examination to provide reasonable assurance that their testimony, like that of other witnesses, is subjected to procedures providing assurance of accuracy. The extent to which a defendant forfeits the privilege by testifying should be related to this rationale for decreased protection because of his testifying. Thus a defendant who testifies should have no right to invoke the privilege regarding questions on cross-examination that the trial court, in the exercise of discretion, determines are necessary to provide the prosecution with a reasonable opportunity to test the defendant's assertions on direct.

If a defendant has testified in his own defense and impermissibly refused to respond to cross-examination in mistaken reliance upon his privilege, what action should or may the trial court take? As in the case where an ordinary witness invokes the privilege on cross-examination,[5] the trial court has substantial discretion as to how to respond. But in view of a defendant's particularly important interest in having his version of the events go to the trier of fact, a trial judge should be especially reluctant to strike the defendant's testimony on direct examination and should do so only after considering and rejecting alternative measures such as striking only part of the testimony on direct examination or directing that the jury consider in assessing the defendant's credibility his improper reliance upon his privilege.

The loss of protection has traditionally been regarded as effective throughout the proceeding in which the accused testifies. During that proceeding the privilege does not reattach if the accused physically leaves the witness stand, and he can be recalled and required to testify again if this is otherwise procedurally proper. On the other hand, testifying in one "proceeding" does not preclude the accused from invoking the privilege in a separate and independent proceeding. A defendant who tes-

---

3. See § 42 supra as to claiming the privilege on cross-examination directed to impeachment.

4. See § 21 supra.

5. See § 134 infra.

tified in one trial is not, for example, barred from relying on the privilege in a second trial on the same charge.

§ 130.   The Privilege of a Witness: (a) Invoking the Privilege

Non-defendant witnesses are privileged only to decline to respond to inquiries, not to be free from those inquiries designed to elicit self-incriminatory responses. The nature of the privilege for non-defendant witnesses means that the requirements for invoking it are somewhat different than those applicable when the holder of the privilege is an accused in a criminal proceeding.

Most importantly, a witness must submit to questioning and invoke the privilege in response to each specific question. A witness has no right to refuse either to appear or to be sworn as a witness. If a witness is asked a series of questions, the witness must ordinarily assert the privilege in response to each one. A "blanket" objection to a line of questioning on self-incrimination grounds generally will not constitute an effective assertion of the privilege. In limited situations, however, such a "blanket objection", as, for example, a "running objection" to an entire "line of questioning", may be effective, at least if specifically accepted by the trial judge.

Courts justify the requirement that witnesses so raise their privilege on the basis of the limited protection afforded witnesses by the privilege in this context and the need to accommodate considerations other than the witnesses' interest in avoiding compelled self-incrimination. Parties to litigation have obvious interests in being able to produce relevant testimony, and society as a whole has an important interest in the accurate and efficient resolution of litigation. The trial judge and not the witness himself must determine whether a witness's claim of the privilege is justified. Requiring specific assertion of the privilege when the testimony or information is sought permits efficient resolution of witnesses' claims in a manner that accommodates these other interests. A claim of the privilege by a witness alerts the court and the parties to the need to immediately inquire into the basis for that claim when the facts are fresh and can most accurately be developed. It also guides that inquiry by identifying the nature of the possible incriminatory risks that must be investigated.

Ordinarily, it is desirable that the jury not know that a witness has invoked the privilege, since neither party to litigation is entitled to draw any inference from a witness's invocation. Therefore, if a party anticipates that his witness will invoke the privilege, he should alert the trial court of this. The witness's invocation and the court's inquiry into the justification for the witness's reliance on the privilege should take place out of the presence of the jury. But where it is not clear in advance whether a witness will invoke the privilege, a trial judge has discretion whether to interrupt the presentation of the case to conduct an anticipatory inquiry or, instead, to proceed despite the risk that the jury will therefore observe the witness's reliance on the privilege.

§ 131.   The Privilege of a Witness: (b) Effect in a Criminal Trial of Prosecution Witness's Reliance on the Privilege

Special problems of potentially constitutional dimensions are presented when the prosecution in a criminal case is permitted to make substantial inquiries before the jury of a witness who responds by relying on the privilege.

In Namet v. United States,[1] the Supreme Court suggested that prosecution misconduct sufficient to render a conviction invalid might occur if the prosecution, knowing that a witness will invoke the privilege, calls that witness before the jury and then makes a "conscious and flagrant attempt to build its case out of inferences arising from use of the [self-incrimination] privilege." Alternatively, such action creates significant risk that the jury will rely upon an inference of the defendant's guilt from the witness's invocation of the privilege or from the questions themselves. This might

§ 131

1.   373 U.S. 179 (1963).

constitute an impermissible use of "testimony" not subject to cross-examination by the defendant. In Douglas v. Alabama,[2] the Court gave constitutional status to the second possibility, holding that a defendant's Sixth Amendment right to effective cross-examination was violated when the prosecution was permitted to extensively question a witness regarding a pretrial statement implicating the defendant and the witness refused on self-incrimination grounds to respond to all questions.

Lower courts apply a multi-factor analysis to determine whether constitutional error is committed under *Namet* and *Douglas* when a prosecution witness is questioned before the jury and invokes his privilege. Among the relevant considerations are the prosecutor's certainty that the witness will invoke the privilege, the number and nature of the questions as to which the privilege is invoked, the importance to the prosecution's case of those matters as to which the jury might have drawn an inference from the witness's invocation of the privilege, whether other evidence has been introduced on those matters, and the giving, and likely effectiveness, of an instruction to the jury to draw no inference from the witness's action.

§ 132.   The Privilege of a Witness: (c) Rights to Be Warned and to Counsel

A witness who is about to lose the privilege against self-incrimination by testifying to self-incriminating facts generally has no "right" to be warned of the privilege and its potential loss by the testimony the witness is about to give.

A trial judge who becomes aware that the questioning of a witness raises the risk that the witness by responding will incriminate himself, however, has substantial discretion as to whether and how to respond. The judge may, for example, stop the questioning briefly to warn the witness that she may decline to give self-incriminating answers and perhaps assure that the witness has a clear opportunity to assert a desire to withhold answers. This is best done out of the presence of the trial jury. The judge may also take more drastic steps as, for example, by temporarily stopping the trial so that the witness may consult with an attorney and even by appointing an attorney to consult with the witness.

Ordinarily, this process protects only the interests of the witness. Noncompliance with any requirements as might apply does not prejudice the legitimate interests of the parties, so they may not complain of the trial judge's failure to take adequate steps to protect the interests of the witnesses.

In a criminal trial when the judge becomes concerned that a defense witness's self-incrimination rights may be placed in unfair jeopardy, however, additional considerations arise. The witness's self-incrimination interests, of course, are no less in such situations. But the accused has a particularly important interest that is also affected, the defendant's Sixth Amendment right to present all potentially exculpatory evidence. As the Supreme Court recognized in Webb v. Texas,[1] trial judges' efforts to protect defense witnesses' interests may impermissibly intrude upon defendants' right to produce evidence.

Perhaps the most that can be generally said with confidence in such situations is that trial judges have a special duty to seek an accommodation between witnesses' self-incrimination interests and defendants' interests in full production of relevant evidence. The judge is not barred from alerting the witness to her self-incrimination right, but the judge's authority to caution the witness "should be exercised sparingly and with great caution." In deciding whether and how to proceed, the judge should consider, among other factors, the actual risk of the witness being prosecuted, and must take special care to assure that any decision not to testify is that of the witness herself. Of course, the prosecution's interest in being able to challenge the credibility of defense testimony must also be given adequate consideration. The witness must therefore be alerted to the duty after testifying on direct

---

2.   380 U.S. 415 (1965).

1.   409 U.S. 95 (1972).

examination to submit to appropriate cross-examination.

§ 133. The Privilege of a Witness: (d) Determination Whether a Specific Response Would Be Incriminatory

Determining whether a specific demanded response would be sufficiently incriminatory to be within the protection of the privilege sometimes presents a difficult task. Often the matter is clear because the question on its face calls for an incriminating response. The difficulties arise from facially innocent questions, as, for example, "Do you know John Bergoti?"

The witness himself, of course, is not the final arbiter of whether his invocation is proper. Rather, the court itself must determine whether the refusal to answer is in fact justifiable under the privilege. Any other position would subordinate the effective operation of the judicial system to the desires of witnesses.

Traditionally, a witness invoking the privilege was required to produce information from which the court could find a sufficient risk of incrimination and perhaps even to convince the court that such a risk existed. In order to sustain the witness's reliance on the privilege the court was required to "see, from the circumstances of the case, and the nature of the evidence which the witness is called to give, that there is reasonable ground to apprehend danger to the witness from his being compelled to answer."

Traditional analysis, however, was been cast into doubt by Hoffman v. United States,[1] which must be the point of reference for modern application of witnesses' Fifth Amendment privilege. "To sustain the privilege," the Supreme Court explained in *Hoffman*, "it need only be evident from the implications of the question, in the setting in which it was asked, that a responsive answer to the question or an explanation of why it cannot be answered might be dangerous because injurious disclosure could result." The trial court erred in refusing to permit Hoffman to refuse to answer the question there at issue, the Court concluded, because "it was not 'perfectly clear,

from a careful consideration of all the circumstances in the case, that the witness is mistaken, and that the answer[s] *cannot possibly* have such tendency' to incriminate."

Despite *Hoffman's* prominence, its precise significance is not entirely clear. The Court's first statement is consistent with traditional doctrine: Unless the court can conclude that further inquiry would create a danger of injurious disclosure it cannot sustain a claim of privilege. If this conclusion cannot be drawn from circumstances already available for scrutiny, the witness has the obligation to bring the necessary circumstances to the attention of the court. But the Court's second statement indicates that a trial judge must permit the witness to refuse to answer in reliance on the privilege *unless* the judge can conclude that the witness's invocation is improper. This, of course, would reallocate at least the burden of producing information and indicates that in the absence of a sufficient factual basis for the conclusion, the claim of privilege must be allowed.

Lower courts disagree on how *Hoffman* is to be read. Some construe it as requiring that a witness's claim to the privilege be sustained unless it is perfectly clear from all the circumstances that the answer to the question cannot possibly have any tendency to incriminate the witness. This suggests that the party seeking the witness's testimony over the witness's claim of the privilege has both the burden of producing information or evidence on which the witness's claim can be evaluated and— once that information or evidence is produced—of persuading the trial judge that the required risk of incrimination is absent. Other courts read *Hoffman* as sometimes at least imposing upon a witness invoking the privilege some obligation to support that claim.

The difficulty with placing any burden on the witness relying on the privilege, of course, is that sometimes meeting this burden will itself require disclosure of self-incriminating facts. In light of this, *Hoffman* is best read as follows: A witness invoking the privilege need not carry a burden of persuasion requiring the

1. 341 U.S. 479 (1951).

witness to persuade the judge that the answer sought would be incriminating. But where the question, considered in light of the evidence in the case and other information properly taken into account, is one which the trial judge could reasonably regard as presenting no more than an imaginary and unsubstantial risk of incrimination, the witness has the burden of putting into the record—by evidence, logical argument, or persuasion—a basis for regarding that conclusion as insufficiently supported. In the words of the Idaho courts, such a witness "must sketch a plausible scenario" under which the answer would be incriminating. Although a witness might produce evidence in support of a claim of the privilege under this approach, such evidence is not necessary. Argument of counsel presenting logical possibilities may well be sufficient.

Whatever the abstract requirements, it is clear that trial judges have considerable flexibility in applying them. Whether to hold a factual hearing is discretionary, although a trial judge would probably act impermissibly in rejecting a witness's claim to the privilege without granting the witness's request for a factual hearing at which he would have an opportunity to establish the basis for his claim. As *Hoffman* itself made clear, the judge is not limited to the formal record in the case but may consider news media reports, general information, and perhaps even specific factual information which he has from other sources. In an effort to minimize the risk that a witness will have to make incriminatory disclosures to establish that he is not required to do so, some courts have entertained *ex parte* submissions.

As in other situations, state courts are of course free to construe state formulations of the privilege as more protective of the underlying interests than the Fifth Amendment as applied in *Hoffman*.

§ 134. Privilege of a Witness: (e) "Waiver" by Disclosure of Incriminating Facts

A witness, unlike an accused in a criminal proceeding, loses the privilege only by actually revealing incriminating facts. In the leading case, Rogers v. United States,[1] the Supreme Court explained that under the well-accepted rule a witness who has voluntarily revealed self-incriminating facts without invoking the privilege cannot invoke that privilege to avoid further disclosure of the details of the incriminating information. To permit a claim of the privilege in such situations, the Court added, "would open the way to distortion of facts by permitting a witness to select any stopping place in the testimony."

Some courts read *Rogers* as directing a relatively mechanical inquiry whether, in view of the witness's prior disclosures, the answer to the question at issue would increase the risk of incrimination. Only if not has the witness lost the right to invoke the privilege in response to the question. Many courts, however, apply a more functional approach based upon Klein v. Harris.[2] In *Klein*, the Second Circuit reasoned that the *Rogers'* rationale should inform the criterion it required be applied. Thus before a witness is found to have lost the ability to invoke the privilege, the court must determine that on the facts of the case "the witness' prior statements have created a significant likelihood that the finder of fact will be left with and prone to rely on a distorted view of the truth."

Rogers itself suggests that a witness's loss of the privilege is based not on waiver principles but rather on the notion that a person not an accused must affirmatively assert the privilege. Nevertheless, courts sometimes refuse to find that disclosure by a witness costs the witness the privilege if the facts show that the witness made the disclosure without awareness of the legal significance of doing so or in a nonvoluntary manner.

The disclosure that results in loss of the privilege's protection is usually disclosure by testimony, but that need not be the case. Courts generally find sufficient disclosure to render the privilege inapplicable in sworn doc-

§ 134
1. 340 U.S. 367 (1951).

2. 667 F.2d 274 (2d Cir.1981).

uments executed by a witness. Informal disclosure, such as in a letter, is probably insufficient.

A witness's loss of the privilege by testifying to incriminating facts applies throughout but not beyond the "proceeding" in which the witness has given the incriminating testimony. This is apparently because the shift in the proceeding sufficiently increases the risk of further incrimination that the witness should be entitled to decide anew whether to disclose incriminating information.

Applying this approach, the courts agree that disclosure of incriminating facts in one trial does not bar a witness from refusing to testify as to those same matters in another trial. More dispute exists concerning the effect of disclosure at an early stage of what is a single unit of litigation. Most courts hold that testimony at a grand jury proceedings, or other pretrial event or hearing does not preclude a witness from invoking the privilege at trial. The District of Columbia courts have taken a different approach. Ellis v. United States[3] held that grand jury disclosure precluded a witness from invoking the privilege at trial, and Tomlin v. United States,[4] reasoning from *Ellis*, held that a person who testified at his own trial thereby waived the privilege when called as a witness in the later trial of another person.

§ 135. Privilege of a Witness: (f) Effect in a Criminal Trial of Witness's Invocation of the Privilege

Several special problems are sometimes presented when a witness in a criminal prosecution invokes the privilege. If the witness has already given testimony damaging to the defendant and invokes the privilege in response to the defendant's cross-examination, the situation implicates defendants' Sixth Amendment right to effective confrontation of witnesses presented against them.

In such situations, the trial court must appraise the impact of the witness's action upon the defendant's ability to test the cred-

ibility of the testimony already given. The assessment must include the nature of the precluded inquiry and the directness of its relationship to critical aspects of the witness's direct testimony, whether the area of inquiry was adequately covered by the other questions that were answered, and the overall quality of the cross-examination viewed in relation to the issues actually litigated at trial. If the witness's invocation of the privilege does preclude effective cross-examination, the witness's testimony on direct examination—or at least that part not subject to challenge by cross-examination—must be struck. On the other hand, if the witness's action does not have this effect, the trial judge can properly take measures short of striking the witness's direct testimony, such as having the witness invoke the privilege before the jury or instructing the jury to consider the testimony in light of the defendant's reduced ability to cross-examine. Trial courts have considerable discretion both in evaluating the effect of witnesses' invocation of the privilege and in fashioning an appropriate remedy.

A somewhat different situation is presented if a defense witness invokes the privilege in response to the prosecution's efforts to cross-examine. The prosecution, of course, is entitled to a fair opportunity to test the credibility of the defense testimony, and in an appropriate case the trial court can properly strike a defense witness's testimony on direct examination. But such action endangers the defendant's Sixth Amendment right to present testimony. Trial judges should consequently be reluctant to impose this drastic remedy. Again, less severe alternatives, such as striking only those portions of the testimony on direct which cannot be adequately tested on cross-examination, should be considered. If, however, the witness's actions frustrate the entire cross-examination process, striking that testimony is permissible and proper.

§ 136 Burdens on Exercise of the Privilege

The Fifth Amendment privilege, according

---

3. 416 F.2d 791 (D.C.Cir.1969).

4. 680 A.2d 1020 (D.C.App.1996).

to Malloy v. Hogan,[1] gives one enjoying it not only the right to remain silent in the face of incriminatory questions but also a right "to suffer no penalty * * * for such silence." Although a criminal defendant may have such a right to be placed at no disadvantage in the criminal prosecution by virtue of invoking the privilege, *Malloy's* language otherwise overstates the Fifth Amendment's protection.

A person who invokes the privilege is entitled to be free of an economic sanction imposed automatically for invoking the privilege. Thus a teacher may not be discharged solely because he invoked his privilege before a congressional committee, an attorney cannot be disbarred because in reliance upon the privilege he refused to produce documents during a judicial investigation into his alleged professional misconduct, a police officer may not be dismissed for refusing to sign a general waiver of immunity during an investigation of the "fixing" of traffic tickets, architects called before grand juries investigating public contracts cannot on the basis of their refusal to waive their privilege be barred from state public contracting for five years, and an officer of a political party cannot be barred from party or public office for five years because he refused to testify or waive immunity when called before a grand jury to testify concerning the conduct of his office.

Nevertheless, under Baxter v. Palmigiano,[2] the Fifth Amendment does not forbid the drawing of adverse inferences against parties to civil actions when they invoke the privilege during that litigation. The inference may be considered in determining whether to penalize the party. It cannot, however, be the sole basis for a decision to do so. Thus in a civil proceeding for issuance of a domestic abuse prevention order, the defendant's refusal to testify in reliance on the privilege permits an adverse inference but this *alone* cannot meet the plaintiff's burden of showing a case for issuance of the order.

Penalty issues most commonly arise when a party to civil litigation invokes the privilege

during discovery. When this occurs, courts have the power to respond appropriately even if the response results in a disadvantage being placed upon the party who invoked the privilege. The purpose of such action, and the objective of the court in fashioning an appropriate response for a particular case, should not be to sanction the party who invoked the privilege but rather to provide a remedy for the party disadvantaged by his opponent's reliance upon the privilege.

Trial courts have considerable discretion in fashioning relief. Dismissal, judgment against the party invoking the privilege or the striking of pleadings is clearly permissible, at least in some situations. But the constitutionally-based need to minimize penalization of the exercise of a fundamental right requires that alternatives, such as delaying the civil litigation pending resolution of criminal matters and excluding evidence on matters about which one party invoked the privilege, be considered first. The remedy imposed should be no more burdensome on the party invoking the privilege than is necessary to prevent unfair and unnecessary prejudice to the other party.

A vigorous penalty is particularly appropriate if a civil plaintiff invokes the privilege, and thus uses the privilege's shield as a sword to force an unfair advantage. Fundamental notions of fairness are violated if a party comes into court seeking relief from another and then relies upon his privilege to conceal information that might defeat his claim. Thus courts properly take particular care to prevent a plaintiff from obtaining relief on facts rendered incomplete by the plaintiff's reliance upon the privilege.

A civil litigant's involuntary involvement in a lawsuit, in contrast, suggests that in fashioning a remedy for his invocation of the privilege more weight be given to his self-incrimination interests. Special efforts are appropriate, for example, when the privilege is invoked by a claimant in a civil forfeiture action brought by the government.

§ 136
1. 378 U.S. 1 (1964).

2. 425 U.S. 308 (1976).

§ 137. The Privilege as Related to Documents and Tangible Items: (a) Limits on Use of "Private" Papers

Boyd v. United States[1] indicated that the Fifth Amendment privilege against compelled self-incrimination prohibited the use in evidence of a person's private papers to prove the person's guilt. The conceptual basis for this position was never entirely clear, but it seemed to rest upon combined Fourth and Fifth Amendment protection.

In Fisher v. United States[2] and decisions following it the Supreme Court has rejected the conceptual basis of *Boyd* by making clear that no violation of the Fifth Amendment privilege occurs in the absence of compulsion to put incriminating thought into the contents of documents. Thus *Boyd's* notion that the Fifth Amendment privilege protects a privacy interest in the contents of certain private or personal document is no longer viable. The privilege, as generally construed, does not protect any interest in the contents of private papers or documents voluntarily created.

Therefore, where officers learned that a suspect had kept a journal in which he had made entries indicating his guilt of a double murder, the suspect had no protected privacy interest in the content of that private document. He consequently was not entitled to resist a subpoena for its production, or to oppose its offer into evidence at his trial, on the ground that the Fifth Amendment prohibits the use against him of the contents of his private papers.

States remain free, of course, to construe state privileges more broadly and as protecting the privacy of personal papers. The New Jersey Supreme Court has construed the state's common law privilege as retaining a *Boyd*-like protection for the content of at least some private papers. Other jurisdictions, however, have shown no inclination to follow this approach.

§ 138. The Privilege as Related to Documents and Tangible Items: (b) Compulsory Production and Incrimination by the "Act of Production"

One in possession of documents or tangible items may have a right under the privilege to refuse a demand—usually made by subpoena—to produce those items. Under Fisher v. United States[1] and United States v. Doe,[2] this is the case, however, only if the act of production involves a self-incriminating testimonial communication.

By producing an item in response to a subpoena a person may make one or more of several explicit or implicit representations: (a) the person believes that items described by the subpoena exist; (b) the person believes that such items are within the person's possession or control; and (c) the person believes that the items produced are within the description of the subpoena. Any such representations are unquestionably testimonial communications. Under *Fisher* and *Doe*, whether the Fifth Amendment applies to a demand for production of items depends upon whether any communications of these sorts as might be involved in a particular case involve a real and appreciable risk of incrimination.

If the information available to the prosecution is such that the item's existence, the person's possession of it, and its authenticity as what the demand calls for are "foregone conclusion[s]," the act of production does not add significantly to the incriminating information available to the government. In this event, testimonial communications involved in production do not create the "real and appreciable risk" of self-incrimination necessary to invoke the privilege,[3] and the privilege provides no basis for refusing the demand for production. If one or more of those matters are not so clearly established, on the other hand, one on whom such a demand for production is made can resist by invoking the Fifth Amend-

§ 137

1.   116 U.S. 616 (1886).

2.   425 U.S. 391 (1976).

§ 138

1.   425 U.S. 391 (1976).

2.   465 U.S. 605 (1984).

3.   See generally § 123 supra.

ment privilege, since the act of production of the item would a testimonial and incriminating admission.

If one on whom a demand for production is made can decline to comply in reliance on the privilege, this basis for refusal to comply can be eliminated by giving the person immunity from the results of the acknowledgments made by the act of production of the item sought. This is the case even it the item is a document with incriminating contents, since one in possession of a document with self-incriminating contents has no Fifth Amendment protection for the contents of those documents.[4]

§ 139. The Privilege as Related to Documents and Tangible Items: (c) "Required Records" and Items Possessed Pursuant to Regulatory Schemes

Compelled production of documents that would otherwise be prohibited by the Fifth Amendment privilege is permitted if those documents are "required records." Further, compelled production of items or even persons may be permitted if the items or persons are in the witness's custody pursuant to a regulatory scheme similar to those making documents required records.

In Shapiro v. United States,[1] the Supreme Court held that the Fifth Amendment privilege against compelled self-incrimination was no barrier to the compelled production of documents that were required records, that is, records that the law requires the witness to keep. As later developed, the *Shapiro* doctrine permits compelled production only if all of three additional requirements be met. First, the purposes of the government's activity that imposes the requirement that the records be kept must be "essentially regulatory." Second, the records required and demanded must be of the sort that the regulated persons or businesses would customarily keep. Third, the records must have some "public aspects."

The first requirement focuses upon the nature of the government's purpose in imposing the regulatory scheme. Usually, the judicial inquiry is simply whether the regulatory scheme is a generally permissible one. If so, a demand for records kept pursuant to it meets the first *Shapiro* requirement. Simply because the government relies in part upon criminal sanctions does not mean that the scheme is not essentially regulatory. However, if the scheme focuses upon those selected for attention because they are suspected of criminal activities or upon conduct which is criminal, the scheme is not regulatory and the exception does not apply.

The second requirement is met if the documents sought are the type of records usually kept in connection with the regulated activity. A subpoena for records and contracts relating to an attorney's representation of a named client called for records within the rule, for example, because these are required and customarily kept by persons engaged in the practice of law.

The third requirement may be the most troublesome to apply, because of uncertainty as to what public aspects must exist and what is required to establish them. Unquestionably, the records need not be "public" in the sense that the general public has access to them or a right of access. Rather, the question is generally posed as whether the records are closely enough related to a sufficiently important "public" interest. In an unusual refusal to apply the required records rule, for example, the Seventh Circuit held that even if the Internal Revenue Code required taxpayers to keep records supporting claims made in tax returns, the limited nature of the taxpayer-Internal Revenue Service relationship was insufficient to give the records the "public aspects" that the *Shapiro* rule requires.[2]

The required records rule is of questionable wisdom. One court has summarized:

> [W]hen the criteria for the required-records exception are met, the exception ap-

---

4. See § 137 supra.

1.　335 U.S. 1 (1948).

2.　United States v. Porter, 711 F.2d 1397, 1405 (7th Cir.1983).

plies regardless of whether the act of producing the requested records would involve self-incriminating testimony by the record holder.

The courts have cited several reasons for [compelling the production of documents under the required-records regardless of whether the act of producing the requested records would involve self-incriminating testimony by the record holder]: (1) a person engaged in a regulated activity in which record keeping is required by statute or law is deemed to have waived the privilege against self-incrimination with respect to the act of producing the required records; (2) the record holder admits little of significance in the way of existence or authentication by producing records that the law requires to be kept in furtherance of public policy; and (3) the public interest in obtaining records required by a regulatory scheme normally outweighs the private interest in nondisclosure because invocation of the privilege frustrates the regulatory purpose of the scheme.[3]

This is essentially a conclusion that the need for disclosure outweighs relatively minimal intrusion upon protected interests caused by compelled production. A balancing analysis of this sort may have been appropriate when *Shapiro* was decided, given the then-current assumption that the Fifth Amendment protected against the self-incriminating *contents* of documents. Such broad protection is perhaps properly limited by balancing analyses of this sort. Now that the federal constitutional privilege applies only to the act of production, however, the quite limited protection afforded self-incrimination interests may not justify limitation by balancing of interests. Nevertheless, the courts have refused to read post-*Shapiro* developments in Fifth Amendment doctrine as superseding the required records rule or so undermining its justification as to demand that it be abandoned.

State courts remain free, of course, to construe their state privileges as embodying no similar exception. They have not, however, done so.

Baltimore City Department of Social Services v. Bouknight[4] suggests that the principle underlying the *Shapiro* required records rule will apply beyond the limited area of production of documents. *Bouknight* upheld the compelled production by Bouknight of a child placed by a juvenile court with her, over her Fifth Amendment objections that by producing the child she would be acknowledging control over the child and that this might aid her prosecution. The Court relied heavily upon *Shapiro*. It explained *Shapiro* as resting on the principle that "[w]hen a person assumes control over items that are the legitimate object of the government's non-criminal regulatory powers, the ability to invoke the privilege is reduced." This same principle, the Court continued, applied in *Bouknight*. By finding the child within the jurisdiction of the juvenile court, the state subjected him to a noncriminal regulatory scheme. When Bouknight accepted custody, she assumed certain obligations attending that custody, including that of producing the child for "inspection."

The required records exception, or at least the principle on which it is based, is obviously not limited to records. It may render the privilege unavailable as a bar to compelled production of other items or even persons where custody of the items or persons is pursuant to a noncriminal regulatory scheme of the same sort as renders documentary records subject to compelled production.

As applied, the required records rule or principle operates to deprive a witness of the power to successfully resist a demand that an item or person be produced. *Bouknight* noted the possibility that in these situations, as where an organizational agent is compelled to produce organizational property despite the self-incriminating effects of doing so,[5] the incriminating testimonial admissions made by the production cannot be used against the

3. State v. Gomes, 648 A.2d 396, 402 (Vt. 1994).
4. 493 U.S. 549 (1990).

5. See § 141 infra, discussing Braswell v. United States, 487 U.S. 99 (1988).

witness. Whether compelled production under the required records approach in fact generates what is in effect use immunity has not been addressed by courts.

§ 140. Privilege as Related to Corporations, Associations, and Their Agents: (a) The Privilege of the Organization

Only natural persons have the Fifth Amendment privilege against compelled self-incrimination. Neither corporations nor unincorporated associations such as labor unions have a privilege.

Many of the rationales for the privilege support its limitation to "natural individuals." Organizations, for example, do not possess the "dignity" which is offended by compelled self-incrimination. An organization cannot be subjected to torture or "equally reprehensible methods that are necessary to compelling self-incrimination or that are invited by the right to do so." Further, a corporation, unlike a natural person, is "a creature of the State" holding privileges subject to the laws of the State and the terms of its charter. Legislatures reasonably reserve a right to investigate such organizations to assure that they have not exceeded their powers and to conduct such investigations by demanding even self-incriminating information from the organizations. If this is not permitted, many necessary investigations into possible abuses by corporations of their immense power would necessarily fail, because such abuses could only be ascertained by information obtained from the organizations themselves.

Thus if a demand for production of documents or items is made upon an organization, the officers or agents of the organization who respond have no right to refuse to respond because doing so will incriminate the organization.

State courts remain free, of course, to construe state privileges as affording protection to such entities. They have not, however, tended to do so.

§ 141. The Privilege as Related to Corporations, Associations, and Their Agents: (b) Agents' Ability to Invoke Their Personal Privilege and the "Collective Entity" Rule

An officer or agent of an association is, of course, protected by that person's own Fifth Amendment privilege against compelled self-incrimination, even though the association itself has no privilege. Such a person's ability to invoke that protection, however, is limited by the so-called "collective entity" rule.

Under the collective entity rule, an organization agent who holds items or documents of the organization may not invoke the person's personal privilege in response to demands for production of the items or documents of the organization.[1] When a corporation custodian produces corporation documents, "the custodian's act of production is not regarded as a personal act, but rather an act of the corporation."

The Supreme Court first justified the collective entity rule on the grounds that significant public interests justified limiting the protection afforded organizational agents by the privilege, and that those agents in effect assumed the risk of this reduced protection by becoming agents of the organization. Permitting a claim of privilege by a corporation agent, the Court explained, would be "tantamount to a claim of privilege by the corporation," and thus would circumvent the privilege's inapplicability to such organizations. This, moreover, "would have a detrimental impact on the Government's efforts to prosecute 'white collar crime,' one of the most serious problems confronting law enforcement authorities." Further, by accepting the position as agent of the organization, a person incurs certain obligations, including that of producing organizational documents regardless of the self-incriminating repercussions.

In Braswell v. United States,[2] the Supreme Court held that the personal protection afforded the organizational agent who is com-

---

§ 141

1. Wilson v. United States, 221 U.S. 361, 382 (1911).

2. 487 U.S. 99 (1988).

pelled to produce organizational items requires that the agent's act of production not be used against him individually. Suppose, for example, the Government subpoenas the records of Corporation A from X, president of that corporation. X produces the records. Later, X is prosecuted and the prosecution wishes to show that X possessed the records and was aware of their contents. To prove this, the prosecution may show: (a) X was president of Corporation A; (b) documents of this sort are generally in possession of and familiar to the president of an organization like Corporation A; and (c) these documents were produced by an agent of Corporation A in response to a subpoena for documents of this sort. But the prosecution may *not* show that X himself personally produced the documents on behalf of Corporation A.

Braswell in effect mandates that an organizational agent who in response to compulsion produces organizational documents or items be given automatic use immunity protecting the agent from the use against him of testimonial communications made by the act of production. Under this approach, the collective entity rule can be regarded as based on the lack of any significant risk of incrimination by whatever testimonial communications are made by production.

The Supreme Court has indicated that the collective entity rule requires the custodian of organizational property to do no more than produce the property or explain under oath the nonproduction of the items. A custodian, the Court said, "may decline to utter upon the witness stand a single self-incriminating word."[3] Subsequently, however, the Court suggested an organizational agent obligated to produce items might also have no right to resist giving testimony merely "auxiliary to the production" of the items because such testimony would not involve an increased risk of incrimination beyond what resulted from the act of production.[4] A witness who has explained nonproduction by testifying the witness does not have the items sought most

likely cannot, however, be compelled to testify as to where the items are now located if that information would be personally incriminating.

A witness is deprived of the right to rely on his personal privilege to resist a demand for documents or items only if there is a collective entity sufficient to invoke the rule. Under Bellis v. United States,[5] whether a unit is sufficient to trigger the rule depends upon whether the unit is recognizable as an entity apart from its individual members, probably on the basis of its performance of organized and institutional activity. *Bellis* added:

> The group must be relatively well organized and structured, and not merely a loose, informal association of individuals. It must maintain a distinct set of organizational records, and recognize rights in its members of control and access to them.[6]

A corporation will generally if not always be a sufficient collective entity. Unincorporated associations present greater difficulties. A labor union, of course, is a sufficient unit to invoke the rule. *Bellis* itself makes clear that a partnership will often be sufficient.

The partnership in *Bellis* was a law firm that had been in existence for nearly fifteen years and had three partners and six employees. It maintained a bank account and held itself out as an entity with an independent institutional identity. Size is relevant but not necessarily determinative, the Court commented. "[A]n insubstantial difference in the form of [a] business enterprise," it continued, should not control. Despite their noncorporate nature, partnerships such as law and stock brokerage firms are often large, impersonal, and perpetual in duration. The personal interest of any particular partner in the financial records of the organization is "highly attenuated." A different case might be presented, the Court noted, if the partnership had been a "small family" one or if "there were some

---

3. Wilson v. United States, supra note 1, 221 U.S. at 385.

4. Curcio v. United States, 354 U.S. 118, 125 (1957).

5. 417 U.S. 85 (1974).

6. Id. at 92–93.

other pre-existing relationship of confidentiality among the partners."

A person loses the right to invoke the person's own privilege only if the demand is for items belonging to the organization held by the person in his capacity as an agent of the entity. With regard to records, the agency rationale for the collective entity rule indicates that agency law provides an appropriate source for standards. Records are organizational ones possessed as an agent of the organization if the person in developing and possessing them acted within the scope of his agency relationship with the entity.

States, of course, remain free to construe state privileges as affording broader protection to organizational agents than is provided by the Fifth Amendment.

§ 142. Removing the Danger of Incrimination by Granting Immunity: (a) In General

The privilege protects only against formal legal liability. Consequently, if the risk of criminal liability is removed by a grant of effective immunity, the privilege no longer applies.

Generally, the availability of immunity to witnesses is closely tied to statutory authority for such immunity and statutorily-provided procedures for conferring and enforcing it. Early statutes sometimes provided for immunity for any witness who testified about a matter, permitting witnesses to insulate themselves from prosecution by volunteering information. Modern statutes, in contrast, tend to provide for immunity only if a witness invokes the privilege, the prosecution seeks a grant of immunity, and the trial judge grants it. This is the case, for example, under the federal statute.

Many courts recognize prosecutors' power to effectively confer "informal" immunity by entering into an agreement with a witness. Unlike most forms of formal immunity, this sort of immunity cannot be imposed on a witness over the witness's refusal to cooperate. Further, a finding that a witness has received such informal immunity is unlikely to trigger the elaborate procedural requirements imposed before prosecution and use of evidence can proceed after a grant of formal immunity. The witness is most likely limited to challenging evidence as either an inadmissible involuntary confession or the inadmissible fruit of such a confession.

Immunity does not protect the witness from prosecution for perjury committed in the giving of the immunized testimony. In such a prosecution, the testimony relied upon as being false may, of course, be used against the witness. It is less clear whether immunized testimony may be used to prove that the witness committed perjury during other testimony, either before or after the immunized testimony. Some authority indicates that a grant of immunity may and perhaps must protect the witness against prosecution for perjury committed prior to the immunized testimony.

Multijurisdictional aspects of immunity create special difficulties, given that testimony may well have incriminating implications in more than one jurisdiction. If state A grants a witness transactional immunity and the witness gives testimony with incriminating implications in state B as well as state A, what flexibility does state B have to prosecute? If state A's grant of transactional immunity had to be given full effect in state B, this would raise serious federalism concerns regarding the right or ability of one state to frustrate the criminal process of another state. But the few cases addressing the matter seem agreed that Fifth Amendment concerns are satisfied if state B, in effect, grants the witness use immunity. While this may impose a significant burden upon state B's prosecutors, this is necessary to protect state A's ability to compel testimony and to enforce its own laws; it does not frustrate state B's right similarly to enforce its own criminal prohibitions.

§ 143. Removing the Danger of Incrimination by Granting Immunity: (b) "Testimonial" Versus "Use" Immunity

Immunity is of two kinds. "Transactional" immunity confers full immunity from prosecution for all offenses related to matters about which the witness testifies, that is, all offenses arising out of the "transaction" that was the subject of the compelled testimony. "Use" immunity, on the other hand, provides no bar to prosecution but protects the witness from use against that witness of the compelled testimony and evidence directly or indirectly derived from that testimony. Some immunity statutes permit only the granting of transactional immunity or only both transactional and use immunity. Others, such as the federal statute, authorize only the granting of use immunity. The Vermont court has construed its statute as authorizing use immunity but also as giving the trial judge discretion to find—on the facts of the particular case—that use immunity would not adequately protect the witness and thus to refuse to compel testimony unless the prosecution seeks transactional immunity.[1]

Counselman v. Hitchcock,[2] decided in 1892, was widely regarded as indicating that the Fifth Amendment privilege permitted compelled testimony over a claim of the privilege only upon a granting of transactional immunity. In Kastigar v. United States,[3] however, the Supreme Court held that a grant of transactional immunity is not necessary in order to compel a witness to testify over an assertion of his privilege. The sole concern of the privilege, reasoned the majority, is the prevention of compulsion to give testimony that leads to the infliction of penalties affixed to criminal acts. "Immunity from the use of compelled testimony, as well as evidence derived directly and indirectly therefrom," it concluded, "affords this protection."

The Kastigar dissenters and other critics of use immunity argue that use immunity is inadequate because, given practical realities, use immunity cannot eliminate or sufficiently minimize the possibility that in actuality compelled testimony will operate to convict the immunized witness. In response, the Kastigar majority held that once a defendant establishes that he has previously testified under a grant of immunity concerning matters related to his prosecution, the prosecution, upon de-fense objection, must affirmatively prove that the evidence it offers against the defendant is derived from a legitimate source wholly independent of the previously compelled testimony. This burden of proof is adequate, the Court concluded, to assure that compelled testimony will not be used to incriminate the witness forced to give it. At such a so-called Kastigar hearing, the prosecution must prove its nonuse of the immunized testimony by a preponderance of the evidence.

Lower courts agree that under Kastigar, the prosecution must prove that it will make no "evidentiary" use of immunized testimony if it proceeds against a witness who has given immunized testimony. All evidence offered at trial and before any indicting grand jury, then, must be shown to have had a source other than—or independent of—the immunized testimony. A general assertion by the prosecution that its evidence has an independent source is not sufficient. Rather, the prosecution must proceed item-by-item and witness-by-witness and demonstrate its source for the proffered testimony. The same is true regarding evidence elicited by cross-examination; Kastigar is violated if a prosecutor's consideration of a defendant's immunized testimony enables the prosecutor to elicit significant testimony on cross-examination of defense witnesses.

When the evidence is testimony of a witness, the prosecution's task is often quite difficult, especially if the evidence shows that the witness has been exposed to the immunized testimony. At least in those situations, the prosecution may be required to proceed line-by-line through the witness's testimony and demonstrate that the substance of the testimony was not affected by the immunized testimony. As a practical matter, the prosecution may be able to meet its burden only if it has "canned" the testimony–by producing and filing a sworn version of it–before the witness was exposed to the immunized testimony.

Lower courts disagree on whether use immunity does–and constitutionally must–

---

§ 143

1.   State v. Ely, 708 A.2d 1332, 1340 (Vt.1997).

2.   142 U.S. 547 (1892).

3.   406 U.S. 441 (1972).

prohibit the prosecution from all "nonevidentiary" use of immunized testimony. Nonevidentiary uses are those that affect the prosecution but not by impacting the substance of evidence used. Thus nonevidentiary use occurs if a prosecutor's decision to prosecute was influenced by immunized testimony or, apparently, if a witness's willingness to testify was so affected. Some courts appear to regard use immunity as sufficient to negate the Fifth Amendment right not to testify to self-incriminating matters only if it prohibits nonevidentiary use.

The prosecution's burden at a *Kastigar* hearing is greatly increased if it must prove that it is making no nonevidentiary use of immunized testimony. Probably the leading decision regarding nonevidentiary use as impermissible, United States v. McDaniel,[4] has been read as holding that proof that prosecutors were exposed to and aware of immunized testimony of the defendant is sufficient to establish that nonevidentiary use was made of that testimony. This is apparently on the rationale that the prosecution cannot, as a practical matter, produce satisfactory evidence that prosecutors so exposed to immunized testimony did not make use of that testimony. Opponents of the nonevidentiary use approach argue, of course, that at least if that approach is applied as required by this reading of *McDaniel*, use immunity effectively precludes prosecution and thus becomes transactional immunity.

A significant number of state courts have construed state constitutions as requiring transactional immunity. Most often, this is based on conclusions that practical difficulties in applying use immunity mean that in actual fact use immunity does not provide adequate assurance that immunized testimony will not be used against the witness in a subsequent prosecution. The Alaska Supreme Court, for example, stressed that faded memories and other difficulties of proof will often make impossible accurate determinations as to whether immunized testimony in fact affected the prosecution's evidence and that no procedural way is available to adequately protect witnesses from nonevidentiary use against them of compelled testimony.

Some courts have found use immunity adequate under state constitutional standards only if it involves safeguards more stringent than those required by *Kastigar* as a matter of Fifth Amendment law. The Pennsylvania Supreme Court, for example, upheld use immunity but only on the condition that the prosecution is required to prove that its evidence "arose *wholly* [from] independent sources" and to prove this by clear and convincing evidence.

4.   482 F.2d 305 (8th Cir.1973).

Chapter 14

CONFESSIONS

Table of Sections

§ 144. "Confessions" and Admissibility

Among the most frequently raised evidentiary issues in criminal litigation are those relating to the admissibility of self-incriminating admissions by the defendant. These issues are the subject of the present chapter.

Traditional analysis sometimes required inquiry into whether a self-incriminating statement by a defendant was a "confession"—a statement admitting all facts necessary for conviction of the crime at issue—or an "admission"—an acknowledgment of one or more facts tending to prove guilt but not of all the facts necessary to do so. Most major limitations upon the admissibility of confessions now also apply to admissions and even exculpatory statements. This chapter, therefore, will assume unless a particular discussion requires otherwise that no distinction is appropriately drawn among self-incriminating acknowledgements.

Confessions are out-of-court statements quite frequently offered to prove the truth of matters asserted therein and thus are potentially subject to exclusion pursuant to the prohibition against hearsay. Nevertheless, there is general agreement that the prosecution is entitled to introduce confessions, although the conceptual basis for this position is somewhat unclear.

211

Given the general principle that defendants' confessions are admissible to prove guilt, confession law becomes primarily a collection of rules that prevent the use of particular categories of confessions. To some extent, some confession law rules are examples of the sort of exclusionary sanctions discussed in Chapter 15. Under these, exclusion of confessions is mandated by a perceived need to implement policies other than the accurate ascertainment of the "truth." For example, the requirement that confessions be excluded if they are shown to be sufficiently related to an unlawful arrest[1] is designed to maximize compliance with the rules governing arrest and prompt presentation.

The traditional voluntariness mandate,[2] on the other hand, is more closely related to the objective of accurate ascertainment of guilt or innocence at trial. Whether the modern voluntariness demand and other confession law requirements—such as the well-known *Miranda* rules[3]—still do and should serve that function, perhaps among others, is a major issue in modern confession law.

§ 145. Corroboration Requirement: (a) In General

American jurisdictions have embraced a requirement that in order for a conviction based upon a confession to be sustained, the confession must have been corroborated by other evidence introduced at trial. The requirement has sometimes been incorporated into statute or court rule. Federal constitutional considerations, however, do not demand it.

There are several quite different formulations of the requirement, some of which are variations of what is often called the requirement of independent proof of the *corpus delicti*. Another, applied by the federal courts and some state tribunals, is a more flexible approach. The two basic approaches are described in the sections that follow.

General Aspects of the Requirement. There is widespread agreement that the requirement, whatever the local formulation of it, applies not only to "confessions", defined as complete and conscious admissions of guilt to a crime, but also to "admissions", acknowledgments of facts relevant to guilt, and even to exculpatory statements, because all involve the risks which the requirement is designed to reduce. The requirement is not limited to statements made to law enforcement officers and consequently applies to statements made to private persons. It does not, however, apply to incriminating statements made prior to or during the offense.

Less agreement exists as to the nature of the requirement. It is clearly a requirement of evidence *sufficiency* to be applied by an appellate court reviewing a conviction, and—apparently—by a trial judge in deciding whether there is sufficient evidence for a case to go to the jury. Is it also a requirement of *admissibility*, demanding that the prosecution produce sufficient corroborating evidence before its proof of a confession is admissible? Certainly some formulations of the requirement assume that it is a demand of admissibility, and courts sometimes discuss it as such a requirement. Whether as so conceptualized it is a meaningful requirement of admissibility is unlikely. A trial judge's discretion regarding the timing of evidence means that if sufficient corroborating evidence is eventually produced by the prosecution, any error in admitting a confession earlier is not reversible error. If the requirement is only one of admissibility, perhaps the prosecution's failure to meet the requirement constitutes trial error mandating a new trial but not acquittal. Agreement that the requirement is always one of evidence sufficiency, however, means that failure to meet it requires acquittal and thus moots any error in admitting a confession.

As a requirement of evidence sufficiency, is the demand only for the court or should the jury be instructed to apply it as well? Wigmore assumes that the trial judge applies the rule

---

§ 144

1. See § 158 infra.

2. See § 148 infra.

3. See §§ 149–153 infra.

first, and if the case goes to the jury the "same question" is then posed for the jury. The jury must then address, "without reference to the judge's ruling, whether the corroboration exists to satisfy them." Some courts certainly regard the jury as playing a role in applying the requirement. At least a few appear to conceptualize the jury's evaluation as the major one, with the judge's ruling merely a preliminary screening decision.

Other courts have taken far different approaches. The Virginia Supreme Court, for example, has held that a defendant is not entitled to have the jury instructed that it should consider whether a confession has been adequately corroborated. Application of the *corpus delicti* rule is for the trial judge, and the jury has no power to "overrule" the judge's decision on that. While the jury passes on the sufficiency of the evidence, which necessarily includes proof of the *corpus delicti,* this task is adequately accomplished under general instructions.[1] Whether under the federal approach a jury issue is ever generated remains unclear.

Rationale for Requirement. The requirement has traditionally been based upon concern that convictions might result from false confessions, and widespread agreement remains that the need to assure accuracy remains at least a major basis for the requirement. There has, however, been no consensus on the nature and sources of inaccuracy that support the rule.

Traditionally and generally, the requirement appears to have a relatively modest objective—protecting against the risk of conviction for a crime that never occurred. Thus the target inaccuracies are very limited. A Maryland court, for example, commented that the requirement serves the limited purpose of preventing a mentally unstable person from confessing to and being convicted of a crime that never occurred.[2]

Often, however, the objectives are stated more broadly although frequently quite generally. The Delaware court, for example, has asserted that its rule "serves to protect those defendants who may be pressured to confess to crimes that they either did not commit or crimes that did not occur."[3] The Washington court has indicated that the rule is designed to combat, first, risks of inaccuracy arising from misinterpretation or misreporting by witnesses who testify to what defendants admitted and, second, risks of inaccuracy with regard to what defendants said. These latter sources of inaccuracy, the court continued, include not only force or coercion but also the possibilities that a confession was "based upon a mistaken perception of the facts or law."[4] The Michigan Supreme Court has indicated that the requirement serves "to minimize the weight of a confession and require collateral evidence to support a conviction,"[5] which it regarded as desirable on the apparent assumption that confessions are of dubious reliability and prosecutors should be encouraged to develop and use other evidence of guilt.

Whether considerations beyond accuracy can also support the requirement is doubtful. It has been argued that the corroboration requirement serves to combat improper police practices in securing confessions generally, and thus serves to discourage law enforcement actions offensive for reasons other than inaccuracy. At best, however, the requirement achieves this objective indirectly, and the function is almost certainly more effectively accomplished by other legal requirements relating to confessions.

Future of Corroboration Requirement. Wigmore maintains that no corroboration rule is needed and that existing requirements are, in the hands of unscrupulous defense counsel, "a positive obstruction to the course of jus-

---

§ 145

1. Watkins v. Commonwealth, 385 S.E.2d 50, 55 (Va. 1989).

2. Crouch v. State, 551 A.2d 943, 944 (Md.App.), cert. denied, 554 A.2d 393 (Md.1989).

3. DeJesus v. State, 655 A.2d 1180, 1202 (Del.1995).

4. City of Bremerton v. Corbett, 723 P.2d 1135, 1139 (Wash.1986).

5. People v. McMahan, 548 N.W.2d 199, 201 (Mich. 1996) (quoting from Hall, General Principles of Criminal Law (2d ed.), ch. VII, p. 226).

tice.''[6] Commentators have generally agreed.

Given the development of other confession law doctrines, especially Fifth Amendment protections as promulgated in *Miranda* and the voluntariness requirement, concerns regarding law enforcement interrogation practices do not provide significant support for the corroboration requirement. Whether courts can retain the doctrine for the purpose of encouraging investigatory techniques other than interrogation with reasonable expectation of success is at best questionable; the corroboration requirement as applied most likely provides little significant pressure for pursuing such alternatives.

Similarly, the requirement as administered is quite unlikely to provide much protection against inaccuracies resulting from mistakes in reporting, suspects' misunderstandings of the law or facts, or pressures too subtle to invoke *Miranda* or voluntariness protection. Any protection the requirement provides against false confessions by mentally disturbed persons could as well be provided by careful scrutiny of the evidence by conscientious judges. The requirement may, however, serve to trigger such scrutiny in appropriate cases by trial judges otherwise too rushed by the press of business to recognize such evidentiary deficiencies.

If a requirement of corroboration is to be retained, the complexity of the *corpus delicti* approach—as discussed in the next section—tends only to detract from the requirement's real function. The Supreme Court's "truthfulness" approach[7] is best designed to pursue the realistic objectives of a corroboration requirement

There is no justification for treating the rule as one related to admissibility of defendant's admissions; the requirement should be only one of evidence sufficiency. If juries are adequately instructed on the prosecution's burden of proof, there is no need to submit the corroboration requirement to those juries. Finally, the rule should be one applied by trial judges and appellate courts, not juries.

Thus a trial judge should have a duty to assure, if the prosecution's case rests for all practical purposes upon the defendant's out-of-court admission, that the prosecution has produced reasonable evidence other than that admission to establish the trustworthiness of the admission or confession.

§ 146. Corroboration Requirement: (b) Independent Proof of the *Corpus Delicti*

The traditional formulation of the corroboration requirement, still applied by most jurisdictions, demands that there be some evidence other than the confession that tends to establish the *corpus delicti*. Generally, the evidence need not do so beyond a reasonable doubt. If sufficient independent evidence exists, that independent evidence *and* the confession may both be considered in determining whether guilt has been proved beyond a reasonable doubt. Only "slight" corroborating evidence is often required, and this can be circumstantial as well as direct.

There is some dispute regarding the definition of *corpus delicti,* which literally means the "body of the crime." To establish guilt in a criminal case, the prosecution must ordinarily show that (a) the injury or harm constituting the crime occurred; (b) this injury or harm was done in a criminal manner; and (c) the defendant was the person who inflicted the injury or harm. Wigmore maintains that *corpus delicti* means only the first of these, that is, "the fact of the specific loss or injury sustained," and does not require proof that this was occasioned by anyone's criminal agency. Some courts have agreed.

Most courts, however, define *corpus delicti* as involving both (a) and (b). This means that the corroborating evidence must tend to show the harm or injury and that it was occasioned by criminal activity. It need not, however, in any manner tend to show that the defendant was the guilty party. Thus in a homicide case, the *corpus delicti* consists of proof that the victim died and that the death was caused by a

---

6. 7 Wigmore, Evidence § 2070 p. 510 (Chadbourn rev. 1978).

7. See § 147 infra.

criminal act, but it need not tend to connect the defendant on trial with that act.

The traditional approach has been to require that the elements of the offense be carefully distinguished and that the corroborating evidence tends to show each of those elements. A growing number of courts, however, are abandoning the strict requirement that the corroborating evidence tend to prove all elements of the *corpus delicti*. Thus the corroborating evidence need only tend to show the "major" or "essential" harm involved in the offense charged and not all of the elements technically distinguished. This tendency is most pronounced in homicide cases, where defendants are often tried for offenses that involve requirements beyond simply the causing of death in a criminal manner.

This approach is somewhat troublesome as applied to certain modern crimes that—unlike homicide offenses—do not involve a single and tangible injury or loss that can readily be characterized as constituting the "major" or "essential" harm involved in the offense. This is arguably the case, for example, where the crime is an inchoate one, such as conspiracy or attempt. Nevertheless, creative analysis in defining the essential features of even such crimes permits application of the modern *corpus delicti* approach to such offenses.

Felony murder cases have posed the problem with special difficulty. Under the traditional application of the *corpus delicti* formulation, the elements of felony murder include the predicate felony as well as the fact of death and the causing of it in a criminal way; thus, corroborating evidence would have to tend to prove that predicate felony. Most courts, however, have balked at this and have held that the corroborating evidence need not tend to prove the predicate felony.

The general rule in felony murder cases is sometimes regarded as reflecting the general principle that elements affecting only the degree or seriousness of the crime are not part of the *corpus delicti* that needs to be corroborated. Thus in a prosecution for burglary that would be first degree burglary because it was committed in the nighttime, the time of the entry could be proved by the confession alone because the time of entry determined only the degree of burglary committed.

Most courts also assume that *mens rea* is part of the *corpus delicti* and must be shown by at least some independent evidence. This has not been critically considered, however, and at least several courts have disagreed. On principle, corroboration should be required since *mens rea* is generally necessary to show that the injury or harm constituting the crime was done in a criminal manner. Given the ease of meeting the requirement, requiring some independent proof—circumstantial, perhaps—from which the necessary mental state can be inferred should not be a difficult burden.

§ 147. Corroboration Requirement: (c) Evidence Establishing Truthfulness

Some courts have rejected the traditional requirement of independent evidence tending to prove the *corpus delicti* of the charged offense in favor of an alternative standard for determining whether a confession is adequately corroborated. This alternative approach is based on the United States Supreme Court's analysis developed in Opper v. United States.[1]

In *Opper*, the Court held as a matter of federal evidence law that a conviction in federal court could not rest upon an uncorroborated confession. The "better rule," *Opper* continued without extensive explanation, would not require that the corroborating evidence establish the *corpus delicti* but rather that it be "substantial independent evidence which would tend to establish the truthfulness of the statement." Some state courts have adopted this position.

The major advantage of the trustworthiness approach is that its flexibility permits it to provide some—and arguably adequate—protection against conviction on the basis of inaccurate confessions while avoiding serious problems sometimes involved in the *corpus delicti* formulation. Application of the *corpus delicti* formulation may have been a relatively simple

§ 147

1. 348 U.S. 84 (1954).

task that accomplished the purpose of the corroboration requirement when crimes were few and were defined in simple and concise terms. But modern statutory criminal law has increased the number and complexity of crimes. Simply identifying the elements of the *corpus delicti* thus provides fertile ground for dispute. Requiring that the corroborating evidence tend to establish each element once the *corpus delicti* is defined may pose an unrealistic burden upon the prosecution without significantly furthering the requirement's objective of providing assurance against conviction on the basis of inaccurate confessions. This is especially the case with regard to crimes that may not have a tangible *corpus delicti,* such as attempt offenses, conspiracy, tax evasion and similar offenses. The modern approach of requiring corroboration of only the "major" or "essential" harm involved in an offense, although conceptually reasonable, may often founder on difficulty in identifying the major or essential harm.

As applied to modern crimes, in summary, the trustworthiness approach is easier than the *corpus delicti* rule to apply, as effective in accomplishing the modest realistic objectives of the requirement, and less likely to lead to occasionally unreasonable results.

§ 148. Voluntariness—In General

The common law rule requiring voluntariness of an out-of-court confession as a condition for admission into evidence was developed only in the mid–1700s. Early discussions made clear that the rationale for the requirement approach was the perceived lack of reliability of statements motivated not by guilt but by a desire to avoid discomfort or to secure some favor.

In its first confession case, Hopt v. Utah,[1] the Supreme Court of the United States adopted as a matter of federal evidence law what it characterized as the well-developed common law requirement of voluntariness.

That requirement, the Court explained, commands that a confession be held inadmissible

> when the confession appears to have been made either in consequence of inducements of a temporal nature, held out by one in authority, touching the charge preferred, or because of a threat or promise by or in the presence of such a person, which, operating upon the fears or hopes of the accused, in reference to the charge, deprives him of that freedom of will or self-control essential to make his confession voluntary within the meaning of the law.[2]

Thirteen years later, in Bram v. United States[3], the Court commented that whenever an issue arises in federal criminal trials as to the voluntariness of a confession, "the issue is controlled by that portion of the Fifth Amendment to the Constitution of the United States, commanding that no person 'shall be compelled in any criminal case to be a witness against himself.' " This, the Court continued, embodied the common law rule of voluntariness.

Because the Fifth Amendment was not held binding on the states until 1964,[4] the *Bram* analysis did not impose the voluntariness requirement upon the states as a matter of federal constitutional law. The Court's 1936 holding in Brown v. Mississippi,[5] however, made clear that a state court conviction resting upon a confession extorted by brutality and violence violated the accused's general right to due process guaranteed by the Fourteenth Amendment. Subsequent cases established that any use in a state criminal proceeding of a coerced confession violated the federal standard. After the Fifth Amendment was applied to the states, the Court characterized the due process standard developed in *Brown* and its progeny as "the same general standard which [is] applied in federal prosecutions, a standard grounded in the policies of the privilege against self-incrimination."[6]

---

§ 148

1. 110 U.S. 574 (1884).
2. Id. at 585.
3. 168 U.S. 532 (1897).

4. See § 116 supra.
5. 297 U.S. 278 (1936).

Despite the traditional emphasis upon the federal constitutional requirement of voluntariness, state constitutional and evidence law in most if not all jurisdictions also imposes similar requirements.

In Blackburn v. Alabama,[7] the Supreme Court explained that "a complex of values underlies the stricture against use by the state of confessions which, by way of convenient shorthand, this Court terms involuntary." The traditional criterion for determining the admissibility of a confession challenged under the federal constitutional voluntariness requirement was articulated by Justice Frankfurter in 1961:

> The ultimate test * * * [is] voluntariness. Is the confession the product of an essentially free and unconstrained choice by its maker? If it is, if he has willed to confess, it may be used against him. If it is not, if his will has been overborne and his capacity for self-determination critically impaired, the use of his confession offends due process.[8]

Physical coercion or the threat of it, of course, necessarily shows that the defendant's will was overborne and his confession involuntary. But the Court was increasingly presented with claims of "psychological" rather than physical coercion. Application of the voluntariness standard became more difficult as cases increasingly relied upon these claims of more subtle influences than were presented by the earlier decisions.

Since 1961 the constitutional question of voluntariness has been carefully distinguished from the question of the accuracy or reliability of particular confessions. In Rogers v. Richmond,[9] the Court held that due process did not permit a trial court to resolve the admissibility of a confession challenged on voluntariness grounds by using "a legal standard which took into account the circumstances of probable truth or falsity." Evidence that a challenged confession (or some subpart of it) is accurate, then, is totally irrelevant to the voluntariness inquiry.

In Colorado v. Connelly,[10] the Court held that the Fourteenth Amendment's due process requirement of voluntariness imposed no absolute requirement that a confession reflect "an essentially free and unconstrained choice" by the defendant. Official and coercive activity "is a necessary predicate to the finding that a confession is not 'voluntary' within the meaning of the Due Process Clause of the Fourteenth Amendment." In the absence of this predicate, a showing that a confession reflected little or no meaningful choice by the defendant—because of private coercion or undisclosed mental impairment, for example—does not does not even raise an issue as to federal due process voluntariness.

Connelly provided little guidance for determining what constitutes the official coercion necessary to require the Fourteenth Amendment analysis to proceed to the mind of the suspect. *Connelly's* facts illustrate the difficulty. Connelly's statement was made in response to hallucinatory voices, but the officer who took it was unaware of Connelly's impairment. The Court summarily concluded that the taking and later the trial use of Connelly's statement to the officer did not violate the Fourteenth Amendment. It appeared to distinguish Blackburn v. Alabama[11] on the basis that in *Blackburn* police learned during interrogation that Blackburn had a history of mental problems. Nevertheless they continued the interrogation and "exploited this weakness with coercive tactics" such as prolonged questioning in a tiny room. Exploitation of a known impairment in a manner that impairs the suspect's ability to decide whether to confess can constitute the coercion necessary for involuntariness.

Pre-*Connelly* Supreme Court case law reflected consideration of numerous factors in evaluating a voluntariness challenge. The

---

6.   Davis v. North Carolina, 384 U.S. 737, 740 (1966).
7.   361 U.S. 199 (1960).
8.   Culombe v. Connecticut, 367 U.S. 568, 602 (1961).
9.   365 U.S. 534 (1961).

10.   479 U.S. 157 (1986).
11.   361 U.S. 199 (1960).

Court gave significant weight to the time of the day or night of the interrogation, the length of interrogation, the quality of the conditions in which the defendant was held before confessing, and similar matters. These have been evaluated in light of various characteristics of the accused that presumably affect the impact of these factors upon the accused. Thus the Court has found suggestion of involuntariness in the accused's youth, physical illness, injury, or infirmity, low educational level, and little or no prior experience with law enforcement practices and techniques. Whether or not officers warned the suspect of his right to silence and explained that right, where there is no specific obligation to do so, is relevant to voluntariness; in any case, the extent of the suspect's actual appreciation of his rights is clearly significant. These factors remain relevant under *Connelly*, but only after official coercive activity has been found.

Nothing in the Supreme Court's due process voluntariness law suggests that voluntariness requires awareness of the legal right to refuse to make a self-incriminating statement. To the contrary, in a general review of voluntariness law, the Court commented that in none of its decisions had the Court required that the prosecution prove "as part of its initial burden" on voluntariness that the defendant was aware of his right to refuse to answer police queries.[12] Although the defendant's awareness of his right is relevant, like nearly all other considerations it is to be considered in evaluating the totality of the circumstances.

Statutory and state constitutional requirements of voluntariness need not, of course, be construed as having the same contents as the due process requirement. As lower courts confront the implications of *Connelly's* limitations on federal due process voluntariness, they may be receptive to arguments that statutory or state constitutional voluntariness requirements are not subject to an absolute requirement of official coercion. Such arguments may find support in pre-*Connelly* state cases imposing absolute requirements that confessing de-

fendants have made meaningful decisions to confess.

§ 149. Self–Incrimination (*Miranda*) Requirements: (a) In General

In 1966, the Supreme Court, clearly dissatisfied with the due process voluntariness requirement, decided Miranda v. Arizona.[1] This decision revolutionized federal constitutional confession law and has become the focus of subsequent confession law development and analysis.

On the doctrinal level, *Miranda's* significance lies, first, in its holding that custodial law enforcement interrogation implicated the Fifth Amendment's privilege against compelled self-incrimination even though police have no legal authority to compel answers to their questions. "As a practical matter," the Court reasoned, "the compulsion to speak in the isolated setting of the police station may well be greater than in courts or other official investigations [where the legal power to compel answers may be exercised]."

The focus of the Court's concern in *Miranda* was what the Court perceived as the "inherently compelling pressures" of custodial interrogation. Without proper safeguards, the Court reasoned, this will inevitably work "to undermine the individual's will to resist and to compel him to speak where he would not otherwise do so freely." Modern in-custody interrogation, it stressed, is "psychologically rather than physically oriented" and inherently involves "compulsion." In the absence of protective devices, therefore, "no statement obtained from the defendant [in this context] can truly be the product of free choice."

To provide the protective devices necessary to protect the privilege in the custodial interrogation context, the Court developed what have come to be characterized as *per se* or "prophylactic" rules. These are requirements that are designed to assure that specific decisions are legally acceptable but which, for protective purposes, apply even to situations where on the facts the suspects' decisions may

---

12. Schneckloth v. Bustamonte, 412 U.S. 218, 226–227 (1973).

1. 384 U.S. 436 (1966).

not have fallen below standards imposed by the law. A confession obtained in violation of these requirements must, as a matter of Fifth Amendment law, be excluded from evidence even if application of voluntariness standards to the particular facts of the case would not lead to a finding that the confession was involuntary.

Although this has been somewhat overshadowed by later developments, it is clear that the *Miranda* Court regarded the major source of protection for those undergoing custodial interrogation to be the right to an attorney. The suspect's Fifth Amendment interests, reasoned the majority, can only be protected by affording the suspect an attendant right to counsel. This means not simply the right to consult with counsel before questioning, "but also to have counsel present during any interrogation * * *." Counsel must be available regardless of the financial ability of the suspect. Consequently, an attorney must be provided at public expense for those indigent defendants who wish the assistance of counsel.

The most well-known *Miranda* requirement is that of warnings. While "no talismanic incantation" of the language used in the opinion is necessary, officers must give the suspect essentially the following admonitions:

> 1. You have the right to remain silent;
>
> 2. Anything you say can [and will] be used against you in court;
>
> 3. You have the right to consult with a lawyer and to have the lawyer with you during interrogation; and
>
> 4. If you cannot afford an attorney, one will be appointed for you prior to any questioning if you so desire.

The first three elements are "absolute prerequisite[s]" to acceptable custodial interrogation. Failure to give even one of them cannot be "cured" by evidence that the suspect was already aware of the substance of the omitted warning[s]. Omission of the fourth element, on the other hand, is not fatal if the suspect was known to already have an attorney or to have ample funds to secure one. If, however, there is any doubt as to the applicability of the fourth element, this will be resolved against the prosecution. The warnings must be given prior to any interrogation.

Neither the right to remain silent nor its attendant right to counsel during interrogation is mandatory. Both are subject to waiver. In all cases where the prosecution offers at trial a self-incriminating statement made during custodial interrogation, it must show a voluntary and intelligent waiver of the privilege against self-incrimination itself. If the statement was made during interrogation at which no lawyer was present on the suspect's behalf, the prosecution must also show an effective waiver of the right to counsel.

Miranda waivers need not be "express," the Court reaffirmed in North Carolina v. Butler. Obviously, evidence that the suspect specifically articulated that she was aware of the right and was choosing not to exercise it constitutes strong, but not necessary, evidence of waiver. At the other extreme, *Miranda* itself makes clear that waiver will not be presumed from a suspect's silence after the warnings or from the fact that the suspect eventually provided a confession. In intermediate situations, the question is whether the evidence before the court regarding what the defendant did and said permits a finding that the prosecution has proved by a preponderance of the evidence that the defendant was aware of the right and both voluntarily and intelligently chose not to exercise it.

Later sections consider in detail the requirements that waivers be both voluntary[2] and intelligent.[3]

Despite the rigor with which the *Miranda* Court fashioned *per se* Fifth Amendment requirements out of the very general language of the constitutional provision, post-*Miranda* decisions have shown no inclination to continue this approach by developing more such requirements.[4] This was made obvious in Moran

---

2. See § 152 infra.

3. See § 153 infra.

4. The one exception is the strict prohibition against approaching a suspect who invokes the right to counsel. See § 151 infra.

v. Burbine,[5] rejecting a *per se* rule requiring police to inform a suspect of an attorney's efforts to reach him. The Court acknowledged that such a rule "might add marginally to *Miranda's* goal of dispelling the compulsion inherent in custodial interrogation." "[O]verriding practical considerations," however, argued against such a rule. The complexity that would accompany any such rule would decrease *Miranda's* clarity and ease of application. Further, such a requirement would cause some suspects to decline to make voluntary but self-incriminating statements and thus "work a substantial and * * * inappropriate shift in the subtle balance struck in [*Miranda*]."

Congress purported, for purposes of federal criminal prosecutions, to "overrule" *Miranda's* basic exclusionary holding. In 1968, as part of the Omnibus Crime Control and Safe Streets Act of 1968, Congress passed what is now Section 3501 of Title 18 of the United States Code.[6] Section 3501(a) provides that in a criminal prosecution brought by the United States or by the District of Columbia, a confession "shall be admissible in evidence if it is voluntarily given." Under section 3501(b), the trial judge determining voluntariness is directed to consider, among other things, whether or not the defendant had been advised that he was not required to make a statement, that any statement made could be used against him, and that he had the right to the assistance of counsel. Also to be considered is whether the defendant was in fact without the assistance of counsel during interrogation and the giving of the confession. But "[t]he presence or absence of any of [these] factors * * * need not be conclusive on the issue of voluntariness of the confession."

This legislation does not attempt to negate the *Miranda* holdings that a suspect undergoing custodial interrogation is entitled to the assistance of counsel or that she is entitled to the four-part warning. It does, however, purport to change *Miranda's* per se exclusion-

ary remedy and to make violations of the suspect's rights merely factors relevant to the voluntariness inquiry which, in turn, determines the admissibility of the confession. The statute remains largely untested in litigation, apparently because federal prosecutors are unwilling to risk convictions by relying on the statute in order to press the federal courts to consider whether the statute exceeded Congressional power.

State courts are, of course, free to read state constitutional self-incrimination provisions as imposing the same requirements which *Miranda* found in the Fifth Amendment privilege. Such action would seem to be a prerequisite to state law holdings that state law imposes more stringent versions of specific *Miranda* requirements than are demanded by Supreme Court case law. A few state courts have explicitly embraced the *Miranda* requirements as independently required by state constitutions.

§ 150. Self–Incrimination (*Miranda*) Requirements: (b) Applicability of *Miranda*—"Custody," "Interrogation," and Exceptions

Miranda v. Arizona[1] applies only if a suspect is in "custody" and is "interrogated." Only if both of these prerequisites exist does a situation present the extreme risk to the suspect's privilege against compelled self-incrimination that justifies the extraordinary protection afforded by the *Miranda* requirements. Each of these terms has become something of a term of art, and their definitions are considered in this section. In addition, the Supreme Court has recognized several exceptional situations in which, despite the existence of both custody and interrogation, either the extreme risks with which *Miranda* is concerned are lacking or those risks are outweighed by countervailing considerations. These exceptions are also addressed here.

Custody. Custody is not limited to "stationhouse custody," but can occur in a sus-

---

5. 475 U.S. 412 (1986).

6. 82 Stat. 197, Title II, § 701(a), codified as 18 U.S.C.A. § 3501.

1. 384 U.S. 436 (1966).

pect's own home. It does not require that the officers' purpose in detaining the suspect relate to the offense which is the subject of the interrogation. On the other hand, not every deprivation of a suspect's liberty constitutes custody.

Custody exists only if the circumstances are such as would cause a reasonable person to perceive that his freedom has been curtailed to a degree associated with a formal arrest. This depends on the objective circumstances of the situation, not on the subjective views of the officer or the suspect. If an officer makes a formal arrest by explicitly informing the suspect that an arrest has been made, of course, this constitutes custody.

In addition, however, a suspect is in custody despite the lack of a formal arrest if the officer detaining the suspect treats him in a manner that a reasonable person would regard as involving an arrest "for practical purposes." Relevant considerations include the length of the detention, any express or implied communication by the officer of the officer's intent to arrest the suspect, and the length, vigor, and subject of questioning and other investigatory efforts by the officer.

Under this approach, a person detained for brief field investigation under what is often called a *Terry* stop is usually not in custody. A motorist subjected to a "traffic stop"—a detention that a reasonable person would perceive as involving issuance of a citation and release—is similarly not in custody.

Interrogation. The meaning of interrogation was addressed in Rhode Island v. Innis,[2] refusing to limit *Miranda* to situations involving "express interrogation:"

> [T]he term "interrogation" under *Miranda* refers not only to express questioning, but also to any words or actions on the part of the police (other than those normally attendant to arrest and custody) that the police should know are reasonably likely to elicit an incriminating response from the suspect.[3]

Whether law enforcement conduct is the "functional equivalent" of express questioning focuses primarily upon the perspective of the suspect. Evidence that the words or conduct at issue were intended by the officer to elicit self-incriminating admissions from the suspect does not itself establish that interrogation took place; it may, however, tend to show that the officer knew or should have known that the words or conduct were sufficiently likely to elicit the desired response.

Applying the *Innis* standard, the Court has been quite reluctant to characterize situations as involving the functional equivalent of express questioning. *Innis* itself illustrates this approach. A comment by one officer to another—"God forbid one of [the neighborhood's impaired children] might find a weapon * * * and * * * hurt themselves."—in a suspect's presence was held in *Innis* not to constitute interrogation; the facts did not establish that the officers should have been aware that their comments would move the suspect to make a self-incriminating admission as to the location of a gun he had hidden in the area. Permitting a suspect's wife to talk to a suspect arrested for the murder of the couple's young son was similarly held not to constitute interrogation.

Even express questions put to a suspect may not constitute interrogation, if—given the other purposes of the questioning—the risk of those questions eliciting a self-incriminating response is minimal. Police inquiry of a suspect whether he would submit to a blood alcohol test, for example, does not constitute "interrogation."[4] No interrogation took place when an officer explained to a suspect how a breathalyzer examination worked, the legal aspects of the applicable Implied Consent Law and then inquired whether he understood and will be willing to submit to the test.[5] Nor was there interrogation when, during a videotaping, an officer instructed the suspect how he was to perform physical sobriety tests and inquired whether the suspect understood the instructions.

---

2.   446 U.S. 291 (1980).

3.   Id. at 301.

4.   South Dakota v. Neville, 459 U.S. 553, 564 n. 15 (1983).

5.   Pennsylvania v. Muniz, 496 U.S. 582, 603 (1990).

Exceptions to Miranda Requirements. Miranda does not apply to some situations involving both custody and interrogation as those are defined under the Court's case law.

If the questioning is done by an officer functioning in an undercover capacity, the Court held in Illinois v. Perkins,[6] *Miranda* has no application. Where a suspect is unaware that he is conversing with his captors, the majority reasoned, the situation does not present the interaction between custody and interrogation creating the risk of coercion that justifies the extraordinary *Miranda* protections. *Miranda* also does not apply, the Court held in New York v. Quarles,[7] in certain situations in which police inquiries are supported by particularly pressing concerns for public safety. Where compliance with *Miranda's* mandates would create an immediate and high risk to public safety, the costs are excessive.

A plurality of the Court in Pennsylvania v. Muniz[8] recognized another exception for "routine booking questions" asked during the processing of an arrested suspect. This exception, which is almost certain to be accepted by a majority of the Court, covers questions designed to elicit biographical data necessary to complete the booking process and to provide pretrial services. Thus in *Muniz, Miranda* was regarded by the plurality as inapplicable to questions concerning Muniz's name, address, height, weight, eye color, date of birth, and current age.

§ 151. Self–Incrimination (*Miranda*) Requirements: (c) Prohibition Against Interrogation

Under certain–and limited–circumstances, *Miranda* gives a person undergoing custodial interrogation a right not to be interrogated at all. Essentially, the right is one to bar officers from attempting to persuade the defendant to make a self-incriminating admission or otherwise give up the right to remain silent. In these situations, the risk of any admission being involuntary is sufficient to justify barring all efforts to elicit such an admission.

As an initial matter, interrogation of a suspect in custody is barred until the person has been adequately warned and has waived the right to counsel's presence during the interrogation. If counsel is in fact present, there is apparently no absolute bar to questioning, even over the objections of the suspect and counsel. The fact that the interrogation was over objection, of course, would be a circumstance tending to show that any admissions ultimately made were involuntary and hence inadmissible.

A suspect who has initially waived counsel may, of course, change his mind. If the suspect during permissible interrogation indicates "in any manner" that he wishes to have the assistance of counsel, interrogation must cease until counsel is present.

In Edwards v. Arizona[1] the Supreme Court held that a suspect who had affirmatively invoked his right to counsel could not be further approached by officers until a lawyer was present, even if that approach did not consist of efforts to persuade him to waive his right but only an inquiry regarding his continued unwillingness to do so. Under *Edwards,* police-initiated inquiries regarding possible admissions or questioning are barred until a lawyer is present. Arizona v. Roberson made clear that a reapproach is impermissible even if it concerns a different offense than that under actual or possible discussion when the suspect invoked his right to counsel. The unacceptable risk that an officer's eagerness to secure the suspect's waiver will result in an involuntary waiver is not eliminated because the reapproach is for a different offense.

After a suspect has initially waived the right to counsel, *Edwards* is triggered only by a clear and unambiguous request for counsel. A suspect's words are sufficiently clear under Davis v. United States[2] only if a reasonable officer hearing them would, given the circum-

---

6. 496 U.S. 292 (1990).

7. 467 U.S. 649 (1984).

8. 496 U.S. 582 (1990).

§ 151

1. 451 U.S. 477 (1981).

2. 512 U.S. 452 (1994).

stances, understand them to be a request for the assistance of counsel. An ambiguous or equivocal reference to counsel that a reasonable officer would at most construe as indicating that the suspect *might* be invoking the right to counsel—such as Davis' statement, "Maybe I should talk to a lawyer."—is of no mechanical significance. Stressing the need for bright lines to guide officers, *Davis* rejected the argument that an ambiguous or equivocal reference to counsel, although not triggering *Edwards'* total bar to reapproaching the suspect, should require officers to limit further inquiries of the suspect to ascertaining whether in fact the suspect does desire to invoke his right to assistance of counsel.

A suspect's request for counsel may be sufficiently limited that continued questioning of some sort does not violate *Edwards*. In Connecticut v. Barrett,[3] for example, Barrett made clear to officers that he would not give a written statement until his lawyer was present, but that he had "no problem" in talking orally with the officers about the incident. This, the Supreme Court held, invoked Barrett's right to counsel only with regard to interrogation designed to produce a written statement. Thus *Edwards* did not bar further interrogation reasonably designed only to elicit an oral statement.

Edwards prohibits only a reapproach by police. If the suspect—without being so reapproached—takes action that demonstrates a desire on the suspect's part for further generalized discussion about the investigation, the *Edwards* bar to further interrogation disappears. In Oregon v. Bradshaw,[4] a plurality held that the suspect's question—"Well, what is going to happen to me now?"—made while he was being transferred from the stationhouse to jail was reasonably interpreted by the officer as evidencing the suspect's desire to open up further discussion concerning the investigation. Although the suspect had previously invoked his right to counsel, police acceptably

again warned him of his rights and, when he waived the right to counsel, interrogated him.

A significant change in circumstances may end an *Edwards* prohibition against reapproaching the suspect. This is most likely to occur if the suspect is released from custody and then rearrested. If, considering the length of interruption of custody and all other relevant considerations, the break in custody would prevent a reasonable person in the suspect's situation from perceiving the officer's reapproach as an effort to circumvent the suspect's previously-expressed desire to deal with the police only though counsel, a reapproach is not a *per se* violation of *Miranda's* demands.

Edwards is triggered only by a suspect's invocation of the *Miranda* right to counsel. A suspect who invokes the right to remain silent but not the right to counsel—as, for example, by asserting, "I have nothing to say."—is not, under Michigan v. Mosley,[5] protected by a *per se* prohibition against reapproach. If after reapproach the suspect waives his rights, however, the situation may require an unusually effective demonstration that the waiver was voluntary.

§ 152. Self–Incrimination (*Miranda*) Requirements: (d) Effectiveness of Waivers—Voluntariness of Waivers

Self-incrimination requirements applicable to custodial interrogation demand effective waivers of suspects' rights to remain silent and, unless lawyers were present, of the right to counsel. Such waivers must be "voluntary" to be effective.

The basic question is whether the standards for determining voluntariness of such waivers are stricter than those imposed by the due process requirements of voluntariness.[1] The fact of custodial interrogation argues for stricter standards than are embodied in due process voluntariness, since suspects' interests are placed at greater risk by custodial interrogation than they are under in those situations to which only the more general due process

---

3. 479 U.S. 523 (1987).

4. 462 U.S. 1039 (1983).

5. 423 U.S. 96 (1975).

1. See § 148 supra.

standard applies. Correspondingly appropriate protection might best be afforded by imposing stricter requirements for determining the acceptability of suspects' decisions to provide the prosecution with evidence or with access to them for questioning without the protection of counsel.

On the other hand, suspects protected by the privilege against self-incrimination as construed in *Miranda* will have been provided warnings, and they are protected against interrogation until they waive their right to counsel. Perhaps these aspects of self-incrimination law provide adequate protection against the increased threat generated by custodial interrogation. Stricter standards for voluntariness, then, may be unnecessary. Moreover, given the difficulty of articulating useful standards in this area, courts may be unable to distinguish meaningfully between two "levels" of voluntariness.

In fact, the Supreme Court has made clear, voluntariness in *Miranda* waiver law is generally the same as in the due process standard. "There is obviously no reason," the Court commented in Colorado v. Connelly,[2] "to require more in the way of a 'voluntariness' inquiry in the *Miranda* waiver context than in the Fourteenth Amendment confession context." No notice was taken of arguments that such reasons exist, no authority was cited, and no discussion was provided.

Specifically, *Connelly* held that a waiver of *Miranda* rights, like a decision to confess under due process voluntariness, need not constitute an exercise of "free will" or "free choice" by the suspect. "Voluntariness" as is required for a *Miranda* waiver is only put into question if the facts show official coercion or overreaching *and,* as a result, the decision was not voluntary in the more ordinary sense of that term.

A showing that the suspect was psychologically impaired or intoxicated, then, does not raise voluntariness issues under *Miranda* waiver law unless officers were aware of and exploited that condition in a manner constitut-

ing official overreaching. If such overreaching is shown, however, those conditions of the suspect are relevant to determining whether the overreaching had sufficient impact upon the suspect to render his waiver decision involuntary under the *Miranda* standard.

The prosecution's burden of showing *Miranda* voluntariness is especially heavy if the suspect was reapproached after earlier invoking his right to remain silent. Under Michigan v. Mosley,[3] the admissibility of any statements so obtained depends upon the effectiveness of that waiver, which in turn depends upon "whether [the suspect's] 'right to cut off questioning' was scrupulously honored.'" What constitutes sufficient respect for this right is not entirely clear.

Mosley itself indicates that among the factors tending to show that the standard was met are: (1) a showing that the first session was noncoercive; (2) a significant time interval between the invocation of the right to silence and the reapproach; (3) reapproach by a different officer than the one who first inquired as to the suspect's willingness to make a statement; (4) changes in circumstances between the two inquiries; (5) a significant difference in the matters of interest to the officers in the two situations; and (6) supplementation of the warnings administered during the second approach with clear explanations that the suspect was under no obligation to answer questions (or even submit to questioning) and could avoid further questioning by simply indicating again that he wished to remain silent. The more the reapproach appears to be an effort to persuade the suspect to submit to questioning about matters concerning which he had previously indicated a desire to remain silent, the more difficult the prosecution's burden becomes. Conversely, the more the reapproach appears to concern matters not covered by the suspect's first invocation of his right to remain silent, the easier is the prosecution's task.

Generally, the prosecution can meet its burden of proving at least a *prima facie* of voluntariness by eliciting from the interrogat-

2. 479 U.S. 157 (1986).

3. 423 U.S. 96 (1975).

ing officer that the suspect had not been threatened or promised anything, and appeared to freely decide for himself to forego the assistance of counsel and to provide an incriminating statement. If the defense introduces evidence suggesting official overreaching and a significant impact of that overreaching upon the suspect, of course, the prosecution may well have to respond with more detailed and persuasive evidence in order to meet its burden of persuasion.

§ 153. Self–Incrimination (*Miranda*) Requirements: (e) Effectiveness of Waivers—Intelligence

The requirement that waivers of self-incrimination rights during custodial interrogation be "intelligent" is separate and distinct from the demand that such waivers be "voluntary." As best defined, the demand that the waivers be intelligent addresses the information of which the suspect must have actually been aware for her decision to be effective.

"Intelligence," as used in *Miranda's* waiver criteria, involves only an understanding of the basic abstract Fifth Amendment rights of which a suspect must be informed: that there is a legal right to remain silent during custodial interrogation; that anything said can be used in evidence to convict her of a crime; that she is entitled to consult with a lawyer and to have a lawyer present during custodial interrogation; and that if she decides to speak to law enforcement officers she is entitled to discontinue such discussion at any time she wishes. It is *not* necessary that she be aware of factual or legal matters bearing upon the wisdom of exercising any of those options. In fact, ignorance of any or all of those matters is totally irrelevant to the effectiveness of the waiver.

Miranda, then, distinguished between the "knowing" nature of decisions, on one hand, and their "wisdom," on the other. The Fifth Amendment, as it applies to custodial interro-

gation, requires only that the decisions be knowing.

Consequently, a defendant who has previously made an incriminating statement which is in fact inadmissible against her need not understand the inadmissibility of that statement in order to effectively waive her rights and again admit those same facts.[1] The Court has strongly hinted that a defendant who acknowledges participation in a robbery under circumstances that, unknown to her, create felony murder liability for a killing committed by a companion has made intelligent waivers of her rights despite ignorance as to the legal effect of the admissions.[2] A suspect's waiver of the right to counsel is not rendered ineffective by ignorance concerning the subjects about which the officers intended to question her if she waived counsel's help. In Moran v. Burbine,[3] the Court held that a suspect's waiver of counsel was not rendered unintelligent by his unawareness that there was a specific attorney ready and willing to represent him during questioning if he wished representation.

In light of Colorado v. Connelly,[4] which held that a *Miranda* waiver can be rendered involuntary only by official coercion,[5] is official coercion also a prerequisite to consideration of the possibility that a *Miranda* waiver is insufficiently intelligent or knowing? The issue was not addressed in *Connelly* itself. *Connelly's* general discussion, however, suggests that official misconduct is necessary. If the "voluntariness" of a waiver is put into issue only by a preliminary showing of official coercion, a similar showing would seem necessary to challenge the "intelligence" of that waiver. Thus *Connelly* apparently means that a trial court need not consider a defendant's claim that because of mental illness or retardation, intoxication or emotional distress she failed to actually understanding the warnings, unless the court first finds that official coercion occurred and played a causal role in this failure to develop the required understanding.

---

§ 153

1. Oregon v. Elstad, 470 U.S. 298, 316–318 (1985).

2. California v. Beheler, 463 U.S. 1121 (1983) (per curiam).

3. 475 U.S. 412 (1986).

4. 479 U.S. 157 (1986).

5. See generally § 152 supra.

The Court's position that an intelligent waiver of *Miranda* rights requires at most only an abstract understanding of those legal matters covered in the *Miranda* warnings serves several purposes. First, it avoids the difficult task of determining and articulating what broader information would be required. Second, it eliminates what would sometimes be an impossible task for the prosecution. Officers in some situations would simply be unable to provide a suspect with sufficient information concerning a crime, their investigation of it, or the suspect's legal position to render any waivers effective. They would, then, be barred from productive interrogation of the suspect. A construction of *Miranda* that so limits officers can reasonably be viewed as excessively solicitous of those interests of suspects that the self-incrimination privilege properly protects.

On the other hand, this position arguably renders *Miranda* ineffective in assuring that suspects' confession decisions reflect what in ordinary terms are "meaningful" decisions. In many situations, awareness of the abstract law would for most persons be only a relatively minor consideration in deciding whether to invoke either or both the rights to representation or counsel.

Assuring that suspects' choices are meaningful in such a broad, tactical sense, however, is most likely beyond the purposes of the *Miranda* requirements. The exceptional risks to suspects' privilege caused by custodial interrogation that justify the *Miranda* requirements probably arise exclusively from potential improper influences on suspects' volition. Custodial interrogation may not pose similarly severe risks to suspects' access to factual information or their abilities to intellectually assimilate or use it. Since the *Miranda* requirements are imposed for reasons at most indirectly related to suspects' ability to make intellectually informed and reasoned decisions, waiver criteria are appropriately formulated so as to require relatively minimal intellectual understanding of facts useful in making "wise" decisions.

States, of course, remain free to construe state constitutional requirements differently and some have done so. Several, for example, have held that police failure to permit an attorney to consult with a client undergoing interrogation renders the client's waivers ineffective.

§ 154. General Right to Counsel Requirements

Miranda and analogous state self-incrimination decisions recognize a right to counsel based upon the privilege against self-incrimination as it applies during custodial law enforcement interrogation. General constitutional rights to counsel, such as that in the Sixth Amendment, focus upon representation at trial, but they also apply to certain pretrial situations in which suspects may make self-incriminating admissions. Since an exclusionary sanction attaches to violations of these rights to counsel, failures to comply with them permit challenges to the admissibility of confessions. Two primary issues are presented: first, under what circumstances is a confessing suspect protected by these general rights to counsel; and second, what protections are afforded a suspect by these provisions?

Sixth Amendment Right to Counsel. The Sixth Amendment applies if adversary judicial proceedings against the suspect have begun and police attempt to deliberately elicit self-incriminating admissions from the suspect. "Deliberate elicitation" of admissions probably differs minimally if at all from "interrogation" as defined in case law under *Miranda*.

When adversary judicial proceedings begin is not entirely clear. Detention by the police or even formal arrest is not sufficient. On the other hand, a formal charge, as by the filing of an indictment, is clearly enough. It is not, however, required. In Michigan v. Jackson,[1] the Court held that an "arraignment", by which it apparently meant an arrested person's post-arrest appearance before a judicial officer, does trigger the Sixth Amendment right. In most situations, this post-arrest appearance will be the definitive point.

§ 154

1. 475 U.S. 625 (1986).

The Sixth Amendment right does not, generally speaking, protect a suspect from being approached in the absence of counsel by officers seeking to persuade him to provide a self-incriminating statement.[2] A suspect entitled to Sixth Amendment protection is apparently entitled to at least the same admonishments required by *Miranda*, although generally not more. The Court has left open the possibility that a waiver of the Sixth Amendment right to counsel may require that the defendant be informed, or perhaps that the suspect know from some source, that the matter has progressed beyond general police investigation to adversary judicial proceedings.

The Sixth Amendment embodies a version of the *Edwards* rule.[3] A suspect who invokes his right to counsel consequently cannot be reapproached by officers. This bar to being approached by law enforcement officers is triggered when during a court appearance a defendant requests generally that counsel be appointed. But the Sixth Amendment right to counsel, unlike *Miranda's* right to representation, is "offense-specific." Therefore, a suspect who has by requesting counsel invoked his Sixth Amendment version of the *Edwards* rule may be approached by officers concerning other offenses as to which matters have not progressed sufficiently so as to give him a Sixth Amendment right to counsel as to those other offenses.[4]

The Sixth Amendment right to counsel during questioning, like the Fifth Amendment right, can be waived. A waiver of the Sixth Amendment right must, of course, be both voluntary and intelligent. The Supreme Court has rejected the arguments that "because a Sixth Amendment right may be involved, it is more difficult to waive than the Fifth Amendment counterpart." Generally, then, a waiver of the Sixth Amendment right to counsel requires no more than an effective waiver of *Miranda* rights.

Sixth Amendment protection differs—and exceeds—Fifth Amendment-*Miranda* protection in three primary ways. First, a suspect whose Sixth Amendment right has attached has a Sixth Amendment right to counsel if efforts are made to elicit a self-incriminating admission from the suspect by a police officer functioning in an undercover capacity or a private citizen acting under the direction of law enforcement officers without disclosing that purpose; *Miranda* does not apply where the interrogator's official status is concealed from the suspect.

Second, the Sixth Amendment right to counsel, unlike *Miranda*, does not require that the suspect be in "custody." Thus a suspect from whom an officer seeks to elicit a self-incriminating admission after the suspect had been released on post-indictment bail is protected by the Sixth Amendment right to counsel.

Finally, if a suspect is in fact represented by counsel and the Sixth Amendment has attached, the Sixth Amendment protects the defendant-counsel relationship more rigorously than it is protected by the Fifth Amendment and *Miranda*. In Moran v. Burbine[5] the Supreme Court indicated that officers' interference with defense counsel's efforts to contact a client undergoing custodial interrogation, although not discovered by the client until later, would render the client's waiver of his right to counsel ineffective. Officers' simple failure to inform such a client that defense counsel is attempting to contact the client would apparently have the same effect.

State Constitutional Rights to Counsel. State courts seeking to impose greater limits upon law enforcement questioning though their state constitutions have tended to rely upon explicit constitutional rights to counsel rather than rights derived from constitutional self-incrimination privileges. This has been the case even if so applying the state rights requires construing them as applicable earlier in the criminal process than the analogous Sixth Amendment right.

2. Patterson v. Illinois, 487 U.S. 285, 290–91 (1988).

3. See § 151 supra.

4. McNeil v. Wisconsin, 501 U.S. 171, 175–76 (1991).

5. 475 U.S. 412 (1986).

State courts' willingness to so apply state constitutional rights has been most common where officers have either or both interfered with counsel's access to a suspect undergoing interrogation or have failed to inform such a suspect of counsel's ready availability. The New York court has vigorously developed that state's right to counsel and held that under certain circumstances a suspect's right to counsel during questioning is "indelible," meaning that it can only be effectively waived in the presence of counsel. The New Jersey court has held that under its right to counsel prosecutors or police cannot—after indictment—initiate conversations with defendants without the consent of defense counsel.

§ 155. Promises Made to Suspects

Early voluntariness law placed particular emphasis on "promises" as among the influences rendering confessions inadmissible. Modern voluntariness standards, self-incrimination demands, and right to counsel requirements have incorporated at least some of this early "promise law."

During the vigorous application of the voluntariness requirement in the early 1800s, what today would be regarded by most courts as quite innocuous references to possible benefits were regarded as *per se* tainting subsequent confessions. Bram v. United States[1] arguably incorporated such an approach into due process voluntariness, on the apparent ground that suspects are particularly sensitive to such inducements and the impact on particular defendants of particular promises is "too difficult to assess."

But in Arizona v. Fulminante[2] the Supreme Court indicated that this early language suggesting a rigid rule that promises render a confession involuntary does not state the current standard for determining the federal constitutional voluntariness of a confession. Instead, the Court approved an approach under which the federal constitution requires no more than that courts consider promises as part of the totality of the circumstances when they determine the voluntariness of defendants' confessions.

Many state courts, sometimes in explicit recognition of *Fulminante*, simply regard promises—whatever the definition of that term—as merely a factor to consider in assessing voluntariness. The ultimate question in such cases, many recognize, is whether the promise or promise-like statement made to the suspect prevented the suspect from making a voluntary and rational decision to confess. How a court is to determine whether a particular promise sufficiently impaired the suspect's decisionmaking, however, is not clear. This is especially the case if a court recognizes—as some have—that the prosecution is not forbidden to buy a confession with an honest promise of consideration, and thus that merely creating and exploiting a desire for leniency is not enough.

Others courts, however, continue to at least articulate the traditional approach, generally without carefully specifying whether it is still accepted as a matter of state constitutional or evidence law. The effect of the rule is mitigated, however, by an increasing willingness to define "promise" narrowly and perhaps artificially to what purport on their faces to be guarantees of some benefit to be delivered if the suspect confesses. What is often characterized as an exhortation to tell the truth, a prediction that confessing will result in more lenient treatment, or even an indication that in return for a confession an officer will "do what he can" or that "things will go easier" are held not to constitute promises. Even if a promise is found, the evidence may not satisfactorily prove that the suspect relied upon it in deciding to confess. Some courts, however, at least sometimes appear to enforce the traditional approach.

There is general agreement that a promise of complete immunity from prosecution or its equivalent in return for a confession will render a resulting confession involuntary. This may also mean that a promise not to pursue charges for the most serious offenses commit-

§ 155
1. 168 U.S. 532 (1897).

2. 499 U.S. 279 (1991).

ted by admitted actions has the same effect. Furthermore, a promise that a confession would be kept confidential has been held to similarly render a confession inadmissible.

What are often called "false promises" are more likely than others to render a confession inadmissible. A promise may be "false" if the interrogator misrepresents the benefit to be derived or does not intend to actually provide the benefit. Apparently the combination of deception and promise increases the strength of the argument for overbearing of the will.

Some approaches emphasize the risk of inaccuracy. Several statutes and some case law provide that confessions are inadmissible if made in response to promises likely to stimulate a false confession by an innocent suspect.

Some discussions of promises holding confessions admissible have emphasized evidence that the defendant first raised the possibility of the benefit which the authorities later promised. Some even suggest that a showing of this sort totally precludes the defendant from later relying on the solicited promise. This may be on the ground that the defendant's initiative shows that the effect of the promise was not such as to impair the defendant's decisionmaking in the manner or degree necessary to render the confession involuntary.

Several courts have suggested that although officers may inform a suspect that cooperation may benefit the suspect, they may not tell that suspect that lack of cooperation—and a failure to confess—may result in harsher treatment. "The first may contribute to the informed nature of the decision. But the second has no legitimate purpose 'and can only be intended to coerce.'" Thus a confession was inadmissible because interrogators told the defendant that if he did not cooperate they would ask for a "lot of jail time" and would make it "real uncomfortable" for him and that they would file a "recommendation that he was uncooperative."

What is really at issue in these cases is the extent to which confession law should attempt to discourage or limit what amounts to plea bargaining between suspects and interrogating law enforcement officers. Suspects are less likely to be represented by counsel in interrogation situations than later when actual plea bargaining occurs, but given their right to counsel this is often as a result of their decision to waive representation. Given suspects' exceptional vulnerability at this point, perhaps some bargaining tactics by police should be discouraged. The case law, however, has failed to articulate a reasonable standard for identifying those deserving of condemnation.

§ 156. Deception of Suspects

Among the most difficult issues raised by confession law is the appropriate effect to be given to evidence that law enforcement officers affirmatively and intentionally deceived the defendant concerning some matter potentially significant to the defendant in making his confession decisions.

If such evidence convincingly demonstrates that the defendant lacked some information necessary to make his confession admissible under the applicable legal standard, of course, the evidence necessarily demonstrates that this legal standard was not met. The legal standards apparently require quite little in terms of a defendant's awareness, however, and this approach therefore gives little significance to proof of deception. Courts sometimes seem open to arguments that deception should have some significance beyond simply "disproving" that the defendant had the awareness required. No consensus has developed, however, on how to implement this.

The uncertain state of the law is almost certainly the result of uncertainty as to why law enforcement deception of suspects might be inappropriate and—if it is inappropriate at all—how inappropriate it is. Is it undesirable because—and thus only when—it might or does lead to an inaccurate confession? Or is it simply "wrong"—perhaps immoral in some sense—for public officials to lie and to exploit those lies? Even if such action is wrong, it is inappropriate enough to demand condemnation by excluding confessions to serious criminal conduct?

The relevance and significance of deception might vary depending upon whether the issue presented is the voluntariness of the confession in the general due process or evidence law sense, the effectiveness of a defendant's waivers of his self-incrimination rights, the effectiveness of a defendant's waiver of his general right to counsel, or whether the deception violated minimal standards of official conduct implicit in the requirement of due process.

Common law voluntariness appears, from the minimal case law available, to have regarded proof of deception as largely if not entirely irrelevant to admissibility. The Supreme Court addressed the issue under Fourteenth Amendment due process voluntariness in Frazier v. Cupp.[1] Officers falsely told Frazier that a companion (Rawls) had been taken into custody and had confessed. Rejecting the attack on the later confession almost offhandedly, the Supreme Court—offering no authority, discussion, or rationale—simply stated, "[T]he fact that the police misrepresented the statements that Rawls had made is, while relevant, insufficient in our view to make this otherwise voluntary confession inadmissible."

In Miranda v. Arizona,[2], the Court, again with no substantive discussion or citation of authority, commented, "[A]ny evidence that the accused was * * * tricked * * * into a waiver [of the Miranda rights] will, of course, show that the defendant did not voluntarily waive his privilege."Although Frazier was decided after Miranda, the Court in Frazier amazingly made no mention of the obvious tension between the implications of the Miranda dictum and the Frazier analysis. In several subsequent cases presenting Miranda issues, the Court has failed to respond to or reach defendants' claims that their Miranda waivers were rendered ineffective by police deception. In Colorado v. Spring,[3] the Court recognized and left open the possibility that affirmative misrepresentations by officers might have significance for the effectiveness of a Miranda waiver beyond its logical relevance to the intelligence of that waiver.

Lower courts have generally not distinguished between the impact of deception on voluntariness as a general requirement and on the effectiveness of waivers. Deceit, it is generally said, is not necessarily sufficient by itself to make an otherwise admissible confession inadmissible, but deception is a factor to consider in determining whether necessarily voluntariness has been demonstrated. Under what circumstances deception is sufficient to tip the scales in favor of involuntariness is not clear. One court has commented that deception will not have this effect simply because it influenced the suspect's decision to confess, "as long as the decision [to confess] results from the suspect's balancing of competing interests." Perhaps the inquiry must be whether the deception and other circumstances so affected the defendant's emotion or reasoning as to prevent the suspect from making a minimally sufficient balance between those considerations militating against the wisdom of confessing and those favoring such action.

Some courts have turned to the risk of deception leading to unreliability as the controlling factor—or at least one of the controlling considerations. Thus "a confession induced by deception or trickery[] is not inadmissible, unless the method used was calculated to produce an untruthful confession or was offensive to due process." The Nebraska court has focused not on the general tendency of the deception used to produce inaccurate confessions, but rather on whether on the facts of the specific case the particular deception used "produced a false or untrustworthy confession."[4]

Several courts have distinguished between deception regarding "intrinsic" facts—facts relating to the crime to which the suspect confessed and the suspect's guilt of it—and misrepresentation as to "extrinsic" facts—facts concerning other matters. Probably the leading decision, Holland v. McGinnis,[5] suggests

§ 156

1.   394 U.S. 731 (1969).

2.   384 U.S. 436 (1966).

3.   479 U.S. 564 (1987).

4.   State v. Nissen 560 N.W.2d 157, 170 (Neb.1997) (per curiam).

5.   963 F.2d 1044 (7th Cir.1992).

that a suspect's deception-induced misunderstanding regarding extrinsic facts is more likely to interject into the suspect's decision to confess considerations that overcome the suspect's will. Intrinsic facts include the suspect's beliefs regarding his actual guilt or innocence, the suspect's moral sense of right and wrong, and the suspect's judgment regarding the amount and strength of incriminating evidence authorities have obtained. To the extent that a suspect is caused to give weight to misunderstood considerations other than these, the deception leading to that misunderstanding creates a particularly high risk, first, of overbearing the suspect's will by distorting what would otherwise be a rational choice whether to confess or remain silent, and, second, that the confession will be unreliable.

Most courts drawing this distinction have held that misrepresentations as to extrinsic facts are simply entitled to more weight as tending to show involuntariness than misrepresentations as to intrinsic facts. The Hawaii Supreme Court, in contrast, indicated that "deliberate falsehoods extrinsic to the facts of the alleged offense, which are of a type reasonably likely to procure an untrue statement or to influence an accused to make a confession regardless of guilt, will be regarded as coercive *per se*, thus obviating the need for a 'totality of circumstances' analysis of voluntariness." Deliberate falsehoods intrinsic to the facts of the offense, in contrast, are to be treated simply as one of the totality of the circumstances to be considered in assessing the voluntariness of a statement.[6]

Deception as to extrinsic facts is illustrated, *Holland* indicated, by the facts of Lynumn v. Illinois,[7] which *Holland* interpreted as involving a misrepresentation to the suspect that if she withheld a confession she was in jeopardy of losing welfare benefits and custody of her children. The extrinsic nature of the facts as to which Lynumn was deceived, *Holland* questionably asserted, meant that the deception was particularly likely to impair the suspect's free choice and cause the suspect, even if innocent, to falsely confess.

Despite the courts' insistence that even deception as to extrinsic facts is at least relevant to the voluntariness of suspects' confession decisions, in actual practice such evidence—especially regarding so-called extrinsic facts—is seldom given much weight and is probably never determinative. At least once deception is characterized as involving extrinsic facts, it is probably logically irrelevant to those characteristics of decisionmaking implicated by the voluntariness requirement and thus of no actual significance to the issue.

§ 157. Delay in Presenting Arrested Person Before Magistrate

Statutes and court rules in virtually every state as well as Rule 5(a) of the Federal Rules of Criminal Procedure require that arrested persons be brought with some dispatch before judicial officers for what, under the Federal Rules, is called the "initial appearance." Controversy continues as to the appropriate effect of violation of the applicable requirement on the admissibility of a confession obtained during the delay. The Supreme Court's development of the so-called *McNabb-Mallory* Rule and Congress's modification of it have served as a basis for analysis.

These cases present two distinguishable issues that are sometimes not separated by the courts. First is whether particular delay is improper, especially if that delay is for purposes of questioning the suspect prior to the appearance before the magistrate and the resulting judicial warnings, appointment of counsel and perhaps release from custody on bail. Second is the effect of delay determined to be improper on the admissibility of a confession given during that improper delay.

McNabb-Mallory Rule. In McNabb v. United States,[1] the Supreme Court held that statements elicited from a defendant during a period in which federal officers had failed to comply with what is now Federal Rule of

---

6. State v. Kelekolio, 849 P.2d 58, 73 (Hawai'i 1993).

7. 372 U.S. 528 (1963).

1. 318 U.S. 332 (1943).

Criminal Procedure 5(a)'s requirement of presentation before a magistrate without "unnecessary delay" were inadmissible at the defendant's subsequent federal criminal trial. This holding, the Court made clear, was not of constitutional dimensions but rather was an exercise of the Court's supervisory power. The impact of this exclusionary requirement was increased by the Court's construction of the substance of the Rule 5(a) requirement. In Mallory v. United States,[2] the Court held that if officers delayed presenting a defendant before a magistrate in order to interrogate him, the delay was "unnecessary" within the meaning of Rule 5(a).

Thus the so-called *McNabb-Mallory* Rule was in part a substantive rule—any delay in presentation for purposes of interrogation was improper under purposes of Rule 5(a)—and in part a remedial rule—a confession obtained during delay that had become unnecessary for Rule 5(a) purposes was for that reason automatically inadmissible. Whether the Court in fact possessed a supervisory power sufficient to support its development of an exclusionary sanction of this sort has been questioned. The Supreme Court has never suggested that the *McNabb-Mallory* Rule or any similar prophylactic rule is required by the federal Constitution. Rather, the Court has assumed that delay is merely a factor in constitutional analysis of the voluntariness of a confession and presumably the effectiveness of waivers of Fifth and Sixth Amendment rights. In any case, a violation of a state prompt presentation requirement does not constitute an automatic violation of any federal constitutional requirement and, generally speaking, goes only to the voluntariness of the confession.

Congressional Modification or Rejection of McNabb–Mallory. In 1968, Congress responded to the *McNabb-Mallory* Rule by enacting what was codified as Section 3501 of Title 18 of the United States Code.[3] Section 3501(c) provides that in a federal criminal prosecution, a voluntary confession made by an arrested person within six hours of arrest or detention "shall not be inadmissible solely because of delay in bringing such person before a magistrate * * *." Under Section 3501(a), a confession "shall be admissible [in a federal prosecution] if it is voluntarily given." Section 3501(b) specifies that among the factors to be considered in determining voluntariness is "the time elapsing between arrest and arraignment of the defendant * * *."

Under § 3501, a confession made within six hours of arrest cannot be excluded from a federal prosecution simply because of delay in presenting the defendant and will be inadmissible only upon a determination that it is involuntary. When a confession given during a period of improper delay lasting longer than the six hour "safe haven" in the statute is less clear. The Ninth Circuit has identified three possible approaches: (a) all confessions given during unreasonable delay that exceeds six hours are inadmissible on that basis alone, that is, *McNabb-Mallory* remains effective regarding such confessions; (b) confessions given during such a period are inadmissible only if, considering all the circumstances including the delay, the confessions are involuntary; and (c) federal courts have discretion to exclude confessions given during such delay on the basis not of traditional voluntariness considerations but rather upon a determination that exclusion would sufficiently serve to encourage prompt presentation or other considerations related to prompt presentation.

Most federal courts have adopted the second of these approaches, finding this analysis most consistent with the statutory scheme. The Ninth Circuit, however, noted that the second approach is problematic because the courts have no guidance as to how delay is to weighed in the voluntariness analysis. It found the third approach as most consistent with the legislative history of the 1968 legislation, but has not had occasion to definitively choose between the last two.[4] The Supreme Court has noted but not addressed the problem.

---

2. 354 U.S. 449 (1957).

3. Pub.L. 90–351, Title II, § 701(a), 82 Stat. 210 (1968), codified as 18 U.S.C.A. § 3501.

4. United States v. Alvarez–Sanchez, 975 F.2d 1396, 1402 (9th Cir. 1992), rev'd on other grounds 511 U.S. 350 (1994).

State Positions. There is wide variation among the approaches taken by the states. The majority, however, treat delay in presentation as merely a factor to consider in determining the voluntariness of decisions made during the delay.

Some state courts, acting under supervisory authority, have adopted state versions of *McNabb-Mallory,* requiring suppression of confessions obtained during delay that has become improper because of failure to present the accused before a judicial officer. This is sometimes qualified by a requirement that the defendant show that the delay caused or at contributed to the defendant's decision to confess. Maximum flexibility is provided by the approach of the Kansas court, which has held that trial courts have broad discretion to fashion and apply remedies for violation of the right of prompt presentation, including exclusion.

Several state legislatures have followed Congress' lead. These jurisdictions provide by statute that delay in presenting a defendant does not by itself render inadmissible those confessions obtained during improper delay.

The Massachusetts Supreme Judicial Court recognized in Commonwealth v. Rosario[5] that the basic question is whether prompt presentation is important enough to protecting suspects' self-incrimination rights to justify enforcing the requirement by excluding all statements made after delay becomes improper. Relying heavily upon the federal statute, the Massachusetts court concluded that *Miranda* and voluntariness requirements were sufficient to protect suspects' self-incrimination rights during brief post-arrest questioning, and therefore otherwise admissible statements made within six hours of arrest are not to be excluded on presentation delay grounds. To minimize the need to define what delays are reasonable, the court held that statements obtained after delay has exceeded six hours are to be excluded, unless the delay is caused by "reasons not attributable to the police, such as a natural disaster."

§ 158. Confessions as "Fruit" of Improper Arrests or Detentions

If a defendant shows that he was improperly arrested or detained prior to making a confession later offered by the prosecution, the confession may be the excludable "fruit" of that arrest or detention. The leading cases are United States Supreme Court decisions addressing claims that confessions are inadmissible because of an arrest made in violation of the Fourth Amendment to the United States Constitution.

Defendants seldom have any difficulty establishing that such a confession is the "but for" result of the detention. The issue then becomes whether intervening circumstances attenuated the taint of that detention. Although the confession must be voluntary within the meaning of the Due Process requirement and *Miranda's* Fifth Amendment demands must be met, neither showing automatically or necessarily establishes attenuation of taint. Compliance with *Miranda,* however, is "an important factor" suggesting attenuation. Several other matters are also relevant.

One is the time between the unreasonable arrest and the making of the confession. Generally, the longer that time, the more likely the taint is to have become attenuated. A second consideration is variously called "the presence of intervening circumstances" or "intervening events." The Court has suggested that presentation of the suspect before a magistrate and the provision of warnings by that magistrate tends to show attenuation. If the intervening events consist of interrogation and other police actions that exploit the custody and are designed to make use of the custody in persuading the defendant to make an incriminating statement, on the other hand, obviously those events suggest that attenuation has not occurred.

A third factor is the extent to which the officers deviated from legal requirements and whether that deviation occurred in a manner causing it to have a particularly severe impact upon the defendant. The final concern is the

---

5. 661 N.E.2d 71 (Mass.1996).

extent to which the officers were motivated by a desire to secure incriminating admissions. Evidence that the officers were so motivated, of course, suggests the absence of attenuation.

§ 159. Evidence Obtained as a Result of Inadmissible Confessions

At early common law, the involuntariness of a confession did not affect the admissibility of other evidence obtained by use of that statement. If, for example, a suspect was coerced into confessing to a murder and also into revealing the location of the murder weapon, the weapon, if located, could be used in evidence. The rationale for this position was that the confession was excluded because of its untrustworthiness. If the "fruits" of that confession were themselves sufficiently probative of the defendant's guilt, the reason for excluding the confession did not extend to that derivative evidence and hence it was admissible. American courts applying the voluntariness requirement adopted this position.

As criminal evidence became permeated with exclusionary flavor after Mapp v. Ohio[1] and *Miranda,* American courts quite uncritically adopted for confession cases the "fruit of the poisonous tree" doctrine as developed in Fourth Amendment case law. This was apparently on the rationale that voluntariness law had come to serve purposes other than assuring the reliability of evidence, and encouraging law enforcement compliance with rules designed to accomplish these broader objectives required exclusion of "fruits" as well as involuntary confessions themselves.

In Oregon v. Elstad,[2] however, the Supreme Court made clear that not all federal constitutional requirements that mandate exclusion of a confession also embody a fruits doctrine requiring the exclusion of derivative evidence. *Elstad* itself held that a noncoercive violation of the prophylactic warning requirements established by Miranda v. Arizona[3] did not invoke a fruit of the poisonous tree approach. Fruit of a poisonous tree, the Court explained, necessarily must be excluded under the federal constitutional exclusionary sanctions only if the poisonous tree is an actual infringement of the suspect's federal constitutional rights. The Fifth Amendment itself prohibits only evidentiary use of compelled confessions. *Miranda's* prophylactic warning requirements are not actual parts of the Fifth Amendment's mandate but rather are judicially developed standards that sometimes require exclusion of a confession not actually "compelled." Therefore, exclusion of the fruits of a violation of these requirements is not constitutionally mandated.

Whether exclusion of fruits would be directed in situations in which it is not automatically mandated, *Elstad* apparently reasoned, depends on whether in those situations exclusion of them is appropriate. Two considerations, it suggested, might dictate a fruits rule in the *Miranda* context—a need to deter violations of the sort shown in the case or a need to assure trustworthy evidence. Neither was found controlling. Since *Miranda* violations are often accidental and do not intrude upon the Fifth Amendment itself, the need for deterrence is somewhat lessened; exclusion of the confession itself meets this reduced need. With regard to trustworthiness, the absence of coercion means that subsequent confessions would not be of questionable accuracy.

Does *Elstad* apply when the *Miranda* violation is not simply a failure to administer the warnings but rather a continuation of interrogation despite the suspect's effort to invoke either the right to counsel or the right to silence? The Court's language can be read as limiting its holding to nonwarning situations. Nevertheless, *Miranda's* bar to interrogation in such situations—where the resulting confession is not involuntary—seems certain not to involve the violation of the Fifth Amendment itself that *Elstad* suggests is necessary to made exclusion of fruits.

If the challenged fruit of a *Miranda* violation is not a subsequent incriminating statement but something else, such as physical

1. 367 U.S. 643 (1961), discussed in § 166 infra.

2. 470 U.S. 298 (1985).

3. 384 U.S. 436 (1966).

evidence, does *Elstad* render the fruits analysis inapplicable? If *Elstad* reflected an analysis similar to attenuation of taint, the voluntariness of the suspect's decision to confess might be critical to the Court's abandonment of the fruits doctrine. No such attenuating voluntary decision intervenes between a confession and discovery of physical evidence, and thus Elstad might be inapplicable where that is the nature of the challenged evidence. *Elstad* does not rest on such an attenuation analysis, however. The Court's articulated rationale in *Elstad* applies as much to nonconfession evidence as to confession evidence itself.

Elstad made clear that if a confession is involuntary, the extraction of it constituted "police infringement of the Fifth Amendment itself" and neither *Elstad* nor its rationale apply. Consequently, at least a subsequent confession given by the defendant is not free from challenge as tainted by the events stimulating the first confession. On the other hand, *Elstad* reaffirmed that a suspect from whom a confession has been coerced is not, as a result, perpetually disabled from thereafter giving an admissible confession. Precisely what standard determines whether a subsequently given confession is suppressible because of successful challenge to the admissibility of the initial confession, however, is not entirely clear. The major question is whether the prosecution establishes admissibility by proving that the second and challenged confession is itself voluntary or whether it must prove more. There are two major possibilities.

First, a defendant may simply need to persuade a court that the prosecution has failed to establish the voluntariness of the challenged subsequent confession. While the Court has left open whether there is a formal presumption that a confession is involuntary if it was given after an initial involuntary statement, the prosecution's burden of proving voluntariness at least imposes a practical need to overcome an inference of involuntariness. As a practical matter, then, the prosecution may need to establish that the influences rendering the first statement involuntary were no longer operative or controlling at the time of the second.

Second, a more conventional fruit of the poisonous tree analysis, as used in Fourth Amendment exclusionary sanction analysis may apply. If the defendant—perhaps aided by a presumption—establishes that "but for" having made the first and involuntary statement the defendant would not have made the second and challenged confession as and when he did, the second confession may become inadmissible fruit unless the prosecution establishes that the taint was attenuated. Whether this approach really differs in substance from the first is by no means clear.

If a defendant challenges nonconfession evidence as the inadmissible result of an involuntary confession, presumably the second approach distinguished above will apply. Such evidence is inadmissible fruit of the involuntary confession if "but for" the confession the evidence would not have been obtained as it was. The prosecution can escape exclusion by showing an exception, such as attenuation of taint or inevitable discovery, applies.

Some state courts have, as a matter of state constitutional law, rejected *Elstad*. After holding that state constitutional law imposes the same limits on police interrogation as *Miranda*, these courts then reason that violation of those state imposed limits triggers a fruit of the poisonous tree analysis. Other state courts, of course, have incorporated *Elstad* into any *Miranda*-like requirement of state law.

§ 160. Judicial Confessions, Guilty Pleas, and Admissions Made in Plea Bargaining

Most confession law involves self-incriminating admissions made by suspects to law enforcement officers during the pre-judicial stages of a criminal investigation. But the prosecution sometimes seeks trial use of self-incriminating admissions made by the defendant during what is essentially the judicial processing of a case. These admissions can usefully be broken down into three categories: "judicial" confessions, guilty pleas, and admissions made in connection with plea bargaining.

Judicial Confessions. A so-called "judicial confession" may consist of a defendant's testimony in a different (and perhaps civil) proceeding or in a prior hearing during the criminal prosecution then being tried. It may also be a "stipulation" or even the pleadings in this or other litigation. Under the general rules governing admissions,[1] these judicial confessions are admissible, subject of course to compliance with such requirements as any right to counsel the defendant may have had at the time.

Guilty Pleas. A defendant's guilty plea and statements made in connection with its offer to and acceptance by the trial court are admissible as admissions. Pleas of guilty to minor offenses may sometimes constitute questionable evidence of actual guilt, but this is best handled by considering on a case-by-case basis the probative value of particular pleas weighed against the risk of undue prejudice likely to arise from their admission into evidence.

Federal Rule 410 and Rule 9 of the Federal Rules of Criminal Procedure, prohibit the use of a withdrawn guilty plea and also bar the use of statements made in the course of proceedings in which such pleas are submitted to and accepted by the trial court. This is apparently on the rationale that permitting use of the plea would frustrate the policy objectives supporting the right to withdraw that plea. State statutes or court rules generally are similar.

Admissions Made in Connection With Plea Bargaining. There is general agreement that admissions made in connection with plea negotiations that do not result in final pleas of guilty must be excluded in order to encourage the desirable or at least necessary process of plea bargaining. This is provided for by Federal Rule 410 and Rule 11(E)(6) of the Federal Rules of Criminal Procedure; state statutes and court rules often address the matter as well, although there is considerable variation among the provisions.

These provisions typically make inadmissible statements made "in the course of plea discussions." Considerable difficulty arises in determining what are "plea discussions," and

when particular statements are made "in the course" of such discussions.

Some provisions, such as the federal ones, limit protection to statements made in connection with discussions with a prosecutor, on the rationale that discussions between law enforcement officers and defendants do not involve the sort of negotiations that should be encouraged by exclusion of admissions made during those negotiations. Thus generally no protection is afforded admissions made to law enforcement officers. Nevertheless, admissions made to a law enforcement officer will be protected if the evidence shows that the officer was acting as the apparently authorized agent of a prosecutor.

Whether a statement was made in the course of plea discussions is often addressed by using a two part inquiry. First, did the defendant make the admission with an actual expectation that he was in the process of negotiating a plea bargain? Second, if so, was that expectation reasonable given the totality of the circumstances? If the applicable provision does not absolutely exclude statements made to law enforcement officers, the fact that the discussion was with such officers rather than a prosecutor is a factor suggesting that any expectation of negotiating a plea bargain was unreasonable. Evidence that the confession was made to someone who had informed the defendant that the person was not in a position to make any deals, of course, suggests the confession is not protected. Perhaps most significantly, the provisions do not extend protection to statements made by defendants who are seeking to obtain leniency or even to begin plea negotiations, where the prosecutors have not entered into discussions of possible quid pro quo exchanges. Similarly, admissions made in the hopes of obtaining information from authorities rather than negotiating a plea bargain are not covered.

These provisions protect only confessions made in the process of reaching a plea bargain. If a bargain is reached and obligates the defendant to make certain statements, those statements are not protected. The provisions' pur-

§ 160

1. See § 266 infra.

pose of encouraging free and open discussion and settlement would not be served by construing them as covering matters developing after settlement was reached. Of course, the plea bargain itself may provide that incriminating admissions made in fulfillment of the bargain will be inadmissible.

The federal provisions permit use in perjury prosecutions of otherwise inadmissible pleas and statements related to pleas and plea negotiations. State provisions often but not always provide similarly. As a result of 1980 amendment, the federal provisions also embody a provision permitting the use of such statements against a defendant when some other statement made in the course of the same plea proceedings or negotiations has been introduced and the statement at issue "ought in fairness be considered contemporaneously with it."

Whether an admission otherwise subject to exclusion may be used to impeach a defendant who testifies is not explicitly addressed under the federal provisions. The original version of Federal Rule 410 contained an explicit but limited exception permitting the use of "voluntary and reliable statements" made in court and on the record, even if they were otherwise inadmissible under Rule 410, but only "where offered for impeachment purposes." Congress eliminated this language in the 1975 amendment of the rule. The Second Circuit has held that this "unusually clear legislative history" demonstrates a Congressional intention "to preclude use of statements made in plea negotiations for impeachment purposes"[2] and other federal courts have agreed. State provisions generally do not address the matter, and the silent provisos are usually read to bar impeachment use of the statements.

§ 161. "Tacit" and "Adoptive" Confessions and Admissions

Under the general rules regarding admissions,[1] the prosecution is generally permitted in a criminal case to prove that an accusatory statement was made in the hearing of the defendant and that the defendant's response was such as to justify the inference that he agreed with or "adopted" the statement. The adopting response may, of course, be an express affirmative agreement with the statement. It may also be conduct from which the defendant's belief in the accuracy of the statement can be inferred; where this is the case, the evidence amounts to what in this text is regarded as an "adoptive" confession. Adoption can be also inferred from the defendant's failure to deny the accusation, so a type of adoptive admission can arise from either silence or an "equivocal response" not a clear denial. Where the accusation is so adopted by the defendant's silence, the evidence thereby rendered admissible, the accusation and the defendant's adopting silence, is a "tacit" confession.

The foundation necessary has been articulated in various ways. Best put, admission requires preliminary proof (1) of an accusatory statement that a person who considered himself innocent would, under the circumstances, deny; (2) that the defendant heard and understood the accusatory statement; (3) that the defendant had the opportunity and ability to deny the statement; and (4) that the defendant manifested his adoption of it or, in the case of a tacit admission, adopted it by his silence.

Here, as in civil litigation, admission is based on the assumption that human nature is such that innocent persons will usually deny false accusations. Critical reconsideration of this assumption, especially as it applies in the criminal context, had led to increasing limitations upon adoptive confessions in criminal litigation. Use of this evidence in criminal trials is also affected by federal and state constitutional considerations. Both of these matters, especially as they concern tacit confessions adopted by defendants' silence, relate to the significance in this context of the requirements imposed by Miranda v. Arizona.[2]

---

2. United States v. Lawson, 683 F.2d 688, 690–693 (2d Cir.1982).

§ 161

1. See § 262 infra as to the nature of admissions.

2. 384 U.S. 436 (1996).

Doyle v. Ohio[3] held that federal Due Process considerations barred cross-examination of a testifying defendant by use of pretrial silence after he was taken into custody and warned pursuant to *Miranda* that he had a right to remain silent. Subsequent Supreme Court decisions made clear that this was based on the unfairness of explicitly representing to a suspect that the suspect has the right to silence and then penalizing the suspect for exercising that right. Consequently, federal Due Process poses no barrier to cross-examination use of silence prior to receipt of the *Miranda* assurance of the right to remain silent. Although the cases dealt with impeachment use, there is no doubt that post-warning silence cannot be used substantively—as the basis of a tacit confession—to prove a suspect's guilt.

Doyle and its progeny explicitly left open "whether or under what circumstances" pre-*Miranda* silence may be protected by the Fifth Amendment and thus unavailable for use as substantive evidence of guilt. Griffin v. California,[4] prohibiting trial comment on a defendant's failure to testify,[5] suggests that a defendant's pretrial silence—if it reflects an assertion of the right to remain silent—must similarly be declared off limits for prosecutorial use at trial.

There can be little doubt that the Fifth Amendment and at least many state provisions give suspects a pretrial right to remain silent, even before custodial interrogation triggers the *Miranda* mandates. Perhaps, however, where the inherently coercive combination of custody and interrogation are lacking, that right—like the right to be free from compelled self-incrimination in general[6]—is one that must be asserted. If so, a suspect's mere silence—that the suspect does not explicitly announce is based on the right to remain silent—is not supported by the right to remain silent. Permitting the prosecution to use that silence as the basis for a tacit confession, therefore, does not burden or penalize an exercise of the self-incrimination right to remain silent.

On the other hand, the message of *Miranda* has been widely disseminated. Most people probable believe—correctly or not—that regardless of whether custodial interrogation is underway they have a general self-incrimination right to remain silent. Given this general perception, silence in pre-*Miranda* situations may often in actual fact reflect reliance upon what the person understands to be the applicable self-incrimination right. Permitting the prosecution to use such silence may often in fact penalize a suspect for exercising at least what the suspect believed was his self-incrimination right.

Courts are split on whether the use of pre-*Miranda* warning silence impermissibly burdens the privilege against compelled self-incrimination. Many regard silence as unprotected when no law enforcement officers were present at the time. When an officer is present, the case for treating silence as reliance on the right of silence is stronger, and the strength of that case increases if the suspect has been taken into custody although not admonished under *Miranda*.

Modern courts considering the admissibility of tacit and adoptive confessions have been increasingly critical of the traditional assumption that silence in the face of an accusation generally reflects agreement with the accusation. Less than unequivocal expressed agreement with the accusation—and especially silence—may—given widespread knowledge of *Miranda*—reflect not agreement but instead a decision to invoke what even an innocent suspect believes to be an available and useful right of silence that may reduce the risk of wrongful prosecution or conviction. The weakness of inference that a failure to unequivocally challenge an accusation reflects agreement with it suggests another reason for questioning the admissibility of such evidence.

Doyle contained language suggesting that the "insolubly ambiguous" nature of silence following *Miranda* warnings was a factor in its holding that prosecutorial use of such silence

---

3. 426 U.S. 610 (1976).

4. 380 U.S. 609 (1965).

5. See generally § 126.

6. See generally §§ 118, 130 supra.

was constitutionally barred. The Court has, however, disclaimed reliance on any such consideration, and the difficulty of choosing the inferences to draw from silence or ambiguous conduct does not seem to affect the federal constitutional admissibility of such evidence.

Such difficulty may, however, affect the admissibility of adoptive or tacit confessions—whether offered for impeachment of a testifying defendant or as substantive evidence of guilt—as a matter of nonconstitutional evidence law. The Supreme Court has held that the minimal probative value of a defendant's silence renders evidence of such silence inadmissible to impeach as a matter of federal evidence law. The Connecticut Supreme Court held that an adoptive admission based on silence is admissible only if no explanation other than assent to the accusatory statement is "equally consistent."[7] Some courts have more severely curtailed prosecution use of tacit admissions. The Alabama Supreme Court, for example, barred all use of either pre-or post-arrest silence, explaining that "neither logic nor common experience any longer support the tacit admission rule, if indeed, either ever supported it."[8]

Others courts have held that admissibility turns on the probative value/risk of undue prejudice balance, and some have encouraged trial judges to engage in more critical appraisals of the competing considerations. The Maryland court, for example, made clear that when the prosecution offers evidence of an accused's prearrest silence following an accusation made in the presence of a law enforcement officer, the trial judge should carefully consider whether the officer's presence, in the circumstances, demonstrates that a reasonable person would not be expected to deny or explain the accusation.[9]

§ 162. Use of Otherwise Inadmissible Confessions for Impeachment

The exclusionary sanctions applicable to confessions are subject to the limitations applicable to exclusionary sanctions generally, including the limitation which often permits the prosecution to use inadmissible evidence to impeach a defendant who testifies in his own defense at trial.[1] Confession law's complexity, and especially the distinction between the voluntariness requirement and other exclusionary rules, results in particular difficulties applying the impeachment exception to confession law.

In a line of cases beginning with Harris v. New York,[2] the Supreme Court has held that the impeachment exception to federal constitutional exclusionary requirements permits the use of confessions obtained in violation of *Miranda* and at least some Sixth Amendment right to counsel requirements for such impeachment purposes. Those obtained in violation of "core" Sixth Amendment demands, however, may be inadmissible even for this purpose.

Harris' impeachment exception to the federal constitutional exclusionary sanctions attaching to confessions does not extend to certain situations in which voluntariness concerns are implicated. In Mincey v. Arizona[3] the Court found constitutional error in the use of an involuntary confession to impeach a testifying defendant. "[A]ny criminal trial use against a defendant of his *involuntary* statement," the Court announced, "is a denial of due process * * *." This is apparently because involuntariness–unlike *Miranda* violations–renders confessions at least somewhat untrustworthy, and consequently less valuable as indicators of defendant perjury. The prosecution's interest in using them for impeachment is therefore reduced. Further, law enforcement activity that has sufficient impact to render confessions involuntary is more offensive to constitutional values than activity that merely violates *Miranda's* prophylactic rules. This increases the need for maximum deterrence, which is provided by excluding the confessions for all purposes. In these cases,

---

7. State v. Vitale, 497 A.2d 956, 961 (Conn.1985).

8. Ex parte Marek, 556 So.2d 375, 381 (Ala.1989).

9. Key–El v. State, 709 A.2d 1305, 1308 (Md. 1998).

§ 162

1. See generally § 183 infra.

2. 401 U.S. 222 (1971).

3. 437 U.S. 385 (1978).

then, the need for full deterrence outweighs the prosecution's reduced interest in using the confessions even for the limited purpose at issue.

As in other exclusionary sanction situations, state courts and legislatures remain free to reject the federal constitutional model and to apply state law exclusionary requirements unqualified by impeachment exceptions. Some have done so.[4]

§ 163. Determining Admissibility and Credibility

The close relationship between some requirements of admissibility and the weight that confession evidence is properly given in determining guilt have generated considerable disagreement on the role of judge and jury in resolving the various issues presented when the prosecution offers evidence of a defendant's confession. Some of the issues, of course, are constitutional ones.

Roles of Judge and Jury. In Jackson v. Denno,[1] the Supreme Court held that the due process clause of the Fourteenth Amendment requires that upon proper demand the trial judge determine the voluntariness of a challenged confession. *Jackson* held constitutionally impermissible what had previously been known as the "New York procedure," under which the trial judge conducted a preliminary inquiry and excluded a challenged confession only if its involuntariness was so clear as to present no issue. If the evidence presented a fair question as to voluntariness or any factual matters relevant to voluntariness, the confession was submitted to the jury with directions to determine voluntariness and to consider the confession on the issue of guilt or innocence only if it was found to be voluntary.

Under the New York procedure, the Court reasoned, jurors might first conclude that a defendant committed the crime charged and then be unable or disinclined to determine the voluntariness of a challenged confession without regard to its accuracy. This would, of course, violate the right to have voluntariness determined without regard to reliability. Alternatively, the jurors might first address the confession and conclude that it was involuntary but reliable; they might then be unable or disinclined to ignore that confession in assessing the sufficiency of the prosecution's evidence on guilt. This would endanger the right to have guilt or innocence determined without consideration of an involuntary confession.

Defendants have no federal constitutional right to jury consideration of claims of involuntariness rejected by trial judges. The Court in Lego v. Twomey[2] found neither a basis for concluding that juries are somehow "better suited" than trial judges to determine voluntariness, nor convincing grounds for regarding trial judges' resolutions of voluntariness challenges as sufficiently unreliable to entitle defendants to "a second forum for litigating [their] claim[s]."

Defendants do have a federal Due Process right to contest the *credibility*—as distinguished from the *voluntariness*—of a confession admitted into evidence. Once the prosecution is permitted to introduce evidence that the defendant made incriminating admissions, the Court held in Crane v. Kentucky,[3] the defendant is entitled to introduce evidence concerning the circumstances under which he made them if those circumstances bear upon the credibility of the admissions.

Federal constitutional considerations, then, permit the trial judge to be given sole responsibility for resolving voluntariness issues. Under this "orthodox" approach, the trial judge resolves all factual disputes and determines voluntariness. No issues related to voluntariness are submitted to the jury. Many jurisdictions follow this procedure.

Federal constitutional requirements also permit what is known as the Massachusetts or "humane" procedure under which the trial judge makes a full inquiry into and determines voluntariness. If the trial judge finds

---

4. See generally, § 183 infra.

§ 163

1. 378 U.S. 368 (1964).

2. 404 U.S. 477 (1972).

3. 476 U.S. 683 (1986).

the challenged confession voluntary, however, the issue of voluntariness is then submitted to the jury for reconsideration, and the jury is instructed to consider the confession on the defendant's guilt only if it first finds it voluntary. A number of jurisdictions take this approach.

The wisdom of this approach is questionable. Most if not all considerations relating to voluntariness will also be relevant to credibility, so the defendant will have an opportunity to present them to the jury. Whether jurors are ever or often able or inclined to distinguish credibility and voluntariness and to disregard a credible but involuntary confession is at best doubtful, and the task of adequately submitting both matters to the jury without confusing the jurors is a difficult and perhaps impossible one. Careful submission of credibility, then, is preferable to the humane procedure.

What is submitted to a jury depends, of course, on the jurisdiction's approach. Under *Crane*, a defendant challenging before the jury the credibility of the prosecution's evidence that he confessed is certainly entitled to adequate jury instructions on the jury's obligation to evaluate credibility. Under nonconstitutional law, juries are often told that they are to consider, in light of all the circumstances, the weight to give to such evidence, and this is probably sufficient under *Crane*.

Some jurisdictions go further at least in certain types of cases, as for example by instructing juries to view with caution evidence that the defendant made an oral admission of guilt or even to so view evidence that the accused made an out-of-court incriminating statement.

Jurisdictions following the humane procedure require juries to address the voluntariness of any self-incriminating statements they find the accuseds made. This is a different task than determining the weight to be given such statements in light of their apparent credibility, and a jury is to be told to first determine voluntariness and then, if it finds the confession voluntary, to consider what if any weight to give to it.

Hearing and Burden of Proof. Jackson means that generally a trial judge is required to hold a hearing on the admissibility of a challenged confession—a "Jackson v. Denno hearing"—if the party against whom it is offered objects and requests such a hearing. A few courts, regarding some confession requirements as too important to fall to defense counsel's default, require that even in the absence of a demand for a hearing, trial judges conduct a hearing, entertain evidence, and determine voluntariness of a proffered confession.

A defendant's federal constitutional right to a fair determination of voluntariness means that a trial judge's conclusion that a challenged confession is voluntary "must appear from the record with unmistakable clarity." It is not constitutionally necessary, however, that the trial judge make formal findings of fact on contested subissues or write a formal opinion. Nevertheless, sound policy and particularly the practicalities of effective appellate review strongly suggest specific findings concerning disputed subquestions of fact as well as a clear ultimate determination of the major issues.

Lego held that when a defendant challenges the prosecution's proffer of a confession, the federal constitution requires that the prosecution prove the voluntariness of the confession but that the prosecution need only establish this by a preponderance of the evidence. Voluntariness does not have to be established beyond a reasonable doubt or even by clear and convincing evidence.

No basis had been presented for believing that traditional determinations of admissibility based on a preponderance of the evidence were unreliable or otherwise "wanting in quality." Whatever might be accomplished by imposing a higher standard, the Court concluded, would be outweighed by the cost of denying juries evidence probative on defendants' guilt or innocence. Fourteen years later, the Court summarily held that the prosecution's burden of proving compliance with Fifth Amendment *Miranda* requirements is no greater.

States remain free to impose higher standards. Many do require the prosecution to establish voluntariness and sometimes compliance with other requirements, such as those imposed by self-incrimination demands, by clear and convincing evidence or even beyond a reasonable doubt.

Chapter 15

THE PRIVILEGE CONCERNING IMPROPERLY OBTAINED EVIDENCE

Table of Sections

§ 164. Introduction

Traditionally, out-of-court impropriety in the manner by which evidence was obtained did not affect its admissibility. This was primarily, of course, because the courts regarded the need for all probative evidence to assure the most accurate resolution of lawsuits as more important than other objectives that might be furthered by excluding relevant evidence. In addition, however, courts' regarded inquiries into possible impropriety in the de-velopment of evidence as too costly and time-consuming to justify whatever other objectives might be furthered by excluding evidence because of impropriety in obtaining it.

Probably the most important recent development in the law of evidence as applied in criminal litigation has been the rejection of this approach and the resulting increase in requirements that evidence be excluded because of the manner in which it was obtained—so-called "exclusionary rules."

Discussions sometimes assume the existence of "the exclusionary rule," suggesting that there is only one remedial requirement involved. This is unfortunate and misleading. Litigation and discussion is often dominated by considerations of the Supreme Court's construction of the Fourth Amendment to the United States Constitution as requiring the exclusion in both state and federal criminal prosecutions of evidence tainted by a violation of that provision. But this ignores that exclusion may be required because evidence was obtained by violating other legal requirements, many of them not embodied in the federal constitution. Moreover, the contents of these exclusionary requirements need not necessarily be the same as that of the Fourth Amendment exclusionary requirement.

Generally, then, discussion best avoids simplistic reference to "the exclusionary rule" as a single rule covering a range of situations. Instead, this area should be conceptualized as containing numerous possible exclusionary rules or sanctions. An exclusionary sanction may attach to any legal requirement that could be violated in the gathering of evidence. There are potentially as many exclusionary sanctions as there are legal requirements of this sort. The Fourth Amendment exclusionary sanction may provide a benchmark for analysis of issues presented by other exclusionary sanctions. But it is important to recognize that other such sanctions may differ in content from the Fourth Amendment's rule. Whether and how they *should* differ are hard issues that tend to be obscured by discussion of "the exclusionary rule."

It is, of course, difficult to separate discussion of exclusionary sanctions from consideration of the underlying rules enforced by these sanctions. Nevertheless, the contents of those rules are not matters of evidence law. Consequently, this chapter focuses upon the exclusionary remedies rather than the underlying legal requirements violated.

Many legal requirements relating to the admissibility of confessions, such as the *Miranda* requirements and directives that an arrested person be promptly presented before a magistrate, are probably exclusionary sanc-

tions within the meaning of this chapter. For convenience, however, these are treated in Chapter 14, devoted generally to confessions.

§ 165. Policy Bases for Exclusionary Sanctions

Exclusionary sanctions result in exclusion of what would otherwise be relevant and competent evidence, and therefore involve a considerable cost. Consequently, they bear a significant burden of justification. Such justification might be provided by several quite different functions which these sanctions might serve.

Promotion of Accurate Results. Can exclusionary rules be defended on the ground that they result in rejection of evidence that might otherwise increase the risk that trials would lead to inaccurate results? Some exclusionary sanctions may be supported, at least to some extent, on this basis. If counsel's presence at lineups reduces the risk of suggestiveness, for example, exclusion of eyewitness testimony tainted by the witness's identification of the defendant at a lineup conducted in violation of this right might to some extent result in rejection of unreliable evidence that might otherwise be credited beyond what can be defended on objective grounds.

Most exclusionary sanctions, however, cannot be supported on these grounds. To the contrary, the fact that the evidence excluded by these requirements is not only relevant and competent but also highly reliable increases the difficulty of justifying the requirements.

Prevention of Future Violations. A major function served by exclusionary sanctions, of course, is the prevention of future violations of the underlying legal requirements. Prevention might be effectuated in at least two quite different ways: deterrence and "education" or "assimilation."

Deterrence consists of motivating persons to consciously choose not to violate legal requirements because of a desire to avoid rendering evidence inadmissible. Usually in exclusionary sanction debates this means encouraging law enforcement officers to comply with legal requirements in a conscious effort to assure the admissibility of the products of their investigative efforts. But detractors of the exclusionary sanction approach argue that any expectation that deterrence will work effectively is naive, because law enforcement officers will often perceive the threat of exclusion as far less meaningful than other considerations influencing their conduct.

Exclusion will be a possibility only if the case is actively contested. Most criminal cases are not ultimately litigated, so the technical admissibility of evidence will not be a consideration. In the infrequent cases in which exclusion becomes a real possibility, the threat materializes only long after the officers' role in the case is finished. A threat to exclude, made in the context of plea bargaining and protracted processing of criminal cases, may be a threat of such minimal and distant significance that it cannot be expected to overcome, in the officers' minds, other considerations that suggest different courses of action.

In actuality, other considerations may be more immediately pressing and make stronger cases for officers' attention. If an officer believes that compliance with legal requirements endangers his personal safety, he is unlikely to ignore that risk because of the possibility of legal challenges to the admissibility of the products of his actions at some distant time. Similarly, the expectations of the officer's peers and immediate supervisors may well conflict with what the law requires and may compete quite effectively with evidentiary rules for the officer's response.

Moreover, the legal requirements with which the officer is expected to comply may be so unclear as to frustrate efforts to ascertain and follow them. Or they may appear to the officer as unrealistic, meaningless or both, and thus invite circumvention.

There is even a risk that to the extent an exclusionary sanction may convey a meaningful deterrent message to law enforcement officers, the result may be that officers will find it most advantageous to completely forego formal prosecution and instead rely upon "street justice" to encourage what they perceive as desirable behavior. If the result of an evidentiary rule is to encourage law enforcement agencies to engage in informal and largely extra-legal activities rather than to encourage them to comply with legal requirements so that prosecution remains possible, the rules have arguably effectuated the worst of all possibilities.

Perhaps the lesson is that generalization about the likely deterrent effect of exclusionary sanctions is difficult or impossible. Some law enforcement activities may be far more subject to being influenced by evidentiary rules than others. Some legal requirements might far more than others lend themselves to effective implementation by means of exclusionary requirements.

Prevention of undesired law enforcement activity, however, may be accomplished in ways other than deterrence. The Supreme Court has noted the possibility that the long-term effect of excluding evidence may be to demonstrate the seriousness with which society regards the underlying legal requirements. This, in turn, may cause law enforcement officers and policymakers to incorporate the requirements into their value system and, presumably, to accept them unconsciously as demanding compliance regardless of the consciously-perceived effect of noncompliance.[1]

How effective exclusionary sanctions are in enforcing various legal requirements in different contexts remains addressed largely on the basis of intuition. Some empirical research has been undertaken, but in part because of severe methodological problems it is inconclusive.

Judicial Integrity Considerations. Exclusionary sanctions might be justified in whole or in part on the basis of what the Supreme Court in Elkins v. United States[2] called "the imperative of judicial integrity." But two very different approaches are sometimes confused in discussions of judicial integrity.

§ 165

1. See Stone v. Powell, 428 U.S. 465, 492 (1976).

2. 364 U.S. 206 (1960).

One argument is that because evidence was improperly obtained, courts' use of that evidence is simply and inherently "wrong" and thus to be avoided. Of course, the nature of the argument means that it is incapable of utilitarian analysis or empirical verification. At its base, it rests upon an intuitive notion of "right" or "integrity." Whether any such notion of "right" can provide strong support for a costly evidentiary rule, of course, is at best problematic.

Another argument often regarded as a judicial integrity consideration has, in contrast, a clearly utilitarian end and thus is—in theory at least—susceptible to efforts to verify it. This approach was articulated by Justice Brandeis in Olmstead v. United States:[3]

> In a government of laws, existence of the government will be imperilled if it fails to observe the law scrupulously * * *. Crime is contagious. If the Government becomes a lawbreaker, it breeds contempt for law; it invites every man to become a law unto himself; it invites anarchy.[4]

This means, he continued, that the government, like a private litigant, should be denied access to the courts if it comes with unclean hands. If the government bases its request for aid from the courts on illegally obtained evidence, "aid is denied despite the defendant's wrong. It is denied in order to maintain respect for law; in order to promote confidence in the administration of justice; in order to preserve the judicial process from contamination."

Essentially, this argument is that if illegally seized evidence is used by the government acting through its courts, government in general and its courts in particular will lose the respect of the governed and will be rendered less able to perform their governing functions. In the case of courts, this means that they will be less able to resolve disputes among citizens.

Despite the rhetorical flourish with which Justice Brandeis demonstrated this argument can be made, it may simply be inconsistent with reality. Whether the courts' ability to command respect and compliance is affected by evidentiary rules is, of course, open to doubt. But to the extent that it is, this argument may distort the effect of those rules. General respect for the judiciary may well suffer when the courts are perceived as ignoring reliable evidence because of impropriety in the manner it was obtained, particularly if doing so requires the acquittal of persons clearly guilty of serious antisocial acts.

Remedy for Wrongs Done in the Illegality. Superficially, at least, exclusionary sanctions would seem to perform a unique and perhaps appropriate remedial function, and thus might be justified on that basis. The law's objective, the argument might run, should be to place a wronged person as close to his previous condition as is feasible. Only an exclusionary sanction can replace such a person in a position in which he need not fear the use against him of the fruits of wrong done to him.

On the other hand, the substance of the underlying legal requirements violated may make clear that persons whose rights are violated have no *legitimate* interest in being free of criminal liability that looms only because of the violations of their rights. If they have no such legitimate interest, the fact that an exclusionary sanction frees them of such liability is of little or no significance.

The right to be free of unreasonable searches, for example, may protect only persons' interest in being free of the privacy invasion occasioned by such searches. That this privacy interest enables them to withhold from the government evidence of their criminal activity would then be at most an undesirable side effect of the privacy right. If the right to be free from unreasonable searches is so conceptualized, no person who is unreasonably searched has a legitimate interest in having the government deprived of the power to use against them evidence found as a result of that search. Their interest in an effective remedy for the violation of their privacy, then, does not include an interest in being returned to a

---

3. 277 U.S. 438 (1928).

4. Id. at 485 (Brandeis, J., dissenting).

condition in which they need not fear the government's use of the discovered evidence against them in a criminal prosecution.

If the underlying legal requirements are so conceptualized, the tendency of exclusionary sanctions to provide unique protection against criminal liability is of no *legitimate* remedial significance. Since the victims of the underlying wrongs have no legitimate interest in being free of the use of the evidence against them, the unique ability of exclusionary sanctions to bring about this result does not significantly support the exclusionary sanctions.

Even if exclusion does tend to some extent at least respond in a logical manner to the harm done, it may not be "appropriate" because it provides an excessive remedy. This is especially the case if exclusion of evidence frustrates the prosecution. Acquittal of a demonstrably guilty person may simply be too heavy a cost even to make a victimized person whole.

§ 166. Federal Constitutional Exclusionary Sanctions: (a) Development

Federal constitutional exclusionary sanctions have served as a model for modern exclusionary requirements. The Supreme Court's case law developing the federal sanctions—and the decisions molding the Fourth Amendment exclusionary requirement in particular—have similarly framed much of the discussion of exclusionary requirements in general.

Exclusion as a response to Federal constitutional illegality in obtaining evidence appears to have originated in confusion concerning the substance of Fourth and Fifth Amendment protection. In Boyd v. United States,[1] an unsuccessful claimant in a forfeiture action sought relief from a judgment of forfeiture on the ground that the trial court erred in receiving into evidence an invoice which the claimant had been compelled to produce by order of the trial court. Both the Fourth and Fifth Amendments were invoked. The Supreme Court held that the compulsory production of the document was subject to scrutiny under the Fourth Amendment. To determine whether it was reasonable, the Court turned to the Fifth Amendment's prohibition against compelled self-incrimination. Finding an "intimate relationship" between the two provisions, the Court concluded that compelled production or other seizure of a person's private books or papers to be used in evidence against him was violative of the Fifth Amendment. Ultimately, the Court held that the admission into evidence of the invoice, given the manner in which it was obtained, violated both the Fourth Amendment prohibition against unreasonable searches and seizures and the Fifth Amendment prohibition against compelled self-incrimination.

Twenty years later, in Adams v. New York,[2] the Court nevertheless refused to require exclusion where only the defendant's Fourth Amendment rights were violated. Such cases were governed by what the Court described as "the weight of authority as well as reason," embodied in the rule that courts will not pause to inquire as to the means by which competent evidence is obtained.

A decade later, however, in Weeks v. United States,[3] the Court embraced exclusion as a Fourth Amendment remedy. The Fourth Amendment as it applied in federal criminal litigation, *Weeks* held, imposed an exclusionary sanction. "If letters and private documents can thus be [improperly] seized and held and used in evidence against a citizen accused of an offense," the Court reasoned, "the protection of the Fourth Amendment declaring his right to be secure against such searches and seizures is of no value, and, so far as those thus placed are concerned, might as well be stricken from the Constitution."

Weeks, of course, was inapplicable to state litigation, and doubt remained even whether the Fourth Amendment itself was binding on the states. In Wolf v. Colorado,[4] the Court for the first time directly addressed these issues. Concluding that the core of the Fourth

§ 166

1. 116 U.S. 616 (1886).

2. 192 U.S. 585 (1904).

3. 232 U.S. 383 (1914).

4. 338 U.S. 25 (1949).

Amendment, the security of one's privacy against arbitrary intrusion by the police, was basic to a free society and therefore implicit in the concept of ordered liberty, the Court held that under Palko v. Connecticut[5] the Fourth Amendment prohibition against unreasonable searches and seizures was enforceable against the States through the Due Process clause of the Fourteenth Amendment.

But *Wolf* then distinguished the prohibition against unreasonable searches and seizures from the exclusionary remedy applied in federal criminal litigation and found the latter not binding on the States. By 1961, however, the Court was prepared to reconsider *Wolf's* second conclusion.

In Mapp v. Ohio,[6] this second holding of *Wolf* was reversed. Since *Wolf*, the majority explained, more than half of those states considering whether to adopt an exclusionary sanction as a matter of state law had decided to do so. The weight of the relevant authority, then, could no longer be said to oppose the *Weeks* rule. More important, however, the Court read experience as contradicting *Wolf's* assumption that remedies other than an exclusionary rule could be relied upon to enforce Fourth Amendment rights. The experience and decisions of the state courts as well as the Supreme Court's own decisions recognized the "obvious futility of relegating the Fourth Amendment to the protection of other remedies * * *" Consequently, the *Weeks* exclusionary rule was held an essential part of both the Fourth and Fourteenth Amendments and therefore binding on the states as well as the federal government.

Mapp was undoubtedly a bold holding made on minimal grounds. Functionally, the Supreme Court read the general terms of the Fourth Amendment as delegating to the federal courts the power to develop remedies appropriate to enforcement of the clear substantive commands of the provision. The framers must have anticipated that the guarantees of the provision be enforceable in federal courts. Since they failed to provide for remedies that enabled this, they must have intended that the courts have authority to develop such remedies as are appropriate given such considerations as the magnitude of the threats posed to the underlying guarantees and the effectiveness of less costly alternatives than exclusion of resulting evidence.

Having determined that an exclusionary sanction was an essential part of the Fourth Amendment right to be free from unreasonable searches and seizures, the Court proceeded to apply it uncritically to other federal constitutional rights. It has made clear, however, that these various federal constitutional exclusionary sanctions are not identical in content.[7]

§ 167. Federal Constitutional Exclusionary Sanctions: (b) Policy Bases and Analytical Approach

As the Supreme Court developed the federal constitutional exclusionary requirements, primarily the Fourth Amendment sanction, it narrowed the policy considerations on which those requirements are based. It has also formulated a consistently-applied approach to framing the subissues raised in developing the contents of those requirements. In the course of this process, the Court has made two—or perhaps three—basic choices regarding the potentially-relevant policy considerations.

First, the Court has made clear that the federal constitutional rules do not serve a significant legitimate remedial function. This is because as the Court envisions the constitutional injuries done, exclusion of evidence simply does not tend to make victims whole. "[T]he ruptured privacy of the victims' homes and effects," it explained in the context of search and seizure law, "cannot be restored. Reparation comes too late."[1]

---

5. 302 U.S. 319 (1937).

6. 367 U.S. 643 (1961).

7. See § 176 infra ("fruit of the poisonous tree" does not apply to Fifth Amendment exclusionary aspect of *Miranda* holdings).

§ 167

1. Linkletter v. Walker, 381 U.S. 618, 637 (1965).

If exclusion of evidence cannot restore the violated privacy, why cannot it at least reduce one effect of the privacy violation by replacing the victim to a position wherein he does not face criminal prosecution based on evidence obtained as a result of the violation of his privacy interests? The Court has not directly addressed this question. But most likely it views the prosecution's possession of and ability to use incriminating evidence as entirely unrelated to the legitimate interests of the defendant. The prosecution has a right to possession of this evidence; the defendant has no ultimate right to withhold it from the prosecution. To the extent that an improper search results in the prosecution being able to implement its interest in obtaining such evidence, the search violates no protected interests, that is, no "rights," of the defendant. The wrong to the defendant consisted entirely of violating his privacy. To the extent that this violation of privacy factually resulted in the prosecution obtaining access to incriminating evidence, this in no way contributes to the constitutionally offensive aspects of the search, that is, those aspects as to which the defendant has a legitimate claim to remedy.

Consequently, to deprive the prosecution of the ability to use this evidence would in no way restore the defendant in a manner to which he has any legitimate claim. His only legitimate claim is for restoration of his violated privacy, which is in no way accomplished by depriving the prosecution of evidence.

The second basic decision made by the Court was adoption of the view that considerations of judicial integrity have only a "limited role" in Fourth Amendment theory and, consequently, in determining the content of the provision's exclusionary mandate. This was accomplished by holding that the "primary meaning" of judicial integrity in this context is such that it is violated when, but only when, courts' use of illegally obtained evidence encourages future violations of the sort that provided the prosecution access to the evidence at issue. Consequently, whether particular use of illegally obtained evidence offends judicial in-

tegrity considerations involves essentially the same question as whether it serves a preventive purpose: will the admission of the evidence encourage future illegality of the sort committed to obtain the evidence at issue?

The third potentially basic policy decision concerns what almost by default has become the basic justification for the federal constitutional requirements—the need to prevent future violations of the underlying constitutional demands. Traditionally, the Court appeared to assume that this would be accomplished by conscious deterrence—law enforcement officers would be motivated by the exclusionary sanction to consciously comply with the constitutional rules. In Stone v. Powell,[2] with regard to the preventive function of the Fourth Amendment exclusionary rule, the Court indicated that the long-term "educative" effect is "[m]ore important[ ]" than the tendency of the threat of exclusion to consciously deter officers from future violations. Nevertheless, it has not followed this pronouncement and in post-*Stone* analyses has assumed that prevention is accomplished primarily if not exclusively by deterrence.

Building on these basic decisions regarding the relevant considerations, the Court has developed a consistent formula for framing specific subissues regarding the content of the federal constitutional exclusionary rules. First articulated in United States v. Calandra,[3] this approach puts the issue as one of proposed expansion of the exclusionary requirement beyond the core demand that evidence obtained as a direct result of activity violating the constitutional requirements be excluded when offered by the prosecution to prove the defendant's guilt in the prosecution's case-in-chief at a criminal trial. The analysis requires identification of, first, the increased effectiveness of the exclusionary sanction in accomplishing its purpose that would result from the proposed expansion, and, second, the costs of doing so. The critical question is whether the incremental increase in effectiveness is worth the cost that must be paid.

---

2. 428 U.S. 465 (1976).

3. 414 U.S. 338 (1974).

Generally, in inquiring into the potential for increased effectiveness the Court focuses upon deterrence and inquires as to the incremental deterrent effect which would be achieved by the proposed expansion. With regard to the costs, of course, the loss of reliable evidence of offenders' guilt is the major concern. But in addition the Court has taken into account other considerations, such as administrative costs and disruption of the criminal justice system in general and criminal trials in particular. In *Calandra*, for example, the specific issue before the Court was whether the Fourth Amendment exclusionary rule should be applied to grand jury proceedings by permitting witnesses to decline to respond to questions based upon information obtained in violation of the witnesses' Fourth Amendment rights. Permitting this, the majority stressed, would require that grand jury investigations be frequently halted for extended inquiries into the manner in which particular information was acquired. The result would be serious interference with the effective and expeditious discharge by grand juries of their historic role and functions.

§ 168. State Constitutional Exclusionary Sanctions

Despite the prominence of *Mapp* and Fourth Amendment case law in exclusionary sanction discussion, the exclusionary remedy was first developed in state constitutional litigation. State decisions provide bases of increasing importance for modern exclusionary sanctions, independent of *Mapp* and its progeny. Proponents of exclusion as a means of enforcing legal requirements, dissatisfied with the Supreme Court's development of federal rights and exclusionary remedies, have increasingly sought to persuade state courts to develop state constitutional rights—and state constitutional exclusionary requirements—as more rigorously protective of those suspected or accused of crime.

States' power to accept or reject an exclusionary approach was confirmed by the Supreme Court in California v. Greenwood.[1] Un-

der California law, the warrantless search of Greenwood's trash constituted an unreasonable search under a state constitutional provision similar to the Fourth Amendment, yet state constitutional law did not require exclusion of the resulting evidence. All agreed that *Mapp* and its rationale did not require, as a matter of Fourth Amendment law, exclusion of evidence obtained in violation of the state constitution but not in violation of any federal provision. Further, the Court held, the Due Process Clause of the Fourteenth Amendment did not bar the state from depriving Greenwood of a remedy for police conduct violating state but not federal constitutional law. California could have defined unreasonable searches as encompassing no more official activity than was covered by the Fourth Amendment. Since the state has the power to permit police activity not barred by the Fourth Amendment, it necessarily also has the lesser included power to prohibit such activity but to enforce that prohibition by means other than excluding evidence from criminal trials.

State constitutional provisions, like their federal counterparts, seldom expressly address the admissibility of evidence obtained in violation of them. When a state court is asked to construe such provisions to require the exclusion of evidence, then, it must choose whether or not to interpret its constitution with the same vigor and flexibility exercised by the Supreme Court in *Mapp*. Thus, state courts are faced with the same basic question as the Supreme Court faced in *Wolf* and *Mapp*—does general language prohibiting certain official conduct require or permit exclusion of evidence resulting from prohibited conduct? Seldom have state courts addressed directly and creatively the difficult question of whether such general constitutional provisions provide the courts with authority to mandate as pervasive and controversial requirements as exclusionary sanctions. Language accepting an exclusionary sanction for violations of state constitutions has sometimes simply offhandedly crept into discussion and become accepted law without any focused and careful consideration as to the propriety of this position. In

§ 168
1. 486 U.S. 35 (1988).

some situations, state judicial attention has been focused upon whether a state exclusionary sanction should be developed as identical in content to federal constitutional exclusionary sanctions, rather than on whether a state exclusionary sanction is even justified. State constitutional exclusionary rules, then, have sometimes developed with little or no careful scrutiny of their propriety or wisdom.

Several courts have addressed in more depth the propriety of construing their state provisions as the Supreme Court construed the Fourth Amendment in *Mapp*. Each has chosen to follow the *Mapp* approach. The most significant consideration in these analyses has been the courts' perceptions that exclusionary sanctions have become generally accepted and thus are appropriately read into a state provision in the absence of a demonstrated reason to read the state provision otherwise. As the intermediate Connecticut appellate court explained in accurately predicting that the state's highest court would recognize a state constitutional exclusionary rule:

> [T]he [exclusionary] rule has gained overwhelming judicial acceptance as the most effective method of guaranteeing the protection against unreasonable invasion of privacy secured by constitutional search and seizure provisions.[2]

Perhaps most amazing is the lack of diversity in the holdings. No highest state court seems recently to have squarely held that a state provision analogous to the Fourth, Fifth or Sixth Amendment does not require exclusion.

A state court's adoption of a state constitutional exclusionary rule, and even its explicit approval of *Mapp's* interpretive approach, does not mean that it is technically or logically bound to follow the Supreme Court's lead in developing the state remedy or even in framing the issues. Most importantly, the state court remains free to redefine for state law purposes the considerations bearing upon how the state remedy will be developed and the comparative importance of those considerations.

The Supreme Court has emphasized the federal constitutional exclusionary sanctions' function in deterring future violations of the substantive requirements of the amendments and has framed exclusionary rule issues so as to tailor the remedies to serve that function. A few state courts have rejected this framework in developing their own state constitutional exclusionary sanctions. The Idaho Supreme Court, for example, has explained:

> We believe that the exclusionary rule should be applied in order to: 1) provide an effective remedy to persons who have been subjected to an unreasonable government search and/or seizure; 2) deter the police from acting unlawfully in obtaining evidence; 3) encourage thoroughness in the warrant issuing process; 4) avoid having the judiciary commit an additional constitutional violation by considering evidence which has been obtained through illegal means; and 5) preserve judicial integrity.[3]

This emphasis on providing an effective remedy has also been embraced by some other courts. While these courts have not extensively developed the bases or significance of this position, it appears to reject the Supreme Court's assumption that exclusion of evidence resulting from official lawlessness does not provide an appropriate remedy to those who suffer privacy intrusions or other harms from that official lawlessness.

State judicial independence in this area has resulted in some restrictive modifications of state constitutions. Florida's state constitutional search and seizure provision has long provided that evidence obtained in violation of it was inadmissible. In 1982, this was supplemented with a specific directive that it be construed "in conformity with" the Supreme Court's construction of the Fourth Amendment, thus limiting exclusion of evidence to those situations in which the evidence "would be inadmissible under decisions of the United States Supreme Court construing the 4th Amendment to the United States Constitution." In the same year, California voters created a state constitutional "Right to Truth-in-

---

2. State v. Brown, 543 A.2d 750, 763 (Conn.App.1988).

3. State v. Guzman, 842 P.2d 660, 672 (Idaho 1992).

Evidence" section providing that except as enacted by a two-thirds vote of both houses of the state legislature, "relevant evidence shall not be excluded in any criminal proceeding." This has effectively deprived the California courts of power to develop state constitutional exclusionary sanctions requiring exclusion of relevant evidence where such exclusion is not mandated by the federal constitution.

§ 169. Exclusion for Nonconstitutional Illegality: (a) In General

Both federal and state constitutional requirements apply only where a defendant establishes that challenged evidence was obtained as a result of a violation of a constitutional rights. But with increasing frequency, defendants are seeking exclusion as a remedy for violation of nonconstitutional legal requirements. When, if ever, exclusion is available on such bases presents a more difficult question than is often recognized. Modern law's acceptance of exclusion as an appropriate remedy for the violation of constitutional requirements has tended too often to lead to uncritical acceptance of exclusion as similarly available upon a showing of any illegality. This is simply not the case.

Challenges to relevant evidence on grounds that it was obtained in violation of nonconstitutional legal requirements raises several distinguishable concerns addressed in the next three sections. First is whether courts have legislatively-provided authority to exclude evidence on these bases.[1] Second is whether courts have autonomous authority to exclude evidence on these grounds.[2] Third is the content of any such exclusionary requirements as exist, given widespread agreement that any exclusionary sanctions in this area are properly more limited than those applied to constitutional violations.[3]

§ 170. Exclusion for Nonconstitutional Illegality: (b) Legislative Requirements

Legislatures unquestionably have authority to direct that legal requirements be imple-

mented by excluding evidence obtained in violation of those requirements, or to give courts of the jurisdiction discretionary power to develop exclusionary remedies. Exercises of this authority may be explicit or implicit, and the two possibilities are best considered separately.

Explicit Legislative Exclusionary Requirements. A few jurisdictions have relatively broad statutory requirements of exclusion. Since 1925, Texas has statutorily excluded from criminal trials evidence obtained in violation of the laws or constitutions of either the United States or Texas. North Carolina has a somewhat narrower provision, requiring the suppression of certain evidence obtained in violation of its Criminal Procedure Act. These provisions, however, are exceptional. Most states have neither any general explicit legislative directive for exclusion of illegally obtained evidence nor explicit delegation to the courts of authority to develop any such exclusionary requirement.

Somewhat more frequently, legislatures have provided exclusionary remedies for particular statutes. The primary example is the federal electronic surveillance statute, which contains its own statutory exclusionary remedy. Under this statute, states are authorized to provide by state law for state law enforcement officers to engage in certain electronic surveillance, and state statutes enacted pursuant to this contain exclusionary requirements similar or identical to that in the federal statute.

Other statutory provisions also sometimes explicitly require exclusion. Exclusion may be authorized indirectly, as in the Oregon "implied consent" statute which provides that it is not to be construed as limiting the introduction of otherwise competent and relevant evidence in any proceeding other than a criminal prosecution for driving while intoxicated.

Implied Legislative Exclusionary Requirements. Legislative authority to exclude evi-

§ 169

1. See § 170 infra.

2. See § 171 infra.

3. See § 172 infra.

dence may sometimes be implied from statutory provisions that lack the sort of explicit requirement discussed above, and courts have recognized this. When a statute is appropriately construed as authorizing or requiring exclusion, however, has proved to be a difficult question for many courts.

In several early cases, the Supreme Court uncritically held that evidence obtained in violation of certain federal statutory requirements must be excluded. It left unclear, however, whether these holdings rested on readings of legislative intent or were rather exercises of the Court's own power to develop exclusionary requirements.

Some lower courts have been willing on quite scant bases to find implied legislative exclusionary requirements. In United States v. Chemaly,[1] for example, the court held that federal legislation limiting currency searches at the border required exclusion of evidence obtained in violation of its terms. Emphasizing the long acceptance among courts of exclusion as a remedy for even nonconstitutional illegality, the court reasoned that Congress assumed that in the absence of an explicit directive to the contrary courts would enforce the statute by excluding evidence obtained in violation of it; therefore, congressional silence regarding exclusionary sanctions was an implied directive that such a remedy be applied. There is a discernible tendency on the part of some courts to pursue this analysis under statutes imposing requirements similar to, but more stringent than, constitutional mandates. This is apparently on the assumption that when a legislature imposes requirements similar to constitutional ones enforced by exclusionary sanctions, it ordinarily assumes that its statutory directives will also be enforced by such sanctions.

Most courts, however, are more reluctant to find unexpressed legislative directives that exclusionary sanctions be available. Several considerations are emphasized. If other statutes passed by the legislative body have expressly directed exclusion, legislative failure to

similarly provide in the statute at issue suggests to many courts a legislative intention that no such remedy be available for statutes silent on the matter. If the overall purpose of legislation is to increase law enforcement power, courts have also reasoned, the legislature is unlikely to have intended to impede this general objective by imposing an exclusionary sanction, and thus courts should be reluctant to read one into such statutes.

On balance, courts should be reluctant to find implied authority in statutes for exclusion of evidence. Exclusion is an exceptionally costly remedy, and its propriety is highly questionable. Legislative silence almost certainly reflects, in most cases, the absence of a consensus that the provisions being enacted are appropriately enforced by such a remedy. Unless there is reasonably clear evidence of such a consensus, generally reflected in the terms of the statute itself, a statute should not be regarded as empowering the courts to exclude evidence obtained in violation of its requirements.

§ 171. Exclusion for Nonconstitutional Illegality: (c) Judicially Developed Requirements

In the absence of legislative or constitutional authorization, courts may nevertheless have independent power to develop and apply exclusionary requirements. This might be based either upon the authority given many courts to promulgate rules relating to procedure and evidence or upon the power claimed by some courts to exercise what is often called "supervisory authority" over litigation and the behavior of some persons whose actions in some way affect that litigation.

Rulemaking Power. Many American courts have power to promulgate rules of evidence and procedure, granted by statute or constitutional provision. This power has been implemented through widespread adoption of evidence rules. Might this power permit a court to promulgate an exclusionary rule appli-

---

§ 170

1. 741 F.2d 1346 (11th Cir.1984), order granting en banc hearing vacated, 764 F.2d 747 (11th Cir.) (en banc).

cable to violation of nonconstitutional, as well as perhaps constitutional, legal requirements?

Such action has been taken by the Alaska Supreme Court, which adopted a general exclusionary rule as part of its Criminal Rules and then incorporated this into its Evidence Rules. Under Alaska Rule of Evidence 412, evidence "illegally obtained" may not be used over proper objection by the defendant in a criminal prosecution "for any purpose," with limited exceptions applicable to perjury prosecutions.

Whether this is an appropriate exercise of the rulemaking power is at best problematic. Rulemaking authority is given to courts in large part because of their exceptional ability to address such matters as how to most efficiently and effectively arrive at accurate resolutions in litigated cases. The extent to which exclusionary requirements will interfere with these interests is, of course, an important consideration in deciding whether an exclusionary sanction is appropriate. But far more important are such considerations as the extent to which violations occur and whether other measures hold reasonable promise of discouraging them. The final decision must balance the costs of an exclusionary sanction and the potential benefits of it. This decision is no more than peripherally within courts' area of particular expertise and is clearly the sort of judgment that is ordinarily for legislative decision. Given the nature of exclusionary sanctions, despite their "evidentiary" form, they are best regarded as beyond general judicial evidentiary and procedural rulemaking authority.

Courts' "Supervisory" Power—The Federal Model. Some American courts have held, or indicated in dicta, that they have supervisory authority over judicial proceedings broader than ordinary rule-making power. This authority may give those courts the power to judicially-develop exclusionary requirements invoked by violation of nonconstitutional legal requirements. Whether such authority exists in particular jurisdictions and, if so, whether it

authorizes such rigorous judicial lawmaking often poses difficult issues.

The most widely-noted model for such authority is the Supreme Court's reliance upon what it has described as its "supervisory power" authority to develop such exclusionary rules for litigation in the lower federal courts. Whether the Court's perception of its power is soundly based is, at best, questionable.

The seminal Supreme Court decision is McNabb v. United States,[1] holding that suppression was required of evidence obtained in violation of what was then the statutory requirement that an arrested person be presented before a magistrate without unnecessary delay. In Rea v. United States,[2] the Court held that a federal officer who had obtained evidence in violation of Rule 41 of the Federal Rules of Criminal Procedure should be enjoined from using that evidence in a state prosecution. Implicitly, *Rea* approved the suppression of this evidence in the federal litigation and explicitly held that Rea was entitled to the additional injunctive relief he sought. Both decisions rested upon what the Court described as its "supervisory power." In *McNabb*, the Court equated an exclusionary rule with other rules of evidence, particularly those, apparently rules of privilege, that are based on considerations other than simply "evidentiary relevance." Development of legal requirements of both sorts, the Court concluded, was permissible pursuant to its "duty" to establish and maintain "civilized standards of procedure and evidence" in the federal courts. *Rea's* discussion went further and suggested that the underlying power was not only to provide for the proper processing of litigation but also to "prescribe standards for law enforcement * * * to protect the privacy of the citizen * * *."

Since *Rea,* the Court has continued to insist that it has such power. It has obviously, however, become more reluctant to exercise it and in fact has not found occasion to do so. In Lopez v. United States,[3] for example, the Court reaffirmed its "inherent power" to ex-

§ 171

1. 318 U.S. 332 (1943).

2. 350 U.S. 214 (1956).

3. 373 U.S. 427 (1963).

clude "material" evidence because of illegality in the manner it was obtained, but commented that this power should be "sparingly exercised." Since Lopez could show no "manifestly improper" conduct by the law enforcement officers, invoking the power in his case would not be justified. In United States v. Caceres,[4] the Court suggested that it had the power to exclude evidence on a "limited individualized approach" for the violation of federal administrative regulations. But exclusion under this power would not be appropriate in the case before it, the Court concluded, since the investigators had made a reasonable, good faith attempt to comply with what they understood to be the applicable legal requirements, and the actions they took would clearly have been permitted had they followed the regulations.

Most recently, the Court in United States v. Payner[5] considered an argument that it should exercise its supervisory power to exclude evidence obtained by "gross illegality" from a person other than the defendant who moved to suppress it. Again reaffirming its supervisory exclusionary power, the Court offered that "Federal courts may use their supervisory power in some circumstances to exclude evidence taken from the defendant by 'willful disobedience of law.'" But it then made clear that the exercise of this power is to be informed by the same considerations and conclusions reached in developing the federal constitutional exclusionary requirements. The Fourth Amendment case law makes clear that as a general rule, the purposes of exclusion are adequately achieved if the remedy is made available to those whose interests were violated by the underlying illegality. This should also apply where exclusion might be justified under the supervisory power, and thus under that power federal courts should not suppress otherwise admissible evidence on the ground that it was unlawfully obtained from a third party not before the court.

Both the scope and legitimacy of the supervisory power as applied and discussed in this line of cases have been severely criticized.

The Supreme Court's refusal, since *McNabb* and *Rea,* actually to exercise what it continues to insist is the federal courts' supervisory power to develop exclusionary rules for nonconstitutional violations suggests that the tribunal is becoming at least ambivalent concerning the legitimacy of this authority.

The lower federal courts continue to assume that some power to develop exclusionary rules exists, perhaps most significantly, implicitly relying on *Rea,* that violations of some of the nonconstitutional requirements for search warrants imposed by Rule 41 of the Federal Rules of Criminal Procedure under some circumstances require or permit exclusion. The courts are, however, increasingly reluctant to exercise this power.

Courts' "Supervisory" Power—State Court Decisions. State courts may also have supervisory powers similar to that invoked in *McNabb-Rea,* and these might be relied upon as a basis for state court developed exclusionary requirements. Generally, however, state courts have engaged in little discussion of this possibility. When state tribunals mention supervisory power, they tend to avoid explicit comment upon whether they possess such power and whether it would support development of exclusionary sanctions. Rather, they simply find that the situations before them are not sufficient to invoke any such sanctions as they might have power to develop. Even state courts embracing such power to exclude evidence generally provide little substantive discussion of the basis for this power and the decision to exercise it in particular situations.

In what is probably the leading state court decision, State v. Pattioay,[6] the Hawaii Supreme Court held that its inherent supervisory authority to prevent and correct "errors and abuses" in the lower courts permitted it to develop exclusionary remedies mandating exclusion of evidence obtained in violation of non-constitutional legal requirements. The power, it cautioned, is to be exercised with restraint and discretion and only in exceptional circumstances.

4. 440 U.S. 741 (1979).
5. 447 U.S. 727 (1980).

6. 896 P.2d 911 (Hawai'i 1995).

Pattioay appeared to conceptualize the use of illegally obtained evidence by parties to litigation in an effort to obtain favorable action by the courts as sufficient abuse of the courts to justify exercise of the supervisory power. This in turn led it to adopt a rationale for exclusion broader than the deterrent-based federal constitutional rules. Use in a criminal trial of evidence tainted by official illegality, it emphasized, "would be to justify the illegality." Even if exclusion does not sufficiently serve to deter illegality of the sort involved, then, such exclusion is justified as a means of precluding judicial "justif[ication]" of the underlying illegality in a manner that would offend notions of what some courts and commentators regard as judicial integrity.

In general, American courts have been insufficiently critical regarding their power, or the lack thereof, to develop exclusionary sanctions for nonconstitutional violations in obtaining evidence. This is no doubt due in large part to the prominence of federal constitutional exclusionary rule case law in any consideration of exclusionary sanction matters. On one hand, this case law encourages an uncritical assumption that courts have power to develop similar exclusionary requirements for nonconstitutional illegality. On the other, resentment at being constitutionally compelled to accept what is regarded by some as an unwise remedy for constitutional violations encourages equally uncritical rejection of exclusion as an authorized remedy where such a remedy is not constitutionally mandated.

Whether the courts of a particular jurisdiction have the power to develop exclusionary sanctions, and whether they should exercise any such power as they may have, must depend in large part upon the nature and breadth of judicial authority in that jurisdiction and the tradition with which it has been developed and applied. Proper resolution of these issues, in any case, requires careful consideration of the argument that the major factors in deciding whether exclusionary sanctions are appropriate are factors that require legislative rather than judicial action.

§ 172. Exclusion for Nonconstitutional Illegality: (d) Substance of Exclusionary Requirements

The exclusionary requirements developed as part of federal constitutional law are, as an initial matter, unqualified. This means that a showing that evidence was obtained as a factual result of a violation of the underlying constitutional requirement demands exclusion of that evidence. Most exclusionary requirements applicable to nonconstitutional violations, on the other hand, are qualified. A right to exclusion, in other words, often demands that a defendant show more than a violation of a nonconstitutional legal requirement and that the challenged evidence was obtained as a factual result of that violation.

The limits or qualifications of these nonconstitutional exclusionary sanctions is developed in this section. Three types of limitations can usefully be distinguished.

First, those nonconstitutional legal requirements whose violation will trigger a possible right to exclusion have sometimes been limited. The case law suggests several approaches towards so limiting exclusionary requirements. Exclusionary requirements could be applied only if the legal requirement applies generally or frequently to official activity designed to collect evidence for use in criminal prosecutions. Given the evidentiary motivation of those affected by the legal requirements, exclusion might be expected to most effectively encourage compliance with the law in these cases.

Exclusion might also be limited to those legal requirements that are related in some sufficient way to constitutional commands. Perhaps the cost of exclusion is justified only if the violated legal requirement protects the same or similar interests as are protected by constitutional rules, although the legal requirement that is violated by infringements is not significant or basic enough to give rise to a constitutional intrusion.

Case law under the federal electronic surveillance regulatory scheme suggests that at least in the context of a set of legislative requirements, exclusion may reasonably be mandated only upon proof of a violation of a statutory requirement directly or importantly related to the underlying legislative objective. Although the federal statutory exclusionary sanction is unqualified, the Supreme Court has held that it is triggered only by those statutory provisions that "directly and substantially implement" the congressional purpose of reasonably limiting use of electronic surveillance techniques. Consequently, failure to secure approval of an application for a surveillance order from the Attorney General or Assistant Attorney General did require exclusion of the resulting evidence, but a failure simply to specify on the documents the official who had in fact authorized the application did not. State exclusionary requirements embodied in similar state electronic surveillance statutes have been similarly construed.

If a legal requirement does not directly and substantially implement a constitutionally-related purpose or the ultimate objective of a legislative scheme, the courts tend to label it "technical" and to treat it as insufficient to trigger an exclusionary sanction.

A second type of limitation upon nonconstitutional exclusionary sanctions makes exclusion available only to those defendants who show more than simply that the evidence at issue was obtained by means of a violation of a sufficient legal requirement. Often the case law requires a showing of either an "intentional" violation of the underlying legal requirement or prejudice in some sense as a result of that violation. As this approach is applied, prejudice means that the defendant suffered the harm that the legal requirement was designed to prevent. When this approach is invoked in response to proof that officers failed to follow nonconstitutional requirements for search warrants, for example, prejudice apparently requires proof that the search would not have occurred had the requirements been met or at least that the search would have been significantly less intrusive if this had been the case.

A similar but more flexible analysis would provide for exclusion only upon proof of a legal violation that was in some sense "substantial." Under a North Carolina statute embodying a demand for a substantial violation of law, determining whether an underlying violation was substantial requires consideration of: (a) the importance of the particular interest protected by the legal requirement; (b) the extent of the deviation from lawful conduct; (c) the extent to which the violation was willful; and (d) the extent to which exclusion will tend to deter future violations of the same sort.

A third type of limitation upon the right to exclusion gives a trial court discretionary authority to exclude evidence where on the facts of the case before the court exclusion is determined to sufficiently further the objectives of exclusionary sanctions to warrant the cost involved. This was the thrust of Commonwealth v. Mason,[1] in which the Pennsylvania Supreme Court explicitly announced that a showing that evidence had been obtained in violation of the Pennsylvania Rules of Criminal Procedure established only that "exclusion *may* be an appropriate remedy." Exclusion is to be in fact ordered only if the trial judge, after considering the nature of the case and the particular facts, determines that exclusion and its costs would be proportional to the benefits to be gained. Trial judges were cautioned to give particular emphasis to the likelihood that exclusion would prevent future misconduct similar to that which gave rise to the violation before the court.

§ 173. Use of Illegally Obtained Evidence in Noncriminal Litigation

Most exclusionary sanction issues arise in criminal litigation. Perhaps because of American courts' increasing acceptance of exclusion as a response to illegality in obtaining evidence, however, litigants sometimes attempt to invoke exclusionary remedies in various types of civil litigation. When, if ever, exclusionary sanctions are appropriate outside of criminal litigation presents a number of difficult questions.

Distinctions here as elsewhere must be drawn among the various exclusionary sanc-

---

§ 172

1. 490 A.2d 421 (Pa.1985).

tions that do or might exist. The Supreme Court's case law addressing the application of the federal constitutional exclusionary requirements outside of criminal litigation provides an attractive model that has been widely but not universally followed in other contexts.

Soon after *Mapp*, the Supreme Court held the Fourth Amendment exclusionary rule applicable in a state proceeding for forfeiture of an automobile on the basis that the vehicle had been used in a crime. Forfeiture was clearly a penalty for a criminal act, the Court reasoned, and it would therefore be incongruous to exclude the evidence in a criminal prosecution but admit it in a forfeiture proceeding based on the same criminal activity.

The matter was addressed again in United States v. Janis,[1] a civil proceeding for a tax refund in which the Government counterclaimed for the unpaid balance of the assessment. The assessment was based upon information concerning Janis' illegal bookmaking activities; that information had been obtained by state law enforcement officers acting pursuant to a defective search warrant but nevertheless in the "good faith" belief that the search was lawful. Use of the evidence was permissible, the Court reasoned, because "exclusion from federal civil proceedings of evidence unlawfully seized by a state criminal law enforcement officer has not been shown to have a sufficient likelihood of deterring the conduct of the state police so that it outweighs the societal costs imposed by the exclusion."

Janis involved an intersovereign situation–the government that committed the illegality in obtaining the evidence was not the same government that sought to use it. Thus the Court's result may have rested in part upon a conclusion that excluding evidence in a *federal* civil proceeding is unlikely to influence *state* officers. In I.N.S. v. Lopez–Mendoza,[2] however, the Court arrived at a similar result in an intrasovereign case. At issue was whether evidence obtained in violation of the Fourth Amendment by federal immigration officers was admissible in a federal civil deportation

proceeding. *Janis*, the Court nevertheless observed, provided the framework for analysis: the likely social benefits of excluding the evidence must be balanced against the likely costs. The intrasovereign nature of the situation suggested that the deterrent benefits were likely to be greater than in *Janis*. But other considerations suggested they would still be quite small: the Government itself disciplines officers who violate the Fourth Amendment and excludes evidence arising from intentional violations, and INS officers know that there is only a small likelihood that any arrestee will actually challenge the officers' actions in a formal proceeding. On the cost side, application of the rule would impede the busy deportation system. Since immigration enforcement often involves continuing violations of the law, application of an exclusionary rule in this context "would require the courts to close their eyes to ongoing violations of the law," a cost of a particularly offensive character. The *Janis* balance, the Court concluded, came out against application of the Fourth Amendment exclusionary rule.

Under *Janis* and *Lopez–Mendoza*, whether the federal constitutional exclusionary rules are applicable in civil litigation turns upon whether the increased prevention of unconstitutional conduct accomplished by application of the exclusionary requirement to civil cases of the sort at issue is worth the costs of so expanding those sanctions. The two decisions suggest that the Court is generally satisfied that sufficient prevention is provided by exclusion of unconstitutionally obtained evidence in criminal litigation. A civil litigant seeking to show that exclusion is justified under *Janis–Lopez–Mendoza* has an extremely difficult task.

Lower courts are understandably hesitant to exclude evidence in civil contexts. Nevertheless, they remain reluctant to characterize the federal constitutional sanctions as never applicable to noncriminal litigation.

There is general agreement that whether the federal constitutional exclusionary rule ap-

§ 173
1. 428 U.S. 433 (1976).

2. 468 U.S. 1032 (1984).

plies in a technically noncriminal proceeding depends upon the type of proceeding and the facts of the case. Several courts have indicated that at least five factors are relevant:

(1) the nature of the noncriminal proceeding;

(2) whether the proposed use of unconstitutionally seized material is intersovereign or intrasovereign;

(3) whether (in intrasovereign situations) the search and the noncriminal proceeding were initiated by the same agency;

(4) whether there is an explicit and demonstrable understanding between the two governmental agencies; and

(5) whether the noncriminal proceeding fell within the "zone of primary interest" of the officers that conducted the search.

The *Janis–Lopez–Mendoza* analysis is most likely to lead to exclusion when unconstitutionally obtained evidence is offered in proceedings which, although "civil," are brought by governmental authorities for what is essentially a public purpose. Governmental activity may be conducted with the prospect of such litigation in mind, and thus exclusion in such litigation may discourage impropriety in the investigatory activity. There is general agreement, for example, that the exclusionary rule applies in proceedings to have a child declared delinquent. Such rules have also been applied in proceedings to collect a "tax" on illegal drugs and a school disciplinary hearing.

Under the *Janis–Lopez–Mendoza* approach, it is quite unlikely that the federal constitutional rules will ever be applicable in civil actions between private parties. If the evidence was wrongfully obtained by public officers, exclusion would not penalize them and officers would not likely be influenced in their future conduct by such exclusion. If the evidence was wrongfully obtained by private persons, the Supreme Court would almost certainly reason that exclusion would at most deter similar private action in the future, a

concern beyond the scope of the underlying federal constitutional rules being enforced.

Most courts, moreover, do not apply the federal constitutional exclusionary rules to school disciplinary proceedings, license revocation proceedings, civil tax assessment or collection proceedings, or even child protection proceedings or actions to compel treatment for impaired persons. Some attempt to draw finer lines; several courts have held that the Fourth Amendment exclusionary rule does not apply under federal Occupational Safety and Health Act proceedings to correct a violation but it does apply to proceedings to punish past violations by assessing penalties for them.

In a plurality portion of the lead opinion, *Lopez-Mendoza* left open the possibility that the Fourth Amendment exclusionary rule might apply in noncriminal actions such as deportation proceedings upon proof that the evidence was obtained by "egregious violations of Fourth Amendment or other liberties that might transgress notions of fundamental fairness and undermine the probative value of the evidence obtained." One court has held that proof of "bad faith"—that the officers should have known their conduct was unreasonable and hence unconstitutional—requires exclusion, even if the violation did not affect the probative value of the evidence at issue. Perhaps if the underlying official activity is particularly offensive, the increased need to discourage such activity justifies the costs of adding to the exclusionary disincentive by rejecting its fruits even in civil litigation.

State courts, of course, are technically free to reject the approach taken in *Janis* and *Lopez-Mendoza* and to construe state constitutional provisions as fully applicable to civil litigation. The Oklahoma Supreme Court exercised this power in Turner v. City of Lawton,[3] holding evidence unconstitutionally obtained inadmissible in an administrative proceeding to dismiss a firefighter. The court accepted the state search and seizure provision as creating a right to exclusion as a necessary remedy for the preceding violation of privacy, regardless of the necessity for exclusion to discourage

3. 733 P.2d 375 (Okl.1986).

future violations of the underlying legal requirements. In order to achieve the remedial
objective of the state exclusionary requirement, then, the Oklahoma court extended its
rule to civil litigation in order to replace the
wronged person as close as possible to his
condition before the wrongful search occurred.

§ 174. Use of Illegally Obtained Evidence in Criminal Proceedings on Matters Other Than Guilt

Evidence may be offered against a criminal defendant in the course of criminal litigation but other than at the trial on guilt or
innocence. It may, for example, be used in an
effort to have pretrial release denied or revoked, at a preliminary hearing to determine
whether a defendant is to be "bound over" for
grand jury consideration or trial, before a
grand jury in support of a proposed indictment
charging the defendant with an offense, at
sentencing in support of a more severe disposition, in support of an effort to revoke probation once granted, or to substantiate a claim
that parole after imprisonment should be denied or revoked. An exclusionary rule's determination that illegally obtained evidence must
be inadmissible to prove defendants' guilt does
not require the further conclusion that such
evidence should be unavailable for any or all of
these or similar purposes.

The Fourth Amendment issue was addressed most extensively in Pennsylvania
Board of Probation v. Scott,[1] in which the
Supreme Court made clear that the critical
question is whether the deterrence benefits of
so expanding the Fourth Amendment exclusionary rule would outweigh the costs incurred. At issue in *Scott* was specifically
whether evidence obtained in violation of the
Fourth Amendment could be used to establish
that a convicted defendant had violated the
conditions of his parole. The costs of requiring
exclusion in parole revocation proceedings
would be exceptionally high, the Court reasoned, indicating that exclusionary rule issues
would delay and impede the necessarily flexible and administrative procedures of parole
revocation.

Probably more important, the deterrent
benefits would most likely be low. Where law
enforcement officers do not know that suspects
are parolees, the remote possibility that this
may be the case—and thus that fruits of misconduct will be unusable for parole violation
purposes—is unlikely to influence the officers.
Regular law enforcement officers who know a
suspect is a parolee are unlikely to be influenced by the admissibility of the fruits of their
actions in parole revocation proceedings. Parole officers specifically charged with parole
concerns, on the other hand, are less likely
than regular officers to perceive themselves
engaged in the "adversarial" process of ferret-
ing out crime, and thus are likely to respond
adequately to less costly alternatives to exclusion, such as departmental training and discipline and civil damage liability.

Scott's assessment of law enforcement officers' motivations is arguably quite naive. The
state court below, like some others, sought a
more sophisticated balance by directing that
the Fourth Amendment exclusionary rule be
applied where—but only where—the defendant challenging the evidence established that
the officer who obtained it knew the suspect
was a parolee. Thus the state court sought to
limit application of the rule to those situations
in which deterrent benefits were most certain.
Rejecting this approach, the Supreme Court
clearly concluded that even in these cases the
potential deterrent benefit was minimal. In
addition, however, it reasoned that a need to
address the officers' awareness in exclusionary
rule litigation would unacceptably increase the
complexity of applying the rule and consequently the costs of doing so.

Scott thus supplemented the earlier holding in United States v. Calandra[2] that the
Fourth Amendment does not require that evidence obtained in violation of its terms be kept
from influencing grand jury decisions to indict.
Together, *Scott* and *Calandra* leave no doubt
that the Supreme Court is firmly convinced

---

§ 174
1. 524 U.S. 357, 118 S.Ct. 2014 (1998).

2. 414 U.S. 338 (1974).

that exclusion at trial from the guilt-innocence process will generally satisfy federal constitutional requirements. Defendants are unlikely to be able to convince the Court that law enforcement officers unaffected by the admissibility of evidence at trial are likely to be sufficiently influenced by its admissibility for other purposes to justify what the Court regards as the considerable cost of expanding the federal constitutional exclusionary demands to proceedings other than the determination of guilt at trial.

The Supreme Court has not addressed the applicability of the federal constitutional exclusionary rules at pretrial stages such as preliminary hearings. In federal litigation, however, Rule 5.1 of the Federal Rules of Criminal Procedure specifically provides that "[o]bjections to evidence on the ground that it was acquired by unlawful means are not properly made at the preliminary examination," and a number of state statutes and rules follow this approach.

Whether the federal constitutional requirements apply in sentencing has also not been resolved by the Court. Almost certainly, however, the Court would reason, under *Scott* and *Calandra*, that whatever minimal incremental deterrence would be achieved by so applying the requirements would be outweighed by the costs. Particular weight would undoubtedly be given to the cost involved in requiring sentencing courts to exercise their considerable discretion without the benefit of all relevant and reliable evidence.

State courts again are free to reject the *Scott-Calandra* approach or the Supreme Court's application of it to some or all nontrial stages of criminal proceedings. An Oregon court has, for example, held that the Oregon constitutional exclusionary requirement, intended not simply to deter but also to adequately vindicate the right to privacy, requires that evidence obtained in an unreasonable search or seizure be excluded from sentencing. Adequate vindication requires assurance that those whose rights are violated be free from

increased punishment based on the fruits of the violations.

§ 175. "Standing" and Personal Nature of Rights

The Fourth Amendment exclusionary rule and most other exclusionary sanctions permit a criminal defendant to seek suppression of evidence only on the basis of a claim that the evidence was obtained in an improper manner that violated the defendant's own rights. Put negatively, this requirement of "standing" precludes a defendant from objecting to evidence on the basis that it was obtained illegally but in a manner that violated only the rights of another person. Courts sometimes suggest that this reflects the "personal" nature of the rights enforced by exclusionary requirements, but in actuality the standing requirement is best conceptualized as an aspect of the exclusionary remedy rather than of the underlying rights.

Fourth Amendment Standing. The Fourth Amendment standing requirement was first developed under pre-*Mapp* law. It was explained in Jones v. United States[1] as based upon language in Rule 41(e) of the Federal Rules of Criminal Procedure authorizing a motion to suppress only by "[a] person aggrieved by an unlawful search and seizure." This was read by the Court as applying the "general principle" that constitutional protections can be claimed only by those parties to litigation that belong to the class of persons for whose sake the constitutional protection is given. The Fourth Amendment exclusionary requirement is not designed to exclude evidence on grounds of unreliability or prejudicial effect. Rather, it is a means of making effective the underlying Fourth Amendment protection against official invasion of privacy and the security of property. "[I]t is," the Court concluded, "entirely proper to require of one who seeks to challenge the legality of a search as the basis for suppressing relevant evidence that he allege, and if the allegation be disputed that he establish, that he himself was the victim of an invasion of privacy." After *Mapp,* this ap-

§ 175
1. 362 U.S. 257 (1960).

proach was incorporated into the Fourth Amendment exclusionary rule as applied to the states.

As first announced and applied, the standing requirement was sometimes read as invoking a distinct body of law distinguishable from that defining the content of the Fourth Amendment's coverage. In Rakas v. Illinois,[2] however, the Supreme Court rejected such an approach and made clear that the inquiry necessitated by the Fourth Amendment standing requirement involves application of the case law defining the scope of Fourth Amendment coverage and, in particular, the extent of a particular defendant's rights under that provision. When a defendant objects to the admissibility of the results of a search or seizure, the standing question is whether, under substantive Fourth Amendment law, the search or seizure violated the rights of the moving defendant.

The Supreme Court has justified the Fourth Amendment's standing limitation in terms of the underlying policy concerns:

> The deterrent values of preventing the incrimination of those whose rights the police have violated have been considered sufficient to justify the suppression of probative evidence even though the case against the defendant is weakened or destroyed. But we are not convinced that the additional benefits of extending the exclusionary rule to other defendants would justify further encroachment upon the public interest in prosecuting those accused of crime and having them acquitted or convicted on the basis of all the evidence which exposes the truth.[3]

Nonconstitutional Federal Exclusionary Requirements. The same approach has been vigorously pursued by the Supreme Court in the context of another, nonconstitutional exclusionary requirement. In United States v. Payner,[4] Court rejected the argument that federal exclusionary requirements based on the courts' supervisory power should not require

standing as did the constitutional requirements. The "same social interests" are implicated by both supervisory power exclusionary requirements and the Fourth Amendment exclusionary rule, it reasoned, and the values assigned to those interests do not change when the basis for the exclusionary sanction is the supervisory power rather than the Fourth Amendment. Consequently, even construction of the supervisory power exclusionary sanction is governed by the Court's conclusion that any increased deterrence that would be provided by abandoning standing is outweighed by the inevitable increased loss of reliable evidence.

The Supreme Court has similarly read statutory exclusionary sanction language as incorporating a requirement of standing. Under the federal electronic surveillance statute, suppression of the results of an improper interception of a covered communication is required upon the motion of any "person against whom the interception was directed." Without discussing the specific terminology chosen by Congress, the Court has held that the legislative history of the statute indicated a Congressional purpose to permit objections to evidence only by persons with standing under existent standing rules.

"Automatic" Standing. Fourth Amendment law had relaxed ordinary standing requirements in limited situations covered by what was characterized as the "automatic" standing rule. Under this rule, a defendant charged with possession of an item at the time of a search or seizure was permitted to challenge that search or seizure regardless of general standing requirements. In part, the automatic standing rule was based on concern that in the cases covered defendants would often have to make an admissible judicial confession of guilt, i.e., possession, to establish standing. Such defendants' testimony establishing standing, given at the hearing on the admissibility of the item, might well be admissible against the defendants at trial. The resulting "dilemma," the Court concluded, was unaccep-

---

2. 439 U.S. 128 (1978).

3. Alderman v. United States, 394 U.S. 165, 174–175 (1969).

4. 447 U.S. 727 (1980).

table. As the Court has recognized in United States v. Salvucci,[5] this part of the rationale was destroyed by Simmons v. United States,[6] holding that testimony given at a motion to suppress evidence is not admissible against the defendant at a subsequent trial. A defendant who, to establish standing, judicially admits possession need not fear that the prosecution will use that admission at trial to establish his guilt.

But the automatic standing rule was also based in part upon perceived offensiveness of contradictory prosecutorial arguments that defendants had close enough relationships to items to be guilty of possession of them but not sufficient relationships to give them standing to challenge the searches by which the prosecution obtained the items. In *Salvucci,* however, the Court concluded that there was no inherent inconsistency between such claims. Since the automatic standing rule had therefore "outlived its usefulness in [the] Court's Fourth Amendment jurisprudence," it was overruled.

The standing requirement is firmly entrenched in the Fourth Amendment and probably in those other exclusionary requirements over which the Supreme Court has substantive development power. But in *Alderman* the Court acknowledged that Congress or states could extend the right of exclusion to persons without standing in the Fourth Amendment sense.

Standing Under State Law Exclusionary Requirements. State courts developing state law exclusionary requirements have generally, but not universally, followed the Supreme Court's Fourth Amendment model. The most dramatic deviation was that of the California Supreme Court, which in 1955 announced that all of the reasons persuading it to adopt exclusionary requirements suggested further that defendants should be able to invoke those requirements regardless of whether they had been the victims of the illegality relied upon.[7]

The California court's rejection of standing rested on several bases. First, the Califor-

nia court sought greater assurance of a deterrent effect than satisfied the Supreme Court, and this was provided by requiring exclusion regardless of the challenging defendant's standing. In addition, however, the California tribunal gave greater weight to judicial integrity considerations than has the Supreme Court. It conceptualized judicial integrity as broader than the Supreme Court's later analysis finding judicial integrity implicated only if judicial use of evidence encourages future violations of the underlying legal requirement. Judicial integrity, as broadly conceptualized, was compromised by use of illegally obtained evidence regardless of whether the victims of the illegality were before the court.

Whatever the controlling rationale, the California approach was nullified by the 1982 amendment to the state constitution barring judicial development of exclusionary sanctions. The Louisiana Constitution, however, continues to be construed as dispensing with any standing requirement.

Several state courts have retained a standing requirement as a matter of state constitutional law but have held that it is more readily met than the Fourth Amendment requirement as construed by the Supreme Court. Both the New Jersey and Vermont courts have held that a defendant need only assert a possessory, proprietary or participatory interest in either the area searched or the item seized in order to have standing. Others have retained the automatic standing rule, sometimes expressing broader misgivings as to other aspects of the Fourth Amendment approach.

§ 176. Scope of Exclusion: (a) Evidence Acquired as a Result of Illegality ("Fruit of the Poisonous Tree")

Some—but not all—exclusionary requirements of federal constitutional law require exclusion not only of evidence obtained as a direct and immediate result of the triggering illegality but also of evidence obtained as a less direct result of that illegality. The relationship between this "fruit of the poisonous tree" rule

---

5.   448 U.S. 83 (1980).
6.   390 U.S. 377 (1968).

7.   People v. Martin, 290 P.2d 855 (Cal.1955).

and what is often regarded as the separate "independent source" rule presents a continuing problem discussed in the next section.

"Fruit of the Poisonous Tree" Rule. In Silverthorne Lumber Co. v. United States,[1] the Supreme Court construed the Fourth Amendment exclusionary rule as requiring exclusion of evidence obtained even as an indirect result of violation of defendants' Fourth Amendment rights. If a defendant establishes a Fourth Amendment violation—a "poisonous tree"—and that evidence was obtained as a factual result of that violation—that the evidence is "fruit" of the poisonous tree—the defendant is entitled to have the evidence excluded unless the prosecution establishes the applicability of an exception to the general requirement of exclusion. American courts have generally—and arguably uncritically—accepted that other exclusionary sanctions must or at least should be similarly defined.

Under this approach, the required link between the illegality and the discovery of the requires only that the evidence would not have been obtained as and when it was "but for" the illegality on which the defendant relies.

If a defendant establishes that law enforcement officers, who possessed adequate basis for a search, were motivated to make a second search by information obtained in a first and unreasonable search, the results of the second search are fruit of the initial illegality. This is so even if the second search was made pursuant to a warrant which was obtained without use of the results of the first and unreasonable search. The challenged evidence would not have been discovered as and when it was, "but for" the first and unreasonable search.

Generally, the taint flows only forward and renders inadmissible only that evidence obtained after, and as a factual consequence of, the unreasonable search. Moreover, part of a search may be reasonable and other parts may be unreasonable. Officers searching pursuant to a valid search warrant, for example,

may search within the terms of the warrant and discover and seize some evidence. But at various times, they may exceed the scope of search authorized by the warrant and during some of these transgressions they may find and seize other evidence. Usually, only that evidence located and seized while the officers were engaged in the unreasonable aspects of the search, that is, while they were acting beyond the authority of the warrant, is tainted by the officers' improper action and thus rendered inadmissible.

Amazingly, the rule developed with little discussion of its rationale or justification. In 1984, however, the Supreme Court retrospectively explained the "core rationale" for the rule in terms of standard Fourth Amendment exclusionary sanction analysis: Although the fruit of the poisonous tree rule increases the cost of the exclusionary sanction, that cost is justified by the need to provide sufficient deterrence assuring adequate disincentive for the prohibited conduct. Only by threatening officers with the inadmissibility of the indirect as well as the direct results of their Fourth Amendment transgressions can adequate incentive for avoiding those transgressions be provided.[2]

Limits on Excludable "Fruit." Insofar as federal constitutional law requires exclusion of fruit of the poisonous tree, there is one indication that at least as applied to some situations the fruits doctrine is qualified by some objective limits on those fruit subject to the exclusionary requirement.

When law enforcement officers violate a defendant's Fourth Amendment rights by unreasonably entering his home to there make an otherwise proper arrest of him, the Supreme Court held in New York v. Harris,[3] that defendant simply cannot challenge the admissibility of statements made by him subsequent to that arrest and after he was removed from his home. This is apparently the case regardless of the strength of his claim that such a statement was caused by the illegal entry and without the prosecution needing to establish

§ 176

1.   251 U.S. 385 (1920).

2.   Nix v. Williams, 467 U.S. 431, 442–443 (1984).

3.   495 U.S. 14 (1990).

the applicability of any exception to the exclusionary requirement.

Harris reflects the Court's conclusion that in the specific context there presented, an adequate balance of deterrence expectations and costs requires that defendants be permitted to challenge the admissibility of some fruits of an unreasonable entry—statements made as a result of that entry and while the defendant is still being detained in the unreasonably entered home. Permitting such defendants' to challenge the admissibility of statements obtained later, however, would trigger loss-of-evidence and increased-litigation costs exceeding whatever marginal deterrence against unreasonable entries of homes might be expected.

Under *Harris*, the fruit of the poisonous tree doctrine is clearly not sacrosanct, even in the Fourth Amendment context. The definition of challengeable fruit may be limited, where that can be done with reasonable clarity and when the characteristics of the type of situation at issue suggest such action as a means of achieving optimum balance between the deterrent benefits and costs of exclusion.

Exclusionary Sanctions With No "Fruits" Rule. In 1985, the Supreme Court made clear that the requirement of exclusion of all evidence obtained as a result of illegality, developed in the Fourth Amendment context, would not be applied to all exclusionary requirements imposed by federal constitutional law.

In Oregon v. Elstad,[4] the Court indicated that under federal constitutional exclusionary sanction law a fruits doctrine *necessarily* applies only where the impropriety—the "poisonous tree"—was an actual infringement of the suspect's federal constitutional rights. In other context, the exclusionary sanction will be construed as extending to "fruits" only if the goals of the underlying constitutional provision invoked indicate a need for such extensive exclusion.

Violations of the requirements of *Miranda,*[5] *Elstad* continued, do not in themselves constitute violations of the Fifth Amendment.

Consequently, where a suspect has given multiple incriminating statements a later statement obtained after compliance with *Miranda* need not be excluded simply upon proof that it was the factual result—or "fruit"—of an earlier *Miranda* violation. The Fifth Amendment privilege against compelled self-incrimination which provided the basis for *Miranda's* judicially-created requirements thus invokes the dual goals of assuring trustworthy evidence and deterring improper police conduct. These goals, *Elstad* concluded, are adequately served by exclusion of only those later and resulting confessions that are involuntary. Thus, the Fifth Amendment exclusionary sanction attached to *Miranda* rights embodies no requirement that all fruit of the poisonous tree be excluded.

Elstad's reasoning suggests that in other contexts, exclusionary requirements attaching to nonconstitutional legal requirements might reasonably be construed as not extending to fruit of the poisonous tree as that as been developed in Fourth Amendment litigation. If the triggering illegality need not be of a constitutional nature, arguably the need for deterrence may be sufficiently low that it cannot support exclusion of all fruits of that illegality.

If the fruits doctrine does not apply, of course, some other standard must be used to determine the scope of taint. In *Elstad,* the Court was able to call into play the voluntariness requirement as an alternative standard. That cannot be done in other contexts.

One possibility is the distinction between primary and derivative evidence applied by some courts in limiting the "inevitable discovery" exception.[6] Exclusion might, then, be limited to the "primary" evidence obtained as the result of illegality. Where the illegality consists of an improper search, those items seized during the search would be "primary" evidence and subject to exclusion. But other items found later by using information obtained during the search would be "derivative" evidence beyond challenge as a result of the improper

---

4.   470 U.S. 298 (1985).

5.   See § 149 supra.

6.   See § 181 infra.

search. Difficulties experienced in applying this distinction in the inevitable discovery context, however, suggest caution in using the concept of primary evidence as an alternative to the fruits doctrine.

§ 177. Scope of Exclusion: (b) Evidence With an "Independent Source"

In Silverthorne Lumber Co. v. United States,[1] the Supreme Court's announcement that even indirect results of unreasonable police activity must be suppressed was accompanied by the comment that this does not necessarily mean that facts acquired in violation of the Fourth Amendment "become sacred and inaccessible." "If," Justice Holmes explained, "knowledge of them is gained from an independent source they may be proved like any others * * *." The "independent source" rule or "concept," based on this comment in *Silverthorne Lumber Co.*—made in close relationship to the Court's articulation of the fruit of the poisonous tree rule—has been a source of some uncertainty in exclusionary rule analysis.

In Murray v. United States,[2] the Supreme Court emphasized that the independent source "concept" has been used in two distinguishable ways. Justice Holmes' *Silverthorne Lumber Co.* dictum used it to describe situations in which the prosecution has both tainted and untainted evidence of a particular fact and offers only the untainted evidence to prove that fact. For example, police might improperly arrest X, question him, and obtain from him an admission to being in the vicinity of V's home the night it was burglarized. But an alert citizen might report to police seeing X in V's neighborhood on the night of the break-in. The fact that the prosecution obtained inadmissible evidence indicating X's presence near the scene of the offense would not bar it from proving his presence, because it could do so by evidence with an "independence source," that is, evidence obtained in a manner not factually related to the improper arrest. This, *Murray* indicated, was the more specific and most important use of the term independent source.

The other and more general use of the term describes situations in which all of the prosecution's evidence of a particular fact is untainted by its improper activity. For example, police might improperly arrest X and question him, but X may not reveal anything about the location of his victim's body. A citizen, however, may report to police that she observed X hide a body in a particular location; police following up on this information might then discover the body. The state's evidence regarding the body is admissible despite the improper arrest of X because that evidence has an independent source.

Conceptually, the *Murray* discussion makes clear, "independent source" is simply a label reflecting a conclusion that particular challenged evidence was not obtained in a manner causally related to the Fourth Amendment violation. The rule or—"concept"—simply describes several ways in which the prosecution can argue that a defendant seeking to invoke the exclusionary rule has not established the necessary causal link between the triggering illegality and the obtaining of the challenged evidence.

§ 178. Effect of Illegality Upon "Jurisdiction" Over Criminal Defendants

The very presence of many criminal defendants before trial courts could be regarded as the "fruit" of earlier official illegality and hence in some way tainted by that activity. This is particularly so when the illegality consists of improper arrests, in the absence of which the defendants would almost certainly have never been apprehended. Nevertheless, there is agreement that ordinary illegality in an investigation does not deprive the trial court of "jurisdiction" in any sense or otherwise interfere with the court's power to proceed with the trial. Thus it does not provide a basis for a motion to dismiss the charges or other relief which automatically ends the proceedings.

As a matter of federal constitutional law, the Supreme Court has held since Ker v. Illi-

§ 177
1. 251 U.S. 385 (1920).

2. 487 U.S. 533 (1988).

nois,[1] decided in 1886, that there is no federal constitutional bar to a court exercising jurisdiction over the person of a criminal defendant regardless of manner in which the presence of the person was obtained. In United States v. Blue,[2] the Court explained why this was not changed by the Court's commitment in *Mapp* and its progeny to exclusionary sanctions as the primary means of implementing many federal constitutional rights:

> Our numerous precedents ordering the exclusion of * * * illegally obtained evidence assume implicitly that the remedy does not extend to barring the prosecution altogether. So drastic a step might marginally advance some of the ends served by exclusionary rules, but it would also increase to an intolerable degree interference with the public interest in having the guilty brought to book.[3]

That interference, of course, would be caused by depriving the prosecution of all possibility of convicting the defendant. Exclusionary sanctions, where applied, always leave open at least the theoretical possibility that the defendant can be convicted by evidence with an independent source.

Reluctance to read exclusionary sanctions as depriving courts of the power to proceed against defendants may affect analysis of other exclusionary sanction issues. In United States v. Crews,[4] for example, the victim made an in-court identification of the defendant, who had been illegally arrested. The Court of Appeals held that the defendant's presence at trial had been used by the prosecution in presenting that testimony; the witness testified that she was comparing her memory of the perpetrator with the defendant's appearance, with which she was familiar because she observed him in the courtroom, and on that basis she concluded that he was the perpetrator. This constituted an impermissible evidentiary use of the fruits of the illegal arrest, the Court of Appeals concluded.

Five members of the Supreme Court, however, rejected this approach and characterized Crews' argument as precluded by *Ker* and its progeny. A holding that a defendant's face can be considered suppressible evidence, Justice White explained, "would be tantamount to holding that an illegal arrest effectively insulates one from conviction for any crime where an in-court identification is essential." This, he concluded, was inconsistent with the rationale of *Ker's* successors. A majority of the Court is strongly committed to the proposition that federal constitutional exclusionary sanctions should not, directly or indirectly, be applied or expanded to completely bar criminal proceedings.

State courts have followed the Supreme Court's federal constitutional approach. Their decisions repeatedly emphasize that the illegality of an arrest or a detention has no effect upon the jurisdiction of the trial court or the state's power to prosecute and convict the defendant, although they have sometimes suggested that extraordinary circumstances–not present in the cases–might support or require dismissal of charges. An isolated defense of the position that an unlawful arrest should fatally taint the jurisdiction of the trial court has been predicated largely upon considerations of broadly-defined judicial integrity:

> By basing the court's jurisdiction on an illegal warrantless arrest of the defendant in his home, the court legitimizes the illegal conduct which produced the arrest. Courts should not be parties to invasions of the constitutional rights of citizens.[5]

§ 179. Exceptions to Exclusion: (a) Attenuation of Taint

The Fourth Amendment exclusionary sanction, and most others modeled upon it, are subject to exception for evidence obtained after the "taint" of the illegality triggering the exclusionary requirement has become "attenuated." Given the nature of this exception, it

§ 178

1. 119 U.S. 436 (1886).
2. 384 U.S. 251 (1966).
3. Id. at 255.

4. 445 U.S. 463 (1980).

5. State v. Smith, 388 N.W.2d 601, 612 (Wis.1986) (Abrahamson, J., concurring).

applies only to "derivative" evidence that is subject to challenge initially only because it is "fruit of the poisonous tree."

This exception, unlike the "independent source" doctrine, does not rest on the lack of an actual causal link between the original illegality and the obtaining of the challenged evidence. Rather, the exception is triggered by a demonstration that the nature of that causal link is such that the impact of the original illegality upon the obtaining of the evidence is such that exclusion is not required *despite* the causal link.

In United States v. Leon,[1] the Supreme Court explained that in the federal constitutional context, the attenuation of taint doctrine is the product of the principles underlying the federal constitutional exclusionary requirements. To some extent, it identifies those cases in which the taint upon evidence is so minimal that admitting the evidence does not compromise the integrity of the court. More importantly, however:

> [T]he "dissipation of taint" concept * * * "attempts to mark the point at which the detrimental consequences of illegal police action become so attenuated that that the deterrent effect of the exclusionary rule no longer justifies its cost."[2]

The attenuation of taint qualification to the federal exclusionary requirements, of course, does not mean that other exclusionary demands must be similarly limited. Nevertheless, court have—perhaps uncritically—assumed that other exclusionary requirements extending to fruit of the poisonous tree are also qualified by a similar limitation.

Generalization as to what is sufficient to establish attenuation of taint is difficult. Most of the Supreme Court case law applies the doctrine to situations in which a confession made by a defendant in custody begun in violation of the Fourth Amendment is challenged as an inadmissible fruit of the arrest. Drawing general standards from those discus-

sions presents some difficulties. Nevertheless, there is frequent agreement that whether the taint of illegality is sufficiently attenuated to render admissible evidence found as a factual result of that illegality is determined by considering three factors: (1) the temporal relationship between the illegality and the discovery of the challenged evidence; (2) the number and nature of "intervening circumstances"; and (3) the purpose and flagrancy of the official misconduct. Often, however, this agreement provides little helpful guidance in making the final judgment. In United States v. Ceccolini,[3] the Court observed that "[o]bviously no mathematical weight can be assigned to any of the [relevant] factors * * *." This is an understatement.

What number and type of intervening circumstances are sufficient to attenuate a particular taint is an especially difficult question. The more intervening events, clearly, the more likely the taint is to have been attenuated. Some case law suggests that if one of the intervening circumstances involves judicial action, this is entitled to particular significance in finding attenuation. The major thread running through the Supreme Court's federal constitutional attenuation cases is arguably the significance of proof that the chain of events involved a voluntary decision by someone to cooperate with investigating authorities. If the decision was that of the defendant, the factor is entitled to particular weight.

The difficulty of applying attenuation analysis is illustrated by the Supreme Court's application of it to the situation in which the challenged evidence consists of the in-court testimony of a witness located by exploitation of information obtained as a result of an improper search or seizure. In *Ceccolini*, the Court refused to adopt a *per se* rule under which such evidence could never be the excludable fruit of a Fourth Amendment violation. But it did hold that the attenuation analysis should be applied in such cases in a manner appropriately accommodated to the situation. When a criminal defendant seeks suppression

---

§ 179

1. 468 U.S. 897 (1984).

2. Id. at 911.

3. 435 U.S. 268 (1978).

of live-witness testimony, "a closer, more direct link between the illegality and that kind of testimony is required," as compared to cases in which exclusion of other kinds of evidence is sought. This apparently means that attenuation is to be more readily found, given that the evidence at issue—eyewitness testimony—is of exceptional importance and therefore exclusion is appropriate only if the facts show a particularly close relationship between the illegality and discovery of the evidence.

§ 180. Exceptions to Exclusion: (b) Intervening Illegal Conduct

If, in response to officers' illegality sufficient to trigger an exclusionary sanction, suspects engage in further criminal conduct, the courts have regarded that further criminal conduct as bases for law enforcement action somehow independent of the initial illegalities. Thus evidence of those further illegalities, or evidence derived from them, is admissible despite the original improper conduct of the officers.

Often the further illegality consists of forcible resistance to the officers' conduct. In the leading decision, United States v. Bailey,[1] the defendant responded to his arguably improper arrest by struggling with the arresting officer. Although "but for" the unlawful arrest the officer would not have observed the defendant's resistance, the constitutional deficiency of the arrest did not require exclusion of evidence regarding the resistance. In a more rigorous application of the analysis, a Texas court applied it to a situation in which a suspect responded to an unlawful search of his car by grabbing the contraband and placing it in his mouth. Although the unlawfulness of the search precluded the prosecution from proving the defendant's possession *before* his criminal effort to destroy the contraband, the *Bailey* analysis permitted the prosecution to prove his criminal possession of it *during and after* his grabbing the drug.

The precise nature of the doctrine being applied in these cases is not clear. Some courts appear to regard the doctrine as simply a specialized application of the attenuation of taint doctrine, under which intervening voluntary criminal conduct usually and perhaps inevitably attenuates the taint of illegality preceding that conduct. This approach, of course, is consistent with the general significance given in attenuation analysis to intervening voluntary conduct.

Other courts appear to regard the doctrine as a separate exception to exclusionary requirements, based on considerations distinguishable from those supporting the attenuation of taint doctrine. *Bailey*, for example, explained that unless authorities are permitted to use evidence of criminal conduct occurring after and because of official transgressions, offenders would be afforded "an intolerable *carte blanche* to commit further criminal acts so long as they are sufficiently connected to the chain of causation started by the police misconduct." This, it concluded, would "too far reaching and too high a price for society to pay" for the deterrence of governmental illegality provided.

The exception is generally assumed to apply only if the defendant engaged in further criminal acts. An unwise response to official illegality that simply reveals a past digression by the defendant will not invoke it.

§ 181. Exceptions to Exclusion: (c) Inevitable Discovery

Many exclusionary requirements are subject to an exception often called the "inevitable discovery" rule. Evidence otherwise inadmissible becomes usable under this exception upon a showing that it not been improperly secured as it was, the prosecution would nevertheless "inevitably" have obtained it in a "legitimate" manner.

Unlike the so-called independent source rule,[1] which is invoked by proof that the challenged evidence was *in actual fact* not obtained as a factual result of the illegality, this excep-

§ 180

1. 691 F.2d 1009 (11th Cir.1982).

§ 181

1. See § 177 supra.

tion rests on proof regarding hypothetical scenarios. This characteristic also distinguishes inevitable discovery from attenuation of taint,[2] which is invoked by a showing regarding the *actual* causal link between the illegal conduct and obtaining the evidence.

Inevitable discovery was incorporated into federal constitutional exclusionary analysis in Nix v. Williams,[3] a Sixth Amendment right to counsel case. The rationale for the exclusionary remedy, the Court reasoned, ordinarily requires only that the prosecution be denied any advantages that might flow from its misconduct. This preventive purpose does not require that the prosecution be put in any worse a position than it would be in had it not committed the primary illegality. Since no reason exists to deny the prosecution any advantage it can establish that it would have enjoyed had its officers eschewed improper action, only an inevitable discovery exception can properly limit the exclusionary requirement as dictated by its rationale.

State courts have tended to construe state exclusionary requirements as qualified by an exception somewhat similar to *Nix's* federal constitutional doctrine. A significant number, however, have been persuaded by the risk that the exception may be misapplied in application to limit the exception more rigorously than the Supreme Court found appropriate in fashioning the exception to the federal constitutional exclusionary sanctions.

The exception is generally agreed to require proof that the prosecution *would*—not *might* or *could*—have obtained the challenged evidence in a proper manner. *Nix* rejected the contention that the nature of the issues posed by the exception requires an unusually high burden of proof on the prosecution. Some state courts, however, have reasoned that the conjecture inherent in application of the exception justifies imposing upon the prosecution the task of proving the exception applies by clear and convincing evidence.

Nix rejected the holdings below that the exception requires a showing that the evidence

was obtained by officers acting in "good faith," reiterating that the purposes of the exclusionary requirement do not justify putting the prosecution in a worse position than it would have occupied had its officers acted properly. Several state courts, however, have required that the officers have acted in good faith. The Alaska Supreme Court, for example, concluded that an unqualified exception poses a sufficient risk of encouraging law enforcement "shortcuts" to demand that as a matter of state constitutional law it be limited to situations in which the officers did not act in bad faith to accelerate the discovery of the challenged evidence.

Some courts have sought to minimize the risk that inevitability will be uncritically found by requiring that the prosecution establish that the legitimate discovery of the evidence would have occurred as a result of an alternative line of investigation that was actually being actively pursued at the time of the illegal conduct. Most reject this requirement, although proof that such an alternative investigation was actually underway strongly supports the contention that it had the independence necessary to trigger the exception.

Clearly some courts are uncomfortable with the inevitable discovery exception, especially as applied to some types of situations, and this discomfort has given rise to a variety of possible limitations on the doctrine. Some discussions suggest that the exception is not to be applied where the illegality is particularly serious or infringes a central aspect of the governing law. Others suggest that it is not to be applied to situations where its application would remove all incentive for those gathering evidence to comply with the legal requirement at issue, or those situations in which excessive speculation would necessarily be involved.

The exception might, as some courts have held, be limited to "derivative" as contrasted with "primary" or "direct" evidence. Under this distinction, direct or primary evidence is that which is actually discovered and seized during the illegal conduct. Derivative evidence, on the other hand, is evidence obtained

---

2.   See § 179 supra.

3.   467 U.S. 431 (1984).

later by means of information derived from illegal conduct. Some courts have limited the exception to evidence of the latter sort. If the exception is limited to derivative evidence, it becomes an exception not to the basic exclusionary requirement but only to the corollary that renders inadmissible all fruit of the poisonous tree. Most courts have refused to limit the exception to derivative evidence, although they have arguably failed to fully explore the possibility that such a limitation might be the most appropriate way of preventing the exception from effectively nullifying some or most of the legal requirements enforced by exclusionary requirements.

§ 182. Exceptions to Exclusion: (d) "Good Faith"

Whether illegally obtained evidence should be excluded if the officers who gathered it mistakenly believed (or could have believed) that their actions complied with legal requirements is perhaps the most controversial issue posed by existing exclusionary requirements. A limited "good faith" exception to the federal constitutional exclusionary rules for some situations of this sort has been recognized by the Supreme Court. State courts and legislatures have sometimes, but not always, followed suit.

Federal Constitutional Exception. In United States v. Leon[1] and Massachusetts v. Sheppard[2] the Supreme Court held that evidence obtained in searches conducted pursuant to defective search warrants was nevertheless admissible if the prosecution established that reasonable officers would have believed the searches constitutionally permissible. Three years later, in Illinois v. Krull,[3] the Court similarly held admissible evidence obtained in a warrantless search upon proof that given an invalid statute purporting to authoring the search, a reasonable officer would have believed the search constitutionally permissible.

The "good faith" label attached to the doctrine developed in *Leon, Sheppard* and *Krull* is arguably misleading. The exception does not require proof that the officers actual-

ly and subjectively—in "good faith," as that term is generally used—believed their actions within constitutional limits. The inquiry is whether under all the circumstances "a reasonably well trained officer" would have known that the actions at issue were constitutionally impermissible. If not, the exception applies whether the officer actually making the search knew the actions were improper. In fact, and despite the general statement of the rule, the exception does not require proof that the officers actually—subjectively—relied on the warrant or legislation.

Emphasizing the preventive purpose of the Fourth Amendment exclusionary rule, *Leon, Sheppard and Krull* reasoned that in at least some situations the rule cannot be expected to deter objectively reasonable law enforcement activity and should not be applied in an effort to do so. This is particularly so, *Leon* continued, where officers have obtained a search warrant. The magistrate has responsibility for determining such matters as whether probable cause exists; officers cannot be expected to question magistrates' resolution of those issues. "Penalizing the officer for the magistrate's errors, rather than his own," the Court concluded, "cannot logically contribute to the deterrence of the Fourth Amendment violations." Similarly, *Krull* reasoned, officers cannot ordinarily be expected to question the judgment of a legislature that passed a statute, so no contribution to deterrence can logically be expected from penalizing the officer for errors of the legislature. Consequently, any benefits derived from excluding evidence in such situations cannot justify the substantial costs of exclusion.

Given that officers' ability to rely on a warrant or legislation must be objectively reasonable, exclusion is required despite a warrant or authorizing statute if the defect in the warrant or statute is so clear that a reasonably well trained officer would recognize it. In the case of reliance upon a warrant, *Leon* added, exclusion is required if the officer in applying

---

§ 182

1.　468 U.S. 897 (1984).

2.　468 U.S. 981 (1984).

3.　480 U.S. 340 (1987).

for the warrant misled the issuing magistrate by including information he knew was false or would have known was false except for his reckless disregard for the truth or if the warrant was issued by a magistrate lacking the impartiality required by the Fourth Amendment.

Under the better view, a warrant can trigger the exception only if the warrant itself was untainted. If the warrant was issued on the basis of excludable evidence, the warrant and evidence obtained pursuant to it are all fruit of the original poisonous tree. Such laundering of tainted information through a magistrate should not render the fruits doctrine inapplicable.

The major issue posed by *Leon, Sheppard* and *Krull* is whether the exception recognized in these cases will be extended to other and perhaps all situations in which reasonable officers would regard their conduct as complying with federal constitutional standards. In such situations, exclusion arguably cannot be expected to significantly increase the quality of evidence-gathering activity, and thus the exception's rationale applies. On the other hand, the difficulty of assuring that reasonable officers could not in fact be expected to act more carefully suggests that the exception might reasonably be limited to situations involving some objectively-reasonable basis for reliance—such as an apparently valid search warrant or a statute authorizing warrantless activity.

The Supreme Court in Arizona v. Evans[4] expanded the *Leon* exception to situations in which a warrant had been issued but withdrawn, although a court employee had failed to notify law enforcement that the warrant was not longer effective. *Evans* in a sense extended the exception to evidence obtained by warrantless law enforcement action. It was, however, clearly limited to situations in which a warrant-issuing court acted in a manner justifying officers' in believing that an effective warrant was outstanding. Whether *Leon, Sheppard, and Krull* will be applied to other and perhaps all situations in which law en-

forcement officers would believe their actions, given the circumstances, reasonable warrantless searches or seizures in Fourth Amendment terms remains unclear.

If the exception applies only to situations in which the reasonableness of the police action is established by a demonstrated error on the part of some entity outside of law enforcement, this suggests that it does not render admissible evidence obtained by officers who erroneously exceed their authority under a valid warrant. The only error in such situations is that of the officers executing the warrant. Arguably, there thus remains sufficient likelihood that exclusion might encourage greater care in ascertaining the existence or effect of warrants.

State Constitutional Requirements. A number of state courts have construed state constitutional requirements as containing no exception identical or similar to the *Leon-Sheppard-Krull* good faith exception to the Fourth Amendment requirement.

These state tribunals have, to some extent, rejected the Supreme Court's assumption that the effect of the exception on the deterrent value of the exclusionary requirement can be measured and that it is acceptable given the cost incurred by the loss of reliance evidence. More importantly, however, some state courts have rejected the Supreme Court's assumption that the deterrent analysis is appropriate, and have found the exception unacceptable given the broader policy bases of state exclusionary requirements. The New Mexico Supreme Court, for example, reasoned that the exception was incompatible with the purpose of the state constitutional requirement "to effectuate in the pending case the constitutional right of the accused to be free from unreasonable search and seizure." "Denying the government the fruits of unconstitutional conduct at trial," the court concluded, "best effectuates the constitutional proscription of unreasonable searches and seizures by preserving the rights of the accused to the same extent as if the government's officers had stayed within the law." In addition, the New Mexico court rea-

---

4. 514 U.S. 1 (1995).

soned, the state provision serves important considerations of judicial integrity, defined more broadly than that consideration in Fourth Amendment analysis, and the exception is inconsistent with this state law objective.

Nonconstitutional Exclusionary Requirements. State statutory exclusionary requirements may be construed as containing no good faith exception. The Georgia Supreme Court has so construed its provision, and the Texas statutory exclusionary rule has an exception limited to evidence obtained in reasonable reliance on warrants actually issued on probable cause.

§ 183. Exceptions to Exclusion: (e) Use of Illegally Obtained Evidence to Impeach Testifying Defendant

Most exclusionary sanctions bar only the use of improperly obtained evidence at trial to prove the guilt of the defendant. Thus they are subject to an exception or qualification that permits the use of such evidence to cross-examine and impeach a defendant who testifies at trial.

In Harris v. New York[1] the United States Supreme Court reaffirmed its pre-Mapp v. Ohio[2] holding in Walder v. United States[3] that the federal constitutional exclusionary requirements permit the use of otherwise inadmissible evidence to impeach a testifying defendant. This has been subsequently reaffirmed. *Harris* rests primarily upon the Court's conclusion that given the deterrence accomplished by excluding evidence offered on guilt, little additional deterrence would be provided by excluding unconstitutionally obtained evidence offered only to impeach the testifying defendant. The value of what little deterrence might be achieved, further, would be outweighed by the exceptionally high and offensive cost of permitting potential perjury to go unchallenged.

If, however, the federal constitutional basis for barring the use of evidence to prove

guilt rests at least in part upon unreliability caused by the illegality, *Walder-Harris* do not permit impeachment use. Thus a confession inadmissible under due process voluntariness standards cannot be used to impeach.

Walder had suggested that impeachment use of unconstitutionally obtained evidence was permissible only if the testifying defendant went beyond simply denying guilt and testified to collateral matters. Such a position would leave a defendant free to present at least a basic contention of innocence without giving up the right to be free from unconstitutionally obtained evidence. *Harris*, however, rejected this approach and thus permits impeachment on the basis of testimony simply denying guilt of the charged crime.

Further, *Harris* and its progeny sometimes allow impeachment on the basis of testimony given on cross-examination as well as on direct. This is permitted, under United States v. Havens,[4] only if the testimony on cross-examination was in response to questions "plainly within the scope of the defendant's direct examination." Whether a defendant's testimony on direct reasonably suggests inquiry by the prosecution on cross-examination into events involving tainted information is "necessarily case specific," and trial judges have considerable discretion in resolving particular cases.

Impeachment is permitted as long as there is some "inconsistency" between the otherwise inadmissible evidence and the defendant's trial testimony. The Supreme Court has suggested that impeachment use must be "otherwise proper," indicating that local rules limiting impeachment might somehow be incorporated into the federal constitutional exception. There seems to be no basis or rationale for constitutionally requiring a state to follow its ordinary cross-examination and impeachment rules when *Harris-Walder* evidence is offered. On the other hand, as a matter of nonconstitutional evidence law, there seems neither basis nor rationale for disregarding

§ 183

1. 401 U.S. 222 (1971).

2. 367 U.S. 643 (1961).

3. 347 U.S. 62 (1954).

4. 446 U.S. 620 (1980).

limits on impeachment simply because the witness is a criminal defendant and the evidence is inadmissible to prove guilt because of constitutional exclusionary requirements.

Only a defendant's personal testimony at trial will trigger the opportunity to use otherwise excluded evidence. In James v. Illinois[5]— by a 5 to 4 vote—the Court declined to expand the exception to permit the use of unconstitutionally obtained evidence to "impeach"—or rebut—defense testimony from witnesses other than the defendant. Such an expanded exception would weaken the deterrent value of the basic exclusionary requirement. Further, permitting such rebuttal use of testimony would discourage defendants from presenting potentially meritorious defensive contentions, since defense counsel lack control over non-defendant witnesses.

State courts addressing the contents of state—generally constitutional—exclusionary requirements have seldom been willing to reject any impeachment exception. Nevertheless, they have expressed concern regarding the scope and effect of exceptions based on the Supreme Court's federal constitutional model. To the extent that state exclusionary requirements rest on broader rationales than the federal constitutional ones, of course, impeachment exceptions may be less appropriate in the state context.

Some state tribunals, responding to such concerns, have adopted impeachment exceptions more limited than *Walder-Harris*. The Vermont Supreme Court, for example, emphasized what it viewed as the need to preserve a defendant's right to an unfettered opportunity to testify in his own defense. On this basis it rejected the *Havens* approach and held that evidence obtained in violation of the state provision could only be used to impeach a defendant's testimony on direct examination. Hawaii, rejecting *Harris* but not *Walder*, held that evidence obtained in an unconstitutional search may not be used to impeach a testifying defendant's testimony "as to his actions," but may be used to contradict testimony regarding "the corroborative circumstances."

---

5. 493 U.S. 307 (1990).

Title 7

RELEVANCY AND ITS COUNTERWEIGHTS

Chapter 16

RELEVANCE

Table of Sections

---

§ 184. Relevance as the Presupposition of Admissibility

In the law of evidence, truth matters. To facilitate judgments based on an accurate understanding of the facts underlying a dispute, the system of proof presupposes that the parties may present to the court or jury all the evidence that bears on the issue to be decided. Of course, many rules, such as those involving privilege, hearsay, and judicial economy, limit this system of free proof and keep probative evidence from the finder of fact. Nevertheless, unless there is some such distinct ground for refusing to hear the evidence, it should be received. Conversely, if the evidence lacks probative value, it should be excluded. Federal Rule of Evidence 402 and the corresponding Uniform Rule adopt these two "axioms" of the common law. These rules succinctly provide that "[a]ll relevant evidence is admissible, except as otherwise provided.... Evidence which is not relevant is not admissible."

§ 185. The Meaning of Relevancy and the Counterweights

To say that relevant evidence is generally admissible, while irrelevant evidence is not, would be of little value without a suitable definition of relevance. This section clarifies the meaning of relevance. It then outlines the factors that can make even relevant evidence inadmissible.

There are two components to relevant evidence: materiality and probative value. Materiality concerns the fit between the evidence and the case. It looks to the relation between the propositions that the evidence is offered to prove and the issues in the case. If the evidence is offered to help prove a proposition that is not a matter in issue, the evidence is immaterial. What is "in issue," that is, within the range of the litigated controversy, is determined mainly by the pleadings, read in the light of the rules of pleading and controlled by the substantive law. Thus, in a suit for worker's compensation, evidence of contributory negligence would be immaterial, whether pleaded or not, since a worker's negligence does not affect the right to compensation. In an action to enjoin the enforcement of a statute prohibiting "partial-birth abortions" as void for vagueness, expert testimony as to a fetus's capacity to sense pain is immaterial, since it relates only to the state's interest in enacting the law and not to the claim of vagueness.

In addition to evidence that bears directly on the issues, leeway is allowed even on direct examination for proof of facts that merely fill in the background of the narrative and give it interest, color, and lifelikeness. Maps, diagrams, charts, and videotapes can be material as aids to the understanding of other material evidence. Moreover, the parties may question the credibility of the witnesses and, within limits, produce evidence assailing and supporting their credibility.

The second aspect of relevance is probative value, the tendency of evidence to establish the proposition that it is offered to prove. Federal Rule and the Revised Uniform Rule of Evidence 401 incorporate these twin concepts of materiality and probative value. They state that " '[r]elevant evidence' means evidence having any tendency to make the existence of any fact that is of consequence to the determination of the action more probable or less probable than it would be without the evidence." A fact that is "of consequence" is material, and evidence that affects the probability that a fact is as a party claims it to be has probative force.

There are at least two ways to think about whether an item of evidence has probative value. First, one can simply ask, "Does learning of this evidence make it either more or less likely that the disputed fact is true?" Take, for example, evidence that a defendant charged with assaulting a neighbor has a reputation for being non-violent. Knowing that someone has this reputation seems to make it less likely that he would commit an assault, presumably because we accept the underlying generalization that fewer people with a reputation for non-violence assault their neighbors than do people with no such reputation. If we denote the reputation evidence as E and the hypothesis that the defendant committed the assault as H, then we can say that the probability of the hypothesis H given the evidence E is less than the probability of H without considering E. In symbols, $P(H|E) < P(H)$. (The vertical bar is read as "given" or "conditioned on," and "<" means "is less than.") Because E changes the probability of the assault, it is relevant.

Sometimes, however, this direct mode of reasoning about the probability of an hypothesis will be more difficult to apply because the effect of E on the probability of H will not be so apparent. A second approach considers the probability of the evidence given the hypothesis, $P(E|H)$, rather than $P(H|E)$. Evidence that is more likely to arise when H is true than when H is not true supports H; evidence that is less likely to arise under H than not-H supports not-H. Evidence of either type is probative of H. But evidence that is just as likely to arise when H is true as when H is false is of no use in deciding between H and not-H—it is irrelevant. In the example of the assault and the reputation for nonviolence, it seems less probable that a person who committed the assault would have such a reputation than that a person who did not commit the assault would have that reputation. Therefore, $P(E|\text{not-H}) > P(E|H)$, and the evidence has probative value—it points toward not-H.

Indeed, the "likelihood ratio" of $P(E|H)$ to $P(E|\text{not-H})$ can be used to quantify the probative value of the evidence E—the larger the ratio, the more strongly the evidence supports the hypothesis H. Consider a behavioral pattern said to be characteristic of abused children. If research established that the behavior is equally common among abused and non-abused children, then its likelihood ratio would be one, and evidence of that pattern would not be probative of abuse. If the behavior were two times more common among abused children, then it would have rather modest probative value. And if it were a thousand times more common among abused children, its probative value would be far greater.

Probative evidence often is said to have "logical relevance," while evidence lacking in substantial probative value may be condemned as "speculative" or "remote." Speculativeness usually arises with regard to dubious projections into the future or questionable surmises about what might have happened had the facts been different. For example, a calculation of lost wages in a wrongful death case that arbitrarily assumes that the deceased's salary would have grown at a constant rate year after year can be excluded as speculative. Remoteness relates not to the passage of time alone, but to the undermining of reasonable inferences due to the likelihood of supervening factors. For example, testimony that the defendant in an automobile accident case was speeding just a few minutes before the collision is relevant to whether defendant was speeding at the moment of the collision, but testimony that defendant exceeded the speed limit two years before the accident is likely to be excluded as too remote. The two-year-old incident offers some indication that the driver was speeding, but many factors affect how fast a driver goes at a particular time, and these factors would change over a two-year period.

Under our system, molded by the tradition of jury trial and predominantly oral proof, a party offers his evidence not *en masse*, but item by item. An item of evidence, being but a single link in the chain of proof, need not prove conclusively the proposition for which it is offered. It need not even make that proposition appear more probable than not. Whether the entire body of one party's evidence is sufficient to go to the jury is one question. Whether a particular item of evidence is relevant to the case is quite another. It is enough if the item could reasonably show that a fact is slightly more probable than it would appear without that evidence. Even after the probative force of the evidence is spent, the proposition for which it is offered still can seem quite improbable. Thus, the common objection that the inference for which the fact is offered "does not necessarily follow" is untenable. It poses a standard of conclusiveness that very few single items of circumstantial evidence ever could meet. A brick is not a wall.

But if even very weak material items of evidence are relevant, what sort of evidence is irrelevant for want of probative value? The long-standing distinction between "direct" and "circumstantial" evidence offers a starting point in answering this question. Direct evidence is evidence which, if believed, resolves a matter in issue. Circumstantial evidence also may be testimonial, but even if the circumstances depicted are accepted as true, additional reasoning is required to reach the desired conclusion. For example, a witness' testimony that he saw A stab B with a knife is direct evidence of whether A did indeed stab B. In contrast, testimony that A fled the scene of the stabbing would be circumstantial evidence of the stabbing (but direct evidence of the flight itself). Similarly, testimony of a witness that he saw A at the scene would be direct evidence that A was there, but testimony that he saw

someone who was disguised and masked, but had a voice and limp like A's, would be circumstantial evidence that the person seen was A.

In terms of this dichotomy, direct evidence from a qualified witness offered to help establish a provable fact can never be irrelevant. Circumstantial evidence, however, can be offered to help prove a material fact, yet be so unrevealing as to be irrelevant to that fact. For instance, evidence that the government awarded a firm a lucrative contract is irrelevant on the issue of whether the firm damaged property leased to it because there is no reason to suppose that firms that handle large government contracts are more likely to damage such property than other lessees.

In short, to say that circumstantial evidence is irrelevant in the sense that it lacks probative value is to say that knowing the evidence does not justify *any* reasonable inference as to the fact in question. Cases involving such evidence are few and far between. That more than one inference could be drawn is not enough to render the evidence irrelevant. Fleeing the scene of a crime, for instance, could mean that the defendant, being conscious of guilt for the crime charged, actually is guilty; or it could mean that defendant is innocent but fled to avoid being apprehended for some other reason entirely. However, the premise that, in general, people who flee are more likely to be guilty than those who do not is at least plausible, and as long as there is some plausible chain of reasoning that leads to the desired conclusion, the evidence is probative of that conclusion. As a result, most evidence seriously offered at trial has *some* probative value. Even when the courts denominate evidence as devoid of probative value, one may often wonder whether the evidence is not more properly excludable on grounds of materiality or insufficient probative value given the countervailing considerations that can bar the use of relevant evidence.

Yet, how can a judge know whether the evidence could reasonably affect an assessment of the probability of the fact to be inferred? In some instances, scientific research may show that the fact in issue is more likely to be true (or false) when such evidence is present than when it is not. Ordinarily, however, the answer must lie in the judge's personal experience, general knowledge, and understanding of human conduct and motivation. If one asks whether an attempted escape by a prisoner charged with two serious but factually unconnected crimes is relevant to show consciousness of guilt of the first crime charged, the answer will not be found in a statistical table of the attempts at escape by those conscious of guilt as opposed to those not conscious of their guilt. The judge can only ask, could a reasonable juror believe that the fact that the accused tried to escape makes it more probable than it would otherwise be that the accused was conscious of guilt of the crime being tried? If the answer is affirmative, then the evidence is relevant. In other situations, the judge may need to consider not only whether the evidence reasonably could support the proposition for which it is offered, but also whether its absence might warrant the opposite inference. That is, where a jury would expect to receive a certain kind of evidence, testimony explaining why that evidence is not available could be helpful and should be considered relevant.

In sum, relevant evidence is evidence that in some degree advances the inquiry. It is material and probative. As such, it is admissible, at least prima facie. But this relevance does not ensure admissibility. There remains the question of whether its value is worth what it costs. A great deal of evidence is excluded on the ground that the costs outweigh the benefits. Rule 403 of the Federal and Revised Uniform Evidence Rules categorize most of these costs. This rule codifies the common law power of the judge to exclude relevant evidence "if its probative value is substantially outweighed by the danger of unfair prejudice, confusion of the issues, or misleading the jury, or by considerations of undue delay, waste of time, or needless presentation of cumulative evidence." Such factors often blend together in practice, but we shall elaborate on them briefly in the rough order of their importance.

First, there is the danger of prejudice. In this context, prejudice (or, as the rule puts it, "unfair prejudice") does not simply mean damage to the opponent's cause—for that can be a sign of probative value, not prejudice.[1] Neither does it necessarily mean an appeal to emotion. Prejudice can arise, however, from facts that arouse the jury's hostility or sympathy for one side without regard to the probative value of the evidence. Thus, evidence of convictions for prior, unrelated crimes might lead a juror to think that since the defendant already has a criminal record, an erroneous conviction would not be quite as serious as would otherwise be the case. A juror influenced in this fashion may be satisfied with a somewhat less compelling demonstration of guilt than should be required. This rationale has been used in innumerable contexts—for example, to preclude inquiry into a medical expert's work in abortion clinics after the expert had testified about the cause of infertility in a woman who used an intrauterine device, to preclude disclosure of the value of stock given to a White House official charged with illegal lobbying, to limit the number and nature of gruesome photographs of murder victims, and to exclude videotapes of an injured plaintiff's rehabilitative therapy or daily activities. Second, whether or not "emotional" reactions are at work, relevant evidence can confuse, or worse, mislead a trier of fact who is not properly equipped to judge the probative worth of the evidence. Third, certain proof and the answering evidence that it provokes might unduly distract the jury from the main issues. Finally, the evidence offered and the counterproof could consume an inordinate amount of time.

Analyzing and weighing the pertinent costs and benefits is no trivial task. Wise judges may come to differing conclusions in similar situations. Even the same item of evidence may fare differently from one case to the next, depending on its relationship to the

§ 185

1. E.g., Foley v. City of Lowell, 948 F.2d 10 (1st Cir.1991) (in a civil rights action against a city for condoning police brutality, the outrageousness of the police conduct on separate occasions "is a hallmark of probative value: the more outrageous the occurrences, the more probable that a policy of tolerance was in place").

other evidence in the case,[2] the importance of the issues on which it bears, and the likely efficacy of cautionary instructions to the jury. Accordingly, much leeway is given trial judges who must fairly weigh probative value against probable dangers. Nevertheless, discretion can be abused, and some appellate courts have urged trial courts to articulate the reasoning behind their relevance rulings. In certain areas, such as proof of character, comparable situations recur so often that relatively particularized rules channel the exercise of discretion. In others, less structured discretion remains prominent. One way or another, however, admissible evidence must satisfy the cost-benefit calculus we have outlined.

2. If other evidence, which does not carry the same dangers with it, could be used to establish the same fact, then the marginal probative value of the evidence in question is slight or non-existent. Old Chief v. United States, 519 U.S. 172 (1997) (in a prosecution for possession of a handgun by a felon, it is error to admit evidence of the name or nature of the defendant's prior conviction for assault causing serious bodily injury when the defendant offers to stipulate to the previous felony conviction); United States v. 88 Cases, More or Less, Containing Bireley's Orange Beverage, 187 F.2d 967, 975 (3d Cir. 1951) (error to introduce pictures of guinea pigs dying in agony from vitamin C deficiency after being put on diet of orange drink); United States v. Layton, 767 F.2d 549 (9th Cir.1985) (tape recording of Jim Jones' remarks that included sounds of children dying in mass suicides in Jonestown, Guyana, was properly excluded, partly because the same substantive point could be established by less inflammatory testimony).

Chapter 17

CHARACTER AND HABIT

Table of Sections

§ 186. Character: In General

Evidence of the general character of a party or witness almost always has some probative value, but in many situations, the probative value is slight and the potential for prejudice large. In other circumstances, the balance shifts the other way. Instead of engaging exclusively in the case-by-case balancing outlined in Chapter 16, however, the courts tend to pass on the admissibility of evidence of character and habit according to a number of rules with myriad exceptions that reflect the recurring patterns of such proof and its usefulness. These rules categorically exclude most "character evidence"—evidence offered solely to prove a person acted in conformity with a trait of character on a given occasion. Character evidence that is not categorically excluded is admissible, subject to the other rules of evidence, including the usual case-by-case balancing of probative value against possible prejudice.

Before turning to the details of the rules, it may be helpful to sketch two general considerations that are central to shaping and applying them. The first is the purpose for which the evidence of character is offered. If a person's character is itself an issue in the case, then character evidence is crucial. But if the evidence of character merely is introduced as circumstantial evidence of what a person did or thought, it is less critical. Other, and probably better, evidence of the acts or state of mind usually should be available. Exclusion is therefore much more likely when the character evidence is offered to help prove that a person acted in one way or another. Thus, Federal and Revised Uniform Evidence Rule 404(a), which basically codify common law doctrine, provide that subject to enumerated exceptions, "[e]vidence of a person's character or a trait of his character is not admissible for the purpose of proving that he acted in conformity therewith on a particular occasion.... "

Federal and Revised Uniform Rule of Evidence 405(a), however, allow opinion testimony as well as reputation testimony to prove character whenever any form of character evidence is appropriate. And, as at common law, when character is "in issue," as discussed in the next section, it also may be proved by testimony about specific acts.

§ 187. Character in Issue

A person's character may be a material fact that under the substantive law determines rights and liabilities of the parties. For example, because truth is a defense in an action for defamation, in an action of slander for the statement that the plaintiff "is in the habit of picking up things," the defendant can introduce evidence of plaintiff's thefts to prove that the statement was true. A complaint for negligence may allege that the defendant allowed an unfit person to use a motor vehicle or other dangerous object, or that an employer was negligent in hiring or failing to supervise an employee with certain dangerous character traits. Likewise, in deciding who should have custody of children, fitness to provide care is of paramount importance. When character has been put in issue by the pleadings in such cases, evidence of character must be brought forth.

In view of the crucial role of character in this situation, the courts usually hold that it can be proved by evidence of specific acts. The Federal and Revised Uniform Rules follow this approach. The hazards of prejudice, surprise and time-consumption implicit in this manner of proof are more tolerable when character is itself in issue than when this evidence is offered as a mere indication that the defendant committed the acts that are the subject of the suit.

Yet, some older cases do not simply permit evidence of specific acts to prove character when it is in issue. They insist on it. But there is no reason to exclude reputation evidence, which ordinarily is the preferred mode of proof of character. Proof by means of opinion testimony is slightly more debatable, but most of the arguments against opinion evidence do not apply when character is in issue. For example, the possibility that specific acts may be inquired into on cross-examination (which may prompt barring specific act evidence when

character is not in issue) is hardly of concern, since the door to such evidence already is open.

The phrase "character in issue" sometimes invites confusion. A defendant in a criminal case generally can bring in evidence of good character to show that he is not the type of person who would have committed to offense charged. Although courts sometimes speak loosely of this strategy as putting the defendant's character in issue, the defendant is using character solely as circumstantial evidence. When the defendant makes his character an issue in this manner, it merely means that the prosecution is allowed to bring forth certain kinds of rebuttal evidence of bad character. It does not justify evidence of specific acts, opinions, and reputation by either party. That free-wheeling approach to character evidence is limited to the unusual situation in which an offense, claim, or defense for which character is an essential element is pled.

§ 188. Character as Circumstantial Evidence: General Rule of Exclusion

Even when a person's character is not itself in issue as defined in the preceding section, litigants may seek to introduce character-type evidence. In ascertaining whether such evidence is admissible, attention to the purpose for which the evidence is offered remains of the utmost importance. In some cases, even though a person's character is not itself in issue, evidence of a character trait may be relevant to proving a material fact that is distinct from whether the person acted in conformity with that trait. Thus, where extortion is charged, the defendant's reputation for violence may be relevant to the victim's state of mind. In these cases the reputation itself, not the character that it tends to prove, is the significant fact; reputation is not used as evidence of how the person with the character traits behaved on a given occasion.

In contrast, evidence that an individual is the kind of person who behaves in certain ways almost always has some value as circumstantial evidence of how this individual acted (and perhaps with what state of mind) in the matter in question. For instance, on average, persons reputed to be violent commit more assaults than persons known to be peaceable. Yet, evidence of character in any form—reputation, opinion from observation, or specific acts—generally will not be received to prove that a person engaged in certain conduct or did so with a particular intent on a specific occasion, so-called circumstantial use of character. The reason is the familiar one of prejudice outweighing probative value. Character evidence used for this purpose, while typically being of relatively slight value, usually is laden with the dangerous baggage of prejudice, distraction, and time-consumption.

At the same time, there are important exceptions to this general rule of exclusion—so many that some writers prefer to state the general rule as one of admissibility subject to exceptions for exclusion. The next six sections consider various applications of the rule of exclusion and the most important exceptions to it.

§ 189. Character for Care in Civil Cases

The rule against using character evidence solely to prove conduct on a particular occasion has long been applied in civil cases, notwithstanding suggestions that exclusion is not justified in this context.[1] The rule is invoked most uniformly when specific act evidence is proffered. Of course, we are speaking of specific acts other than those at bar. No doubt, evidence that someone acted negligently says something about that person's character. But we are concerned here with character as circumstantial evidence, that is, as evidence of a propensity to behave in a certain way which, in turn, makes it more likely that such behav-

ior occurred on the occasion in question. A previous accident or negligent act that does something more than show character or predisposition may be admissible. Negligence cases illustrate the point. Evidence of negligent conduct of the defendant or his agent on other occasions may reflect a propensity for negligent acts, thus enhancing the probability of negligence on the occasion in question, but this probative force has been thought too slight to overcome the usual counterweights.[2] The same applies to evidence of other negligent acts of the plaintiff, as well as other instances of careful conduct.

Most courts also reject proof of an actor's character for care by means of reputation evidence or opinion testimony. In the past, a minority of courts had admitted these types of evidence, often under the guise of evidence of "habit," when there were no eyewitnesses to the event. A few even did so if there were eyewitnesses with conflicting stories. The Federal and revised Uniform Rules do not make such fine distinctions. The prevailing pattern is to exclude all forms of character evidence in civil cases when the evidence is employed merely to support an inference that conduct on a particular occasion was consistent with a person's character.

This pattern persists despite psychological studies of "accident proneness." It had been argued that scientific research establishing that drivers with inadequate training, defective vision, and certain attitudes and emotional traits are at risk for automobile accidents should prompt a relaxation of the rule against evidence of character for negligence. The argument seems to be that because a small number of drivers with identifiable characteristics account for the bulk of the accidents, they must

---

§ 189

1. The Model Code and the Uniform Rules, prior to the 1974 revision, permitted the use of character evidence to prove conduct in civil cases, except on the issue of negligence. Whether the rule should bar a civil defendant from proving his good character when the allegations against him state a criminal offense also has engendered debate, see infra § 192, as has its application to civil assault and battery cases in which the identity of the first attacker is in dispute. See infra § 193. In 1994, Congress added Fed. R. Evid. 415, which makes admissible other acts of sexual assault or child molestation in "a civil case in which a

claim for damages or other relief is predicated on a party's alleged commission of conduct constituting an offense of sexual assault or child molestation."

2. Moorhead v. Mitsubishi Aircraft Int'l, 828 F.2d 278 (5th Cir.1987) (error to admit pilot's low marks at flight school refresher course); Thornberg v. Perleberg, 158 N.W.2d 188, 191 (N.D. 1968) (improper for plaintiff in automobile accident case to ask defendant driver on cross-examination, "you have a constant record of accidents and traffic violations, do you not?").

drive improperly as a routine matter, and this provides a better than usual basis for inferring that the accident in issue resulted from such negligent driving. Presumably, the reform would be to admit evidence of previous accidents combined with proof that the particular driver fits the "accident proneness" profile.

A somewhat different proposal asks that aggregate and individual data concerning the actions of physicians should be admissible in malpractice cases. For example, in deciding whether the removal of a patient's appendix was unnecessary surgery, the jury might be invited to consider whether the defendant physician performs appendectomies far more frequently than his colleagues. Although evidence of previous accidents or similar happenings should not be freely admitted, a suitable expert testifying about a departure from the customary standard of care should be permitted to rely on such information and to explain this analysis to the jury. Moreover, where the statistically measured departure from the customary pattern is itself so great as to make it plain that the defendant is behaving differently from the norm, this statistic should be provable. Conversely, a defendant might wish to establish statistically that a pattern is within the normal range. The statistical pattern can be proved without going into the prejudicial, distracting, or time-consuming details of other incidents. The value of the evidence is greatest in cases where each surgery or other event, viewed in isolation, could be a matter of reasonable professional judgment. In these situations, the need for such evidence justifies taking the risks associated with defendant's seeking to prove reasonable care in each of the other incidents.

§ 190. Bad Character as Evidence of Criminal Conduct: Other Crimes

If anything, the rule against using character evidence to prove conduct on a particular occasion applies even more strongly in criminal cases. Unless and until the accused gives evidence of his good character, the prosecution may not introduce evidence of (or otherwise seek to establish) his bad character. The evidence of bad character would not be irrelevant,

but particularly in the setting of the jury trial, the dangers of prejudice, confusion and time-consumption outweigh the probative value.

This broad prohibition includes the specific and frequently invoked rule that the prosecution may not introduce evidence of other criminal acts of the accused unless the evidence is introduced for some purpose other than to suggest that because the defendant is a person of criminal character, it is more probable that he committed the crime for which he is on trial. As Federal and revised Uniform Rule (1986) 404(b) put it:

> Evidence of other crimes, wrongs, or acts is not admissible to prove the character of a person in order to show that he acted in conformity therewith. It may, however, be admissible for other purposes, such as proof of motive, opportunity, intent, preparation, plan, knowledge, identity or absence of mistake or accident.

As the rule indicates, there are numerous uses to which evidence of criminal acts may be put, and those enumerated are neither mutually exclusive nor collectively exhaustive. Subject to such caveats, examination is in order of the principal purposes for which the prosecution may introduce evidence of a defendant's bad character. Following this listing, some general observations will be offered about the use of other crimes evidence for these purposes. The permissible purposes include the following:

(1) To complete the story of the crime on trial by placing it in the context of nearby and nearly contemporaneous happenings. For example, in a prosecution for the murder of one child, the state was allowed to show that the defendant shot the child along with his other children and his wife while they were asleep. The phrases "same transaction" or, less happily, "res gestae" often are used to denote such evidence. This rationale should be applied only when reference to the other crimes is essential to a coherent and intelligible description of the offense at bar.

(2) To prove the existence of a larger plan, scheme, or conspiracy, of which the crime on trial is a part. For example, when a criminal steals a car to use it in a robbery, the

automobile theft can be proved in a prosecution for the robbery. Although some courts construe "common plan" more broadly, each crime should be an integral part of an overarching plan explicitly conceived and executed by the defendant or his confederates. This will be relevant as showing motive, and hence the doing of the criminal act, the identity of the actor, or his intention.

(3) To prove other crimes by the accused so nearly identical in method as to earmark them as the handiwork of the accused. Much more is demanded than the mere repeated commission of crimes of the same class, such as repeated murders, robberies or rapes. The pattern and characteristics of the crimes must be so unusual and distinctive as to be like a signature. For example, in *Rex v. Smith*, the "brides of the bath" case, George Joseph Smith was accused of murdering Bessie Mundy by drowning her in the small bathtub of their quarters in a boarding house. Mundy had left all her property to Smith in a will executed after a bigamous marriage ceremony. The trial court allowed the prosecution to show that Smith "married" several other women whom he drowned in their baths after they too left him their property. In all the drownings, Smith took elaborate steps to make it appear that he was not present during the drownings. The Court of Criminal Appeal affirmed the resulting conviction on the ground that the evidence in connection with Mundy's death alone made out a prima facie case, and the other incidents were properly admitted "for the purpose of shewing the design of the appellant."

(4) To show, by similar acts or incidents, that the act in question was not performed inadvertently, accidentally, involuntarily, or without guilty knowledge. *Rex v. Smith* falls in this category. The death of one bride in the bath might be an accident, but three drownings cannot be explained so innocently. Another classic example of the "improbability" logic is the "baby farming" case of *Makin v. Attor-*

ney General of New South Wales. The remains of thirteen infants were discovered in places where John and Sarah Makin were living or had lived, and the Crown charged the Makins with the murder of two of these children. One was identified by his clothing and hair. His mother testified that the Makins had agreed to adopt her son in exchange for only three pounds. The jury convicted the Makins of murdering the boy whose remains had been identified. On appeal, the couple argued that all the evidence concerning other missing children should not have been admitted. The Privy Council rejected this argument. Although its opinion did little to explain the basis for this conclusion, counsel for the Crown had stressed that "the recurrence of the unusual phenomenon of bodies of babies having been buried in an unexplained manner in a similar part of premises previously occupied" implied that the deaths were "wilful and not accidental." In these cases, the similarities between the act charged and the extrinsic acts need not be as extensive and striking as is required under purpose (3), and the various acts need not be manifestations of an explicit, unifying plan, as required for purpose (2).

(5) To establish motive. The evidence of motive may be probative of the identity of the criminal or of malice or specific intent. This reasoning commonly is applied in cases in which a husband charged with murdering his wife had previously assaulted or threatened her, evincing not merely a general disposition toward violence, but a virulent hostility toward a specific individual.

An application of this principle to cases in which the defendant is charged with conduct that interferes with the enforcement of the law enables the prosecution to prove that the defendant committed a crime that motivated the interference.[1] Finally, a variation of the reasoning permits proof of a consciousness of guilt as evidenced by criminal acts of the accused that are designed to obstruct justice or to avoid punishment for a crime.

---

§ 190

1. Grandison v. State, 506 A.2d 580, 605 (Md.1986) (indictment in federal narcotics case admissible in state prosecution for hiring an assassin to kill witness in federal

case); State v. Helling, 391 N.W.2d 648 (S.D.1986) (prior DWI convictions admissible to show motive for flight from accident and fabrication of "phantom driver" story).

(6) To establish opportunity, in the sense of access to or presence at the scene of the crime or in the sense of possessing distinctive or unusual skills or abilities employed in the commission of the crime charged. For example, a defendant charged with a burglary in which a sophisticated alarm system was deactivated might be shown to have neutralized similar systems in the course of other burglaries.

(7) To show, without considering motive, that defendant acted with malice, deliberation, or the requisite specific intent. Thus, weapons seized in an arrest have been held admissible to show an "intent to promote and protect" a conspiracy to import illicit drugs.

(8) To prove identity. Although this is indisputably one of the ultimate purposes for which evidence of other criminal conduct will be received and frequently is included in the list of permissible purposes for other-crimes evidence, it is rarely a distinct ground for admission. Almost always, identity is the inference that flows from one or more of the theories just listed. The second (larger plan), third (distinctive device), and sixth (motive) seem to be most often relied upon to show identity. Certainly, the need to prove identity should not be, in itself, a ticket to admission. In addition, the courts tend to apply stricter standards when the desired inference pertains to identity as opposed to state of mind.

(9) To show a passion or propensity for unusual and abnormal sexual relations. Initially, proof of other sex crimes was confined to offenses involving the same parties, but many jurisdictions now admit proof of other sex offenses with other persons, at least as to offenses involving sexual aberrations. Federal Rules of Evidence 413 and 414, added by Congress in 1994, allow the broadest conceivable use of "similar crimes" in sexual assault and child molestation cases, making "evidence of defendant's commission" of other such offenses "admissible . . . for its bearing on any matter to which it is relevant."

Unlike the other purposes for other-crimes evidence, the sex-crime exception flaunts the general prohibition of evidence whose only purpose is to invite the inference that a defendant who committed a previous crime is disposed toward committing crimes, and therefore is more likely to have committed the one at bar. Although one can argue for such an exception in sex offense cases in which there is some question as to whether the alleged victim consented (or whether the accused might have thought there was consent), a more sweeping exception is particularly difficult to justify. It rests either on an unsubstantiated empirical claim that one rather broad category of criminals are more likely to be repeat offenders than all others or on a policy of giving the prosecution some extra ammunition in its battle against alleged sex criminals.

(10) To impeach an accused who takes the witness stand by introducing past convictions.

A number of procedural and other substantive considerations also affect the admissibility of other crimes evidence pursuant to these ten exceptions. To begin with, the fact that the defendant is guilty of another relevant crime need not be proved beyond a reasonable doubt. The measure of proof that the defendant is guilty of the other crime has been variously described, ranging from "sufficient . . . to support a finding by the jury," to "a preponderance," to "substantial," to "clear and convincing." If the applicable standard is satisfied, then the other crimes evidence should be potentially admissible even if the defendant was acquitted of the other charge.

Second, the connection between the evidence and the permissible purpose should be clear, and the issue on which the other crimes evidence is said to bear should be the subject of a genuine controversy. For example, if the prosecution maintains that the other crime reveals defendant's guilty state of mind, then his intent must be disputed. Thus, if the defendant does not deny that the acts were deliberate, the prosecution may not introduce the evidence merely to show that the acts were not accidental. Likewise, if the accused does not deny performing the acts charged, the exceptions pertaining to identification are unavailing.

Finally, even if one or more of the valid purposes for admitting other crimes evidence is appropriately invoked, there is still the need to balance its probative value against the usual counterweights described in § 185. When the sole purpose of the other crimes evidence is to show some propensity to commit the crime at trial, there is no room for ad hoc balancing. The evidence is then unequivocally inadmissible—this is the meaning of the rule against other crimes evidence. But the fact that there is an accepted logical basis for the evidence other than the forbidden one of showing a proclivity for criminality does not preclude the jury from relying on a defendant's apparent propensity toward criminal behavior.[2] Accordingly, most authority recognizes that the problem is not merely one of pigeonholing, but of classifying and then balancing. In deciding whether the danger of unfair prejudice and the like substantially outweighs the incremental probative value, a variety of matters must be considered, including the strength of the evidence as to the commission of the other crime, the similarities between the crimes, the interval of time that has elapsed between the crimes, the need for the evidence, the efficacy of alternative proof, and the degree to which the evidence probably will rouse the jury to overmastering hostility.

§ 191. Good Character as Evidence of Lawful Conduct: Proof by the Accused and Rebuttal by the Government

The prosecution, as we saw in the preceding section, generally is forbidden to initiate evidence of the bad character of the defendant merely to imply that, being a bad person, he is more likely to commit a crime. This rule, in turn, is a corollary of the more general proscription on the use of character as circumstantial evidence of conduct. Yet, when the table is turned and the defendant in a criminal case seeks to offer evidence of his good character to imply that he is unlikely to have committed a crime, the general rule against propensity evidence is not applied. In both situations, the character evidence is relevant circumstantial evidence, but when the accused chooses to rely on it to exonerate himself, the problem of prejudice is altogether different. Now, knowledge of the accused's character may prejudice the jury in his *favor*, but the magnitude of the prejudice or its social cost is thought to be less. Thus, the common law and the Federal and Revised Uniform Rules of Evidence permit the defendant, but not the government, to open the door to character evidence.

Not all aspects of the accused's character are open to scrutiny under this exception. The prevailing view is that only pertinent traits— those involved in the offense charged—are provable. One charged with theft might offer evidence of honesty, while someone accused of murder might show that he is peaceable, but not vice versa. A few general traits, like being law-abiding, seem relevant to almost any accusation.

The common law has vacillated as regards the methods of establishing the good character of the accused. A rule of relatively recent origin limits proof to evidence of reputation for the pertinent traits. This constraint prevents a witness from giving a personal opinion and also prohibits testimony concerning specific acts or their absence.

The Federal and Revised Uniform Evidence Rules reinstate the earlier common law approach. Rule 405(a) provides, in part, that:

> In all cases in which evidence of character or a trait of character of a person is admissible, proof may be made by testimony as to reputation or by testimony in the form of an opinion.

This liberalization was not achieved without debate. It allows expert opinion testimony about an accused's character traits, subject to the court's residual power to screen for prejudice, distraction, and time-consumption. Nevertheless, like the common law rules, it does not allow evidence of particular incidents. For example, a federal inspector charged with accepting a bribe can call a character witness to show his reputation for being honest, but he

---

2. Dunn v. United States, 307 F.2d 883, 886 (5th Cir. 1962) ("one cannot unring a bell; after the thrust of the saber it is difficult to say forget the wound").

may not call other meat packers to testify that he did not solicit bribes from them.

Where reputation evidence is employed, it may be confined to reputation at approximately the time of the alleged offense. Traditionally, only testimony as to the defendant's reputation in the community where the accused resided was allowed, but increasing urbanization has prompted the acceptance of evidence as to reputation within other substantial groups of which the accused is a constantly interacting member, such as the locale where defendant works.

When defendant does produce evidence of his good character as regards traits pertinent to the offense charged, whether by way of reputation or opinion testimony, he frequently is said to have placed his character "in issue." The phrase is misleading. That a defendant relies on character witnesses to indicate that he is not predisposed to commit the type of crime in question does not transform his character into an operative fact upon which guilt or innocence may turn. Defendant simply opens the door to proof of certain character traits as circumstantial evidence of whether he committed the act charged with the requisite state of mind.

Ordinarily, if the defendant chooses to inject his character into the trial in this sense, he does so by producing witnesses who testify to his good character. By relating a personal history supportive of good character, however, the defendant may achieve the same result.[1] Whatever the method, once the defendant gives evidence of pertinent character traits to show that he is not guilty, his claim of possession of these traits—but only these traits—is open to rebuttal by cross-examination or direct testimony of prosecution witnesses. The prosecution may cross-examine a witness who has testified to the accused's reputation to probe the witness' knowledge of the community opinion, not only generally, but specifically as to whether the witness "has heard" that the defendant has committed particular prior criminal acts that conflict with the reputation vouched for on direct examination. Likewise, if a witness gives his opinion of defendant's character, then the prosecution can allude to pertinent bad acts by asking whether the witness knew of these matters in forming his opinion.[2]

This power of the cross-examiner to re-open old wounds is replete with possibilities for prejudice. Accordingly, certain limitations should be observed. The general responsibility of trial courts to weigh probative value against prejudice does not vanish because reference to other crimes or wrongs takes the form of insinuation or innuendo rather than concrete evidence. The extent and nature of the cross-examination demands restraint and supervision. Some questions are improper under any circumstances. For instance, questions about the effect of the current charges on reputation or opinion usually are barred on the ground that it is unfairly prejudicial to ask the witness to indulge in a hypothetical assumption of the defendant's guilt. As a precondition to cross-examination about other wrongs, the prosecutor should reveal, outside the hearing of the jury, what the basis is for believing in the rumors or incidents he proposes to ask about. The court then should determine whether there is a substantial basis for the cross-examination. When cross-examination is allowed, a jury instruction explaining the limited purpose of the inquiry may be advisable.

The other prosecutorial counterthrust to the defendant's proof of good character is not so easily abused. The government may produce witnesses to swear to defendant's bad reputation or, currently in most jurisdictions, their opinion of defendant's character. As with defense character witnesses, the strictures concerning pertinent traits and remoteness apply.

§ 191

1. Courts generally allow a defendant leeway "to let the jury know who he is." State v. Stokes, 523 P.2d 364, 366 (Kan.1974) ("background information" and "biographical data" such as "place of birth, education, length of residence in the community, length of marriage, size of family, occupation, place of employment, service in armed forces" are not character evidence entitling prosecution to respond with evidence of bad character).

2. Government of Virgin Islands v. Roldan, 612 F.2d 775, 778 (3d Cir.1979) (proper for government to ask on redirect whether witness who testified on cross that defendant "is a man that never bother anybody" knew of defendant's previous murder conviction).

The courts had divided over the admissibility as rebuttal evidence of judgments of convictions for recent crimes displaying the same traits, but with the adoption of the federal rules, few jurisdictions allow any proof of specific instances of misconduct as rebuttal evidence.

§ 192. Character in Civil Cases Where Crime Is in Issue

As explained above in § 191, in criminal cases the law relaxes its ban on evidence of character to show conduct to the extent of permitting a defendant to produce evidence of good character. It is not unusual in civil litigation, however, for one party to accuse another of conduct that amounts to a criminal offense. For instance, much of the conduct that is the subject of civil antitrust, securities, and civil rights cases as well as a substantial proportion of more traditional civil actions, could also provide grist for the public prosecutor's mill.

Where the homologous crimes are largely regulatory or administrative, it may seem inappropriate to accord the civil party the same dispensation given criminal defendants whose lives or liberties are in jeopardy. But what of the party whose adversary's pleading or proof accuses him of what would be an offense involving moral turpitude, as in an action for conversion, a complaint arising from an alleged incident of police brutality, or a suit for a breach of a fire insurance policy in which the insurer refuses to pay because it believes that the insured set the fire? Some courts have thought that the damage that may be done to the party's standing, reputation and relationships warrants according the civil defendant the same special dispensation. These courts therefore permitted the party to introduce evidence of good reputation for the traits involved.

But this has never been the majority view. Since the consequences of civil judgments are less severe than those flowing from a criminal conviction, most courts have declined to pay the price that the concession would demand in terms of possible prejudice, consumption of time, and distraction from the issue. Although the balance may be arguable, the Federal and Revised Uniform Rules of Evidence adhere to the majority position. Rule 404 bars evidence of character in civil cases to show how a person probably acted on a particular occasion.

§ 193. Character of Victim in Cases of Assault, Murder, and Rape

A well established exception to the rule forbidding character evidence to prove conduct applies to homicide and assault cases in which there is a dispute as to who was the first aggressor. Under this exception, the accused can introduce evidence of the victim's character for turbulence and violence. The evidence must be directed to the victim's reputation or opinion rather than to specific acts. In response, the prosecution may adduce evidence that the victim was a characteristically peaceful person.

Federal and Revised Uniform Evidence Rule 404(a)(2) address such situations. They speak to "pertinent" character traits of the victims of crimes generally and specifically to the trait of nonviolence in homicide cases. They exempt from the usual rule of exclusion

> Evidence of a pertinent trait of character of the victim of the crime offered by the accused, or by the prosecution to rebut the same, or evidence of the character trait of peacefulness of the victim offered by the prosecution in a homicide case to rebut evidence that the victim was the first aggressor.

That the character of the *victim* is being proved renders inapposite the usual concern over the untoward impact of evidence of the defendant's poor character on the jury's assessment of the case against the defendant. There is, however, a risk of a different form of prejudice. Learning of the victim's bad character could lead the jury to think that the victim merely "got what he deserved" and to acquit for that reason. Nevertheless, at least in murder and perhaps in battery cases as well, when the identity of the first aggressor is really in doubt, the probative value of the evidence ordinarily justifies taking this risk.

In some jurisdictions, a claim of self-defense may not trigger, in itself, the prosecution's power to introduce rebuttal evidence of the victim's non-violent nature. By one view, such counterproof is allowed only when the accused opens the door specifically by evidence of the victim's character for belligerence. The rule quoted above clearly follows the contrary view in homicide cases. Since a dead victim cannot attest to his peaceable behavior during the fatal encounter, the last clause of Rule 404(a)(2) provides that whenever the accused claims self-defense and offers *any* type of evidence that the deceased was the first aggressor, the government may reply with evidence of the peaceable character of the deceased.

A similar exception to the general rule against the use of character to prove conduct pertained to the defense of consent in sexual assault cases. In the past, the courts generally admitted evidence of the victim's character for chastity, although there were diverging lines of authority on whether the proof could be by specific instances and on whether the prosecution could put evidence of chastity in its case in chief.

In the 1970s, however, nearly all jurisdictions enacted criminal "rape shield" laws "to protect rape victims from degrading and embarrassing disclosure of intimate details about their private lives, to encourage reporting of sexual assaults, and to prevent wasting time on distracting collateral and irrelevant matters."[1] The reforms ranged from barring all evidence of the victim's character for chastity to merely requiring a preliminary hearing to screen out inadmissible evidence on the issue.

Federal Rule of Evidence 412 lies between these extremes. As originally promulgated, Rule 412 applied only to prosecutions for sexual assault. Reversing the traditional preference for proof of character by reputation, in criminal cases the rule bars all reputation and opinion evidence of the victim's past sexual conduct, but permits evidence of specific incidents if certain conditions are met. Procedurally, the proponent of the evidence ordinarily must give written notice before trial, and the court must conduct an *in camera* hearing before admitting the disfavored evidence. Substantively, in criminal cases Rule 412 distinguishes between evidence of past sexual behavior of the victim with the accused and sexual conduct involving other individuals. If the evidence pertains to past conduct with an accused who claims consent, it may be admitted to prove or disprove consent. But if the evidence pertains to acts of the victim with other individuals, the defendant may use it only to prove that someone else was the "the source of semen or injury." Finally, the rule specifies that if the constitution mandates it, the defendant may introduce evidence of the victim's prior sexual conduct.

Resort to an undefined, residual provision to avoid an otherwise unconstitutionally sweeping ban on proof of the victim's character is inferior to an articulation of the full range of allowable uses of sexual history evidence. It places trial courts in the awkward position of having to make constitutional rulings rather than being able to apply a self-contained and structured rule of evidence. Be that as it may, a few cases have identified circumstances in which a defendant is constitutionally entitled to introduce evidence of an alleged victim's sexual conduct under the due process or confrontation clauses. For example, in *Olden v. Kentucky*,[2] the Supreme Court held that a rape defendant's right to confront his accusers entitled him to inquire into the alleged victim's cohabitation with another man to show that she had a reason to falsely accuse the defendant.[3]

A 1994 amendment extends the federal rape shield law to all civil cases "involving alleged sexual misconduct." This augmented rule surely reaches civil suits for sexual assaults that could be (or were) the subject of criminal actions, and it probably extends to

§ 193

1. United States v. Torres, 937 F.2d 1469, 1472 (9th Cir. 1991).

2. 488 U.S. 227 (1988).

3. A state court had prevented this inquiry, not on the basis of a rape shield law, but on the ground that it was unfairly prejudicial because the jury would have learned that the victim, a white woman, was living with a black man.

civil rights claims for sexual harassment. However, the shield is weaker in the civil context than in criminal cases, where the rule excludes all evidence of the victim's sexual character—no matter how probative—that is not within the categorical exceptions. In contrast, Rule 412(b)(2) adopts a balancing test with the scales tilted against admission. It forbids admission of any type of evidence for sexual disposition unless the "probative value substantially outweighs the danger of harm to any victim and of unfair prejudice to any party."

Under state laws, evidence of the victim's sexual experience generally is admissible, upon notice, for specified purposes: to demonstrate that the victim, having had previous voluntary sexual relations with defendant, consented to the alleged attack; that the victim has a motive falsely to accuse defendant; that the witness characteristically fantasizes sexual assaults; that the witness knowingly brings false accusations of sexual misconduct; that a young child who gave a detailed account of a sexual assault already possessed the knowledge to do so; or that someone else may have been the source of semen or trauma to the witness.

A recurring difficulty under all the statutes arises in determining the conduct that is shielded from inquiry. The shield laws certainly apply to direct evidence of other acts of sexual intercourse or contact, for these laws are intended to protect victims from the embarrassment of having to disclose intimate sexual details. Concern for personal privacy and for not discouraging victims from complaining extends as well to private behavior that implies sexual intercourse or contact, such as the use of contraceptives or the presence of venereal disease. As one moves to conduct that is less directly linked to sex acts, however, the applicability of a rape shield law becomes more arguable. Should modes of dress or prior accusations of rape be considered "sexual conduct" or "sexual behavior" that is exempt from inquiry or proof? The statutes and cases are divided.

The rape shield laws have withstood constitutional attacks. They reflect the judgment that most evidence about chastity has far too little probative value on the issue of consent to justify extensive inquiry into the victim's sexual history. Given the recognition of this notion in the case law emerging during the period preceding their enactment, however, whether special rape shield laws were necessary to alter the law is questionable. Furthermore, there is scant evidence that the reforms have achieved the goals of increasing reports or convictions of rapes. Thus, the true value of the rape shield laws may be symbolic rather than instrumental.

§ 194. Evidence of Character to Impeach a Witness

The familiar practice of impeaching a witness by producing evidence of bad character for veracity amounts to using a character trait to prove that a witness is testifying falsely. As such, it is a true exception to the policy against admitting evidence of a character trait solely to show action in conformity with that trait. The chapter on impeachment discusses the scope of this exception.

§ 195. Habit and Custom as Evidence of Conduct on a Particular Occasion

Although the courts frown on evidence of traits of character when introduced to prove how a person or organization acted on a given occasion, they are more receptive to evidence of personal habits or of the customary behavior of organizations. To understand this difference, one must appreciate the distinction between habit and character. The two are easily confused. People sometimes speak of a habit for care, a habit for promptness, or a habit of forgetfulness. They may say that an individual has a bad habit of stealing or lying. Evidence of these "habits" would be identical to the kind of evidence that is the target of the general rule against character evidence. Character is a generalized description of a person's disposition, or of the disposition in respect to a general trait, such as honesty, temperance or peacefulness. Habit, in the present context, is more specific. It denotes one's regular response to a repeated situation. If we speak of a character for care, we think of the person's tendency to act prudently in all the varying situations of life—in business, at home, in handling automobiles and in walking across the street. A habit, on the other hand, is the person's regular practice of responding to a particular kind of situation with a specific type of conduct. Thus, a person may be in the habit of bounding down a certain stairway two or three steps at a time, of patronizing a particular pub after each day's work, or of driving his automobile without using a seatbelt. The doing of the habitual act may become semi-automatic, as with a driver who invariably signals before changing lanes.

Evidence of habits that come within this definition has greater probative value than does evidence of general traits of character. Furthermore, the potential for prejudice is substantially less. By and large, the detailed patterns of situation-specific behavior that constitute habits are unlikely to provoke such sympathy or antipathy as would distort the process of evaluating the evidence.

As a result, many jurisdictions accept the proposition that evidence of habit is admissible to show an act. These courts only reject the evidence categorically if the putative habit is not sufficiently regular or uniform, or if the circumstances are not sufficiently similar to outweigh the dangers of prejudice, distraction and time-consumption. The Federal, Revised Uniform, and Model Rules all follow this pattern. A few state courts, however, exclude evidence of habit altogether. Others admit it only if there are no eyewitnesses to testify about the events that are said to have triggered the habitual behavior.

Even the jurisdictions that are reluctant to accept evidence of personal habits are willing to allow evidence of the "custom" of a business organization, if reasonably regular and uniform. This may be because there is no confusion between character traits and business practices, as there is between character and habit, or it may reflect the belief that the need for regularity in business and the organizational sanctions which may exist when employees deviate from the established procedures give extra guarantees that the questioned activity followed the usual custom. Thus, evidence that a letter was written and signed in the course of business and put in the regular place for mailing usually will be admitted to prove that it was mailed.

The existence of the personal habit or the business custom may be established by a knowledgeable witness's testimony that there was such a habit or practice. Evidence of specific instances may also be used. Naturally, there must be enough instances to permit the finding of a habit, the circumstances under which the habit or custom is followed must be present, and, as always, there are the limitations for cumulativeness, remoteness, unnecessary inflammatory quality, and so on.

Chapter 18

SIMILAR HAPPENINGS AND TRANSACTIONS

Table of Sections

§ 196. Other Claims, Suits, or Defenses of a Party

Should a party be permitted to cast doubt on the merits of the claim at bar by demonstrating that an opponent has advanced similar claims or defenses against others in previous litigation? Inescapably, two conflicting goals shape the rules of evidence in this area. Exposing fraudulent claims is important, but so is protecting innocent litigants from unfair prejudice. The easy cases are those in which one of these considerations clearly predominates. If the evidence reveals that a party has made previous, very similar claims and that these claims were fraudulent, then almost universally the evidence will be admissible despite the dangers of distraction and time-consumption with regard to the quality of these other claims, and despite the general prohibition on using evidence of bad character solely to show conduct on a given occasion. At the other pole, if the evidence is merely that the plaintiff is a chronic litigant with respect to all sorts of claims, the courts consider the slight probative value overborne by the countervailing factors. This evidence they usually exclude.

In between lie the harder cases. Suppose the evidence is that the party suing for an alleged loss, such as fire damage to his property or personal injury in a collision, has made many previous claims of similar losses. The evidence surely is relevant. The probability of so many similar accidents happening to the same person by chance alone can be vanishingly small. Yet, rare events do happen. There will always be some people who suffer the slings and arrows of outrageous fortune. In itself, this fact gives no indication of prejudice. Presumably, a jury can come to a reasonable judgment as to the relative likelihood of the alternatives. Nevertheless, there is a form of prejudice inherent in this situation. The jury may disapprove of a person precisely because that person is litigious. The judge, balancing probative value against prejudice, should admit the evidence only if there is a basis for concluding that the other claims were fabricated.

This foundation could be supplied by distinct evidence of fraud, or it might be inferred when the probability of coincidence seems so negligible as to leave fraud as the only plausible explanation. The likelihood of repeated, substantially identical claims depends on the number of claims and the probability of each incident. In addition, the degree of similarity among the claims is important, inasmuch as a series of disparate but bona fide claims seems more likely than a string of very similar ones.

So far, we have discussed evidence of a party's other claims introduced to raise a question about the instant claim or suit. Evidence of a witness' past accusations or defenses introduced to attack the veracity of that witness presents comparable problems. In these situations, a litigant might seek to prove that the other accusations have been false as circumstantial evidence that the testimony just delivered is also false. Although this is a species of character evidence to show conduct, it usually will be admissible to impeach the witness. Even without proof that the other accusations were false, the very fact that the witness repeatedly accuses many others of the same kind of behavior may seem too extraordinary to be explained as a mere coincidence. The logic and issues here are perfectly analogous to those already addressed with regard to the filing of repeated, similar suits or claims. However, in keeping with the customary relaxation of the standard of admissibility on cross-examination, it is generally easier to elicit admissions about the other claims on cross-examination than it is to introduce the evidence by the testimony of the proponent's witnesses.

§ 197. Other Misrepresentations and Frauds

In cases alleging fraud or misrepresentation, proof that the defendant perpetrated similar deceptions frequently is received in evidence. Such admission is not justified on the theory of "once a cheat, always a cheat," for

that would contravene the ban on using character traits solely as propensity evidence of conduct on the occasion. Rather, at least one of three well entrenched alternate theories typically is available. To begin with, evidence of other frauds may help establish the element of knowledge—by suggesting that defendant knew that the alleged misrepresentation was false or by indicating that defendant's participation in an alleged fraudulent scheme was not innocent or accidental.

Second, the evidence may be admissible with respect to the closely related element of intent to deceive. When other misrepresentations are used to show intent or knowledge, they need not be identical nor made under precisely the same circumstances as the one in issue.

Finally, if the uttering of the misrepresentations or the performance of the fraudulent conduct is contested, then other misrepresentations or fraudulent acts that are evidently part of the same overall plan or scheme may be admissible to prove the conduct of the defendant. The requirement of a common plan or scheme is well recognized, but it appears to be of questionable value in civil cases. When there is conflicting testimony as to the making of the misrepresentation at issue, the value of evidence of other, very similar misrepresentations—whether or not part of the same plan or scheme—in resolving the controversy should be sufficient to outweigh the danger of prejudice. As it is, the courts often manage to discern a larger plan when the various acts could well be described as separate transactions.[1]

---

§ 197

1. For example, in In re Brandon's Estate, 433 N.E.2d 501 (N.Y.1982), the Appellate Division had upheld the admission of two prior judgments of undue influence "as tending to establish a common scheme or plan under which appellants inveigle into Murphy's place of residence aged and ailing residents of her nursing home for the purpose of stripping them of their life savings." Noting that the courts often are too ready to find a common plan, the Court of Appeals rejected this reasoning. It explained that "[u]nlike the intent exception, mere similarity between the acts is an insufficient predicate for admissibility under the common scheme or plan exception. * * * Indeed, there must be such a clear concurrence of common features—i.e., time, place and character—that 'the various

acts are naturally to be explained as caused by a general plan of which they are the individual manifestations.'" Id. at 504. Here, it concluded, "there was no showing that the [prior] incidents had any direct connection, either in fact or in Mrs. Murphy's mind, with the fraud or undue influence visited upon Alice Brandon." Despite the striking similarities in the treatment of three elderly women, the Court of Appeals determined that the incidents could well be characterized as "separate and independent transactions entered into as the occasion arose." Id. at 505. With *Brandon*, compare Baldwin v. Warwick, 213 F.2d 485, 486 (9th Cir.1954) (testimony that defendants had drugged the drinks of other real estate agents and then won heavily from them at cards admissible to show an "overall scheme" that included drugging plaintiff's drinks

§ 198.   Other Contracts and Business Transactions

Evidence concerning other contracts or business dealings may be relevant to prove the terms of a contract, the meaning of these terms, a business habit or custom, and occasionally, the authority of an agent. As to many of these uses, there is little controversy. Certainly, evidence of other transactions between the same parties readily is received when relevant to show the meaning they probably attached to the terms of a contract. Likewise, when the existence of the terms is in doubt, evidence of similar contracts between the same parties is accepted as a vehicle for showing of a custom or continuing course of dealing between them, and as such, as evidence of the terms of the present bargain. Also, when the authority of an agent is in question, other similar transactions that the agent has carried out on behalf of the principal are freely admitted.

In the past, many courts had balked when contracts *with others* were offered to show the terms or the making of the contract in suit. It is hard to understand why any hard and fast line should be drawn. As an historical matter, these decisions perhaps may be explained as manifestations of the perennial confusion between the sufficiency of an item of evidence to prove the proposition for which it is offered and its relevance to that proposition. In addition, these decisions reflect the beguiling power of the mystical phrase *res inter alios acta*. Yet, it seems clear that contracts of a party with third persons may show the party's customary practice and course of dealing and thus supply useful insights into the terms of the present agreement. Indeed, even if there are but one or two such contracts, they may be useful evidence. When, in a certain kind of transaction, a business has adopted a particular mode of handling a bargaining topic or standardized feature, such as warranty, discount or the like, it is often easier for it to cast a new contract in the same mold than it is to work out a new one. Moreover, some practices become so accepted in an industry that they may shape the meaning of most contracts in that field. As to these, evidence in the form of contracts or transactions involving neither of the parties may nevertheless be probative of the commercial relationship that exists between the parties.

Inasmuch as there is no general danger of unfair prejudice inherent in evidence of other business transactions, strict rules or limits on admissibility are inappropriate. The courts should admit such evidence in all cases where the testimony as to the terms of the present bargain is conflicting and where the judge finds that the risk of wasted time and confusion of issues does not substantially outweigh the probative value of the evidence of the other transactions. Many jurisdictions therefore leave evidence of other contracts or business dealings to the trial judge to evaluate on a case by case basis.

§ 199.   Other Sales of Similar Property as Evidence of Value

When the market value of property needs to be determined, the price actually paid in a competitive market for comparable items is an obvious place to look. Indeed, when presented with the sometimes wildly disparate estimates of professional appraisers, courts have remarked that the sales prices of comparable properties are the best evidence of value. The testimony of witnesses with first-hand knowledge of other sales, or reliable price lists, market reports, or the like may be received to show the market price.

The less homogeneous the product, the more difficulty there is in measuring market value in this way. Thus, cases involving land valuation, especially condemnation cases, frequently discuss the admissibility of evidence of other sales. A dying rule excludes the evidence entirely save in exceptional circumstances. The dominant view gives the judge discretion to admit evidence of other sales. The inquiry focuses on whether these sales have been suffi-

at various bars at which plaintiff shook dice with defendants after having shown them certain real estate); Kabel

v. Brady, 519 So.2d 912 (Ala.1987) (representations to patients that Medicare covers chiropractic services).

ciently recent, and whether the other land is sufficiently nearby and alike as to character, situation, usability, and improvements, as to make it clear that the two tracts are comparable in value. A weaker standard for similarity applies when the other sales are used as the basis for an expert judgment as to value instead of being introduced as independent evidence of value.

Since the value sought is what, on average, a willing buyer would have paid a willing seller, prices on other sales of a forced character, such as execution sales or condemnation awards for other tracts, generally are inadmissible. Many courts also exclude the condemnor's evidence of prices it paid to other owners on the theory that sales made in contemplation of condemnation do not approximate the relevant market price. Other courts, following what seems the better reasoned view, allow such evidence in the judge's discretion.

Of course, any other sale must be genuine, and the price must be paid or substantially secured. Although actual sale prices rather than asking prices typically are required, unaccepted offers made by a party may be admissible as statements of a party-opponent. Furthermore, unaccepted offers are admitted more easily when the offeror is available for examination or when there have been no consummated sales.

§ 200. Other Accidents and Injuries

The admissibility of evidence of other accidents and injuries is raised frequently in negligence and product liability cases. In light of the prejudice that such evidence can carry with it, and because of the rule that evidence of other accidents or their absence is not admissible solely to show a character or propensity for careful or careless behavior, most judges will scrutinize it carefully. Usually, a non-propensity purpose and a showing of sufficient similarity in the conditions giving rise to the various accidents is required. In practice, the various permissible purposes tend to blend together in that more than one typically is available, but for clarity of analysis we shall try to isolate each valid purpose for admitting evidence of other accidents.

To begin with, the evidence may be admissible to prove the existence of a particular physical condition, situation, or defect. For instance, the fact that several persons slipped and fell in the same location in a supermarket can help show that a slippery substance was on the floor. At the same time, this proof is a bit sensational. Unless the defendant strenuously disputes the presence of the condition, the court may reject the evidence of the similar accidents as unduly prejudicial and cumulative.

Second, the evidence of other accidents or injuries may be admissible to help show that the defect or dangerous situation caused the injury. Thus, instances in which other patients placed on the same drug therapy contracted the same previously rare disease is circumstantial evidence that the drug caused the disease in plaintiff's case. As typically developed at trial, such evidence of other accidents is a crude version of a retrospective epidemiologic study. Since many unsuspected factors could contribute or cause the observed effects, the conditions of the other injuries and the present one must be similar. Although the use of evidence of other accidents to prove the existence of a condition (the first purpose listed above) can overlap the use of the evidence to prove that the condition caused plaintiff's injuries, ordinarily, the need to use the evidence for this second purpose is plainer. Causation is frequently in genuine dispute, and circumstantial evidence may be of great value in pursuing this elusive issue. Thus, receptivity to evidence of similar happenings to show causation is heightened when the defendant contends that the alleged conduct could not possibly have caused the plaintiff's injury.

Third, and perhaps most commonly, evidence of other accidents or injuries may be used to show the risk that defendant's conduct created. If the extent of the danger is material to the case, as it almost always is in personal injury litigation, the fact that the same conditions produced harm on other occasions is a natural and convincing way of showing the hazard. The requirement of substantial similarity is applied strictly here.

Finally, the evidence of other accidents commonly is received to prove that the defendant knew, or should have known, of the danger. Of course, if defendant's duty is absolute, this theory is inapposite. In negligence cases, however, the duty is merely to use reasonable care to maintain safe conditions. Even in many strict product liability cases, demonstrating that the product is defective or unreasonably dangerous for its intended use requires an analysis of foreseeable risks.

When the evidence of other accidents is introduced to show notice of the danger, subsequent accidents are not admissible under this rationale. The proponent probably will want to show directly that the defendant had knowledge of the prior accidents, but the nature, frequency or notoriety of the incidents may well reveal that defendant knew of them or should have discovered the danger by due inspection. Since all that is required is that the previous injury or injuries be such as to call defendant's attention to the dangerous situation that resulted in the litigated accident, the similarity in the circumstances of the accidents can be considerably less than that which is demanded when the same evidence is used for one of the other valid purposes.

Having surveyed the utility of a history of accidents in establishing liability, we now consider the admissibility of a history of safety for exculpatory purposes. One might think that if proof of similar accidents is admissible in the judge's discretion to show that a particular condition or defect exists, or that the injury sued for was caused in a certain way, or that a situation is dangerous, or that defendant knew or should have known of the danger, then evidence of the absence of accidents during a period of similar exposure and experience likewise would be receivable to show that these facts do not exist in the case at bar. Indeed, it would seem perverse to tell a jury that one or two persons besides the plaintiff tripped on defendant's stairwell while withholding from them the further information that another thousand persons descended the same stairs without incident.

Yet, many decisions lay down just such a general rule against proof of absence of other accidents. Admittedly, there are special problems with proving the nonexistence of something. In particular, an absence of complaints does not necessarily mean that accidents have not been occurring. "Those who stumble without falling may be too busy to register a complaint, and complaints to one employee may not be passed on to the person who testifies that he has not heard of any trouble. Also, the condition of areas continually changes. The plaintiff may in fact be among the first to encounter a newly dangerous situation."[1] While these factors should be considered in balancing probative value against the usual counterweights, they do not justify a flat rule of exclusion. In some cases, excluding such proof of safety may be justified on the ground that the persons passing in safety were not exposed to the same conditions as those that prevailed when the plaintiff's injury occurred. The evidence of a thousand safe descents down the stairs would be far less convincing if it were revealed that all of these were made in daylight, while the two or three accidents occurred at night in poor lighting. However, the possibility that a very general safety record may obscure the influence of an important factor merely counsels for applying the traditional requirement of substantial similarity. When the experience sought to be proved is so extensive as to be sure to include an adequate number of similar situations, the similarity requirement should be considered satisfied.

Neither can the broad proscription be justified by the other considerations that affect the admissibility of evidence. The problems of prejudice and distraction over "collateral issues" seem much more acute when it comes to proof of other accidents than when evidence of an accident-free history is proffered. Indeed, the defendant will seldom open this door if there is any practical likelihood that the plaintiff will dispute the safety record.

Consequently, few recent decisions can be found applying a general rule of exclusion. A

§ 200

1. Richard O. Lempert & Stephen A. Saltzburg, A Modern Approach to Evidence 210 (2d ed. 1983).

large number of cases recognize that lack of other accidents may be admissible to show (1) absence of the defect or condition alleged, (2) the lack of a causal relationship between the injury and the defect or condition charged, (3) the nonexistence of an unduly dangerous situation, or (4) want of knowledge (or of grounds to realize) the danger.

Chapter 19

INSURANCE AGAINST LIABILITY

Table of Sections

§ 201. Insurance Against Liability

A formidable body of cases holds that evidence that a party is or is not insured against liability is not admissible on the issue of negligence. This doctrine rests on two premises. The first is the belief that insurance coverage reveals little about the likelihood that one will act carelessly. Subject to a few pathological exceptions, financial protection will not diminish the normal incentive to be careful, especially where life and limb are at stake. Similarly, the argument that insured individuals or firms are more prudent and careful, as a group, than those who are self-insurers seems tenuous, and also serves to counteract any force that the first argument may have. Thus, the relevance of the evidence of coverage is doubtful. In addition, there is concern that the evidence would be prejudicial—that the mention of insurance invites higher awards than are justified, and conversely, that the sympathy that a jury might feel for a defendant who must pay out of his own pocket could interfere with its evaluation of the evidence under the appropriate standard of proof. Although empirical research into these possible forms of prejudice yields no clear answers, the "shallow pocket" hypothesis seems better supported.

Despite these concerns and the general rule that evidence of the fact of insurance coverage is inadmissible to show negligence or reasonable care, such evidence frequently is received. As with the exclusionary rules discussed in Chapters 17 (Character and Habit) and 18 (Similar Happenings and Transactions), the evidence may be admitted for some other purpose, providing of course that its probative value on this other issue is not substantially outweighed by its prejudicial impact. The purposes for which such evidence may be offered are several. Federal and Revised Uniform Rule 411, which begins with declaration that "[e]vidence that a person was or was not insured against liability is not admissible upon the issue whether the person acted negligently or otherwise wrongfully," lists most of them. It states that "[t]his rule does not require the exclusion of evidence of insurance against liability when offered for another purpose, such as proof of agency, ownership or control, or bias or prejudice of a witness."

The fact that persons rarely purchase liability insurance to cover contingencies for which they are not responsible makes the evidence relevant to questions of agency, ownership, and control. The fact of insurance can be relevant to the bias of a witness in a number of ways. For example, the witness may be an investigator or other individual employed by the insurance company. Cross-examination affords the usual means of revealing the relationship between the company and the witness.

Plainly, these purposes do not exhaust the possibilities. Evidence of insurance may be admitted when it is an inseparable part of an admission of a party bearing on negligence or damages. And, there are some less common uses.

Furthermore, there are two other ways in which the fact of insurance can be brought home to the jury. Witnesses have been known to make unexpected and unresponsive references to insurance. In these situations, the judge may declare a mistrial, but it is a rare case in which he will do more than strike the reference and instruct the jury to ignore it. Finally, in the examination of prospective jurors, most jurisdictions allow questions about employment by or interest in insurance companies.

Despite its nearly universal acceptance, the wisdom of the general prohibition on injecting insurance into the trial, as it currently operates, is questionable. When the rule originated, insurance coverage of individuals was exceptional. In the absence of references to insurance at trial, a juror most probably would not have thought that a defendant was insured. Today, compulsory insurance laws for motorists are ubiquitous, and liability insurance for homeowners and businesses has become the norm. Most jurors probably assume that defendants are insured. Yet, few courts will allow a defendant to show that he is uninsured, unless the plaintiff has opened the door to such evidence. At a minimum, such a defendant, and indeed any party, should be entitled to an instruction that there has been no evidence as to whether or not any party is insured because the law is that the presence or absence of insurance should play no part in the case.

More fundamentally, the underlying soundness of the general rule forbidding disclosure of the fact of insurance has been the object of scathing criticism. Stripped to its essentials, the debate is not really over the application of the doctrines of relevancy and its counterweights. Hardly anyone questions the premise that the evidence is irrelevant to the exercise of reasonable care. Neither does anyone contend that a party has a right to put irrelevant evidence into the record. Rather, the arguments for the abandonment of the policy

of secrecy are either pragmatic or idealistic. The pragmatic argument is straightforward. The conspiracy of silence is hard to maintain. Its costs include extensive and unnecessary arguments, reversals, and retrials stemming from elusive questions of prejudice and good faith. This state of affairs might be tolerable if the revelations of insurance were truly fraught with prejudice. But, as we have suggested, most jurors probably presuppose the existence of liability insurance anyway, and the heart of the policy of nondisclosure is surrendered when jurors are examined about their connection with insurance companies. Consequently, the extent to which evidence of coverage or its absence is prejudicial is unclear. Even the direction in which such prejudice might work is obscure. In sum, the rule has become a hollow shell, expensive to maintain and of doubtful utility.

The other principal argument against the rule of secrecy is more difficult to evaluate, but standing alone, it is less persuasive. It arises from a certain conception of fairness—a conception that holds that the jury should know who the "real" parties in interest are. The insurance company, which under its policy has the exclusive right to employ counsel, defend the suit, and control the decision as to settling or contesting the action, is a party in all but name. Unfortunately, this argument begs the question. If the substantive law is that the depth of the defendant's pocket has nothing to do with liability or damages, then why should the jury be apprised of this fact? To be sure, in many cases the relative wealth of the parties is manifest. A multinational corporation cannot disguise itself as a struggling member of the proletariat. But where admittedly irrelevant characteristics can be removed from the courtroom without great strain, it is hard to see why they should be retained. In the end, therefore, it is the more pragmatic analysis that should be decisive. The benefits of a half-hearted policy of secrecy are not worth the costs. If disclosure of the fact of insurance really is prejudicial, the corrective is not a futile effort at concealment, but the usual fulfillment by the court of its function of explaining to the jury its duty to decide according to the facts and the substantive law, rather than upon sympathy, ability to pay, or concern about proliferating litigation and rising insurance premiums.

Chapter 20

EXPERIMENTAL AND SCIENTIFIC EVIDENCE

Table of Sections

§ 202. Pretrial Experiments

The dominant method of factual inquiry in the courts of law is observational. Witnesses relate what they have seen under naturally occurring conditions, and the judge or jury, observing the witnesses, accepts or rejects their stories with varying degrees of confidence. In many fields of science, naturalistic observations of people or things are also a principal means of gathering information (though the observations are made in a more structured fashion and are presented and analyzed in a different way). In other scientific disciplines, the major method for collecting data involves manipulating the environment. In its simplest and ideal form, a controlled experiment screens out or holds constant all extraneous variables so that the experimenter can measure the impact of the one factor of interest.

The opportunities for applying the experimental method to factual controversies that arise in litigation are immense, but they generally go unrecognized and unused. Some of the more frequently encountered types of experiments are tests of the composition or physical properties of substances or products, tests of the flammability or explosive properties of products, tests of the effects of drugs and other products on human beings or other organisms, tests of firearms to show characteristic, identifying features, or capabilities, tests of the visibility of objects or persons under certain conditions, tests of the speed of moving vehicles and of the effectiveness of brakes, headlights or other components. Some of these experiments can be simple affairs, such as driving an automobile along a stretch of road to determine where a particular object on the road first becomes visible. Others are more complicated, requiring sophisticated machinery, statistical analysis of the results, or other specialized knowledge or procedures. Testimony describing the experiments may be received as substantive evidence, or it may form the basis for an expert opinion. Although scientific or engineering experts conduct most pretrial experiments, the simplest experiments are often the most convincing, and scientific sophistication is not always necessary or cost-effective.[1]

Pretrial experiments will be admitted as evidence if their probative value is not substantially outweighed by the usual counterweights of prejudice, confusion of the issues, and time consumption. The only form of prejudice that might operate in this context is that of giving experimental results more weight than they deserve. As discussed in the next section, this can be a barrier to admissibility when the interpretation of the experiment would require expert scientific testimony. The extent to which the presentation will be distracting or time-consuming will vary from case to case. As for probative value, the courts often speak of the need for similarity between the conditions of the experiment and those that pertained to the litigated happening. The burden of showing substantial similarity is on the proponent.

In practice, however, the similarity requirement is not applied to all pretrial experiments, or if it is nominally applied, the notion of "similarity" becomes almost infinitely flexible. In the words of one state supreme court, "[s]ubstantial similarity does not require identity of conditions, but only that degree of similarity which will insure that the results of the experiment are probative."[2] The requirement is at its strictest when the experiment expressly seeks to replicate the event in question to show that things could (or could not) have happened as alleged. But even in these case-specific experiments, differences between the experimental and actual conditions that only could make it harder for the experiment to be favorable to the proponent should be no obstacle to admission. Furthermore, an event can never be perfectly reenacted or simulated. There are too many details to keep track of, and some defy precise re-creation. For example, the human agent in the happening to which the experiment pertains may be deceased, the vehicle may be destroyed, the surrounding circumstances may be known only vaguely, or the process of duplicating what actually happened may be too dangerous. Consequently, although the similarity formula is sometimes overrigidly applied, most courts recognize that the requirement is a relative one. If enough of the obviously important factors are duplicated in the experiment, and if the failure to control other possibly relevant variables is justified, the court may conclude that the experiment is sufficiently enlightening that it should come into evidence. This determination typically is subject to review only for an abuse of discretion.

On the other hand, the similarity requirement either is not applied or is highly diluted when the pretrial experiment does not purport to replicate the essential features of a particular happening. There are many perfectly acceptable experiments of this nature. For example, if one party contends that certain acts or omissions could not produce—under any circumstances—the result in question, then the other party may conduct an experiment to falsify this hypothesis. Of course, the closer the experiment is to the conditions that actually pertained, the more useful the experiment will be, but merely refuting the opposing party's sweeping claim may be sufficiently valuable to make the evidence admissible. Similarly, the proponent may offer to prove that something was not the cause of the actionable result by means of an experiment showing that some other agent can bring about the same result. Finally, the experiment may be

§ 202

1. Johnson for Johnson v. Young Men's Christian Ass'n, 651 P.2d 1245, 1248–49 (Mont.1982) (tossing diving ring into pool at location where drowning victim was found and timing how long it took two boys to retrieve it "supported the conclusion that it took one to one and one-half minutes to retrieve the victim from the pool," an elapsed time too short to have caused permanent brain damage); Larson v. Meyer, 161 N.W.2d 165 (N.D.1968)

(whether tractor could pull milk truck out of rut without overturning).

2. Hermreck v. State, 956 P.2d 335, 339 (Wyo.1998) (holding admissible an experiment using a ten-year-old girl on a 20″ bicycle to determine how long it would take a seven-year-old boy on a 16″ bicycle to go from a standing start at the side of the road to the place where defendant's truck struck the bicycle).

introduced solely to illustrate or demonstrate a scientific principle or empirical finding that a jury, perhaps with the aid of an expert witness, can apply to the specifics of the case. Thus, experiments showing general properties of materials are admitted without confining the experiments to the conditions surrounding the litigated situation. Most of these analyses are referred to as tests rather than experiments. When this label is attached, the question becomes one, not of similarity, but of authentication—making sure that the right material was tested and that it underwent no essential alterations before testing. With all these limited purpose experiments, the issue, as always, is whether, on balance, the evidence will assist the jury.

At a conceptual level, the "substantial similarity" standard is somewhat frustrating. Its value lies in calling attention to the possible effect of differences on the implications of an experiment for the situation at bar. However, the requisite degree of similarity is not always obvious. One could say that when experiments reveal properties or traits that clearly apply under a wide range of conditions, substantial similarity is present even if the conditions are quite different. After all, there is little point in controlling for irrelevant conditions, and if physical theory indicates that the gross differences are superficial and inconsequential, the circumstances are similar in the relevant respects. More generally, whenever the marginal benefits of a more refined experiment do not exceed the marginal costs and the experiment is probative, the substantial-similarity requirement should be deemed satisfied.

Although some opinions adopt such an approach to finding substantial similarity, others treat the requirement as stating a preference for duplicating conditions to the greatest extent feasible. Yet, many useful experiments fall short of this Procrustean demand, and the courts that speak in these terms usually do not exclude an experiment just because a slightly more fastidious one could have been conducted. One device that they use to achieve a

sensible result is to accept experiments elucidating "properties" as falling outside the rule demanding maximum similarity. Nevertheless, these cases rarely provide an analysis of what makes the experimental findings pertain to general properties or traits and why a more detailed simulation is unnecessary. For instance, in *Council v. Duprel*,[3] the Supreme Court of Mississippi held an experiment with herbicides admissible, because it "was not an effort to duplicate the conditions existing on appellant's farm" but merely an attempt "to establish the fact that 2,4–D is far more destructive to cotton than 2,4,5–T." Of course, the question for the jury was whether 2,4–D was more destructive on *appellant's* farm, and an experiment could have been designed to control for possible differences in soil conditions, humidity, and other variables. But if the herbicidal quality of the chemical is largely independent of these variables, it can be considered a general property, and controlling for those variables would have been of little value. Thus, deciding when an experiment is acceptable as an investigation of a "property" as opposed to a recreation of the conditions of the accident involves the same inquiry as deciding when the experimental conditions are substantially similar to the ones of interest.

In short, whether the experiment is an overt effort at re-creation or a simple study of general properties, the core question is whether matching the variables that are different would make the experiment so much more revealing as to be worth the additional effort and expense. Focusing directly on marginal costs and benefits gives some definition to the substantial similarity test; indeed, it makes that language superfluous.

Some courts distinguish between experiments commissioned for a specific lawsuit and those undertaken solely to obtain scientific knowledge of greater generality. The latter have the advantage of being untainted by any interest in the litigation. Of course, scientists rarely are devoid of self-interest or biases, but the process of exposing one's work to the scrutiny of the scientific community through publi-

3. 165 So.2d 134 (Miss.1964).

cation acts as an important check. In recent years, this has led many courts to emphasize the importance of "peer review."

But many of the case-specific experiments that are the subject of this section do not lend themselves to publication in scholarly journals. Instead, courts must look to other indicia of reliability. Some courts simply have asked whether an expert's work reflects "the degree of care that [such an expert] would use in his scientific work, outside the context of litigation."[4] Because such post hoc inquiries can be difficult to undertake, however, it might be more fruitful to consider procedures to improve the design and implementation of case-specific experiments *before* they are conducted. Consideration might be given to excluding experiments unless the adversary has had reasonable notice, an opportunity to make suggestions, and to be present during the experiment. Also worthy of consideration is appointment by the court of an impartial person to conduct or supervise an experiment. Such prophylactic procedures could lead to findings that would invite much less in the way of time-consuming or distracting attack and defense at trial.

§ 203. Scientific Tests in General: Admissibility and Weight

To deal effectively with scientific evidence, attorneys must know more than the rules of evidence. They must know something of the scientific principles as well. While they can rely on suitably chosen experts for advice about the more arcane points, they must have a sufficient grasp of the field to see what is essential and what is unnecessary detail and verbiage if they are to develop or counteract the evidence most effectively. In this chapter, we cannot explore in any depth the vast body of knowledge that comes into play in the forensic applications of science and medicine. Only a superficial sampling of a few areas will be attempted. We shall focus on some of the problems that can arise in making measurements and in interpreting data. Sections 204

through 207 deal with laboratory, clinical, or field tests (organized somewhat arbitrarily by scientific discipline) in which statistical analysis of the data does not play a major role. Sections 208 through 211 concern studies in which statistical analyses are prominent. In the remainder of this section, we discuss some general points concerning the admissibility of all such evidence and the weight that it should receive.

Most of the case law centers on the threshold question of admissibility. The principles of relevancy outlined in Chapter 16 are as applicable to scientific evidence as to any other kind, and the doctrines governing all expert testimony discussed in Chapter 3 operate here as well. The screening of scientific evidence under these general principles can be described as "relevancy-plus-helpfulness" review, or more, simply a relevancy analysis. However, many courts apply a more specialized rule for admissibility when expert witnesses are called to testify about scientific tests or findings. Two approaches are dominant—"general acceptance" and "scientific soundness." Under the former, the proponent must show that the scientific community agrees that the principles or techniques on which the expert relies are capable of producing accurate information and conclusions. Under the latter standard, general acceptance remains an important consideration, but the court must consider other factors to decide for itself whether the expert's methodology is scientifically valid. Both the "general acceptance" and the "scientific soundness" test require a binary determination. Evidence either possesses the necessary quality and is admissible (subject to the other rules of evidence), or it lacks the essential quality and is inadmissible. In contrast, the relevancy-plus standard considers the *degree* of general acceptance, the *extent* of scientific soundness, and still other factors in evaluating probative value.

The notion of a special rule for scientific evidence originated in 1923 in *Frye v. United States*.[1] *Frye* was a murder prosecution in

---

4. Sheehan v. Daily Racing Form, Inc., 104 F.3d 940, 942 (7th Cir.1997) (criticizing a statistical analysis).

1. 293 Fed. 1013 (D.C.Cir.1923).

which the trial court rebuffed defendant's effort to introduce results of a "systolic blood pressure test," a forerunner of the polygraph. On appeal, the defendant relied on the traditional rule governing expert testimony, but the Court of Appeals for the District of Columbia, without explanation or precedent, superimposed a new standard:

> Just when a scientific principle or discovery crosses the line between the experimental and demonstrable stages is difficult to define. Somewhere in this twilight zone the evidential force of the principle must be recognized, and while courts will go a long way in admitting expert testimony deduced from a well-recognized scientific principle or discovery, the thing from which the deduction is made must be sufficiently established to have gained general acceptance in the particular field in which it belongs.

The opinion did not state clearly whether "the thing" that needed "to have gained general acceptance" was the link between conscious insincerity and changes in blood pressure or the ability of an expert to measure and interpret the changes, or both. The court concluded, however, that the deception test lacked the requisite "standing and scientific recognition among physiological and psychological authorities."

Many courts adopted the *Frye* standard in the ensuing years with scant discussion. Polygraphy, graphology, hypnotic and drug induced testimony, voice stress analysis, voice spectrograms, various forms of spectroscopy, infrared sensing of aircraft, retesting of breath samples for alcohol content, psychological profiles of battered women and child abusers, post traumatic stress disorder as indicating rape, penile plethysmography as indicating sexual deviancy, astronomical calculations, blood group typing, and DNA testing all have fallen prey to its influence. In the jurisdictions that follow *Frye*, the proponent of the evidence must prove general acceptance by surveying scientific publications, judicial decisions, or practical applications, or by presenting testimony from scientists as to the attitudes of their fellow scientists.

Especially since the early 1970s, however, the *Frye* standard has been subjected to critical analysis, limitation, modification, and finally, outright rejection. Some courts found the *Frye* standard satisfied in the teeth of expert testimony that the technique in question was too new and untried and the test results too inconclusive for court use. While asserting the continuing vitality of the *Frye* standard, other courts held that general acceptance goes to the weight rather than the admissibility of the evidence. Still others reasoned that the standard applies only to tests for truthfulness, to relatively esoteric applications of science, to the "hard sciences" or to very general principles or methodology rather than to the body of studies or results being applied to reach a conclusion in the case at bar. Many opinions simply ignored the standard, and many others blithely equated it with a requirement of showing the accuracy and reliability of the scientific technique. Finally, in the 1970s and 1980s, a strong minority of jurisdictions expressly repudiated *Frye*.

The adoption of the Federal Rules of Evidence intensified the retreat from *Frye*. These rules do not explicitly distinguish between scientific and other forms of expert testimony, and they do not mention general acceptance. Rule 702 majestically provides that "[i]f scientific, technical, or other specialized knowledge will assist the trier of fact to understand the evidence or to determine a fact in issue, a witness qualified as an expert by knowledge, skill, experience, training, or education, may testify thereto * * * ." Some courts construed the omission of any direct reference to "general acceptance" as evincing a legislative intent to overturn the well-established common law requirement.

Although the much more convincing view is that the rules left the viability of the general acceptance standard open to further common law development, in *Daubert v. Merrell Dow Pharmaceuticals, Inc.*,[2] the Supreme Court determined that the federal rules "su-

---

2. 509 U.S. 579 (1993).

perseded" *Frye* and "displaced" general acceptance as "the exclusive test for admitting expert scientific testimony." Plaintiffs in *Daubert* were two young children born with missing or malformed limbs. Together with their parents, they sought damages from the maker of Bendectin, a drug approved by the Food and Drug Administration as safe and effective for the relief of nausea and vomiting during pregnancy. Plaintiffs' case foundered when they were unable to point to any published epidemiological studies concluding that Bendectin causes limb reduction defects. The district court granted summary judgment for Merrell Dow, and the Ninth Circuit Court of Appeals affirmed on the theory that under *Frye*, there could be no admissible expert testimony of causation without some peer-reviewed, published studies showing a statistically significant association between exposure to Bendectin and limb reduction defects. Having determined that *Frye* no longer governed, the Supreme Court remanded the case to the court of appeals, which adhered to its original decision on other grounds.

However, the Supreme Court did not simply hold, as had the courts in a significant minority of federal and state jurisdictions, that with *Frye*'s demise, the relevancy-plus standard governs scientific expert testimony. Instead, it read into the phrase "scientific * * * knowledge" in Rule 702 a requirement of a "body of known facts or * * * ideas inferred from such facts or accepted as truths on good grounds" in accordance with "the methods and procedures of science." In addition, the Court emphasized that scientific analysis must "fit" the facts of the case.[3] The Court then offered an abstract discussion of how the requirement of scientifically "good grounds" might be satisfied. It suggested inquiring into such matters as the degree to which a theory has been tested empirically, the extent to

which it has been "subjected to peer review and publication," the rate of errors associated with a particular technique, and the extent of acceptance in the scientific community.

Frye's general acceptance standard and *Daubert*'s scientific soundness inquiry do not exhaust the range of "tests" for scientific evidence, and neither opinion offers any reasons for choosing among the many possibilities. Proponents of the general acceptance test argue that it assures uniformity in evidentiary rulings, that it shields juries from any tendency to treat novel scientific evidence as infallible, that it avoids complex, expensive, and time-consuming courtroom dramas, and that it insulates the adversary system from novel evidence until a pool of experts is available to evaluate it in court. Most commentators agree, however, that these objectives can be met with less drastic constraints on the admissibility of scientific evidence. In addition to the *Daubert* approach of looking directly to reliability or validity rather than to the presence or absence of general acceptance, it has been suggested that a panel of scientists rather than judges screen new developments for validity or acceptance, that a substantial acceptance test be substituted for the general acceptance standard, that scientific evidence be admitted freely, coupled with testimony of an expert appointed by the court if it finds that the testimony would be subject to "substantial doubt in peer review by the scientific community," and that the traditional standards of relevancy and the need for expertise—in other words, the relevancy-plus analysis—should govern.

The last method for evaluating the admissibility of scientific evidence is the most appealing. General scientific acceptance is a proper condition for taking judicial notice of scientific facts, but it is not suitable as a determinant of the admissibility of scientific

---

3. Id. at 591. Whether the necessary "fit" is something more than what is required under the general doctrine of the inadmissibility of irrelevant evidence (see supra § 184) is not apparent from the Court's opinion. In a later toxic tort case, the Court used language that might be employed to give additional content to "fit." In General Elec. Co. v. Joiner, 522 U.S. 136 (1997), the majority observed that "[a] court may conclude that there is simply too great an

analytical gap between the data and the opinion proffered." Thus, proof that a chemical causes tumors in mice at very high doses might be relevant to whether the chemical is a human carcinogen at low dosages (see supra § 185), but the extrapolation from across species and dosages might constitute "too great an analytical gap" to provide the requisite "fit."

evidence. Any relevant conclusions supported by a qualified expert witness should be received unless there are distinct reasons for exclusion. These reasons are the familiar ones of prejudicing or misleading the jury or consuming undue amounts of time.

This traditional approach to the evidence does not make scientific testimony admissible on the say-so of a single expert. Neither does it go to the other extreme of insisting on a fully formed scientific consensus. It permits general scientific opinion of both underlying principles and particular applications to be considered in evaluating the worth of the testimony. In so treating the yeas and nays of the members of a scientific discipline as but one indication of the validity, accuracy, and reliability of the technique, the traditional balancing method focuses the court's attention where it belongs—on the actual usefulness of the evidence in light of the full record developed on the power of the scientific test.

Furthermore, unlike the general acceptance and scientific soundness standards, the relevancy approach is sensitive to the perceived degree of prejudice and unnecessary expense associated with the scientific technique in issue. Not every scrap of scientific evidence carries with it an aura of infallibility. Some methods, like bitemark identification and blood splatter analysis, are demonstrable in the courtroom. Where the methods involve principles and procedures that are comprehensible to a jury, the concerns over the evidence exerting undue influence and inducing a battle of the experts have less force.[4] On the other hand, when the nature of the technique is more esoteric, as with some types of statistical analyses and biochemical tests, when subjective judgments are misleadingly presented as hard science, or when the inferences from the

scientific evidence sweep broadly or cut deeply into sensitive areas, a stronger showing of probative value should be required. This could result in the categorical exclusion of certain types of evidence, such as polygraphic lie detection polygraph and statements made while under the influence of a "truth" serum. By attending to such considerations, the rigor of the requisite foundation can be adjusted to suit the nature of the evidence and the context in which it is offered.

Using a legal standard that recognizes that scientific validity and acceptance are matters of degree rather than yes-or-no judgments diminishes the severity of many of the problems that have plagued the general acceptance and scientific soundness standards. Courts in *Frye* and *Daubert* jurisdictions have been forced to draw (and tempted to manipulate) an often obscure line between "scientific" evidence and other expert or lay testimony. Focusing at the outset on the costs and benefits of the particular evidence makes it less crucial to decide exactly when evidence is so "scientific" or "novel" that the special test for novel scientific evidence applies. Similarly, predictability is not easily attained in the face of ambiguity and disagreement as to how general the acceptance in the scientific community must be, who can speak for that community, and the "particular field" to which the scientific evidence belongs and in which it must be accepted. Although such issues arise under any effort to assess the probative value of scientific evidence, they are far less critical when a court can consider the number of fields in which a technique is used, the rigor required in those fields, and the degree of its acceptance in those fields, without having to label the technique as generally accepted or not.[5] Finally, attending

---

4. Ex parte Dolvin, 391 So.2d 677 (Ala.1980) ("physical comparisons" admitted); People v. Marx, 126 Cal.Rptr. 350 (Cal.App.1975) (bitemark analysis admitted); State v. Hall, 297 N.W.2d 80 (Iowa 1980) (blood spatter analysis admitted).

5. In theory, *Daubert* can be applied to reach the same results as the broader relevancy analysis proposed here. Indeed, some courts have seen the opinion as confirming the relevancy approach applied in opinions predating *Daubert*. E.g., State v. O'Key, 899 P.2d 663 (Or.1995). Certainly, in rejecting general acceptance as the touchstone of

admissibility, the *Daubert* opinion encourages more flexible treatment of scientific evidence. As introduced by the Court, the scientific soundness threshold is arguably quite low—it could be read to exclude only "subjective belief or unsupported speculation" and "inference[s] or assertion[s] [not] derived by the scientific method." 509 U.S. at 590. Evidence that clears this low hurdle then would be assessed under the usual helpfulness and relevancy standards. See id. at 591 & 595. This framework would be equivalent to starting with the relevancy standard. See State v. Porter, 698 A.2d 739 (Conn.1997) (adhering to

to the probative value of conclusions as well as methodologies softens the brittle distinction between the two that has proved awkward to apply in both *Frye* and *Daubert* jurisdictions.

Of course, it might be argued that the relevancy-plus approach is no less amorphous and manipulable than the general acceptance and scientific soundness standards. There is truth in this charge, but courts and commentators have identified the varied considerations that determine the balance of probative value and prejudice of scientific evidence.[6] Applying these to various types of scientific evidence offers a more honest and sensitive basis for making admissibility decisions than the more cramped tests that have characterized this area of the law of evidence.

Whatever the standard for admissibility may be in a particular jurisdiction, arguments as to the weight that the jury should give to the evidence will be important. Indeed, skills in building cases with admissible scientific evidence and demolishing these same structures have become valuable as the forensic applications of science have grown more commonplace. Attention to possible infirmities in the collection and analysis of data can cut superficially impressive scientific evidence down to its proper size. To begin with, one might consider the process by which the forensic scientist makes raw measurements. Does subjective judgment play any role? If so, do different experts tend to find very different measured values, so that the measurement process is unreliable? Are the variations randomly distributed about some true mean, or are they biased in one direction or another, so that even if they are reliable, their accuracy is suspect? Then there are problems of interpretation. Is the quantity being measured the real item of interest, or at least a suitable proxy for that variable? In brief, considering the probable errors introduced at each stage of the scientific analysis, is the final result likely to be reliable, accurate, and meaningful?[7] The remainder of this chapter describes particular scientific (and pseudo-scientific) tests and studies both with regard to these weight-related factors and to the validity of the reasoning of the scientific experts who bring their specialized knowledge and training to the courtroom.

Before turning to particular areas and types of scientific evidence, however, one additional feature of scientific evidence deserves mention. The fundamental problem of scientific expert testimony is that judges and juries are compelled to evaluate scientific claims with little or no prior knowledge of the field. We call scientists in because they have knowledge that legal decisionmakers lack, then we ask those decisionmakers to evaluate intelligently that mysterious knowledge. How can they perform this task without becoming "am-

---

exclusionary rule for polygraph evidence even assuming that polygraphic lie detection satisfies *Daubert*). In practice, however, courts applying *Daubert* can set the soundness bar considerably higher, and it is not hard to present the "scientific method" as demanding rigorous validation and extensive publication. See Foster & Huber, Judging Science: Scientific Knowledge and the Federal Courts (1997).

6. See State v. O'Key, 899 P.2d 663 (Or.1995); United States v. Downing, 753 F.2d 1224 (3d Cir.1985). Building on various state and federal opinions, one former state supreme court justice outlined the following factors for consideration in weighing probative value against possible prejudice:

(1) the potential error rate in using the technique, (2) the existence and maintenance of standards governing its use, (3) presence of safeguards in the characteristics of the technique, (4) analogy to other scientific techniques whose results are admissible, (5) the extent to which the technique has been accepted by scientists in the field involved, (6) the nature and breadth of the inference adduced, (7) the clarity and simplicity with which the technique can be described and its results explained, (8) the extent to which the basic data are verifiable by the court and jury, (9) the availability of other experts to test and evaluate the technique, (10) the probative significance of the evidence in the circumstances of the case, and (11) the care with which the technique was employed in the case.

McCormick, Scientific Evidence: Defining a New Approach to Admissibility, 67 Iowa L.Rev. 879, 911–12 (1982) (footnotes omitted).

7. The term "validity" often is used to denote these last two qualities. That is, a valid technique or measuring device returns reasonably accurate values of the variables that the scientist purports to be measuring. A valid method or measure is reliable, but not all reliable (consistent) measures are valid. Although courts commonly use the term "reliability" to mean "that which can be relied upon" for some purpose such as establishing probable cause or crediting a hearsay statement, when experts testify as to "reliability," it may be well to keep this distinction in mind.

ateur scientists"? Procedures permitting and encouraging professional scientists to contribute their expertise to screening and assessing scientific evidence can help resolve this conundrum. In particular, requiring adequate pretrial disclosure of the witness's scientific reasoning in written form for review by other scientists could be valuable. And, a century of calls for court-appointed, testifying experts or expert advisers or managers may be having some effect.

§ 204. Particular Tests: Physics and Electronics: Speed Detection and Recording

Forensic applications of physics and electronics include motor vehicle accident reconstruction, analysis of tape recordings, and detecting and recording speed and other aspects of the movements of vehicles. This section surveys the evidentiary features of speed detection and recording devices.

The branch of classical mechanics that deals with the motion of objects is called kinematics. The physicist defines average velocity as the distance travelled along a given direction in a specified time period divided by the length of this time period. Speed is the absolute value of velocity. (The difference between speed and velocity is that the latter includes information as to the direction of travel, while the former merely states how fast the object moved.) Acceleration is the change in velocity for a unit of time divided by the time elapsed. It states how quickly an object is speeding up, slowing down, or changing direction. Measuring such quantities without some mechanical aid is difficult to do accurately, although it can be easy enough to ascertain whether one vehicle is moving faster or slower than another. A more elaborate application of these principles of kinematics to the detection and conviction of traffic offenders is recorded in an English case at the turn of the century in which a constable took readings from a watch with a second hand. A progression of more sophisticated timing mechanisms followed, culminating in the Visual Average Speed Computer and Record (VASCAR). When a suspected violator's vehicle reaches a clearly

marked point, such as an intersection, the operator activates the timer. When the police car reaches the same point, the operator activates a mechanism for recording the distance the police car travels as measured by its odometer. When the target vehicle reaches a second clearly marked point down the road, the police officer shuts off the timer, and when the police car arrives at this second point, he turns off the distance switch. The computer divides the measured distance by the measured time elapsed and displays this average speed.

Initially, the courts required expert testimony concerning the principles and operation of the VASCAR. However, the kinematic principles, which date back to the time of Galileo and Newton, are so well established that they, like the ability of an electronic computer to divide two numbers, easily can be the subject of judicial notice. The more serious issue, which goes to the weight (and in an extreme case, the admissibility) of the evidence, is the accuracy of the device under operational conditions. Errors can arise from a poorly calibrated odometer, from turning on and off the switches at the wrong times, and so on. A foundation indicating that the device is properly calibrated and the operator well trained in its use is usually required.

A speed detector and recorder not so closely tied to police work is the tachograph. It consists of a tachometer and a recording mechanism that furnishes, over time, the speed and mileage of the vehicle to which it is attached. It is used on trains, trucks and busses. Its readings have been admitted in civil and criminal cases, on a showing the particular device works accurately and an identification of which portion of the record generated pertains to the events in issue.

A more advanced kinematic recording instrument is the aircraft flight recorder. It records time, airspeed, altitude, attitude (orientation of axes relative to some reference line or plane, such as the horizon), magnetic heading, vertical acceleration, and other instrument readings. These records can be extremely valuable in analyzing aircraft crashes. Admissibility turns on evidence of authenticity and expert testimony to explain how the machine operates and to interpret the marks on the chart.

Radar equipment provides another means of measuring velocity. Military or aircraft pulse-type radar uses the velocity-distance-time relationships previously discussed. The radar antenna transmits microwave radiation in pulses. The equipment measures the time it takes for a pulse to reach the target and for its echo to return. Since the radiation travels at a known speed (the speed of light), this fixes the distance to the target. The changes in the distances as determined from the travel times of later pulses permit the target's velocity to be computed. Police radar relies on different principles. In its simplest form, the radar speedmeter used by police agencies transmits a continuous beam of microwaves of uniform frequency, detects the reflected signals, and measures the difference in frequency between the transmitted and reflected beams. It converts this frequency difference into a number for the speed of the object that has reflected the radiation. This conversion is based on the phenomenon known as the Doppler effect. Electromagnetic radiation coming from an object moving relative to the observer is shifted to a higher frequency if the object is approaching, and to a lower frequency if the object is receding. For the range of velocities of interest in traffic court, the extent of this Doppler shift is directly proportional to the relative speed. When the radar set is at rest relative to the ground (earth's surface), it therefore gives the speed of the vehicle being tracked.

A more complicated version of the Doppler shift detector processes signals received at two distinct frequencies. This refinement allows the unit to be used conveniently in a moving vehicle. The shift in frequency of the beam as reflected off the road surface gives the speed of the police vehicle. The shift in frequency as reflected off the target vehicle gives its speed relative to the police car. In effect, circuitry in the radar unit adds the relative speed to the police car's speed to yield the ground speed of the target.

Most of the early cases admitting radar evidence of speeding involved testimony showing not only that the target car had been identified and that a qualified operator had obtained the reading from a properly functioning device, but also explaining the Doppler effect, its application in the radar speedmeter, and the scientific acceptance of this method of measuring speed. Within a few years, the courts began to take judicial notice of the underlying scientific principles and the capability of the device to measure speed with tolerable accuracy. Expert testimony on these subjects is no longer essential.

The question of what must be proved to establish that the specific instrument was operating accurately has provoked more controversy. Decisions range from holdings that the evidence is inadmissible without independent verification of the accuracy of the system at the time and place of the measurement to holdings that lack of evidence of testing goes to the weight but not the admissibility of the results. In many jurisdictions, statutes provide for admissibility and specify the requisite type of showing of accuracy. Revelations that police radar units operating under field conditions may not be as reliable as had once been assumed underscore the importance of demonstrating the accuracy of the equipment.

Regardless of whether the jurisdiction has a particularized rule for the extent and type of testing needed for admissibility, evidence pertaining to the accuracy of the reading is admissible. There are many ways in which errors can creep into the system. Stationary radar readings will be wrong if the transmission frequency changes, if the receiver misevaluates the frequency difference, if the radar is not held motionless, or if radiation from another source is attributed to the suspect's vehicle. Moving radar, being a more complex device, has more room for error. Acceleration of the patrol car, "cosine error," and "shadowing" can lead the instrument to underestimate the patrol car's speed, and hence to overstate the target vehicle's speed.[1]

---

§ 204

1. "Cosine error" can arise when the radar echo comes from a target that is not directly in front of the radar unit.

It results from the fact that the Doppler shift is a function of the component of the relative velocity along the line of

Some of these potential sources of error can be minimized or excluded by careful operating procedures and on-site tests. These include the use of tuning forks vibrating at frequencies such that their linear motions will cause the speedometer to register particular speeds if it is receiving properly, use of an internal, electronically activated tong for the same purpose, and simply checking that, when aimed at another police car, the radar reading corresponds with that car's speedometer reading. Of course, after a few years of use, tongs may not vibrate at the presumed frequency, an internal oscillator may need adjustment, and a car's speedometer may not be accurate. At least on the question of admissibility, however, most courts recognize that independent errors are unlikely to be identical. They tend to hold that some combination of these methods is sufficient to warrant admissibility. Furthermore, a number of decisions, sometimes aided by statute, hold that tested radar readings can amount to proof beyond a reasonable doubt.

Yet another device uses a laser to generate pulses of infrared radiation about every billionth of a second. Like pulse radar, this laser-based speed detection device measures the reflection times of the pulses to determine the speed of the reflecting object via the distance-time-velocity formulas. The physical principles that the device relies on are eminently sound, and the only possible ground for questioning the scientific basis of such speed measurements is whether the instrument properly implements them. At this time, only a handful of court opinions on the admissibility of this type of scientific evidence have been published. When the prosecution has mounted a serious effort to prove that the device can measure vehicular speed accurately, the evidence has been deemed admissible.

§ 205. Particular Tests: Biology and Medicine: Drunkenness and Blood, Tissue, and DNA Typing

The forensic applications of the biological sciences and medicine are far too extensive and varied to be discussed fully here, but we shall consider two groups of laboratory tests of biological samples that commonly provide crucial evidence. These are chemical tests for drunkenness and immunogenetic and other tests for blood, tissue and DNA types.

A. *Drunkenness.* Physiologically, the amount of alcohol in the brain determines the degree of intoxication. Except in an autopsy, however, a direct measurement of this quantity is not feasible. Nevertheless, samples of blood, urine, saliva, or breath can be taken, and the alcohol level in these samples can be measured. Using these measurements to determine whether a person is intoxicated raises two technical problems—the accuracy of the measurement itself and the relationship between the concentration of alcohol in the sample and the degree of intoxication. There is room for concern on both these points.

Analysis of blood samples gives the most accurate and reliable results. Various chemical techniques are available to measure the concentration of ethyl alcohol in the sample. When proper laboratory procedures are followed and the sample is correctly obtained and preserved, these give reliable estimates. Of course, there is always room for error in these measurements, but the more fundamental problem lies in moving from an estimated value for the blood alcohol concentration (BAC) to a correct statement about the degree of intoxication during the crucial period. Even where the measured values are reliable and accurate, substantial variability in tolerances for alcohol, absorption rates, and clearance rates, both among individuals and within the same individual from one situation to another, complicates efforts to deduce the true extent of intoxication at the time of an arrest or accident. In particular, one cannot assume that BAC inevitably is higher at the time of an accident than it is afterwards, at the time of testing, for the concentration rises after drinking, then drops. Extrapolations based on direct measurements of BAC therefore seem more perilous than is generally recognized, and

sight. "Shadowing" occurs when the reflection indicating the speed of the police car comes from slow-moving objects

rather than stationary ones.

there have been suggestions that BAC be measured at several different times to ascertain whether the first reading is from the early period of rising BAC or the later period of declining BAC. However, even with two measurements, the situation may not be clearcut.

Determinations resting exclusively on concentration of alcohol contained in a sample of breath (BrAC) are even more questionable. Again, the problem is not the accuracy of the instrumentation as maintained and used in laboratory studies, and arguments that particular instruments are not generally accepted or sufficiently accurate for the purpose of determining BrAC usually fail. As with tests of blood, errors can arise from field operating conditions, individual biological variability, and extrapolation to the time in question, but there is a further problem with breath testing. A formula must be used to convert BrAC to BAC. Traditionally, a single number is used as a multiplier in making this conversion, but the true value of this parameter is debatable. Certainly, the conversion ratio varies among individuals and even within the same individual over time. Although most studies suggest that the conventional figure of 2100 tends to understate the blood alcohol level, a small fraction of individuals will have blood alcohol concentrations that are lower than those deduced from this value.

These cautions concerning the scientific proof do not necessarily make the blood and breath test evidence inadmissible. On the contrary, when the tests are properly conducted and analyzed, the evidence can be of great value in deciding questions connected with intoxication. Since the links from breath alcohol concentration to blood alcohol level to intoxication, as well as the accuracy of measurements made under ideal conditions are well established, under the usual principles governing scientific evidence, the test results should be admissible if founded on a showing of authenticity and satisfactory care in the collection of the sample and its analysis. Expert testimony ordinarily would be needed to establish that the party with the measured or inferred BAC was intoxicated during the period in question.

In the context of traffic offenses, however, specialized statutes and regulations provide shortcuts to the application of the common law principles and evidence codes in determining the admissibility of blood and breath test evidence. The Uniform Vehicle Code illustrates some common provisions. In proceedings involving driving or control of a vehicle while under the influence of intoxicating liquor, it makes chemical test evidence of BAC admissible as long as it is obtained by certified persons following procedures that the state department of health has prescribed. If the procedures are sufficiently rigorous, then the results of this testing can trigger two rebuttable presumptions: if BAC at the relevant time was .08% or more, that the individual was under the influence; and if BAC was .05% or less, that he was not. An intermediate reading is deemed "competent evidence" for consideration along with the other evidence in the case. In most jurisdictions, a party offering test results pursuant to such a statute must lay a foundation by producing witnesses to explain how the test is conducted, to identify it as duly approved under the statutory scheme, and to vouch for its correct administration in the particular case. By the early 1980s, as concern with the carnage due to drunken driving escalated, nearly all states placed still more emphasis on chemical testing by enacting "per se" laws making it a crime to drive while having a BAC or a BrAC in excess of a specified amount. Some of these statutes seek to circumvent the introduction of evidence exposing the problem of converting BrAC to BAC by redefining the offense in terms of breath rather than blood alcohol. Indeed, to avoid the need to present or consider testimony extrapolating from later to earlier measurements, some statutes even redefine the offense to consist of having a given BAC or BrAC within several hours after operating a motor vehicle. The typical result is a potentially confusing mosaic of laws and rules in which a set of overlapping offenses with various statutory provisions for admitting evidence of BAC or BrAC in traffic cases is superimposed on the more general evidence code or common law rules.

B. *Blood, Tissue, and DNA Types.* Another group of chemical tests—those that identify blood, tissue and DNA types—are often the subject of courtroom testimony. Elucidating the biochemical mechanisms by which a multicellular organism distinguishes between self and non-self—between its own cells and foreign substances—is a major research problem in biology. The topic is fundamental to understanding the way in which the body responds to infections from microorganisms, to grafts of foreign tissues or materials, and to blood transfusions, and it is central to the study of allergies, tumors, and autoimmune diseases. Research in this field reveals that sticking out of the surface of cells are various molecules, called in this context, antigens. For instance, individuals with type A blood have the molecule known as an A antigen on their red blood cells.[1] The red blood cells are not the only ones to possess antigens. Human Leucocyte Antigens (HLA) are found on the surface of most human cells, and there is an elaborate nomenclature for these. The full set of antigens that a cell possesses thus distinguishes it from the cells of other organisms. It is conceivable that each person is uniquely identifiable in this way. In addition to the immunologically crucial antigens, cells and bodily fluids contain chemicals such as enzymes and other proteins that can differ from one person to another.

Most enzymes and serum proteins are identified by a technique called electrophoresis, in which an electric field is applied to separate the molecules according to their electric charge. Although electrophoresis is a standard technique in biochemistry, its application to aged or dried blood stains was marked by controversy. Difficulties arose because thin gel multisystem testing is used only in crime laboratories, because few outside investigations of the effects of aging and environmental contamination were undertaken, and because crime laboratories did not submit to routine proficiency testing. Nevertheless, almost all appellate courts that encountered challenges to electrophoretic identifications concluded that both the multisystem and the more generally used electrophoretic procedures are scientifically accepted and that the findings can be admitted into evidence.

A different type of test is used to detect antigens. The antigens react with other biologically produced molecules, called antibodies. Serologic tests consist of exposing a suspected antigen to its corresponding antibody and observing whether the expected reaction occurs. Errors involving misinterpretation, mislabeling, poor reagents, and the like are always possible, but workers in this field report that with stringent procedures and quality control standards, the risk of error can be made very small.

The forensic use of these tests arises principally in two areas—identifying the perpetrators of violent crimes or sexual offenses from traces of blood or semen and ascertaining parentage in child support cases, criminal cases, and other litigation. In general, the courts have moved from an initial position of mistrust of such evidence to the present stage of taking judicial notice of the scientific acceptance or acceptability of serologic and related tests. From the outset, it was recognized that if the suspect's antigens do not match those in the sample found at the scene of a crime, then the incriminating trace does not consist of his blood. For a considerable time, however, there was a difference of judicial opinion concerning evidence of a match. Since some combinations of antigens are relatively common, a few courts dismissed the positive test results for these antigens as irrelevant. The better view—and the overwhelming majority position—is that positive findings are neither irrelevant nor so inherently prejudicial as to justify a rule against their admission.[2]

---

§ 205

1. We are simplifying for ease of exposition. In fact, there are several distinct antigens that are included within type A blood. Consequently, the type A blood group can be divided into various subgroups corresponding to the presence or absence of the particular antigens. Ignoring subdivisions, type B blood corresponds to the B antigen, type AB to the combination of the A and B antigens, and type O blood lacks both the A and B antigens.

2. In one leading case, Shanks v. State, 45 A.2d 85 (Md.1945), the accused was charged with rape. The state proved that blood found on the coat of the accused, like that of his alleged victim, was type O. The defendant argued that since 45% of the population had type O blood,

Serologic tests have been used for the last half-century in paternity litigation. The underlying logic is based on a few principles of human genetics. Roughly speaking, portions of the DNA contained in the chromosomes of the nucleus of a cell—the genes—direct the synthesis of proteins. Different versions (or alleles) of these genes oversee the synthesis of the different antigens. Consequently, by ascertaining which antigens are present in an individual (the phenotype), one learns something about that individual's alleles (the genotype). As such, the antigens can be thought of as genetic markers. Knowing the phenotypes of the child, mother, and putative father and applying the laws of inheritance, a geneticist can say whether it would be possible for a child with the observed phenotype to have been born to the mother and the alleged father. That is, the medical expert can state that whoever the biological father was must have had certain genetic characteristics, which can be compared to those that the alleged father has. In this way, a man falsely accused—one who does not have the necessary characteristics—can be excluded.

With an appropriate foundation, such negative test results are nearly always admissible, although the weight accorded to an exclusion varies. A few cases can be found upholding liability despite serologic proof of nonpaternity. Perhaps the most notorious involved the comedian Charlie Chaplin. In most states, however, a properly conducted blood test that excludes the defendant is conclusive.

Positive immunogenetic findings are another matter. The traditional rule in this country was that serologic tests are inadmissible for this purpose. At one time, when only a few, widely shared antigens were known, this approach made some sense. For example, under the early ABO system, a positive test result merely meant that the accused was, on average, one of the 87% of the male population possessing the requisite genotypes. Such evidence is not very probative, and the fear that

the jury would give it more weight than it deserved, cloaked as it was in the garb of medical expertise, prompted many courts to exclude it as unduly prejudicial. For decades, however, this situation has been changing steadily. With the plethora of genetic markers now known, it is commonplace to determine that the biological father has immunogenetic traits shared by one in several thousand men of the same race. Many laboratories are equipped to test reliably for enough antigens that such positive test results are simply too probative to be ignored.

As a result, evidence that the accused has immunogenetic traits that are consistent with the claim that he is the biological father is received regularly. In most states, this is a consequence of statutory innovation. In other instances, it is an example of the common law lugubriously digesting a technological advance. The battle over the admissibility of serologic and related tests to prove paternity is over, but disputes over efforts to give an exact statement of the "probability of paternity" linger.[3]

Red blood cell grouping, blood serum protein and enzyme analysis, and HLA typing can go a long way toward identifying individuals, but they have been overshadowed by forensic adaptations of DNA technology. There is no single method of DNA typing. As with conventional immunogenetic testing, the probative value of the laboratory findings depends on the procedure employed, the quality of the laboratory work, and the genetic characteristics that are discerned. We shall describe some of these procedures and the theory that lies behind them, and then consider the developing case law.

DNA is found in all nucleated cells, including those in bodily fluids such as blood and saliva. The DNA molecule has two long strands that spiral around one another, forming a double helix. Within the double helix are units, called nucleotide bases, that link one

---

the evidence should have been excluded as too remote. The court reasoned that "[t]he objection of remoteness goes to the weight of the evidence rather than its admissibility. To exclude evidence merely because it tends [only] to establish a possibility * * * would produce curious results not heretofore thought of. [T]hat the accused was somewhere

near the scene of the crime would not, in itself, establish a probability [exceeding .5] that he was guilty, but only a possibility, yet such evidence is clearly admissible as a link in the chain." Id. at 87.

3. See infra § 211.

strand to the other, like the steps of a spiral staircase. There are four of these bases, which can be referred to by their initials, A, T, G and C. The A on one strand pairs with T on the other, and the G bonds to C. The lengthy sequence of AT and GC "stairs" within the DNA includes all the genes and control sequences (for turning certain genes on and off). The genes are stretches of base pairs whose order determines the composition of proteins and related products synthesized by various cells. Oddly enough, however, much of the DNA in human beings has no known function. But whether functional or not, essentially all the DNA in all of an individual's bodily cells are faithful copies of the DNA in the fertilized cell that grew into that individual.

Examining cell surface antigens (such as the ABO and HLA systems) or blood serum enzymes or proteins gives some information about the DNA sequences that code for these particular substances—if the markers differ, then the underlying DNA must differ. In contrast, DNA typing works with the DNA molecule itself and is not limited to identifying variations in coding sequences. With appropriate "DNA probes," one can detect differences in the base pair sequences anywhere in the DNA molecules of human cells. A probe is a short piece of a single strand of DNA with a radioactive or other readily identifiable component attached, like a tag on a suitcase. If the bases in the target DNA are in an order complementary to those in the probe, the probe will bind to that DNA.

Because 99.9 percent of the DNA sequence in any two people is identical, the technical challenge is to detect the relatively rare stretches of DNA, also called alleles, that vary among individuals. Two categories of procedures are in use. In PCR-based testing, small portions of DNA molecules are "amplified" by heating and cooling with an enzyme called DNA polymerase. Even if the sample contains only a small number of DNA molecules to start with, the polymerase induces a chain reaction that generates millions of identical fragments. Various procedures then can be used to characterize these small DNA fragments. For instance, in one technique the am-

plified DNA is "spotted" onto a membrane, and a probe added. If the sequence complementary to the probe is present, the probe will bind to it. If a molecule that changes color is used to tag the probe, the DNA with the targeted sequence will show up as a colored dot or blot. The analyst simply looks to see whether the dot, and hence the allele, is present. This test resembles serologic tests in giving a categorical answer—either the allele is present or it is not. This form of analysis detects alleles that result from variations in genes such as those in the HLA system.

Other discrete DNA alleles can be investigated with the aid of PCR. Considerable variability occurs with STRs (short tandem repeats). STRs consist of repeated occurrences of a core pattern of a few bases, such as (AATG)(AATG)(AATG).... Depending on the number of repeats, these portions of DNA differ in their lengths—the more repeats, the longer the allele. The number of repeats can be detected with a form of electrophoresis. As with serologic tests, however, a single allele may be common in the population, and hence not especially revealing. Of course, a series of probes can narrow the percentage of the population that could have been the source of the sample, and testing for ten or so STRs often is feasible—and very discriminating.

The typing procedure that dominated the first decade or so of forensic DNA cases is known as RFLP (restriction fragment length polymorphism) testing. It involves "digesting" DNA into fragments with enzymes ("restriction enzymes") from bacteria, separating the restriction fragments according to length by gel electrophoresis, blotting the array of fragments onto a nylon membrane, tagging the fragments with a radioactive probe, then placing X-ray film to the membrane to give an image with dark bands at the locations of the tagged fragments. The process can be repeated with other probes, and each probe yields a picture (known as an autoradiogram) with one or two bands. There will be one band if DNA in the sample came from a person who inherited the same allele from each parent; but more commonly, there will be two bands per probe because the individual inherited one allele from one parent and a different allele from the other parent. The locations of the bands from all the probes is the DNA "profile."

With RFLP testing, the region within the long DNA molecules that are profiled depends on the particular combination of probe and restriction enzyme. Within some regions are stretches of DNA known as VNTRs (variable number of tandem repeats). Like STRs, VNTRs result from repetitions of core sequences. However, the repeated units are much longer (about 30 to 60 base pairs), and so are the alleles (which can consist of many thousands of base pairs). A probe that detects the core repetitive sequence will detect these variable length fragments. Because the number of repeating units at a VNTR locus varies greatly within a population, the probes that detect this type of repetitive DNA are exquisitely informative. However, gel electrophoresis is not capable of measuring the lengths of VNTRs down to the level of a single repeat unit. This limitation makes for some complications in deciding whether two VNTR bands "match" and how many people in the general population might be found to have similarly matching bands.

A major advantage of the polymerase chain reaction over conventional immunogenetic and RFLP testing is that it requires very little biological material, and it permits smaller (more degraded) DNA fragments to be analyzed. PCR-based procedures also can be automated and take less time to complete. For such reasons, they are expected to dominate forensic testing in the years to come.

The judicial reception of DNA evidence can be divided into at least five phases. The first phase was one of rapid acceptance. Initial praise for RFLP testing in homicide, rape, paternity, and other cases was effusive. Indeed, one judge proclaimed "DNA fingerprinting" to be "the single greatest advance in the 'search for truth' * * * since the advent of cross-examination." In this first wave of cases, expert testimony for the prosecution rarely was countered, and courts readily admitted RFLP findings.

In a second wave of cases, however, defendants pointed to problems at two levels—controlling the experimental conditions of the analysis, and interpreting the results. Some scientists questioned certain features of the procedures for extracting and analyzing DNA employed in forensic laboratories, and it became apparent that declaring matches or nonmatches among the RFLPs due to VNTR loci in two samples is not always trivial. Despite these concerns, most cases continued to find forensic RFLP analyses to be generally accepted, and a number of states provided for admissibility of DNA tests by legislation. Concerted attacks by defense experts of impeccable credentials, however, produced a few cases rejecting specific proffers on the ground that the testing was not sufficiently rigorous. Moreover, a minority of courts, perhaps concerned that DNA evidence might well be conclusive in the minds of jurors, added a "third prong" to the general acceptance standard. This augmented *Frye* test requires not only proof of the general acceptance of the ability of science to produce the type of results offered in court, but also of the proper application of an approved method on the particular occasion. Such matters, however, are better handled not as part of the special screening test for scientific evidence, but as aspects of the balancing of probative value and prejudice.

A different attack on DNA profiling begun in cases during this period proved far more successful and led to a third wave of cases in which many courts held that estimates of the probability of a coincidentally matching VNTR profile were inadmissible. These estimates relied on a simplified population-genetics model for the frequencies of VNTR profiles, and some prominent scientists claimed that the applicability of the mathematical model had not been adequately verified. A heated debate on this point spilled over from courthouses to scientific journals and convinced the supreme courts of several states that general acceptance was lacking. A 1992 report of the National Academy of Sciences proposed a more "conservative" computational method as a compromise, and this seemed to undermine the claim of scientific acceptance of the less conservative procedure that was in general use.

In response to the population-genetics criticism and the 1992 report came an outpouring of critiques of the report and new studies of the distribution of VNTR alleles in many population groups. Relying on the burgeoning literature, a second National Academy panel concluded in 1996 that the usual method of estimating frequencies of VNTR profiles in broad racial groups was sound. In the corresponding fourth phase of judicial scrutiny of DNA evidence, the courts almost invariably returned to the earlier view that the statistics associated with VNTR profiling are generally accepted and scientifically valid.

The fifth phase of the judicial evaluation of DNA evidence is well underway. As results obtained with the new PCR-based methods enter the courtroom, it becomes necessary to ask whether each such method rests on a solid scientific foundation or is generally accepted in the scientific community. The opinions are practically unanimous in holding that the more commonly used PCR-based procedures satisfy these standards.

In sum, in little more than a decade, DNA typing has made the transition from a novel set of methods for identification to a relatively mature and well studied forensic technology. However, one should not lump all forms of DNA identification together. New techniques and applications continue to emerge. These range from the use of new genetic systems and new analytical procedures to the typing of DNA from plants and animals. Before admitting such evidence, it will be necessary to inquire into the biological principles and knowledge that would justify inferences from these new technologies or applications.

§ 206. Particular Tests: Psychology: Lie Detection, Drugs, Hypnosis, Eyewitness Testimony, Profiles, and Syndromes

The law and its procedures have long attracted the interest of psychologists. Although the preeminent contributions of psychologists and psychiatrists as expert witnesses have come in presenting clinical diagnoses or evaluations in criminal and other cases, at this point, we shall describe less conventional forensic applications. Specifically, this section surveys issues arising from expert testimony about physiological indicators of deception, "truth" drugs and hypnosis, eyewitness identifications, and "profiles" of certain types of offenders or victims.

A. *Detection of Deception.* Popular belief has it that lying and consciousness of guilt are accompanied by emotion or excitement that expresses itself in bodily changes—the blush, the gasp, the quickened heartbeat, the sweaty palm, the dry mouth. The skilled cross-examiner may face the witness with his lies and involve him in a knot of new ones, so that these characteristic signs of lying become visible to the jury. This is part of the demeanor of the witness that the jury is told it may observe and consider upon credibility.

Internal stress also has been thought to accompany the process of lying. It is said that more than 4,000 years ago the Chinese would try the accused in the presence of a physician who, listening or feeling for a change in the heartbeat, would announce whether the accused was testifying truthfully. The modern "lie detectors" operate on the same general principle. While an interrogator puts questions to the suspect, the polygraph monitors and records several autonomic physiological functions, such as blood pressure, pulse rate, respiration rate and depth, and perspiration (by measuring skin conductance). In the most commonly used procedure, the "diagnosis" is made by comparing the responses to "control" questions with the reactions to "relevant" questions. Control questions attempt to force the subject to lie about some common transgression. In an embezzlement case, for instance, a control question might be, "Have you ever stolen anything?" A relevant question is one that relates to the particular matter under investigation. If the autonomic disturbances associated with the relevant items seem greater or more persistent, then the subject is judged to be dissembling. In making this judgment, most federal and local law enforcement agencies employ some type of numerical scoring system. Other analysts apply a less structured procedure and insist that polygraphic lie detection is a "clinical judgment" that depends on "intrinsic emotional states," "medical conditions," and "unique" interviews.

The validity and reliability of the control question test are hotly contested. Polygraph examiners claim that, properly administered, it is a highly effective means of detecting deception, and they cite figures such as 92%, 99%, and even 100% for its accuracy. Although some controlled experiments and other studies have been interpreted as showing that such accuracy is possible, most psychologists reviewing the literature are not impressed with these bold assertions. They see methodological flaws undermining the conclusions, they suggest figures in a much lower range, and they point out that the percentage figures of "accuracy" are inappropriate measures of validity. Attempts to determine the rate of false positives—of saying that someone is lying when he is actually telling the truth—also have been controversial. Some writers claim that these errors rarely occur, but there are also studies and analyses that put the expected rate of false positives in excess of 35%. The skeptics also dispute the underlying theory. At best, the control question technique registers physiological correlates of anxiety, which is not the same thing as consciousness of guilt or lying. Questions can provoke inner turmoil even when they are answered truthfully. As one critic has put it, "the polygraph pens do no special dance when we are lying."[1] In addition, there are numerous countermeasures that a suspect can use to mislead the analyst, some of which are said to be effective and difficult to detect. It is feared that if the polygraph came into widespread use in court cases, these could cause the rate of false negatives—saying that the suspect is telling the truth when he is lying—to become intolerably high.

Another group of devices that measure a physiological response to detect when a person is consciously concealing knowledge are the voice stress analyzers. They analyze the frequency spectrum of a speaker's voice to detect subaudible, involuntary tremors said to result from emotional stress. The scientific literature on these lie detection devices indicates that they have no validity.

The courts have not greeted the modern methods of lie detection with enthusiasm. Indeed, *Frye v. United States*, the case that announced the general-acceptance standard for the admissibility of scientific evidence, involved a primitive version of the polygraph. In the succeeding decades, many courts treated the early decision as if it established that polygraph results were inadmissible regardless of any improvements in the technology. With the erosion of the general-acceptance requirement and the explosive growth of polygraphy in American government and business, however, a substantial number of courts have been willing to take a fresh look at the evidentiary value of the most commonly used polygraph tests. Three principal positions on admissibility have emerged, with considerable back and forth movement into and out of each category. First, there is the traditional rule that the test results are inadmissible when offered by either party, either as substantive evidence or as relating to the credibility of a witness. As a corollary, the willingness or unwillingness of a party or witness to submit to examination is also inadmissible. Second, a substantial minority of jurisdictions have carved out an exception to the rule of unconditional exclusion. In these jurisdictions the trial court has the discretion to receive polygraph testimony if the parties stipulated to the admission of the results prior to the testing and if certain other conditions are met. Third, in a small number of jurisdictions, admissibility even in the absence of a stipulation is said to be discretionary with the trial judge. Even in these jurisdictions, however, admission of unstipulated results is so rare as to be aberrational.

The widespread and strongly rooted reluctance to permit the introduction of polygraph evidence is grounded in a variety of concerns. The most frequently mentioned is that the technique is not generally accepted in the scientific community or is "unreliable" due to

§ 206

1. David Lykken, as quoted in Kleinmuntz & Szucko, on The Fallibility of Lie Detection, 17 Law & Soc'y Rev.

85, 88 (1981).

inherent failings, a shortage of qualified opera-tors, and the prospect that "coaching" and practicing would become commonplace if the evidence were generally admissible. Because there is intense disagreement in the literature as to the premise that even a truly expert polygrapher is capable of distinguishing truth-ful statements from intentional falsehoods in realistic situations at rates significantly above chance levels, admissibility under the *Frye* test is, at best, doubtful. Likewise, whether polyg-raphy possesses the modicum of demonstrated validity demanded under the federal rules as interpreted in *Daubert v. Merrell Dow Phar-maceuticals, Inc.*, is open to grave question.

Yet, the decisive arguments against admis-sion go beyond the search for the artificial level of "acceptance" or "reliability" com-pelled by *Frye* and *Daubert*. After all, a great deal of lay testimony routinely admitted is at least as unreliable and inaccurate, and other forms of scientific evidence involve risks of instrumental or judgmental error. Rather, the more compelling argument against admissibili-ty adjusts the requisite quantum of acceptance or validity to the type of evidence in question. If the probative value of polygraph readings is slight (or would be if barriers to admissi-bility were dropped), then their value easily is outweighed by the countervailing consider-ations. These counterweights are the danger that jurors would be unduly impressed with the "scientific" testimony on a crucial and typically determinative matter, that judicial and related resources would be squandered in producing and coping with the expert testimo-ny, and that routine admissibility would put undesirable pressure on defendants to forfeit the right against self-incrimination.

Some of these concerns may be overstated, and the miscellaneous other reasons that courts sometimes give for excluding polygraph

tests may not withstand analysis.[2] Nonethe-less, it would seem that opening up the matter to the discretion of the trial courts—without providing more detailed standards than the usual balancing prescription—could lead to untoward results. Nor is the "stipulation-only" approach satisfactory.[3] Whether poly-graph testimony should be admitted is doubt-ful, but if it is to be received, clear standards should be developed as to whether such testi-mony is admissible solely for impeachment purposes, how important the testimony must be in the context of the other evidence in the case for admissibility to be warranted, what level of training and competence examiners should have, what precautions should be taken against deceptive practices on the part of ex-aminees, and what procedures would be best to give an independent or opposing expert a meaningful opportunity to view or review the examination and analysis. When all is said and done, the game simply does not seem worth the candle. A categorical rule of exclusion is a logical and defensible corollary to the general principles of relevancy.[4]

B. *Drugs and Hypnosis.* Psychologists and psychiatrists have used hypnosis and hyp-notic drugs for diagnosis and therapy. Resort to these techniques became prevalent in the treatment of traumatic war neuroses during World War II, and the methods have been applied to the treatment of hysterical amnesi-as, catatonic conditions, and psychosomatic disorders. They have also been employed to test the truthfulness of a witness' testimony as well as to enhance recall.

Although the scientific study of hypnosis began over 200 years ago, a single, satisfactory explanation of the phenomenon has yet to emerge. The scientific studies do make it clear, however, that people who are hypnotized or

---

2. It sometimes is said that polygraph results would not aid the jury because the credibility of a witness is susceptible to resolution without expert testimony. Talk of "prejudice to the jury process," People v. Anderson, 637 P.2d 354, 362 (Colo.1981), may reflect this cramped view of the scope of expert testimony in addition to the previ-ously catalogued concerns. The real issue, of course, is not whether juries can decide which witnesses to believe with-out polygraph testing, but rather how much such testing would enhance those decisions—and at what cost.

3. Recognizing that the presence of a stipulation does not enhance the validity or reliability of the examiner's conclusions, many courts have declined to relax their traditional exclusionary rule to recognize stipulations.

4. Being founded in part on the reasonable judgment that the evidence uniformly is low in probative value, the "per se" rule constitutionally can be applied to exclude evidence that a defendant in a criminal case passed a polygraph test. United States v. Scheffer, 523 U.S. 303 (1998).

given "truth serum" do not always tell the truth. Indeed, subjects have been known to feign, quite convincingly, a hypnotized state. Even though some studies suggest that in certain circumstances hypnosis can enhance memory, the effect is not well established in experimental studies, and it is clear that hypnosis can *alter* memory. Hypnotized persons are highly suggestible, and some authorities believe that when a hypnotist encourages a subject to relate everything he can possibly remember, the subject produces fragments and approximations of memory in an effort to be cooperative. In addition, the subject may accept as his own recollections distortions inadvertently suggested by the hypnotist. Finally, the hypnotic session may reinforce the witness' confidence in erroneous memories.

Forensic applications of hypnosis can generate a variety of constitutional and evidentiary issues. A party may seek admission of statements a witness made while under hypnosis or narcoanalysis to show directly the existence of certain facts, to impeach or buttress credibility, or to show the basis for a psychiatric or psychological opinion. Similarly, a party may offer the in-court testimony of a witness even though this testimony may be influenced or "tainted" by this person's prior exposure to such interrogation.

The courts have been most reluctant to admit such statements or testimony. In the first case to raise the issue, a California court stated in 1897 that "the law of the United States does not recognize hypnotism."[5] Since then the courts nearly always have excluded statements made under hypnosis or narcoanalysis, regardless of whether these statements are offered as substantive evidence or as bearing on credibility.

Posthypnotic testimony as to recollections enhanced or evoked under hypnosis has produced more divergent holdings. A few courts have said that such testimony is generally admissible, with objections as to its accuracy bearing on the weight that the finder of fact should give it. But even in these jurisdictions there is a tendency to insist on rigorous safe-

guards for the hypnotically refreshed memories to be admissible. The far more prevalent view is that testimony about the posthypnotic memories is inadmissible, although the once hypnotized witness may be permitted to testify to memories demonstrably held prior to hypnosis, and in *Rock v. Arkansas*,[6] the Supreme Court held that the constitution precludes categorical exclusion of the hypnotically refreshed testimony of a criminal defendant who cannot present a meaningful defense without that testimony.

Typically, the courts adopting a strict exclusionary rule rely on the *Frye* test of general scientific acceptance, although the same result could be reached by examining scientific validity under *Daubert* or inquiring directly into the relative costs and benefits of the testimony. Indeed, the more modern cases support their invocation and application of the general acceptance standard by examining scientific testimony or literature on the value of hypnosis for recovering memories and by referring to the usual concerns with scientific evidence— its suspected tendency to over-awe the jury and to consume time and resources—in a matter of particular sensitivity.

When an expert uses narcoanalysis or hypnosis to determine whether a subject is insane, incompetent, or mentally incapacitated, the case for admissibility is much stronger. A few courts have excluded expert opinions based on these techniques, but this position seems difficult to defend even under the restrictive general acceptance standard. Most courts recognize that the opinions of the experts may be admitted and that the revelation of the details of what the subject said while under hypnosis or drugs is within the trial judge's discretion. Thus, the trial court may permit the expert to give an explanation of the underlying information along with an opinion, but still curb the introduction of the statements made under hypnosis or narcoanalysis.

C. *Eyewitness Testimony*. For many years, expert testimony has been received to show that mental disorders may have affected the testimony of eyewitnesses. In the 1970s,

---

5. *People v. Ebanks*, 49 P. 1049, 1053 (Cal.1897) (excluding testimony about statements given under hypnosis).

6. 483 U.S. 44 (1987).

criminal defendants also began to call on psychologists to offer expert opinions on the factors that ordinarily influence the reliability of eyewitness identifications. Typically, the expert testifies to generalizations from experiments in which students or other subjects have witnessed a film or other enactment or description of the kind of events that are the subjects of courtroom testimony. In such studies, the accuracy of the recall of faces or facts is then tested under a variety of conditions. The overall findings indicate that such witnesses often make mistakes, that they tend to make more mistakes in cross-racial identifications as well as when the events involve violence, that errors are easily introduced by misleading questions asked shortly after the witness has viewed the simulated happening, and that the professed confidence of the subjects in their identifications bears no consistent relation to the accuracy of these recognitions.

Testimony about such research findings has been received in some cases and rejected in others. Given the extreme deference usually accorded trial court decisions on the need for expert testimony, these decisions seem almost invariably to be upheld. Although a handful of courts have held that exclusion of expert testimony on highly pertinent aspects of eyewitness identifications constitutes an abuse of discretion or that this testimony is not categorically excluded, many of the appellate opinions display a distinct distaste for such testimony. These opinions argue that since an appreciation of the limitations on eyewitnesses' perceptions and memory is within the ken of a lay jury, broad brush psychological testimony about these mechanisms would not appreciably assist the jury. They point also to the standard concerns with scientific evidence—that lay jurors will overstate its importance and that its introduction will entail undue expense and confusion.

Some courts are dubious of the scientific validity of the psychological research. The more poorly reasoned opinions speak of invading the province of the jury.

The matter cannot be disposed of this easily. Concern over the reliability of eyewitness testimony lies at the heart of the Supreme Court's right to counsel and due process decisions in cases involving lineups and other pretrial identification procedures. It may well be that without some counteracting influence, juries give too much weight to the witness's assertions of recognition. To contend that juries know how to evaluate the reliability of the identifications without expert assistance, while simultaneously maintaining that the assistance would have too great an impact on the jury's deliberations, smacks of makeshift reasoning. Admittedly, there are dangers—some obvious and some subtle—in translating laboratory and classroom demonstrations of witness fallibility into conclusions about the accuracy of a particular witness's identification in a real life setting. Nevertheless, it would seem that the researchers have something to offer, and that where a case turns on uncorroborated eyewitness recognition, the courts should be receptive to expert testimony about the knowledge, gleaned from methodologically sound experimentation, concerning the factors that may have produced a faulty identification. Although the researcher must be circumspect in stating inferences about a particular witness's testimony,[7] the pertinent research findings should assist the jury in evaluating a crucial piece of evidence. While expert testimony on the psychology of eyewitness identifications may not be necessary or appropriate in many cases, in those instances where the case turns on the eyewitness testimony and the expert's assistance could make a difference, the scientific knowledge generally should be admitted, either through expert testimony or judicial instructions concerning factors affecting eyewit-

---

7. Loftus, Eyewitness Testimony 200 (1979) ("Any psychologist who attempted to offer an exact probability for the likelihood that a witness was accurate would be going far beyond what is possible"). Although there is no longer any specific prohibition on allowing an expert to express an opinion on an "ultimate" fact, the need to avoid undue prejudice can justify curtailing testimony.

Thus, it has been held that it is proper to allow a clinical psychologist to "testify regarding those factors which he believed could influence eyewitness identifications," but to prevent him "from stating to the jury his own opinion as to the reliability of [the particular] identification." Hampton v. State, 285 N.W.2d 868, 872 (Wis.1979).

ness accuracy that are important to assessing the identification in question and that are not well understood by most jurors.

D. *Profiles and Syndromes.* Psychological studies sometimes show a correlation between certain traits or characteristics and certain forms of behavior. When this is the case, one can construct a diagnostic or predictive "profile" for such behavior. For instance, retrospective analysis of individuals apprehended while smuggling drugs through airports shows that these persons tend to arrive from major points of distribution, to have little or no luggage with them, to look nervously about, to arrive in the early morning, and to have large amounts of cash in small bills. Studies of "accident prone" persons indicate that such factors as having poor eyesight, being relatively young or old, and acting impulsively, aggressively or rebelliously are prevalent in this group. Physicians regard certain patterns of physical injuries in children, which they designate the "battered child syndrome," as indicating repeated physical abuse. Indeed, we all evaluate information in the light of some such "profiles." Jurors, for example, can be said to bring to the courtroom their preconceived "profiles" which they then apply to decide who is lying and who is telling the truth, and who is likely to have committed an offense and who is innocent. Although there is no fundamental difference between the psychological and medical profiles and the more common, impressionistic ones, some of the former may have been derived in a more systematic and structured way, and some may have been tested by verifying that they give correct diagnoses or predictions when applied to new cases. The correlations obtained in such prospective studies measure the validity of the profiles.

Particularly in criminal cases, litigants have sought to introduce expert testimony as to the scientifically constructed or validated profiles. The "battered woman syndrome"[8] has been invoked by women to support pleas of self-defense in murder cases, to buttress defenses of duress in cases in which they aided their abusive partners in criminal activity, to explain inconsistencies in a woman's testimony or statements, and in various other situations. Prosecutors in sexual abuse cases have relied on the "rape trauma syndrome"[9] to negate a claim of consent, to explain conflicting statements or actions of the complainant, to prove criminal sexual penetration, and defendants have introduced evidence that a complainant did not experience the syndrome's symptoms. In sexual abuse cases involving children, prosecutors have relied on a similar "sexual abuse accommodation syndrome" for children to prove the fact of abuse or to explain the child's delay in reporting the abuse, his or her retraction of the accusation, or other behavior apparently inconsistent with abuse. They also have relied on expert testimony that children who report sexual abuse generally are truthful. In child abuse and homicide cases, prosecutors have called witnesses to establish that defendants exhibited the "battering parent syndrome." And defendants accused of sexual offenses have offered testimony to the effect that they did not fit the profiles for sexual offenders.

When the plaintiff or the government offers evidence that the defendant fits an incriminating profile, it may be excluded under the rule that prohibits evidence of character to show conduct on a particular occasion.[10] Yet, arguably the rule should not bar admission in all such cases. After all, the rule rests on the premise that the marginal probative value of character evidence generally is low while the potential for distraction, time-consumption and prejudice is high. Where the profile is not

---

8. Many courts and commentators quickly embraced the theories of "cycles" and "learned helplessness" propounded in Walker, The Battered Woman (1979). But see Faigman, Note, The Battered Woman Syndrome and Self–Defense: A Legal and Empirical Dissent, 72 Va. L. Rev. 619, 647 (1986) (since "the leading research suffers from significant methodological and interpretive flaws," "[t]he prevailing theories of battered woman syndrome have little evidentiary value in self-defense cases").

9. The "rape trauma syndrome" is a form of post-traumatic stress disorder (PTSD). The latter condition is listed in American Psychiatric Association, Diagnostic and Statistical Manual of Mental Disorders 236 (3d ed. 1980). It has been suggested that since there is no rape-specific syndrome, the phrase "rape trauma syndrome" should be avoided. State v. Taylor, 663 S.W.2d 235 (Mo.1984).

10. See supra § 190.

itself likely to arouse sympathy or hostility, the argument for applying the rule against character evidence to prove conduct on a particular occasion is weakened. Conversely, if it were shown that the profile was both valid and revealing—that it distinguishes between offenders and non-offenders with great accuracy—then the balance might favor admissibility. It is far from clear, however, that any existing profile is this powerful.

When the profile evidence is used defensively (to show good character, to restore credibility, or to prove apprehension in connection with a claim of self-defense), it falls under an exception to the rule against character evidence.[11] Admissibility then should turn on the extent to which the expert testimony would assist the jury viewed in the light of the usual counterweights.[12] The qualifications of the expert, the degree of acceptance in the appropriate scientific community, the reliability and validity of using the profile, and the need for the evidence in light of what most jurors know about the behaviors in question, and whether the expert crosses the line between the general and the specific[13] or tries to evaluate the truthfulness of the witness or a class of witnesses,[14] thus affect the admissibility and of course the weight of the profile evidence. For example, it is not clear how the "battered woman syndrome" helps show the reasonableness of the use of deadly force within the traditional doctrine of self-defense. The effect of the syndrome evidence in such situations is to redefine the substantive law. This result suggests the need for a stronger scientific base than now exists for the expert testimony.

In some ways, profile evidence resembles expert testimony, considered earlier in this section, describing the results of psychological research into eyewitness identifications. In both instances, the expert provides background information that might contradict lay impressions and that the jury can apply to the case at hand, if persuaded to do so. Perhaps

the greater receptivity of the appellate courts to psychological profile evidence stems from the fact that this type of testimony seems more like the clinical assessments routinely received from psychologists and physicians. In addition, considering the subject matter of most of the psychological profiles that have come to the attention of the courts, it is likely that a growing sensitivity to women's and children's issues has played a major role.

§ 207. Particular Tests: Criminalistics: Identifying Persons and Things

Many of the techniques of scientific criminal investigation, or criminalistics, are aimed at identifying people or things. Fingerprinting, studying the trajectories and characteristics of bullets and firearms, examining questioned documents, detecting and identifying poisons and other drugs, microscopically comparing hair samples and fibers, and matching blood stains are among the better known examples. In addition, there is a vast array of less familiar techniques for detecting and analyzing what might be called "trace evidence" of criminal or other activity. These include other applications of microanalysis, forensic odontology, anthropology, entomology, and somewhat esoteric chemical and physical tests used in connection with fingerprints, firearms, glass fragments, hair, paints, explosions and fires, questioned documents, and recordings.

While these methods are unquestionably of great value in many investigations, their use in the courtroom can pose problems. Perhaps to emphasize the scientific quality of the analysis, or merely in an effort to be as precise as possible, expert witnesses may state the results or implications of their tests in quantitative, probabilistic terms—a practice that causes difficulty for the courts. Furthermore, a few of these analytic procedures or tests are themselves specially adapted or developed for forensic purposes and well known primarily in law enforcement circles. Consequently, the

---

11. See supra §§ 191 & 194.

12. See supra § 203.

13. Many courts allow some generalized or "social framework" testimony but exclude expert opinions on the

applicability of the profile or the credibility of a witness in a given case.

14. State v. Lindsey, 720 P.2d 73, 76 (Ariz.1986) (error to allow testimony that "[t]he one statistic that I have found [was] that it was possibly one percent that lied").

test of general scientific acceptance does not always work well in this context, and this incongruity can result in important opinions on the standards governing the admissibility of scientific evidence.

The spectrographic analysis of human voices illustrates this last point. Complex sound waves, such as those involved in speech, can be understood mathematically as sums of simple waveforms of various frequencies. The frequency spectrum of such a sound wave is, in effect, a list of each such constituent frequency and its relative importance in describing the composite sound. Since the 1940s or 1950s, electronic devices that analyze sound waves into these frequency components have been available. A spectrogram is a graphic representation of this information, that is, a picture of the frequency spectrum of a sound wave. In the 1960s, it was proposed that the spectral characteristics of a speaker's voice could identify that speaker. The theory behind this suggestion was that individuals have different but largely stable patterns in the way they manipulate their lips, teeth, and so on in speaking. From the outset, this hypothesis has been controversial. If it is false, then comparisons of spectrograms should not produce consistently correct identifications. Despite a few early (and seemingly extravagant) claims of accurate identifications, subsequent studies providing better approximations of realistic forensic conditions report misidentifications at rates ranging from 18% (12% false negatives and 6% false positives) to 70 and 80% (including 42% false positives). Many scientists therefore doubt the reliability and validity of the current technique.

Most courts applying the general scientific acceptance test to voice spectrographic evidence have held the evidence inadmissible. In fact, this evidence has inspired some of the most spirited and thoughtful defenses of the general acceptance standard for scientific evidence. On the other hand, faith in the method and a belief that jurors will not find it overly impressive have prompted some courts to bend the *Frye* test to the breaking point to conclude that the evidence should be admissible. Whatever standard may be applied, however, it

seems that until further research makes the validity of the technique plainer, the courts will remain divided over the admissibility of voice spectrographic identification.

§ 208. Statistical Studies: Surveys and Opinion Polls

Samuel Johnson once remarked that "You don't have to eat the whole ox to know the hide is tough." In the past, courts required litigants to dismember and devour an ox or two to prove a point. However, with the development and implementation of scientific survey methods, the courts are much more receptive to proof based on sample data. The Federal and Uniform Rules sweep aside traditional hearsay objections and allow the evidence to come in, if it is reasonably reliable, as the basis for an expert opinion. Specially commissioned surveys or samples have been used to support motions for a change of venue in response to pretrial publicity, to show consumer perceptions in trademark and misleading advertising cases, to unmask community standards in obscenity prosecutions, and for numerous other purposes. Advocates have also relied on pre-existing research involving sample data in product liability, food and drug, environmental, and other cases. The modern opinions have said that case-specific surveys are generally admissible if they are conducted according to the principles accepted by social scientists and statisticians for gathering and analyzing survey data. This section therefore attempts to give an overview of these principles—adherence to which affects the weight as well as the admissibility of survey evidence. In a great many cases, courts have carefully examined whether the conclusions of the survey researchers rest on data collected in such a way as to permit fair inferences about the relevant factual questions.

Although many refinements are possible, the basic ideas behind scientific survey techniques are simple enough. The researcher tries to collect information from a manageable portion (a sample) of a larger group (a population) to learn something about the population. Usually some numbers are used to characterize the population, and these are called parameters. For example, the proportion of all consumers who would mistake one product for another because of a similarity in the brand names is a population parameter. Sample data lead to statistics, such as the proportion of the persons in the sample who are confused by the similarity. These sample statistics are then used to estimate the population parameters. If 50% of the sample studied exhibited confusion between the products with the similar brand names, then one might conclude that 50% of the population would be confused. Under some circumstances, statistical methods enable the researcher not only to make an estimate, but to state the probability that such an estimate would differ from the unknown parameter by a given amount—that is, to quantify the error that may be lurking in the estimate.

Sampling underlies almost every pertinent research effort. Descriptive surveys, like those introduced in connection with change of venue motions, are almost always confined to a sample of the entire population. Surveys looking for causal explanations (such as a survey of homicide rates in states that do and states that do not have capital punishment) usually involve samples. Even experiments designed to investigate causation, such as a trial of a new drug, typically produce only sample data. Many such surveys are nonverbal. Since an employer's records can be inspected, no one needs to poll the current employees to obtain data on the distribution of wages paid to men as opposed to women. Other surveys are personal or verbal, as we know from experience with survey interviewers and written questionnaires.

What factors are likely to make such surveys produce accurate as opposed to misleading estimates? We can identify two major categories of errors: random errors and non-random errors. There are many potential sources of non-random, or systematic errors. In personal surveys, these include the specification of the population to be sampled, the technique for eliciting responses, the wording of the questions, the method for choosing and finding respondents, and the failure to pose questions that address the proper issues. Unless those sources of non-random er-

ror cancel each other out, any estimates made on the basis of the sample data will be biased. Making the sample size larger offers no protection against bias. It only produces a larger number of biased observations.

Random errors arise at two levels. The first is with respect to the observations on each unit sampled. In a nonverbal study, a measuring instrument (such as an instrument to determine breath alcohol content) might well give slightly different readings even on identical samples. A person seeking to get rid of an interviewer may say whatever pops into mind. The process for making individual measurements or observations is rarely perfectly reliable. The second kind of random error results from variability from one sample to the next. One sample of air expelled from the lungs may be slightly different from the next in its concentration of alcohol. Even though great care may be taken to assure that the people selected for interviews are representative of the population, there can be no guarantee that another sample selected by the same procedure would give identical responses. As such, even if all the answers or measurements are individually free from error, sampling variability remains a source of statistical, or chance error.

If methods known as probability sampling are employed, however, the magnitude of the sampling error (but not of the non-random errors) can be estimated. Probability sampling also has been shown to be very effective in producing representative samples. The reason is that unlike human beings, blind chance is impartial. Probability sampling uses an objective chance process to pick the sample. It leaves no discretion to the interviewers. As a result, the researcher can compute the chance that any particular unit in the population will be selected for the sample. Stated another way, a probability sample is one in which each unit of the sampling frame has a known, nonzero probability of being selected. Other samples, either "convenience" samples or "quota" samples, do not have this property, and they are acceptable only in special circumstances. A common type of probability sampling is simple random sampling, in which every unit has the same probability of being sampled. It amounts to drawing names at random without replacement.

The statistics derived from observations or measurements of random samples permit one to estimate the parameters of the population. In a consumer confusion survey for instance, some proportion of the sample of consumers who are interviewed will indicate confusion between the products. If the sample is a simple random sample, and if there are no non-random errors, then this sample proportion is an unbiased estimator of the proportion for all consumers. But it is only an estimate. Another random sample probably would not include precisely the same persons, and it probably would produce a slightly different proportion of responses indicating confusion. There is no single figure that expresses the extent of this statistical error. There are only probabilities. If one were to draw a second random sample, find the proportion of confused consumers in this group, then do the same for a third random sample, a fourth, and so on, one would obtain a distribution of sample proportions fluctuating about some central value. Some would be far away from the mean, but most would be closer. Pursuing this logic in a rigorous way, the statistician computes a "confidence interval" and gives an "interval estimate" for the population proportion. The analyst may report that at a 90% confidence level, the population proportion is 50% plus or minus 10%. This means that if the same method for drawing samples and interviewing the customers were repeated a very large number of times, and if a 90% confidence interval were computed about each sample, 90% of the resulting interval estimates would be correct. This many would include the population proportion, whatever that number happens to be.

Although testimony as to confidence intervals often is received in cases involving survey evidence, its meaning apparently remains obscure in many cases. Note that a confidence of, say, 90% does not necessarily mean that the interval estimate has a 90% probability of being correct. Strictly speaking, all that the classical statistical methodology reveals is that the particular interval was obtained by a method that gives intervals that would capture the true proportion in 90% of all possible samples. But each such interval estimate could be different. Thus, the "confidence" pertains to the process rather than to any particular result. Despite this difficulty in interpreting a confidence interval, the technique does give the finder of fact some idea of the risk of error in equating the sample proportion to the population figure. If the interval is small, even for a high level of "confidence," then the sample proportion is reasonably accurate, at least in the sense that taking more, or larger samples probably would give similar results.

The width of the confidence interval depends on three things. For a given sample, there is a trade-off between the level of confidence and the narrowness of the interval. One can be sure that the population proportion lies somewhere between zero and one. The confidence is 100%, but the interval is so broad as to be useless. Lowering the confidence level narrows the range of the estimate, but there is more risk in concluding that the population value lies within the narrower interval. Second, for a given confidence and a fixed sample size, the width of the interval depends on how homogeneous the population is. If nearly every consumer would be confused (or nearly no one would be), then there will be minimal sampling variability, since almost all the possible samples can be expected to look alike. Hence, the confidence interval for any sample will be very narrow. On the other hand, if the population is highly variable, then there are more chances to draw aberrant samples, and the computed confidence interval for any sample will be larger. Third, whatever the makeup of the population, larger samples give more reliable results than smaller ones. However, the point of diminishing returns rapidly is reached in that adding the same amount to the sample size does little to narrow the confidence interval. It is wrong to believe that one always needs to sample a substantial proportion of a large population to obtain an accurate estimate of a population parameter.

In assessing the statistical error of a survey, therefore, the courts should look to the interval estimates rather than to untutored intuitions as to how large a sample is needed. Deciding what level of confidence is appropriate in a particular case, however, is a policy question and not a statistical issue. Finally, in making use of surveys, it is important to remember that the statistical analysis does not address the non-random sources of error. A small confidence interval is not worth much if the data collection is badly flawed.

§ 209. Statistical Studies: Correlations and Causes: Statistical Evidence of Discrimination

Survey evidence, as we described it in the previous section, involves sampling from some population, deriving statistics from the sample data, and offering some conclusion about the population in light of these sample statistics. In this section, we describe applications and extensions of this approach used to supply and interpret evidence on the issue of causation. When causation is at issue, advocates have relied on three major types of information—anecdotal evidence, observational studies, and controlled experiments. Anecdotal reports can provide some information, but they are more useful as a stimulus for further inquiry than as a basis for establishing association or causation. Observational studies can establish that one factor is associated with another, but considerable analysis may be necessary to bridge the gap from association to causation. Controlled experiments are ideal for ascertaining causation, but they can be difficult to undertake.

"Anecdotal evidence" means reports of one kind of event following another. Typically, the reports are obtained haphazardly or selectively, and the logic of "post hoc, ergo propter hoc" does not suffice to demonstrate that the first event causes the second. Consequently,

while anecdotal evidence can be suggestive, it can also be quite misleading. For instance, some children who live near power lines develop leukemia; but does exposure to electrical and magnetic fields cause this disease? The anecdotal evidence is not compelling because leukemia also occurs among children who have minimal exposure to such fields. It is necessary to compare disease rates among those who are exposed and those who are not. If exposure causes the disease, the rate should be higher among the exposed, lower among the unexposed. Of course, the two groups may differ in crucial ways other than the exposure. For example, children who live near power lines could come from poorer families and be exposed to other environmental hazards. These differences could create the appearance of a cause-and-effect relationship, or they could mask a real relationship. Cause-and-effect relationships often are quite subtle, and carefully-designed studies are needed to draw valid conclusions. Thus, some courts have suggested that attempts to infer causation from anecdotal reports are inadmissible as unsound methodology under *Daubert v. Merrell Dow Pharmaceuticals, Inc.*[1]

Typically, a well-designed study will compare outcomes for subjects who are exposed to some factor—the treatment group—and other subjects who are not so exposed—the control group. A distinction must then be made between controlled experiments and observational studies. In a controlled experiment, the investigators decide which subjects are exposed to the factor of interest and which subjects go into the control group. In most observational studies, the subjects themselves choose their exposures. Because of this self-selection, the treatment and control groups of observational studies are likely differ with respect to important factors other than the variable whose

§ 209

1. 509 U.S. 579 (1993). See, e.g., Haggerty v. Upjohn Co., 950 F.Supp. 1160, 1163–64 (S.D.Fla.1996) (holding that reports to the Food and Drug Administration of "adverse medical events" involving the drug Halcion and "anecdotal case reports appearing in medical literature * * * can be used to generate hypotheses about causation, but not causation conclusions" because "scientifically valid cause and effect determinations depend on controlled

clinical trials and epidemiological studies"); Cartwright v. Home Depot U.S.A., Inc. 936 F.Supp. 900, 905 (M.D.Fla. 1996) (excluding an expert's opinion that latex paint caused plaintiffs' asthma, in part because "case reports * * * are no substitute for a scientifically designed and conducted inquiry"); Casey v. Ohio Med. Prods., 877 F.Supp. 1380, 1385 (N.D.Cal.1995); Schmaltz v. Norfolk & W. Ry. Co., 878 F.Supp. 1119, 1122 (N.D.Ill.1995).

effects are of primary interest. (These other factors are called confounding variables or lurking variables.) With studies on the health effects of power lines, family background is a possible confounder; so is exposure to other hazards.

Whether the data come from observational or experimental studies, the conclusions that can be drawn will involve further statistical assessments. Parties in environmental and product liability cases typically rely on statistical reasoning to establish that a chemical or other agent is carcinogenic or toxic. In civil rights cases, parties seeking to prove (or disprove) that a class or an individual has been subjected to unlawful discrimination may find statistical evidence useful. In antitrust litigation, a party may use statistical analysis to show illegal conduct and its effects. In business litigation generally, a party may apply statistical techniques to estimate lost profits or other damages resulting from illegal conduct. In these and other sorts of cases, the statistics, and inferences drawn from them, usually will be admissible via the testimony of a suitably qualified expert.

The weight that may be given such testimony will depend, of course, on the skill of counsel and the ability and preparation of the witness. In addition, the methods that the expert uses to analyze and interpret that data, so as to assist the court or jury in understanding it, may be of great importance in determining the outcome. This section outlines one of the statistical concepts most frequently encountered in connection with sophisticated statistical proofs. Because most cases addressing the usefulness of this concept arose in the context of discrimination issues, we shall draw on a few of the developments in this area to illustrate some general points about the presentation of statistical evidence.

The courts have relied heavily on statistical evidence in cases in which a criminal defendant alleges that he was indicted by an unconstitutionally selected grand jury or an unconstitutionally empaneled petit jury. There is no constitutionally permissible basis for systematically excluding, say, members of defendant's race from the population of citizens who are eligible for jury duty. Where direct evidence of discrimination is unavailable, or where additional proof is desired, statistical methods have been pressed into service. The usual procedure is to compare the proportion of the persons eligible for jury service who are in the class allegedly discriminated against with the corresponding proportion appearing on jury venires or pools. Substantial underrepresentation over a significant period of time is taken as evidence of discrimination.

In early cases, the courts made purely intuitive assessments of the disparity in the proportions. More recent cases use formal statistical reasoning to evaluate the quantitative evidence. The logic begins from the assumption that selection of potential jurors is a random process, like blindly drawing differently colored marbles from an urn, in which the chance that a person in the protected class will be selected is the same in each instance. Under the "null" hypothesis, which is consistent with the position that there is no discrimination, the probability of picking a member of the protected class each time is simply the overall proportion of these individuals in the eligible population. The alternative to this hypothesis is not always specified clearly, but usually amounts to the claim that the chance of picking a protected class member is not equal to the population proportion. The statistical analyst calculates the probability that so few members of the protected class would be chosen for jury service if each selection were made by the random process described above with the parameter stated in the null hypothesis. This probability is called a "P-value." It states the chance that the observed disparity would result from bad luck, or coincidence. If it is very small, it is taken to indicate that the null hypothesis is implausible. If the P-value, or probability of the data given the assumptions behind the null hypothesis, is large, it is taken to indicate that this hypothesis of no discrimination is consistent with the data. The P-value thus serves as an index of the statistical force of the quantitative evidence—the smaller the P-value, the more unlikely it is that the statistical disparity was the result of the chance process.

But the P-value is not the only such index, and some statisticians do not think that it is the best. One problem with its use in court is the tendency of some expert witnesses or judges to assume that because there is an arbitrary convention of insisting on P-values of .05 or less before labelling scientific findings "statistically significant," this same number should be required before the factfinder may rely on the quantitative results. If the P-value is not to be misleading, its meaning must be clearly understood. The factfinder must realize that the P-value is not itself evidence. Neither is it a statement of how large the observed underrepresentation is. It is merely one measure of the probative force of statistical evidence, and an incomplete measure at that. This is not to deny that it is a useful concept. Properly understood, it may assist the court or jury in assessing the statistical evidence.

This approach also is used in employment discrimination cases. There is more difficulty in defining the relevant population from which employees are drawn, there are more variables to consider, the sample sizes tend to be smaller, and the mechanics of computing P-values may differ, but the meaning of the P-value and of "statistical significance" is the same. When complicated statistical models are used to account for the effects of many variables, however, many subtle errors are possible, and an uncritical acceptance of the estimates derived from these models and their calculated P-values can be misleading. In short, for this form of scientific testimony, the battle is not usually over the admissibility of statistical evidence in general or over the use of concepts like the P-value to assess the evidence. Rather, the battlelines are drawn when it comes to the admissibility of obviously flawed applications, to the weight that should be given the evidence, and to transforming methods and conventions of statistical inference into rules of law.

§ 210. Probabilities as Evidence: Identification Evidence Generally

The previous two sections discussed the use of probability calculations in connection with statistical studies. When the statistical analyst takes properly collected sample data, computes some statistics such as a proportion, a difference between two means, or a regression coefficient, and calculates a P-value or a confidence interval for each such statistic, the courts are willing to rely on the probabilities in assessing the force of the statistical evidence. Especially in criminal cases, however, the courts are substantially more reluctant to admit probability calculations intended to show the identity of a wrongdoer. This section examines the admissibility of probability calculations relating to the myriad forms of identification evidence—eyewitness testimony, blood tests, fingerprints, bitemarks, questioned document examinations, microanalysis, and so on. The next section focuses on the role of probability calculations in paternity litigation.

In one important sense, all evidence is statistical. Admittedly, courts sometimes suggest that evidence about a class of objects cannot be used to support a conclusion about a particular member of the class. But we rely on such evidence all the time. Law schools admit students with high grades and test scores because they have had favorable experiences with other such students, surgeons perform drastic operations on patients because they have had beneficial effects in some proportion of cases in the past, legislatures enact statutes making it an offense to drive with a blood alcohol concentration exceeding an amount seen to impair the functioning of a sample of persons, and juries tend to convict or acquit defendants because of hunches or beliefs about how certain classes of people behave, and they award damages in wrongful death cases with the assistance of mortality tables that reflect the experiences of many other men or women.

So, too, any expert giving any opinion on whether the scientific test identifies the defendant as being the person who left the incriminating trace, such as a fingerprint, bullet, or bloodstain, necessarily bases this conclusion on an understanding or impression of how similar the items being compared are and how common it is to find items with these similarities. If these beliefs have any basis in fact, it is to be found in the general experience of the criminalists or more exacting statistical studies of these matters. In brief, the reluctance to allow testimony or argument about probabilities must be justified, if at all, on the basis of something other than an undifferentiated claim about the logical weakness of relying on probabilities derived from statistics about other persons or things. In fact, a variety of more conventional concerns about "probability evidence"—a term that is something of a misnomer[1]—surface in the decisions in this area. These relate to the probative value of the explicit quantification and the tendency of the seemingly impressive numbers to mislead or confuse the jury.

To begin with, for more than a hundred years there have been attempts to compute the probability of observing a conjunction of certain incriminating characteristics by assuming that each characteristic is statistically independent and that the probabilities of these presumably independent characteristics could be obtained by introspection. In what may be the most notorious of these cases, police apprehended a man and a woman fitting descriptions supplied by eyewitnesses near the scene of a robbery. The prosecutor proposed figures for the frequencies of such things as an interracial couple in a car, a girl with a pony tail, a partly yellow automobile, a man with a mustache, and so on. A mathematics professor testified to the rule that the joint probability of a series of independent events is the product of the probabilities of each event. Applying this rule to the "conservative estimates" that he had propounded, the prosecutor concluded that there was but one chance in 12 million that any couple possessed the distinctive characteristics of the defendants, and he argued that "the chances of anyone else besides these defendants being there, * * * having every similarity, * * * is something like one in a billion."[2]

In these cases, the appellate courts hold that it is error to admit such testimony on the ground that the hypothesized values used in computing the probability of the joint event

are sheer speculation. In addition, some opinions decry the use of the multiplication rule for the probabilities of independent events when there is reason to believe that the events are dependent. Because the computations have little basis in fact and are presented in the guise of expert analysis, they are excluded under the principle that their prejudicial impact clearly outweighs their probative value.

In another group of cases, there are some data for calculating the joint probability. While many forensic experts are content to describe the points of similarity between the incriminating traces and material taken from the defendant or his belongings and to leave it to the jury to decide how unlikely it would be to find all these similarities by mere coincidence, from time to time, the experts testify to vanishingly small probabilities. The appellate responses to estimates that have some empirical basis are more divided. When statistical independence of characteristics is established, multiplication of individual probabilities is allowed. In the exceptional case that finds error in the admission of computations that the court considers well founded, the rationale seems to be that the jury would misconstrue the meaning of the probability or overemphasize the number, or that it would be too difficult to explain its true meaning.

In evaluating these decisions, it is important to distinguish between explicit calculations of the probability of guilt or coincidence and the presentation of relevant background statistics. If the offender, whoever he or she might have been, left a bloodstain at the scene of the crime that matches the defendant's blood types, the scientific evidence cannot be interpreted intelligently without some knowledge of how frequently these blood types occur in the relevant population. We have already remarked that if the expert offers any conclusion as to whether the defendant left the incriminating trace, he or she is relying, either explicitly or *sub rosa,* on estimates of these

§ 210

1. The phrase "probability evidence" is used as a convenient shorthand for testimony or argument involving probability calculations. The probabilities are not themselves evidence. They are numbers ranging from zero to

one that may be used in drawing conclusions from the statistical or other evidence.

2. People v. Collins, 438 P.2d 33 (Cal.1968).

quantities. Without being informed of such background statistics, the jury is left to its own speculations. Where the available data do not permit a reasonable calculation, but it is obvious that the match is probative, this may be tolerable. But where reasonable estimates of the population frequencies are available, they should not be kept from the jury. Thus, courts routinely admit testimony estimating such frequencies, often without objection. To be sure, there are risks in this policy. A juror who hears that only one out of every five, or for that matter, one out of every 10,000 persons, possesses the traits that characterize the true offender, may be tempted to subtract this statistic from one to arrive at the incorrect conclusion that the remainder is the probability that the defendant is guilty. Nevertheless, it should not be so difficult for defense counsel to correct any such misapprehension by pointing out that the frequency estimate merely establishes that the defendant is one member of a class of persons who have the incriminating characteristics. The distribution of these characteristics in the population at large simply determines whether this class of persons whom the scientific evidence would identify as a possible offender is large or small.

In principle, a statistician could do more than state the frequency at which the scientific tests would implicate persons. First, in those cases in which the identifying characteristics were not the very basis on which the defendant was picked from the general population, the expert could be explicit about the P-value for the findings. Second, valiant efforts have been made to calculate conditional probabilities pertaining to the number of people in some populations who have the incriminating characteristics. Indeed, the opinion in *People v. Collins* sported a mathematical appendix purporting to show that the conditional probability of there being more couples with the characteristics of the Collins's given that there was at least one such couple was 0.41. One could imagine admitting testimony about these probabilities. Finally, and perhaps most satisfying from the mathematical standpoint, it has been proposed that the expert apply Bayes' rule to show jurors how the frequency data would

increase a previously established probability that the person tested is the one who left the incriminating traces. This proposal has been attacked on both philosophical and practical grounds. It has been said in reply that the pragmatic objections are the more persuasive. Certainly, having an expert testify to the "probability of guilt" given the evidence would be inadvisable. But whether the benefits of using this method of statistical inference solely to educate the jury by displaying the probative force of the evidentiary findings would be worth the costs in terms of time-consumption and possible confusion is a closer question. Outside of the parentage testing area, however, Bayesian calculations rarely are seen in court.

In general, it appears that the explicit use of the theories of probability and statistical inference, either as a basis for the opinions of the experts themselves or as a course of education for jurors in how to think about scientific identification evidence, remains controversial. As long as counsel and the experts do not try to place a scientific seal of approval on results not shown to be scientifically based, however, it would seem that there is room for some judicious use of these theories to put the identification evidence in reasonable perspective.

§ 211. Probabilities as Evidence: Paternity Testing

Problems of questioned or disputed parentage have plagued mankind, perhaps ever since the origin of the species. The Talmud tells of a case in which a widow married her brother-in-law before the required three-month waiting period after the death of her husband. She gave birth to a child scarcely six months later. The rabbis reasoned that either the child was a full term baby fathered by the deceased husband or a premature child of the second husband. Since the mother had shown no visible signs of pregnancy three months after her first husband's death, the matter was not easy to settle. As one rabbi said, "it is a doubt."

Many legislators, courts, and commentators have concluded that genetic and statistical methods permit such doubts to be dispelled. In section 205(B) we described the methods of detecting genetic markers and the principles of human genetics that allow this information to be applied to resolve cases of disputed parentage. We saw that a majority of states now admit the results of blood and tissue typing tests not merely to exclude the alleged father as the biological father, but, when he is not excluded, to help prove that he is the father. In most, if not all of these jurisdictions, an expert may go beyond reporting the positive test findings. To assist the trier of fact in interpreting these positive results, the expert, under generally applicable evidentiary principles, may give reliable estimates of the frequencies that characterize the distribution of the pertinent genetic markers in the male population. That is, if the population data warrant it, the expert may testify to the proportion of men that the test would exclude—a parameter that is sometimes converted into the "probability of exclusion." To this extent, the procedures are essentially the same as those that apply to scientific identification evidence generally.

Yet, many experts believe that testimony limited to the test results and the probability of exclusion is incomplete and sometimes misleading. They would prefer to testify to "the probability of paternity," and almost all jurisdictions allow such testimony in civil cases. Yet, even though most states have statutes that permit positive test results to be received into evidence, not all of these statutes say whether the probabilities derived from the test results also are admissible. At the other extreme, a few statutes—of dubious value—not only allow such testimony, but rely on the "probability of paternity" to trigger a presumption of paternity. In the absence of a statute explicitly authorizing the expert to give the "probability of paternity," admissibility should turn on whether probability testimony is sufficiently likely to aid the jury in properly assessing the probative value of the positive findings. To answer this question, one must first understand what the "probability of paternity" is. For this reason, this section indicates how this probability is computed. It then

argues that one version of this approach is not suited for courtroom use and suggests some alternative methods of assisting the jury or court to weigh the positive test results along with the other evidence in the case to reach a decision as to paternity. Finally, it discusses special concerns that have been raised about probability computations involving DNA typing. It concludes with the suggestion that in most cases, testimony as to the numerical probability of paternity is no longer necessary.

The probability of paternity, as conventionally computed, is a deceptively simple application of an elementary result in probability theory discovered by the Reverend Thomas Bayes in the nineteenth century. Bayes' formula can be interpreted as showing the effect of a new item of evidence on a previously established probability. Suppose we let B stand for the event that the alleged father is the biological father, we let Odds(B) designate the odds in favor of this event (before we learn the outcome of the laboratory tests), and we use the letter T to denote the test evidence (the phenotypes of the mother, child and father). Many testifying experts who realize how the probability of paternity is calculated take the prior odds to be 1 (that is, 50–50) on the theory that doing so shows that they are neutral as between plaintiff and defendant. Although this conception of "neutrality" cannot withstand examination, adopting these odds does amount to assuming that the accusation of paternity is as likely to be true as to be false. Bayes' rule tells us how to update these odds to account for the test results T. In particular, it says to multiply the prior odds by a quantity called the likelihood ratio to produce the new odds that the alleged father is the biological father, which we write as $\text{Odds}(B|T)$, for the odds of B given the test results T. In symbols, $\text{Odds}(B|T) = \text{LR} \times \text{Odds}(B)$, where LR is an abbreviation for likelihood ratio. For the standard assumption that the prior odds are 1, the posterior odds of paternity are just $\text{Odds}(B|T) = \text{LR}$.

This likelihood ratio can be computed as the ratio of two probabilities. The numerator is the probability that the phenotypes T would be found if the alleged father really were the biological father. The denominator is the probability that the phenotypes T would be found if the alleged father were not the biological father. In other words, the likelihood ratio states how many times more likely it is that the tests would show the phenotypes T if the alleged father were the biological father than if he were not. It often is referred to as the "paternity index." The computation of the numerator is relatively simple. It is just the probability that a man with the phenotypes of the alleged father and a woman with the mother's phenotypes would produce an offspring with the child's phenotypes. The computation of the denominator is trickier. The denominator is the probability that a man other than the alleged father would produce an offspring with the child's phenotypes. But which man? Some "alternative men" could not produce this type of child. They are the ones whom the tests would exclude. Others would have the same probability of producing this type of child as does the alleged father. These are the ones who have the same phenotypes that he does. Still others would produce this type of child with other probabilities. Their phenotypes differ from the alleged father's but are still consistent with the genotypes of the biological father. The conventional solution is to invent a "random man"—a hypothetical entity whose genotypes (and hence phenotypes) are a kind of average across all these men. Assuming that the estimates of the population allele frequencies are completely free from error, the computation can proceed.

Suppose, for example, that given the estimated allele frequencies, it is 5,000 times more likely to obtain a child with the observed phenotypes from a man with the alleged father's phenotypes than from the imaginary "random man." Bayes' formula then states that $\text{Odds}(B|T) = 5,000 \times \text{Odds}(B)$. For prior odds of 1, this means that the odds that the alleged father is the biological father are 5,000 to 1. The corresponding probability of paternity is $5000/5001 = .9998$, or 99.98%. These are the kind of numbers of which the experts testifying to the "probability of paternity" speak.

Should the results of these calculations ever be admissible? Resorting to the "random man" to form the likelihood ratio and postulating prior odds of 1 create problems for any courtroom presentation. It is tempting to dismiss the choice of the prior odds as contrived, speculative, and lacking any scientific basis. It sounds like some of the classic cases in which an expert multiplied together probabilities that had no basis in fact. Here, however, there are some hard data suggesting that these prior odds understate the incidence of truthful accusations of paternity and therefore favor the alleged father, who would be the objecting party.

Nonetheless, to serve up any single number computed in this fashion as "the" probability of paternity connotes more than the mathematical logic can deliver. Most persons hearing that the probability of paternity is 99.98% would think that the alleged father's role in the affair is conclusively confirmed. Indeed, the experts have developed standardized phrases, which they call "verbal predicates," to characterize the numbers. Yet, in view of the way in which the "probability of paternity" is calculated, many men—all those who share the alleged father's phenotypes—would have had "probabilities of paternity" of 99.98% had they been tested. Some non-excluded men might have even higher "probabilities of paternity." In more than one case, a man later shown to be sterile had a "probability of paternity" of this magnitude as determined from HLA typing. Unless an expert can somehow explain that the calculated "probability of paternity" is not the chance that the alleged father, as distinguished from all other possible fathers, is the biological father, the expert should not be allowed to put this "probability" before the jury. Furthermore, it would appear that any accurate explanation of why the "probability of paternity" does not mean the probability that the alleged father, rather than any other man, is the biological father, and then of what it does mean, would be hopelessly confusing. Consequently, testimony as to the "probability of paternity," computed with a fixed and undisclosed prior probability of one-half, should not be allowed. Such testimony seems unable to fulfill its only legitimate function—assisting the jury in weighing the positive test results along with the other evidence in the case. The same rule of exclusion should apply to the "verbal predicates" that some experts attach to probabilities of paternity.

This rule would not prohibit the introduction of the genetic evidence and an explanation of its significance. The fact that competently performed genetic tests prove the alleged father's phenotypes to be consistent with the claim of paternity is always relevant and useful evidence. The strength of this evidence, like other forms of identification evidence, can be shown to some extent by testimony about the probability of exclusion or related concepts. There is also a strong argument for using a Bayesian approach to help the jury evaluate the evidence. Instead of viewing the evidence from the position of a laboratory, which, having nothing else to go on, is driven to such artifacts as using prior odds of one, one can adjust the focus to the trial, where other evidence is available to the decisionmaker. As noted in section 210, the expert could show the jury how the test results would affect not merely a prior probability of one-half, but a whole spectrum of prior probabilities. It could be made clear to the jurors that the purpose of this exposition is not to compel them to assign a prior probability to the other evidence in the case, but to permit them to gauge the strength of the positive test findings and to weigh these findings, along with the other evidence, in the manner that they think best. By using variable instead of fixed prior odds, the expert can display the statistical force of the evidence without attempting to quantify—on the basis of incomplete information—the one thing that the jury must decide with the benefit of all the evidence in the case: the probability of paternity.

Even if an illustrative rather than a fixed prior probability is used to generate the probability of paternity, however, it is important to recognize that the likelihood ratio does not include all the information pertinent to assessing the laboratory findings. As we have described it (and as it typically computed), this ratio assumes that there is no ambiguity or doubt about the determination of phenotypes and the frequencies of the related genotypes in the relevant population.

Although these assumptions are defensible in some cases involving red blood cell, HLA or serum protein tests, they have been questioned with regard to probabilities of paternity that include certain types of DNA tests. The traditional paternity tests, which detect gene products, can be supplemented by tests of the genetic material itself. The overall logic of the probability calculation—multiplying prior odds by a likelihood ratio—is the same, but restriction fragment length polymorphism (RFLP) matching entails measurement error that poses problems in declaring a match and in determining population frequencies for specific bands. In principle, this uncertainty can be incorporated into the likelihood ratio for single-locus VNTR probes. Furthermore, RFLP testing is giving way to discrete allele systems that are more easily interpreted.

In criminal cases, a widespread criticism of DNA profiling was that the validity of the assumption of statistical independence of bands detected with VNTR probes had not been established. This argument occasionally proved effective for DNA-based paternity tests as well. With the debate about population structure having come to closure, however, reliance on the statistical independence of the DNA characteristics should not impede probability-of-paternity computations.

Even so, the need for these computations is open to doubt. With the exquisite power of DNA probes to discriminate individual characteristics detailed calculations of the troublesome "probability of paternity" may be beside the point. The full panoply of conventional genetic tests and DNA tests can produce posterior probabilities well in excess of 0.99 for virtually *any* plausible prior probability in the ordinary case. As a result, it has been suggested that:

> [W]e are approaching the point where explicit statistical analysis can be relegated to the background. Today, exclusions rarely are interpreted in terms of a paternity index or a probability of paternity, presumably because these numbers are so

close to zero as to give no more guidance to a judge or jury than a simple statement that if the test results are correct, then it is practically impossible for the tested man to be the father. Likewise, an inclusion for which the paternity index is clearly astronomical perhaps may be more profitably described as demonstrating that it is practically impossible for the putative father to be anything but the biological father.

Title 8

DEMONSTRATIVE EVIDENCE

Chapter 21

DEMONSTRATIVE EVIDENCE

Table of Sections

---

§ 212. Demonstrative Evidence in General

There is a type of evidence which consists of things, e.g., weapons, whiskey bottles, writings,[1] and wearing apparel, as distinguished from the assertions of witnesses (or hearsay declarants) about things. Most broadly viewed, this type of evidence includes all phenomena which can convey a relevant firsthand sense impression to the trier of fact, as opposed to those which serve merely to report secondhand the sense impressions of others. Thus, for example, demeanor evidence, i.e. the bearing, expression, and manner of a witness while testifying, is an instance of the type of evidence here considered, but the statements which he utters are not.

Evidence from which the trier of fact may derive a relevant firsthand sense impression is almost unlimited in its variety. As a result, the problem of satisfactorily labeling and classifying such evidence has proved a difficult one, and it will be seen variously referred to as real, autoptic, demonstrative, tangible, and objective. The present treatment continues the long-standing practice of referring to the generic class which includes all evidence which is neither testimonial nor documentary as "demonstrative." However, it should be noted that, though convenient for many purposes, the use of this, or any, single term to denominate all such evidence can potentially be confusing, for in fact not all tangible exhibits are offered for the same purpose or received on the same theory. For example, an item may be offered on the theory that it actually played a part in the transaction or occurrence in litigation, and thus that the trier of fact may perceive a relevant fact from it irrespective of whether any witness testifies to that fact. By contrast, an item may be offered on the theory that it merely "illustrates" facts testified to by a witness. As discussed subsequently, this distinction becomes important in assessing the sufficiency of the foundation offered for a particular exhibit, and perhaps should be more carefully observed in certain other contexts. Some, though by no means all, courts label evidence of the first type "real," and of the second type "illustrative," and this terminolo-

---

§ 212

1. Writings, except insofar as they contain statements which the writing is offered to prove, are examples of the present subject. They have, however, developed rules of their own which are treated independently. See Ch. 22 (authentication) and Ch. 23 (documentary originals).

gy will be employed here where it is necessary to mark the distinction.

Since "seeing is believing," and demonstrative evidence appeals directly to the senses of the trier of fact, it is today universally felt that this kind of evidence possesses an immediacy and reality which endow it with particularly persuasive effect. Largely as a result of this potential, the use of demonstrative evidence of all types has increased dramatically during recent years, and the trend seems certain to continue in the immediate future. At the same time, demonstrative evidence remains the exception rather than the rule, and its use raises certain problems for a juridical system the mechanics of which are essentially geared to the reception of *viva voce* testimony by witnesses. Some of these problems are so commonly raised by the offer of demonstrative evidence, and are so frequently made the bases of objections to its admission, that they deserve preliminary note.

It has already been noted that evidence from which the trier of fact may derive his own perceptions, rather than evidence consisting of the reported perceptions of others, possesses unusual force. Consequently, demonstrative evidence is frequently objected to as prejudicial, a term which is today generally defined as suggesting "decision on an improper basis, commonly, though not necessarily, an emotional one." A great deal of demonstrative evidence has the capacity to generate emotional responses such as pity, revulsion, or contempt, and where this capacity outweighs the value of the evidence on the issues in litigation, exclusion is appropriate.

Again, even if no essentially emotional response is likely to result, demonstrative evidence may convey an impression of objective reality to the trier. Thus, the courts are frequently sensitive to the objection that the evidence is "misleading," and zealous to insure that there is no material differential between objective things offered at trial and the same or different objective things as they existed at the time of the events or occurrences in litigation.

Further, and apart from its bearing on the issues of the case, demonstrative evidence as a class presents certain essentially logistical difficulties for the courts. Since the courts are basically structured, architecturally and otherwise, to receive the testimony of witnesses, the presentation of demonstrative evidence may require that the court physically move to receive it, or that unwieldy objects or paraphernalia be introduced into the courtroom, actions which may occasion delay and confusion. Finally, while oral testimony is easily incorporated into a paper record for purposes of appellate review, demonstrative evidence will sometimes be insusceptible to similar preservation and transmission.

The cogency and force of the foregoing objections to the introduction of demonstrative evidence will obviously vary greatly with the nature of the particular item offered, and the purpose and need for its introduction in the particular case. Since the types of demonstrative evidence and the purposes for which it is sought to be introduced are extremely varied, it is generally viewed as appropriate to accord the trial judge broad discretion in ruling upon the admissibility of many types of demonstrative evidence.

Despite its great variety, certain classifications of demonstrative evidence appear both valid and useful. First, like other evidence, it may be either direct or circumstantial. If a material issue in the case is whether an object does or does not possess a perceptible feature, characteristic, or quality, the most satisfactory method of demonstrating the truth of the matter will ordinarily be to produce the object so that the trier of fact may perceive the quality, or its absence, for himself. Thus, where a party seeks damages for the loss of a limb or for an injury leaving a disfiguring scar, exhibition of the person will constitute direct evidence of a material fact. Similarly, exhibition of the chattel purchased in an action for breach of warranty will, at least if the quality or characteristic warranted is a perceivable one, constitute direct evidence on the issue of condition. In these cases no process of inference, at least in the ordinary sense, is required. Similarly, exhibition of a person to establish such facts as race and age may perhaps also be considered examples of demonstrative evidence of a direct sort, though the immediate perceptibility of these qualities may on occasion be subject to more doubt.

Demonstrative evidence may also be offered for its circumstantial value, i.e., as the basis for an inference beyond those facts which are perceivable. Such is the case when the exhibition of a person is made for the purpose of demonstrating his relationship to another, as in a filiation proceeding. The use of demonstrative evidence is even more clearly circumstantial when articles of clothing worn at the time of his arrest by the defendant in a robbery prosecution are exhibited to the jury to demonstrate their conformity with the descriptions of the robber given by witnesses.

The practical significance of the foregoing distinction lies in the fact that direct evidence, because of its eminently satisfactory character, will generally be admitted even where it is likely to occasion some prejudice or physical difficulty. Thus, gruesome photographs which directly show a material fact have been held properly admitted in innumerable criminal cases, often without regard to their obvious capacity to inflame the jury. The better view, reflected in some recent decisions, is that the admission even of demonstrative evidence which directly portrays material facts calls for the exercise of judicial discretion.

When circumstantial evidence is involved, in the present context as elsewhere, the trial judge will generally be viewed as possessing a broader discretionary power to weigh the probative value of the evidence against whatever prejudice, confusion, surprise and waste of time are entailed, and to determine admissibility accordingly. The desirability of judicial discretion to deal with highly individual situations is particularly well illustrated by the frequently recurring question of the admissibility of photographs portraying a murder victim or the decedent in a wrongful death case as they were "in life." Both the materiality and the potential prejudicial effect such photographs will vary markedly with the type of case in which they are offered, a fact which renders the careful use of judicial discretion indispensable.

As with other circumstantial evidence, of course, demonstrative evidence offered for its circumstantial value may give rise to more than one inference. Thus introduction of a firearm taken from the defendant on his arrest and shown to be similar to that used in the commission of the offense charged may imply both that the defendant was the robber and that the defendant is a dangerous individual given to carrying firearms. If a permissible inference is present, admission will generally be upheld, a limiting instruction being deemed sufficient to prevent any untoward damage.

Again, demonstrative evidence may be classified as to whether the item offered did or did not play an actual and direct part in the incident or transaction giving rise to the trial. Objects offered as having played such a direct role, e.g., the alleged weapon in a murder prosecution, are commonly called "real" or "original" evidence and are to be distinguished from evidence which played no such part but is offered for illustrative or other purposes. It will be readily apparent that when real evidence is offered an adequate foundation for admission will require testimony first that the object offered is *the* object which was involved in the incident, and further that the condition of the object is substantially unchanged. If the offered item possesses characteristics which are fairly unique and readily identifiable, and if the substance of which the item is composed is relatively impervious to change, the trial court is viewed as having broad discretion to admit merely on the basis of testimony that the item is the one in question and is in a substantially unchanged condition. On the other hand, if the offered evidence is of such a nature as not to be readily identifiable, or to be susceptible to alteration by tampering or contamination, sound exercise of the trial court's discretion may require a substantially more elaborate foundation. A foundation of the latter sort will commonly entail testimonially tracing the "chain of custody" of the item with sufficient completeness to render it reasonably probable that the original item has neither been exchanged with another nor been contaminated or tampered with. It should, however, always be borne in mind that foundational requirements are essentially require-ments of logic, and not rules of art. Thus, e.g., even a radically altered item of real evidence may be admissible if its pertinent features remain unaltered.

Real evidence consisting of samples drawn from a larger mass are also generally held admissible, subject to the foregoing require-ments pertaining to real evidence generally, and subject to the further requirement that the sample be established to be accurately representative of the mass. Further, where a mass of material is offered in toto, it will generally be sufficient for the witness to de-scribe the mass and not each constituent item.

Demonstrative evidence, however, is by no means limited to items which may properly be classed as "real" or "original" evidence. It is today increasingly common to encounter the offer of tangible items which are not them-selves contended to have played any part in the history of the case, but which are instead tendered for the purpose of rendering other evidence more comprehensible to the trier of fact. Examples of types of items frequently offered for purposes of illustration and clarifi-cation include models, maps, photographs, charts, and drawings. If an article is offered for these purposes, rather than as real or original evidence, its specific identity or source is generally of no significance whatever. In-stead, the theory justifying admission of these exhibits requires only that the item be suffi-ciently explanatory or illustrative of relevant testimony in the case to be of potential help to the trier of fact. Whether the admission of a particular exhibit will in fact be helpful, or will instead tend to confuse or mislead the trier, is a matter commonly viewed to be within the sound discretion of the trial court.

§ 213.   Maps, Models, and Duplicates

Among the most frequently utilized types of illustrative evidence are maps, sketches, dia-grams, models and duplicates. Unlike real evi-dence, the availability of which will frequently depend upon circumstances beyond counsel's control, opportunities for the use of the types of demonstrative evidence here considered are limited only by counsel's ability to recognize

them. The potential of these aids for giving clarity and interest to spoken statements has brought about their widespread use, which will undoubtedly continue in the future.

While all jurisdictions allow the use of demonstrative items to illustrate and explain oral testimony, there is some diversity of judi-cial opinion concerning the precise evidentiary status of articles used for this purpose. Thus, while most jurisdictions treat items used to illustrate testimony as fully admissible, a few have singled out such items for distinct treat-ment. Of the various restrictions which have been imposed, the most supportable is that which limits jury access to illustrative items during deliberation. But there would appear to be no reason why this policy, even if adopted, necessitates denying "admission" to such items.

Even in the majority of jurisdictions where there is no apparent bar to, or restric-tion upon, their full admission, it is not un-common for maps, models, etc., to be displayed and referred to without being formally offered or admitted into evidence. While no absolute prohibition would seem to be justified concern-ing such informal use of illustrative items, numerous appellate courts have commented upon the difficulties created on appeal when crucial testimony has been given in the form of indecipherable references to an object not available to the reviewing court. By the more common, and clearly preferable practice, illus-trative objects will be identified by the witness as substantially correct representations and will be formally introduced as part of the wit-ness' testimony, in which they are incorporat-ed by reference. When the record is not so perfected many courts have presumed that the illustrative items and testimony referring to them support the verdict, making it in the interest of both parties to clarify the record.

Illustrative exhibits may often properly and satisfactorily be used in lieu of real evi-dence. As previously noted, articles actually involved in a transaction or occurrence may have become lost or be unavailable, or wit-nesses may be unable to testify that the arti-cle present in court is the identical one they have previously observed. Where only the generic characteristics of the item are significant no objection would appear to exist to the introduction of a substantially similar "duplicate." While the matter is generally viewed as within the discretion of the trial court, it has been suggested that it would constitute reversible error to exclude a duplicate testified to be identical to the object involved in the occurrence. On the other hand, if there is an absence of testimony that the object to be illustrated ever existed, the introduction of a "duplicate" may foster a mistaken impression of certainty and thus merit exclusion.

Models, maps, sketches, and diagrams (as distinguished from duplicates) are by their nature generally not easily confused with real evidence, and are admissible simply on the basis of testimony that they are substantially accurate representations of what the witness is endeavoring to describe. Some discretionary control in the trial court is generally deemed appropriate, however, since exhibits of this kind, due to inaccuracies, variations of scale, etc., may on occasion be more misleading than helpful. Nevertheless, when the trial court has exercised its discretion to admit, it will only rarely be found in error, at least if potentially misleading inaccuracies have been pointed out by witnesses for the proponent, or could have been exposed upon cross-examination.

§ 214. Photographs, Movies, and Sound Recordings

The principle upon which photographs are most commonly admitted into evidence is the same as that underlying the admission of illustrative drawings, maps and diagrams. Under this theory, a photograph is viewed merely as a graphic portrayal of oral testimony, and becomes admissible only when a witness has testified that it is a correct and accurate representation of relevant facts personally observed by the witness. Accordingly, under this theory, the witness who lays the foundation need not be the photographer, nor need he know anything of the time, conditions, or mechanisms of

the taking. Instead he need only know about the facts represented or the scene or objects photographed, and once this knowledge is shown he can say whether the photograph correctly and accurately portrays these facts. Once the photograph is thus verified it is admissible as a graphic portrayal of the verifying witness' testimony, into which it is incorporated by reference. If the photograph fails to portray the relevant facts with complete accuracy, such as where changed conditions have been brought about by lapse of time or other factors, the photograph may still be admissible in the trial court's discretion if the changes are not so substantial as to be misleading.

The foregoing doctrine concerning the basis on which photographs are admitted is clearly a viable one and has undoubtedly served to facilitate the introduction of the general run of photographs. It is doubtful, however, whether this theory should be pressed to its logical limits, as some few courts have done, by limiting photographs admitted on this basis to "illustrative" status and denying them "substantive" effect. This distinction has been cogently criticized, and in any event does not seem to warrant the procedural consequences seen to flow from it. A majority of jurisdictions have either rejected the distinction explicitly or ignored it altogether.

The products of certain applications of the photographic process do not readily lend themselves to admission in evidence on the foregoing theory.[1] X-ray photographs are a common example, and are of course constantly admitted, despite the fact that no witness has actually viewed the objects portrayed. The foundation typically required for X-rays is calculated to demonstrate that a reliable scientific process was correctly utilized to obtain the product offered in evidence. Earlier recognized only sporadically, this same approach has in recent years found greatly increased acceptance as applied to various products of the photographic process. Under this doctrine, commonly referred to as the "silent witness" theory of

§ 214

1. Comment, Photographic Evidence—Is There a Recognized Basis for Admissibility? 8 Hast.L.J. 310 (1957) (noting that scenes photographed by infrared flash or by electronically triggered surveillance cameras are not seen by any potential witness.)

admission, photographic evidence may draw its verification, not from any witness who has actually viewed the scene portrayed on film, but from other evidence which supports the reliability of the photographic product. Most commonly, such evidence has been directed at establishing the validity of the photographic process by means of a foundation closely resembling that required for the admission of the products of other scientific processes. However, it has been pointed out that other types of foundation may properly support the admission of "silent witness" evidence. Today the "silent witness" doctrine affords an alternative route to the introduction of photographic evidence in virtually all jurisdictions. However, since the foundation required will generally be more elaborate than the relatively simple one sufficient under the traditional theory, resort to the latter remains preferable where circumstances permit.

The interest and vividness of photographs may be heightened by utilization of various techniques of photography, such as having the photographs taken in color, or having them enlarged so that pertinent facts may be more readily observed. While the use of these techniques clearly increases the number of factors subject to distortion, the basic standard governing admission of photos generally remains applicable. Thus color and enlarged photographs have generally been viewed as admissible provided the photo represents the scene depicted with substantial accuracy.

A somewhat more troublesome problem is presented by posed or artificially reconstructed scenes, in which people, automobiles, and other objects are placed so as to conform to the descriptions of the original crime or collision given by the witnesses. When the posed photographs go no further than to portray the positions of persons and objects as reflected in the undisputed testimony, their admission has long been generally approved. Frequently, however, a posed photograph will portray only the version of the facts supported by the testimony of the proponent's witness. The dangers inherent in this situation, i.e., the tendency of the photographs unduly to emphasize certain testimony and the possibility that the jury may

confuse one party's reconstruction with objective fact, have led some courts to exclude photographs of this type. The orthodox theory of photos as merely illustrated testimony, however, can be viewed to support the admission of any photo reflecting a state of facts testified to by a witness and the current trend would appear to be to permit even photos of disputed reconstructions in some instances.

Motion pictures, when they were first sought to be introduced in evidence, were frequently objected to and sometimes excluded on the theory that they afforded manifold opportunities for fabrication and distortion. Even those older decisions which upheld the admission of motion pictures appear to have done so on the basis of elaborate foundation testimony detailing the methods of taking, processing, and projecting the film. More recently, however, it appears to have become generally recognized that, as with the still photograph, the reliability and accuracy of the motion picture need not necessarily rest upon the validity of the process used in its creation, but rather may be established by testimony that the motion picture accurately reproduces phenomena actually perceived by a witness. Under this theory, though the requisite foundation may, and usually will, be laid by the photographer, it may also be provided by any witness who perceived the events filmed. Of course, if the foundation testimony reveals the film to be distorted in some material particular, exclusion is the proper result.

The "silent witness" theory of admissibility is as fully applicable to the motion picture as to the still photograph, and in fact many of the explicit applications of that theory have been with reference to movies.

Both the "pictorial testimony" and "silent witness" doctrines previously discussed will readily be seen to be equally applicable to the newer technology of the videotape, despite the fact that the latter operates upon quite different principles. The videotape has several practical advantages over the motion picture, and in fact seems largely to have displaced it as the common mechanism for presenting representations of motion to the trier of fact. While the admissibility of videotape evidence has sometimes been specifically provided for by rule or statute, such treatment should not be a necessary precondition to reception of this type of evidence.

Judicial discretion in the admission or exclusion of representation of action is constantly emphasized in the decisions, and is perhaps largely attributable to the fact that the presentation of this kind of evidence will involve considerable expenditure of time and inconvenience. At the same time, however, when motion pictures are offered which reproduce the actual facts or original events in controversy, such as films of an allegedly incapacitated plaintiff shoveling snow or playing baseball, or post-arrest films of an allegedly intoxicated driver, the cogency of the evidence is such that the taking of considerable time and trouble to view the evidence would appear amply warranted.

Somewhat more difficult questions are posed by moving pictures taken of an injured party pursuing ordinary day-to-day activities, offered for the purpose of bringing home to the trier of fact the implications and significance of the injury for which damages are sought. With respect both to their relevance and to the possible objections which may legitimately be raised against them, these films are closely akin to bodily demonstrations of injuries in court. Both species of evidence therefore ought to be governed by the same rule, to wit, both should be admissible only in the sound discretion, and under the strict control, of the trial court.

A still different set of problems is presented by photographs or videotapes which do not portray original facts in controversy, but rather represent one party's staged reproduction of those facts. Here the extreme vividness and verisimilitude of pictorial evidence is truly a two-edged sword. For not only is the danger that the jury may confuse art with reality particularly great, but the impressions generated by the evidence may prove particularly difficult to limit or, if the film is subsequently deemed inadmissible, to expunge by judicial instruction. The latter difficulty may be largely eliminated by a preliminary viewing by the court in chambers, and the decided cases suggest that this expedient is widely employed.

Experiments and demonstrations must today be mentioned in the present context because of the frequency with which these are currently filmed or taped so that the jury may observe the results rather than merely having them reported. While the fact of filming does not alter the basic principles applicable to experiments and demonstrations, it does raise the additional problem that the evidence may be presented in such a way as to cause the jury to confuse the filmed event with the actual one in litigation. Thus, where the film or tape appears to present a replication of the original event it will generally be required that the experiment be conducted under substantially similar circumstances. Where the purpose of the evidence is not to present a graphic reproduction of the event and there is little chance of jury confusion, this similarity requirement is not imposed. Experiments intended to demonstrate the nature or capacity of physical objects are generally placed in this latter category, and films and tapes of such experiments have frequently been admitted.

In recent years technology has added a new weapon to the arsenal to the trial lawyer in the form of the computer graphic. To the extent that the computer graphic represents simply a new type of illustrative evidence, its admissibility has logically been viewed by the courts as controlled by the principles discussed here. Where the sole objective of the computer animation is to render visual and thus more understandable the verbal descriptions of witnesses, the computer graphic can easily be justified by the same theory underlying illustrative evidence generally. In such cases a witness or witnesses vouches for the accuracy of the representation and may be cross-examined concerning it. However, continued advances in the technology make it necessary to distinguish between merely illustrative uses of the computer graphic and even more sophisticated applications in which the computer is used to "model" phenomena and thus to provide the equivalent of experimental scientific data which is either sought to be introduced directly or to be used by an expert to form an opinion. These latter applications, to be sure, may also be admissible, but only after satisfying rules not generally applicable to demonstrative evidence.

Sound recordings will sometimes be offered as an integral part of a motion picture, or videotape, raising the possibility that the visual portrayal is admissible while the recording is not. The common sense expedient in such cases, suggested by some decisions, is to suppress the sound. When a sound recording consists of spoken words, questions concerning the "best evidence" rule and the rule of completeness may be raised. Where a sound recording itself does constitute the "best evidence," it is not uncommon to find a transcript of the recorded words offered to assist the jury in following the recording. Clearly such transcripts can serve a beneficial demonstrative function where no question exists as to the accuracy of the transcription, but serious theoretical and practical problems arise when a legitimate question is presented as to what words the recording contains.

Sound recordings may also be offered as reproducing relevant nonverbal sounds, and when this is the purpose the considerations potentially affecting admissibility are substantially similar to those relating to motion pictures. Thus, the recording will generally be admitted if a witness testifies that the recording as played is an accurate reproduction of relevant sounds previously audited by the witness. On occasion, too, sound recordings may be admitted upon a foundation analogous to that sometimes recognized for films taken by surveillance cameras. This will consist of a showing of the accuracy and completeness of the recording by scientific and corroborative evidence.

§ 215. Bodily Demonstrations: Experiments in Court

The exhibition of a wound or physical injury, e.g., the injury sustained by a plaintiff in a personal injury action, will frequently be the best and most direct evidence of a material fact. Not surprisingly, therefore, exhibitions of physical injuries to the jury are commonly allowed. In most jurisdictions the matter is

viewed as subject to the discretion of the trial court, but has sometimes been said to be a matter of right on the part of the injured party. Further, in those jurisdictions which hold the matter to be discretionary, a trial court is rarely reversed for permitting a bodily exhibition. Thus, when the exhibition is permitted no abuse of discretion is generally found present even though the injury displayed was particularly shocking, or even where the injury's nature or existence need not have been proved because it has been admitted.

The physical characteristics of a person may also constitute relevant evidence in a criminal prosecution. For example, the scars or physical condition of the victim may tend to prove the nature of an assault, or a physical trait of a person may be relevant to prove or disprove the identity of the perpetrator of an offense. Though some awkwardness is encountered in treating persons as exhibits, bodily exhibitions for purposes such as those indicated are viewed as within the trial court's discretion and have frequently been allowed. When the prosecution desires to exhibit traits of the defendant, the question has long been considered under the heading of self-incrimination and the demonstration allowed so long as it may be classed as "non-testimonial." Similarly, it has generally been held that it is open to the defendant to display his physical characteristics to the trier of fact without incurring the necessity of taking the stand.

Judicial opinion has been somewhat more divided concerning the propriety of going beyond the mere exhibition of an injury or physical condition by having the injured person perform actions or submit to manipulation by a physician. The dangers inherent in demonstrations of this latter type include undue emotional response on the part of the jury and the fact that manifestations of pain and impairment of function are easily feigned and difficult to test by cross-examination. Nevertheless, this matter too is commonly left to the discretion of the trial courts, and that discretion is frequently exercised in favor of permitting the demonstration. Occasional cases have, however, held the allowance of a particular demonstration to be an abuse of trial court discretion, a fact which may suggest that the tactic is a somewhat hazardous one for the party utilizing it.

In addition to active demonstrations of physical injuries, in-court reenactment of material events by witnesses has been held permissible to illustrate testimony.

Whether demonstrations in the form of experiments in court are to be permitted is also largely subject to the discretion of the trial judge. Unlike experiments performed out of court, the results of which are generally communicated testimonially, in-court experimentation may involve considerable confusion and delay, and the trial judge is viewed as in the best position to judge whether the game is worth the candle. Simple demonstrations by a witness are usually permitted, and may be strikingly effective in adding vividness to the spoken word.

In addition to the limitations arising from the desirability of orderly and expeditious proceedings, in-court experiments are held to the same basic requirement of similarity of conditions which is applicable to experimental evidence generally. This requirement may be particularly difficult to meet under courtroom conditions, and many proposed courtroom experiments have been held properly excluded on this ground. Nevertheless, the well-planned courtroom experiment may provide extremely striking and persuasive evidence, and the opportunities for utilizing such experiments should not be overlooked.

§ 216. Views

The courts, like the prophet, have sensibly recognized that if a thing cannot be brought to the observer, the observer must go to the thing. Venturing forth to observe places or objects which are material to litigation but which cannot feasibly be brought, or satisfactorily reproduced, within the courtroom, is termed a "view." While statutes or court rules concerning views are in effect in nearly all states, it is frequently said that even without express statutory authorization there is an in-

herent power in the trial judge to order a view by the jury, or, in a judge-tried case, to take a view personally. This power extends to views of personalty, realty, and to criminal as well as civil cases.

Since a view is often time-consuming and disruptive of the ordinary course of a trial, the trial judge is in most instances vested with a wide leeway of discretion to grant or refuse a view. It is to be noted, however, that a number of state statutes provide that in certain types of cases, notably eminent domain, either party is entitled to a view upon request as a matter of right. Where the grant of a view is discretionary with the trial court, as is usually the case, factors which are commonly stated to be appropriate for consideration by the court in determining whether to a grant a view include the importance to the issue of the information to be gained by the view, the extent to which this information has or could have been secured from maps, photographs, or diagrams, and the extent to which the place or object to be viewed has changed in appearance since the controversy arose.

The appropriate procedures to be followed in connection with views are widely regulated by statute. At common law, and generally in civil cases today, the presence of the trial judge at a view is not required, the more common practice being for the jury to be conducted to the scene by "showers," expressly commissioned for the purpose. Unauthorized views by one or more jury members are of course improper and will generally constitute reversible error. Attendance at the view by the parties and their counsel is generally permitted though subject to the discretion of the trial judge. The judge in a bench trial may take a view, though to do so without allowing the parties to attend invites a claim of error. In criminal cases, the rights of the defendant to have the judge present at the view, and to be present personally, are frequently provided for by statute. Moreover, when testimony is taken at the view, or the view itself is deemed to constitute evidence, the right of the defendant to be present in all probability possesses a constitutional underpinning.[1]

Statutory and constitutional considerations aside, the advisability of trial court attendance at views is strongly suggested by the numerous cases in which unauthorized comments, obviously hearsay, have been made to the jury, or other improper events have occurred during the course of the view. Presence of the trial judge would seem to afford the best guarantee available against the occurrence of events of this nature. On the other hand, where the trial judge is present to rule on admissibility, and provision for preparation of a proper record is made, there would appear no inherent vice in receiving testimony or allowing demonstrations or experiments during a view. These practices, however, have often been looked upon with disfavor by appellate courts, and some jurisdictions appear to hold reception of testimony or experiments during a view improper under any circumstances.

Closely related to the above questions is the troublesome problem of what evidentiary status a view possesses. A large number of jurisdictions, probably a majority, holds that a view is not itself evidence, but is only to assist the trier of fact in understanding and evaluating the evidence. This doctrine undoubtedly rests in large part upon the consideration that facts garnered by the jury from a view are difficult or impossible to embody in the written record, thus rendering review of questions concerning weight or sufficiency of the evidence impracticable. At the same time, however, this doctrine ignores the fact that many other varieties of demonstrative evidence are to some extent subject to the same difficulty, and further that it is unreasonable to assume that jurors, however they may be instructed, will apply the metaphysical distinction suggested and ignore the evidence of their own senses when it conflicts with the testimony of the witnesses. Commentators have uniformly condemned the downgrading of views to nonevidentiary status, and a substantial number of courts holds a view to be evidence like any other. The latter position appears to be the preferable one, at least when modified by the caveat that where the question is one of sufficiency, a view alone cannot logically be considered to constitute sufficient evidence of a fact the establishment of which ordinarily requires the introduction of expert testimony.

§ 217. Exhibits in the Jury Room

Under modern American practice it is common to allow many types of tangible exhibits to be taken by the jury for consideration during the deliberations, provided that the exhibits have been formally admitted into evidence. The question whether a particular exhibit may be taken by the jury is widely viewed as subject to discretionary control by the trial judge, but in some jurisdictions jury access to at least certain types of exhibits is apparently made mandatory either by judicial holding or legislative enactment.

The current practice extends, unlike that at common law, to written exhibits generally except for those which are testimonial in nature, such as depositions, dying declarations in writing, etc. The reason underlying this latter exception is that writings which are merely testimony in a different form should not, by being allowed to the jury, be unduly emphasized over other purely oral testimony in the case. As an exception to the exception, however, written or recorded confessions in criminal cases, despite their obvious testimonial character, are in many jurisdictions allowed to be taken by the jury, apparently on the theory that their centrality in the case warrants whatever emphasis may result.

---

§ 216

1. In Snyder v. Commonwealth of Massachusetts, 291 U.S. 97 (1934) the Supreme Court held, four justices dissenting, that due process had not been denied a defendant who was refused the opportunity to be present at a view, even if it were assumed that the right of confrontation guaranteed by the Sixth Amendment is "reinforced" by the Fourteenth. Thus, even though the Confrontation Clause has now been held operative against the states by virtue of the Fourteenth Amendment, Pointer v. Texas, 380 U.S. 400 (1965), the defendant appears to have no federally guaranteed right to attend a view in every instance. The Court, however, carefully limited its holding in *Snyder* to the facts of that case. These included the fact that a view is not deemed evidence in Massachusetts, that no oral testimony was taken at the view, and that the judge, court reporter, and also defendant's counsel were present.

The practice of allowing nontestimonial written evidence generally to be taken by the jury would appear to be supported by many of the same considerations which underlie the so-called "Best Evidence Rule." Legal rights and liabilities are frequently a function of particular words and figures, and may be drastically affected by seemingly minor variations in phraseology. Thus crucial documents, such as deeds, contracts, or ledger sheets may frequently be of vital help to the jury. On the other hand, where a writing is of only minor relevance, despatch to the jury may induce an emphasis upon it out of proportion to its intrinsic worth.

The case for allowing the jury to take with it tangibles other than writings is somewhat weaker, at least if in-court examination of the tangible by the jury has been had. As noted in an earlier section, demonstrative evidence has peculiar force which arguably does not stand in need of yet additional augmentation. Further, the relevant characteristics of many tangible exhibits are sufficiently gross as not to require the close perusal appropriate to writings, while at the other end of the spectrum there appears some anomaly in allowing independent jury inspection of tangibles the relevant features of which are so fine as to require expert exposition and interpretation. Nevertheless, the sending of tangible exhibits to the jury room is today probably so well established as to be practically irreversible.

A major problem stemming from relatively free jury access to tangible exhibits other than writings is that of controlling jury use of them for purposes of experimentation. The general limitations upon the introduction of evidence of experiments obviously become largely meaningless if the jury is allowed to conduct experiments of its own devising in the jury room. In attempting to distinguish between proper and improper jury use of tangible exhibits, the most commonly drawn distinction is between experiments which constitute merely a closer scrutiny of the exhibit and experiments which go "beyond the lines of the evidence" introduced in court and thus constitute the introduction of new evidence in the jury room. The decisions reached under the aegis of this rubric are perhaps not totally reconcilable. Most courts, however, emphasize the immunity of jury-conducted experiments from adversary scrutiny as their preeminently objectionable feature. Thus it would seem correct to say that jury experimentation is improper if reasonable grounds existed for an adversary attack on the experiment by the complaining party and, in addition, if nothing transpiring during the in-court proceedings rendered such an attack inappropriate. Specifically, experiments which are merely reruns of in-court experiments, or which use techniques of examination not markedly different from those employed during trial are not generally held to fall within the proscribed class. On the other hand, jury experiments utilizing techniques or equipment substantially different from any employed in court tend to be held error, at least where counsel has not specifically acquiesced in the experiment, such as by arguing that the jury should be allowed certain tools.

Title 9

WRITINGS

Chapter 22

AUTHENTICATION

Table of Sections

§ 218. General Theory: No Assumption of Authenticity

The concept of authentication, although continually used by the courts without apparent difficulty, seems almost to defy precise definition. Some writers have construed the term very broadly, as does Wigmore when he states that "when a claim or offer involves impliedly or expressly any element of *personal connection with a corporeal object,* that connection must be made to appear * * *."[1] So defined, "authentication" is not only a necessary preliminary to the introduction of most writings in evidence, but also to the introduction of various other sorts of tangibles. For example, an article of clothing found at the scene of a crime can hardly constitute relevant evidence against the defendant unless ownership or previous possession of the article is shown. Since authentication of tangibles other than writings, has been treated elsewhere, however,

the term authentication will here be used in the limited sense of proof of authorship of, or other connection with, writings.

It is clear that the relevancy of a writing to a particular issue raised in litigation will frequently be logically dependent upon the existence of some connection between that writing and a particular individual. If Y sues X for libel and attempts to introduce into evidence a writing containing libelous statements concerning Y, it will readily appear that the writing is relevant only if some connection between the writing and X exists, as where X authored or published it. The real question, however, is not whether such a connection is logically necessary for relevancy, but rather what standards are to be applied in determining whether the connection has been made to appear. In some instances testimony concerning a writing will be offered rather than the

---

§ 218

1. 7 Wigmore, Evidence § 2129 at 564 (Chadbourn rev. 1978).

writing itself. Where this is permissible through the operation of the so-called "best evidence" rule or its exceptions, is the requirement of authentication excused? The answer should necessarily be that it is not, for the connection between the writing and the individual is rendered no less logically significant because of the form of evidence concerning the writing.

In the everyday affairs of business and social life, it is the custom to look merely at the writing itself for evidence as to its source. Thus, if the writing bears a signature purporting to be that of X, or recites that it was made by X, we assume, nothing to the contrary appearing, that it is exactly what it purports to be, the work of X. At this point, however, the law of evidence has long differed from the common sense assumption upon which each of us conducts her own affairs. Instead it adopts the position that the purported signature or recital of authorship on the face of a writing will *not* be accepted as sufficient preliminary proof of authenticity to secure the admission of the writing in evidence. The same attitude has traditionally extended as well to the authority of agents, with the result that if an instrument recites that it is signed by A as agent for P, not only must additional proof be given that A actually did the signing, but also of the fact that she was P's agent and authorized to sign.

The principal justification urged for this judicial agnosticism toward the authorship of documents is that it constitutes a necessary check on the perpetration of fraud. Thus it is quite conceivable that the libelous writing previously adduced by way of example is not the work of X but of some third person who, for reasons of her own, wishes to embroil X in difficulties, or to libel Y without suffering any adverse consequences. It is also possible that Y has fabricated the writing to provide herself with a cause of action.

Another possibility against which traditional authentication is sometimes suggested to guard is that of mistaken attribution of a writing to one who fortuitously happens to possess the same name, etc., as the author.

On the other side of the coin, requiring proof of what may correctly be assumed true in 99 out of 100 cases is at best time-consuming and expensive. At the worst, the requirement will occasionally be seen to produce results which are virtually indefensible.

Thus, while traditional requirements of authentication admittedly furnish some slight obstacles to the perpetration of fraud or occurrence of mistake in the presentation of writings, it has frequently been questioned whether these benefits are not outweighed by the time, expense, and occasional untoward results entailed by the traditional negative attitude toward authenticity of writings.

§ 219. Authentication by Direct Proof: (a) In General

The simplest form of direct testimony authenticating a writing as that of X, is the production of a witness who swears that he saw X sign the offered writing. Other examples would be the testimony of X, the signer, acknowledging execution, or the admission of authenticity by an adverse party in the present action, either made out of court and reported by another witness or shown by the party's own letter or other writing, or in the form of the party's testimony on the stand. It is generally held that business records may be authenticated by the testimony of one familiar with the books of the concern, such as a custodian or supervisor, who has not made the record or seen it made, that the offered writing is actually part of the records of the business.

§ 220. Authentication by Direct Proof: (b) Requirement of Production of Attesting Witnesses.

Our rules about the production of subscribing witnesses are survivals of archaic law. They have their origins in Germanic practice earlier than jury trial, when pre-appointed transaction-witnesses were the only kind of witnesses that could be summoned or heard in court. When jury trial came in, the attesting witnesses at first were summoned along with the jurors themselves, and this practice seems to have lingered until the middle fifteen hundreds. The rule in its modern common law form requires, when a document signed by subscribing witnesses is sought to be authenticated by witnesses, that an attesting witness must first be called, or all attesters must be shown to be unavailable, before other witnesses can be called to authenticate it.

The requirement has no application where the foundation for introducing the document is the opponent's judicial admission of its genuineness, either by stipulation of the parties in writing or in open court, or under modern rules and statutes by the opponent's failure to deny the genuineness of the writing. Though it has been suggested that extra-judicial admissions also, if in writing, might properly be held to dispense with the production of attesters, such American authority as exists seems to deny that extra-judicial admissions of any sort have this effect.

The requirement is that the attesting witnesses be called before other authenticating witnesses are heard, but it is not required that the attesters give favorable testimony establishing the writing. So even if they profess want of memory or even deny that they attested, the writing may be established by other proof, and conversely if they support the writing, other proof may establish that it is not authentic. Moreover, since the party calling the attester is required by law to do so, the prohibition upon impeaching one's own witness is held inapplicable.

This requirement of calling particular persons, or accounting for them, to authenticate the writing is often inconvenient, and of doubtful expediency, and various exceptions have been carved out by the courts, as for ancient documents, writings only "collaterally" involved in the suit, and for certified copies of recorded conveyances, where the original is not required to be produced. A more sweeping reform, generally effected by statute but on occasion by judicial decision, has been to dispense with the requirement of calling attesting witnesses except when the writing to be offered is one required by law to be attested.

§ 221. Authentication by Direct Proof: (c) Proof of Handwriting

A witness is placed on the stand. "Will you state whether you are acquainted with the handwriting of X?" "I am." "Will you look at this letter (or this signature) and tell me whether it is in the handwriting of X?" "It is." These or similar questions and answers are part of the familiar routine of authenticating writings, a routine which might be supposed to possess a rationale until note is taken of the qualifications typically required to be shown as part of his testimony by the witness through whom such a foundation is laid. These qualifications are minimal to say the least. Thus it is generally held that anyone familiar with the handwriting of a given person may supply authenticating testimony in the form of his opinion that a writing or signature is in the handwriting of that person. Adequate familiarity may be present if the witness has seen the person write, or if he has seen writings *purporting* to be those of the person in question under circumstances indicating their genuineness. Examples of the latter situation include instances where the witness has had an exchange of correspondence with the person, or has seen writings which the person has asserted are his own, or has been present in an office or other place where genuine writings of a particular person in the ordinary course of business would naturally be seen. Finally, it is not required that the authenticating witness' identification be categorical in nature.

The same assumptions which underlie lay witness authentication based upon familiarity with individual handwriting may be seen to justify another well-established doctrine, that of authentication by handwriting specimens or "exemplars." The common law limited the use of exemplars for comparison purposes to writings otherwise admissible in the case, but this rule has generally been modified by rule or statute to allow handwriting samples to be admitted solely for the purpose of comparison. Some conflict of authority exists concerning the standard by which the authenticity of such specimens is to be determined. Once admitted, however, an apparent majority of jurisdictions hold that the genuineness of other offered writings alleged to be the work of the same author becomes a question for the trier of fact who may, but need not, be assisted in this task by expert comparisons. Analogous holdings may be found in the relatively rarer cases of authentication by typing technique or word usage patterns (psycholinguistics), both of which, like handwriting identification, proceed on the basis of comparisons between the document in question and exemplars of known origin.

Demonstration is available, if demonstration is thought to be needed, that evidence of the foregoing varieties is essentially meaningless in cases where the authenticity is actually disputed. If a writing is in fact questioned no layperson is competent to distinguish a skilled forgery from a genuine writing. Certainly it is incredible that an unskilled layman who saw the person write once a decade before could make such a differentiation. In the event of an actual controversy over genuineness, both logic and good advocacy demand a resort to evidence of greater reliability and persuasiveness, principally, according to the prevalent view, the testimony of bona fide handwriting experts.[1]

The minimal qualifications required of the ordinary witness authenticating a writing by identification of handwriting are defensible only on the basis that no more than one in a hundred writings is questioned. The current permissive standards allow the admission of the general run of authentic documents with a minimum of time, trouble, and expense. The latter argument, however, may prove too much, since even greater savings in these commodities might safely be achieved by simply presuming the authenticity of writings for purposes of admissibility in the absence of proof raising a question as to genuineness.

§ 222. Authentication by Circumstantial Evidence: (a) Generally

As has been seen there are various ways in which writings may be authenticated by direct evidence. Nevertheless, it will frequently occur that no direct evidence of authenticity of any type exists or can be found. Resort must then be had to circumstantial proof and it is

clear that authentication by circumstantial evidence is uniformly recognized as permissible. Certain configurations of circumstantial evidence have in fact been so frequently held to authenticate particular types of writings that they have come to be recognized as distinct rules, e.g., the ancient documents rule, the reply doctrine, etc. These more or less formalized rules are treated in succeeding sections.

It is important to bear in mind, however, that authentication by circumstantial evidence is not limited to situations which fall within one of these recurrent patterns. Rather, proof of any circumstances which will support a finding that the writing is genuine will suffice to authenticate the writing.

§ 223. Authentication by Circumstantial Evidence: (b) Ancient Documents

A writing which has been in existence for a number of years will frequently be difficult to authenticate by direct evidence. Where the maker of an instrument, those who witnessed the making, and even those familiar with the maker's handwriting have over the course of years died or become unavailable, the need to resort to authentication by circumstantial evidence is apparent. The circumstances which may, in a given case, raise an inference of the genuineness of an aged writing are of course quite varied, and any combination of circumstances sufficient to support a finding of genuineness will be appropriate authentication. Facts which may be suggested as indicative of genuineness include unsuspicious appearance, emergence from natural custody, prompt recording, and, in the case of a deed or will, possession taken under the instrument. Age itself may be viewed as giving rise to some inference of genuineness in that an instrument is unlikely to be forged for fruition at a time in the distant future.

The frequent necessity of authenticating ancient writings by circumstantial evidence, plus the consideration that certain of the above facts probative of authenticity are com-

§ 221

1. Handwriting comparisons for the purpose of determining authenticity has long been generally accepted as a

proper subject for expert testimony. See § 207.

monly found associated with genuine older writings, have led the courts to develop a rule of thumb for dealing with the question. Under the common law form of this rule a writing is sufficiently authenticated as an ancient document if the party who offers it produces sufficient evidence that the writing is thirty years old, that it is unsuspicious in appearance, and further proves that the writing is produced from a place of custody natural for such a document. The Federal Rules of Evidence and most state derivatives continue the rule but reduce the required documentary age to twenty years.[1] In addition to the foregoing requirements, some jurisdictions, if the writing is a dispositive one such as a deed or a will, impose the additional condition that possession must have been taken under the instrument. The documents which may be authenticated under the rule here described, however, are not limited to dispositive instruments, and the rule has been applied to allow authentication of a wide variety of writings.

In the case of a writing which purports to be executed by an agent, executor, or other person acting under power or authority from another, proof of the facts which authenticate the writing as an ancient document gives rise to a presumption that the person signing was duly authorized.

It should be borne in mind that, despite the utility of the rule here discussed, it is merely a rule of authentication, the satisfaction of which does not necessarily guarantee the admission of the writing authenticated. Thus, it is sometimes forgotten that a writing may be proved perfectly genuine and yet remain inadmissible as being, e.g., hearsay or secondary evidence. This source of confusion is compounded by a partial overlap between the requirements of the present rule and those of the distinct doctrine which holds that recitals in certain types of ancient instruments may be received as evidence of the facts recited. The latter doctrine, however, constitutes an exception to the rule against hearsay and is quite

distinct from the present rule concerning authentication. It is discussed in another place.[2]

The preferable and majority view is that satisfaction of the ancient document requirements will serve to authenticate an ancient copy of an original writing. And a fresh certified copy of an instrument of record for thirty years will prove the ancient writing, though perhaps with the additional qualification that before the copy can come in, the original documents rule must be satisfied by showing the unavailability of the original. Admission of a writing as an ancient document does, however, dispense with the production of attesting witnesses.[3]

§ 224. Authentication by Circumstantial Evidence: (c) Custody

If a writing purports to be an official report or record and is proved to have come from the proper public office where such official papers are kept, it is generally agreed that this authenticates the offered document as genuine. This result is founded on the probability that the officers in custody of such records will carry out their public duty to receive or record only genuine official papers and reports, and thus it is the official duty to record and maintain the document, rather than the duty to prepare it, which constitutes the document a public record. Similarly, where a public office is the depository for private papers, such as wills, conveyances, or income tax returns, the proof that such a purporting deed, bill of sale, tax return or the like has come from the proper custody is usually accepted as sufficient authentication. This again can be sustained on the same principle if it appears that the official custodian had a public duty to verify the genuineness of the papers offered for record or deposit and to accept only the genuine.

As is discussed in a subsequent section,[1] any need for testimonial proof of production from proper official custody is today frequently avoided by resort to certification procedures or

---

§ 223

1. Fed.R.Evid. 901(b)(3).
2. See § 323 infra.
3. See § 220 supra.

§ 224

1. See § 228 infra.

"self-authentication." However, it is significant to note that such procedures are not exclusive or mandatory, and that proof of the facts necessary to secure admission of a public record may be made by any witness with competent knowledge.

As is true with ancient documents, the question of the authenticity of official records should not be confused with the ultimate admissibility of such records. It is quite possible for a public record to be perfectly genuine, and yet remain inadmissible for some distinguishable reason, e.g., that it is excludable hearsay.

Some question exists whether the rule which accepts, as prima facie genuine, documents which are shown to emerge from official custody should be extended beyond the field of public duty and recognized as to writings found in private custody. Since the circumstances of private custody are infinitely more varied than those of public custody, a new rule in an already rule-ridden area seems inadvisable. No such rule, in fact, is needed, provided that, in their discretion, courts recognize that proof of private custody, together with other circumstances, is frequently strong circumstantial evidence of authenticity. In the present day, this approach will readily accommodate the modern tendency to retain documents and records in computer memory. Thus, while presence in a computer file will constitute some indication of a connection with the person or persons having ordinary access to that file, much will depend on the surrounding facts and circumstances, and it is reasonable to require that these include some additional evidence of authenticity.

§ 225. Authentication by Circumstantial Evidence: (d) Knowledge: Reply Letters and Telegrams

When a letter, signed with the purported signature of X, is received "out of the blue," with no previous correspondence, the traditional "show me" skepticism of the common law trial practice[1] prevails, and the purported signature is not accepted as authentication, unless authenticity is confirmed by additional facts.

One circumstance recognized as sufficient is that in which the letter discloses knowledge that only the purported signer would be likely to have. Moreover, a convenient practice recognizes that if a letter has been written to X, and the letter now offered in evidence purports to be written by X and purports to be a reply to the first letter (that is either refers to it, or is responsive to its terms) and has been received without unusual delay, these facts authenticate it as a reply letter. This result may be rested upon the knowledge-principle, mentioned above. In view of the regularity of the mails the first letter would almost invariably come exclusively into the hands of X, or those authorized to act for him, who would alone know of the terms of the letter. It is supported also by the fact that in common experience we know that reply letters do come from the person addressed in the first letter.

The same principles appear potentially applicable to electronic mail, which is increasingly replacing more traditional means of communication and which will undoubtedly come to figure prominently in litigation in the near future. For purposes of authentication, e-mail can be viewed as roughly analogous to an unsigned letter written on letterhead stationery. In both instances, the indication of the source of the communication is susceptible to misappropriation and unauthorized use, and, accordingly, some further evidence of authenticity should arguably be required. Should such additional evidence be permitted to take the form that the communication to be authenticated is a timely response to an earlier message addressed to the purported sender?

In its traditional application, the reply letter doctrine rests upon the presumed regularity and dependability of the mails to provide the likelihood that the author of the response did in fact receive the original communication. Thus, it is also open to the proponent to show that the original message was communicated in some other manner, and that a reply was timely received. If the reply letter doctrine is

§ 225

1. See § 218 supra.

applied to e-mail, no problem whatever is encountered if the message sought to be authenticated is an e-mail response to a communication shown to have been mailed or otherwise conventionally delivered. However, if the message sought to be authenticated is an e-mail response to an original e-mail message, the rationale of the doctrine requires that the reliability of e-mail be assumed to approximate that of the post office, and that the probability of unauthorized interception of e-mail is not substantially greater than with conventional mail. This assumption seems justified.

It is hoped that authentication of e-mail under the reply letter doctrine will proceed more rapidly than was the case with an earlier technological advance, the telegraph. The early decisions, apparently on the grounds that employees of the telegraph company also knew the contents of the original message, and that telegrams went astray more frequently than the mails, refused to apply the doctrine to reply telegrams. In retrospect, this hesitancy seems extreme, and the modern decisions accept the inference of authenticity of the reply telegram as sufficient.

When the reply letter purports to be signed by an agent or other representative of X, the addressee of the first letter, the authority of the signing representative is presumed.

The first step in authentication of the reply letter is to prove that the first letter was dated and was duly mailed at a given time and place addressed to X. Seemingly oral testimony to these facts should suffice as to the first letter if the reply letter refers to it by date.[2] If, however, the reply letter only refers to it by reciting or responding to its terms, then since the terms of the first letter become important,[3] probably it would be necessary to satisfy the Best Evidence Rule. If X, as usually would be the case, is the party-opponent, and has the first letter in his hands, it would be necessary to give him notice to produce it, before a copy could be used to prove its terms.[4]

§ 226. Authentication by Circumstantial Evidence: (e) Telephone Messages and Other Oral Communications

Modern technology makes commonplace the receipt of oral communications from persons who are heard but not seen. The problems of authentication raised by these communications are substantively analogous to the problems of authenticating writings. Thus, if the witness has received, e.g., a telephone call out of the blue from one who identified himself as "X", this is not sufficient authentication of the call as in fact coming from X. The requisite additional proof may take the form of testimony by the witness that he is familiar with X's voice and that the caller was X. Or authentication may be accomplished by circumstantial evidence pointing to X's identity as the caller, such as if the communication received reveals that the speaker had knowledge of facts that only X would be likely to know. These same modes of authentication are also recognized where communications have been received by radio.

Whatever the means of transmission, oral communications today will frequently be perpetuated in some type of recording. Where such is the case the authentication of the communication is likely to be facilitated simply because otherwise unavailable proof of various kinds may be generated by use of the recording. At the same time, the use of recordings in turn raises a variety of additional problems. These include disputes over the completeness and audibility of the recording, whether and under what conditions transcripts of the recording should be made available to the jury, and, finally, what constitutes adequate authentication of a transcript. In addition, it should be noted that many courts have insisted upon a foundation for recordings which appears disproportionately demanding given the modest objectives of authentication. Finally, since the recordings treated here are almost invariably statements, it must be constantly born in mind that authentication is by no means a guarantee of admissibility, and that

---

2. See § 233 infra.
3. See § 233 infra.

4. See § 239 supra.

recordings will often raise evidentiary problems other than authentication.[1]

A somewhat easier problem is presented when the witness testifies that she placed a telephone call to a number listed to X, and that the person answering identified himself as X. In such a situation the accuracy of the telephone system, the probable absence of motive to falsify and the lack of opportunity for premeditated fraud all tend to support the conclusion that the self-identification of the speaker is reliable. Thus most courts today view proof of proper placing of a call plus self-identification of the speaker as sufficient proof of authenticity to admit the substance of the call. Moreover, it is likewise held that where it is shown that the witness has called the listed number of a business establishment and spoken with someone purporting to speak for the concern with respect to matters within its ordinary course of business, it is presumed that the speaker was authorized to speak for the employer.

§ 227. Functions of Judge and Jury in Authentication

If direct testimony of the authorship of a writing or of an oral statement is given, this is sufficient authentication and the judge has no problem on that score.[1] The writing or statement comes in, if not otherwise objectionable. When the authenticating evidence is circumstantial, however, the question whether reasonable men could find its authorship as claimed by the proponent may be a delicate and balanced one as to which the judge must be accorded some latitude of judgment.[2] Accordingly, it is often said to be a matter of discretion. It must be noticed, however, that authenticity is not to be classed as one of those preliminary questions of fact conditioning admissibility under technical evidentiary rules of competency or privilege. As to these latter, the trial judge will permit the adversary to introduce controverting proof on the preliminary issue in support of his objection, and the judge

will decide this issue, without submission to the jury, as a basis for his ruling on admissibility.[3] On the other hand, the authenticity of a writing or statement is not a question of the application of a technical rule of evidence. It goes to genuineness and conditional relevance, as the jury can readily understand. Thus, if a prima facie showing is made, the writing or statement comes in, and the ultimate question of authenticity is left to the jury.

§ 228. Escapes From the Requirement of Producing Evidence of Authenticity: Modern Theory and Practice

As the foregoing sections clearly imply, the authentication of writings and other communications by formal proof may prove troublesome, time consuming, and expensive even in cases where no legitimate doubt concerning genuineness would appear to exist. The ultimate explanation for the continuing insistence upon the furnishing of such proof, justifiable only upon assumptions which accord very little with common sense, is of course obscure. It may be speculated, however that in part the explanation is to be found in various procedural devices which afford escape from authentication requirements. Use of these devices will avert some of the impatience which might otherwise be engendered by formal authentication requirements. The legislatures, too, have frequently nibbled at the problem by enacting statutes relieving the rigors of authentication in what would otherwise be particularly troublesome contexts. Among these "escapes from authentication," the following are particularly noteworthy.

Requests for Admission. Under the practice in the Federal courts as provided by Rules 36 and 37(c) of the Federal Rules of Civil Procedure, and under analogous rules or statutes in many states, a party may serve upon an adversary a written request for admission of the genuineness of any relevant document described in the request. If the adversary un-

§ 226
1. See, e.g., § 214 supra, Ch. 23 infra.

§ 227
1. See §§ 219–221 supra.

2. See §§ 222–226 supra.
3. See § 53 supra.

reasonably fails within a specified time to serve an answer or objection, genuineness is admitted. If genuineness is denied and the requesting party thereafter proves the genuineness of the document at trial, the latter may apply for an order of court requiring the adversary to pay her the reasonable costs of making the authenticating proof.

Securing Admission at Pretrial Conference. Under Rule 16 in the Federal courts, and under analogous rules and statutes in many states, it is provided that a pretrial conference of the attorneys may be called by the court to consider among other things, "the possibility of obtaining admissions of fact and of documents which will avoid unnecessary proof." Of course, similar stipulations often are secured in informal negotiation between counsel, but a skillful judge may create at a pretrial conference an atmosphere of mutual concession unusually favorable for such admissions. This function of the pretrial practice has been considered one of its most successful features.

Statutes and Rules Requiring Special or Sworn Denial of Genuineness of Writing. A provision of practice acts and rules of procedure may require that when an action is brought upon a written instrument, such as a note or contract, copied in the complaint, the genuineness of the writing will be deemed admitted unless a sworn denial be included in the answer.

Writings Which "Prove Themselves:" Acknowledged Documents, Certified Copies, and Law Books Which Purport to be Printed by Authority. There are certain kinds of writings which are said to "prove themselves" or to be "self-identifying." In consequence one of these may be tendered to the court and, even without the shepherding angel of an authenticating witness, will be accepted in evidence for what it purports to be. This convenient result is reached in two stages. First, by statutes which often provide that certain classes of writings, usually in some manner purporting to be vouched for by an official, shall be received in evidence "without further proof." This helpful attribute is most commonly given by statute to (1) deeds, conveyances or other instruments, which have been acknowledged by the signers

before a notary public, (2) certified copies of public records, and (3) books of statutes which purport to be printed by public authority.

But in the first two of these classes of writings, which can qualify only when the acknowledgment is certified by a notary or the copy certified by the official who has custody of the record, how is the court to know without proof that the signature or seal appearing on the writing is actually that of the official whose name and title are recited? This second step is supplied by the traditional doctrines which recognize the seal or signature of certain types of officers, including the keeper of the seal of state, judicial officers, and notaries public, as being of themselves sufficient evidence of the genuineness of the certificate.Moreover in many state codes particular provisions supplement or clarify tradition by specifying that the seals or signatures of certain classes of officialdom shall have this self-authenticating effect.

Federal Rules of Evidence. The concept of self-authentication, previously recognized by statute in the case of the certain relatively limited classes of writings noted above, is given an expanded ambit of operation by the Federal Rules of Evidence. Rule 902 accords prima facie authenticity not only to those types of writings such as acknowledged writings and public records which have commonly enjoyed such treatment by statute but also to various other types of writings not previously so favored. Among these new classes of self-authenticating writings are included books, pamphlets and other publications issued by public authority, newspapers and periodicals, and trade inscriptions and labels indicating ownership, control or origin. Presumptive authenticity, as provided for by the rule, does not preclude evidentiary challenge of the genuineness of the offered writing, but simply serves to obviate the necessity of preliminary authentication by the proponent to secure admission. This common sense approach was long overdue and might well be extended to apply to all writings purporting to have a connection with the party against whom offered.

The concept of self-authentication was subsequently extended dramatically in federal criminal proceedings by enactment of a statute which confers self-authenticating effect on foreign records of regularly conducted activity which are certified by the custodian in accordance with the statute.[1] This development in turn motivated the Conference of Commissioners on Uniform State Laws to amend Uniform Rule 902 to provide for self-authentication of "certified" business records, domestic as well as foreign.

§ 228

1. 18 U.S.C.A. § 3506.

Chapter 23

THE REQUIREMENT OF THE PRODUCTION OF THE ORIGINAL WRITING AS THE "BEST EVIDENCE"

Table of Sections

§ 229. The "Best Evidence" Rule

Thayer[1] tells us that the first appearance of the "best evidence" phrase, is a statement in 1700 by Holt, C.J. (in a case in which he admitted evidence questioned as secondary) to the effect that "the best proof that the nature of the thing will afford is only required."[2] This statement given as a reason for receiving evidence, that it is the best which can be had—a highly liberalizing principle—not surprisingly gives birth to a converse and narrowing doctrine that a man must produce the best evi-

dence that is available—second-best will not do. And so before 1726 we find Baron Gilbert in one of the earliest treatises on Evidence saying, "the first and most signal rule in relation to evidence is this, that a man must have the utmost evidence the nature of the fact is capable of * * *."[3] Blackstone continues the same broad generalizing and combines both the positive and negative aspects of the "best evidence" idea when he says, " * * * the best evidence the nature of the case will admit of shall always be required, if possible to be had; but if not possible then the best evidence that

---

§ 229

1. Thayer, Preliminary Treatise on Evidence at the Common Law 489 (1898).

2. Ford v. Hopkins, 1 Salk. 283, 91 Eng.Rep. 250 (1700).

3. Gilbert, Evidence (2d ed.) 4, 15–17, quoted Thayer, op. cit. 490.

can be had shall be allowed."[4] Greenleaf in this country in 1842 was still repeating these wide abstractions.

Thayer, however, writing in 1898, points out that these broad principles, though they had some influence in shaping specific evidence rules in the 1700s, were never received as adequate or accurate statements of governing rules, and that actually "the chief illustration of the Best Evidence principle, the doctrine that if you would prove the contents of a writing, you must produce the writing itself" is an ancient rule far older than any notion about the "best" evidence. While some modern opinions still refer to the "best evidence" notion as if it were today a general governing legal principle most would adopt the view of modern textwriters that there is no such general rule. The only actual rule that the "best evidence" phrase denotes today is the rule requiring the production of the original writing.

§ 230. Original Document Rule

The specific context in which it is generally agreed that the best evidence principle is applicable today should be definitely stated and its limits clearly defined. The rule is this: in proving the terms of a writing, where the terms are material, the original writing must be produced unless it is shown to be unavailable for some reason other than the serious fault of the proponent. The discussion in the following sections is directed to adding content to this basic framework.

§ 231. The Reasons for the Rule

Since its inception in the early 18th century, various rationales have been asserted to underlie the "best evidence rule." Many older writers have asserted that the rule is essentially directed to the prevention of fraud. Wigmore, however, vigorously attacked this thesis on the analytical ground that it does not square with certain recognized applications and non-applications of the rule. Most modern commentators follow his lead in asserting that the basic premise justifying the rule is the

central position which the written word occupies in the law. Because of this centrality, presenting to a court the exact words of a writing is of more than average importance, particularly in the case of operative or dispositive instruments such as deeds, wills or contracts, where a slight variation of words may mean a great difference in rights. In addition, it is to be considered (1) that there has been substantial hazard of inaccuracy in some of the commonly utilized methods of making copies of writings, and (2) oral testimony purporting to give from memory the terms of a writing is probably subject to a greater risk of error than oral testimony concerning other situations generally. The danger of mistransmitting critical facts which accompanies the use of written copies or recollection, but which is largely avoided when an original writing is presented to prove its terms, justifies preference for original documents.

At the same time, it has long been observed that the opportunity to inspect original writings may be of substantial importance in the detection of fraud. Not surprisingly, then, prevention of fraud has long been sporadically cited as at least an ancillary justification for the rule, and the Federal and Uniform Rules of Evidence clearly incorporate this view. And some modern authorities go so far as to assert that fraud prevention constitutes the principal current justification for the rule. For unless this additional justification is accepted, there would appear little reason to apply the rule, as is frequently done, to copies produced by modern copying techniques which virtually eliminate any possibility of mistransmission. To accept fraud prevention as the exclusive basis for the rule, however, forces reexamination of the question raised by Wigmore, why is the rule not equally applicable to chattels?

Finally, one leading opinion intimates that the rule should be viewed to protect not only against mistaken or fraudulent mistransmissions but also against intentional or unintentional misleading through introduction of selected portions of a comprehensive set of writings to which the opponent has no access.

---

4. Blackstone, Commentaries 368, quoted Thayer op. cit. 491.

This seems to engraft upon the best evidence rule an aspect of completeness not heretofore observed.

Whatever rationale is viewed to support the rule, it will be observed that the advent of modern discovery and related procedures under which original documents may be examined before trial rather than at it, have substantially reduced the need for the rule. Though it has been pointed out that at present limitations on the availability of these alternatives leaves the original documents rule a continuing and important sphere of operations, it is foreseeable that further extensions of discovery practice will ultimately render the rule obsolete.

§ 232. What Are Writings? Application to Objects Inscribed and Unscribed

A rule which permitted the judge to insist that all evidence must pass the court's scrutiny as being the "best" or most reliable means of proving the fact would be a sore incumbrance upon the parties, who in our system have the responsibility of proof. In fact, as we have seen, no such general scrutiny is sanctioned, but only as to "writings" is a demand for the "best," the original, made.[1] This limitation on the ambit of the rule rests largely on the practical realization that writings exhibit a fineness of detail, lacking in chattels generally, which will often be of critical importance. Prevention of loss of this fine detail through mistransmission is a basic objective of the rule requiring production of documentary originals.

But while writings may be generally distinguished from other chattels with respect to the amount and importance of the detail they exhibit, chattels bearing more or less detailed inscriptions are far from uncommon. Thus, when an object such as a policeman's badge, a flag, or a tombstone bears a number or legend the terms of which are relevant the problem is raised as to whether the object shall be treated as a chattel or a writing. It is here clearly

unwise to adapt a purely semantic approach and to classify the object according to whether its written component predominates sufficiently to alter the label attached to it in common parlance. At the same time, however, it would seem also unnecessary to classify as writings, as apparently do the Federal and Revised Uniform Rules, any object which carries an inscription of any sort whatsoever. In the final analysis, it is perhaps impossible to improve upon Wigmore's suggestion, followed by a number of courts, that the judge shall have discretion to apply the present rule to inscribed chattels or not in light of such factors as the need for precise information as to the exact inscription, the ease or difficulty of production, and the simplicity or complexity of the inscription.

Within this general framework, certain types of chattels warrant specific mention. Thus, sound recordings, where their content is sought to be proved, so clearly involve the identical considerations applicable to writings as to warrant inclusion within the present rule. Somewhat more questionable are the provisions of the Federal and Revised Uniform Rules of Evidence which bring photographs within the rule in those relatively rare instances in which their contents are sought to be proved. However, while it is difficult to accept that photographs of objects exhibit more intricacy of detail than do the objects photographed, there does exist a rationale for bringing photographs within it where their contents are sought to be proved. Certainly, the original of a photograph may afford indices of chicanery which secondary evidence of its contents would not betray, and this is likely to be of unusual importance where photographic products are offered "to speak for themselves." An obvious example of such an application is the X-ray, which has frequently been held to be within the rule even though no writings in the usual sense are displayed.

These and other extensions of the rule[2] (such, for example, as copyright or defama-

---

1. See § 229 supra.

2. In copyright and defamation cases the "contents" of a picture may well be argued to be material and sought to be proved. And, though no letters or figures are involved,

tion cases), admittedly appealing in certain contexts, nevertheless possess the major disadvantage that they sacrifice the cardinal limiting principle of the common law rule, its non-applicability to evidence other than writings. Once this limitation is breached, the rule is easily extended to other non-verbal graphic representations which exhibit a wealth of detail, after which no easily identifiable bar remains to demands for the production of virtually any complex chattel as the "best evidence."

§ 233. What Constitutes Proving the Terms

It is apparent that this danger of mistransmission of the contents of the writing, which is the principal reason for the rule, is only important when evidence other than the writing itself is offered for the purpose of proving its terms. Consequently, evidence that a certain document is in existence or as to its execution or delivery is not within the rule and may be given without producing the document.

In what instances, then, can it be said that the terms of a writing are sought to be proved, rather than merely its identity, or existence? First, there are certain writings which the substantive law, e.g., the Statute of Frauds, the parol evidence rule, endow with a degree of either indispensability or primacy. Transactions to which substantive rules of this character apply tend naturally to be viewed as written transactions, and writings embodying such transactions, e.g., deeds, contracts, judgments, etc., are universally considered to be within the present rule when actually involved in the litigation. Contrasted with the above described types of writings are those, essentially unlimited in variety, which the substantive law does not regard as essential or primary repositories of the facts recorded. Writings of this latter sort may be said merely to happen to record the facts of essentially nonwritten transactions. Testimony descriptive of nonwritten transactions is not generally considered to be within the scope of the present rule

and may be given without producing or explaining the absence of a writing recording the facts. Thus, evidence of a payment may be given without production of the receipt, or evidence of a marriage without production of the marriage certificate.

While, however, many facts may be proved without resort to writings which record them, the party attempting to prove a fact may *choose* to show the contents of a writing for the purpose. Thus, for example, a writing may contain a recital of fact which is admissible under an exception to the hearsay rule. Here the recited fact might possibly be established without the writing, but if the contents are relied upon for the purpose, the present rule applies and oral testimony as to its contents will be rejected unless the original writing is shown to be unavailable.

Distinguishable from the situation in which the witness undertakes to state the fact based upon what he has seen in a writing, is the situation in which the witness testifies that the fact did not occur because relevant records contain no mention of it. This negative type of testimony is usually held not to constitute proof of contents and thus not to require production of records. But it will be seen that care in the application of this exception is required, since testimony as to what does not appear may easily involve a questionable description by the witness of the details which do appear. Perhaps a better approach would be to treat such "non-entry" testimony as a form of summary, which in fact it is, and to subject it to the safeguards employed in that context.

It has long been held that records too voluminous to be conveniently produced and examined in court may be summarized and their import testified to by a witness, usually an expert, who has reviewed the entirety. The Federal and Revised Uniform Rules of Evidence recognize and clarify this helpful practice, and also provide appropriate safeguards by requiring that the originals be made available for examination and copying by other

---

it may reasonably be concluded that the high desirability of intricate detail in such cases warrants application of the rule. See Seiler v. Lucasfilm, Ltd., 797 F.2d 1504 (9th Cir.

1986) (Rule held applicable in copyright action to bar admission of "reconstructions" of original drawings of science fiction creations).

parties. These requirements, of course, tacitly assume that reasonable notice be given of the intent to offer summaries. And, since the summaries admitted under this rule are being introduced substantively in place of the matters summarized, it has reasonably been held that a foundation is required for such evidence which establishes both the admissibility of the underlying data and the accuracy of the summary.

Certain criticisms may be leveled at the commonly applied distinction between facts the legal efficacy of which is affected by reduction to writing, and facts which are legally effective whether or not contained in a writing. Thus it has been suggested that in modern law there are few if any instances in which a writing is anything more than a recordation of some nonwritten fact. For example, a written contract, it may be contended, merely records the operative legal fact, which is the agreement of the parties. Moreover, the distinction has proved a difficult one to apply, and does not adequately serve to reconcile various common applications and nonapplications of the rule. Thus it is commonly held that oral evidence of a witness's prior testimony is receivable even though that testimony is embodied in a transcript. But when a confession has been both orally made and reduced to writing, numerous courts require the writing. Dying declarations both spoken and reduced to writing have produced a similar contrariety of opinion.

Perhaps the most satisfactory solution to the problem would be to abandon the distinction between transactions essentially written and nonwritten and allow the application of the rule to turn upon the trial judge's determination of such factors as the centrality of the writing to the litigation, the importance of bringing the precise words of the writing before the trier, and the danger of mistransmission or imposition in the absence of the original. The result would simply be to merge the present confusing and confused doctrine with the collateral documents exception discussed below, or at least to enlarge the scope of the latter.

§ 234. Writings Involved Only Collaterally

At nearly every turn in human affairs some writing—a letter, a bill of sale, a newspaper, a deed—plays a part. Consequently any narration by a witness is likely to include many references to transactions consisting partly of written communications or other writings. A witness to a confession, for example, identifies the date as being the day after the crime because he read of the crime in the newspaper that day, or a witness may state that he was unable to procure a certain article because it was patented. It is apparent that it is impracticable to forbid such references except upon condition that the writings (e.g., the newspaper, and the patent) be produced in court. Recognition of an exception exempting "collateral writings" from the operation of the basic rule has followed as a necessary concession to expedition of trials and clearness of narration, interests which outweigh, in the case of merely incidental references to documents, the need for perfect exactitude in the presentation of these documents' contents.

While writings are frequently held to be collateral within the meaning of the present exception, the purposes for which references to documents may be made by witnesses are so variegated that the concept of collateralness defies precise definition. Three principal factors, however, should, and generally do, play a role in making the determination of collateralness. These are: the centrality of the writing to the principal issues of the litigation; the complexity of the relevant features of the writing; and the existence of genuine dispute as to the contents of the writing. Evaluation and weighting of these factors in the particular instance may perhaps best be left to the discretion of the trial judge, and as elsewhere in the application of this essentially administrative rule, exercise of that discretion should be reviewed only for grave abuse.

§ 235. Which Is the "Writing Itself" That Must Be Produced? Telegrams, Counterparts

What should be the application of the basic rule where two documents, X and Y, exist,

X having been created first and Y being some variety of reproduction of X? Copies, of course, are frequent and in most cases the document first prepared will be the one whose initial production is required by the rule. But the problem is not always so simple. For example, X may be a telegram written by the sender and handed to the company for transmission; or X may be a libelous handwritten letter given to a stenographer for copying and sending, and Y the letter actually received by the addressee; or X may be a ledger sheet in the creditor's books and Y the account rendered made up therefrom and sent to the debtor. Today X may be the document prepared in an office and Y the facsimile copy transmitted to the addressee over a phone line.

In any of the above cases, if a party in court offers document Y in evidence, what determines whether the document is "the writing itself" offered to prove its own terms, or merely a "copy" offered to establish the terms of X? The answer here clearly does not depend upon the chronology of creation or the ordinary semantic usage which would denominate Y as a "copy." Instead it will depend upon the substantive law of contracts, defamation, property, and the like. The question to be asked, then, is whether, under the substantive law, the creation, publication, or other use of Y may be viewed as affecting the rights of the parties in a way material to the litigation. If the answer to this question is affirmative, the fact that Y happens to be a copy of another writing is completely immaterial. There are, then, many instances in which the terms of "copies" are the facts sought to be proved.

It will also frequently occur that a written transaction, such as a contract or deed, will be evidenced by several counterparts or identical copies, each of which is signed by the parties or, at any rate, intended to be equally effective as embodying the transaction. Such multiple counterparts are frequently termed "duplicate (or triplicate, etc.) originals". Each of these counterparts is admissible as an "original" without producing or accounting for the others, but before secondary evidence may be resorted to, all of the counterparts must be shown to be unavailable.

§ 236. Reproductions: Carbons: Printed and Multigraph Copies: Photo and Xerographic Copies

The treatment of copies under the rule requiring the production of the original document can only properly be understood when viewed in light of the technological history of copying itself. In its earliest stages, the rule appears to have developed against a background of copying performed by individuals of the Bob Cratchit sort, transcribing manually not always under the best of conditions. Errors under such circumstances were routinely to be expected. Only marginally greater reliability was to be found in the so-called letter-press. Here the original was written or typed in copying ink or with copying pencil. Presumably influenced by the infirmities present in such modes of copying, the courts generally declined to accept subsequently created copies as equivalent to originals.

The advent of carbon paper, however, made possible the creation of copies of substantially greater reliability and legibility. Here, since the copy is made by the same stroke as the original, there was an apparent factual distinction between these copies and copies produced subsequent to the original by the older methods. It moreover became common, as it is today, to create multiple counterparts of a contract or transaction through the use of carbon paper, with each copy duly signed either through the same medium or individually. What makes such writings counterparts, of course, is the signing with intent to render each co-equal with the others, and the doctrine of counterparts can therefore hardly apply to a retained carbon copy which is not intended as a communication at all. However, the fact that many true counterparts are made by the use of carbons coupled with the notion that writings generated simultaneously by the same stroke are in some way superior, has caused a great number of courts to treat all carbons as if they were duplicate originals, i.e., as admissible without accounting for the original.

More comprehensibly, there is warrant for believing that the courts will accept as primary evidence of the contents of a given book or a given issue of a newspaper any other book or newspaper printed from the same sets of fixed type, or the same plates or mats. A like result should be reached as to all copies run off from the same mat by the multigraph, lithoprint or other duplicating process.

In the present day, copying by various photographic and other processes has become commonplace, replacing the carbon for many purposes. Various types of photographic copying, of course, produce facsimiles of an extremely high degree of verisimilitude, and thus might have been expected, as have carbons, to win recognition as duplicate originals. In fact, an early judicial step in this direction was taken in a celebrated federal court of appeals decision which held that "recordak" photographs of checks which had been paid, preserved by a bank as part of its regular records were admissible under the Federal Business Records Act. Subsequently, a uniform act was prepared under which photographic copies, regularly kept, of business and public records are admissible without accounting for the original.[1] This act has been widely adopted.[2] In the cases, however, in which photographs of writings have been offered to show the terms of the original, without the aid of specific statutes, they have been almost uniformly treated as secondary evidence, inadmissible unless the original is accounted for.

The resulting state of authority, favorable to carbons but unfavorable to at least equally reliable photographic and xerographic reproductions, appears inexplicable on any basis other than that the courts, having fixed upon simultaneous creation as the characteristic distinguishing of carbons from copies produced by earlier methods have on the whole been insufficiently flexible to modify that concept in the face of newer technological methods which fortuitously do not exhibit that characteristic. Insofar as the primary purpose of the original documents requirement is directed at securing accurate information from the contents of material writings, free of the infirmities of memo-

ry and the mistakes of hand-copying, we may well conclude that each of these forms of mechanical copying is sufficient to fulfill the policy. Insistence upon the original, or accounting for it, places costs, burdens of planning, and hazards of mistake upon the litigants. These may be worth imposing where the alternative is accepting memory or hand-copies. They are probably not worth imposing when risks of inaccuracy are reduced to a minimum by the offer of a mechanically produced copy.

At the same time, however, if the original documents requirement is conceded to be supported by the ancillary purpose of fraud prevention, it will be seen that even copies produced by photographic or xerographic processes are not totally as desirable as the original writing. Many indicia of putative fraud such as watermarks, types of paper and inks, etc., will not be discernable on the copy. The most reasonable accommodation of the purposes of the basic rule to modern copying to date would appear to be that of the Federal Rules of Evidence. Under Federal Rule 1001(4) copies produced by photography or chemical reproduction or equivalent techniques are classed as "duplicates," and, under Rule 1003 are declared admissible as originals unless a genuine question is raised as to the authenticity of the original or it appears under the circumstances that it would be unfair to admit the duplicate in lieu of the original.

An even more recent challenge to the flexibility of the rule requiring documentary originals has appeared in the form of machine readable records stored on punch cards or magnetic tape. Obviously, where records are originally deposited in such media nothing akin to a conventional documentary original will be created. To the credit of the courts, records there stored have generally fared well in the face of objection predicated on the original document rule, and machine printouts of such records have been admitted. Similar treatment has also been accorded hardcopy

---

§ 236

1. Uniform Photographic Copies of Business and Public Records as Evidence Act, 9A U.L.A. 584.

2. 14 U.L.A. (1980). Following preparation of the uniform act, its substance was expressly incorporated into the Federal Business Records Act, now 28 U.S.C.A. § 1732.

printouts of images displayed on a computer screen.

§ 237. Excuses for Nonproduction of the Original Writing: (a) Loss or Destruction

The production-of-documents rule is principally aimed, not at securing a writing at all hazards and in every instance, but at securing the best *obtainable* evidence of its contents. Thus, if as a practical matter the document cannot be produced because it has been lost or destroyed, the production of the original is excused and other evidence of its contents becomes admissible. Failure to recognize this qualification of the basic rule would in many instances mean a return to the bygone and unlamented days in which to lose one's paper was to lose one's right. Recognition of the same qualification also squares with the ancillary purpose of the basic rule to protect against the perpetration of fraud, since proof that failure to produce the original is due to inability to do so tends logically to dispel the otherwise possible inference that the failure stems from design.

Loss or destruction may sometimes be provable by direct evidence but more often the only available evidence will be circumstantial, usually taking the form that appropriate search for the document has been made without discovering it. It would appear that where loss or destruction is sought to be proved by circumstantial evidence of unavailing search, the declarations of a former custodian as to loss or destruction may be admitted to show the nature and results of the search, though if offered as direct evidence of loss or destruction itself such declarations would be incompetent as hearsay.

Where loss or destruction is sought to be shown circumstantially by proof of unsuccessful search, it is obvious that the adequacy of the showing will be largely dependent upon the thoroughness and appropriateness of the search. It was laid down in certain early decisions that when the writing is last known to have been in a particular place or in the hands of a particular person, then that place must be searched or the person produced, and state-

ments to the same effect are to be found in modern decisions. It is believed, however, that these statements are best considered as general guides or cautions, rather than strict and unvarying rules. Virtually all jurisdictions view the trial judge as possessing some degree of discretion in determining the preliminary question as to whether it is feasible to produce the original document. Such discretion is particularly appropriate since the character of the search required to show probability of loss or destruction will, as a practical matter, depend on the circumstances of each case. Factors such as the relative importance of the document and the lapse of time since it was last seen have been seen to bear upon the extent of search required before loss or destruction may be inferred. The only general requirement, however, should be that all reasonable avenues of search should be explored to the extent that reasonable diligence under the circumstances would dictate.

If the original document has been destroyed by the person who offers evidence of its contents, the evidence is not admissible unless, by showing that the destruction was accidental or was done in good faith, without intention to prevent its use as evidence, he rebuts to the satisfaction of the trial judge, any inference of fraud.

§ 238. Excuses for Nonproduction of the Original Writing: (b) Possession by a Third Person

When the writing is in the hands of a third person who is within the geographical limits of the trial court's subpoena power, the safest course is to have a writ of subpoena duces tecum served on the possessor summoning him to bring the writing to court at the trial, though some decisions will excuse resort to subpoena if the possessor is privileged not to produce it, and others suggest that proof of a hostile or unwilling attitude on his part will be a sufficient excuse.

If the writing is in the possession of a third person out of the state or out of the reach of the court's process, a showing of this fact alone will suffice, in the view of many courts, to excuse production of the writing. This practice has the merit of being an easy rule of thumb to apply, but the basic policy of the original document requirement would tend to support the view of a substantially equal number of courts that a further showing must be made. These latter courts require that, before secondary evidence is used, the proponent must show either that he has made reasonable but unavailing efforts to secure the original from its possessor, or circumstances which persuade the court that such efforts, had they been made, would have been fruitless.

§ 239. Excuses for Nonproduction of the Original Writing: (c) Failure of Adversary Having Possession to Produce After Notice

A frequently used method of showing that it is impracticable for the proponent to produce the original writing is to prove, first, that the original is in the hands of his adversary or under his control, and second, that the proponent has notified him to produce it at the trial and he has failed to do so. Observe that the notice is without compulsive force, and is designed merely to account for nonproduction of the writing by the proponent, and thus to enable him to use secondary evidence of the writing's terms. If the proponent actually needs the production of the original itself he will resort to subpoena duces tecum or under modern rules the motion for an order to produce. But when the notice is offered as an excuse for resorting to secondary evidence the adversary cannot fairly complain that he was only given opportunity, not compelled, to make the writing available.

An oral notice may be sufficient, but the safest and almost universal practice is to give written notice beforehand to the party or his attorney, describing the particular documents, and then to call upon the adversary orally at the trial for the writings requested. It is held that the nature of the complaint or of the defense may constitute a sufficient implied notice that the pleader is charging the adversary with possession of the original and that he

considers its production essential. As to the time of serving notice it is sufficient if it allows the adversary a fair opportunity under the existing circumstances to produce the writing at the trial. Accordingly, if it appears at the trial itself that the adversary has the original paper in the courtroom, an immediate notice then and there is timely.

Some exceptions, under which notice is unnecessary before using secondary evidence of a writing in the adversary's possession, have been recognized. The first is well sustained in reason. It dispenses with the need for notice when the adversary has wrongfully obtained or fraudulently suppressed the writing. The others seem more questionable. There is a traditional exception that no notice is required to produce a writing which is itself a notice. This is understandable in respect to giving notice to produce a notice to produce, which would lead to an endless succession of notices, but there seems little justification for extending the exception, as the cases do, to notices generally. Finally an exception is made by the majority view for writings in the hands of the accused in a criminal prosecution. Under this view, secondary evidence may be received without notice to the accused to produce. The logic of deriving this position, as seems to have been done, from the privilege against self-incrimination is dubious. For while a demand upon the accused to produce which is delivered before the jury clearly has a tendency to coerce the defendant and thus cheapen the privilege,[1] there is no logical necessity that the demand be so delivered. Since the object of notice is to protect against imposition upon the opponent, and since this object may be achieved in the case of the criminal defendant by notice before trial, the minority view under which the prosecution must give notice as a necessary precondition to the use of secondary evidence seems the fairer and more reasonable stand.

§ 240. Excuses for Nonproduction of the Original Writing: (d) Public Records

If the contents of the judgment of a court or of an executive proclamation are to be

---

§ 239

1. As to compelling production generally by an accused, see § 128 supra.

proved, shall the proponent be required to produce the original writing? The accepted view is that, in general, public and judicial records and public documents are required by law to be retained by the official custodian in the public office designated for their custody, and courts will not require them to be removed. To require removal would be inconvenient for the public who might desire to consult the records and would entail a risk of loss of or damage to the official documents. Accordingly, statutes and rules have provided for the issuance of certified copies and for their admission in evidence in lieu of the original. In addition, examined copies, authenticated by a witness who has compared it with the original record, are usually receivable.

§ 241. Preferences Among Copies and Between Copies and Oral Testimony

The basic policy of the original document requirement is that of specially safeguarding the accuracy of the presentation in court of the terms of a writing. If the original is unavailable does the same policy require a preference among the secondary methods of proving the terms? Some means of proof are clearly more reliable than others. In order of reliability the list might go something like this: (1) a mechanically produced copy, such as a photograph or xerograph, a carbon, a letter-press copy, etc., (2) a firsthand copy by one who was looking at the original while he copied (immediate copy, sworn copy), (3) a copy, however made, which has been compared by a witness with the original and found correct (examined copy), (4) a secondhand or mediate copy, i.e., a copy of a firsthand copy, (5) oral testimony as to the terms of the writing, with memory aided by a previously made memorandum, and (6) oral testimony from unaided memory. There are many additional variations.

There is one rule of preference that is reasonable and is generally agreed on by the courts, namely, that for judicial and other public records, a certified, sworn or examined copy is preferred, and other evidence of the terms of the record cannot be resorted to unless the proponent has no such copy available, and the

original record has been lost or destroyed so that a copy cannot now be made.

As to writings other than public records, there are two general approaches to the problem. First there is the view, fathered by some of the English decisions and early espoused by a minority of the American cases, that "there are no degrees of substantive evidence." This position has the virtues of simplicity and easiness of application. In addition, it may be observed that failure to apply the basic rule as between varieties of secondary evidence leaves unimpaired a substantial practical motivation to produce more satisfactory secondary evidence where it appears to exist. This practical motivation, of course, stems from apprehension of the adverse inference which may be drawn from failure to produce more satisfactory secondary evidence indicated to exist and not shown to be unavailable. These considerations have led the draftsmen of most modern codes of evidence to adopt the so-called "English" view.

The opposing view, once the majority "American" rule, recognizes a distinction between types of secondary evidence, with a written copy being preferred to oral testimony. This view possesses the common sense merit that even poor copies are likely to contain more detail than the recollection of the best witness. As an additional justification, it may be argued that there is some incongruity in pursuing the policy of accurately obtaining the terms of writings by structuring a highly technical rule to that end, only to abandon the objective upon a showing of the original's unavailability. But whatever its merits, the adherents of this rule have been reduced to distinctly minority status by the widespread adoption of evidence codes following the pattern of the Federal and Uniform Rules of Evidence which, as earlier noted, do not recognize degrees of secondary evidence.

§ 242. Adversary's Admission as to the Terms of a Writing

Many American courts have followed the lead of Baron Parke's decision in Slatterie v. Pooley and have held admissions by a party opponent admissible to prove the terms of a writing. Upon reflection, however, it will be seen that Baron Parke's decision squares rather poorly with the primary modern day policy in favor of obtaining the contents of writings with accuracy. The evidence determined admissible in Slatterie v. Pooley was actually at two removes from the writing itself, being a witness' report of the defendant's comment. Perhaps the policy of holding admissible any admission which a party-opponent chooses to make will suffice to justify the first step, but the second frequently raises the possibility of erroneous transmission without corresponding justification. Accordingly, some American decisions have rejected testimony relating oral admissions concerning contents of writings.

It will be observed, however, that the second possibility of mistransmission noted above is effectively eliminated where no testimonial report of the admission is required. Thus, the desirable solution, towards which it is believed the decisions may be drifting, is to receive admissions to evidence a document's terms (1) when the admission itself is in writing and is produced in evidence, or (2) when the party himself, on the stand in this or some other trial or hearing, makes the admission about the contents of the writing or concedes that he made such an admission on a former occasion. Oral testimony by a witness that he heard the party's admission as to the terms of the writ-

ing, despite the authority of Slatterie v. Pooley, should be excluded.

§ 243. Review of Rulings Admitting Secondary Evidence

It will be seen from the earlier sections of this chapter that the requirement of the production of original writings, with the several excuses for nonproduction and the exceptions to the requirement itself, make up a fairly complex set of regulations for administration by the trial judge. Mistakes in the application of these rules are, understandably, not infrequent. The purpose of this system of rules, on the other hand, is simple and practical. That purpose is to secure the most reliable information as to the contents of documents, when those terms are disputed. A mystical ideal of seeking "the best evidence" or the "original document," as an end in itself is no longer the goal. Consequently when an attack is made, on motion for new trial or on appeal, upon the judge's admission of secondary evidence, it seems that the reviewing tribunal, should ordinarily make inquiry of the complaining counsel, "Does the party whom you represent actually dispute the accuracy of the evidence received as to the material terms of the writing?" If the counsel cannot assure the court that such a good faith dispute exists, it seems clear that any departure from the regulations in respect to secondary evidence must be classed as harmless error.

Title 10

THE HEARSAY RULE AND ITS EXCEPTIONS

Chapter 24

THE HEARSAY RULE

Table of Sections

§ 244. The History of the Rule Against Hearsay

In an oft-quoted passage, Wigmore calls the rule against hearsay "that most characteristic rule of the Anglo–American Law of Evidence—a rule which may be esteemed, next to jury trial, the greatest contribution of that eminently practical legal system to the world's methods of procedure."[1] How did this rule come about?

The development of the jury was, no doubt, an important factor. In its earlier forms, the jury was in the nature of a committee or special commission of qualified persons in the neighborhood to report on facts or issues in dispute. So far as necessary, its members conducted its investigations informally among those who had special knowledge of the facts. Attesting witnesses to writings were summoned with the jurors and apparently participated in their deliberations, but the practice of calling witnesses to appear in court and testify publicly about the facts to the jury is a late development in jury trial. Though something like the jury existed at least as early as the 1100s, this practice of hearing witnesses in court does not become frequent until the later 1400s. The movement is gradual thereafter to the present conception that the normal source of proof is not the private knowledge or investigation of the jurors but the testimony of witnesses in open court. In the 1500s it becomes, though not yet the exclusive source of proof, the normal and principal one.

A consciousness of need for exclusionary rules of evidence did not begin to appear until this period of the emergence of witnesses testifying publicly in court. Admittedly, even early witnesses to writings were required to speak only of "what they saw and heard,"[2] and this requirement would naturally be applied to the

---

§ 244

1. 5 Wigmore, Evidence § 1364, at 28 (Chadbourn rev. 1974).

2. Thayer, Preliminary Treatise on Evidence 101, 519 (1898).

new class of testifying witnesses. But when the witness has heard the statement of X out of court that X has seen an injury inflicted by a blow with a sword, and offered it as evidence of the blow, a new question was presented. Certainly, the earlier requirement of knowledge must have predisposed the judges to skepticism about the value of hearsay.

The value of hearsay and its sufficiency as proof is the subject of discussion in this gestation period. Through the reigns of the Tudors and the Stuarts, a drumfire of criticism and objections by parties and counsel against evidence of oral hearsay declarations gradually increases. While the evidence was constantly admitted, the confidence in its reliability was increasingly questioned. It was derided as "a tale of a tale"[3] or "a story out of another man's mouth."[4] Parallel with this increasingly discredited use of casual oral hearsay was a similar development with respect to transcribed statements made under oath before a judge or judicial officer, not subject to cross-examination by the party against whom it is offered. In criminal cases in the 1500s and down to the middle 1600s, the main reliance of the prosecution was the use of such "depositions" to make out its case. As oral hearsay was becoming discredited, uneasiness about the use of "depositions" began to take shape, first in the form of a limitation that they could only be used when the witness could not be produced at the trial. Neither the lack of an oath nor the unreliability of the report of the oral statement can be urged against such evidence, but only the absence of cross-examination and observation of demeanor.

During the first decade after the Restoration, the century or so of criticism of hearsay had its final effect in decisions rejecting such evidence, first as to oral hearsay and then as to depositions. Wigmore finds that the period between 1675 and 1690 is the time of crystallization of the rule against hearsay. For a time, the rule was qualified by the notion that hearsay, while not independently admissible, could be received to confirm other evidence, and this

qualification survived down to the end of the 1700s in the limited form of admitting witnesses' prior consistent statements to corroborate their testimony.

Whether the rule against hearsay was, with the rest of the English law of evidence, in fact "the child of the jury"[5] or the product of the adversary system may be of no great contemporary significance. The important point is that the rule against hearsay taking form at the end of the seventeenth century was neither a matter of immemorial usage nor an inheritance from Magna Charta but was a relatively late development of the common law.

Holdsworth thinks that the immediate influences leading to the crystallization of the rule against hearsay, at the particular time in the late 1600s when this occurred, were first, a strong dictum by Coke in his Third Institute denouncing "the strange conceit that one may be an accuser by hearsay," and second, the rejection of the attempt to naturalize in English law the two-witness requirement of the canon and civil law and the consequent urge to provide some compensating safeguard. As noted earlier, a century of increasing protests against the use of hearsay had preceded the establishment of the rule. However, most of the specific weaknesses of hearsay, which were the underlying reasons for the adoption of the rule and which have explained its survival, were not clearly acknowledged until after the beginning of the 1700s when the newly established rule came to be rationalized by the judges and the text writers.

§ 245. The Reasons for the Rule Against Hearsay; Exceptions to the Rule

The factors upon which the value of testimony depends are the perception, memory, narration, and sincerity of the witness. (1) *Perception*. Did the witness perceive what is described and perceive it accurately? (2) *Memory*. Has the witness retained an accurate impression of that perception? (3) *Narration*. Does the witness' language convey that im-

---

3.   Colledge's Trial, 8 How.St.Tr. 549, 663 (1681).
4.   Gascoigne's Trial, 7 How.St.Tr. 959, 1019 (1680).

5.   Thayer, supra note 2, at 47, 180.

pression accurately? (4) *Sincerity*. Is the witness, with varying degrees of intention, testifying falsely?

In order to encourage witnesses to put forth their best efforts and to expose inaccuracies that might be present with respect to any of the foregoing factors, the Anglo–American tradition evolved three conditions under which witnesses ordinarily are required to testify: oath, personal presence at the trial, and cross-examination. The rule against hearsay is designed to insure compliance with these ideal conditions, and when one of them is absent, the hearsay objection becomes pertinent.

In the hearsay situation, two "witnesses" are involved. The first complies with all three of the ideal conditions for the giving of testimony but merely reports what the second "witness" said. The second "witness" is the out-of-court declarant whose statement was not given in compliance with the ideal conditions but contains the critical information.

Oath. Among the earliest of the criticisms of hearsay, and one often repeated in judicial opinions down to the present, is the objection that the out-of-court declarant who made the hearsay statement commonly speaks or writes without the solemnity of the oath administered to witnesses in a court of law. The oath may be important in two aspects. As a ceremonial and religious symbol, it may induce a feeling of special obligation to speak the truth, and it may also impress upon the witness the danger of criminal punishment for perjury, to which the judicial oath or an equivalent solemn affirmation would be a prerequisite condition. Wigmore considered the oath requirement incidental and not essential and supported his argument by reference to the practice of excluding hearsay statements made under oath. But the fact that the oath is not the only requirement of the rule against hearsay does not prove it is unimportant. Similarly, the fact that the oath lacks the power that it had in an earlier age does not mean it no longer has significance; although affirmation is now commonly permit-

ted as a substitute, the oath (or affirmation) requirement for witnesses remains firm.

Personal presence at trial. Another long asserted objection is the lack of opportunity for observation of the out-of-court declarant's demeanor, with the light that this may shed on credibility. In addition, the solemnity of the occasion and possibility of public disgrace can scarcely fail to impress the witness, and testifying falsely becomes more difficult if the person against whom it is directed is present.

Moreover, personal presence eliminates the danger that the witness reporting the out-of-court statement may do so inaccurately. Also, reporting the spoken word is likely subject to special dangers of inaccuracy beyond the fallibility common to all reproduction from memory of matters of observation, and the risk of such inaccuracy is one of the weaknesses of hearsay. As Wigmore points out, however, not all hearsay is subject to this danger. Written statements can be produced in court and can be tested with reasonable accuracy for genuineness and freedom from alteration. Moreover, as Morgan notes, the reporting in court of spoken words for nonhearsay purposes, as in proving the making of an oral contract or the utterance of a slander, is subject to this same risk of misreporting. Neither argument seems conclusive. Moreover, no general distinction is made between written and spoken hearsay.

Cross-examination. The lack of any opportunity for the adversary to cross-examine the absent declarant whose out-of-court statement is reported is today accepted as the main justification for the exclusion of hearsay. As early as 1668, hearsay was rejected because "the other party could not cross-examine the party sworn."[1] Judicial expressions stress this as a principal reason for the hearsay rule. Cross-examination, as Bentham pointed out, was a distinctive feature of the English trial system, and the one that most contributed to the prestige of the institution of jury trial. He called it "a security for the correctness and completeness of testimony."[2] The nature of this safe-

---

§ 245

1. 2 Rolle's Abr. 679, pl. 9 (1668).

2. Rationale of Judicial Evidence, b. II, ch. IX, and b. III, ch. XX (1827).

guard which hearsay lacks is indicated by Chancellor Kent: "Hearsay testimony is from the very nature of it attended with all such doubts and difficulties and it cannot clear them up. 'A person who relates a hearsay is not obliged to enter into any particulars, to answer any questions, to solve any difficulties, to reconcile any contradictions, to explain any obscurities, to remove any ambiguities; he entrenches himself in the simple assertion that he was told so, and leaves the burden entirely on his dead or absent author.' "[3] In perhaps his most famous remark, Wigmore described cross-examination as "beyond any doubt the greatest legal engine ever invented for the discovery of truth."[4]

Hearsay that is admitted. Eminent judges have spoken of the "intrinsic weakness" of hearsay, but the unreliability of hearsay can be easily overstated. Hearsay is not by its inherent nature unworthy of any reliance in a judicial proceeding. The contrary is proved by the fact that courts are constantly admitting hearsay evidence under the numerous exceptions to the hearsay rule. If otherwise inadmissible hearsay evidence is received without objection, it typically may be considered and, if apparently reliable, is sufficient to sustain a verdict or finding of fact. Also, hearsay is widely used to establish probable cause, and more generally, much of our learning comes in the form of hearsay.

Hearsay evidence exhibits a wide range of reliability, some mere third-hand rumors to sworn affidavits of credible observers and ranging virtually from the highest to the lowest levels of trustworthiness. Although a wide range of reliability is found in most testimonial or circumstantial evidence, which is similarly based upon the frailties of human perception, memory, narration, and veracity, such evidence is not subject to a general rule of exclusion. The effort to adjust the rules of admissibility to variations in the reliability of hearsay has been a major motivating factor in the movement to liberalize evidence law.

Nevertheless, broad support exists for a general policy of requiring that testimony be given by witnesses in open court, under oath, and subject to cross-examination, which is the objective of the rule against hearsay. The problem lies in the operation of the rule that excludes evidence as a means of effectuating that policy.

§ 246. A Definition of Hearsay

A definition cannot furnish in a sentence or two ready answers to all the complex problems of an extensive field, such as hearsay. It can, however, provide a helpful general focus, mark a starting point, and serve as a memory aid in arranging some of the solutions.

The definition of hearsay in Rule 801 of the Federal Rules of Evidence, which is in effect in the federal courts and is followed by most states, has two major components. First, a "statement" is defined as "(1) an oral or written assertion or (2) nonverbal conduct of a person, if it is intended by the person as an assertion." Second, "hearsay" is defined as "a statement, other than one made by the declarant while testifying at the trial or hearing, offered in evidence to prove the truth of the matter asserted." This definition is affirmative in form; it says that an out-of-court assertion, offered to prove the truth of the matter asserted, is hearsay. For example, witness W reports on the stand that declarant D has stated that X was driving a car at a given time and place. The proponent is trying with this evidence to prove that X did so act. The out-of-court assertion is being offered to prove the truth of the matter asserted, and by definition, it is hearsay.

The definition does not in terms say that everything not included within the definition is not hearsay, but that was the intended effect of the rule, according to the Advisory Committee's Note. The rule's definition means, therefore, that out-of-court conduct is not hearsay if it is not an assertion or, even if it is assertive, it is not offered to prove the truth of the matter asserted.

---

3. Coleman v. Southwick, 9 John. 50 (N.Y.1812).

4. 5 Wigmore, Evidence § 1367, at 32 (Chadbourn rev. 1974).

Despite the importance of forms of the word "assert" to the meaning of hearsay, that term is nowhere defined. What does it mean? The contemporary dictionary meaning is to state positively or strongly.[1] However, in the pre-Rule world of evidence, the word "assert" carried no connotation of being positive or strong. A favorite of writers in the field for at least a century and a half, the word simply means *to say that something is so,* e.g., that an event happened or that a condition existed. Unfortunately, this definition is nowhere set out, and as a consequence contemporary courts sometimes exclude from the hearsay definition questions or imperative statements simply because they are not directly assertive.

Another formulation of the definition of hearsay that is different from the federal model is sometimes used. It measures the out-of-court statement against the policy underlying the hearsay rule and classifies as hearsay statements whose evidentiary value depends upon the credibility of the declarant without the assurances of oath, presence, or cross-examination. While the assertion-oriented definition of hearsay used by the Federal Rules and the definition based on the dangers behind the rule (sometimes termed declarant-oriented) often reach the same result, they also sometimes differ. This treatise in its original edition advanced the assertion-oriented approach and has continued to do so throughout its subsequent revisions, although later editions have moderated the approach somewhat.

When conduct or statements are not assertive or when they are assertive but are not used to prove the truth of the matter asserted, the statement should generally not be treated as hearsay because it does not fit the literal definition and because under these circumstances the danger of insincerity is usually significantly reduced. Although not perfect, this approach is relatively simple to apply and reaches a reasonable result in most situations even as judged by the rule's underlying policy.

However, analysis based on whether the statement is used to prove the specific point asserted is sometimes inadequate. Where a realistic appraisal of the statement and its circumstances reveal that the danger of insincerity has not been meaningfully reduced, hearsay treatment is appropriate. However, the burden should be on the opponent to show that an exception to the normal application of the hearsay definition should be recognized. These general principles will be further applied in the succeeding sections and particularly in the analysis of "implied assertions" in § 250.

Not in presence of party against whom offered. A remarkably persistent bit of courthouse folklore is that statements are inadmissible if not made in the presence of the party against whom they are offered. As the above discussion reveals, this objection is not related to the basic concept of hearsay. The presence or absence of the party against whom an out-of-court statement is offered has significance only in a few situations, e.g., when a statement spoken in the party's presence is relied upon to establish notice,[2] or when failure to deny a statement is the basis for claiming that the party adopted the statement.[3]

§ 247. Distinction Between Hearsay Rule and Rule Requiring Firsthand Knowledge

There is a rule, more ancient than the hearsay rule but having some kinship in policy, that should be distinguished from it. This rule is that witnesses are qualified to testify to facts susceptible of observation only if it appears that they had a reasonable opportunity to observe the facts.[1] Thus, if a witness testifies that on a certain day a flight arrived on time at X airport and from her other testimony it appears she was not in X at that time and could therefore only have spoken from conjecture or report of other persons, the proper objection is not hearsay but want of personal knowledge. Conversely, if the witness testi-

§ 246

1. Webster's Third New International Dictionary (1993).

2. See § 249, infra.

3. See § 262, infra.

§ 247

1. See § 10 supra.

fies that his brother *told* him that he came in on the flight and it arrived on time, the objection for want of knowledge of when the plane arrived is inappropriate. The witness purports to speak from his own knowledge of what his brother said, and as to this, he presumably had knowledge. If the testimony in this latter case was offered to show the time of the plane's arrival, the appropriate objection is hearsay.

The distinction is one of the form of the testimony, whether the witness purports to give the facts directly upon his or her own credit (though it may appear later that the statement was made on the faith of reports from others) or whether the witness purports to give an account of what another has said and this is offered to establish the truth of the other's report. However, when either from the phrasing of the testimony or from other sources, the witness appears to be testifying on the basis of reports from others, although not to their statements, the distinction loses much of its significance, and courts may simply apply the label "hearsay."

§ 248. Instances of the Application of the Hearsay Rule

A few examples of the rejection of evidence under the general hearsay rule excluding extra-judicial assertions offered to prove the facts asserted will indicate the scope of its operation. Evidence of the following oral statements has been excluded: on the issue whether deceased had transferred his insurance to his new automobile, testimony that he said he had made the transfer; to prove that veniremen had read newspaper articles, testimony of deputy sheriff that attorney said that one venireman said that another had read the articles; to prove that driver was driving with consent of insured owner, testimony that owner said after the accident that the driver had his permission; in rebuttal of defense of entrapment, criminal reputation of defendant to show predisposition; to show defendant's control of premises where marijuana was found, testimony of police officer that neighbors said person of same name occupied the premises; and

statements of child to social workers describing sexual abuse.

Instances of exclusion of written statements as hearsay when offered in court as evidence of their truth are likewise frequent. Thus, the following have been determined to be hearsay: written estimates of damages or cost of repairs made by an estimator who did not appear as a witness; written appraisal of stolen trailer by appraiser who did not testify; invoices from third parties as independent evidence of the making of repairs; the written statement of an absent witness to an accident; newspaper accounts as proof of the facts reported; statements in will that testator's second wife had agreed to devise property to his children as proof of that agreement; medical report by a physician who did not testify to prove that plaintiff had sustained injuries in a subsequent accident; and manufacturer's advertising claims as proof of product's reliability.

§ 249. Some Out-of-Court Utterances That Are Not Hearsay

The hearsay rule forbids evidence of out-of-court assertions to prove the facts asserted in them. If the statement is not an assertion or is not offered to prove the facts asserted, it is not hearsay. A few of the more common types of nonhearsay utterances are discussed in the present section.

Verbal acts. When a suit is brought for breach of a written contract, no one would think to object that a writing offered as evidence of the contract is hearsay. Similarly, proof of oral utterances by the parties in a contract suit constituting the offer and acceptance which brought the contract into being are not evidence of assertions offered testimonially but rather verbal conduct to which the law attaches duties and liabilities. Other obvious instances are evidence of the utterance by the defendant of words relied on as constituting a slander or deceit for which damages are sought.

Verbal parts of acts. The legal significance of acts taken alone and isolated from surrounding circumstances may be unclear. Thus, the bare physical act of handing over money to another person is susceptible of many interpretations. The possibilities include: loan, payment of a debt, bribe, bet, gift, and no doubt many other kinds of transactions. Explanatory words which accompany and give character to the transaction are not hearsay when under the substantive law the pertinent inquiry is directed only to objective manifestations rather than to the actual intent or other state of mind of the actor. As used by most courts, the "verbal parts of acts" concept has been tightly limited to words that constitute operative legal conduct and renders the doctrine an adjunct to the verbal acts doctrine. A narrow range for this doctrine seems appropriate.

Utterances and writings offered to show effect on hearer or reader. A statement that D made a statement to X is not subject to attack as hearsay when its purpose is to establish the state of mind thereby induced in X, such as receiving notice or having knowledge or motive, or to show the information which X had as bearing on the reasonableness, good faith, or voluntariness of subsequent conduct, or on the anxiety produced. The same rationale applies in self-defense cases to proof by the defendant of communicated threats by the person killed or assaulted. If offered to show the defendant's reasonable apprehension of danger, the statement is not offered for a hearsay purpose because its value does not depend on its truth.

In the situations discussed above, the out-of-court statement will frequently have an impermissible hearsay aspect as well as a permissible nonhearsay aspect. For example, an inspector's statement that a customer's tires are defective admitted to establish notice of the defective condition (with other proof being required to establish the condition) is susceptible of being used improperly by the trier of fact as proof that the tires were in fact defective. Unless the need for the evidence for the proper purpose is substantially outweighed by the danger of improper use, the appropriate result is to admit the evidence with a limiting instruction.[1]

§ 249

1. See §§ 59 & 185 supra.

One area where abuse may be a particular problem involves statements by arresting or investigating officers regarding the reason for their presence at the scene of a crime. The officers should not be put in the misleading position of appearing to have happened upon the scene and therefore should be entitled to provide some explanation for their presence and conduct. They should not, however, be allowed to relate historical aspects of the case, such as complaints and reports of others containing inadmissible hearsay. Such statements are sometimes erroneously admitted under the argument that the officers are entitled to give the information upon which they acted. The need for this evidence is slight, and the likelihood of misuse great. Instead, a statement that an officer acted "upon information received," or words to that effect, should be sufficient.

Prior inconsistent and consistent statements used to affect credibility. A common technique to impeach the credibility of a witness is to show that on a prior occasion the person made a statement inconsistent with his or her testimony on the stand.[2] The theory of impeachment does not depend upon the prior statement being true and the present one false. Instead, the mere fact that the witness stated the facts differently on separate occasions is sufficient to impair credibility. By "blowing hot and cold," doubts are raised as to the truthfulness or accuracy of both statements. Thus, the prior statement is not offered for its truth and is not hearsay. It is important to note that as a consequence of the theory of admissibility, statements offered under this theory may not be used for their truth and do not constitute substantive evidence. Similarly, once a witness' testimony has been impeached, prior consistent statements may be offered under some circumstances in rehabilitation,[3] and when offered for this limited purpose, they are also nonhearsay.

Indirect versions of hearsay statements; group statements. If the purpose of testimony

2. See § 34 supra.

3. See § 47 supra.

is to use an out-of-court statement to prove the truth of facts stated, the hearsay objection cannot be eliminated by eliciting the content of the statement in an indirect form. Thus, when offered as proof of the facts asserted, testimony regarding "information received" by the witness and the results of investigations made by other persons are properly classified as hearsay.

Statements of collective or group decisions presented by the testimony of one of the group should be treated similarly except where expert opinions are involved. For example, when the statement involves a decision reached after consultation by a group of doctors, the opinion reached and the statements of others supporting it should be admissible because the expert opinion rule allows such opinions to be based on reliable although inadmissible evidence.[4] However, the statements of other experts should still not received for their truth but only to support the opinion.[5]

Reputation. In the earlier stages of jury trial, when the jurors were expected to seek out the facts by neighborhood inquiries (instead of having the witnesses bring the facts through their testimony in court), community reputation was a frequent source of information for the jurors. When in the late 1600s the general doctrine excluding hearsay began to take form,[6] the use of reputation either directly by the jurors or through the testimony of the witnesses was so well established in certain areas that exceptions to the hearsay rule for reputation in those areas was soon recognized.

Reputation is a composite description of what the people in a community have said and are saying about a matter. A witness who testifies to reputation testifies to a generalized version of a series of out-of-court statements. Whether reputation is hearsay depends on the same tests applied to evidence of other out-of-court statements and sometimes may not be hearsay at all. Thus, in an action for defamation where an element of damages is injury to the plaintiff's reputation, evidence that the plaintiff's reputation was bad before the slander is not hearsay when presented regarding damages. Proof of reputation in the community offered as evidence that some person there had knowledge of the reputed facts is similarly not hearsay.

On the other hand, evidence of reputation is hearsay when offered to prove the truth of the fact reputed and hence depends for its value on the veracity of the collective asserters. It should be excluded when it fits within no exception. However, several hearsay exceptions have been recognized for reputation as to character and certain other issues.[7]

Prior statements of witnesses offered for the truth; admissions of party-opponents. Some prior statements of witnesses offered for their truth and admissions by party-opponents are excluded from the hearsay rule by the Federal Rules under theories separate from the definition of hearsay discussed above. These statements are discussed in later sections.[8]

§ 250. Conduct as Hearsay and "Implied Assertions"

Nonverbal conduct. The examination thus far into what is and is not hearsay has been confined to out-of-court words, either spoken or written. Under the definition in § 246, if they constitute an assertion and are offered as proof that the matter asserted happened or existed, they are hearsay.

In some situations, non-verbal conduct may be just as assertive as words. If, in response to a question "Who did it?," one of the auditors held up her hand, no one would contend that this gesture could be treated as different from an oral or written statement. Other illustrations are the act of pointing to a particular person in a lineup as the equivalent of saying "That's the person," or the sign language used by persons with impaired speech or hearing. These are clear instances of "non-verbal conduct of a person * * * intend-

---

4. See § 15 supra; Fed.R.Evid. 703.

5. See § 342.3 infra.

6. See § 244 supra.

7. See § 322 infra.

8. See § 251 infra (prior statements), Chap. 25 infra (admissions).

ed by the person as an assertion," which under our hearsay definition receives the same treatment as oral or written assertions. The only difference is that an oral or written assertion is assumed in the first instance to have been intended as such by virtue of being assertive in form, while in the case of the nonverbal conduct an intent to assert must be found by the judge as a precondition to classification as hearsay.

In other situations, the conduct is just as clearly nonassertive. Thus, an uncontrollable action or reaction by its very nature precludes any intent to make an assertion. Two cases illustrate the difference. In the first, an officer testified he went to the murder suspect's home and asked defendant's wife for the shirt he was wearing when he arrived home after the murder was committed. She handed the officer a shirt on which blood stains were later found.[1] In the second case, a murder suspect was described by witnesses as wearing a jacket with a fur-lined collar. The officer who arrested defendant at his home testified that he asked defendant if he had a jacket with a fur-lined collar, and that defendant turned to his wife and said, "I don't have one like that, do I dear?" His wife fainted.[2] In the first case, the suspect's wife was found to have intended to assert that the shirt produced was the one requested, and therefore her conduct was hearsay. In the second, the conduct was considered nonassertive and hence not hearsay. The disputed area lies between these extremes.

Nonassertive Nonverbal Conduct. The celebrated 19th century case of Wright v. Tatham[3] is focal point of this debate. By will, John Marsden, a country gentleman, had left his estate to one Wright, who had risen from a menial station to the position of steward and general man of business for Marsden. The legal heir, Admiral Tatham, brought proceedings to recover the manors of the estate, alleging that Marsden was not competent to make a will. Defendant Wright, supporting the will,

offered in evidence several letters that had been written to the deceased by third persons who were no longer alive.

The theory of the offer was that the letters indicated the writers' belief that Marsden was mentally competent from which it might be inferred that he was in fact competent. The letters were admitted and the will sustained. However, upon retrial after reversal, the letters were excluded, and the verdict was against the will. The House of Lords ended eight years of litigation by upholding the ruling that the letters were inadmissible as equivalent to hearsay evidence of the opinions of the writers. The holding was perhaps most pithily put by Baron Parke in these words:

> The conclusion at which I have arrived is, that proof of a particular fact which is not of itself a matter in issue, but which is relevant only as implying a statement or opinion of a third person on the matter in issue, is inadmissible in all cases where such a statement or opinion not on oath would be of itself inadmissible; and, therefore, in this case the letters which are offered only to prove the competence of the testator, that is the truth of the implied statements therein contained, were properly rejected, as the mere statement or opinion of the writer would certainly have been inadmissible.[4]

To describe the evidence in Wright v. Tatham as "implied statements," i.e. implied assertions, as suggested by Baron Parke is to prejudge the issue, for it is to extrajudicial assertions that the hearsay rule applies.

Before turning to the letters actually at issue in the case, let us examine one of the best known examples used by the House of Lords. That is the nonverbal conduct of a deceased captain embarking on a ship with his family after he conducted a full inspection of it to establish its seaworthiness. The line of reasoning suggested is that (a) the captain's con-

---

§ 250

1. Stevenson v. Commonwealth, 237 S.E.2d 779 (Va. 1977).

2. People v. Clark, 86 Cal.Rptr. 106 (Cal.App.1970).

3. 7 Adolph. & E. 313, 112 Eng.Rep. 488 (Exch.Ch. 1837), and 5 Cl. & F. 136 (H.L.1838).

4. 7 Adolph. & E. at 388, 112 Eng.Rep. at 516.

duct tends to prove that he believed the ship to be seaworthy and (b) from this belief, the conclusion might be drawn that the ship was in fact seaworthy. This, the judges said, was the equivalent of an out-of-court statement by the captain that the ship was seaworthy and hence inadmissible hearsay. Functional equivalence can, however, be misleading. The vital element of intent to assert does not appear to be present in the example.

After Wright v. Tatham, the hearsay issue often went unrecognized, and when noticed, the earlier cases tended to favor the objection. Now, however, Federal Rule 801(a) and numerous decisions treat nonverbal conduct as nonhearsay unless an intent to assert is shown.

Is this result consistent with the policies that underlie the hearsay rule? The question should be answered through an evaluation of the dangers that the hearsay rule is designed to guard against, i.e., imperfections of perception, memory, narration, and particularly sincerity. Such an analysis rejects the view that nonassertive nonverbal conduct, from which may be inferred a belief, from which in turn may be inferred the happening of the event which produced the belief, is the equivalent of an assertion that the event happened and hence hearsay. Prior to raising their umbrellas, people do not say to themselves in soliloquy form, "It is raining," nor does the motorist go forward on the green light only after making an inward assertion, "The light is green." The conduct offered in the one instance to prove it was raining and in the other that the light was green involves no intent to communicate the fact sought to be proved, and purposeful deception is much less likely in the absence of intent to communicate. True, the threshold question whether communication was intended may on occasion present difficulty, yet the probabilities against intent are generally so great as to justify putting the burden of establishing it upon the party urging the hearsay objection.

Even though the risks arising from purposeful deception may be slight or nonexistent in the absence of intent to communicate, the objection remains that the actor's perception and memory are untested by cross-examination for the possibility of honest mistake. However, in contrast to the risks from purposeful deception, those arising from the chance of honest mistake seem more sensibly to be factors useful in evaluating weight and credibility rather than grounds for exclusion. Moreover, the kind of situation involved is ordinarily such as either to minimize the likelihood of flaws of perception and memory or to present circumstances lending themselves to their evaluation. While the suggestion has been advanced that conduct evidence ought to be admitted only when the actor's behavior has an element of significant reliance as an assurance of trustworthiness, a sufficient response here too is that the factor is one of evaluation, not a ground for exclusion. Moreover, undue complication ought to be avoided in the interest of ease of application. The same can be said with respect to the possibility that the conduct may be ambiguous so that the trier of fact will draw a wrong inference. Similar arguments exclude nonassertive verbal conduct from the hearsay rule although the analysis is generally more difficult and the reduction of hearsay dangers somewhat less clear.

Silence as hearsay. One aspect of the conduct-as-hearsay problem is presented by cases where a failure to speak or act is offered to support an inference that conditions were such as would evoke silence or inaction in a reasonable person. The cases are likely to fall into two classes: (1) evidence of absence of complaints from other customers as disproof of claimed defects of goods or food or from other persons who would have been affected, as disproof of a claimed injurious event or condition, and (2) evidence from members of a family that a particular member never mentioned an event or claim to or disposition of property, to prove nonoccurrence or nonexistence. Often the presence of an arguable hearsay question is neither noted nor discussed.

Although common law cases were divided as to the hearsay status of this kind of evidence, the evidence is not hearsay under the definition of hearsay in Section 246 because it is not intended as an assertion. Support for admissibility, aside from any question of hearsay, may be stronger in the cases of absence of complaints than in other cases of silence. The other cases present a variety of situations, some of which suggest motivations for silence other than nonoccurrence of the disputed event that call for evaluation of whether the probative value of the evidence is outweighed by its prejudicial effect. Silence as an admission by a party-opponent is treated elsewhere.

So-Called "Implied Assertions"; Out-of-court assertions not offered to prove the truth of the matter asserted. The preceding discussion relates to hearsay aspects of nonassertive nonverbal conduct. The actual issue in Wright v. Tatham, on which the discussion is largely based, involved verbal conduct that was, in a measure at least, assertive—letters that made some affirmative statements. They raise the hearsay status of certain types of assertive conduct.

If one of the letters had said, "Marsden, you are competent to make a will," it would clearly fall within the definition of hearsay as an out-of-court assertion offered to prove the truth of the matter asserted, but that was not the case. The letters, though assertive in form, were not offered to prove the truth of what was asserted. The letter from the cousin describing conditions found on his voyage to America, for example, was not offered as evidence of conditions in America but as evidence that the writer believed Marsden to be of reasonable intelligence, from which belief competency might be inferred. Under these conditions, should the evidence be treated as hearsay?

Although the application of the principle is sometimes complicated, the basic answer under the Federal Rules and contemporary judicial analysis is that an out-of-court assertion is not hearsay if offered as proof of something other than the matter asserted. The theory is that questions of sincerity are generally reduced when assertive conduct is "offered as a basis for inferring something other than the matter asserted."[5] This argument is somewhat less compelling than for nonasser-

tive conduct since an intent to make some assertion is present, and the danger of insincerity regarding indirect uses of the statement can never be entirely discounted. However, this risk is generally not so great as to mandate treatment as hearsay when the intent does not embrace the inference suggested, and the likelihood of purposeful deception is accordingly substantially reduced.

Clearly, the contemporary definition of hearsay is less inclusive than logical and analytical possibilities would allow and elimination of all hearsay dangers would require. Relatively early in his career, noted evidence scholar Edmund Morgan suggested:

A comprehensive definition of hearsay * * * would include (1) all conduct of a person, verbal or nonverbal, intended by him to operate as an assertion when offered either to prove the truth of the matter asserted or to prove that the asserter believed the matter asserted to be true, and (2) all conduct of a person, verbal or nonverbal, not intended by him to operate as an assertion, when offered either to prove both his state of mind and the external event or condition which caused him to have that state of mind, or to prove that his state of mind was truly reflected by that conduct.[6]

He subsequently concluded that a definition of hearsay expanded to the outer limits suggested by logic and analysis was undesirable, with needless complication of the hearsay rule that outweighed any supposed advantage. Similarly, the contemporary resolution of the issues involved in "implied assertions" reflect ultimately a compromise between theory and the need for a relatively simple and workable definition in situations where hearsay dangers are generally reduced.

Knowledge. On an issue whether a given person was alive at a particular time, evidence that she said something at the time would be proof that she was alive. Whether she said, "I am alive," or "Hi, Joe," would be immaterial; the inference of life is drawn from the fact

---

5. Adv.Comm. Note, Fed.R.Evid. 801(a).

6. Morgan, Hearsay and Non–Hearsay, 48 Harv.L.Rev. 1138, 1144 (1935).

that she spoke, not from what was said. No problem of veracity is involved. In terms of the definition of hearsay, even the first statement is not offered to prove what is asserted because its relevance does not depend upon its content.

This analysis may be extended to declarations evincing knowledge, notice, or awareness of some fact. Conversation about a matter demonstrates on its face that the person was aware of it, and veracity does not enter into the situation. Caution is appropriate, however, since the self-proving aspect is limited strictly to what is said. Thus, the statement, "I know geometry," establishes no more than that the speaker is aware of the term "geometry," not that she has command of that subject. On the other hand, if the statement is itself a proposition of geometry, it is self-evident that the speaker knows some geometry; whether the statement is prefaced with "I know" is immaterial.

When the existence of knowledge is sought to be used as the basis for a further inference, the hearsay rule may be violated. That possibility becomes a reality when the purpose of the evidence of knowledge is to prove the existence of the fact known. Statements of memory or belief are not generally allowed as proof of the happening of the event remembered or believed, since allowing the evidence would destroy the hearsay rule.[7] For this purpose, knowledge is indistinguishable from memory and belief. However, drawing from evidence of knowledge an inference other than the existence of the fact known will occasionally be possible.

For example, evidence that a person made statements showing knowledge of matters likely to have been known only to a specific person is receivable as tending to prove the identity of the declarant. A similar nonhearsay use of knowledge is illustrated by Bridges v. State.[8] In that case, a child victim gave a description of the house and its surroundings and of the room and its furnishings where the crime occurred. Other evidence showed that the description fit the house and room where the defendant lived. At a superficial level the evidence, which was used to help identify the defendant as the perpetrator, depends for its value upon the observation, memory, and veracity of the child and thus shares some of the hazards of hearsay. Significantly, the testimony has value independent of these factors. Other witnesses established the physical characteristics of the locale, and the child's testimony was not used for that purpose. *Assuming* other possible sources of her knowledge have been eliminated—as the court determined—the only remaining inference was that she had acquired that knowledge by being in the defendant's room. Evidence of this sort is thus not hearsay.

§ 251. Prior Statements of Witnesses as Substantive Evidence

The traditional view has been that a prior statement, even one made by the witness, is hearsay if it is offered to prove the matters asserted therein. Of course, this categorization has not precluded using the prior statement for other purposes, e.g., to impeach the witness by showing a self-contradiction if the statement is inconsistent with his testimony[1] or to support credibility when the statement is consistent with the testimony and logically helps to rehabilitate.[2] But the prior statement has traditionally been admissible as substantive evidence to prove the matter asserted therein only when falling within an established exception to the hearsay rule. This position has come under substantial attack on both logical and practical grounds.

The logic of the orthodox view is that the previous statement of the witness is hearsay since its value rests on the credit of the declarant, who, when the statement was made, was not (1) under oath, (2) in the presence of the trier, or (3) subject to cross-examination.

The counter-argument goes as follows: (1) The oath is no longer a principal safeguard of

---

7. See § 276 infra.
8. 19 N.W.2d 529 (Wis.1945).

1. See § 34 supra.
2. See § 49 supra.

the trustworthiness of testimony. Affidavits, although under oath, are not exempted from the hearsay rule. Moreover, of the numerous exceptions where evidence is admitted despite being hearsay, only prior testimony must have been under oath. (2) With respect to allowing the trier of fact to observe the demeanor of the witness while making the statement, Judge Learned Hand cogently stated: "If, from all that the jury see of the witness, they conclude that what he says now is not the truth, but what he said before, they are none the less deciding from what they see and hear of that person and in court."[3] (3) The principal method for achieving credibility is clearly cross-examination, and this condition is largely satisfied. As Wigmore, who originally adhered to the traditional view, observed: "Here, however, by hypothesis the witness is present and subject to cross-examination. There is ample opportunity to test him as to the basis for his former statement. The whole purpose of the hearsay rule has been already satisfied."[4]

The question remains whether cross-examination must take place at the time when the statement is made to be effective. The orthodox view urges:

> The chief merit of cross-examination is not that at some future time it gives the party opponent the right to dissect adverse testimony. Its principal virtue is the immediate application of the testing process. Its strokes fall while the iron is hot. False testimony is apt to harden and become unyielding to the blows of truth in proportion as the witness has opportunity for reconsideration and influence by the suggestions of others * * *.[5]

Yet, with inconsistent statements, the witness by definition has changed his or her story; rather than hardening, the story has yielded to something between the giving of the statement and the time of testifying; and the circumstances most frequently suggest that the "something" which caused the change was an improper influence.

An additional persuasive factor against the orthodox rule is the superior trustworthiness of earlier statements based on the general proposition that recency aids memory. The prior statement is always nearer and usually very much nearer to the event than is the testimony. The fresher the memory, the fuller and more accurate it is. The requirement of the hearsay exception for memoranda of past recollection, that the matter have been recorded while fresh in memory,[6] is based precisely on this principle.

These various considerations led to a substantial movement to abandon the orthodox view completely. The Model Code of Evidence provided: "Evidence of a hearsay declaration is admissible if the judge finds that the declarant * * * is present and subject to cross-examination."[7] Substantial support for this position began to appear in the decisions.

Under the Model Code/Wigmore position, all prior statements of witnesses, regardless of their nature, would be exempt from the ban of the hearsay rule. This complete rejection of the orthodox rule resulted in uneasiness that a practice might develop among lawyers whereby a carefully prepared statement would be offered in lieu of testimony, merely tendering the witness for cross-examination on the statement. The practice seems not to have materialized in the jurisdictions where the orthodox rule was rejected, but the potential for abuse nevertheless remained.

As a consequence, the Advisory Committee on Federal Rules of Evidence adopted an intermediate position, neither admitting nor rejecting prior statements of witnesses *in toto* where the "declarant testifies and is subject to cross-examination concerning the statement," but exempting from classification as hearsay certain prior statements thought by circumstances to be generally free of the danger of abuse. Under Federal Rule of Evidence 801(d)(1), the exempt statements are (A) inconsistent statements "given under oath sub-

---

3.   Di Carlo v. United States, 6 F.2d 364 (2d Cir.1925).

4.   3A Wigmore, Evidence § 1018, at 996 (Chadbourn rev. 1970).

5.   State v. Saporen, 285 N.W. 898, 901 (Minn.1939).

6.   See § 281 infra.

7.   Model Code of Evidence Rule 503(b).

ject to the penalty of perjury at a trial, hearing, or other proceeding, or in a deposition"; (B) consistent statements "offered to rebut an express or implied charge against the declarant of recent fabrication or improper influence or motive"; and (C) statements of identification.

(A) Prior inconsistent statements. The witness who has told one story earlier and another at trial has invited a searching examination of credibility through cross-examination and re-examination. The reasons for the change, whether forgetfulness, carelessness, pity, terror, or greed, may be explored by the adversaries in the presence of the trier of fact, under oath, casting light on which is the true story and which the false. Certainly, evidence of a prior inconsistent statement, when declarant is on the stand to explain it if he or she can, has the major safeguards of examined testimony. In addition, admitting it as substantive evidence avoids use of a limiting instruction that the jury is unlikely to follow.

When is a prior statement inconsistent?[8] Where a witness no longer remembers an event, a prior statement describing that event should not be considered inconsistent. Yet the tendency of unwilling or untruthful witnesses to seek refuge in a claim forgetfulness is well recognized. Hence the judge may be warranted in concluding under the circumstances the claimed lack of memory of the event is untrue and in effect an implied denial of the prior statement, thus qualifying it as inconsistent. The case law readily accepts this position.

As originally drafted by the Advisory Committee and transmitted to the Congress by the Supreme Court, the Federal Rule contained no requirement as to the conditions under which the prior inconsistent statement must be made. However, Congress imposed limitations, adding the language "given under oath subject to the penalty of perjury at a trial, hearing, or other proceeding, or in a deposition." The result of the limitation is to confine substantive use of prior inconsistent statements virtually to those made in the course of judicial proceed-

ings, including grand jury testimony, although allowing use for impeachment without these limitation.

(B) Prior consistent statements. While prior consistent statements are hearsay by the traditional view and inadmissible as substantive evidence, they have nevertheless been allowed a limited admissibility for the purpose of supporting the credibility of a witness, particularly to show that a witness whose testimony has allegedly been influenced told the same story before being influenced. Federal Rule of Evidence 801(d)(1)(B) goes further and exempts from the hearsay rule prior consistent statements that are "offered to rebut an express or implied charge against the declarant of recent fabrication or improper influence or motive." In Tome v. United States,[9] the Supreme Court concluded that the rule imposes a timing requirement and admits only those statements "made before the charged recent fabrication or improper influence or motive."[10] One frequently encountered situation involves prior consistent statements by a government witness accused by the defendant with providing testimony to gain favor regarding the witness' own criminal liability. When the witness is under investigation at the time such statements were made, they are generally excluded because the motive to fabricate has already arisen.

Although the issue is not entirely resolved, the Federal Rule's exemption of some prior consistent statements from the hearsay rule under rigid requirements does not mean that other consistent statements failing those requirements are inadmissible when they only affect credibility. The most clearly accepted use of consistent statements for rehabilitation purposes is to clarify or rebut prior inconsistent statements that have been used to impeach the witness.

(C) Statements of identification. When A testifies that on a prior occasion B pointed to the accused and said, "That's the man who robbed me," the testimony is clearly hearsay.

---

8. See § 34 supra as to the requirement of inconsistency in prior statements used for impeachment.

9. 513 U.S. 150 (1995).

10. Id. at 156.

If, however, B is present in court, testifies to the prior identification, and is available for cross-examination, the case fits within the present section. Admissibility of the prior identifications has long-standing case law support, often in the older cases without recognition of the hearsay problem. Justification is found in the unsatisfactory nature of courtroom identification and by the constitutional safeguards that regulate out-of-court identifications arranged by the police. Evidence of such a pre-trial identification is usually permitted even when the witness cannot make an in-court identification.

The requirement of cross-examination. With respect to each of the categories of prior statements discussed above, the Federal Rule requires that declarant testify at the trial or hearing and be "subject to cross-examination concerning the statement." The meaning of the witness being subject to cross-examination has been vigorously debated for both prior inconsistent statements and statements of identification. Bogus and real claims of lack of memory, denials, and acknowledgments of both the underlying event and the prior statement appear in various combinations. Until United States Supreme Court's decision in United States v. Owens,[11] some of the possible scenarios described were seen to create difficult problems for adequate cross-examination under either the rule or Confrontation Clause.

Owens, which dealt with a prior identification by a witness who could not recall the crime at issue because of head injuries he suffered during it, and cases applying its analysis to prior inconsistent statements, have ended the debate. The Court concluded that the requirements of both the hearsay rule and the Confrontation Clause are satisfied as long as the witness takes the stand and responds willingly to questions. Judicial restrictions on cross-examination and claim of privilege would threaten meaningful cross-examination, but lack of memory does not. Lower courts have extended the analysis of *Owens* to statements involving prior inconsistent statements and to

feigned lack of memory. Because *Owens* found cross-examination adequate in one of the most difficult fact patterns, few plausible challenges remain.

§ 252. Constitutional Problems of Hearsay: Confrontation and Due Process

The constitutional issues related to admission of hearsay focus primarily on the Confrontation Clause of the Sixth Amendment, which applies to the states through the Fourteenth Amendment. The clause requires "that in all criminal prosecutions, the accused shall enjoy the right * * * to be confronted with the witnesses against him." In addition, nearly every state constitution has a similar provision.

The Confrontation Clause is applicable only to criminal prosecutions and may be invoked only by the accused. However, the values served by confrontation are so basic that elements of its requirements are occasionally extended as a matter of due process to persons other than the accused in a criminal case.

Certain facets of the right of confrontation and the right to due process, while relevant to the values sought to be protected by the hearsay rule, do not bear directly upon it. Of these facets, one is the right of an accused to be present at every stage of the trial. Another is the defendant's right to cross-examine witnesses who appear and testify against the defense.[1] A related right is to disclosure by the prosecution of material exculpatory evidence as an element of due process. The right to counsel is a thread running through much of this constitutional fabric.

Turning to examination of the relationship between the hearsay rule and constitutional right of confrontation, the similarity of their underpinnings is evident. The hearsay rule operates to preserve the ability of a party to confront adverse witnesses in open court. The Confrontation Clause does the same for an accused in a criminal case. The hearsay rule has numerous exceptions and so does the

---

11. 484 U.S. 554 (1988).

1. See § 19 supra.

Confrontation Clause. To what extent do these exceptions overlap?

In the late 1700s when confrontation provisions were first included in American bills of rights, the general rule against hearsay had been accepted in England for a hundred years, but it was equally well established that under certain circumstances hearsay might be admitted. One could certainly argue that the purpose of the American provision was to guarantee the maintenance in criminal cases of the hard-won principle of the hearsay rule, without abandoning the accepted exceptions which had not been questioned as to fairness, but forbidding especially the practice of using depositions taken in the absence of the accused. This latter practice was subsequently abandoned by the English judges and forbidden by statute.

One of the major issues in the ongoing debate about the impact of the Confrontation Clause on the admission of hearsay is whether it recognizes the validity of the traditional hearsay rule and its exceptions, roughly according the body of rules a constitutional status, or whether it stands largely independent of the body of rules and substantially limits the introduction of evidence admissible under the rule and its exceptions. The recent decisions of the Supreme Court indicate adoption of the first of these two positions and demonstrate an effort by the Court to simplify and diminish the impact of the Confrontation Clause as an independent restraint on the admission of hearsay. If the clause constitutionalizes the hearsay rule, secondary questions are: how it does so, and whether modern expansions of rules violate the constitutional limitation.

The Supreme Court's progression toward its present view of the relationship of the hearsay rule and the Confrontation Clause effectively began with the case of California v. Green.[2] In Green, the Court established one prong of current Confrontation Clause analysis. It concluded that the clause did not limit the introduction of prior statements of witnesses actually produced at the trial for full cross-examination, and it recognized in United States v. Owens[3] that, generally absent limitations by the trial court on cross-examination or the witness' invocation of a privilege, the opportunity to cross-examine would be found constitutionally adequate.

A decade later in Ohio v. Roberts,[4] the Court stated a two-part test for the admission of hearsay under the Confrontation Clause that appeared to be generally applicable. First, "the prosecutor must either produce, or demonstrate the unavailability of, the declarant whose statements it wishes to use against the defendant."[5] Second, if the declarant is unavailable, the statement must have been made under circumstances providing sufficient "indicia of reliability." The Roberts Court further noted that sufficient reliability to satisfy the Confrontation Clause "can be inferred without more in a case where the evidence falls within a firmly rooted hearsay exception. In other cases, the evidence must be excluded at least absent a showing of particularized guarantees of trustworthiness."[6]

In United States v. Inadi,[7] the Court backed away from, or clarified, the apparent general requirement of unavailability announced in Roberts. The Court concluded that the prosecutor need not produce or demonstrate the unavailability of a conspirator whose statement was used against the accused, and it limited the Roberts requirement to instances involving the use of the prior testimony exception, which has always required a showing of unavailability. In the case of coconspirator's statements, the Court found that such statements "provide evidence of the conspiracy's context that cannot be replicated, even if the declarant testifies to the same matters in court."[8] The Court also noted that the benefits of an unavailability rule for coconspirator declarants would be slight and the burdens substantial, and concluded that "the

2. 399 U.S. 149 (1970).
3. 484 U.S. 554 (1988).
4. 448 U.S. 56 (1980).
5. Id. at 65.

6. Id.
7. 475 U.S. 387 (1986).
8. Id. at 395.

Confrontation Clause does not embody such a rule."[9] White v. Illinois[10] applied the same analysis to hearsay admitted under the exception for spontaneous declarations and for statements made in the course of receiving medical care, finding that the Confrontation Clause imposed no unavailability requirement. Indeed, the analysis of *Inadi* and *White* appear to mean that unavailability is not required as to any statement admissible under a hearsay exception based on a theory that the out-of-court is superior to what is likely to be produced in court, i.e., all exceptions under Federal Rule of Evidence 803.

Inadi and *White* leave undisturbed prior analysis of the impact of the Confrontation Clause on the showing of unavailability required for hearsay exceptions that mandate unavailability, such as former testimony. Other decisions dictate a reasonably rigorous test under the Constitution for unavailability when hearsay is offered under one of these exceptions by the prosecution in a criminal case.

The Court has also clarified the other prong of the *Roberts* test regarding the definition of "firmly rooted" hearsay exceptions that will automatically satisfy "indicia of reliability" requirement. In Bourjaily v. United States,[11] the Court ruled that the co-conspirator "exception" was firmly enough rooted in our jurisprudence that a court need not independently inquire into the reliability of such statements. The definition of "firmly rooted," it concluded, rested on the exception's longevity and widespread acceptance, not on an individualized assessment of the exception's reliability.

The Court has addressed as well how "indicia of reliability" is to be judged for exceptions that are not firmly rooted. In Idaho v. Wright,[12] it examined statements of a child to a doctor that were admitted under Idaho's residual hearsay exception, which is not a "firmly rooted" exception for Confrontation Clause purposes. Accordingly, statements may be constitutionally admitted under the residu-

al exception only if supported by a finding of "particularized guarantees of trustworthiness." The Court ruled that the search for such guarantees was limited to the totality of circumstances "that surround the making of the statement and that render the declarant particularly worthy of belief"[13] and expressly rejected the use of evidence corroborating the truth of a hearsay statement to provide the guarantee of trustworthiness.

In summary, hearsay falling within a traditional or "firmly rooted" exception to the rule will be admissible under the Confrontation Clause. Where the exception does not require unavailability because of the theoretical superiority of the out-of-court statement, the Constitution does not require it. Where unavailability is constitutionally required, the Confrontation Clause will in some situations require a more rigorous demonstration of unavailability by the prosecution than the hearsay rules require. Where the hearsay is offered by the prosecution under a residual exception, "particularized guarantees of trustworthiness" must be shown, which is not identical to meeting the "equivalent circumstantial guarantees of trustworthiness" requirement of the Federal Rules and their state counterparts. In addition, the prosecution must establish the trustworthiness of the statement itself, rather than depending on its likely truth in light of corroborating circumstances. Newly created statutory hearsay exceptions should also be subject to the test set forth in *Wright* until widespread acceptance and longevity render such exceptions firmly rooted.

Some of the questions still remain for the Supreme Court. To what extent will the Confrontation Clause limit expansion of traditional hearsay exceptions to nontraditional circumstances? For example, is a state free to apply the traditional exception for public records to permit the introduction of police reports against the accused in a criminal case, and is the exception for statements of medical diagnosis or treatment firmly rooted when applied

---

9. Id. at 400.

10. 502 U.S. 346 (1992).

11. 483 U.S. 171 (1987).

12. 497 U.S. 805 (1990).

13. Id. at 820.

to statements made only for diagnosis without any concern for treatment? Could a state dispense with a traditional requirement of unavailability for declarations against interest? Although a few significant issues remain, the above discussion should have made clear that the Court has provided a categorical resolution for most major Confrontation Clause objections whereby the hearsay decision typically resolves the constitutional question.

In contrast to the right of confrontation, which results in exclusion when ruled to be applicable to an item of hearsay, the Due Process Clause may require the admission of otherwise inadmissible hearsay if of sufficient reliability and importance. In Chambers v. Mississippi,[14] the Supreme Court ruled that due process was denied where several confessions exculpating the accused given under circumstances that provided considerable assurances of their reliability were excluded and where the accused was prohibited from cross-examining the confessing person because of the state's "voucher rule." Although the decision appeared to present intriguing possibilities, it was limited to the facts presented and has not proven to be a significant catalyst of further developments.

§ 253. The Hearsay Exceptions Where Declarant Is Unavailable; Admission of Hearsay as a Consequence of Wrongful Procurement of Unavailability

One of the basic challenges to the hearsay rule is how to effectuate through the procedure of excluding evidence a policy of requiring that testimony be given in open court, under oath, and subject to cross-examination. Some of the difficulty arises from the wide variation in the reliability of evidence that is classified as hearsay. The traditional solution has been to recognize numerous exceptions where "circumstantial guarantees of trustworthiness" justify departure from the general rule excluding hearsay. These exceptions are the subject of several of the chapters that follow.

The pattern that has evolved divides the hearsay exceptions into two groups. In the first, the availability or unavailability of the declarant is not a relevant factor: the exception is applied without regard to it. In the second group, unavailability is a requirement of the exception. The theory of the first group is that the out-of-court statement is as reliable or more reliable than would be testimony in person so that producing the declarant would involve pointless delay and inconvenience. The theory of the second group is that, while live testimony would be preferable, the out-of-court statement will be accepted if the declarant is unavailable. To a large extent, the division is the product of history and experience, and as might be expected of a body of law created by deciding cases as they randomly arose, it is not completely consistent. Nevertheless, the division has stood the test of time and use and offers a substantial measure of predictability. Although the number of the exceptions may at first glance appear extremely complex, many are encountered only rarely, and the actual working collection numbers approximately a dozen.

The importance accorded unavailability in the scheme of hearsay exceptions requires that it be considered in some detail. Although general practice is to speak loosely of unavailability of the witness, the critical factor is actually the unavailability of the witness' testimony. Witnesses may be physically present in court but their testimony nevertheless unavailable. Of course, if unavailability is procured by the party offering the hearsay statement, the requirement is not satisfied. Depositions are briefly discussed in the latter portions of this section.

Federal Rule of Evidence 804(a) provides a convenient list of the five generally recognized unavailability situations, which are examined below:

(1) Exercise of privilege. The successful exercise of a privilege not to testify renders the witness unavailable within the scope of the privilege.

---

14. 410 U.S. 284 (1973).

(2) Refusal to testify. If a witness simply refuses to testify, despite all appropriate judicial pressures, he or she is practically and legally unavailable.

(3) Claimed lack of memory. A claim of lack of memory made by the witness on the stand can satisfy the unavailability requirement. If the claim is genuine, the testimony is simply unavailable by any realistic standard. The earlier cases, however, indicated concern that the claimed lack might not be genuine, particularly in former testimony cases where the witness learns that the adversary has discovered new fuel for cross-examination or for other reasons seeks refuge in forgetfulness. However, this problem is of no great moment when the parallel to the witness who refuses to testify is recognized. The witness who falsely asserts loss of memory is refusing to testify in a way that attempts to avoid a collision with the judge. Under the language of the Federal Rule, the witness must testify regarding a lack of memory and is subject to cross-examination. If that claim is determined to be false, the witness is subject to contempt proceedings, though perhaps less effectively than in cases of simple refusal. An assertion of loss of memory clearly may constitute unavailability. If the forgetfulness is only partial, the appropriate solution would appear to be resort to present testimony to the extent of recollection, supplemented with the hearsay testimony to the extent required.

(4) Death; physical or mental illness. Death was the form which unavailability originally assumed with most of the relevant exceptions. Physical disability to attend the trial or testify is a recognized ground. Mental incapacity, including failure of faculties due to disease, senility, or accident, is also recognized as a basis for unavailability. The relative scarcity of decisions passing upon the required degree of permanency of either physical and mental incapacity suggests that most of the cases are handled by granting a continuance. Where the disability is not permanent, unavailability should be determined by the judge, with due regard for the prospects for recovery, the importance of the testimony, and the interest in prompt administration of justice. Under the influence of the Confrontation Clause, a higher standard of disability may be required in criminal cases for witnesses testifying against the accused.

(5) Absence. Absence of the declarant from the hearing, standing alone, does not establish unavailability. Under the Federal Rule, the proponent of the hearsay statement must in addition show an inability to procure declarant's attendance (a) by process or (b) by other reasonable means. State requirements vary, especially with respect to the latter. Furthermore, the requirements of the Confrontation Clause must be satisfied.

(a) *Process.* The relevant process is subpoena, or in appropriate situations, writ of habeas corpus ad testificandum. If a witness is beyond the reach of process, obviously process cannot procure attendance. Substantial differences in the reach of process exist between civil and criminal cases. For example, service of a civil subpoena may be relatively limited, while a criminal subpoena may be served anywhere in the country and under some circumstances even abroad. Although in state courts process in civil cases will usually not be effective beyond state boundaries, all states have enacted the Uniform Act To Secure the Attendance of Witnesses from Without a State in Criminal Proceedings, which in effect permits extradition of witnesses from another state in criminal cases. If a witness against the accused in a criminal case is within the reach of process, the prosecution must resort to process in both state and federal cases.

If a witness cannot be found, process obviously cannot be effective. The proponent of the hearsay statement must, however, establish that the witness cannot be found. For witnesses testifying against the accused, the prosecution must demonstrate a substantial effort, described as a "good-faith effort." A lesser showing may be adequate as to other witnesses in criminal and in civil cases, where confrontation requirements do not apply.

(b) *Other Reasonable Means.* In addition to inability to procure attendance by process, the Confrontation Clause requires the prosecution, before introducing a hearsay statement of the type where unavailability is required, also to show that declarant's attendance cannot be procured through good-faith efforts by other means. Here the standard is one of diligence. In Barber v. Page,[1] the Confrontation Clause was held to require a state prosecutor, before using at trial the preliminary hearing testimony of a witness presently incarcerated in a federal penitentiary in an adjoining state, to take appropriate steps to induce the federal authorities to produce him at the trial. When the witness is beyond the reach of process for reasons other than imprisonment, the least that would seem to satisfy confrontation requirements is a request to appear coupled with reimbursement for travel and subsistence expenses. When the Confrontation Clause does not apply, i.e. civil cases and defense witnesses in criminal cases, the authorities are divided as to whether attempts must be made to induce the witness to attend voluntarily. The Federal Rule requires an effort through reasonable means, while others demand only a showing that the witness is beyond the reach of process.

When absence is relied upon as grounds of unavailability, the Federal Rule imposes a further requirement that inability to take the deposition of the missing witness also be shown.

Admission of Hearsay as a Consequence of Wrongful Procurement of Unavailability. As noted earlier, the final sentence of Rule 804(a) states that a witness is not legally unavailable if the justification for that unavailability "is due to the procurement or wrongdoing of the proponent of the statement for the purpose of preventing the witness from attending or testifying." The language of the Rule requires a specific purpose to render the witness unavailable but does not require wrongful conduct.

Federal Rule of Evidence 804(b)(5) carries the above concept one step further. The Rule, which became effective in 1997, admits hearsay against a party who, directly or through others, engages in purposeful wrongful conduct that procures the witness' unavailability. This provision is unique among hearsay exceptions in admitting evidence without a guarantee of trustworthiness, based on a theory that the opponent's purposeful wrongful action forfeits any objection.

Depositions. Unavailability may appear as a requirement at two different stages in connection with depositions: (1) the right to take a deposition may be subject to certain conditions of which the most common is unavailability to testify at the trial, or (2) the right to use a deposition at the trial in place of the personal appearance of the deponent is usually conditioned upon unavailability. The matter is largely governed by statute or rule.

The use of depositions in criminal cases requires particular consideration in view of the higher standards of confrontation applicable to evidence presented against an accused. Legislation providing for depositions in criminal cases is in effect in a number of jurisdictions. No constitutional problems arise when the deposition is to be taken and used by the accused. When, however, the deposition is to be used *against* the accused, the unavailability standards of Barber v. Page, previously discussed, are applicable. If these standards are met, a meaningful opportunity to confront and cross-examine must also be provided, with its concomitant right to counsel, when the deposition is taken.

Children. Particularly in sexual abuse cases, receiving testimony from children often presents difficult questions of unavailability for purposes of the application of both a hearsay exception and the Confrontation Clause. In some jurisdictions, a finding of incompetence will make a witness unavailable. Other courts have found unavailability based upon the inability of the child to remember the events. Often, a finding of unavailability is justified based upon a determination that testifying will cause emotional trauma to the child and that the child is therefore unavailable. Courts finding the child unavailable within the meaning of the hearsay rule have usually also found any Confrontation Clause requirement of unavailability satisfied.

§ 253

1.   390 U.S. 719 (1968).

Some states have enacted statutes permitting either the introduction of videotaped statements or closed-circuit testimony based upon a finding that the child would suffer emotional or mental distress if required to testify in open court. Maryland v. Craig[2] held an individualized finding of potential serious emotional distress sufficient to permit a child to give testimony via closed circuit television outside the physical presence of the accused but subject to cross-examination. The development of technologies that permit high quality audiovisual links and thus would allow simultaneous examination of witnesses at long distances with considerable advantages in terms of cost savings and convenience to witnesses will challenge traditional conceptions of in person confrontation.

2.   497 U.S. 836 (1990).

Chapter 25

ADMISSIONS OF A PARTY–OPPONENT

Table of Sections

§ 254. Nature and Effect

"Anything that you say can be used against you." This familiar phrase provides a convenient starting point for the examination of admissions as evidence.

Admissions are the words or acts of a party or a party's representative that are offered as evidence by the opposing party. They may be *express* admissions, which are statements of the opposing party or an agent whose words may fairly be used against the party, or admissions by *conduct*. The major theories that have historically explained and supported the probativity and admissibility of admissions are discussed below.

Morgan's view was that admissions are received as an exception to the hearsay rule. Exceptions to the hearsay rule usually are justified on the ground that evidence meeting the requirements of the exception possesses special reliability and often special need, such as the unavailability of the declarant. However, no objective guaranty of trustworthiness is furnished by the admissions rule. The party is not required to have firsthand knowledge of the matter declared; the declaration may be self-serving when made; and the declarant is probably sitting in the courtroom. As Morgan himself admitted, "The admissibility of an admission made by the party himself rests not upon any notion that the circumstances in which it was made furnish the trier means of evaluating it fairly, but upon the adversary theory of litigation. A party can hardly object that he had no opportunity to cross-examine himself or that he is unworthy of credence save when speaking under sanction of an oath."[1]

Wigmore, after noting that the party's declaration generally has the probative value of any other person's assertion, argued that it had a special value when offered *against* the party. In that circumstance, the admission discredits the party's statements inconsistent with the present claim asserted in pleadings and testimony, much like a witness impeached by contradictory statements. Moreover, admissions pass the gauntlet of the hearsay rule, which requires that extra-judicial assertions be excluded if there was no opportunity for the opponent to cross-examine because it is the opponent's own declaration, and "he does not need to cross-examine himself." Wigmore added that the hearsay rule is satisfied because the party "now as opponent has the full opportunity to put himself on the stand and explain his former assertion."[2]

Strahorn suggested a further theory that classified all admissions when offered against a party, whether words or acts, as *conduct* offered as circumstantial evidence rather than for its assertive, testimonial value. This circumstantial value is, as noted by Wigmore, the quality of inconsistency with the party's present claim.

On balance, the most satisfactory justification of the admissibility of admissions is that they are the product of the adversary system, sharing on a lower level the characteristics of admissions in pleadings or stipulations. Under this view, admissions need not satisfy the traditional requirement for hearsay exceptions that they possess circumstantial guarantees of trustworthiness. Rather admissions are outside the framework of hearsay exceptions, classed as nonhearsay, and excluded from the hearsay rule.

Federal Rule 801(d)(2), which excludes admissions from the hearsay rule, defines an admission as a statement offered against a party that is:

(A) the party's own statement, in either an individual or a representative capacity, or (B) a statement of which the party has manifested an adoption or belief in its truth, or (C) a statement by a person authorized by the party to make a statement concerning the subject, or (D) a statement by the party's agent or servant concerning a matter within the scope of the agency or employment, made during the existence of the relationship, or (E) a statement by a coconspirator of a party during the course and in furtherance of the conspiracy.

Regardless of the precise theory, admissions of a party are received as substantive evidence of the facts admitted and not merely to contradict the party. As a result, no foundation by first examining the party, as required for impeaching a witness with a prior inconsistent statement,[3] is mandated for admissions.

When the term admission is used without any qualifying adjective, the customary meaning is an evidentiary admission, that is, words in oral or written form or conduct of a party or a representative offered in evidence against the party. *Evidentiary* admissions are to be distinguished from *judicial* admissions. Judicial admissions are not evidence at all. Rather, they are formal concessions in the pleadings in the case or stipulations by a party or counsel that have the effect of withdrawing a fact from issue and dispensing wholly with the need for proof of the fact.[4] Thus, a judicial admission, unless allowed by the court to be withdrawn, is conclusive in the case, whereas an evidentiary admission is not conclusive but is subject to contradiction or explanation.

Confessions of crime are a particular kind of admission, governed by special rules discussed in the chapter on confessions.[5] An admission does not need to have the dramatic

---

1. Morgan, Basic Problems of Evidence 265–266 (1963).

2. 4 Wigmore, Evidence § 1048, at 5 (Chadbourn rev. 1972).

3. See Fed.R.Evid. 613(b); supra § 37.

4. See infra § 257.

5. See supra Ch. 14.

effect or to be the all-encompassing acknowledgment of responsibility that the word confession connotes. Admissions are simply words or actions inconsistent with the party's position at trial, relevant to the substantive issues in the case, and offered against the party. Moreover, while generally received in evidence because of their typically significant probative value, admissions may be excluded if their probative value is substantially outweighed by the prejudicial impact.

A type of evidence with which admissions may be confused is evidence of declarations against interest. The latter, treated under a separate exception to the hearsay rule,[6] must have been against the declarant's interest when made. Although most admissions are against interest when made, no such requirement is applied to admissions. For example, if a person states that a note is forged and then later acquires the note and sues upon it, the previous statement may be introduced as an admission although the party had no interest when he or she made the statement. Hence the common phrase "admissions against interest" is an invitation to confuse two separate theories of admitting hearsay and erroneously engraft an against-interest requirement on admissions.

Other distinctions between admissions and declarations against interest are that admissions must be the statements of a party to the lawsuit, and they must be offered against the party opponent. By contrast, declarations against interest need not be made by a party but may be made by some third person, and they may be offered by either party.[7] Finally, the declaration against interest exception admits the statement only when the declarant has become unavailable as a witness, while unavailability is not required of admissions.

§ 255. Testimonial Qualifications: Mental Competency; Personal Knowledge

In some instances, the mental capacity of a declarant making an admission must be considered. Statements by badly injured persons,

possibly under sedation, are an example. While older decisions examined the capacity of the declarant and excluded the evidence if capacity was seriously in issue, the trend in decisions was to view the question as one of weight rather than admissibility and was carried further by the adoption of rules that eliminated formal competency requirements.[1] The adversary roots of admissions suggest this reasoning should be applied with caution to statements by children, but substantive rules of tort liability may provide acceptable standards of responsibility for such admissions.

The requirement that a witness speak from firsthand knowledge is applicable to hearsay declarations generally and on rare occasions has been applied to admissions. However, the traditional view that firsthand knowledge is not required for admissions is accepted by the vast majority of courts and adopted by the Federal Rules.

The elimination of firsthand knowledge as a requirement is supported by several arguments. When people speak against their own interest, it is generally to be supposed that they have made an adequate investigation. While this disserving feature might attach to most admissions, we have seen that admissions are competent evidence though not against interest when made, and as to these, the argument does not apply. Nevertheless, the vast majority of admissions that become relevant in litigation concern some matter of substantial importance to declarants upon which they would likely have informed themselves, and as a result, such admissions possess greater reliability than the general run of hearsay, even when not based on firsthand observation. Moreover, the possibility is substantial that the declarant may have significant information that the opponent cannot prove. The validity of dispensing with firsthand knowledge for admissions by agents has been questioned by some commentators, but courts have not drawn a distinction.

---

6. See infra § 316.

7. See infra § 316.

§ 255

1. See Fed.R.Evid. 601; supra § 62.

§ 256. Admissions in Opinion Form; Conclusions of Law

If the lack of firsthand knowledge of the party does not exclude an admission, then neither should the opinion rule. As discussed earlier,[1] the purpose of the latter rule is to regulate the in-court interrogation of a witness so as to elicit answers in a more concrete form rather than in terms of inference. In its modern form, it is a rule of preference for more concrete answers, if the witness can give them, rather than a rule of exclusion.

Thus, the rule limiting lay opinions, which is designed to promote the concreteness of answers on the stand, is grotesquely misapplied to out-of-court statements such as admissions where the declarant's statements are made without thought of the form of courtroom testimony. While counsel may reframe the question in the preferred form if an objection is sustained to testimony in court, the rule can only be applied by excluding an out-of-court statement. Accordingly, the prevailing view is that admissions in the form of opinions are competent.

Another argument sometimes made to exclude opinions within admissions is that they constitute conclusions of law. Most often this issue arises in connection with statements of a participant in an accident that the mishap was the speaker's fault. While conceivably a party might give an opinion on an abstract question of law, such are not the typical statements actually offered. Instead, the statements normally include an application of a standard to the facts. Thus, they reveal the facts as the declarant thinks them to be, to which the standard of "fault" or other legal or moral standard involved in the statement was applied. In these circumstances, the factual information conveyed should not be ignored merely because the statement may also indicate the party's assumptions about the law. However, the legal principle may conceivably be so technical as to deprive an admission of significance, or the party may indeed give an opinion regarding solely an abstract issue of law. In those situations, exclusion is warranted. Also,

it should be remembered that evidentiary admissions are subject to explanation.

§ 257. Admissions in Pleadings; Pleas of Guilty

The final pleadings upon which the case is tried state the contentions of each party as to the facts, and by admitting or denying the opponent's pleading, they define the factual issues that are to be proved. Thus, the court must look to the pleadings as part of the record in passing on the relevancy of evidence and to determine the issues to be submitted to the jury. For these purposes, the pleadings need not be offered in evidence. They are used as judicial and not as evidentiary admissions, and they are conclusive until withdrawn or amended.

A party may also seek to use a portion of an adversary's final pleading as a basis for arguing the existence of some subordinate fact or as the foundation for an adverse inference. Some courts permit the party to do this by quoting or reading the pleading as part of the record, while others require that the party, in order to make this use of the final pleading, introduce the relevant passage from the opponent's pleading as part of its own evidence during the course of the trial. Such a requirement may be preferable in that it allows the pleader to give explanatory evidence, such as that the allegation was made through inadvertence or mistake, and avoids the possibility of a surprise inference from the pleading in closing argument.

Subject to the qualifications developed later in this section, pleadings are generally usable against the pleader. As noted earlier, if they are the effective pleadings in the case, they have the standing of judicial admissions. Amended, withdrawn, or superseded pleadings are no longer judicial admissions but may be used as evidentiary admissions. A party's pleading in one case may generally be used as an evidentiary admission in other litigation. These same principles apply to the use in a subsequent trial of counsel's oral in-court statements representing the factual conten-

1. See supra § 18.

tions of the party, even including assertions made during opening statement.

How closely is it necessary to connect the pleading with the party against whom it is to be introduced as an admission? Certainly if it is shown to have been sworn to, or signed by, the party that would be sufficient. More often, however, the pleading is prepared and signed by counsel, and the older view was that statements contained in such pleadings were presumed to be merely "suggestions of counsel" unless other evidence was produced that they were actually sanctioned by the client. The dominant position, however, is that pleadings shown to have been prepared or filed by counsel employed by the party are prima facie regarded as authorized by the client and are entitled to be received an admissions. The party opposing admission may offer evidence that the pleading was filed upon incorrect information and without his or her actual knowledge, but, except in extraordinary circumstances, such a showing goes only to the weight and not to the admissibility of the pleading.

An important exception to the use of the pleadings as admissions must be noted. A basic problem which attends the use of written pleadings is uncertainty whether the evidence as it actually unfolds at trial will prove the case described in the pleadings. Traditionally a failure in this respect, i.e., a variance between pleading and proof, could bring disaster to the pleader's case. As a safeguard against developments of this kind, the common law permitted the use of counts, each a complete separate statement of a different version of the same basic claim, combined in the same declaration to take care of variance possibilities. The same was done with defenses. Inconsistency between counts or between defenses was not prohibited; in fact it was essential to the successful use of the system. Also essential to the system was a prohibition against using allegations in one count or defense as admissions to prove or disprove allegations in another.

Under the influence of the Field Code of 1848, the view prevailed for a time that there could exist only one set of facts in a case and that inconsistent statements and defenses were therefore not allowable. Nevertheless, uncertainty as to how a case will in fact develop at trial is now recognized as a reality, with a concomitant need for some procedure for dealing with problems of variance. The modern equivalent of the common law system is the use of alternative and hypothetical forms of statement of claims and defenses, regardless of consistency. It can readily be appreciated that pleadings of this nature are directed primarily to giving notice and lack the essential character of an admission. To allow them to operate as admissions would frustrate their underlying purpose. Hence the decisions with seeming unanimity deny them status as judicial admissions, and generally disallow them as evidentiary admissions.

Some courts have exhibited sensitivity to the potential unfairness involved in admitting pleadings where a more skillful pleader would have avoided the pitfalls of creating an admission, particularly where the pleading at issue concerned the conduct of third parties. Another approach is to recognize the potential of an inconsistent pleading to prejudice unfairly a party or to be overvalued in relation to its true probative worth, excluding the pleading in appropriate cases after balancing the relevant factors. A final possible exception, not widely recognized, is denial of status as an admission to amended, withdrawn, or superseded pleadings on the theory that to admit them into evidence contravenes the policy of liberality in amendment.

A recurring question is whether a plea of guilty to a criminal charge should be allowed in evidence in a related civil action. Generally the evidence is admitted. While a plea of guilty to a traffic offense is in theory no different from a plea of guilty to other offenses, recognition that people plead guilty to traffic charges for reasons of convenience and with little regard to guilt or collateral consequences has led some commentators to argue against admissibility, but courts have generally rejected these arguments. In jurisdictions where allowed, pleas of *nolo contendere* or *non vult* are generally regarded as inadmissible, and in fact that attribute is a principal reason for use of such pleas.

A related question involves whether a plea of guilty can be introduced as an admission in a criminal case where the accused is allowed to withdraw the guilty plea and is subsequently tried on the charge. The result depends on the resolution of competing considerations of policy. On the one hand, a plea of guilty if freely and understandingly made is so likely to be true that to withhold it from the jury seems to ask them to do justice without knowledge of very important evidence. On this basis, some courts have received admissions in civil cases, leaving it to the adversary to rebut or explain. The competing concern is that if the withdrawn plea is admitted the effectiveness of the withdrawal itself is substantially impaired. In addition, admitting the guilty plea virtually compels the accused to explain why it was initially entered, with resultant encroachment upon the privilege against self-incrimination and intrusion into sensitive areas of the attorney-client relationship. The drafters of the Federal Rules accepted the policy arguments against receiving evidence of a withdrawn guilty plea, and Rule 410 excludes such evidence in both civil and criminal cases.

§ 258. Testimony by the Party as an Admission

While testifying on pretrial examination or at trial, a party may admit some fact that is adverse, and sometimes fatal, to a cause of action or defense. If the party's admission stands unimpeached and uncontradicted at the end of the trial, like unimpeached and uncontradicted testimony generally, it is conclusive against the party. Frequently this situation is what the courts are referring to when they say somewhat misleadingly that a party is "bound" by his or her own testimony. The controversial question is whether the party is "bound" by such testimony in the sense that the party will not be allowed to contradict it with other testimony, or if contradictory testimony has been received, the judge or jury is nevertheless required to accept as true the party's disserving testimony as a judicial admission.

Three main approaches are reflected in the decisions, which to some extent tend to merge and do not necessarily lead to different results in particular situations. First, some courts take the view that a party's testimony in this respect is like the testimony of any other witness called by the party, and the party is free to elicit contradictory testimony from the same witness or to call other witnesses to contradict the statement. Obviously, however, the problem of persuasion may be a difficult one when the party seeks to explain or contradict his or her own words, and equally obviously, the trial judge would often be justified in ruling on a motion for directed verdict that reasonable minds could only believe the party's disserving statement.

Second, others take the view that the party's testimony is not conclusive against contradiction except when testifying unequivocally to matters in his or her "peculiar knowledge." These matters may consist of subjective facts, such as the party's own knowledge or motivation, or they may consist of objective facts observed by the party.

Third, some courts adopt the doctrine that a party's disserving testimony is to be treated as a judicial admission, conclusive on the issue, so that the party may not bring other witnesses to contradict the admission, and if the party or the adversary does elicit such conflicting testimony, it will be disregarded. This third rule often comes with a number of qualifications and exceptions. For example, the party is free to contradict, and thus correct, his or her own testimony; only when the party's own testimony taken as a whole unequivocally affirms the statement does the rule of conclusiveness apply. Also, the rule is inapplicable when the party's testimony may be attributable to inadvertence or to a misuse of language, is merely negative in effect, is explicitly uncertain or is an estimate or opinion rather than an assertion of concrete fact, or relates to a matter as to which the party could easily have been mistaken, such as the swiftly moving events just preceding a collision in which the party was injured.

Of these three approaches the first seems preferable in policy and most in accord with the tradition of jury trial. It rejects any restrictive rule and leaves the evaluation of the party's testimony and the conflicting evidence to the judgment of the jury, the judge, and the appellate court, with only the standard of reason to guide them.

The second theory, binding as to facts within the party's "peculiar knowledge," is based on the assumption that as to such facts the possibility that the party may be mistaken largely disappears. If the facts are subjective ones (e.g., knowledge, motivation), the likelihood of successful contradiction is slight, but even then the assumption may be questionable. "Often we little note nor long remember our 'motives, purposes, or knowledge.' There are few if any subjects on which plaintiffs are infallible."[1]

The third theory is also of doubtful validity. The party's testimony, uttered by a layman in the stress of examination, cannot with justice be given the conclusiveness of the traditional judicial admission in a pleading or stipulation, deliberately drafted by counsel for the express purpose of limiting and defining the facts in issue. Again, a general rule of conclusiveness necessitates an elaboration of qualifications and exceptions, which represents an unfortunate transfer to the appellate court of some of the traditional control of the jury by the trial judge, or in a nonjury case of the judge's factfinding function. Also, the moral emphasis is wrong. In the early cases where the rule of conclusiveness first appeared, judges were outraged by apparent attempts by parties to play fast and loose with the court. However, this is far from being the typical situation of the party testifying to disserving facts. Instead of the unscrupulous party, it is either the one who can be pushed into an admission by the ingenuity or persistence of adverse counsel or the unusually candid or conscientious party willing to speak the truth regardless of its consequences who is penalized by the rule of conclusiveness.

§ 259. Representative Admissions; Coconspirator Statements

When a party to the suit has expressly authorized another person to speak, it is an obvious and accepted extension of the admission rule to admit against the party the statements of such persons. In the absence of express authority, how far will the statements of an agent be received as the principal's admission by virtue of the employment relationship? The early texts and cases used as analogies the doctrine of the master's substantive responsibility for the acts of the agent and the notion then prevalent in evidence law that words accompanying a relevant act were admissible as part of the *res gestae*. Together, these concepts produced the inadequate theory that the agent's statements could be received against the principal only when made at the time of, and in relation to, some act then being performed in the scope of the agent's duty.

A later theory that gained currency was that the admissibility of the agent's statements as admissions of the principal was measured by precisely the same tests as the principal's substantive responsibility for the conduct of the agent, that is, the words of the agent would be received as the admissions of the principal if they were spoken within the scope of the authority of the agent to speak for the employer. This formula made plain that the statements of an agent employed to give information (a so-called "speaking agent") could be received as the employer's admissions, and the authority to act, e.g., the authority of a chauffeur to drive a car, would not carry with it automatically the authority to make statements to others describing the duties performed.

These tests were most frequently used to exclude statements made by employees involved in an accident to someone at the scene regarding the accident when the statement was not made in furtherance of the employer's interest but rather as the employee's description of what occurred. Exclusion represents the logical application of these tests, but the assumption that the determinant of the master's responsibility for the agent's *acts* should be the test for using the agent's statements as *evidence* against the master is a shaky one.

---

§ 258

1. Alamo v. Del Rosario, 98 F.2d 328, 332 (D.C.Cir. 1938).

The rejection of such post-accident statements coupled with the admission of the employee's testimony on the stand resulted in preferring the weaker to the stronger evidence. Typically the agent is well informed about acts in the course of the business, the statements are offered against the employer's interest, and while the employment continues, the employee is not likely to make the statements unless they are true. Moreover, if admissions are viewed as arising from the adversary system, responsibility for statements of one's employee is consistent with that theory. Accordingly, even before adoption of the Federal Rules, the predominant view was to admit a statement by an agent if it concerned a matter within the scope of the declarant's employment and was made before that relationship was terminated. Of course, admissibility of the traditional authorized statement was continued.

Federal Rule 801(d)(2)(C) & (D), following the expansive view described in the preceding paragraph, admits statements offered against a party "by a person authorized by the party to make a statement concerning the subject," and "by the party's agent or servant concerning a matter within the scope of the agency or employment, made during the existence of the relationship."

The party offering evidence of the alleged agent's admission must first prove that the declarant is an agent of the adverse party and the scope of that agency. This may be done directly by the testimony of the asserted agent, or by anyone who knows, or by circumstantial evidence. Traditionally, courts held that evidence of the purported agent's past declarations asserting the agency could not be considered in deciding whether an agency relationship existed. By contrast, the Federal Rule permits such statements to be used by the trial judge in deciding the agency issue but states explicitly that standing alone they are insufficient to establish it. If the preliminary fact of the declarant's agency is disputed, the question is one to be decided by the court under Rule 104(a).

The question also arises whether to be an admission a statement by an agent must be made to an outsider rather than to the principal or to another agent. Typical instances are the railway employee's report of an accident or a letter to the home office from a manager of a branch office of a bank. Historically, though plainly made in the scope of authority, some courts refused to admit such statements unless they were adopted by the principal. Others admitted them even if made in-house. The courts that excluded such statements relied chiefly on the fact that the doctrine of *respondeat superior* does not apply to transactions between the agent and the principal, determining the hearsay question by the rules of substantive liability of principals. However, other analogies could just as reasonably control, such as the fact that statements made by a party not intended for the outside world—entries in a secret diary, for example—are receivable as admissions.

Reliability also favored admissibility of such in-house statements. While slightly less reliable as a class than the agent's authorized statements to outsiders, intra-organization reports are generally made as a basis for some action, and when this is so, they share the reliability of business records. They will only be offered against the principal when they admit some fact damaging to the principal, and this kind of statement by an agent is likely to be trustworthy. No special danger of surprise, confusion, or prejudice from the use of the evidence is apparent.

The drafters of the Federal Rules found the arguments in favor of receiving such in-house admissions persuasive. The expansion has been held to apply both to statements by agents authorized to speak and by those authorized only to act for the principal.

While the Federal Rule greatly expands the scope of statements within a corporation that will qualify as admissions, it leaves a number of difficult issues to be resolved by analysis of the individual facts of the situation. For example, statements made by corporate employees that are admissions of the corporation are not automatically vicarious admissions of other employees of the corporation, and a specific showing of agency between the two is required. Also, while firsthand knowledge is not required for vicarious admissions of corporate employees, uncertainty about the identity of the person who was the source of a statement may result in exclusion because of a failure to establish that the statement concerned a matter within the scope of the declarant's employment as opposed to "mere gossip."

The general principles developed above are applied in the remainder of this section to special categories of agents and to types of vicarious admissions that are frequently encountered:

Attorneys. If an attorney is employed to manage a party's conduct of a lawsuit, the attorney has *prima facie* authority to make relevant judicial admissions by pleadings, by oral or written stipulations, or by formal opening statement, which unless allowed to be withdrawn are conclusive in the case. Such formal and conclusive admissions, which are usually framed with care and circumspection, are sometimes contrasted with an attorney's oral out-of-court statement, which have been characterized as "merely a loose conversation." Some courts take the view that the client is not "bound" as to such "casual" statements of counsel made outside of court. The use of the word "bound" is obviously misleading. The issue is not whether the client is "bound," as he or she is by a judicial admission, but whether the attorney's extrajudicial statement is admissible against the client as a mere evidentiary admission made by an agent.

A desire to protect the client and the attorney against the hazard of counsel's ill-advised statements produced a tendency in the older cases to restrict introduction of such statements more than those by other types of agents. More recent cases generally measure the authority of the attorney to make out-of-court admissions by the same tests of express or implied authority as would be applied to other agents, and when they meet these tests, admit them as evidentiary admissions. These admissions occur, for example, in letters or oral conversations made in the course of efforts for the collection or resistance of claims,

or settlement negotiations, or the management of any other business in behalf of the client.

Partners. A partner is an agent of the partnership for the conduct of the firm's business. Accordingly, when the existence and scope of the partnership have been proved, the statement of a partner made in the conduct of the business of the firm is receivable as the admission of the partnership. What of statements of a former partner made after dissolution? The cases are divided, but since a continuing power is recognized in each former partner to do such acts as are reasonably necessary to wind up and settle the affairs of the firm, one former partner should be regarded as having authority to speak for the others in making statements of fact as are reasonably incident to collecting the claims and paying the debts of the firm. Beyond this, it seems that one partner's admissions should be competent only against that partner.

Coconspirator. Conspiracies to commit a crime or an unlawful or tortious act are analogous to partnerships. If A and B are engaged in a conspiracy, the acts and declarations of B occurring while the conspiracy is actually in progress and in furtherance of the design are provable against A, because they are acts for which A is criminally or civilly responsible as a matter of substantive law. But B's declarations may also be introduced against A as representative admissions to prove the truth of the matter asserted. Only statements of the latter sort are at issue within this section on representative admissions. However, courts have seldom discriminated between declarations offered as conduct constituting part of the conspiracy and declarations offered as vicarious admissions of the facts declared. Instead, even when offered as admissions, courts have generally imposed the same test applicable to statements that form part of the conduct of the crime, namely that the declaration must have been made while the conspiracy was continuing and must have constituted a step in furtherance of the venture. Federal Rule 801(d)(2)(E) is consistent with the foregoing analysis, treating as an admission, "a statement by a coconspirator of a party during the course and in furtherance of the conspiracy."

Literally applied, the "in furtherance" requirement calls for exclusion of statements possessing evidentiary value solely as admissions. Under this requirement, statements that merely recount prior events in the conspiracy are not admissible, but the line of admissibility is not always clear since historical statements that advance the goals of the conspiracy are admissible. Courts have generally placed more emphasis on the "during the course" requirement and generously interpreted whether it furthered the conspiracy. Some parallel can be seen between the liberal admissibility of coconspirator statements and admission against the principal of statements relating to the subject of the agency even though the agent was not authorized to make a statement.

The requirement that the statement be made "during the course" of the conspiracy calls for exclusion of admissions and confessions made after the termination of the conspiracy, which generally is held to occur with the achievement or failure of its primary objectives. The "in furtherance" requirement has a similar effect. Questions arise, of course, as to when termination occurs. Under some circumstances, the duration of the conspiracy is held to extend beyond the commission of the principal crime to include closely connected disposition of its fruits or concealment of its traces, as in the case of police officers engaged in preparing a false report to conceal police participation in a burglary, disposal of the body after a murder, or continuation of a racketeering enterprise that involved on-going concealment to effectuate the scheme. In Krulewitch v. United States,[1] the Supreme Court held inadmissible a coconspirator's statement regarding concealment efforts after arrest of the participants and established the position of the federal courts. *Krulewitch* was cited with approval in the Advisory Committee Note to Federal Rule 801(d)(2)(E), and attempts to ex-

pand the "concealment phase" to include all efforts to avoid detection have generally not been accepted. While statements made after the termination of the conspiracy are inadmissible, subsequent acts which shed light upon the nature of the conspiratorial agreement have been held admissible.

Preliminary questions of fact with regard to declarations of coconspirators are governed by Federal Rule 104(a) and must be established by a preponderance of the evidence. The Supreme Court changed longstanding practice in Bourjaily v. United States[2] by holding that the putative coconspirator statement itself can be considered by the trial court in determining whether a conspiracy exists and its scope. However, the statement is not sufficient by itself to establish these facts under the Federal Rules.

Statements of government agents in criminal cases. In a criminal prosecution, statements by the agent of an accused may generally be admitted against the accused, but statements by agents of the government are often held inadmissible against the government. "This apparent discrimination is explained by the peculiar posture of the parties in a criminal prosecution—the only party on the government side being the government itself whose many agents and actors are supposedly uninterested personally in the outcome of the trial and are historically unable to bind the sovereign."[3] A more plausible explanation is the desirability of affording the government a measure of protection against errors and indiscretions on the part of at least some of its many agents.

The cases ruling against admissibility involve statements by agents at the investigative level, with statements by government attorneys after the initiation of proceedings being held admissible. An admissibility dividing line based on the agent's position in the government may properly balance the conflicting in-

---

§ 259

1. 336 U.S. 440 (1949).

2. 483 U.S. 171 (1987).

3. United States v. Santos, 372 F.2d 177, 180 (2nd Cir.1967).

terests involved. While Federal Rule 801(d)(2) does not specifically address the question, it is very hard to find any support in its language or structure for a blanket exclusion of statements by government agents. However, a balancing approach of the type suggested above appears consistent with its basic approach and the various policy concerns involved.

§ 260. Declarations by "Privies in Estate," Joint Tenants, Predecessors in Interest, Joint Obligors, and Principals Against Surety

Historically, courts accepted the notion that "privity," or identity of interest between the declarant and a party justified introduction of the statement of the declarant as an admission of the party. Thus, the declaration of one joint tenant or joint owner against another could be received, but the distinction derived from the law of property was applied so strictly in this context that statements of a tenant in common, a co-legatee or co-devisee, or a co-trustee were excluded.

The more frequent and important application of this property analogy was the use of declarations of a predecessor in title to land, personalty, or choses in action against a successor. The successor was viewed as acquiring an interest burdened with the same liability of having declarations used against him or her as could have been used against the predecessor. The declarations had to relate to the declarant's transactions, intent, or interest in the property, and they must have been made while the declarant was the owner of the interest now claimed by the successor. Under this theory, courts received the declarations of grantors, transferors, donors, and mortgagors of land and personalty against the transferees and mortgagees; of decedents against their representatives, heirs, and next of kin; of a prior possessor against one who claims prescriptive title relying on such prior possession; and of former holders of notes and other choses in action against their assignees. Of course, concepts such as bona fide purchaser and hold-

er in due course may make the evidence irrelevant and therefore inadmissible.

Similarly, when two parties are jointly liable as obligors, the declarations of one were sometimes receivable as an admission against the other. However, the element of authorization to speak in furtherance of the common enterprise, as in the case of agency, partnership, or conspiracy, can hardly be spelled out from the mere relationship of joint obligors, and admissibility of declarations on this basis has been criticized. In fact, most of the cases found in support involve the special situation of declarations of a principal offered as admissions against a surety, guarantor, indemnitor, or other person secondarily liable. These declarations were usually held admissible.

Morgan criticized importing into the law of evidence the property doctrines of identity of interest and privity of estate:

> The dogma of vicarious admissions, as soon as it passes beyond recognized principles of representation, baffles the understanding. Joint ownership, joint obligation, privity of title, each and all furnish no criterion of credibility, no aid in the evaluation of testimony.[1]

Following Morgan's view, the Model Code omitted any provision for admitting these declarations, and the Federal Rules followed the same pattern. Most meritorious statements will qualify as declarations against interest, vicarious admissions of agents, or some other hearsay exception more soundly grounded than on the privity concept.

§ 261. Admissions by Conduct: (a) Adoptive Admissions

One may expressly adopt another's statement. That is an explicit admission like any other and calls for no further discussion. In this treatise, the term adoptive admission is used somewhat restrictively to apply to evidence of other conduct of a party manifesting

---

§ 260

1. Morgan, Admissions, 12 Wash.L.Rev. 181, 202 (1937).

circumstantially the party's assent to the truth of a statement made by another.[1]

Adoptive admissions under the Federal Rules are governed by Rule 801(d)(2)(B). In conformity with traditional practice, it provides that a statement is not hearsay if offered against a party and is "a statement of which the party has manifested an adoption or belief in its truth."

The fact that the party declares that he or she has heard that another person has made a given statement is not alone sufficient to justify finding that the party has adopted the third person's statement. The circumstances surrounding the party's declaration must be examined to determine whether they indicated an approval of the statement.

The question of adoption often arises in life and accident insurance cases when the defendant insurance company offers a statement, such as the certificate of the attending physician or the coroner's report, which the plaintiff beneficiary attached to the proof of death or disability. The fact that the beneficiary tendered it as an exhibit accompanying a formal statement of "proof" presented for the purpose of having the company pay the claim would appear to be enough to secure its admission. In actuality, however, the surrounding circumstances often show that an inference of adoption would be most unrealistic. This is clear when the beneficiary expressly disavows the accompanying statement, and it seems that exclusion of the attached statement should likewise follow when the statements of the beneficiary in the proofs are clearly contrary to those in the exhibits. Moreover, when the company's agent prepared the proof for signature and procured the accompanying documents, as is frequently done as a helpful service to the beneficiary, the inference of adoption of statements in the exhibits should not be drawn if the agent has failed to call the beneficiary's attention to inconsistencies between the proof and the exhibits. By similar reasoning, furnishing a copy of an examining physician's report to the opponent under the

requirement of a discovery rule should not be considered an adoption. The argument for exclusion is particularly strong if accompanying statements, such as the certificate of the attending physician regarding particular facts, are required under the terms of the policy. In such cases, the statements are not attached at the choice of the beneficiary, and the sponsorship generally to be inferred from a voluntary tendering of another's statement cannot be made.

Does the introduction of evidence by a party constitute an adoption of the statements of witnesses so that they may be used against the party as an admission in a subsequent lawsuit? The answer ought to depend upon whether the particular circumstances warrant the conclusion that adoption in fact occurred and not upon the discredited notion that a party vouches for its own witnesses. When a party offers in evidence a deposition or an affidavit to prove the matters stated therein, the party knows or should know the contents of the writing so offered and presumably desires that all of the contents be considered on its behalf since only the portion desired could be offered. Accordingly, it is reasonable to conclude that the writing so introduced may be used against the party as an adoptive admission in another suit.

With respect to oral testimony, however, the inference of sponsorship of the statements is not always so clear. Nevertheless, here too circumstances may justify the conclusion that, when the proponent placed the witness on the stand to prove a particular fact and the witness so testified, the party has created an adoptive admission of the fact that may be admitted in a later suit. But how is the party offering the testimony in the later suit to show that a given statement of the witness at the former trial was intended to be elicited by the party who called the witness or was contrary to or outside that intention? The form and context of the question would usually, but not always, give the clue. In view of the prevailing practice of interviewing one's witnesses before

§ 261

1. Admissions by silence are treated separately in § 262.

putting them on the stand, it would seem that a practical working rule would admit against the proponent the direct testimony of its own witness as presumptively elicited to prove the facts stated, in the absence of counter proof that the testimony came as a surprise to the interrogator or was repudiated in the course of argument. By contrast, testimony elicited on cross-examination may be drawn out to reveal the witness' errors and dishonesty and should not be assumed to have been relied on by the examiner as evidence of the facts stated. To constitute an adoptive admission, reliance must be affirmatively established.

In the main, preliminary factual issues arising with regard to whether a statement was adopted are to be decided as questions of conditional relevancy under Rule 104(b).

Similar to adoptive admissions are the instances where the party has referred an inquirer to another person whose anticipated statements the party accepts in advance. However, these admissions by reference to a third person are probably more properly classifiable as representative or vicarious admissions, rather than adoptive.[2]

§ 262. Admissions by Conduct: (b) Silence

When a statement is made in the presence of a party containing assertions of facts which, if untrue, the party would under all the circumstances naturally be expected to deny, failure to speak has traditionally been received as an admission. Whether the justification for receiving the evidence is the assumption that the party has intended to express its assent and thus has adopted the statement or that the probable state of belief can be inferred from the conduct is probably unimportant. Since it is the failure to deny that is significant, an equivocal or evasive response may similarly be used against the party on either theory, but if the total response adds up to a clear-cut denial, this theory of implied admission is inapplicable.

Despite the offhand appeal of this kind of evidence, courts have often suggested that it be received with caution, an admonition that is especially appropriate in criminal cases. Several characteristics of the evidence should be noted. First, its nature and the circumstances under which it arises often amount to an open invitation to manufacture evidence. Second, ambiguity of inference is often present. Silence may be motivated by many factors other than a sense of guilt or lack of an exculpatory story. For example, silence may be valued. As indicated at the beginning of this chapter, everyone knows that anything you say can be used against you. Third, *Miranda*'s constitutional limitations apply to the use of this type of evidence in criminal cases, but only if the suspect is interrogated by the police while in custody. Fourth, while in theory the statement is not offered as proof of its contents but rather to show what the party accepted, the distinction is indeed a subtle one; the statement is ordinarily highly damaging and of a nature likely to draw attention away from the basic inquiry whether acquiescence did in fact occur.

Despite the array of circumstances raising doubts regarding the reliability of this kind of evidence, the Supreme Court has not found any absolute federal constitutional barriers against its use other than those imposed in some circumstances by *Miranda*. Nevertheless, courts have evolved a variety of safeguards against misuse: (1) the statement must have been heard by the party claimed to have acquiesced; (2) it must have been understood by the party; and (3) the subject matter must have been within the party's knowledge. At first glance, this requirement may appear inconsistent with elimination of the firsthand knowledge requirement for admissions. However, a person cannot reasonably be expected to deny a matter on which he or she has no knowledge, lacking the incentive or the ability to dispute the accusations. (4) Physical or emotional impediments to responding must not be present. (5) The personal makeup of the speaker, e.g., young child, or the person's relationship to the party or the event, e.g., bystander, may be such as to make it unreason-

---

2. See generally supra § 259.

able to expect a denial. (6) Probably most important of all, the statement itself must be such as would, if untrue, call for a denial under the circumstances. Beyond the constitutional issues that can be raised, the fact that the police are present when an accusatory statement is made may constitute a critical circumstance that eliminates the naturalness of a response.

The above list is not an exclusive one, and other factors will suggest themselves. The essential inquiry in each case is whether a reasonable person under the circumstances would have denied the statement, with answers not lending themselves readily to mechanical formulations.

Most preliminary questions of admissibility in connection with admissions by acquiescence fall within the category of conditional relevancy. While some preliminary issues involved with admissions by silence are entrusted to final determination by the court, questions such as whether the statement was made in the person's hearing and whether there was an opportunity to reply should be submitted for jury determination if the court concludes sufficient evidence has been introduced so that a reasonable jury could find that those facts have been established.

Failure to Reply to Letter or other Written Communication. If a written statement is given to a party and read in the presence of others, the party's failure to deny its assertions may be received as an admission, when under the circumstances it would be natural for the person to deny them if he or she did not acquiesce. The principle in operation here is similar to the failure to deny an oral statement. Moreover, if a party receives a letter containing several statements, which he or she would naturally deny if untrue, and states a position as to some of the statements but fails to comment on the others, this failure will usually be received as evidence of an admission to those omitted.

More debatable is the question whether the failure to reply at all to a letter or other written communication should be received as

an admission by silence. Certainly such a failure to reply will often be less convincing than silence in the face of an oral charge. Indeed, a "general rule" is sometimes announced that failure to answer a letter generally does not constitute an admission. The negative form of the rule unfortunately tends toward over-strict rulings excluding evidence of material value. The preferable view is that the failure to reply to a letter containing statements which it would be natural under all the circumstances for the addressee to deny if he or she believed them untrue is receivable as evidence of an admission by silence. Two factors particularly tend to show that a denial would be naturally forthcoming: first, where the letter was written as part of a mutual correspondence between the parties, and second, where the proof shows that the parties were engaged in some business, transaction, or relationship which would make it improbable that an untrue communication about the transaction or relationship would be ignored.

The most common instance of this latter situation is the transmission by one party to a business relationship to the other of a statement of account or a bill. Failure to question such a bill or statement is uniformly received as evidence of an admission of its correctness. On the other hand, if the negotiations have been broken off by one party's taking a final stand, thus indicating a view that further communication would be fruitless, or if the letter was written after litigation was instituted, these circumstances tend to show that failure to answer should not be received as an admission.

§ 263. Admissions by Conduct: (c) Flight and Similar Acts

"The wicked flee when no one pursues."[1] Many acts of a defendant after the crime seeking escape are received as admissions by conduct, constituting circumstantial evidence of consciousness of guilt and hence of the fact of guilt itself. In this class are flight from the scene, from one's usual haunts, or from the jurisdiction after the crime; assuming a false

§ 263
1. Proverbs 28:1 (New Rev. Standard).

name; changing appearance; resisting arrest; attempting to bribe arresting officers; forfeiture of bond by failure to appear or departure from the trial while it is proceeding; escapes or attempted escapes from confinement; and suicide attempts by the accused.

If the flight is from the scene of the crime, evidence of it seems to be wholly acceptable as a means of locating the accused at the critical time and place. However, in many situations, the inference of consciousness of guilt of the particular crime is so uncertain and ambiguous and the evidence so prejudicial that one is forced to wonder whether the evidence is not directed to punishing the "wicked" generally rather than resolving the issue of guilt of the offense charged. Particularly troublesome are the cases where defendant flees when sought to be arrested for another crime, is wanted for another crime, or is not shown to know that he or she is suspected of the particular crime. Some courts appear to accept a general sense of guilt as sufficient. Perhaps the most troublesome cases involve attempted suicide.

Many cases currently adopt the rubric that the probative value of flight

> as circumstantial evidence of guilt depends upon the degree of confidence with which four inferences can be drawn: (1) from the defendant's behavior to flight; (2) from flight to consciousness of guilt; (3) from consciousness of guilt to consciousness of guilt concerning the crime charged; and (4) from consciousness of guilt concerning the crime charged to actual guilt of the crime charged.[2]

Increasingly, courts look with particular care at the timing of the flight relative to the offense and the strength of the inference that in fleeing the defendant was aware of, and motivated by fear of apprehension for, a particular offense. The potential for prejudice of flight evidence should also be weighed against its probative value. Critical scrutiny of the balance between the often weak probative value of this type of evidence and its prejudicial impact is appropriate in each case.

While the great bulk of the decisions involve criminal prosecutions, flight also finds recognition in civil actions.

§ 264. Admissions by Conduct: (d) Failure to Call Witnesses or Produce Evidence; Refusal to Submit to a Physical Examination

When it would be natural under the circumstances for a party to call a particular witness, or to take the stand as a witness in a civil case, or to produce documents or other objects in his or her possession as evidence and the party fails to do so, tradition has allowed the adversary to use this failure as the basis for invoking an adverse inference. An analogous inference may be drawn if a party unreasonably declines to submit, upon request, to a physical examination or refuses to furnish handwriting exemplars.

Most of the controversy arises with respect to failure to call a witness. The classic statement is:

> [I]f a party has it peculiarly within his power to produce witnesses whose testimony would elucidate the transaction, the fact that he does not do it creates the presumption that the testimony, if produced, would be unfavorable.[1]

The cases fall into two groups. In the first, an adverse inference may be drawn against a party for failure to produce a witness reasonably assumed to be favorably disposed to the party. In the second, the inference may be drawn against a party who has exclusive control over a material witness but fails to produce him or her, without regard to any possible favorable disposition of the witness toward the party. Cases in the second group are increasingly less frequent due to the growth of discovery and other disclosure requirements. In either group, if the testimony of the witness would be merely cumulative, the inference is unavailable.

Despite an abundance of cases recognizing the inference, refusal to allow comment or to

---

2. United States v. Myers, 550 F.2d 1036, 1049 (5th Cir.1977).

§ 264
1. Graves v. United States, 150 U.S. 118, 121 (1893).

instruct rarely results in a reversal, while erroneously instructing the jury on the inference or even an erroneous argument by counsel much more frequently requires retrial. The appellate courts often counsel caution. A number of factors support a conservative approach. Conjecture or ambiguity of inference is often present. The possibility that the inference may be drawn invites waste of time in calling unnecessary witnesses or in presenting evidence to explain why they were not called. Failure to anticipate that the inference may be invoked entails substantial possibilities of surprise. Finally, the availability of modern discovery and other disclosure procedures serves to diminish both its justification and the need for the inference. In recognition of these factors, courts often require early notice from a party expecting to make a missing witness argument or intending to request such an instruction.

If a witness is "equally available" to both parties, courts often state that no inference springs from the failure of either to call the witness. This statement can hardly be accurate, as the inference may be allowed when the witness could easily be called or subpoenaed by either party. What is meant instead is that when the witness would be as likely to be favorable to one party as the other, no inference is proper. However, equality of favor is nearly always debatable, and although the judge thinks the witness would be equally likely to favor either party, perhaps both should be permitted to argue the inference.

A party may be at liberty to call a witness, but may have a privilege against the witness being called by the adversary, as when in a criminal case the accused may call his or her spouse but the state may not. Similarly, it may be clear that all the information that a witness has is subject to a privilege which the party may exert, such as the doctor-patient privilege. In these situations probably the majority of courts would forbid an adverse inference from a failure to call.[2] Of course, an inference from the failure of the criminal defendant to take the stand is constitutionally forbidden.[3] The

policy considerations with respect to comment upon the exercise of evidentiary privileges are discussed elsewhere.[4]

The specific procedural effect of the inference from failure to call a witness is seldom discussed. Some courts have said that the party's failure to call the witness or produce the evidence creates a "presumption" that the testimony would have been unfavorable. It is usually phrased in terms, however, of "may" rather than "must" and seemingly could at most be only a "permissive," not a mandatory presumption.[5] Moreover, unlike the usual presumption, it is not directed to any specific presumed fact or facts which are required or permitted to be found. The burden of producing evidence of a fact cannot be met by relying on this "presumption." Rather, its effect is to impair the value of the opponent's evidence and to give greater credence to the positive evidence of the adversary upon any issue upon which it is shown that the missing witness might have knowledge.

Instead, most courts speak of the party's failure to call the witness as creating an "inference." Some of these courts consider that the party has a right to have such inference explained in the instructions on proper request while others consider that the instruction is proper but not required. Still others condemn an instruction as a comment on the evidence. Of course, all courts permit counsel to argue the inference where it is an allowable one.

In jurisdictions where the judge retains the common law power to comment on the evidence, a fair comment on failure to produce witnesses or evidence is traditionally allowable. Permitting judicial discretion to instruct on the inference is appropriate. However, a practice that gives a party a right to such instruction is undesirable because it tends to lead to the development of elaborate rules defining the circumstances when the right exists. Making instruction a matter of right does have the advantage of focusing past experience

---

2. See supra § 74.1.

3. See supra § 132.

4. See supra § 74.1.

5. See discussion of these terms infra in Ch. 36.

on the problem presented at the trial, but the cost of complex rules far outweighs the gain.

A web of rules also can develop by tightly controlling counsel's argument on the inference. It is wiser to hold that if an argument on failure to produce proof is fallacious, the remedy is the answering argument and the jury's good sense. Thus, the judge should be required to intervene only when the argument, under the general standard, can be said to be not merely weak or unfounded, but unfair and prejudicial.

§ 265. Admissions by Conduct: (e) Misconduct Constituting Obstruction of Justice

We have seen in the preceding section that a party's failure to produce evidence that he or she is free to produce or withhold may be treated as an admission. As might be expected, wrongdoing by the party in connection with its case amounting to an obstruction of justice is also commonly regarded as an admission by conduct. By resorting to wrongful devices, the party is said to provide a basis for believing that he or she thinks the case is weak and not to be won by fair means, or in criminal cases that the accused is conscious of guilt. Accordingly, the following are considered under this general category of admissions by conduct: a party's false statement about the matter in litigation, whether before suit or on the stand; subornation of perjury; fabrication of documents; undue pressure by bribery, intimidation, or other means to influence a witness to testify favorably or to avoid testifying; destruction or concealment of relevant documents or objects; attempt to corrupt the jury; and hiding or transferring property in anticipation of judgment.

Of course, it is not enough to show that someone did the acts charged as obstructive. The actor must be connected to the party, or, in the case of a corporation, to one of its superior officers. Moreover, the circumstances of the act must manifest bad faith. Mere negligence is not enough, for it does not sustain the inference of consciousness of a weak cause.

A question may well be raised whether the relatively modest probative value of such evidence is not often outweighed by its prejudicial effect. The litigant who would not like to have a stronger case must indeed be a rarity. The real underpinning of the rule of admissibility may be a desire to impose swift punishment, with a certain poetic justice, rather than concern over niceties of proof. In any event, the evidence is generally admitted, despite incidental disclosure of another crime.

What is the probative reach of these various kinds of "spoliation" admissions beyond their great tactical value in darkening the atmosphere of the party's case? They should entitle the proponent at least to an instruction that the adversary's conduct may be considered generally as tending to corroborate the proponent's case and to discredit that of the adversary. This result is worthwhile in itself, and it carries with it the corresponding right of the proponent's counsel to argue these inferences.

However, a crucial and perplexing question remains whether the adverse inference from the party's obstructive conduct substitute for evidence of a fact essential to the adversary's case. Certainly, the primitive impulse to answer "yes" is strong, and an analogy has been suggested to the practice under statutes and rules permitting the court to enter a default against a party who refuses to provide discovery. When the conduct points toward an inference about a particular specific fact, as in the case of bribing an attesting witness to be absent or destroying a particular document, there is likely to be a greater willingness to allow an inference of that fact although the only available information regarding it is the proponent's claim in the pleadings. Where the conduct is not directed toward suppression of any particular fact, as in attempts to "buy off" the prosecution, to tamper with the jury, or to defeat recovery by conveyance of property, an inference as to the existence of a particular fact not proved is more strained. Without adverting to this distinction, many decisions have supported the general doctrine that the inference from obstructive conduct will not satisfy the need for proof of a particular fact essential to the proponent's case.

Some recent cases have indicated a willingness to rethink these traditionally established principles. Several cases have found intentional actions that result in the destruction of evidence either to shift the burden of proof or to provide affirmative evidence on a critical issue. A few cases have proposed a separate tort for spoliation of evidence. This area of the law appears to be in flux, and the patterns of the new order are not yet clear.

§ 266. Admissions by Conduct: (f) Offers to Compromise Disputed Claim in Civil Suits and Plea Negotiations in Criminal Cases

In general. Arguably an offer to accept a sum in compromise of a disputed claim might be used against the party as an admission of the weakness of the claim. Conversely, an offer by the adversary to pay a sum in compromise might be used against that party as an admission of the weakness of his or her position. In either situation, general agreement exists that the offer of compromise is not admissible on the issue of liability, although the reason for exclusion is not always clear.

Two grounds for the rule of inadmissibility are advanced: lack of relevancy and policy considerations. First, the relevancy of the offer will vary according to circumstances, with a very small offer of payment to settle a very large claim being much more readily construed as a desire for peace rather than an admission of weakness of position. Relevancy would increase, however, as the amount of the offer approaches the amount claimed. Second, the policy argument is the promotion of settlement of disputes, which would be discouraged if offers of compromise were admitted. Resting the rule on this latter basis has the advantage of avoiding difficult questions of relevancy. On this ground, the principle should protect one who made the offer and is a party to the suit in which the evidence is offered.

To invoke the exclusionary rule, an actual dispute must exist, preferably some negotiations, and at least an apparent difference of view between the parties as to the validity or amount of the claim. An offer to pay an admitted claim is not privileged since there is no policy of encouraging compromises of undisputed claims, which should be paid in full. If the validity of the claim and the amount due are undisputed, an offer to pay a lesser sum in settlement or to pay in installments would accordingly be admissible.

What is excluded? The offer is excluded, as well as any suggestions or overtures of settlement. How far do any accompanying statements of fact made by either party during oral negotiations or correspondence looking to settlement share the privilege? The historically accepted doctrine held that an admission of fact in the course of negotiations was not privileged, unless it was stated hypothetically ("we admit for the sake of the discussion only"), expressly made "without prejudice," or inseparably connected with the offer so that it could not be correctly understood without considering the two together.

The traditional doctrine of denying the protection of the exclusionary rule to statements of fact had serious drawbacks. It discouraged freedom of communication in attempting compromise and involved difficulties of application. As a result, the trend has been to extend the protection to all statements made in compromise negotiations, and this result is accomplished by the second sentence of Federal Rule 408, which is reproduced in its entirety in the footnote.[1]

---

§ 266

1. The rule states:

Evidence of (1) furnishing or offering or promising to furnish, or (2) accepting or offering or promising to accept, a valuable consideration in compromising or attempting to compromise a claim which was disputed as to either validity or amount, is not admissible to prove liability for or invalidity of the claim or its amount. Evidence of conduct or statements made in compromise negotiations is likewise not admissible. This rule does not require the exclusion of any evidence otherwise discoverable merely because it is presented in the course of compromise negotiations. This rule also does not require exclusion when the evidence is offered for another purpose, such as proving bias or prejudice of a witness, negativing a contention of undue delay, or proving an effort to obstruct a criminal investigation or prosecution.

The rule is designed to exclude the offer of compromise only when it is tendered as an admission of the weakness of the offering party's claim or defense, not when offered for another purpose. Thus, for example, the rule does not call for exclusion when the compromise negotiations are offered to explain delay in taking action or failure to seek employment to mitigate damages, to show the extent of legal services rendered in conducting them, to establish bias, or to show the terms of compromise in another dispute that are part of the current case. Similarly, using the evidence of an effort to settle a civil case is not barred to prove an effort to obstruct a criminal prosecution. As in other situations where evidence is admissible for one purpose but not for another, the probative value for the proper purpose must be weighed against likelihood of improper use, with due regard to the probable efficacy of a limiting instruction.[2] Use of statements made in compromise negotiations to impeach the testimony of a party, which is not specifically treated in Rule 408, is fraught with danger of misuse of the statements to prove liability, threatens frank interchange of information during negotiations, and generally should not be permitted.

A completed compromise agreement, discussed below, may also be admissible for another purpose. For example, a defendant in a personal injury case may call a witness who was injured in the same collision. If the witness has made a claim against the defendant inconsistent with the witness' present favorable testimony, the claim may be proved to impeach the witness. Furthermore, if the witness has been paid or promised money in compromise of his or her claim, this may be shown as evidence of bias or used more generally to impeach.

Evidence of present party's compromise with third persons. In an action between plaintiff (P) and defendant (D), a compromise offer or a completed compromise by D with a third person having a claim similar to P's arising from the same transaction may be relevant as showing D's belief in the weakness of the defense in the present action. Nevertheless, the same consideration of policy which prompts exclusion of a compromise offer made by D to P, namely the danger of discouraging such compromises applies here. Accordingly, the prevailing view is that the compromise offer or payment made by the present defendant is privileged when offered as an implied admission of liability.

Effect of acceptance of offer of compromise. If an offer of compromise is accepted and a contract is thus created, the party aggrieved may sue on the contract and obviously may prove the offer and acceptance. Moreover, if after such a contract is made and the offering party repudiates it, the other may elect to sue on the original cause of action and here again the repudiating party may not claim privilege against proof of the compromise. The shield of the privilege does not extend to the protection of those who repudiate the agreements, which the privilege is designed to encourage.

Compromise evidence in criminal cases. The policy of protecting offers of compromise in civil cases does not extend to efforts to stifle criminal prosecution by "buying off" the prosecuting witness or victim. On the other hand, the legitimacy of settling criminal cases by negotiations between prosecuting attorney and accused, whereby the latter pleads guilty in return for some leniency, has been generally recognized. Effective criminal law administration would be difficult if a large proportion of the charges were not disposed of by guilty pleas. Public policy accordingly encourages compromise, and as in civil cases, that policy is furthered by protecting from disclosure at trial not only the offer but also statements made during negotiations.

Federal Rule 410 excludes from civil and criminal cases as evidence against a defendant who made a plea or participated in the plea discussions (1) guilty pleas which were later withdrawn, (2) nolo contendere pleas, (3) statements made in the course of entering the plea under Rule 11 of the Federal Rules of Criminal Procedure or comparable state procedures, and (4) statements made in the course

---

2. See supra § 59.

of plea discussions with a prosecuting attorney which did not result in a plea of guilty or which result in a plea that was later withdrawn. The rule allows such statements to be admitted for completeness in some instances and in prosecutions for perjury regarding such statements.

The original version of the rule did not explicitly state that its protection extended only to negotiations between the accused and the prosecutor. As a result, some decisions held that efforts to make deals with a considerable variety of federal law enforcement officers were within the rule. The rule accordingly was amended as stated above to make clear that only negotiations "with an attorney for the prosecuting authority" fall within its protection.

While the rule permits use of statements made as part of plea negotiations for certain limited purposes, impeachment of the defendant's subsequent testimony is not one of those permissible purposes. However, in United States v. Mezzanatto,[3] the Supreme Court held that impeachment was permissible if the plea agreement was drafted to waive the defendant's objection. If the transaction on which the prosecution is based also gives rise to a civil cause of action, a compromise or offer of compromise to the civil claim should be privileged when offered at the criminal trial if no agreement to stifle the criminal prosecution was involved.

§ 267. Admissions by Conduct: (g) Safety Measures After an Accident; Payment of Medical Expenses

Remedial Measures. After an accident causing injury, the owner of the premises or the enterprise will often take remedial measures, such as repairing a defect or changing safety rules. Are these new safety measures, which might have prevented the injury, admissible to prove negligence as an implied acknowledgment by conduct that due care required that these measures should have been taken before the injury? Particularly when the

remedial measures follow the injury immediately, they may be very persuasive of the owner's belief as to the precautions required by due care before the accident. Nevertheless, courts at one time occasionally asserted that the evidence was irrelevant for this purpose. While such remedial changes permit varying explanations, some of which are consistent with due care, the evidence would often meet the usual standards of relevancy if treated only as raising issues of the admissibility of circumstantial evidence and admission by conduct.[1]

The predominant reason for excluding such evidence, however, is not lack of probative significance, but rather a policy not to discourage safety measures. Courts exclude evidence of various types of remedial measures taken after an injury when offered as admissions of negligence or fault, and in some jurisdictions, defects in a product or its design or a need for warning or instruction. These include: repairs and alterations in construction; installation of new safety devices, such as lights, gates, or guards; changes in rules and regulations or the practice of the business; and the dismissal of an employee charged with causing the injury. However, when the remedial measures are taken by a third person, the policy ground for exclusion is absent, and the evidence, if otherwise admissible, is not excluded.

The ingenuity of counsel in suggesting other purposes has made substantial inroads upon the general rule of exclusion. Thus evidence of subsequent repairs or changes has been admitted as evidence of the defendant's ownership or control of the premises or duty to repair; as evidence of the possibility or feasibility of preventive measures; as evidence to explain that the situation at the time of accident was different when the jury has observed the scene at a later time; as evidence of what was done later to show that the earlier condition as of the time of the accident was as plaintiff claims; to impeach testimony of adversary's witnesses; and as evidence that the

---

3. 513 U.S. 196 (1995).

1. See supra § 185.

faulty condition later remedied was the cause of the injury by showing that after the change the injurious effect disappeared. Federal Rule 407, which is generally consistent with the foregoing discussion, is set out in the footnote.[2]

As noted earlier, not discouraging remedial measures is the principal reason for the rule excluding evidence that such measures were taken. Liberal admission of remedial measure evidence for purposes other than as an admission of negligence seriously undercuts the basic policy of the rule. Hence Rule 407 specifically requires that, when the evidence is offered for another purpose, that purpose must be controverted. Ownership, control, and feasibility of precautionary measures are mentioned as illustrations of other purposes. If the other purpose is not controverted, the evidence is inadmissible. The fact that the other purpose is controverted should not be taken as a guarantee of admissibility; the possibility of misuse of the evidence as an admission of fault still requires a balancing of probative value and need against potential prejudice under Rule 403. The availability of other means of proof is an important factor in this balancing process.[3]

The provision of the rule that permits evidence of remedial measures to be admitted for impeachment is of particular concern in that, if applied expansively, it could "swallow up" the rule. At the same time, impeachment should be permitted in some situations, such as when the witness' testimony constitutes, not simply a general denial of negligence, but a claim that is directly contradicted by the remedial conduct.

Whether subsequent remedial measures should be excluded in product liability cases

has been debated in the courts. Ault v. International Harvester Company[4] led the movement against application in such cases. The departure is based primarily on a rejection of the assumption that admitting the evidence discourages remedial steps when the enterprise involved is a large manufacturer and a general desire to spread the cost of injuries. A number of state courts have followed *Ault*. The federal courts, by contrast, generally disagreed, and a 1997 amendment to Federal Rule 407 made explicit that the rule applies to product liability cases tried in the federal courts.

The admissibility of recall letters has been approached in somewhat similar vein, as the first step in the taking of remedial steps. The courts have divided on the question. Those admitting the letters often take the view that the action should not be protected since it is not likely to be deterred because undertaken under regulatory command and not voluntarily.

PRE 409

Payment of medical expenses. Similar considerations of doubtful relevancy and of public policy underlie the general exclusion of evidence of payment or offers to pay medical and like expenses of an injured person. Federal Rule 409 is in general conformity with the prior case law.

Unlike compromise negotiations, where the discussion of issues is an essential part of the process and requires protection against disclosure, communications are unnecessary to the providing of care. Accordingly, they are unprotected. Also, if the offer to pay is relevant to an issue other than liability for the injury, exclusion is not required by this doctrine.

---

2. The rule states:

When, after an injury or harm cause by an event, measures are taken which, if taken previously, would have made the event less likely to occur, evidence of the subsequent measures is not admissible to prove negligence, culpable conduct, a defect in a product, a defect in a product's design, or a need for a warning or instruction. This rule does not require the exclusion of

evidence of subsequent measures when offered for another purpose, such as proving ownership, control or feasibility of precautionary measures, if controverted, or impeachment.

3. See supra § 185.

4. 528 P.2d 1148 (Cal.1974).

Chapter 26

SPONTANEOUS STATEMENTS

Table of Sections

§ 268. Res Gestae and the Hearsay Rule

The term *res gestae* seems to have come into common usage in discussions of admissibility of statements accompanying material acts or situations in the early 1800s. At this time, the theory of hearsay was not well developed, and the various exceptions to the hearsay rule were not clearly defined. In this context, the phrase *res gestae* served as a convenient vehicle for escape from the hearsay rule in two primary situations. First, it was used to explain the admissibility of statements that were not hearsay at all.[1] Second, it was used to justify the admissibility of statements that today come within the four exceptions discussed in this chapter: (1) statements of present sense impressions, (2) excited utterances, (3) statements of present bodily condition, and (4) statements of present mental states and emotions.

Initially the term *res gestae* was employed to denote words that accompanied the principal litigated fact, such as the murder, collision, or trespass. However, usage developed to the point where the phrase seemed to embody the notion that evidence of any relevant act or condition might also bring in the words that accompanied it. Two main policies or motives are discernible in this recognition of *res gestae* as a password for the admission of otherwise inadmissible evidence. One is a desire to permit each witness to tell his or her story in a natural way by reciting all that happened at the time of the narrated incident, including those details that give it life and color. Events occur as a seamless web, and the naturalness with which the details fit together gives confirmation to the witness' entire account. The other policy, emphasized by Wigmore and those following his leadership, is the recogni-

§ 268

1. See infra § 269.

tion of spontaneity as the source of special trustworthiness. This quality of spontaneity characterizes to some degree nearly all the types of statements which have been labeled *res gestae*.

Commentators and courts have criticized use of the phrase *res gestae*. Its vagueness and imprecision are apparent. Moreover, traditional limitations on the doctrine, such as the requirement that it be used only in regard to the principal litigated fact and the frequent insistence of concurrence (or at least a close relationship in time) between the words and the act or situation, have restricted its usefulness as a tool for avoiding unjustified application of the hearsay rule. Historically, however, the phrase served its purpose. Its very vagueness made it easier for courts to broaden its coverage and thus permit the admissibility of certain statements in new situations. However, the law has now reached a stage where expanding admissibility is better done in other ways. The ancient phrase can be jettisoned, with due acknowledgment that it served an era in the evolution of evidence law.

§ 269. Spontaneous Statements as Nonhearsay: Circumstantial Proof of a Fact in Issue

The types of spontaneous statements discussed in this chapter are often treated by courts as hearsay, and thus to be admissible, they must come within an exception to the general rule excluding hearsay. In many cases, however, this maneuver is unnecessary because the statements are not hearsay in the first place. As suggested in an earlier section,[1] hearsay is generally defined as assertive statements or conduct offered to prove what is asserted. But many so-called spontaneous statements are in fact not assertive statements or, if assertive, are not offered to prove the truth of the assertion. For example, it is clear that the statements, "I plan to spend the rest of my life here in New York" and "I have lost my affection for my husband" are hearsay when offered to prove the plan to remain in New York or the loss of affection. On the other hand, statements such as "I have been happier in New York than in any other place," when offered to show the speaker's intent to remain in New York, and "My husband is a detestable wretch," offered to show lack of affection for the husband, will or will not be classed as hearsay, depending upon the position taken with respect to the long debated question whether "implied assertions" are to be treated as hearsay.[2]

If the statement offered in evidence is not classed as hearsay, then no further consideration of the exceptions developed in this chapter is required. If, however, it is considered hearsay, then these exceptions may become pertinent to admissibility. Indeed, often the hearsay definition question is almost entirely academic, for statements offered to prove the declarant's state of mind are admissible under a rather broad exception even if hearsay.

§ 270. "Self–Serving" Aspects of Spontaneous Statements

The notion that parties' out-of-court statements could not be evidence in their favor because of the "self-serving" nature of the statements seems to have originated with the now universally discarded rule forbidding parties to testify. When this rule of disqualification for interest was abrogated by statute, any sweeping rule of inadmissibility regarding self-serving statements should have been regarded as abolished by implication.

The hearsay rule excludes all hearsay statements unless they fall within some exception to the rule. Thus, no specific rule is necessary to exclude self-serving out-of-court statements if not within a hearsay exception. If a statement with a self-serving aspect falls within an exception to the hearsay rule, the judgment underlying the exception that the assurances of trustworthiness outweigh the dangers

---

§ 269

1.   See supra § 246.

2.   See supra § 250.

inherent in hearsay should be taken as controlling, and the declaration should be admitted despite its self-serving aspects.

Historically, most courts agreed that this was the proper approach when the self-serving statement fell within one of the well-established exceptions, such as the exclusion of business records, excited utterances, and spontaneous statements of present bodily sensations or symptoms. However, with regard to the somewhat more recently developed exceptions, such as statements of present state of mind or emotion, less agreement existed. Some courts applied a purported general rule of exclusion of self-serving statements in this area. Others rejected any blanket rule of exclusion, although the self-serving aspects of the declaration were taken into account in applying a requirement that the statements must have been made under circumstances of apparent sincerity.

The Federal Rules covering hearsay exceptions for spontaneous statements, discussed in the remaining sections of this chapter, make no special provision for self-serving statements. What is clear, however, is that since spontaneity is the principal, and often the only, guarantee of trustworthiness for the exceptions in this chapter, its absence should result in exclusion of the statement. Circumstances indicating a lack of spontaneity, which may be related to the self-serving character of the statement, are accordingly extremely important to the determination of admissibility.

Although reference to spontaneity is helpful, the difficult issue remains: may courts properly exclude statements because of doubts about the sincerity of the declarant as evidenced by the self-serving nature of the statement? Judicial consideration of credibility is not theoretically prohibited in determining an issue of preliminary-fact-finding of the type involved in admitting or excluding hearsay. The chief problem with this approach under hearsay rules modeled on the Federal Rules is legislative intent. The rules give no authoriza-

tion to such considerations, and indeed the omission of a requirement found in the original Uniform Rule that the statement must not be made in "bad faith" indicates a contrary legislative intent. Moreover, in some other exceptions, the self-serving character of a statement, appearing in the form of motive to falsify, is specified as a ground for exclusion.[1]

A somewhat more comfortable place for the general exercise of such judicial judgment is under the balancing of probativity and prejudice authorized by Federal Rule 403, although this home is hardly secure since neither the rule itself nor its history gives explicit authorization. Nevertheless, in exercising discretion to exclude evidence where the danger of prejudice, confusing the issues, misleading the jury, or wasting time outweighs its probative value, circumstantial or direct evidence revealing a self-serving motive should logically have a place.[2] Rarely, however, should statements of substantial importance to the case be excluded even under this rule based upon judicial doubts about the declarant's motivation. Under the structure of the Federal Rules, judgments about credibility should generally be left to the jury rather than preempted by a judicial determination of inadmissibility. Leaving the issue to the jury is particularly appropriate when the credibility issue can be readily appreciated by the jury, as is generally the case when the reason to question credibility rests upon the declarant's self-serving motivation.

§ 271. Unexcited Statements of Present Sense Impressions

Although Wigmore's creative work did much to clarify the murky concept of *res gestae*, his analysis of spontaneous declarations may have led to one unfortunate restricting development of this exception. Professor Thayer, reviewing the *res gestae* cases in 1881, concluded that this was an exception based on the contemporaneousness of statements. He read the law as creating an exception for statements "made by those present when a thing

---

§ 270

1. E.g., accident reports, infra § 288, and police reports, infra § 296.

2. See generally supra § 185.

took place, made about it, and importing what is present at the very time * * *.''[1] Wigmore, however, saw as the basis for the spontaneous exclamation exception, not the contemporaneousness of the exclamation, but rather the nervous excitement produced by the exposure of the declarant to an exciting event.[2] As a result, the American law of spontaneous statements shifted in its emphasis from what Thayer had observed to an exception based on the requirement of an exciting event and the resulting stifling of the declarant's reflective faculties. As Professor Morgan noted, this shift was unfortunate. Given the danger of unreliability caused by the very emotional impact required for excited utterances, it makes little sense to admit them while excluding other out-of-court statements that may have equal assurances of reliability and lack the inherent defects of excited utterances.

Under Morgan's leadership, arguments were made for restoring Thayer's view of the law by recognizing another exception to the hearsay rule for statements concerning nonexciting events that the declarant was observing while making the declaration. Although these statements lack whatever assurance of reliability is produced by the effect of an exciting event, other factors offer safeguards. First, since the report concerns observations being made at the time of the statement, possible errors caused by a defect of the declarant's memory are absent. Second, a requirement that the statement be made contemporaneously with the observation means that little or no time is available for calculated misstatement. Third, the statement will usually have been made to a third person (the witness who subsequently testifies to it), who was also present at the time and scene of the observation. Thus, in most cases, the witness will have observed the situation and thus can provide a check on the accuracy of the declarant's statement and furnish corroboration. Moreover, since the declarant will often be available for cross-exami-

nation, his or her credibility will be subject to substantial verification before the trier of fact.

The courts generally did not rush to the support of the proposed exception for unexcited statements of present sense impressions. A considerable number continued to admit contemporaneous statements under *res gestae* language without emphasis on the presence or absence of an exciting event. In a large proportion of these decisions, an arguably exciting event was present. However, cases recognizing the exception for unexcited statements of present sense impressions began to emerge. The case most commonly cited to illustrate judicial recognition of the exception is Houston Oxygen Co. v. Davis.[3] Although an apparently exciting event transpired, the opinion disclaimed reliance upon it and instead expressly based its decision upon the exception for unexcited declarations of present sense impressions. A more compelling case on its facts, decided in the same year, is Tampa Electric Co. v. Getrost.[4] Judicial acceptance gradually gained momentum. The relative infrequence of such cases results from the fact that unexciting events do not often give rise to statements that later become relevant in litigation.

Instead, the rulemaking process provided the principal impetus for recognition of the hearsay exception for unexcited statements of present sense impressions. The Model Code of Evidence and the original Uniform Rules included such an exception. Federal Rule 803(1) provides a hearsay exception, without regard to the availability of the declarant, for ''a statement describing or explaining an event or condition made while the declarant was perceiving the event or condition, or immediately thereafter.''

Like all hearsay exceptions and exclusions other than admissions,[5] present sense impressions and excited utterances require that the declarant have firsthand knowledge, which can sometimes be proved entirely by the statement. These two exceptions otherwise differ in a number of important respects. First, no ex-

---

§ 271

1. Thayer, Bedingfield's Case—Declarations as a Part of the Res Gesta, 15 Am.L.Rev. 1, 83 (1881).

2. 6 Wigmore, Evidence § 1747 (Chadbourn rev. 1976).

3. 161 S.W.2d 474 (Tex.1942).

4. 10 So.2d 83 (Fla.1942).

5. See supra § 255.

citing event or condition is required for present sense impressions. Second, while excited utterances "relating to"[6] the startling event or condition are admissible, present sense impressions are limited to "describing or explaining" the event or condition perceived. Tighter correspondence between observation and statement is appropriate given the theory underlying the present sense impression exception. Although fabrication and forgetfulness are reduced by the absence of time lapse between perception and utterance, the lack of a startling event makes the assumption of spontaneity difficult to maintain unless the statements directly pertain to perception. Third, although the time within which an excited utterance may be made is measured by the duration of the stress caused by the exciting event,[7] the present sense impression statement may be made only while the declarant was actually "perceiving" the event or "immediately thereafter." This shortened period is also consistent with the weaker guarantee of trustworthiness of the present sense impression. While principle might seem to call for a limitation to exact contemporaneity, some allowance must be made for the time needed for translating observation into speech. Thus, the appropriate inquiry is whether sufficient time elapsed to have permitted reflective thought.

Some commentators have suggested that corroboration by an "equally percipient" witness should be a further requirement for admitting statements of present sense impression into evidence. The proposal represents a significant departure from the general pattern of exceptions to the hearsay rule. The only instance in which a requirement of corroboration is found is where a statement against penal interest by a third person—a third-party confession—is offered to exculpate an accused person. There, the common law had a firmly established position against admission. In order to increase the acceptability of a change of that position, the Advisory Committee incorporated into Federal Rule 804(b)(3) a requirement that the hearsay statement must

be corroborated.[8] The present sense impression exception presents no such need. Its underlying rationale offers sufficient assurances of reliability without the additional requirement of corroboration, and the Federal Rule and most courts have not required it.

The limitation of the exception in terms of time and subject matter does usually insure that the witness who reports the making of the statement will have perceived the event or at least observed circumstances strongly suggesting it. This aspect is certainly an added assurance of accuracy, but a general justification for admission is not the same as a requirement. The matter is better left for consideration by the finder of fact as going to weight and sufficiency rather than becoming a complicating admissibility requirement.

§ 272. Excited Utterances

While historically often lumped together with the amalgam of concepts under the term *res gestae*,[1] an exception to the hearsay rule for statements made under the influence of a startling event is now universally recognized. Formulations of the exception differ, but all agree on two basic requirements. First, there must be an occurrence or event sufficiently startling to render inoperative the normal reflective thought processes of the observer. Second, the statement of the declarant must have been a spontaneous reaction to the occurrence or event and not the result of reflective thought. These two elements, which define the essence of the exception, together with a third requirement that the statement "relate to" the event, discussed later, determine admissibility.

The rationale for the exception lies in the special reliability that is furnished when excitement suspends the declarant's powers of reflection and fabrication. This factor also serves to justify dispensing with any requirement that the declarant be unavailable because it suggests that testimony on the stand,

---

6. See infra § 272.

7. See infra § 272.

8. See infra § 318.

1. See supra § 268.

given at a time when the powers of reflection and fabrication are operative, is no more (and perhaps less) reliable than the out-of-court statement.

The entire basis for the exception is, of course, subject to question. While psychologists would probably concede that excitement minimizes the possibility of reflective self-interest influencing the declarant's statements, they have questioned whether this might be outweighed by the distorting effect of shock and excitement upon the declarant's observation and judgement. Despite these questions concerning its justification, the exception is well established.

The sufficiency of the event or occurrence as an exciting event is usually easily resolved. Physical violence, though often present, is not required. An automobile accident, pain or an injury, an attack by a dog, a fight, seeing a photograph in a newspaper, and a wide range of other events may qualify. The courts look primarily to the effect upon the declarant, and if satisfied that the event was such as to cause adequate excitement, the inquiry is ended.

A somewhat more serious issue is raised by the occasional requirement of proving the exciting event by some proof in addition to the statement itself, which certainly can be considered.[2] Under generally prevailing practice, the statement itself is considered sufficient proof of the exciting event, and therefore the statement is admissible despite absence of other proof that an exciting event occurred. Some courts, however, have taken the position that an excited utterance is admissible only if other proof is presented which supports a finding of fact that the exciting event did occur. The issue has not yet been resolved under the Federal Rules. Fortunately, only a very few cases need actually confront this knotty theoretical problem if the courts view what constitutes independent evidence broadly, as they should where the circumstances and content of the statement indicate trustworthiness.

The question most frequently raised when a purported excited utterance is offered involves the second requirement. In all cases, the ultimate question is whether the statement was the result of reflective thought or whether it was rather a spontaneous reaction to the exciting event. Initially, it is necessary that the declarant be affected by the exciting event. The declarant need not actually be involved in the event; an excited utterance by a bystander is admissible. However, if the identity of the bystander-declarant is undisclosed, the courts have been reluctant to admit such statements, principally because of uncertainty that foundational requirements, including the impact of the event on the declarant, have been satisfied.

Probably the most important of the many factors entering into this determination is the temporal element. If the statement occurs while the exciting event is still in progress, courts have little difficulty finding that the excitement prompted the statement. But as the time between the event and the statement increases, courts become more reluctant to find the statement an excited utterance. However, passage of time viewed in isolation is not an entirely accurate indicator of admissibility. For example, while courts have held statements made twelve or more hours after a physical beating to be the product of the excitement caused by the beating, other courts have held statements made within minutes of the event not admissible.

A useful rule of thumb is that where the time interval between the event and the statement is long enough to permit reflective thought, the statement will be excluded in the absence of some proof that the declarant did not in fact engage in a reflective thought process. Testimony that the declarant still appeared "nervous" or "distraught" and that there was a reasonable basis for continuing emotional upset will often suffice. The nature of the exciting event and the declarant's concern with it are obviously relevant. Thus, a statement made by the victim's wife one hour after a traffic accident was held admissible where the husband was still in the emergency room and his wife was still concerned about his condition.

---

2. See supra § 53.

Other factors may indicate the opposite conclusion. Although not grounds for automatic exclusion, evidence that the statement was made in response to an inquiry or was self-serving is an indication that the statement was the result of reflective thought. Where the time interval permitted such thought, those factors might swing the balance in favor of exclusion. Proof that the declarant performed tasks requiring relatively careful thought between the event and the statement provides strong evidence that the effect of the exciting event had subsided. Because of the wide variety of factual situations, appellate courts have recognized substantial discretion in trial courts to determine whether a declarant was still under the influence of an exciting event at the time of an offered statement.

Whether the excited utterance must concern the exciting event and the strictness of the necessary relationship between the exciting event and the content of the statement was the subject of historical disagreement. Murphy Auto Parts Co. v. Ball[3] set out one of the major positions in this debate, arguing that a requirement that the statement "explain or illuminate" the event was, if "mechanically and narrowly construed," a "spurious element." Instead, failure to describe the exciting event should be a factor in evaluating the spontaneity of the statement. Under that test, the statement following an accident of the driver that he had to call on a customer and was in a hurry to get home, which went to the issue of agency, was admissible.

Federal Rule 803(2) takes a different approach. The rule *requires* a connection between the event and the content of the statement, but it defines that connection broadly as "relating to" the event. This terminology is intended to extend beyond merely a description or an explanation of the event. The courts have been quite liberal in applying this requirement. The formulation used by Rule 803(2) has the advantage of simplicity while at the same time preserving the trustworthiness gained by requiring a relationship between the exciting event or condition and the resulting statement. It also permits clarification of the difference in theory between excited utterances and statements of present sense impressions, discussed in the preceding section.

Another major issue frequently encountered with excited utterances is whether the declarant meets the tests of competency for a witness. In a modified manner, the witness is required to have firsthand knowledge.[4] Direct proof of observation is not necessary; if the circumstances appear consistent with opportunity by the declarant, the requirement is met. If there is doubt, the question should be for the jury.[5] Especially in cases where the declaration is of low probative value, however, the statement is usually held inadmissible if there is no reasonable suggestion that the declarant had an opportunity to observe.

On the theory that there is a countervailing assurance of reliability in the excitement of the event, the other aspects of competency are not applied. Thus, an excited utterance is admissible despite the fact that the declarant was a child and would have been incompetent as a witness for that reason, or the declarant was incompetent by virtue of mental illness.

Courts have occasionally argued that an excited utterance must not be an opinion. Such a blanket limitation is unjustified in view of the nature and present standing of the opinion rule.[6] Where the declarant is an in-court witness, requiring testimony in concrete terms rather than conclusory generalizations is appropriate. But in everyday life, people often talk in conclusory terms, and when these statements are later offered in evidence, the declarant's words obviously cannot be changed to more specific language. Here, as elsewhere, the opinion rule should be applied sparingly, if at all, to out-of-court speech. Nevertheless, courts have sometimes excluded excited utterances on the grounds that they violate the opinion rule, especially in situations in which the declarants' statements place blame on themselves or others. Despite possible danger

---

3. 249 F.2d 508, 511–12 (D.C.Cir.1957).

4. See supra § 10.

5. See supra §§ 53, 58.

6. See supra § 18.

that these opinions may be given exaggerated weight by a jury, the need for knowledge of the facts usually outweighs this danger, and the better view admits excited statements of opinion.

§ 272.1   Excited Utterances and Other Hearsay Exceptions in Sexual Abuse Cases

Rape cases and other sexual offenses, particularly those involving minors, raise a number of difficult hearsay issues. Several different exceptions may be involved, including statements for the purpose of medical diagnosis and the catchall exception, which are treated elsewhere.[1] The application of the excited utterance exception and several new specific exceptions developed to deal with issues involved with the prosecution of offenses against children are examined here.

Before moving into modern developments, one historical artifact should be noted. Historically, out-of-court statements that a rape victim made a complaint were admissible to corroborate the assault. In terms of a time requirement, the complaint must have been made without a delay that was either unexplained or inconsistent with the occurrence of the offense, which is generally less demanding than would imposed under a typical excited utterance analysis. The theory of admissibility was that the statement rebuts an inference that, because the victim did not immediately complain, no crime had in fact occurred. Accordingly, if the victim did not testify, evidence of the complaint was not admissible, and only the fact that a complaint was made could be admitted. Some jurisdictions continue to recognize a role for this exception.

Moving to modern practice, particularly where children are the victims of sexual offenses, many courts have liberally interpreted the allowable period of time between the exciting event and the child's description of it. The theory of these courts is that the general psychological characteristics of children typically extend the period that is free of the dangers of conscious fabrication. In addition, a growing number of states have enacted specific hearsay exceptions to cover the situations where children are involved as witnesses or victims. One of the advantages of this latter approach is that it reduces the pressure to distort the traditional time limitations of the excited utterance exception to deal with this difficult set of cases.

The new exception is illustrated by the Washington statute, which became a model for many other states. It admits a child's extrajudicial statement if (1) the court finds after a hearing that the time, content, and circumstances of the statement provide sufficient indicia of reliability, and (2) the child either testifies at the proceeding or is unavailable as a witness and, if unavailable, corroborative evidence is produced to support trustworthiness.

States have also undertaken a major effort to ameliorate the trauma associated with the judicial process by changing the mechanics of the trial in child abuse and related cases. Part of this process has involved the development of new methods of receiving testimony, some of which include the development of new hearsay exceptions. Drawing on a broad base of statutory and other material, the drafters of the Uniform Rules added Rule 807. The rule exempts from the ban of the hearsay rule the audio-visually recorded statement of a child victim or witness describing an act of sexual abuse or physical violence if the court finds that (1) the minor will suffer severe emotional or psychological stress if required to testify in open court; (2) the time, content, and circumstances of the statement provide sufficient circumstantial guarantees of trustworthiness; and (3) other enumerated requirements are followed regarding the conduct of the recording process. Presence of judge, accused, or counsel is not required or apparently contemplated; any person may conduct the interview. However, before the admission of a statement under the rule, the court, on defendant's request, shall provide for further questioning of the minor in a manner as the court may direct. Finally, the rule provides that admission of a

---

§ 272.1

1. See infra §§ 277–78 & 324.

statement under these provisions does not preclude the court from permitting any party to call the child as a witness if the interests of justice require it.

Another provision of Uniform Rule 807 permits the taking of testimony by either deposition recorded by audio-visual means or by contemporaneous examination communicated to the courtroom by closed-circuit television if the court concludes the child will suffer severe emotional or psychological harm if required to testify in open court. The court may order the testimony to be taken outside the presence of any party, including the defendant, if it finds such presence would contribute to the likelihood of harm to the child. The court must locate any party excluded so that he or she can see and hear the testimony of the child and can consult with counsel but not be seen by the child.

These provisions raise constitutional issues involving the Confrontation Clause. The most common issue—whether the child witness may be shielded from facing the defendant while testifying is constitutionally resolved if based upon an individualized finding that the child will suffer trauma otherwise.[2] A second issue is presented by a version of the Uniform Rules that permits the creation and introduction of a recording of the child's statement as part of the state's case, which is made without the opportunity for contemporaneous cross-examination by defense counsel. Although one court upheld such a statute, it has been found unconstitutional by several others. Further refinements may be expected as courts and legislatures seek to accommodate the special needs for preservation and presentation of the testimony of child victims or witnesses and the constitutional commands of Due Process and the Confrontation Clause.

§ 273. Statements of Physical or Mental Condition: (a) Statements of Bodily Feelings, Symptoms, and Condition

Statements of the declarant's present bodily condition and symptoms, including pain and other feelings, offered to prove the truth of the statements, have been generally recognized as an exception to the hearsay rule.

Special reliability is provided by the spontaneous quality of the declarations, assured by the requirement that the declaration purport to describe a condition presently existing at the time of the statement. This assurance of reliability is not always effective in that some of these statements describing present symptoms are almost certainly calculated misstatements. Nevertheless, a sufficiently large percentage are undoubtedly spontaneous to justify the exception.

Being spontaneous, the hearsay statements are considered of greater probative value than the present testimony of the declarant. Moreover, the alternative of insisting upon the in-court testimony of the declarant, when available, promises little improvement since cross-examination and other methods of exposing deliberate misrepresentation are relatively ineffective. Together, these factors of trustworthiness and necessity not only provide a basis for admitting statements of this type but also justify dispensing with any requirement of unavailability of the declarant.

Despite earlier indications to the contrary, declarations of present bodily condition do not have to be made to a physician in order to satisfy the present exception. Any person hearing the statement may testify to it. The exception is, however, limited to descriptions of present condition and therefore excludes description of past pain or symptoms, as well as accounts of the events furnishing the cause of the condition.

Federal Rule 803(3) defines a hearsay exception, without regard to the unavailability of the declarant, for "a statement of the declarant's then existing * * * physical condition (such as * * * pain and bodily health) * * *." Not only does the rule mandate that the statement must be spontaneous by its requirement that the statement describe a "then existing" physical condition, but the Advisory Committee's Note indicates that the rule is a specialized application of the broader rule recognizing a hearsay exception for statements describing a present sense impression, the cornerstone of which is spontaneity. If cir-

---

2. Maryland v. Craig, 497 U.S. 837 (1990).

cumstances demonstrate a lack of spontaneity, exclusion should follow.

§ 274. Statements of Physical or Mental Condition: (b) Statements of Present Mental or Emotional State to Show a State of Mind or Emotion in Issue

The substantive law often makes legal rights and liabilities hinge upon the existence of a particular state of mind or feeling. Thus, such matters as the intent to steal or kill, or the intent to have a certain paper take effect as a deed or will, or the maintenance or transfer of the affections of a spouse may come into issue in litigation. When this is so, the mental or emotional state of the person becomes an ultimate object of inquiry. It is not introduced as evidence from which the person's earlier or later conduct may be inferred but as an operative fact upon which a cause of action or defense depends. While a state of mind may be proved by the person's actions, the statements of the person are often a primary source of evidence.

In many instances, statements used for this purpose are not assertive of the declarant's present state of mind and are therefore not hearsay.[1] Courts, however, have tended to lump together arguably hearsay statements asserting the declarant's state of mind with those arguably nonhearsay that tend to prove state of mind circumstantially, applying a general exception to the hearsay rule and ignoring the possibility that many of these statements could be treated as nonhearsay.

As with statements of bodily condition, the special assurance of reliability for statements of present state of mind rests upon their spontaneity and resulting probable sincerity.[2] The guarantee of reliability is assured principally by the requirement that the statements must relate to a condition of mind or emotion existing at the time of the statement. In addition, some formulations of the exception require that the statement must have been made under circumstances indicating apparent sincerity, although Federal Rule 803(3) imposes no such explicit condition.[3]

Such statements are also admitted under a version of the same necessity argument that supports most hearsay exceptions. Often no better way exists to prove a relevant mental or physical condition than through the statements of the individual whose condition is at issue. Even with cross-examination, the alternative of using the declarant's testimony is not likely to be a better, and perhaps an inferior, manner of proof. If the declarant were called to testify, "his own memory of his state of mind at a former time is no more likely to be clear and true than a bystander's recollection of what he then said."[4] As a result, unavailability of declarant is not required.

Common examples of statements used to prove mental state at the time of the statement include: statements of intent to make a certain place the declarant's home offered to establish domicile, statements expressive of mental suffering to prove that element of damages, statements by customers regarding anger to prove loss of good will, statements of patients regarding lack of knowledge of risk of taking medication in malpractice suit, statements of willingness to allow one to use the declarant's automobile offered to prove that the car was used with the owner's consent, statements accompanying a transfer of property showing intent, or lack of intent, to defraud creditors, statements of ill will to show malice or the required state of mind in criminal cases, and statements showing fear.

Although the statement must describe a state of mind or feeling existing at the time of the statement, the evidentiary effect of the statement is broadened by the notion of the continuity in time of states of mind. For example, if a declarant asserts on Tuesday a then-existing intention to go on a business trip the next day, this will be evidence not only of the intention at the time of the statement, but also of the same purpose the next day when

---

§ 274

1. See supra § 246.
2. See supra § 273.

3. See generally supra § 270.

4. Mutual Life Ins. Co. v. Hillmon, 145 U.S. 285, 295 (1892).

the declarant is on the road. Continuity may also look backwards. Thus, when there is evidence that a will has been mutilated by the maker, the declarant's subsequent statements of a purpose inconsistent with the will are received to show his or her intent to revoke it at the time it was mutilated. Similarly, whether payment of money or a conveyance was intended by the donor as a gift may be shown by statements of intent existing at the time of the statement whether made before, at the time of, or after the act of transfer. The duration of states of mind or emotion varies with the particular attitudes or feelings at issue and with the cause, and the court may require some reasonable indication that in light of all the circumstances, including the proximity in time, the state of mind was the same at the material time. Whether a state of mind continues is a decision for the trial judge.[5]

Declarations such as those involved here frequently include assertions other than state of mind. For example, the victim may assert that the defendant's acts caused the state of mind. The truth of those assertions may coincide with other issues in the case, as where the defendant is charged with acts similar to those described. In such circumstances, the normal practice is to admit the statement and direct the jury to consider it only as proof of the state of mind and to disregard it as evidence of the other issues.[6] Compliance with this instruction is probably beyond the jury's ability and almost certainly beyond their willingness. Where substantial evidence has been admitted on the other act, probably little harm results. However, where the mental state is provable by other available evidence and the danger of harm from improper use by the jury of the offered declarations is substantial, the trial judge should exclude the statements or prohibit the witness from giving the reasons for the state of mind.

Federal Rule 803(3) covers statements of "the declarant's then existing state of mind, emotion, sensation * * * (such as intent, plan,

motive, design, mental feeling * * *)." The rule is generally consistent with the hearsay exception as developed by the courts at common law.

Insanity. A main source of proof of mental competency or incompetency is the conduct of the person in question, showing normal and abnormal response to the circumstances of his or her environment. By this test, every act of the subject's life, within reasonable limits of time, would be relevant to the inquiry. Whether the conduct is verbal or nonverbal, assertive or nonassertive, is inconsequential. It is offered as a response to environment, not to prove anything that may be asserted, and is accordingly not hearsay.[7] Thus, whether declarant says "I am King Henry the Eighth" or "I believe that I am King Henry the Eighth" is insignificant. Both are offered as evidence of irrationality, and niceties of form should not determine admissibility. If, nevertheless, it is argued that abnormal conduct can be simulated, thereby becoming assertive and therefore hearsay, a short answer is that in that event the evidence would be admissible under the present hearsay exception. Such inquiries are largely superfluous, and courts should spend little effort determining whether the statement is nonhearsay or is admissible hearsay evidence showing an abnormal state of mind.

§ 275. Statements of Physical or Mental Condition: (c) Statements of Intention Offered to Show Subsequent Acts of Declarant

As the previous sections made clear, statements of mental state are generally admissible to prove the declarant's state of mind when that state of mind is at issue. But the probative value of a state of mind obviously may go beyond the state of mind itself. Where a state of mind would tend to prove subsequent conduct, can the two inferential processes be linked together, with the declarations of state of mind being admitted as proof of the con-

---

5. See generally supra § 53.

6. The legitimacy of inferring from state of mind the happening of the act claimed to have caused the state of mind is discussed in infra § 276.

7. See supra §§ 246, 250.

duct? For example, can the declarant's statements indicating an intent to kill be admitted to prove not only intent but also that the declarant did in fact subsequently commit the murder? The answer involves concerns of both hearsay and relevancy.

These issues are somewhat more difficult than the matter of admissibility of statements to show only the state of mind. The special reliability of the statements is less in the present situation since it is significantly less likely that a declared intention will be carried out than it is that a declared state of mind is actually held. A statement of intention to kill another is much stronger proof of malice toward the victim at the time of the statement (or subsequently) than it is proof that the declarant committed the murder. Nevertheless, a person who expresses an intent to kill is undeniably more likely to have done so than a person not shown to have had that intent. The accepted standard of relevancy, i.e., more probable than without the evidence,[1] is easily met.

Statements of state of mind are now recognized as admissible to prove subsequent conduct. Thus, out-of-court statements that tend to prove a plan, design, or intention of the declarant may be received, subject to the usual limitations as to remoteness in time and perhaps apparent sincerity[2] common to all statements of mental state, to prove that the plan, design, or intention of the declarant was carried out by the declarant.

The leading case is Mutual Life Insurance Co. v. Hillmon,[3] which concerned a suit on life insurance policies by the wife of the insured, Hillmon. The principal issue was whether Hillmon had in fact died; a body had been found at Crooked Creek, Kansas, and the parties disputed whether the body was that of Hillmon. Plaintiff's theory was that Hillmon left Wichita, Kansas about March 5, 1879 with a man named Brown and that on the night of March 18, 1879, while Hillmon and Brown were camped at Crooked Creek, Hillmon was killed by the accidental discharge of a gun. The de-

fendants, on the other hand, maintained that another individual named Walters had accompanied Hillmon and that the body found at Crooked Creek was Walters'.

Defendants offered testimony that on or about March 5, 1879 Walters wrote to his sister that "I expect to leave Wichita on or about March 5, with a certain Mr. Hillmon."[4] An objection to this and similar evidence was sustained. The United States Supreme Court reversed on the ground that the evidence of the letters should have been admitted:

> The letters * * * were competent, not as narratives of facts communicated to the writer by others, nor yet as proof that he actually went away from Wichita, but as evidence that, shortly before the time when other evidence tended to show that he went away, he had the intention of going, and of going with Hillmon, which made it more probable both that he did go and that he went with Hillmon, than if there had been no proof of such intention.[5]

Although Federal Rule 803(3) does not explicitly address the question of admitting intent for the purpose of proving the doing of the intended act, the Advisory Committee stated that it was to continue. Statements for this purpose are currently routinely admitted. However, a number of subsidiary problems remain to be considered under the rule and the common law decisions.

The suggestion has been made that unavailability of the declarant should be a requirement. In fact, in virtually all the cases admitting the statements of intent as proof of the doing of the intended act, the declarant has been unavailable, and it may well be that the resulting need for the evidence influenced the courts in the direction of admissibility. However, neither the decisions nor the Federal Rule require unavailability.

---

§ 275

1. See supra § 185.
2. See supra § 274.

3. 145 U.S. 285 (1892).
4. Id. at 288.
5. Id. at 295–296.

In a somewhat similar vein, in virtually all the cases admitting the evidence the intent stated was quite concrete, e.g., to do a specific act at a specific time. Again, this quality of specificity is not generally stated as a requirement, but probative value is undeniably enhanced by its presence. Its absence not only detracts from probative value but, in its vague generality, may tend to stray into areas of character evidence that is inadmissible against a criminal defendant.

The danger of unreliability is greatly increased when the action sought to be proved is not one that the declarant could have performed alone, but rather is one that required the cooperation of another person. If completion of a plan or design requires not only the continued inclination and ability of the declarant to complete it, but also the inclination and ability of someone else, arguably the likelihood that the design or plan was completed is substantially less. In *Hillmon* itself, Walters' successful completion of his plan to leave Wichita depended upon the continued willingness of Hillmon to have Walters as a companion and upon Hillmon's willingness and ability to leave at the time planned. However, all parties agreed that Hillmon did in fact go to Crooked Creek, and the Supreme Court had no occasion to consider this aspect of the case.

The issue is made more difficult when the cooperative actions between the declarant and another are themselves at issue. For example, in the homicide prosecution of Frank, a witness testifies that on the morning of the killing the victim said, "I am going out with Frank tonight." While this tends to prove the victim's acts, it also tends to prove that the defendant "went out" with the victim, a fact very much in issue. Despite some objection, courts have admitted these statements. The result is that the statement is used as proof of the other person's intent and as proof that this intent was achieved. The additional dangers present here have, however, prompted some courts to impose additional restrictions or requirements. These include: instructing the jury to consider the evidence only to prove the conduct of the declarant, requiring independent evidence to establish the defendant's con-

duct, permitting the declaration to be used only to explain the declarant's intent, and limiting use of such statements to cases where the declarant is dead or unavailable and to situations where both the statement of intent is shown to be serious and the event is realistically likely to be achieved.

Acceptance of the use of statements of state of mind to prove subsequent conduct and recognition of occasions for its application by the courts have differed among types of situations. In will cases, for example, previous declarations of intention are received as evidence of the decedent's later conduct when those acts are at issue. Such statements are admissible on issues of forgery, alteration, contents of a will, and whether acts of revocation were done by the testator. Despite early decisions to the contrary, or decisions greatly restricting their use, statements of intent to commit suicide have been admitted when offered by the accused in homicide cases to prove that the victim took his or her own life and similarly in insurance cases to show suicide. Historically, there has been some greater resistance, however, to admitting threats of a third person to commit the act with which the accused is charged as evidence that the act was committed by the third person and therefore not by the accused. Greater liberality should follow under the Federal Rules since Rule 803(3) provides no basis to restrict admission of threats by others, and the Federal Rules' flexible approach to relevancy should provide fewer reasons to treat this as a special class of evidence.

Homicide and assault cases present other special problems. If the accused asserts self-defense and knows of threats of the victim against the accused, these threats are admissible to prove the accused's apprehension of danger and its reasonableness. When used for this purpose, the statements of the victim are not hearsay. But uncommunicated threats pose a more serious problem. They are only admissible to show the victim's intention to attack the accused and further that the victim carried out this intention, thus committing the first act of aggression in the fatal altercation. Fear that juries will abuse the evidence has led some courts to admit proof of uncommunicated threats only under qualification. No qualification appears in the Federal Rule 803(3), and under its influence, changes in the qualifications imposed can be anticipated. However, even under the Federal Rule, courts can certainly impose reasonable restrictions on admissibility of such statements to reduce dangers of confusion and misleading under relevancy concerns, which provide the principal focus for determining admissibility of these statements rather than the hearsay doctrine.

The matter of the admissibility of declarations of state of mind to prove subsequent conduct is a far different question from that of the sufficiency of these statements, standing alone, to support a finding that the conduct occurred. In the typical case, it is reasonable to hold that the declarations are themselves insufficient to support the finding and therefore that statements of intention must be admitted in corroboration of other evidence to show the acts.

§ 276. Statements of Physical or Mental Condition: (d) Statements of State of Mind to Show Memory or Belief as Proof of Previous Happenings

As was seen in the preceding section, under the *Hillmon* doctrine, statements of intent to perform an act are admissible as proof that the act was in fact done. By contrast, a statement by the declarant that he or she had in fact done that act would be excluded under this exception to the hearsay rule. Thus Walters' statement that he intended to go to Crooked Creek is admissible, but a later statement by him that he had been to Crooked Creek would be excluded. As a matter of common experience, this result seems wrong. The first statement, which is admissible, appears inferior as evidence to the second, which would be excluded. While both statements involve the truthfulness of the declarant, the first statement involves the further risk that supervening events may prevent the stated intent from being accomplished. Minds are changed; tick-

ets are lost; popular sayings, literature, and experience are filled with plans that went awry. Accordingly, the argument goes, if the inferior evidence of intent is admitted as proof that the act was done, the superior statement that the act was in fact done should certainly be admitted. In other words, hearsay statements of memory or belief should be admitted as proof that the matter remembered or believed did happen.

Forty years after *Hillmon,* in Shepard v. United States,[1] the Supreme Court dealt with an aspect of this argument. In *Shepard,* the trial court had admitted in a murder prosecution testimony that the victim, the wife of the physician-defendant, had stated to a nurse, "Dr. Shepard has poisoned me." Reversing, the Supreme Court rejected the argument that the statement was admissible as a declaration of state of mind:

> [*Hillmon*] marks the high water line beyond which courts have been unwilling to go. It has developed a substantial body of criticism and commentary. Declarations of intention, casting light upon the future, have been sharply distinguished from declarations of memory, pointing backwards to the past. There would be an end, or nearly that, to the rule against hearsay if the distinction were ignored.

> The testimony now questioned faced backward and not forward in its most obvious implications. What is even more important, it spoke to a past act by someone not the speaker.[2]

In more formal hearsay terms, forward-looking statements of intention are admitted while backward-looking statements of memory or belief are excluded because the former do not present the classic hearsay dangers of memory and narration. The weakness inherent in forward-looking statements—the uncertainty that the intention will be carried out—may lead to exclusion, but this is under the relevancy doctrine rather than hearsay analysis.

Nevertheless, after the decision in *Shepard,* the blanket exclusion of statements of

---

§ 276

1. 290 U.S. 96 (1933).

2. Id. at 105–106.

memory or belief to prove past events was the subject of some re-examination. From the blanket exclusion of statements of memory or belief to prove past events, the courts carved out an area of admissibility for statements by a testator made after the execution of an alleged will. Thus, the testator's statements that he or she has or has not made or revoked a will or made a will of a particular purport were excepted from the ban of the hearsay rule by a preponderance of the decisions. Impetus to recognize such an exception is furnished by the unavailability of the testator who best knew the facts and often was the only person with that knowledge. Special reliability is suggested by the undeniable firsthand knowledge and lack of motive to deceive, though the possibility may exist that the testator wished to deceive his or her relatives. Federal Rule 803(3) explicitly allows the introduction of a statement of memory or belief to prove the fact remembered or believed if it "relates to the execution, revocation, identification, or terms of declarant's will."

Various types of efforts have been made to permit broader admissibility of hearsay in this general area. A few statutes have allowed receipt of statements by deceased persons made in good faith and upon personal knowledge before the commencement of the action. The Model Code of Evidence went much further by allowing any hearsay statement by an unavailable declarant. The original Uniform Rules proposed a narrower exception. Although statements of "memory or belief to prove the fact remembered or believed" were generally excluded, statements were admissible if made by an unavailable declarant describing an event or condition recently perceived while the declarant's recollection was clear and made in good faith prior to the commencement of the action.

As proposed by the Supreme Court, the Federal Rules included an exception for recent perception with the added limitation that the statement must not have been made in response to the instigation of a person engaged in investigating, litigating, or settling a claim.

The entire provision was eliminated by Congress, but limited to civil cases, it is included in the Revised Uniform Rules. Either the Uniform Rule or the proposed federal rule has been adopted in a handful of states. In addition, California has created a new hearsay exception that admits statements regarding past threats made to unavailable declarants where the threat is recorded in writing or electronically or was reported to a police officer.

A recurring problem arises in connection with the admissibility of accusatory statements made before the act by the victims of homicide. If the statement is merely an expression of fear—i.e., "I am afraid of D"—no hearsay problem is involved, since the statement falls within the hearsay exception for statements of mental or emotional condition. This does not, however, resolve the question of admissibility. The victim's emotional state must relate to some legitimate issue in the case. For example, the victim's emotional state may permit the inference of some fact of consequence, such as lack of consent where the prosecution charges that the killing occurred during the commission of either a kidnapping or rape.

However, the most likely inference that jurors may draw from the existence of fear, and often the only logical inference that could be drawn, is that some conduct of the defendant, probably mistreatment or threats, occurred and caused the fear. The possibility of over-persuasion, the prejudicial character of the evidence, and the relative weakness and speculative nature of the inference, all argue against admissibility as a matter of relevance.[3] Moreover, even if the judgment is made that evidence of fear standing alone should be admitted, statements of fear are rarely stated pristinely. Instead, that state of mind usually assumes the form either of a statement by the victim that the accused has made threats, from which fear may be inferred, or perhaps more likely a statement of fear because of the defendant's threats. Not only does the evidence possess the weaknesses suggested above for expressions of fear standing alone, but in addition it seems unlikely that juries can resist

---

3. See supra § 185.

using the evidence for forbidden purposes in the presence of specific disclosure of misconduct of the defendant.

In either event, the cases have generally excluded the evidence. While the same pressing need for the evidence may be present as that which led to the development of the hearsay exception for dying declarations, the case for trustworthiness is much weaker, and need alone is not a sufficient basis for a hearsay exception. Exclusion is not universal, however,

4. See supra § 272 & infra Ch. 32.

for in some circumstances statements may be admissible under other hearsay exceptions, such as that for excited utterances or dying declarations.[4] Moreover, the decedent's fear may be relevant for other legitimate purposes beyond proof of the defendant's act or state of mind. Also, such statements are admissible where the defense claims self-defense, suicide, or accidental death because in each of those situations the decedent's fear helps to rebut aspects of the asserted defense.

Chapter 27

STATEMENTS FOR THE PURPOSE OF MEDICAL DIAGNOSIS OR TREATMENT

Table of Sections

---

§ 277. Statements of Bodily Feelings, Symptoms, and Condition: (a) Statements Made to Physicians Consulted for Treatment

Statements of a presently existing bodily condition made by a patient to a doctor consulted for treatment[1] have almost universally been admitted as evidence of the facts stated, and even courts that otherwise limited the admissibility of declarations of bodily condition have admitted statements made under these circumstances. Since statements made to physicians are usually made in response to questions, many are not spontaneous. Instead, their reliability is assured by the likelihood that the patient believes that the effectiveness of the treatment depends on the accuracy of the information provided to the doctor, which may be termed a "selfish treatment motivation."

As this exception developed, many courts extended it to include statements made by a patient to a physician concerning *past* symptoms because of the strong assurance of reliability. This expansion is generally sound, as patients are likely to recognize the importance to their treatment of accurate statements of past, as well as present, symptoms. Some courts continued, however, to admit the testimony only for the limited purpose of explaining the basis for the physician's conclusion rather than to prove the fact of the prior symptoms.[2]

A major issue involving the scope of the exception is the treatment of statements made to a physician concerning the cause or the external source of the condition to be treated. In some cases, the special assurance of reliability—the patient's belief that accuracy is essential to effective treatment—also applies to statements concerning the cause. Moreover, a physician who views cause as related to diagnosis and treatment might reasonably be expected to communicate this to the patient and perhaps take other steps to assure a reliable response. However, the result is different when statements as to causation enter the realm of establishing fault. Generally neither the patient nor the physician is likely to re-

---

§ 277

1. Statements made to nontreating physicians are discussed in infra § 278.

2. Bases for expert opinions are discussed in supra § 15.

gard them as related to diagnosis or treatment. In such cases, the statements lack any assurance of reliability based on the declarant's interest in proper treatment and should properly be excluded. "Thus a patient's statement that he was struck by an automobile would qualify, but not his statement that the car was driven through a red light."[3]

Federal Rule 803(4) provides a hearsay exception, regardless of availability of declarant, for

> [s]tatements made for purpose of medical diagnosis or treatment and describing medical history, or past or present symptoms, pain, or sensation, or the inception or general character of the cause or external source thereof insofar as reasonably pertinent to diagnosis or treatment.

The statement need not have been made to a physician; one made to a hospital attendant, ambulance driver, or member of the family may qualify if intended by the patient to secure treatment. Psychologists and social workers have been included within the exception. Nor does the rule require that the statement concern the declarant's condition, and statements by others, most often close family members, may be received if the relationship or the circumstances give appropriate assurances. The rule is broadly drawn as to subject matter, including medical history and descriptions of past and present symptoms, pain, and sensations. The test for admissibility is whether the subject matter of the statements is reasonably pertinent to diagnosis or treatment—an apparently objective standard. Descriptions of cause are similarly allowed if they are medically pertinent, but statements of fault are unlikely to qualify. A related use of the exception to establish the identity of the perpetrator in sexual assault cases is examined in the next section.

§ 278. Statements of Bodily Feelings, Symptoms, and Condition: (b) Statements Made to Physicians Consulted Only to Testify

Historically, many courts drew a sharp line between statements made to physicians consulted for treatment and those made to physicians consulted solely with the anticipation that the physician would testify for the declarant. Courts were hesitant to admit statements made to doctors consulted only for diagnosis because when the declarant does not anticipate that the effectiveness of treatment depends upon the accuracy of his or her statement, the traditional underlying rationale for the exception—a selfish treatment interest—does not exist. Indeed, if the declarant anticipates that enhancement of symptoms will aid in the subsequent litigation, an affirmative motive may exist to falsify or at least to exaggerate.

The precise nature of the restrictions upon statements made to doctors not consulted for treatment differed among the jurisdictions, although a very common pattern permitted the doctor to recite the statements of the declarant for the limited purpose of providing a basis for the doctor's medical opinion. The dubious propriety of these restrictions was probably responsible for the restrictive view taken by the courts as to what constituted consultation solely for purposes of obtaining testimony. An inquiry was made to determine whether there was any significant treatment motive; if this existed, an additional motive to obtain testimony was ignored.

The Federal Rule abandons these restrictions. The Advisory Committee concluded that permitting statements to be admitted as a basis for a medical expert's opinion but not for their truth was likely to be a distinction lost on juries and rejected the limitation. The general reliance upon "subjective" facts by the medical profession and the ability of its members to evaluate the accuracy of statements made to them is considered sufficient protection against contrived symptoms. Within the medical profession, the analysis of the rule appears to be that facts reliable enough to be relied on in reaching a diagnosis have sufficient trustworthiness to satisfy hearsay concerns.

---

3. Adv.Comm. Note, Fed.R.Evid. 803(4).

The result also has its practical dimension. Under prior practice, contrived evidence was avoided at too great a cost and in substantial departure from the realities of medical practice. Rule 803(4) eliminates any differences in the admissibility of statements made to testifying, as contrasted with treating, physicians. Here, as with statements made for treatment, the test for admissibility is whether the statement is medically pertinent to the diagnosis.

The changes in the hearsay exception for statements made for medical diagnosis or treatment have had their biggest impact in cases of child sexual abuse. In this area, a number of courts have admitted a broad range of statements by children, including statements identifying a particular individual as the perpetrator of the offense. This evidence is admitted under the rationale that such information is pertinent to treatment of the abused child. Statements have been received when made in a number of different situations and to a rather broad array of professionals, although some courts have developed limitations where non-physicians are involved. These uses of the expanded hearsay exception challenge the wisdom of its extension to cover statements made without any treatment purpose and may raise constitutional problems regarding the right of confrontation in criminal cases.[1]

§ 278

1. See supra § 253.

Chapter 28

RECORDS OF PAST RECOLLECTION

Table of Sections

§ 279. History and Theory of the Exception

By the middle 1600s it had become customary to permit a witness to refresh a failed memory by looking at a written memorandum and to testify from a then-revived memory.[1] Frequently, while examination of the writing did not revive memory, the witness recognized the writing as one that he or she had prepared and was willing to testify on the basis of the writing that the facts recited in it were true. By the 1700s this later procedure was also accepted as proper, although the theoretical difficulty of justifying the new practice was often avoided by labeling it with the somewhat ambiguous term of "refreshing recollection," which clearly was not strictly accurate. Beginning in the early 1800s, courts began to distinguish between the two situations and to recognize that the use of past recollection recorded was a far different matter from permitting the witness to testify from a memory refreshed by examining a writing.

As the rule permitting the introduction of past recollection recorded developed, it had four requirements: (1) the witness must have had firsthand knowledge of the event, (2) the written statement must be an original memo-randum made at or near the time of the event while the witness had a clear and accurate memory of it, (3) the witness must lack a present recollection of the event, and (4) the witness must vouch for the accuracy of the written memorandum.

With some refinements, this exception appears as Rule 803(5) of the Federal Rules of Evidence with no formal unavailability of the declarant specified. It reads as follows:

> A memorandum or record concerning a matter about which a witness once had knowledge but now has insufficient recollection to enable the witness to testify fully and accurately, shown to have been made or adopted by the witness when the matter was fresh in the witness' memory and to reflect that knowledge correctly. If admitted, the memorandum or record may be read into evidence but may not itself be received as an exhibit unless offered by an adverse party.

The usefulness of the hearsay exception is apparent from the huge variety of items the courts have admitted into evidence under its sponsorship.

---

§ 279

1. See supra § 9.

Whether recorded recollection should be classed as a hearsay exception or as not hearsay is debatable since the reliability of the assertions rests upon the veracity of a witness who is present and testifying.[2] Which way the argument is decided seems not to have affected the requirements for admissibility, however, and it is convenient to treat recorded recollection as a hearsay exception since at least some failure of memory is required.

Should the writing be admitted into evidence and be allowed to be taken to the jury room? Some difference of opinion is apparent. However, the testimonial character of the writing makes a strong argument against the practice, just as depositions are generally not given to the jury.[3] Federal Rule 803(5) solves the problem by resort to the ancient practice of reading the writing into evidence but not admitting it as an exhibit unless offered by the adverse party.

§ 280. Firsthand Knowledge

The usual requirement of firsthand knowledge[1] that applies to witnesses and hearsay declarants is also enforced in regard to past recollection recorded. Thus, where an inventory was offered and the witness produced to lay the necessary foundation testified that it had been made only partly from his own inspection and partly from information provided by an assistant, the inventory was inadmissible.

§ 281. Record Made While the Witness' Memory Was Clear

Despite some cases suggesting the contrary, the exception as generally stated requires that there be a written formulation of the memory. Federal Rule 803(5) uses the somewhat broader terms "memorandum or record," which, for example, a videotape or audio recording would satisfy. Moreover, the original must be produced or accounted for as is generally required when the contents of

documents are sought to be proved.[1] However, the record need not have been prepared by the witness personally if the witness read and adopted it. Multiple-participant situations are considered further in § 283.

The record must have been prepared or recognized as correct at a time close enough to the event to ensure accuracy. Some opinions use the older strict formulation that requires the writing to have been either made or recognized as correct "at or near the time" of the events recorded. This requirement finds some support in psychological research suggesting that a rapid rate of memory loss occurs within the first two or three days following the observation of an event. However, the trend is toward accepting the formulation favored by Wigmore, which would require only that the writing be made or recognized at a time when the events were fairly fresh in the mind of the witness. The formula of Federal Rule 803(5) is "when the matter was fresh in the witness' memory." The cases vary as to the length of time lapse allowable, and while the period of time between the event and the making of the memorandum or record is a critically important factor, a mechanical approach, looking only to the length of time that has passed rather than focusing on indications that the memory remains fresh, should not be employed.

§ 282. Impairment of Recollection

The traditional formulation of the rule requires that the witness who made or recognized it as correct must testify that he or she lacks any present memory of the event and therefore is unable to testify concerning it. A few courts took a more relaxed position, suggesting that, although the witness retain more present recollection than allowed under the traditional requirement, the prior recorded statement was more complete and more reliable than testimony based upon the witness'

---

2. Compare the treatment of prior inconsistent statements of a witness in supra § 251 and § 252 (Confrontation Clause issues).

3. See supra § 217.

§ 280

1. See supra § 10.

§ 281

1. See generally supra Ch. 23.

memory. An occasional case has supported complete abandonment of the requirement, arguing that failure of memory adds nothing to the credibility of the statement.

Clouded by the passage of time, present recollection is often less accurate than a statement made at a time when recollection was fresh and clear. However, complete abandonment of the requirement that the witness must have some memory impairment would likely encourage the use of statements carefully prepared for litigation under the supervision of claims adjusters or attorneys or under other circumstances casting significant doubt upon the reliability of the statement.

These competing concerns are accommodated by phrasing the requirement not in absolute terms but as a lack of sufficient present recollection to enable the witness to testify fully and accurately. This standard of the Federal Rule has gained increasing judicial adherents in preference to a total elimination of any requirement of impaired memory.

Is the requirement of "insufficient recollection to enable the witness to testify fully and accurately" satisfied when an apparently reluctant witness seeks to avoid testifying to a particular fact by claiming no memory? A number of courts have answered this question affirmatively. Perhaps that result does no great violence to the underlying hearsay concerns since the witness is still required to establish the accuracy of the statement and is available for at least some limited cross-examination. However, whether this pattern meets the literal requirement of the rule that the witness "has insufficient recollection" or is consistent with either the historical function of this exception or the legislative intention of its framers is far from clear.

§ 283. Proving the Accuracy of the Record; Multi–Party Situations

As a final assurance of reliability, either the person who prepared the writing or one who read it at a time close to the event must testify to its accuracy. This may be accomplished by a statement that the person presently remembers recording the fact correctly or remembers recognizing the writing as accu-

rate at an earlier time. Also, if present memory is inadequate, the requirement may be met by testimony that the declarant knows it is correct because of a habit or practice to record such matters accurately or to check them for accuracy. At the extreme, some courts find sufficient testimony that the individual recognizes his or her signature and believes the statement correct because the witness would not have signed it if he or she had not believed it true at the time.

No particular method of proving the accuracy of the memorandum is prescribed by Federal 803(5), which merely requires that it be "shown * * * to reflect that knowledge correctly." However, the witness must acknowledge at trial the accuracy of the statement. An assertion of its accuracy in the acknowledgment line of a written statement or such an acknowledgment made previously under oath is not sufficient.

Courts have been relatively liberal in finding that the witness has acknowledged the accuracy of a prior statement, particularly where the witness is apparently hostile or reluctant to testify but does not repudiate the statement. A special danger of misuse of the exception occurs when this weak proof of the statement's accuracy operates in combination with the argument, discussed in the preceding section, that reluctance to testify satisfies the exception's requirement that a witness have insufficient memory of the event. The statement as recorded by the second party may not have accurately reflected the declarant's knowledge, particularly as to details, and the limited examination of a reluctant declarant may not produce its correction.

Typically, past recollection recorded involves one person, with a single witness making the original observation, recording it, and verifying its accuracy. When the verifying witness did not prepare the report but merely examined it and found it accurate, the matter involves a cooperative report, but the substantive requirements of the exception can be met by the testimony of the person who read and verified the report. A somewhat different type of cooperative report is involved when one person orally reports facts to another person, who writes them down. A store clerk or time-keeper, for example, may report information to a bookkeeper. In this situation, courts have held the written statement admissible if the person reporting the facts testifies to the correctness of the oral report (although at the time of the testimony, the detailed facts cannot be remembered) and the recorder of that statement testifies to faithfully transcribing the oral report. While subject to some ambiguity because of inartful drafting by Congress, the Federal Rule continues to permit admission of such multi-party statements.

Chapter 29

REGULARLY KEPT RECORDS

Table of Sections

§ 284. Admissibility of Regularly Kept Records

Regularly kept records may be offered in evidence in many different situations, although in most the record is offered as evidence of the truth of its terms. In such cases the evidence is hearsay, and some exception to the hearsay rule must be used if the record is to be admitted. Often no special exception is needed, however, as the record comes within the terms of another exception. For example, if the record was made by a party to the suit, it is admissible against that party as an admission.[1] If the entrant is produced as a witness, the record may be used to refresh memory,[2] or it may be admissible as a record of past recollection.[3] Sometimes the record may be admissible as a declaration against interest.[4] The present chapter is concerned with those situations in which a specific exception to the hearsay rule for regularly kept records is employed.

§ 285. The Origin of the Regularly Kept Records Exception and the Shopbook Vestige

By the 1600s in England, a custom emerged in the common law courts of receiving the "shop books" of tradesmen and craftsmen as evidence of debts for goods sold or services rendered on open accounts. Since most tradesmen were their own bookkeepers, the rule permitted a reasonable means of avoiding the harsh common law rule preventing a party from appearing as its own witness. Nevertheless, theoretical objections to the self-serving nature of this evidence, apparently coupled with abuse of it in practice, led to a statutory curb in 1609 that limited the use of a

---

§ 284

1. See generally supra § 254.
2. See generally supra § 9.

3. See generally supra Ch. 28.
4. See generally infra Ch. 33.

party's shopbooks to a period of one year after the debt was created unless a bill of debt was given or the transaction was between merchants and tradesmen. The higher courts refused to recognize the books at all after the year had elapsed, although in practice such evidence was received in the lower courts with small claims jurisdiction.

During the 1700s, a broader doctrine began to develop in the English common law courts. At first, this doctrine permitted only the use of regular entries in the books of a party by a deceased clerk, but it was expanded to cover books regularly kept by third persons who had since died. By 1832, the doctrine was firmly grounded, and its scope was held to include all entries made by a person, since deceased, in the ordinary course of the maker's business.

The development of the doctrine in America was less satisfactory, however. In the colonies, limited exceptions for the books of a party based on the English statute of 1609 and Dutch practice were in force. In addition to requiring that the entries be regularly made at or about the time of the transaction and as a part of the routine of the business, other common restrictions were that (1) the party using the book not have had a clerk, (2) the party file a supplemental oath to the justness of the account, (3) the books bear an honest appearance, (4) each transaction not exceed a certain limited value, (5) witnesses testify from their experience in dealing with the party that the books are honest, (6) the books be used only to prove open accounts for goods and services furnished the defendant (thus making them unavailable for proof of loans and goods and services furnished under special contract or furnished to third persons on defendant's credit), and (7) other proof be made of the delivery of some of the goods.

Not until the early 1800s did the American equivalent of the English general exception for regular business entries by deceased persons emerge. As the doctrine gained acceptance, however, often no provision was made for the "shop books" of a party, whose admis-

sibility continued to be controlled by the restrictive statutes. This failure made little sense, especially in view of the fact that abolition of the party's disqualification as a witness[1] removed the justification for treating the books of a party as a special problem. Most courts today take the reasonable position that the remaining shop book statutes are alternative grounds for admissibility.

§ 286. The Regularly Kept Records Exception in General

The hearsay exception for regularly kept records is justified on grounds of trustworthiness and necessity that underlie other hearsay exceptions. Reliability is furnished by the fact that regularly kept records typically have a high degree of accuracy. The regularity and continuity of the records are calculated to train the recordkeeper in habits of precision; if of a financial nature, the records are periodically checked by balance-striking and audits; and in actual experience, the entire business of the nation and many other activities function in reliance upon records of this kind. The impetus for receiving these hearsay statements at common law arose when the person or persons who made the entry, and upon whose knowledge it was based, were unavailable because of death, disappearance, or other reason.

The common law exception had four elements: (1) the entries must be original entries made in the routine of a business, (2) the entries must have been made upon the personal knowledge of the recorder or of someone reporting the information, (3) the entries must have been made at or near the time of the transaction recorded, and (4) the recorder and the informant must be shown to be unavailable. If these conditions were met, the business entry was admissible to prove the facts recited in it.

The regularly kept records exception had evolved within the context of simple business organizations, using the typical records of a double-entry system of journal and ledger. In this setting, the common law requirements were not unduly burdensome. Control and

1. See supra § 65.

management of complex organizations require correspondingly complicated records, however, and business, government, and other institutions were becoming increasingly intricate. While the theory of the exception was sound, some of the common law requirements were incompatible with modern conditions. The limitation to records of a business was unduly restrictive. The requirement of an original record was inconsistent with modern developments in record keeping. The need to account for nonproduction of all participants in the process of assembling and recording information was a needless and disruptive burden in view of the unlikelihood that any of those involved would remember a particular transaction or its details. Also, what witnesses were required to lay the necessary foundation for the records was sometime uncertain. Since the courts seemed unable to resolve these difficulties, relief was sought in legislation, and even before the enactment of the Federal Rules, the exception was governed by statute or rule virtually everywhere.

The Commonwealth Fund Act and the Uniform Business Records as Evidence Act provided the principal models for the early legislative reforms. Their essential features are now incorporated in Federal Rule 803(6), which provides a hearsay exception, without regard to unavailability of declarant, as follows:

> A memorandum, report, record, or data compilation, in any form, of acts, events, conditions, opinions, or diagnoses, made at or near the time by, or from information transmitted by, a person with knowledge, if kept in the course of a regularly conducted business activity, and if it was the regular practice of that business activity to make the memorandum, report, record, or data compilation, all as shown by the testimony of the custodian or other qualified witness, unless the source of information or the method or circumstances of preparation indicate lack of trustworthiness. The term "business" as used in this paragraph includes business, institution, association, profession, occupation, and calling of every kind, whether or not conducted for profit.

§ 287. Types of Records; Opinions; Absence of Entry

The usual statement of the business records exception to the hearsay rule suggests that oral reports are not within it, even if the other requirements for admissibility are met. The common law cases tended to speak in terms of entries in account books.[1] The Commonwealth Fund Act used the terms "writing or record," the Uniform Act spoke of "record," and Federal Rule 803(6) includes a "memorandum, report, record, or data compilation." Of these, only the term "report" in the Federal Rule is arguably broad enough to include an oral report, and the provision that the report be "kept" negates the idea that oral reports are within the rule. Nevertheless, the English position is that oral reports may qualify under the exception, and some American courts have admitted oral reports on the basis of a partial analogy to business records.

Under the common law exception, the entries were required to be original entries and not mere transcribed records or copies. This restriction was based on the assumption that the original entries were more likely to be accurate than subsequent copies or transcriptions. In business practice, however, daily transactions, such as sales or services rendered, are customarily noted upon slips, memorandum books, or the like by the person most directly concerned. Someone then collects these memoranda and from them makes entries in a permanent book, such as a journal or ledger. In these cases, the entries in the permanent record sufficiently comply with the requirement of originality. They would certainly be admissible if the slips or memoranda disappeared and should be admissible as the original permanent entry without proof as to the unavailability of the tentative memoranda. This practice also serves the interest of convenience, since it is much easier to use a ledger or similar source than slips or temporary

1. See supra § 285.

memoranda when the inquiry concerns the state of an entire account. Of course, the slips or memoranda would also be admissible if they should be offered. The Federal Rule does not require that the entry be original, but allows "any form."

With regard to opinions in business records, two types of issues arise. The first concerns lay opinions or conclusions, which are largely conclusory forms of expression. The opinion rule should be restricted to governing the manner of presenting live testimony where a more specific and concrete answer can be secured if desired[2] and should have little application to the admissibility of out-of-court statements, including business records. The second and more difficult issue regards expert opinions within business records. Federal Rule 803(6) specifically provides that an admissible regularly kept record may include "opinions," which will ordinarily be expert opinions. Such opinions should be governed by the ordinary restrictions on expert qualifications and proper subjects for expert opinions. In § 293, these issues are examined for hospital records.

Sometimes the absence of an entry relating to a particular transaction is offered as proof that no such transaction took place. For example, a car rental agency's records showing no lease or rental activity for a certain vehicle may be offered to prove that the defendant, found in possession of the car, stole it. Courts have generally admitted the evidence for this purpose, and Federal Rule 803(7) specifically so provides.

§ 288. Made in the Routine of a "Business"; Accident Reports; Reports Made for Litigation; Indications of Lack of Trustworthiness

The early cases construed the requirement of a "business" literally and excluded, for example, records kept in connection with loans made by an individual not in the business of loaning money to others on the basis that they were not concerned with "business." The Commonwealth Fund Act defined "business" much more expansively to "include business,

profession, occupation and calling of every kind." The Uniform Act added "operation of institutions, whether carried on for profit or not."

In Federal Rule 803(6), the term includes "business, institution, association, profession, occupation, and calling of every kind, whether or not conducted for profit." Applying to a "memorandum, report, record, or data compilation, in any form," of a "business" broadly defined, this rule has broad scope. It has been held to encompass such diverse items as a diary of tips kept by a blackjack dealer, notations on calendar of daily illegal drug sales, performance evaluations of hospital employees, a hospital's scrapbook of newspaper articles showing visiting hours, restaurant "guest check" with defendant's name written on it, videotape made by prison of removal of prisoner from his cell, a bill of lading, an automobile lease by dealer, a logbook of malfunctions of a machine, loan counselor's notes of telephone conversations with defendant, and an appraisal of a painting for purposes of insurance. These examples are all in addition to account books and their counterparts, which might more readily fall within the usual concept of business records. Hospital records are specially treated below in § 293 and computer-stored records are the subject of § 294.

Records, such as diaries, if of a purely personal nature not involved in declarant's business activities, do not fall within the rule, but if kept for business purposes are within the rule. Memoranda of telephone conversations are treated similarly. The breadth of the exception is also demonstrated by cases holding that the activity need not be legal for the record to qualify. Some church records are covered by the business records exception, while those related to the family history of members are the subject of Federal Rule 803(11).

Under the English rules, both the matter or event recorded and the recording of it must have been performed pursuant to a duty to a third person. Under American law, conduct in

---

2. See § 18 supra.

the regular course of the business is required instead.

How far Rule 803(6) goes in requiring not only that the record must be made in the regular course of a business but that it "be the regular practice of that business to make the memorandum" is disputed. What might be termed nonroutine records, which are nevertheless made in the course of regularly conducted activities, are the focus of concern here. Unusual records, often outside the expertise assured by a business routine, are properly excluded for that reason. Other records of this type will be properly excluded because of motivational concerns arising from the fact they were generated for litigation purposes, discussed immediately below. While an occasional court has focused on the apparent intention of Congress as reflected in the wording of the rule that the making of the memorandum be the "regular practice," the general focus is much more on whether the basic concern of trustworthiness is met for nonroutine records.

An important set of concerns revolves around the purpose of the report and the circumstances of its preparation, particularly reports of accidents. The seminal case is Palmer v. Hoffman,[1] a suit against railroad trustees arising out of an accident at a railroad crossing. The engineer of the train involved was interviewed two days after the accident by a representative of the railroad and a representative of the state public utilities commission and signed a statement giving his version of the incident. He died before trial, and the statement was offered by the defendants, who contended that the railroad obtained such statements in the regular course of its business. Affirming the trial court's exclusion of the report, the Supreme Court stated:

> [The report] is not a record made for the systematic conduct of the business as a business. An accident report may affect that business in the sense that it affords information on which the management may act. It is not, however, typical of entries made systematically or as a matter

of routine to record events or occurrences, to reflect transactions with others, or to provide internal controls * * *. Unlike payrolls, accounts receivable, accounts payable, bills of lading and the like, these reports are calculated for use essentially in the court, not in the business. Their primary use is in litigating, not in railroading.[2]

Consequently, the report was held not to have been made "in the regular course" of the business within the meaning of the federal statute then providing for the admissibility of business records.

While *Palmer* has been subject to various interpretations, the most reasonable reading is that it did not create a blanket rule of exclusion for accident reports or similar records kept by businesses. Rather, it recognized a discretionary power in the trial court to exclude evidence which meets the letter of the exception, but which under the circumstances appears to lack the reliability business records are assumed ordinarily to have. The existence of a motive and opportunity to falsify the record, especially in the absence of any countervailing factors, is of principal concern. The Federal Rule incorporates this reading of *Palmer* by permitting admission of reports that otherwise comply with the requirements of the rule, "unless the source of information or the method or circumstances of preparation indicate lack of trustworthiness." When records are prepared in anticipation of litigation, they will often lack the requisite trustworthiness.

Police reports and records can, of course, meet the requirements for the regularly kept records exception to the hearsay rule, but they also qualify under the hearsay exception for public records and reports.[3] Federal Rule 803(8) contains certain restrictions upon the use of police reports in criminal cases, and the question has arisen whether those restrictions can be avoided by offering police reports under the regularly kept records exception, which

§ 288

1. 318 U.S. 109 (1943).

2. Id. at 113–114.

3. See generally infra Ch. 30.

imposes no such limitations. The answer, while complicated, is generally "no." This subject is discussed in greater detail in § 296 infra.

§ 289. Made at or Near the Time of the Transaction Recorded

A substantial factor in the reliability of any system of records is the promptness with which transactions are recorded. The formula of Federal Rule 803(6) is "at or near the time." Whether an entry made subsequent to the transaction has been made within a sufficient time to render it within the exception depends upon whether the time span between the transaction and the entry was so great as to suggest a danger of inaccuracy by lapse of memory. In addition, the failure to make a timely record may suggest nonregularity in the making of the statement and may indicate motivational problems related to records prepared for litigation purposes.

§ 290. Personal Knowledge; All Participants in Regular Course of Business

The common law exception for regularly kept records required that the entries have been made by one with personal knowledge of the matter entered or upon reports to the maker by one with personal knowledge. The entrant was required to be acting in the regular course of business, and if the information was supplied by another, that person also was required to be acting in the regular course of business. If the information was transmitted through intermediaries, they were subject to the same requirement. The application of the regular course requirement to all participants in the process of acquiring, transmitting, and recording information was consistent with, indeed mandated by, the theory of the hearsay exception.

Early legislation did not deal clearly with whether the information must initially be acquired by a person with firsthand knowledge and whether that person and all others involved in the process must be acting in the regular course of the business. The Common-

wealth Fund Act required that the record be "made in the regular course of * * * business" and provided that "other circumstances * * *, including lack of personal knowledge by the entrant or maker, may be shown to affect its weight, but they shall not affect its admissibility." The Uniform Act also required that the record be "made in the regular course of business," and in addition required that "in the opinion of the court, the sources of information, method and time of preparation were such as to justify its admission." Federal Rule 803(6) requires that the record be "made * * * by, or from information transmitted by, a person with knowledge, if kept in the course of a regularly conducted business activity."

Assuming, as is reasonable, that "knowledge" means firsthand knowledge, then Rule 803(6) answers the first part of the above question affirmatively, to the effect that the person who originally feeds the information into the process must have firsthand knowledge. Also, the person making the record must be in the regular course of business, Rule 803(6) using the term "kept" to describe records produced in the regular course of business.

Any doubts about drafting should be resolved by referring to the underlying theory of the exception, namely, a practice and environment encouraging the making of accurate records. If any person in the process is not acting in the regular course of the business, then an essential link in the trustworthiness chain fails, just as it does when the person feeding the information does not have firsthand knowledge. Johnson v. Lutz,[1] the leading case on this point, was decided under the New York version of the Commonwealth Fund Act, which held inadmissible a police officer's report insofar as it was not based upon his personal knowledge but on information supplied by a bystander. Courts generally followed its analysis for various formulations of the exception, including Federal Rule 803(6). Thus, if information going from observation to final recording is to be received under this exception, all parts of the process must be conducted under

§ 290

1. 170 N.E. 517 (N.Y.1930).

a business duty. One alternative is for someone within the organization to verify the accuracy of the information provided by the "outsider."

Also, when the matter recorded itself satisfies the conditions of some other hearsay exception, the requirement that the person initially acquiring the information must be acting in the regular course of the business does not apply. For example, a police officer may include in a report of an automobile accident a damaging statement by one of the drivers, who later becomes a party to litigation. The statement qualifies as an admission, and the report may be used to prove it was made. That the officer has no firsthand knowledge of the correctness of the statement is immaterial if it was the officer's responsibility to record this type of information. These issues are discussed further in connection with multiple hearsay.[2]

Direct proof that the maker of the statement had actual knowledge may be difficult, and proving specifically the identity of the informant with actual knowledge may be impossible. Evidence that it was someone's business duty in the organization's routine to observe the matter will be prima facie sufficient to establish actual knowledge. This principle does not dispense with the need for personal knowledge, but permits it to be proved by evidence of a routine practice and a reasonable assumption that such practice was followed with regard to a particular matter, or by other appropriate circumstances.

§ 291. Unavailability

Historically, if the person who made a business record was present as a witness, the record could be used to refresh recollection, or if that person could not recall the facts, the record might be admissible as past recollection recorded. If, however, the witness could not be produced in court, then these alternative avenues to admissibility for the business record could not be used. A need for a special hearsay exception for business records in such cases was apparent. Unfortunately, as sometimes

happens, the reason why the rule came into existence became a requirement, in this instance a requirement of unavailability.

The process of calling a series of participants, only to have them testify that referring to the business record did not refresh their recollection, or at best to give rote testimony that it was their practice to be accurate, was a waste of the court's time and disruptive to the business involved with no corresponding benefit. Yet no other response could reasonably be expected from participants in the keeping of business records under modern conditions. The reliability of the record could be shown by evidence other than the testimony of participants, as had been done when a participant was unavailable. Accordingly, unavailability virtually disappeared as a requirement under common law decisions. Federal Rule 803(6) does not require unavailability, and the unavailability requirement has now almost entirely disappeared from American jurisdictions.

§ 292. Proof; Who Must Be Called to Establish Admissibility

The demise of the requirement of unavailability had its intended impact upon the method of proving business records. No longer was it necessary to call each available participant and exhaust the possibility of refreshing memory or establishing the record as past recollection recorded. Any witness with the necessary knowledge about the particular recordkeeping process could testify that the regular practice of the business was to make such records, that the record was made in the regular course of business upon the personal knowledge of the recorder or of someone reporting in the regular course of business, and that the entries were made at or near the time of the transaction. The Uniform Act provided that the foundation might be laid by "the custodian or other qualified witness," and this language is incorporated in Federal Rule 803(6).

Perhaps the most commonly used foundation witness is a person in authority in the recordkeeping department of the business. Whether or not such a person falls within the

---

2. See infra § 324.1.

term "custodian" may be questioned, but certainly he or she is "a qualified witness." In fact, anyone with the necessary knowledge is qualified; this witness need not have firsthand knowledge of the matter reported or actually have prepared the report or observed its preparation.

Problems may arise when one business organization seeks to introduce records in its possession but actually prepared by another. Obviously, mere possession or "custody" of records under these circumstances does not qualify employees of the possessing party to lay the requisite foundation, and transmittal of information by the custodian regarding the contents of records in the custodian's possession does not qualify the recipient to lay the foundation. However, when the business offering the records of another has made an independent check of the records, has integrated them into their own business operation, or can establish accuracy by other means, the necessary foundation may be established.

In order to facilitate the introduction of regularly kept records, Congress enacted a statute providing a certification procedure for foreign records in criminal cases. However, generally the foundation for the record cannot be established without a witness appearing at trial and testifying, but amendments have been proposed that would change this result for the Federal Rules.

§ 293. Special Situations: (a) Hospital Records

In the past, specific statutory authority governed the admission of hospital records. Although some courts hesitated to expand the business record exception to hospital records, they are now admissible upon the same basis as other regularly kept records. This result is appropriate, for the safeguards of trustworthiness of records of the modern hospital are at least as substantial as the guarantees of relia-

bility of records of business establishments generally.

History. Under standard practice, a trained attendant at hospitals enters upon the record a "personal history," including an identification of the patient, an account of the present injury or illness, and the events and symptoms leading up to it. This information, which may be obtained from the patient directly or from a companion, is elicited to aid in the diagnosis and treatment of the patient's injury or disease. Is this history admissible to prove assertions of facts it may contain? Two layers of hearsay are involved here, with the first being the use of the hospital record to prove that the statement was made. The primary issue is whether the specific entry involved was an entry made in the regular course of the hospital's business. If the subject matter falls within matters that under hospital practice are regarded as relevant to diagnosis or treatment or other hospital business, it is within the regular course of business.[1] If, on the other hand, the subject matter does not relate to those concerns, the making of the entry is not within the regular course of the hospital's business, and thus it is not admissible even for the limited purpose of proving that the statement was made.

Assuming that the hospital record is admissible to prove that the statement contained in the history was made, is this statement admissible to prove the truth of assertions made in it? In accordance with the general rule, the business record exception cannot support admission of the history because the declarant's action in relating the history was not part of a business routine of which he or she was a regular participant. However, if as is generally the case the history comes within one of the other exceptions to the hearsay rule, it is admissible.[2] The statements may, for example, constitute statements for the purpose of diagnosis or treatment,[3] admissions of a

---

§ 293

1. See supra §§ 277–278.

2. See infra § 324.1.

3. See supra Ch. 27.

party opponent,[4] dying declarations,[5] declarations against interest,[6] or excited utterances.[7]

Diagnostic statements. Professional standards for hospital records contemplate that entries will be made of diagnostic findings at various stages. These entries are clearly in the regular course of the operations of the hospital. The problem which they pose is one of the admissibility of "opinions."[8] In the hospital records area, the opinion is usually one of an expert who would unquestionably be permitted to give it if personally testifying. While the requirement of qualification does not disappear, if the record is shown to be from a reputable institution, it may be inferred that regular entries were made by qualified personnel in the absence of any indication to the contrary.

When an expert opinion is offered by a witness personally testifying, the expert is available for cross-examination on that opinion. If the opinion is offered by means of a hospital record, no cross-examination is possible. Consequently, courts historically tended to limit the scope of opinions that could be introduced by this method. Ordinary diagnostic findings customarily based on objective data and not presenting more than average difficulty of interpretation were usually admitted, but diagnostic opinions that on their face were conjectural were often excluded.

Given that Federal Rule 803(6) specifically includes opinions or diagnoses, this historical distinction based on whether the opinion is objective or conjectural does not appear to survive, at least directly. However, admissibility of all such entries is not assured. First, where indications of lack of trustworthiness are shown, which may result from a lack of expert qualifications or from a lack of factual support, exclusion is warranted. Moreover, inclusion of opinions or diagnoses within the rule only removes the bar of hearsay. In the

absence of the availability of the expert for explanation and cross-examination, the court may conclude that probative value of this evidence is outweighed by the danger that the jury will be misled or confused.[9] This concern is particularly significance if the opinion involves difficult matters of interpretation and a central dispute in the case, such as causation. Under these circumstances, a court operating under the Federal Rules, like earlier courts, is likely to be reluctant to permit a verdict to be reached on the basis of an un-cross-examined opinion and may require that the witness be produced.

Privilege. In most states, patients have been afforded a privilege against disclosure by physicians of information acquired in attending the patient and necessary for diagnosis and treatment.[10] While hospital records are generally privileged to the extent that they incorporate statements made by the patient to the physician and the physician's diagnostic findings, application of the privilege to information obtained by nurses or attendants is more complicated. On one hand, privilege statutes should arguably be strictly construed, and most do not mention nurses or attendants. On the other hand, information is usually gathered and recorded by them as agents of the physician and for the purpose of aiding the physician in treatment and diagnosis. The answer lies in interpreting the underlying privilege. If it would bar the direct testimony of a nurse or attendant, it should bar use of their hearsay statement under this exception; if it would not, such statements in hospital records should not be privileged.

§ 294. Special Situations: (b) Computer Records

Even though the scrivener's quill pens in original entry books have often been replaced

---

4. See supra Ch. 25.
5. See infra Ch. 32.
6. See infra Ch. 33.
7. See supra § 272.

8. See supra § 287.
9. See generally supra § 185.
10. See supra Ch. 11.

by computer records, the theory behind the reliability of regularly kept business records remains the same. Provided a proper foundation is laid, computer-generated evidence is no less reliable than original entry books and should be admitted under the exception.

With the explosive development of electronic data processing, most business records are now processed by computers. Although some commentators initially argued that evidence rules should be amended to add a rule specifically governing computer-generated evidence, this suggestion was not followed. Instead, Federal Rule 803(6) applies to a "data compilation, in any form," terminology intended to include records stored in computers, and courts and legislatures have judged the admissibility of such records by the hearsay exception for regularly kept records. Generally courts have dealt competently with the admissibility of such evidence by applying Rule 803(6) or its common law or statutory counterparts.

The usual conditions for the exception are applicable.[1] The differences between traditional record-keeping methods and sophisticated electronic equipment, however, require some further exploration of foundation requirements. While paper records can be inspected and the process of keeping the record can often be tracked in a step-by-step manner, electronically processed data is not a visual counterpart of the machine record and is not subject to inspection until it takes the form of a printout.

The theory of trustworthiness supporting the regularly kept records exception assumes a reliable method for entering, processing, storing, and retrieving data. Moreover, the rule excludes statements when "the source of information or the method or circumstances of preparation indicate lack of trustworthiness." Issues may arise at any of the stages of the handling of the data regarding (1) computer hardware, (2) software or programming, and (3) accuracy or security.

Serious problems are rarely presented regarding computer hardware because most computer equipment used to produce records otherwise meeting the requirements of the exception is both standard and highly reliable, with few data errors resulting from defects in equipment. Testimony regarding equipment ordinarily need only describe the function that each unit performs in the process and that each is adequate for the purpose. Excursions into theory are not required or ordinarily appropriate.

Human factors involved in the programming of the computer and the development of software afford more frequent potential for errors. However, the trend here is not to require the proponent of the statement to call the programmer to lay the foundation for admission. With regard to questions of inaccuracy and data security, courts have not imposed rigid requirements. Thus, in the typical case, the proponent is not initially required to show periodic testing for programming errors or the elimination of all possibilities of data alteration or errors in data entry or programming.

While a well-laid foundation will touch upon each of the general areas noted above, the trend among courts has been to treat computer records like other business records and not to require the proponent of the evidence initially to show trustworthiness beyond the general requirements of the rule. The fact that the organization relies upon the record in the regular course of its business may itself provide sufficient indication of reliability, absent realistic challenge, to warrant admission.

As noted in an earlier section, in order to qualify under the hearsay exception for regularly kept records, a record must have been made in the regular course of business, and documents made for use in litigation frequently do not meet that requirement. Because of the motivation factor, such records typically lack the trustworthiness contemplated by the exception.[2] Also, the regularly kept records exception requires that entries must be made

§ 294

1. See supra §§ 286–290.

2. See supra § 288.

at or near the time of the event recorded.[3] The application of these general principles to the creation of a computer printout raise several specific problems. These issues are presented by a computer printout that is made (1) long after the data were entered into the system and (2) after litigation has commenced.

The question as to the timeliness of the creation of the record is answered by observing that the time requirement refers to when the entry into the data bank was originally made, not the time the printout was produced. With regard to documents prepared for use in litigation, the arrangement of the data in a form designed to aid litigation should not result in exclusion if the data and the retrieval processes are themselves reliable. For example, when information is recorded in the computer in the sequence in which it was received rather than organized by customers or transactions, reordering the data by computer should not present a barrier to its admission greater than a

manual collation of related business records would. The evidence should not be rejected merely because it is not a visual counterpart of the electronic record. However, the court must consider whether the process producing the printout is reliable and whether the record may have been compromised by that process.

Another specific issue encountered with regard to computer records is whether records that are self-generated by the computer are hearsay at all. A frequently encountered example of a record of this type is the trace report produced by telephone company computers when tracking a call made to a specific number. Because such records are not the counterpart of a statement by a human declarant, which should ideally be tested by cross-examination of that declarant, they should not be treated as hearsay, but rather their admissibility should be determined on the basis of the reliability and accuracy of the process involved.

---

3. See supra § 289.

Chapter 30

PUBLIC RECORDS, REPORTS, AND CERTIFICATES

Table of Sections

§ 295. The Exception for Public Records and Reports: (a) In General

The common law developed an exception to the hearsay rule for written records and reports of public officials under a duty to make them, made upon firsthand knowledge of the facts. These statements are admissible as evidence of the facts recited in them. The common law formulation of this hearsay exception has been broadened by decisions, statutes, and rules, discussed in the sections that follow. The most important of these modern formulations of the exception is the Federal Rule.

Federal Rule 803(8) provides, without regard to the declarant's availability, a hearsay exception for the following:

> Records, reports, statements, or data compilations, in any form, of public offices or agencies, setting forth (A) the activities of the office or agency, or (B) matters observed pursuant to duty imposed by law as to which matters there was a duty to report, excluding, however, in criminal cases matters observed by police officers and other law enforcement personnel, or (C) in civil actions and proceedings and against the Government in criminal cases, factual findings resulting from an investigation made pursuant to authority granted by law, unless the sources of information or other circumstances indicate lack of trustworthiness.

The special trustworthiness of official written statements is found in the declarant's official duty and the high probability that the duty to make an accurate report has been performed.[1] The possibility that public inspection of some official records will reveal any inaccuracies and cause them to be corrected (or will deter the official from making them in the first place) has been emphasized by the English courts, which have imposed a corresponding requirement that the official statement be one kept for the use and information of the public. This limitation has been criticized, and the American courts have not

---

§ 295

1. See also supra § 286 concerning regular entries.

adopted it. Although public inspection might provide a modest additional assurance of reliability, strictly limiting admissibility to records that are open to public inspection would be unwise because many documents with sufficiently reliability to justify admission would be excluded.

The impetus for the development of this hearsay exception is the inconvenience of requiring public officials to appear and testify concerning the subject matter of their records and reports. Not only would this disrupt the administration of public affairs, but it almost certainly would create a class of official witnesses. Moreover, given the volume of business in public offices, the official written statement will usually be more reliable than the official's memory. For these same reasons, the declarant's unavailability is not required. The convenience of proof by certified copy,[2] the simplicity of foundation requirements,[3] and the lack of need for the testimony of a custodian, make the official records exception an attractive choice over business records when an available option.

§ 296. The Exception for Public Records and Reports: (b) Activities of the Office; Matters Observed; Investigative Reports; Restrictions on Prosecutorial Use

Under Federal Rule 803(8) matters falling within the hearsay exception for public records and reports are divided into three groups, which track the common law and statutory background.

(A) Activities of the office. The first group includes the oldest and most straightforward type of public records, records of the activities of the office itself. An example is the record of receipts and disbursements of the Treasury Department. In addition to the assurances of reliability common to public records and reports generally, this group has the assurances of accuracy that characterize business records and are routinely admitted.

(B) Matters observed pursuant to duty. The second group consists of matters observed and reported, both pursuant to duty imposed by law. Rainfall records of the National Weather Service are illustrative. This general category of records is relatively uncontroversial except when the matter is observed by a police officer or other law enforcement personnel, discussed in the concluding portion of (C) below.

(C) Investigative reports. In Beech Aircraft Corporation v. Rainey,[1] the Supreme Court resolved an issue that had previously divided lower federal courts. It rejected a narrow interpretation of "factual findings" and held that "factually based opinions and conclusions" could be included within the exception.[2] Under the exception, a wide range of agency findings are admissible.

The Court noted that the primary protection against admission of unreliable evidence was the Rule's provision directing exclusion of all elements of the report—both factual and evaluative—if the court determines that they lack trustworthiness. In making the determination of trustworthiness, the four factors to be examined include: the timeliness of the investigation, the skill or experience of the investigator, whether a formal hearing was held, and the bias of the investigator. To be admissible, the record is not required to satisfy all four requirements, and if the record facially satisfies the requirements of the rule, the opponent has the burden to demonstrate lack of trustworthiness.

As the name indicates, these reports embody the results of investigation and accordingly are often not the product of the declarant's firsthand knowledge, required under most hearsay exceptions. Nevertheless, the nature and trustworthiness of the information relied upon, including its hearsay nature, is important in determining the admissibility of the report. Also, the statement must constitute the conclusion of a governmental agency as

---

2. See supra § 240.

3. See supra § 224.

§ 296

1. 488 U.S. 153 (1988).

2. Id. at 163.

opposed to a mere accumulation of information, and it must not be an interim or preliminary document.

Restrictions on use by prosecution in criminal cases. As submitted by the Supreme Court and enacted by the Congress, clause (C) of the Federal Rule prohibits the use of investigative reports as evidence against the accused in a criminal case. The limitation was included because of "the almost certain collision with confrontation rights which would result" from using investigative reports against the accused.[3]

As transmitted by the Supreme Court to the Congress, clause (B) simply provided for including in the public records and reports exception "matters observed pursuant to duty imposed by law." In the course of debate on the floor of the House, concern was expressed that the provision might allow the introduction against the accused of a police officer's report without producing the officer as a witness subject to cross-examination. Accordingly, the provision was amended by adding the italicized words to read "(B) matters observed pursuant to duty imposed by law *as to which matters there was a duty to report, excluding, however, in criminal cases matters observed by police officers and other law enforcement personnel.*" It was enacted as so amended.

The amendment raises a number of questions of varying importance. (1) Can the accused in a criminal case use a report falling under (B)? Clearly the criminal defendant can use an investigative report which falls under (C). However, the language of (B) appears to prohibit the admission of all records of matters observed in criminal cases, which, if read literally, would exclude use by the defense as well as the prosecution. This meaning is not what Congress had in mind, and the cases have construed the provision to permit the defendant to introduce police reports under clause (B). (2) Who are "other law enforcement personnel"? In its broadest form, this term has been construed to include "any officer or em-

ployee of a governmental agency which has law enforcement responsibilities."[4] In specific, "law enforcement personnel" has been held to include a Customs Service chemist analyzing the seized substance in a narcotics case, border inspectors, and I.R.S. agents, but not a city building inspector, medical examiner, or judge. This second inquiry has, however, become somewhat less important as the courts have developed the exceptions examined below for routine or nonadversarial governmental records and for circumstances where the declarant testifies at trial. (3) Does the limitation of clause (B) apply to routine records? The courts have consistently answered that Congress did not intend to exclude observations characterized as "objective" and "nonadversarial" even though contained in law enforcement reports.

(4) Can the limitation of (B) and also that of (C) be avoided by resorting to some other hearsay exception? This question arises when the statement satisfies the requirements of some other hearsay exception that does not prohibit the use of police records and reports or investigative reports against the accused. For example, police reports can often meet the exception for recorded past recollection, and laboratory tests of materials have often been admitted as business records. Neither of these hearsay exceptions contains limitations like those of Rule 803(8)(B) & (C).

The case first considering this issue answered with an unequivocal and uncompromising "no." It concluded that Congress meant to exclude law enforcement and investigative reports against defendants in criminal cases whatever route around the hearsay rule was chosen.[5] However, subsequent consideration by other courts has led to direct disagreement by some and to a number of exceptions. First, the limitations of (B) and (C) will not be extended to other hearsay exceptions if the maker is produced as a witness and subject to cross-examination since the essential purpose of Congress was to avoid admission of evidence not subject to cross-examination. Second, this

---

3.   Adv.Comm. Note, Fed.R.Evid. 803(8)(C).

4.   United States v. Oates, 560 F.2d 45, 68 (2d Cir. 1977).

5.   Id. at 78.

limitation is inapplicable to proof of the absence of an entry in a governmental record.

§ 297. The Exception for Public Records and Reports: (c) Vital Statistics

If the requirement that the out-of-court declarant must have an official duty to make the report were strictly enforced, such matters as a minister's return upon a marriage license indicating that the ceremony had been conducted and the report of an attending physician as to the fact and date of birth or death would not be admissible. Consequently this requirement has been relaxed with regard to matters involving various general statistics. Where the report was made to a public agency by one with a professional, although not necessarily an "official," duty to make the report, such as a minister or a physician, the courts have generally admitted the record to prove the truth of the reporter's statement. An alternative approach is to regard the maker of the report as acting as an official for purposes of making the report. However, the mere fact that a report is required by law is not sufficient to convert it into a public report. The person making the report—a motorist, for example, completing a required accident report—can scarcely be regarded as acting in a temporary official capacity or under a professional duty.

The law concerning records of vital statistics is largely statutory, and states generally have enacted legislation on the subject. Federal Rule 803(9) covers records in any form of births, deaths, and marriages, if the report is made to a public office pursuant to requirements of law. While the rule looks largely to local law to determine the duty to make the report and for its content, it should not be regarded as borrowing and incorporating the local law as to admissibility. The federal rule governs that issue.

As to routine matters, such as place and date of birth or death and "immediate" cause of death, such as drowning or gunshot wound, admissibility is seldom questioned. However,

entries in death certificates as to the "remote" cause of death, such as suicide, accident, or homicide, usually are made on the basis of information obtained from other persons and predictably involve the questions that have been raised with regard to investigative reports generally, and courts have divided on admissibility. When conclusions of this type are involved, the provisions of Rule 803(8), which is equally applicable and involves a much more careful treatment of the issues, should be applied. Thus, the restrictions on using police and investigative reports against accused persons contained in Federal Rule 803(8)(B) & (C) should be applied to this aspect of records of vital statistics. Similar tests for the admissibility of investigative reports under Federal Rule 803(8)(C), such as the expertise and motivation of the preparer and the sources of information used, should prevail.

§ 298. The Exception for Public Records and Reports: (d) Judgments in Previous Cases, Especially Criminal Convictions Offered in Subsequent Civil Cases

Since reports of official investigations are admissible under the official written statement exception, the judgment of a court, made after the full investigation of a trial, should likewise be admissible in subsequent litigation to prove the truth of those facts necessarily determined in the first action. Guilty pleas and statements made in the course of litigation may constitute declarations against interest[1] or admissions of a party-opponent[2] and under those exceptions avoid the bar of the hearsay rule. Where the doctrines of res judicata, collateral estoppel, or claim or issue preclusion make the determinations in the first case binding in the second, a judgment in the first case is not only admissible in the second, but it is conclusive against the party as a matter of substantive law. However, the courts were often unwilling to admit judgments in previous cases if neither res judicata nor collateral estoppel applied under the theory that they are hearsay.

§ 298
1. See infra Ch. 33.

2. See supra Ch. 25. As to guilty pleas, see especially § 257.

A variety of reasons have been advanced for this rule. Civil cases often involve numerous issues and determining what issues were decided by a judgment may be difficult. This argument, however, should only require that one offering a judgment establish first that the judgment in fact determined an issue relevant to the instant litigation. Another argument advanced is that the party against whom the judgment is offered may not have had an opportunity to be present and participate in the first action. In many cases, the party will in fact have been present and have had not only an opportunity but a strong motive to defend. However, the appropriate question is not the party's opportunity to have been present at the official investigation but whether that investigation provided adequate assurance of reliability.

The argument against admissibility has particular merit for judgments offered against a criminal defendant. When that judgment was rendered against another, admitting it would violate the defendant's constitutional right of confrontation. Admitting civil judgments rendered against the defendant directly raises constitutional issues as well.

Other arguments against admissibility of prior judgments relate to the danger of undue prejudice and the need for orderly administration of trials. Also juries may have difficulty grasping the distinction between a prior judgment offered as evidence and one that is conclusive, giving the judgment binding effect even if this is contrary to substantive law. A final argument is that if prior judgments are admissible parties offering them will rely heavily on them and not introduce significant other evidence with the result that the evidence available in the second case does not support a reliable decision. These arguments have caused many courts to exclude a prior civil judgment offered in a subsequent civil case when offered under a public records and reports exception.

By contrast, most courts admit a prior conviction for a serious criminal offense in a subsequent civil action. With serious offenses, the party against whom the judgment is offered was generally the defendant in the criminal case and therefore had not only the opportunity but also the motive to defend fully. In addition, because of a heavier burden of proof, a criminal judgment requires significantly more reliable evidence than a judgment in a civil case. The trend was most obvious when the judgment was offered in a subsequent civil case in which the convicted defendant sought to benefit from his criminal offense—for example, a convicted arsonist sues to recover upon his fire insurance policy. The strong desire to prevent this result undoubtedly influenced courts to admit the judgment of conviction, and some courts also held it was conclusive in the civil case. Courts soon moved to a general admissibility of a prior criminal conviction in a civil action against the party who was previously the criminal defendant.

Often the exception is limited to convictions for serious offenses under the theory that convictions for misdemeanors do not represent sufficiently reliable determinations to justify dispensing with the hearsay objections. Judgments of acquittal, however, are still inadmissible in large part because they may not present a determination of innocence, but rather only a decision that the prosecution has not met its burden of proof beyond a reasonable doubt.

Federal Rule 803(22), quoted in the footnote,[3] is generally consistent with these trends and has a number of significant features. First, only criminal judgments of conviction are included. Judgments in civil cases are not included, their effect being left to the law of res judicata or preclusion. Second, it covers only serious crimes, i.e., punishable by death or imprisonment for more than one year, thus

---

3. The rule states:

Evidence of a final judgment, entered after a trial or upon a plea of guilty (but not upon a plea of nolo contendere), adjudging a person guilty of a crime punishable by death or imprisonment in excess of one year, to prove any fact essential to sustain the judgment, but

not including, when offered by the Government in a criminal prosecution for purposes other than impeachment, judgments against persons other than the accused. The pendency of an appeal may be shown but does not affect admissibility.

eliminating problems associated with convictions of lesser crimes. Third, the rule does not apply to judgments of acquittal. Fourth, when offered by the government in criminal prosecutions, judgments of conviction of persons other than the accused are admissible only for purposes of impeachment. When the judgment of conviction is offered in a civil case, however, it is treated as are investigative reports generally, and there is no restriction as to the parties against whom the evidence is admissible. Fifth, judgments entered on pleas of nolo contendere are not included within the exception.[4] Finally, the provision merely removes the hearsay bar from a qualifying judgment and does not purport to dictate the use to be made of the judgment once admitted. Applicable rules of res judicata or preclusion will be given effect. Otherwise the evidence may be used "substantively" or for impeachment, as may be appropriate.

§ 299. The Exception for Official Certificates: (a) In General

For purposes of the law of evidence, a certificate is a written statement issued to an applicant by an official that recites certain matters of fact. It is not a part of the public records of the issuing office, although a common form of certificate is a statement that a document to which it is attached is a correct copy of such a record.[1] The common law was strict about admitting certificates as hearsay exceptions, for the most part requiring statutory authority.

The relation between certification and a public record may be illustrated by proof of marriage. If the celebrant of a marriage issues a certificate that the marriage was performed and gives it to the parties, this document is not a public record, and admission in evidence must be under some other hearsay exception. If, however, the celebrant makes a "return" of the license, i.e., a redelivery to the issuing official with an endorsement of the manner in which the authority was exercised, then the return becomes a part of the public record and is admissible under that hearsay exception.

Federal Rule 803(12) provides a hearsay exception for certificates of marriage and similar ceremonies performed by the clergy, public officials, or others authorized to perform the ceremony where the certificate is issued at the time of the act or within a reasonable time thereafter. Certification is also provided for a large variety of matters by statutes, with corresponding provisions for admissibility in evidence. Federal Rule 802 continues the effectiveness of such statutes.

§ 300. The Exception for Official Certificates: (b) Certified Copies or Summaries of Official Records; Absence of Record

When a purported copy of a public record is presented in court accompanied by a certificate that the purported copy is correct, a two-layered hearsay problem is presented. First, is the public record within the hearsay exception for that kind of record? Second, is the certificate within the hearsay exception for official certificates? The first question has been considered in the earlier sections of this chapter. The second question involves a specialized application of the certification procedure discussed generally in the immediately preceding section.

The early common law generally required a statutory duty to certify. However, the Supreme Court long ago rejected this position with respect to certification of copies of public records, and the American common law rule remains that a custodian has, by virtue of the office, the implied duty and authority to certify the accuracy of a copy of a public record in the custodian's official possession. The usual practice is to prove public records by copy certified as correct by the custodian, and many statutes so provide. Federal Rule 1005 allows proof of public records by copy, without producing or accounting for the original,[1] and Rule 902(4) provides for authentication by certificate.

---

4. See supra § 257.

§ 299

1. Certification of copies of public records receives further treatment in infra § 300.

§ 300

1. See supra § 240.

In the absence of a statute to the contrary, the usual view has been that the authority to certify copies of public records is construed literally as requiring a copy and does not include paraphrases or summaries. Thus a certificate saying "our records show X" is not admissible to prove X.

By analogy to the rule that nonoccurrence of an event may be proved by a business record containing no entry of the event where the practice was to record such events,[2] proof of nonoccurrence may be made by absence of an entry in a public record where such matters are recorded.However, absence of the entry or record could at common law be proved only by testimony of the custodian. This limitation has been modified by many statutes, and Federal

Rule 803(10) defines a hearsay exception for a certification in accordance with Rule 902 or for testimony that a diligent search failed to disclose a record, report, or entry used to prove the absence of the record, report, or statement or the nonoccurrence or nonexistence of a matter which should otherwise have been recorded. The rule is phrased to include not only proving nonoccurrence of an event of which a record would have been made, but also the non-filing of a document allowed or required by law to be filed. Courts have insisted that the requirement of a "diligent search" must be satisfied but have not required that a specific form of words be used to meet that requirement.

---

2. See supra § 287.

Chapter 31

TESTIMONY TAKEN AT A FORMER HEARING OR IN ANOTHER ACTION

Table of Sections

§ 301. Introduction

Upon compliance with requirements designed to guarantee an adequate opportunity for cross-examination and after showing that the witness is unavailable, testimony given previously may be received in the pending case. The prior testimony may have been given during a deposition or at a trial. It may have been received in a separate case or in an earlier hearing of the present case.

Depending upon the precise hearsay definition used, this evidence, which is usually called "former testimony," could be classified as an exception to the hearsay rule or considered as nonhearsay under the theory that the requirements of the hearsay concept have been met. The former view is accepted generally today; the latter was espoused by Wigmore.[1] In this treatise, former testimony is classified as a hearsay exception under the general definition of hearsay developed earlier that treats as hearsay all prior statements offered for their truth.[2]

Cross-examination, oath, the solemnity of the occasion, and the accuracy of modern methods of recording testimony all combine to give former testimony a high degree of reliability. Accordingly, to allow its use only upon a showing of unavailability may seem to relegate former testimony to an undeserved second-class status. The result is, however, explained by the strong preference to have available witnesses testify in open court.

This exception was one widely regulated by statute. The predecessor statutes have generally been replaced by rules like Federal Rule 804(b)(1), which upon a showing of unavailability, excepts from the hearsay rule:

§ 301

1. 5 Wigmore, Evidence § 1370 (Chadbourn rev. 1974).

2. See supra § 246.

Testimony given as a witness at another hearing of the same or a different proceeding, or in a deposition taken in compliance with law in the course of the same or another proceeding, if the party against whom the testimony is now offered, or, in a civil action or proceeding, a predecessor in interest, had an opportunity and similar motive to develop the testimony by direct, cross, or redirect examination.

Former testimony may often be admitted without meeting the requirements discussed in this chapter, which are applicable only when the evidence is offered under this exception. When the former testimony is offered for some nonhearsay purpose—to show the commission of the act of perjury, to show that testimony against the accused furnished the motive for retaliation against the witness, to refresh recollection, or to impeach a witness at the present trial by proving that earlier testimony was inconsistent—the restrictions of the hearsay exception do not apply. Likewise, if offered for a hearsay purpose but under some other exception, e.g., as the admission of a party-opponent or past recollection recorded, only the requirements of the other exception must be satisfied.

§ 302. The Requirement of Oath and Opportunity for Cross–Examination; Confrontation and Unavailability

To be admitted under this hearsay exception, former testimony must have been given under the sanction of an oath or affirmation. More frequently at issue is the requirement that the party against whom the former testimony is now offered, or perhaps a party in like interest,[1] must have had a reasonable opportunity to cross-examine.

Actual cross-examination is not required if the opportunity was afforded and waived. Whether cross-examination was conducted or waived, admissibility under this exception is not judged by the use made of the opportunity to cross-examine but rather the availability of

the opportunity. This point is amply demonstrated in cases holding that the opportunity to cross-examine at a preliminary hearing in a criminal case provides sufficient opportunity even though few litigants, for a number of reasons, fully exercise that opportunity. However, circumstances may differ sufficiently between the prior hearing and the present trial to bar admission under this requirement, as where questions on a particular subject would have been largely irrelevant at the earlier proceeding. Moreover, as discussed in later sections, the opportunity to cross-examine must have been such as to render the cross-examination actually conducted or the decision not to cross-examine meaningful in the light of the circumstances prevailing when the former testimony was given.[2]

If a right to counsel exists when the former testimony is offered, a denial of counsel when the testimony was taken renders it inadmissible. However, a general finding of ineffective representation at the prior hearing does not automatically require rejection of the testimony; the adequacy of the cross-examination under the facts must be determined. Improper judicial interference may render the opportunity to cross-examine inadequate. However, restrictions upon cross-examination do not have this consequence unless very substantial, some courts holding that they must render the testimony inherently unreliable. Similarly, the fact that a party was less able to impeach the witness at the prior hearing will ordinarily not bar its later use under this exception.

The opportunity to cross-examination is not construed literally; rather the party must have the opportunity to develop the testimony through questioning. Thus, if a party calls and examines a witness and this testimony is offered against that same party in a subsequent trial, the witness' testimony may be admitted.

If evidence is offered under the former testimony exception to the hearsay rule, it is offered as a substitute for testimony given in person in open court, and the strong policy

---

§ 302

1. See infra § 303 for discussion of when parties are "in like interest."

2. See infra § 304.

favoring personal presence requires that una-vailability of the witness be shown before the substitute is acceptable. If the witness is pres-ent in court and is available for cross-examina-tion, his or her former testimony may be ad-mitted under some circumstances as a prior statement of a witness.[3] Exclusion of prior testimony for reasons relating to availability will generally occur only when the witness is absent from court but is not unavailable as defined by evidence rules or the Confrontation Clause. Unavailability under the hearsay rule and problems of confrontation, which are is-sues common to a number of hearsay excep-tions, are discussed elsewhere.[4]

§ 303. Identity of Parties; "Prede-cessor in Interest"

The haste and pressure of trials cause lawyers and judges to speak in catchwords or shorthand phrases to describe evidence rules. Thus "identity of parties" is often spoken of as a requirement for the admission of former testimony. It is a convenient phrase to indicate a situation where the underlying requirement of adequacy of the present opponent's opportu-nity for cross-examination would usually be satisfied. But as a *requirement,* identity of parties (or, for that matter, identity of issues[1]) is hardly a useful generalization. It both ob-scures the true purpose of the requirement and must be hedged with too many qualifica-tions to be helpful.

Historically, courts recognized a number of situations where identity of parties has not been required. An important inroad upon strict identity of parties results from the recog-nition, developed under Wigmore's guidance, that it is only the party *against* whom the former testimony is now offered whose pres-ence as a party in the previous suit is signifi-cant. Second, if both the proponent and oppo-nent of the evidence were parties in the former proceedings where the testimony was taken, the presence of additional parties in either or both proceedings is immaterial. Third, identity

of parties is not required as to a party against whom prior testimony is offered when that party is a successor in interest to the corre-sponding party in the former suit. This notion, to which the label "privity" is attached, is considered to offer adequate protection to the party opposing admission. Finally, if the party against whom the former testimony is now offered, though not a party to the former suit, actually cross-examined the witness (personal-ly or by counsel) about the relevant matters or was accorded a fair opportunity for such cross-examination and had a like motive for such examination, then the former testimony may be received.

The next step in this progression away from the formalistic requirement of identity of parties would be to treat neither identity of parties nor privity as requirements, but merely as means to an end. Under this view, if a party in the former suit had a motive similar to the present party to cross-examine about the sub-ject of the testimony and was accorded an adequate opportunity for such examination, the testimony could be received against the present party. Identity of interest in the sense of motive, rather than technical identity of cause of action or title, would satisfy the test. Under this perspective, the argument that it is unfair to force upon a party another's cross-examination or decision not to cross-examine loses its validity with the realization that other hearsay exceptions involve no cross-examina-tion whatsoever and that the choice is not between perfect and imperfect conditions for the giving of testimony but between imperfect conditions and no testimony at all.

Exactly how Federal Rule 804(b)(1) should be interpreted regarding these issues remains unclear. As sent to Congress by the Supreme Court, the prior testimony exception would have taken the next step described above and admitted prior testimony if the party against whom that testimony was offered, or a party "with similar motive and interest" had an

---

3. See supra § 251.

4. See supra §§ 252, 253.

1. See infra § 304.

opportunity to examine the witness.[2] The House Judiciary Committee, however, objected to this formulation on the ground that "it is generally unfair to impose upon the party against whom the hearsay evidence is being offered responsibility for the manner in which the witness was previously handled by another party."[3] Accordingly, it substituted a requirement that "the party against whom the testimony is now offered, or in a civil action or proceeding a *predecessor in interest,* had an opportunity and similar motive" to examine the witness,[4] and this version of the rule was enacted.

While the impact in civil litigation of this congressional modification is cloudy, one point is clear: when the testimony is offered against a criminal defendant, the defendant must have been a party to the former proceeding. The rule as enacted eliminates doubts under the Confrontation Clause raised by the Court's version, which would have allowed examination by a substitute. However, by its literal terms the rule insists on identity of prosecution also, which would appear to bar a defendant in a federal prosecution from introducing exculpatory testimony from a related state case given by an unavailable witness. Exclusion of such evidence implicates due process considerations, and quite likely was not intended by Congress.

For civil cases this unfortunately oblique legislative history is more troubling, providing no definitive meaning for the term "predecessor in interest." As enacted, the rule requires that there have been opportunity to examine the witness by the party against whom now offered or by a "predecessor in interest" with similar motive. The explanation offered by the report of the House Committee is only modestly helpful. After asserting the general unfairness of requiring a party to accept another's examination of a witness, quoted above, the report stated, "The sole exception to this, in the Committee's view, is when a party's prede-

cessor in interest in a civil action or proceeding had an opportunity and similar motive to examine the witness. The committee amended the Rule to reflect these policy determinations."[5] In adding the language regarding a predecessor in interest, the House Committee presumably meant to make some change. The Senate Committee, however, characterized the difference between the version transmitted by the Supreme Court and that developed by the House Committee as "not great,"[6] and the Conference Committee remained silent on this point.

This state of legislative history has left little concrete guidance in determining congressional intent. Apparently, the House Subcommittee that drafted this modification intended it to require a "formal relationship" between the parties. How much weight to give such obscure indications of legislative intent is unclear, particularly since even the Senate Judiciary Committee appeared not to understand the significance of the modification, which suggests no Congressional "meeting of the minds." However, to ignore entirely the addition of the predecessor in interest language and construe the provision precisely as it was before that change would not be sensible. Thus, those courts that have read the language to mean no more than the general requirement that the prior party have a similar interest appear to have misconstrued the provision. On the other hand, interpreting the actions of Congress to require a strict privity approach, while not unreasonable, appears too rigid.

Courts construing the "predecessor in interest" language have taken several discrete approaches that appear consistent with the murky intent of Congress. One interesting approach is the so-called community of interest analysis. This approach requires some connection—some shared interest, albeit far less than a formal relationship—that helps to insure

---

2. 56 F.R.D. 183, 321.

3. House Comm. on Judiciary, H.R.Rep. No. 650, 93d Cong., 1st Sess. 15 (1973) reprinted in 1974 U.S.Code Cong. & Admin.News 7075, 7088.

4. Id. (emphasis added).

5. Id.

6. Senate Comm. on Judiciary, S.Rep. No. 1277, 93d Cong., 2d Sess. 28 (1974), reprinted in 1974 U.S.Code Cong. & Admin.News 7051, 7074.

adequacy of cross-examination. A second approach appears consistent with congressional concerns about fairness and is even more broadly applicable than the community of interest analysis. It requires courts to insure fairness directly by seriously considering whether the prior cross-examination can be fairly held against the later party. The testimony can be excluded if the objecting party shows that the cross-examination was inadequate by, for example, setting out the additional questions or lines of inquiry that he or she would have pursued. The opportunity to challenge the adequacy of the prior cross-examination directly, while ostensibly available in all situations, is not applied with rigor where there is no change in the identity of the party between the different proceedings.[7] The suggested interpretation accomplishes all that we know for certain was intended by the published legislative history—an interpretation of the term predecessor in interest that makes it fair to hold the present party responsible for the actions of another.

§ 304. Identity of Issues; Motive to Cross-Examine

Questions of identity of the issues involved in the former and present proceedings often arise in association with questions about identity of parties. This is to be expected because any supposed requirement of identity of issues is, like the rule about parties,[1] merely a means of fulfilling the policy of securing an adequate opportunity and sufficient motive for cross-examination.

While occasionally stated as a requirement that the issue in the two suits must be the same, the policy underlying this exception does not require that all the issues (any more than all the parties) in the two proceedings must be the same. At most, the issue on which the testimony was offered in the first suit must be the same as the issue upon which it is offered in the second. Additional issues or differences with regard to issues upon which the former testimony is not offered are of no consequence.

Moreover, insistence upon precise identity of issues, which might have some appropriateness if the question were one of res judicata or estoppel by judgment, is out of place with respect to former testimony where the question is not of binding anyone but merely of salvaging the testimony of an unavailable witness. Accordingly, even before the enactment of the Federal Rules, the trend was to demand only "substantial" identity of issues.

Thus, neither the form of the proceeding, the theory of the case, nor the nature of the relief sought need be the same between the proceedings. Such formalism is not warranted by a policy of insuring adequacy of opportunity and motive for cross-examination. For example, in criminal cases where the first indictment charges one offense (robbery) and the second alleges another distinct offense (murder of the person robbed), that the two indictments arise from the same transaction is usually considered sufficient. The requirement has become, not a mechanical one of identity or even of substantial identity of issues, but rather that the issues in the first proceeding, and hence the purpose for which the testimony was offered, must have been such as to produce an adequate motive for testing on cross-examination the credibility of the testimony. How this requirement has been applied gives definition to the general rule.

In criminal cases, one important pattern involves introducing testimony from the preliminary hearing at trial; analogously, in a civil case, testimony from a discovery deposition is admitted. In another frequently encountered situation, testimony given against the accused in an earlier criminal trial is offered against the same accused in a civil case to which the criminal defendant is a party. Prior testimony is generally admitted in these situations.

By contrast, cases examining the admissibility of prior grand jury testimony of a witness against the government reach mixed results. The typical fact pattern involves a witness who testified before the grand jury giving testimony that in some aspect excul-

---

7. See infra § 304 regarding preliminary hearings.

§ 304

1. See supra § 303.

pates the defendant and is unavailable at trial, usually because the witness asserted the Fifth Amendment privilege against self-incrimination. In United States v. Salerno,[2] the Supreme Court rejected the view that "adversarial fairness" requires admission of such testimony obtained by the government under a grant of immunity regardless of whether the "similar motive" test of Rule 804(b)(1) is satisfied.

Militating against admission, the government may be still investigating the crime and not yet be the opponent of the witness. It faces a relatively low burden of proof and has little incentive to contest an exculpatory statement if the case is strong and challenging the statement would reveal still secret information. On the other hand, the commitment to prosecute may be clear and the challenge of the exculpatory testimony obvious, yielding strong motivation to challenge it. Although generally resting their results on specific facts that go to the existence of a "similar motive," the Circuits appear divided as to whether in typical grand jury situations exculpatory testimony meets this requirement of the Rule.

Courts do not require that the party at the earlier proceeding actually have conducted a full cross-examination of the witness. The cases emphatically hold that judgments to limit or waive cross-examination at that earlier proceeding based on tactics or strategy, even though these judgments were apparently appropriate when made, do not undermine admissibility. Instead, the courts look to the operative issue in the prior proceeding, and if basically similar and if the opportunity to cross-examine was available, the prior testimony is admitted. However, at some extreme point, differences in the nature of the proceeding, the stakes involved, and even factual details with regard to the same core issue will result in exclusion of the prior testimony.

§ 305. The Character of the Tribunal and of the Proceedings in Which the Former Testimony Was Taken

If the accepted requirements of an oath, adequate opportunity to cross-examine on sub-

stantially the same issue, and present unavailability of the witness are satisfied, then the character of the tribunal and the form of the proceedings are immaterial, and the former testimony should be received. Accordingly, when these conditions are met, testimony has been received when taken before an arbitrator or a committing magistrate at a preliminary hearing, in a sworn examination before the comptroller by the corporation counsel of a person asserting a claim against a city, at a driver's license revocation hearing or a broker's license revocation hearing, at a Coast Guard hearing or a hearing on motion to suppress, in a bankruptcy proceeding, or at a deposition in a foreign country. Because some of the above requisites were missing, testimony given in the course of a coroner's inquest or a legislative committee hearing has been excluded. Also, exclusion in particular situations may be mandated by statute.

Some courts have held that, if the court in the former proceeding lacked jurisdiction of the subject matter, the former testimony is inadmissible, but others have concluded that the fact that the court may ultimately be held to lack power to grant the relief sought does not deprive it of power to compel attendance of witnesses and to administer oaths, and accordingly the former testimony was held admissible. A glaring usurpation of judicial power would call for a different ruling, but where the first court has substantial grounds for believing that it has authority to entertain the proceeding, and the party called upon to cross-examine should consider that the existence of jurisdiction is reasonably arguable, the guarantees of reliability are present. The question should be viewed, not as one of limits of jurisdiction, but whether the sworn statement of a presently unavailable witness was made under such circumstances of opportunity and motive for cross-examination as to make it sufficiently trustworthy to be received in evidence.

§ 306. Objections and Their Determination

May objections to the former testimony, or parts thereof, which could have been asserted

---

2. 505 U.S. 317 (1992).

when it was given, be made for the first time when offered at the present trial? There are sweeping statements in some opinions that this may always be done and in others that it is never allowable. The more widely approved view, however, is that objections which go merely to the form of the testimony—as on the ground of leading questions, unresponsiveness, or opinion—must be made at the original hearing when errors can be corrected. On the other hand, objections that go to the relevancy or the competency of the evidence may be asserted for the first time when the former testimony is offered at trial.

Whether the former testimony meets the requirements of the hearsay exception rule may depend on a question of fact. For example, is the witness unavailable? This and other preliminary questions of fact are to be decided by the court.[1] The declarant, whose former testimony is introduced, may be impeached as if he or she were a witness.[2]

§ 307. Methods and Scope of Proof

When only a portion of the former testimony of a witness is introduced by the proponent, the result may be a distorted and inaccurate impression. Under the rule of completeness, the adversary is entitled to introduce such other parts as fairness requires and to have them introduced at that time rather than waiting until the presentation of his or her own case.

Four methods of proof can be used to admit prior testimony.

1. Any firsthand observer of the giving of the former testimony may testify to what was said from *unaided memory*. This and the next method were frequently used before court stenographers became commonplace. The reporting witness need not profess to be able to give the exact words of the former witness but must satisfy the court that he or she is able to give the substance of all that the former witness has said, both on direct and cross-examination, about the subject matter relevant to the present suit.

2. A firsthand observer may testify regarding the former testimony by using a memorandum, such as counsel's or the stenographer's notes or transcript, to *refresh the present memory* of the witness.[1]

3. A witness who has made written notes or memoranda of the testimony at the time of the former trial, or while the facts were fresh in his or her recollection, and who will testify that he or she knows that they are correct, may use the notes as memoranda of *past recollection recorded*.[2]

4. In most states, the official stenographer's transcribed notes of the testimony are admitted when properly authenticated as evidence of the fact and purport of the former testimony, either by statute or under the hearsay exception for *official written statements*.[3] Although sound advocacy would make proof by any other form almost unthinkable where transcript or an official mechanical recording of the testimony exists, no rule of preference exists in most states to require an official transcript or recording over the unaided memory of a witness to the testimony, for example.

§ 308. Possibilities of Improving Existing Practice

In earlier editions, this treatise argued that hearsay admitted under the former testimony exception should be admitted regardless of the availability or unavailability of the declarant because few exceptions measure up in terms of the reliability of statements under former testimony. However, given the Supreme Court's analysis of the Confrontation Clause that treats former testimony as perhaps uniquely inferior hearsay and requires for that reason a showing of unavailability,[1]

§ 306
1. See generally supra § 53.
2. See infra § 324.2.

§ 307
1. As to refreshing recollection generally, see supra § 9.

2. See generally supra §§ 279–283.
3. For the requirements of this exception, see supra Ch. 30.

§ 308
1. United States v. Inadi, 475 U.S. 387, 394 (1986).

such change has no real prospects of being accepted when the prior testimony is offered against the criminal defendant.

In spite of the Supreme Court's characterization of prior testimony as a weaker form of live testimony, according second-class status to former testimony is incongruous. The anomaly is apparent when prior testimony is compared to hearsay exceptions that possess generally inferior guarantees of trustworthiness, such as declarations of present bodily or mental state, or excited or spontaneous utterances, where no showing of unavailability is required. The fears that the proponent of prior testimony would routinely resort to the use of such testimony when witnesses are available appears overblown, and when the witness is available, the opponent is able to conduct meaningful cross-examination under Rule 806 even if the declarant is not called on direct examination.[2]

Improvement would be gained from a procedure under which prior testimony is admitted in civil cases after giving the opposing party notice of intent to offer the testimony, thus affording an opportunity to produce the witness in person if desired and if the witness is available. The matter might even be left to the ordinary processes of discovery, with no formal notice procedure at all.

A second area where reform regarding the admissibility of prior testimony should be considered concerns the application of the predecessor in interest concept. Under Federal Rule 804(b)(1), prior testimony is admissible in civil cases "if the party against whom the testimony is now offered or * * * a predecessor in interest, had an opportunity and similar motive to develop the testimony." A very substantial issue is raised by the meaning of predecessor in interest and in particular whether the concept applies to situations where no economic or legal relationship exits between the parties.[3]

This problem in defining a predecessor in interest might be avoided if the courts recognized explicitly that the dimensions of the opportunity and motive to cross-examine may differ between the situation where the party itself was involved in the previous litigation and one where an unrelated party conducted the cross-examination. In the former situation, as exemplified by the use of preliminary hearing testimony against criminal defendants at trial, parties have been, and should be, held responsible for previous strategic or tactical judgments and just plain poor lawyering. By contrast, in the situation where the parties are unconnected, the quality of the cross-examination should be scrutinized more carefully. Even if opportunity and motive for cross-examination are adequate, the costs of poor lawyering should not be imposed on a separate party. If courts become willing to examine directly and meaningfully the adequacy of the testing of the prior testimony, issues about what constitutes a predecessor in interest will become much less important.

2. See infra § 324.2.

3. See supra § 303.

Chapter 32

DYING DECLARATIONS

§ 309. Introduction

Of the doctrines that authorize the admission of special classes of hearsay, the doctrine relating to dying declarations is the most mystical in its theory and traditionally among the most arbitrary in its limitations. The notion of the special likelihood of truthfulness of deathbed statements was widespread long before the recognition of a general rule against hearsay in the early 1700s. Not surprisingly, nearly as soon as we find a hearsay rule, we also find an exception for dying declarations.

§ 310. Requirements That Declarant Must Have Been Conscious of Impending Death and That Declarant Must Be Unavailable

The popular reverence for deathbed statements flows from two important limitations upon the dying declaration exception as developed at common law. Unlike several other limitations, which will be discussed in the next section, these two were arguably rational even though they restricted the exception too tightly.

The first was that the declarant must have been conscious that death was near and certain when making the statement. The declarant must have lost all hope of recovery. A belief in a probability of impending death would arguably make most people strongly disposed to tell the truth and hence guarantee the needed special reliability, but belief in the certainty of impending death, not its likelihood or probability, is the formula that was rigorously required. Perhaps this limitation reflected some lack of confidence in the reliability of "deathbed" statements generally.

The description of the declarant's mental state in Federal Rule 804(b)(2) is less emphatic than in the common law cases, merely saying "while believing that declarant's death was imminent." Evidence that would satisfy the common law would clearly satisfy the rule, and a growing number of courts have recognized that a lesser showing will suffice.

Often this belief in the imminence of death is proved by the declarant's own statements of belief at the time—an expression of a "settled hopeless expectation"—but the declarant need not have made such a statement.

463

The belief may be shown circumstantially by the apparent fatal quality of the wound, by the statements made to the declarant by doctors or others of the hopelessness of the condition, or by other circumstances. These preliminary questions of fact are to be determined by the court.[1]

The second historical limitation was that the declarant must be dead when the evidence is offered. However, the Federal Rules do not require that the declarant must be dead, only unavailable, which of course includes death.[2] Since the declarant need not die from the wounds or injuries, the length of time between a statement and death could not be dispositive of the statement's admissibility under the exception. Even under the earlier formulations, death was not required to have followed at any very short interval after the declaration. The critical issue throughout is the declarant's belief in the nearness of death at the time of the statement, not the actual swiftness with which death ensues after the statement or the immediacy of the statement after the injury.

§ 311. Limitation to the Use in Criminal Homicide Cases and Subject Matter Restrictions

If the courts in their creation of rules about dying declarations had stopped with the limitations discussed above, the result would have been a narrow, but rational and understandable, exception. The requirement of consciousness of impending death arguably tends to guarantee a sufficient degree of special reliability, and the requirement that the declarant must have died and thus be unavailable as a witness provides an ample showing of the necessity for the use of hearsay. This simple rationale of dying declarations sufficed until the beginning of the 1800s, and these declarations were admitted in civil and criminal cases without distinction and seemingly without untoward results. The subsequent history of the rule is an object lesson in the use of precedents to preserve and fossilize earlier judicial mistakes.

The first error occurred in limiting admissibility to homicide prosecutions. Sergeant East, in his widely used treatise, Pleas of the Crown, wrote regarding dying declarations:

> Evidence of this sort is admissible in this case on the fullest necessity; for it often happens that there is no third person present to be an eye-witness to the fact; and the usual witness on occasion of other felonies, namely, the party injured himself, is gotten rid of.[1]

East's statement was seized upon for a purpose not intended, namely, an announcement that the sole justification of the admission of dying declarations is the necessity of punishing murderers who might otherwise escape for lack of the testimony of the victim. This need may exist, but the proposition that the use of dying declarations should be limited to instances where it exists surely does not follow. Nevertheless, this proposition was further developed into a series of largely arbitrary limiting rules.

The first of these was the rule that the use of dying declarations was limited to cases of criminal homicide. Although the English courts in the 1700s had not done so, subsequent decisions refused to admit dying declarations in civil cases, whether death actions or other civil cases, or in criminal cases other than those charging homicide as an essential part of the offense. For example, in a rape prosecution, the declarations were held inadmissible even though the victim died before trial. Probably this restriction proceeded from a sense that dying declarations both rest on a somewhat questionable guarantee of trustworthiness and constitute a dangerous kind of testimony, which a jury is likely to handle too emotionally. However, these dangers are not likely to be less serious in a murder prosecution, where the statements are admitted, than they are in a civil action for wrongful death or

---

§ 310

1. See generally supra § 53.
2. Unavailability is discussed in supra § 253.

§ 311

1. East, 1 Pleas of the Crown 353 (1803).

in a prosecution for rape, where they were excluded.

As proposed by the Supreme Court, the exception for dying declaration was not restricted to any particular type of case. However, led by the House Judiciary Committee, Congress amended the exception and limited it to prosecutions for homicide and civil actions or proceedings. Thus, under the Federal Rule, dying declarations are inadmissible in criminal cases other than homicides.

The concept of necessity, limited to protection of the state against the slayer who might go free because of the death of his victim, produced another consequence. This was the further limitation that not only must the charge be homicide, but the defendant in the present trial must have been charged with the death of the declarant. When a marauder shot a man and his wife at the same time but the defendant was tried separately for the husband's murder, the dying declaration of the wife identifying the defendant as the assailant was excluded under this doctrine. Wigmore could not imagine "a more senseless rule of exclusion."[2] No such limitation appears in the Federal Rule.

A third limitation regarding the subject matter was conceptually sound, but its early formulations were sometimes arbitrary, i.e., declarations were admissible only insofar as they related to the circumstances of the killing and to the events more or less nearly preceding it in time and leading up to it. Under this version, declarations about previous quarrels between the accused and the victim would be excluded, while transactions between them leading up to and shortly before the present attack would be received. Some limitation as to time and circumstances is appropriate to enhance trustworthiness, but proper phrasing is difficult. Federal Rule 804(b)(2) requires only that the statement be one "concerning the cause or circumstances of what the declarant believed to be impending death." Statements identifying an attacker are clearly admissible under this terminology,

and those describing prior threats by, or fights and argument with, such person also meet its requirements. Within this more liberal framework, decisions to exclude may be made in terms of remoteness and prejudice under Rule 403.[3]

Finally, in some jurisdictions, dying declarations are limited with regard to statements elicited by leading questions. However, no blanket limitation against statements in response to questions is generally recognized or appropriate.

§ 312. Admissible on Behalf of Accused as Well as for Prosecution

The historical limitation of dying declarations to homicide cases, based on the extreme necessity in those cases of admitting the statements of the decedent *and* the sense of rough justice that admitting such statements against the murderer was only fair, might have led some courts to restrict dying declarations only to use by the prosecution. However, the unfairness of such a result was too apparent, and they have long been received on behalf of the defendant as well.

§ 313. Application of Other Evidentiary Rules: Personal Knowledge; Opinion; Rules About Writings

Other principles of evidence law present recurrent problems in their application to dying declarations. If the declarant did not have adequate opportunity to observe the facts recounted, the declaration will be rejected for lack of firsthand knowledge. When there is room for doubt as to whether the statement is based on knowledge, the question is for the jury. Expressions of suspicion or conjecture are to be excluded, however.

The knowledge requirement has sometimes been confused with the opinion rule, and this confusion may have led courts to make the statement that opinions in dying declarations will be excluded. The traditional opinion rule, designed as a regulation of the manner of questioning of witnesses in court, is entirely inappropriate as a restriction upon out-of-

---

2.   5 Wigmore, Evidence § 1433, at 281 n.1 (Chadbourn rev. 1974).

3.   See supra § 185.

court declarations.[1] Accordingly, most courts, including some that have professed to apply the opinion rule here, have admitted statements in which the declarant attributes purpose or lack of justification to the other party, which at one time would have been excluded as opinions if spoken by a witness on the stand.

Another problem is the application of the so-called best evidence rule.[2] Often the dying victim will make one or more oral statements about the facts of the crime and, in addition, may make a written statement, or the person hearing the statement may write it down and have the declarant sign it. When must the writing be produced or its absence be explained? Any separate oral statement is clearly provable without producing a later writing, but the terms of a written dying statement cannot be proved as such without producing or accounting for the writing.[3] What if the witness who heard the oral statement, which was taken down and signed, offers to testify to what he or she heard? Wigmore argued that the execution of the writing does not call into play the parol evidence rule since that rule is limited to contracts and other "legal acts."[4] To a limited degree, a some courts ruled otherwise. They did not exclude evidence of other oral statements made on the same occasion which were not embraced in the writing, but oral declarations embodied in a writing signed or adopted by the deceased were provable only by producing the written statement, if available. The result might be justified by the need for accuracy in transmitting to the tribunal the exact terms of this very important statement. However, these restriction do not have a justification in modern evidence rules, and whether such limitations continue in any jurisdiction is unclear.

§ 314. Instructions Regarding the Weight to Be Given to Dying Declarations

Historically, commentators and courts frequently theorized as to the weight properly to be given to dying declarations. As a result, the practice has grown up in some states of requiring or permitting the judge to instruct the jury that these declarations are to be received with caution or that they are not to be regarded as having the same value and weight as sworn testimony. In other jurisdictions, such instructions have been held to be improper. Others have considered it proper to direct the jury that they should give the dying declaration the same weight as the testimony of a witness.

While there may be merit in a standardized practice of giving cautionary instructions, the direction to give the declaration a predetermined fixed weight seems of questionable wisdom. The weight of particular dying declarations depends upon so many factors varying from case to case that no standardized instruction will fit all situations. Certainly in jurisdictions where the judge retains common law power to comment on the weight of the evidence, the dying declaration is an appropriate subject for individualized comment. But where the judge lacks this power, as in most states, the wiser practice is to leave the weight of the declaration to the arguments of counsel, the judgment of the jury, and the consideration of the judge on motion for new trial.

§ 315. Suggestions for Changes in the Exception

In a remarkably forward-looking decision involving an action by the executor of the seller to recover on a land sale contract, the Kansas Supreme Court was confronted with a dying statement of the seller of "the truth about the sale."[1] Admission required departure from traditional common law limitations in that the case was civil, not a criminal homicide prosecution, and the statement did not relate to the cause or circumstances of death. In admitting the evidence, the court stated: "We are confronted with a restrictive rule of evi-

---

§ 313

1. See supra § 18.

2. See supra Ch. 23.

3. See supra § 233.

4. 5 Wigmore, Evidence § 1450(b), at 314 (Chadbourn rev. 1974).

§ 315

1. Thurston v. Fritz, 138 P. 625 (Kan.1914).

dence commendable only for its age, its respectability resting solely upon a habit of judicial recognition, formed without reason, and continued without justification.''

As observed in earlier sections of this chapter, there has been some willingness to expand admissibility with respect to the type of case, as witnessed by the Revised Uniform Rules (1986), which would admit dying declarations in all cases. The exclusion of such hearsay under the Federal Rules from criminal cases other than prosecutions for homicide because of Congressional concern about the reliability of this form of hearsay seems to strike the wrong balance. Only a sense of very rough justice will admit statements in the most serious type of cases because the murder of the witness threatens to rob the court of valuable testimony but exclude them because of questionable trustworthiness in less serious criminal prosecutions. Under the terms of the Federal Rule, the need for the testimony is frequently just as great in non-homicide cases because the declarant, while not a murder victim, must be unavailable to testify. As a result, extension of the exception to other criminal cases would appear appropriate.

While the limitation on statements admissible under the exception to the circumstances of the declarant's death was not in the original Uniform Rules, it is a requirement of the Federal Rule, and departure from this limitation is found only in occasional rules and statutes. The restriction is generally sound because the connection between these circumstances and the statement helps to enhance its trustworthiness by reducing the dangers of poor memory and insincerity.

Chapter 33

DECLARATIONS AGAINST INTEREST

Table of Sections

§ 316. General Requirements; Distinction Between Declarations Against Interest and Admissions

Traditionally, two main requirements have been imposed on the statement against interest exception: first, either the declaration must state facts that are against the pecuniary or proprietary interest of the declarant or the making of the declaration itself must create evidence that would harm such interests;[1] second, the declarant must be unavailable at the time of trial.[2] Under the theory that people generally do not lightly make statements that are damaging to their interests, the first requirement provides the safeguard of special trustworthiness justifying most of the exceptions to the hearsay rule. The second is largely an historical development but operates usefully as a limiting factor. As with hearsay exceptions generally,[3] the declarant must have had firsthand knowledge. Minor qualifications may be added, such as, the interest involved must not be too indirect or remote.

While sometimes erroneously called an admission against interest, this exception and the admission exclusion[4] are distinct. The traditional distinctions developed by Wigmore[5] are generally followed. Thus, the admissions of a party-opponent may be introduced without satisfying any of the requirements for declarations against interest. First, while frequently admissions are against interest when made, they need not be and may, in fact, have been self-serving at that time.[6] Second, the party making the admission need not be, and seldom is, unavailable.[7] Third, the party making the admission need not have had personal knowledge of the fact admitted.[8] Accordingly, when the opponent offers a statement of a party, it should be submitted as, and tested by, the requirements for parties' admissions and not those for declarations against interest. On the other hand, statements of nonparties, which may not be introduced as admissions, may be admitted if they are against interest and if the

---

§ 316

1. See infra §§ 317–319.
2. See infra § 320.
3. See, e.g., supra §§ 280, 290, 313.
4. See supra Ch. 25.

5. 5 Wigmore, Evidence § 1475 (Chadbourn rev. 1974); C.J.S. Evidence § 217(b).
6. See supra § 254; infra § 319.
7. See supra § 254.
8. See supra § 255.

declarant is unavailable. Moreover, since the Federal Rules do not recognize admissions by persons in "privity" with parties,[9] the instant exception provides one of the principal alternative methods for introducing damaging statements made by a party's predecessor.

The Federal Rules preserve the hearsay exception as broadly developed at common law with respect to statements against pecuniary or proprietary interest and expand the definition to include statements against penal interest. Rule 804(b)(3) admits statements of unavailable declarants as follows:

> A statement which was at the time of its making so far contrary to the declarant's pecuniary or proprietary interest, or so far tended to subject the declarant to civil or criminal liability, or to render invalid a claim by the declarant against another, that a reasonable person in the declarant's position would not have made the statement unless believing it to be true. A statement tending to expose the declarant to criminal liability and offered to exculpate the accused is not admissible unless corroborating circumstances clearly indicate the trustworthiness of the statement.

§ 317. Declarations Against Pecuniary or Proprietary Interest; Declarations Affecting Claim or Liability for Damages

The traditional field for this exception has been that of declarations against proprietary or pecuniary interest. Common instances of the former are acknowledgments that the declarant does not own certain land or personal property, or has conveyed or transferred it. Moreover, a statement by one in possession that he or she holds an interest less than complete ownership has traditionally been regarded as a declaration against interest, though it is obviously ambiguous in that it claims some rights.

The clearest example of a declaration against pecuniary interest is an acknowledgment that the declarant is indebted. Here the

declaration, standing alone, is against interest on the theory that to owe a debt is against one's financial interest. This theory is routinely followed even though it may not be applicable in particular circumstances. Less obviously an acknowledgment of receipt of money in payment of a debt owing to the declarant is also traditionally classed as against interest. Here the fact of payment itself is advantageous to the receiver, but the acknowledgment of it is regarded as against interest because it is evidence of the reduction or extinguishment of the debt. Of course, a receipt for money which the receiver is to hold for another is an acknowledgment of a debt. Similarly, a statement that one holds money in trust is against interest.

The exception as developed by English courts narrowly focused it in the areas of debt and property, but the American cases extended the field of declarations against interest to include acknowledgment of facts which would give rise to a liability for unliquidated damages for tort or seemingly for breach of contract. The exception was also extended to statements of facts impairing a defense to a claim of damages otherwise available to the declarant.

Federal Rule 804(b)(3) is broadly drawn to include statements against pecuniary or proprietary interest in general, and more specifically those tending to subject declarant to civil liability, without being limited to tort or contract, and those tending to invalidate a claim by the declarant against another. This aspect of the rule thus occupies the entire area developed by the common law except for some of the more fanciful English decisions in tenancy cases.

§ 318. Penal Interest; Interest of Prestige or Self-Esteem

In 1844 in the Sussex Peerage Case,[1] the House of Lords determined that a declaration confessing a crime committed by declarant was not receivable as a declaration against interest. This decision was influential in confining the

---

9. See supra § 260.

1. 11 Cl. & F. 85, 8 Eng.Rep. 1034 (1844).

development of this exception to the hearsay rule within narrow materialistic limits. It was generally followed in this country in criminal cases for many years. Courts, while not repudiating the limitation, have sometimes justified admission of a third person's confession of crime in the civil context on the basis that the particular crime was also a tort and thus the statement was against material interest by exposing the declarant to liability for damages.

The practice of excluding third-person confessions in criminal cases certainly cannot be justified on the ground that an acknowledgment of facts rendering one liable to criminal punishment is less trustworthy than an acknowledgment of a debt. The motivation for the exclusion was no doubt a different one, namely, the fear of opening the door to a flood of witnesses testifying falsely to confessions that were never made or testifying truthfully to confessions that were false. This fear was based on the likely criminal character of the declarant and the witness who would recount the alleged statement, reinforced by the requirement that declarant must be unavailable, which would make perjury easier to accomplish and more difficult to punish.

Wigmore rejected the argument of the danger of perjury, since that danger is one that attends all human testimony, and concluded that "any rule which hampers an honest man in exonerating himself is a bad rule, even it if also hampers a villain in falsely passing for an innocent."[2] Under this argument, accepted by Justice Holmes in a famous dissent,[3] courts began to relax the rule of exclusion of declarations against penal interest in particular situations or generally. The inclusion of declarations against penal interest in the Federal Rule 804(b)(3) has given great impetus to the use of this exception, and most of the recent case law and literature dealing with declarations against interest has centered on this aspect and its concomitant problems.

During the course of the expansion of the hearsay exception to include declarations against penal interest, the situation principally

examined was whether a confession or other statement by a third person offered by the defense to *exculpate* the accused should be admissible. The traditional distrust of declarations against penal interest had evolved in that setting, and as a result, the Federal Rule included a prohibition against admitting an exculpatory statement in evidence "unless corroborating circumstances clearly indicate the trustworthiness of the statement." While the possibility was recognized that statements against penal interest by third parties inculpating both the declarant and the defendant might also be offered by the prosecution to *inculpate* the accused, prior to the adoption of the Federal Rules the possibility of their admissibility was raised infrequently in cases or the literature. Under Rule 804(b)(3), admission of such statements has been relatively common. The issues involved in statements against penal interest made by third parties have raised a number of difficult issues, which will be examined in the next section.

Whether the hearsay exception for declarations against interest should be enlarged to include declarations against "social" interests has been debated. Traditionally, interests of this nature were not regarded as sufficiently substantial to ensure reliability. However, following the pattern of the original Uniform Rule, the Federal Rule, as proposed by the Supreme Court, included statements tending to make the declarant "an object of hatred, ridicule, or disgrace," but it was deleted from the rule by Congress. The provision was reinstated in the Revised Uniform Rule (1986) and has been adopted in a handful of states.

§ 319. Determining What Is Against Interest; Confrontation Problems

(a) The time aspect. As observed at the beginning of this chapter, the theory underlying the hearsay exception for declarations against interest is that people do not make statements that are harmful to their interests without substantial reason to believe that the statements are true. Reason indicates that the harm must exist at the time the statement is

---

2. 5 Wigmore, Evidence § 1477, at 359 (Chadbourn rev. 1974).

3. Donnelly v. United States, 228 U.S. 243, 277–78 (1913) (Holmes, J., dissenting).

made; otherwise it can exert no influence on declarant to speak accurately and truthfully. That the statement later proves to be damaging—or, for that matter, beneficial—is without significance. Rather, the motivation and the statement must be contemporaneous.

(b) The nature of the statement. Under Rule 804(b)(3), the statement must be such "that a reasonable person in the declarant's position would not have made the statement unless believing it to be true," in view of the statement's adversity to declarant's interest. The interests involved are the declarant's pecuniary, proprietary, or penal interest. With regard to the latter, the statement need not be a confession, but it must involve substantial exposure to criminal liability.

(c) "Collateral" statements and Williamson. In the archetypal case of Higham v. Ridgway,[1] an entry in the record book of a midwife was introduced showing a charge for attendance upon the mother for birth of a child together with an entry six months later showing payment of the charge offered to prove the date of birth of an individual. The court said the entry payment "was in prejudice of the party making it." However, although the entry of payment may have been against interest, the issue in the case was not payment, but the birth six months earlier. To this the court replied, "By the reference to the ledger, the entry there [of the birth] is virtually incorporated in the other entry [of payment], of which it is explanatory." In civil cases such as Higham v. Ridgway, admission of an associated statement may have been acceptable, even though not itself against interest, if it was closely connected to the statement against interest.

However, the generally sound decision to recognize statements against penal interest as qualifying under the exception put substantial new pressures on this element of the exception. When the contextual statement is not about a birth noted in the doctor's bill, but rather is an incriminating statement offered by the prosecution against the accused found

in a statement against the interest of a third party, both trustworthiness issues and the Confrontation Clause move unavoidably to the forefront.

In Williamson v. United States,[2] the Court resolved the most difficult issues presented by contextual statements by focusing on the definition of "statement" as used in this rule. It concluded that the principle behind the rule pointed to a narrow reading to the term—"a single declaration or remark" rather than "a report or narrative"—because only as to the more narrow meaning does the rationale hold that not particularly honest people make self-incriminatory statements only if they believe them to be true. Indeed, one of the most effective ways to lie is to mix falsehood with truth; to mix within a larger report the exculpatory with the self-incriminating. The text of the Rule, the Court concluded, supports that result and overcame ambiguous Advisory Committee comments.[3] The result is that only the specific parts of the narrative that inculpate qualify. The determination of whether a statement in this narrow sense is self-incriminatory requires examination of context.

Williamson noted that under the new test statements against interest by third parties can continue to be admitted against the defendant where the statement does not mention the defendant directly but either logical inferences or the operation of law makes it incriminating to the defendant. Also, statements mentioning a defendant may also be admissible if a reasonable person in the declarant's position would realize that being linked to others implicated the declarant in another crime. Applying *Williamson*, federal courts have most frequently admitted third party statements that inculpate a defendant where two general conditions are satisfied: (1) the statement was made to a private person and does not seek to curry the favor of law enforcement authorities, and (2) it does not shift blame.

Finally, the majority noted that "the very fact that a statement is genuinely self-inculpatory—which our reading of Rule 804(b)(3) re-

---

§ 319
1. 10 East 109, 103 Eng.Rep. 717 (K.B.1808).

2. 512 U.S. 594 (1994).
3. Id. at 603.

quires—is itself one of the 'particularized guarantees of trustworthiness' that makes a statement admissible under the Confrontation Clause."[4] The limitation that the part of the statement that inculpates another individual must actually inculpate the declarant renders many statements that might otherwise violate the Confrontation Clause inadmissible as a matter of hearsay law. However, because *Williamson* focused on admissibility under the Federal Rules of Evidence, it was binding only on the federal courts. Nevertheless, a number of states quickly adopted its analysis, and the Court's subsequent decision in Lilly v. Virginia[5] effectively imposes under the Confrontation Clause limitations of the type required by *Williamson* when such statements are offered in state criminal prosecutions.

(d) The factual setting. Whether a statement was against interest "can only be determined by viewing it in context"[6] and will often require a delicate examination of the circumstances under which it was made. That determination may depend on outside facts that existed at the time the statement was made that were reasonably known by the declarant but may not be disclosed in the statement. For example, whether a statement that declarant is a member of a certain partnership is against his or her pecuniary interest depends upon whether the firm is clearly solvent or is on an uncertain economic footing. Likewise, a statement that one has a contract to purchase a commodity, such as wheat, at a certain price is against or for interest depending upon the price in the market at the time of the statement.

The setting in which the statement is made is of particular importance where statements against penal interest are offered to inculpate the accused. If the declarant was in police custody when he or she made the statement, the statement or parts of it implicating others very likely were made to curry favor even if it also inculpates the declarant. However, courts have not treated being in custody as conclusively establishing that the statement is self-serving if it is voluntarily given, strongly

incriminating of the declarant, and shows no indication of currying favor.

A relation of trust and confidence between speaker and listener could militate against awareness that making the statement might be against declarant's interest. The possibility of disclosure appears to be enough. Instead, in the context of statements against penal interest, greater significance is attached to the fact a statement made to private individuals, rather than to law enforcement authorities, was not likely made for the purpose of currying favor.

(e) Corroboration. Both the proper role for, and definition of, corroboration for statements against interest is almost hopelessly confused. Federal Rule 804(b)(3) makes third party statements that exculpate the defendant admissible only if "corroborating circumstances clearly indicate the trustworthiness of the statement." Although not in the text of the rule, many of the federal circuits have likewise imposed a corroboration requirement for third party statements that inculpate the defendant.

Turning first to statements that exculpate the defendant, the federal courts have disagreed on whether the corroboration requirement applies to the veracity of the in-court witness testifying that the statement was made in addition to the clearly required showing that the statement itself is trustworthy. As a matter of standard hearsay analysis, the credibility of the in-court witness regarding the fact that the statement was made is not an appropriate inquiry. However, given the strong legislative concern over the possibility of perjured testimony that the exculpatory statement was made, it is not obvious that courts err in considering this factor as a matter of special statutory intent for this exception.

Corroboration of the trustworthiness of the out-of-court declaration should generally focus on the circumstances of the making of the statement and the motivation of the declarant. Occasionally, reasonably objective factors such as whether the declarant was in the

---

4. Id. at 605.

5. 119 S.Ct. 1887 (1999).

6. *Williamson*, 512 U.S. at 603.

vicinity of the crime and had any motivation to commit it, may affirmatively or negatively corroborate the statement. Significantly, the rule does not require that the statements themselves be independently proved to be accurate; rather it requires only that corroborating circumstances indicate trustworthiness.

The corroboration requirement for inculpatory statements is likely to disappear in the wake of the Supreme Court's *Williamson* decision. The federal courts imposed this requirement chiefly to satisfy a perceived need to protect the Confrontation Clause concerns raised when inculpatory statements by a third party are offered against the defendant. Although Justice O'Connor's opinion reserved judgment on whether a corroboration requirement should be read into the rule, the Court is very unlikely to impose such a requirement to satisfy the Confrontation Clause given its requirement that the statement be "genuinely self-inculpatory," which meets the requirements of the Clause.

(e) Motive: Actual state of mind of declarant. In strictest logic, attention in cases of declarations against interest, as with other hearsay exceptions, should focus on the actual state of mind produced in the declarant by the supposed truth-inducing circumstances, and a "reasonable-person" standard should not be the focus of attention. That, of course, is not the case. The usual standard is that found in Federal Evidence Rule 804(b)(3): "that a reasonable person in the declarant's position would not have made the statement unless believing it to be true." Difficulties of proof, probabilities, and the unavailability of the declarant all favor the accepted standard. However, statements of a declarant disclosing his or her ostensible actual mental state should certainly be received and should control in an appropriate case.

The exception has often been stated as requiring that there have been no motive to falsify. This is too sweeping, and the limitation can probably best be understood merely as a qualification that even though a statement must be against interest in one respect, if it appears that declarant had some motive, whether of self-interest or otherwise, which was likely to lead to misrepresentation of the facts, the statement should be excluded.

§ 320. Unavailability of the Declarant

The Federal Rule and the vast majority of the states require unavailability. While the requirement of unavailability followed its own course of development at common law with respect to declarations against interest, as was the case with other hearsay exceptions requiring unavailability of the declarant, the pattern is now largely standardized. Unavailability requirements are discussed in detail in § 253.

Chapter 34

VARIOUS OTHER EXCEPTIONS AND THE FUTURE OF THE RULES ABOUT HEARSAY

Table of Sections

§ 321. Learned Treatises, Industry Standards, and Commercial Publications

When offered to prove the truth of matters asserted in them, learned writings, such as treatises, books, and articles regarding specialized areas of knowledge, are clearly hearsay. Nevertheless, Wigmore argued strongly for an exception for such material.[1] According to his view, permitting such sources to be proved directly would not be as great a change as might at first be supposed because much of the testimony of experts consists of information they have obtained from such sources. Also, admitting the sources would greatly improve the quality of information presented. Wigmore concluded that learned treatises had sufficient assurances of trustworthiness to justify equating them with the live testimony of an expert. First, authors of treatises have no bias in any particular case. Second, they are acutely aware that their material will be read and evaluated by others in their field, and accordingly feel a strong pressure to be accurate.

Virtually all courts permit some use of learned materials in the cross-examination of an expert witness. Historically, several patterns had developed. Most courts permitted use where the expert relied upon the specific material in forming the opinion given during direct examination. Some of these courts extended the rule to situations in which the witness admitted to having relied upon some general authorities although not the particular impeaching material. Other courts required only that the witness acknowledge that the

§ 321

1. 6 Wigmore, Evidence §§ 1690–1692 (Chadbourn rev. 1976).

material offered for impeachment was a recognized authority in the field and permitted use of the material on that basis despite the fact that the witness may not have personally relied upon it. Finally, some courts permitted use of such material to impeach without regard to whether the witness relied upon or acknowledged the authority of the source if either the cross-examiner established, or the court judicially noticed, the general authority of the material.

Traditionally, the material used to impeach was not admissible as substantive evidence received for its truth. Instead, its only impact was upon the witness' competency or the accuracy of the opinions rendered. Under the common law development of the practice, most courts were unwilling to adopt a broad exception to the hearsay rule for treatises and other professional literature. Although not finding them compelling, Wigmore recognized a number of arguments that could be made against recognizing an exception: (a) professional skill and knowledge shift rapidly, so printed material is likely to be out of date; (b) a trier of fact is likely to be confused by being exposed to material designed for the professionally-trained reader; (c) the opportunity to take sections of material out of context creates a danger of unfair use; and (d) most matters of expertise are really matters of skill rather than academic knowledge of the sort put in writing and therefore personally-appearing witnesses are likely to be better sources of evidence than written material. In Wigmore's view, the only arguably meritorious objection was the basic hearsay objection that the author is not available for cross-examination, but he concluded this concern was outweighed by the need for the evidence and the other assurances of accuracy.

The Federal Rules addressed these various issues by creating a hearsay exception for "learned treatises." Federal Rule 803(18) provides:

> To the extent called to the attention of an expert witness upon cross-examination or relied upon by the expert witness in direct examination, statements contained in published treatises, periodicals,

or pamphlets on a subject of history, medicine, or other science or art, established as a reliable authority by the testimony or admission of the witness or by other expert testimony or by judicial notice. If admitted, the statements may be read into evidence but may not be received as exhibits.

The rule is broadly worded as to subjects—"history, medicine, or other science or art"—and is sufficient to include standards and manuals published by government agencies and industry or professional organizations. The rule requires that the reliability of the publication must be established, which demonstrates that it is viewed as trustworthy by professionals in the field. Authoritativeness can be established by the expert of either party or by judicial notice.

The rule also requires that the publication must be called to the attention of an expert on cross-examination or relied upon by the expert in direct examination. This provision is designed to ensure that the materials are used only under the sponsorship of an expert, who can assist the fact finder and explain how to apply the materials. This policy is furthered by the prohibition against admission as exhibits, which prevents sending the materials to the jury room.

While Rule 803(18) defines a hearsay exception, its requirements have an impact beyond hearsay concepts, in effect setting the general standards for the use of such documents to impeach. At the same time the rule has this impact beyond the hearsay area, satisfying its requirements does not automatically guarantee admissibility. Documents that meet the terms of the rule are still excluded if their probative value is outweighed by their prejudicial impact or potential to confuse or mislead.

Courts have developed a somewhat related hearsay exception that includes publications such as reports of market prices, professional directories, city and telephone directories, and mortality and annuity tables used by life insurance companies. The justification for this exception is that the motivation for accuracy is high, and public acceptance depends upon reliability.

Federal Rule 803(17) defines a hearsay exception for such publications, covering "market quotations, tabulations, lists, directories, or other published compilations, generally used and relied upon by the public or by persons in particular occupations." While the precise definition of this exception is somewhat difficult, other than by example, some of its basic characteristics are clear. The list must be published in written form and circulated for use by others; it must be relied upon by the general public or by persons in a particular occupation; and it must pertain to relatively straightforward objective facts.

§ 322. Reputation as to Character; Statements, Reputation, and Judgments as to Pedigree and Family History; Reputation Concerning Land Boundaries and General History

A. *Reputation as to Character*

Evidence regarding pertinent traits of character are admitted both to prove conduct in conformity with those traits and to impeach the credibility of witnesses, and in modern evidence law, these traits may be proved by evidence of reputation or opinion.[1] Proof of the trait by reputation raises a hearsay issue, which has traditionally been resolved by a hearsay exception that readily admitted such evidence. Federal Rule 803(21), which deals only with the hearsay aspect of the issue, recognizes an exception that admits reputation among associates or in the community when used to establish character.

B. *Statements, Reputation, and Judgments as to Pedigree and Family History*

One of the oldest exceptions to the hearsay rule encompasses statements concerning family history, such as the date and place of birth and death of members of the family and facts about marriage, descent, and relationship. Under the traditional rule, declarations are admissible when made by the person

whose family situation is at issue and by other members of the family. Under a liberal view adopted by some courts, declarations by non-family members with a close relationship to the family are also admitted. These statements were admissible, however, only upon a showing that the declarant is unavailable, that the statement was made before the origin of the controversy giving rise to the litigation in which the statement is offered (i.e., *ante litem motam*), and that there was no apparent motive for the declarant to misrepresent the facts.

Under the strict traditional view, the relationship of declarant to the family had to be proved by independent evidence, but this requirement did not apply where declarant's own family relationships were the subject of the hearsay statement. Firsthand knowledge by declarant of the facts of birth, death, kinship, or the like was not required. The general difficulty of obtaining other evidence of family matters, reflected in the unavailability requirement, furnished impetus for the hearsay exception. Reliability was assured by the probability that absent a motive to fabricate, discussions with relatives (and others intimately associated) regarding family members would be accurate.

Federal Rule of Evidence 804(b)(4) continues the requirement of unavailability of the declarant[2] and provides a hearsay exception for

(A) A statement concerning the declarant's own birth, adoption, marriage, divorce, legitimacy, relationship by blood, adoption, or marriage, ancestry, or other similar fact of personal or family history, even though declarant had no means of acquiring personal knowledge of the matter stated; or (B) a statement concerning the foregoing matters, and death also, of another person, if the declarant was related to the other by blood, adoption, or marriage or was so intimately associated with the other's family as to be likely to

---

§ 322

1. See Fed.R.Evid. 404, 405 & 608; supra § 43.

2. As to unavailability, see generally supra § 253.

have accurate information concerning the matter declared.

The rule follows the liberal view in allowing statements by intimate associates of the family. It eliminates the traditional requirements that the statement have been made *ante litem motam* and without motive to misrepresent, leaving these aspects to be treated as questions of weight, or excluded under Rule 403 in extreme cases.[3] The narrow view of what is included in family history is continued.

The traditional hearsay exception went beyond the statements described above and allowed the use of contemporary records of family history, such as entries in a family Bible or on a tombstone, even though the author may not be identifiable. Federal Rule 803(13) follows this pattern in providing a hearsay exception irrespective of the declarant's availability for statements "concerning personal or family history contained in family Bibles, genealogies, charts, engravings on rings, inscriptions on family portraits, engravings on urns, crypts, or tombstones, or the like."

Matters of family history traditionally have also been provable by reputation in the family and sometimes in the community. Federal Rule 803(19) continues this pattern. It covers:

> Reputation among members of a person's family by blood, adoption, or marriage, or among a person's associates, or in the community, concerning a person's birth, adoption, marriage, divorce, death, legitimacy, relationship by blood, adoption, or marriage, ancestry, or other similar fact of his personal or family history.

The exception requires reputation among family members or members of the community to establish such facts and not simply assertions by individuals. In addition, Rule 803(23) permits admission of judgments as "proof of matters of personal family or general history, or boundaries, essential to the judgment, if the same would be provable by evidence of reputation."

C. *Reputation Regarding Land Boundaries and General History*

When the location of boundaries of land is at issue, reputation is admitted to prove that location. Traditionally, the reputation not only had to antedate the beginning of the present controversy, but also it had to be "ancient," i.e., to extend beyond a generation. Some recent cases suggest that the requirement is only that the monuments or markers of the original survey must have disappeared. Federal Rule 803(20) dispenses completely with a requirement that the reputation be ancient or that the passage of time have rendered other evidence of the boundaries unavailable.

Reputation is also admissible to prove a variety of facts which can best be described as matters of general history. Wigmore suggested that the matter must be "one as to which it would be unlikely that living witnesses could be obtained."[4] Rule 803(20) does not impose that requirement, although by use of the term "history" some requirement of substantial age is imposed. In addition, the matter must be one of general interest, so that it can accurately be said that there is a high probability that the matter underwent general scrutiny as the community reputation was formed. Thus, when the navigable nature of a certain river was at issue, newspaper accounts and histories describing its use during the nineteenth century were admissible to prove reputation for navigability at that time.

In addition to these well-developed exceptions, reputation evidence is sometimes admitted under statute or local law to prove a variety of other miscellaneous matters. These include ownership of property, financial standing, and maintenance of a house as an establishment for liquor-selling or prostitution.

§ 323. Recitals in Ancient Writings and Documents Affecting an Interest in Property

One method of authenticating a writing is to show that it is at least twenty years old, is

---

3. See supra § 185.

4. 5 Wigmore, Evidence § 1597, at 561 (Chadbourn rev. 1974).

unsuspicious in appearance, and came from a place of custody natural for such a writing.[1] Indeed, historically the "ancient documents" rule related only to authentication, but American courts began recognizing a hearsay exception for written statements that met these requirements. Thus, what originated as an aspect of authentication also became an exception to the hearsay rule in some jurisdictions.

Necessity, which produced the special authentication rule, was the primary stimulus for this hearsay exception. After passage of a long period of time, witnesses are unlikely to be available or, if available, are unlikely to recall reliably the events at issue.

As to assurances of trustworthiness, the mere age of the writing offers little assurance of truth since the prevalence of lying is unlikely to have changed much in twenty years. Advocates of the exception argue, however, that sufficient assurances of reliability exist. First, the dangers of mistransmission are minimized since the rule applies only to written statements. Second, the age requirement virtually assures that the assertion was made before the beginning of the present controversy. Consequently, it is less likely that the declarant had a motive to falsify, and, in any case, the statements are almost certainly uninfluenced by partisanship. Finally, some additional assurance of reliability is provided by insistence, insofar as practicable, that the usual qualifications for witnesses and out-of-court declarants be met. As a result, the writing is inadmissible if the declarant lacked the opportunity for firsthand observation of the facts asserted.[2] Finally, the writing must not be suspicious on its face.

Well before the drafting of the Federal Rules, a number of courts accepted a hearsay exception for recitals in an ancient deed. Thus, recitals of the contents and execution of an earlier instrument, of heirship, and of consideration were commonly received to prove those facts. Arguably these cases involve unusual assurances of reliability, especially where possession has been taken under the deed, and

the exception could be limited to them. However, a number of courts applied the exception to other types of documents, and the Federal Rule 803(16) followed suit, creating an exception for statements in "a document in existence twenty years or more the authenticity of which is established." While the rule itself contains no limitation as to the kind of document that may qualify, as long as it is at least twenty years old and properly authenticated,[3] several limitations are imposed that provide additional assurance of trustworthiness. The declarant is subject to the general requirement of firsthand knowledge, and by virtue of the authentication requirements, the document must not be suspicious in appearance, which supports its reliability.

A somewhat related hearsay exception is recognized by Federal Rule 803(15), which covers statements contained in a document "purporting to establish or affect an interest in property if the matter stated was relevant to the purpose of the document, unless dealings with the property since the document was made have been inconsistent with the truth of the statement or the purport of the document." This exception imposes no requirement of age of the document, but it is limited to title documents, such as deeds, and to statements relevant to the purpose of the document.

The circumstances under which documents of a dispositive nature are executed, the character of the statements that will qualify, and the inapplicability of this exception if subsequent dealings have been inconsistent with the truth of the statement or the purport of the document, are considered sufficient guarantees of trustworthiness. A companion rule deals with the evidentiary status of such documents that have been recorded.

§ 324. The Residual Hearsay Exceptions

Despite the extensive array of specific hearsay exceptions in the Federal Rules, the Advisory Committee felt it "presumptuous to

---

§ 323

1. See supra § 223.

2. See generally supra §§ 10, 247.

3. See supra § 223.

assume that all possible desirable exceptions to the hearsay rule have been catalogued and to pass the hearsay rule to oncoming generations as a closed system." Therefore, it proposed for both available and unavailable declarants a residual or catchall exception for statements "having comparable circumstantial guarantees of trustworthiness." Cautioning against wholesale modification of the established system of hearsay exceptions by unrestricted admission under the residual exceptions, the Committee observed, "They do not contemplate an unfettered exercise of judicial discretion, but they do provide for treating new and presently unanticipated situations which demonstrate a trustworthiness within the spirit of the specifically stated exceptions."[1]

The House Judiciary Committee deleted the provisions entirely, believing they injected too much uncertainty into the law and arguing that additional hearsay exceptions should be created by amending the rules. The Senate Committee responded by suggesting further restrictions on the proposed exceptions, and they were enacted as modified.

In arguing to restore these exceptions after the House deleted them, the Senate Judiciary Committee stated that it intended that the residual exceptions should be used "very rarely, and only in exceptional circumstances."[2] Although occasionally this language is quoted by a court in supporting its decision to exclude hearsay offered under a catchall exception, resort to the exception has been very substantial. Perhaps most surprising is that the predominant use of the exceptions in federal courts, at least as reflected in the reported cases, has been by the prosecution in criminal cases.

In 1997, the two residual exceptions were combined into a single rule, a change that the Advisory Committee stated was not intended to change the meaning of the rules. Rule 807 provides:

> A statement not specifically covered by Rule 803 or 804 but having equivalent circumstantial guarantees of trustworthiness, is not excluded by the hearsay rule, if the court determines that (A) the statement is offered as evidence of a material fact; (B) the statement is more probative on the point for which it is offered than any other evidence which the proponent can procure through reasonable efforts; and (C) the general purposes of these rules and the interests of justice will best be served by admission of the statement into evidence. However, a statement may not be admitted under this exception unless the proponent of it makes known to the adverse party sufficiently in advance of the trial or hearing to provide the adverse party with a fair opportunity to prepare to meet it, the proponent's intention to offer the statement and the particulars of it, including the name and address of the declarant.

The rule contains five requirements, three of which impose substantial limitations on the admission of hearsay. They are considered below.

Equivalent circumstantial guarantees of trustworthiness In applying the residual exceptions, the most important issue is whether the statement offers "equivalent circumstantial guarantees of trustworthiness" to those found in the various other specific hearsay exceptions. In making the admissibility determination, courts frequently compare the circumstances surrounding the statement to the closest hearsay exception. They also focus on idiosyncratic factors of the particular statement that suggest trustworthiness. However, since the specific exceptions themselves vary widely in their trustworthiness, a rather substantial variation in the types of statements admitted under the residual exceptions has developed, with variation in approach further encouraged by the deferential "abuse of discretion" standard of appellate review.

Although the factors supporting and undermining trustworthiness are extremely var-

---

§ 324

1. Adv. Comm. Note, Fed.R.Evid. 803(24).

2. Senate Comm. on Judiciary, S.Rep. No. 1277, 93d Cong., 2d Sess. 18–20 (1974), reprinted in 1974 U.S.Code Cong. & Admin.News 7051, 7065–66.

ied and occur in numerous combinations, certain recurring factors are particularly significant to the determination of admissibility. Among these factors are: whether the declarant had a motivation to speak truthfully or otherwise; the spontaneity of the statement, including whether it was elicited by leading questions, and generally the time lapse between event and statement; whether the statement was under oath; whether the declarant was subject to cross-examination at the time the statement was made; the relationship between the declarant and the person to whom the statement was made; whether the declarant has recanted or reaffirmed the statement; whether the statement was recorded and particularly whether it was videotaped; and whether the declarant's firsthand knowledge is clearly demonstrated. One factor that should *not* be considered in evaluating the trustworthiness of the statement is the credibility of the person testifying to having heard it.

The availability of the declarant to be cross-examined also may support the admissibility of statements that otherwise would be found insufficiently trustworthy to be received. On the other hand, the availability of the declarant to testify as a superior alternative to the hearsay and a basis for exclusion is discussed below under the "Necessity" heading.

The most controversial additional factor to show trustworthiness is corroboration of the statement by other evidence that shows its accuracy. This factor does not bear upon declarant at the time the statement was made but in retrospect offers support to its truthfulness. The Supreme Court's opinion in Idaho v. Wright[3] casts doubt on whether corroboration can properly be used to demonstrate "equivalent circumstantial guarantees of trustworthiness" to that of the enumerated exceptions. Although *Wright* decided only an issue regarding the Confrontation Clause, it adopted a view of hearsay law to resolve the constitutional issue, and that view restricts the analysis of trustworthiness to the circumstances surrounding the making of the statement and

would exclude any consideration of corroboration by external facts to establish the accuracy of the statement. Nevertheless, some courts continue to use corroboration as a factor establishing trustworthiness of hearsay admitted under a catchall exception when the confrontation issue is otherwise resolved. Although state courts, which are not bound by the Supreme Court's interpretation of federal law, are entitled to follow this path, the decision of some federal courts to disregard *Wright's* hearsay analysis appears questionable. However, even in the federal courts, the proper outcome is not entirely clear because it rests on the meaning of "equivalent circumstantial guarantees of trustworthiness" in the rule, and the Court in *Wright* did not address the statutory interpretation question at all.

"Necessity" A second factor given varying significance by the opinions is the requirement that the statement must be "more probative on the point for which it is offered than any other evidence the proponent can procure through reasonable efforts." Many courts interpret this as a general necessity requirement. However, it does not mean that the hearsay evidence must be essential. Indeed, some courts view the requirement as providing a basis for a trial court to evaluate the need for the statement in the case as compared to the costs of obtaining alternative evidence. Others view it as imposing a requirement of diligence. The requirement also has the effect of imposing a rough "best evidence" requirement on the exception in the sense that where live testimony of the declarant is available and the the out-of-court statement is not superior, the exception cannot be used.

Notice Another substantial requirement of the rule is that notice be given sufficiently in advance of trial to enable the adverse party to prepare to meet the hearsay evidence. While occasionally strict compliance with this requirement is enforced, courts generally have been willing to dispense with notice if the need for the hearsay arises shortly before or during the trial, and possible injustice is avoided by

---

3.　497 U.S. 805 (1990).

the offer of a continuance or other circumstances.

Other requirements The remaining requirements lettered (A) and (C) in the rules, have had no appreciable impact upon the application of the residual exception. Provision (A), requiring that the statement be offered as evidence of a material fact, is a restatement of the general requirement that evidence must be relevant. Requirement (C), that the general purposes of the rules and the interests of justice will be served by admitting the evidence, in effect restates Rule 102.

"Near Miss" The rule states that it applies to "statements not specifically covered by" any of the specific exceptions. What this language means with respect to statements that narrowly, but clearly, fail to qualify under one of the enumerated exceptions is often characterized by the term "near miss." Does the failure to meet the exception result in automatic disqualification or stand generally as a strong factor supporting admissibility because little else is needed to establish equivalent trustworthiness? The almost unanimous opinion of courts is that failing to qualify under an enumerated exception does not disqualify admission under the residual exception.

Frequent Applications of the Exception Courts have employed the exception most extensively in admitting statements made by child witnesses, particularly in sexual abuse cases. They emphasized factors such as the spontaneity and consistency of the statement, the general proposition that young children do not invent allegations of the type involved, the unusualness of explicit sexual knowledge by a young child, or use of childish terminology to describe sex. Statements tend to be excluded in cases where the court found that they were made in response to leading questions by poorly trained interrogators.

Beyond child sexual abuse cases, the residual exception has been used to admit hearsay in an extraordinarily varied array of cases associated with all the frequently used hearsay exceptions. For example, hearsay has been received under this exception involving grand jury testimony, statements to police officers by victims, prior testimony cross-examined by unrelated parties, statements made with death approaching but not imminent, and statements made by private citizens to public agencies or businesses.

§ 324.1 Hearsay Within Hearsay; Multiple Hearsay

"On principle it scarcely seems open to doubt that the hearsay rule should not call for exclusion of a hearsay statement which includes a further hearsay statement when both conform to the requirements of a hearsay exception."[1] The common law followed this reasoning, and under Federal Rule 805, multiple levels of hearsay are admissible "if each part of the combined statements confirms with an exception to the hearsay rule provided in these rules."

In the usual situation, two stages of inquiry are involved. First, does the primary statement qualify under a hearsay exception? If so, the hearsay rule allows its use to prove that the included statement was made, which may end the inquiry. Ordinarily, however, the included statement will be offered to prove the truth of the facts that it asserts. In that event, the second stage of inquiry is required: Does the included statement also qualify under a hearsay exception? If the answer again is in the affirmative, the requirements of Rule 805 are met. However, if the included statement is inadmissible, the rule is not satisfied, and the statements are excluded.

Police reports of accident investigations frequently provide examples of multiple hearsay, with admissibility depending upon the nature of the secondary statement. The primary statement—the written report of the officer—is admissible generally as a public record. Statements of individuals made to the officer either qualify under various exceptions, such as excited utterances or dying declarations, or they fail to meet any additional excep-

§ 324.1

1. Adv.Comm.Note, Fed.R.Evid. 805, 56 F.R.D. 183, 329.

tion and must be excluded as violating the principle. It is violated, for example, when a police officer testifies that A stated that B confessed to the crime. Although B's confession to A—the included statement likely qualifies as an admission or a statement against interest, A's statement to the police officer— the primary statement—appears to meet no hearsay exception.

Another frequently encountered version of the multiple hearsay problem involves a regularly kept business record that includes a further hearsay statement. If both the primary and the included statements are by persons acting in the routine of the business, then both are admitted under the regularly kept records exception, and no further exception need be invoked. However, if the person whose statement is included is not acting in the routine of the business, it is inadmissible unless another exception is available.

An argument could be made that even if the included statement met some other hearsay exception, the primary statement could not qualify under a hearsay exception because the regularly kept records exception requires that the informant must be produced in the routine of the business. This position has not been accepted, but instead the recorder must have a business duty to record the information provided by the outsider.

The requirement of a duty to record will lead to a different result depending upon the nature of the business involved. For instance, a hospital intake worker has an interest in a narrower and different type of information when talking to an assault victim about the circumstances surrounding the injury than a police officer. The statement that the victim was shot by a person of a particular race would not be material to the hospital's business and not admissible through the business records exception when made to a hospital employee even if the included statement met another hearsay exception. By contrast, the same statement would be highly relevant to a police officer's duties in locating the assailant, and accordingly the primary statement should be admissible as a public record when offered by the accused.

One of the statements might constitute an admission, which at common law was considered a hearsay exception. Since admissions are not classed as hearsay under the Federal Rules, the question arises whether an admission may qualify as a hearsay exception for purposes of the multiple hearsay rule. One answer has been that admissions are within the spirit and purpose of the rule. An easier answer may be that only one level of hearsay exists since an admission is not hearsay under the Federal Rules, and if the other statement satisfies an exception, no further hearsay difficulty remains.

§ 324.2 Impeachment of Hearsay Declarant

When a hearsay statement is introduced, often the declarant does not testify. It is, however, ultimately the declarant's credibility that determines the value that should be accorded to the statement. How should that credibility be attacked or, where appropriate, supported?

Federal Rule 806 provides:

> When a hearsay statement, or a statement defined in Rule 801(d)(2), (C), (D), or (E), has been admitted in evidence, the credibility of the declarant may be attacked, and if attacked may be supported, by any evidence which would be admissible for those purposes if declarant had testified as a witness. Evidence of a statement or conduct by the declarant at any time, inconsistent with the declarant's hearsay statement, is not subject to any requirement that the declarant may have been afforded an opportunity to deny or explain. If the party against whom a hearsay statement has been admitted calls the declarant as a witness, the party is entitled to examine the declarant on the statement as if under cross-examination.

The rule effectively treats the hearsay declarant a witness for impeachment purposes. It covers both statements admitted under hearsay exceptions and admissions, but it does not apply to statements that are nonhearsay and not admitted for their truth.

The declarant may be impeached by any of the standard methods of attacking credibility, including prior convictions, inconsistent statements, bias or interest, and character for untruthfulness. With regard to impeachment by prior inconsistent statements, the rule eliminates the requirement, otherwise applicable to statements made by witnesses who testify in person,[1] that an opportunity be afforded for them to explain or deny the inconsistency. When the declarant does not take the stand, the procedure for conducting the impeachment should be relaxed, but restrictions in other rules are not eliminated.

If the declarant takes the stand, the Rule permits an adverse party to examine on the statement "as if under cross-examination," which permits use of leading questions. When the statement is admitted against a criminal defendant, the accused can invoke the compulsory process clause to require assistance in securing the declarant's presence.

§ 324.3 Basis for Expert Opinion as a Quasi–Hearsay Exception

Under Federal Rule 703, an expert may base an opinion on facts or data that are not "admissible in evidence" if of a type reasonably relied upon by experts in the field. An expert often should be allowed to disclose to the jury the basis for an opinion because otherwise the opinion is left unsupported with little way for evaluation of its correctness. In those situations, the expert may testify to evidence even though it is inadmissible under the hearsay rule, but allowing the evidence to be received for this purpose does not mean it is admitted for its truth. It is received only for the limited purpose of informing the jury of the basis of the expert's opinion and therefore does not constitute a true hearsay exception. As a result, where it constitutes the only evidence on a critical issue—such as the identity of the assailant in a child sexual abuse case—this distinction will prove decisive.

Probably more often the difference between limited admissibility and admission for the truth of the statement is of little significance and threatens no harm. For instance, if the underlying data has no direct relevance to the dispute in the case or if the facts it concerns, although relevant, have already been proved through other admissible evidence, allowing the jury to hear the inadmissible data from the expert will have no significant consequences.

Unfortunately, although limiting instructions are appropriate and required when requested, jurors may be unable or unwilling to follow them. Thus, in those instances where the inadmissible facts or data would have an important impact if used for the truth and would therefore be subject to abuse, a danger exists of Rule 703 improperly becoming a "backdoor" hearsay exception. This danger caused the Advisory Committee on the Federal Rules in 1998 to propose an amendment to the Federal Rules that would continue to allow inadmissible evidence to be used to form the basis of the opinion but would restrict the situations under which it can be presented to the jury. The proposed amendment states that "[i]f the facts or data are otherwise inadmissible, they shall not be disclosed to the jury by the proponent of the opinion or inference unless their probative value substantially outweighs their prejudicial effect." Even before, this proposal, the inadmissible data was subject to exclusion for prejudice or irrelevancy.[1] The proposed amendment would increase the burden on the proponent before the expert may disclose the underlying inadmissible evidence to the jury.

§ 325. Evaluation of the Present Rules

In his evidence treatise published in 1842, Professor Greenleaf wrote:

The student will not fail to observe the symmetry and beauty of this branch of the law * * * and will rise from the study of its principles convinced, with Lord Erskine, that "they are founded in the charities of religion,—in the

---

§ 324.2

1. Fed.R.Evid. 613(b). See generally supra § 37.

§ 324.3

1. See generally supra § 185.

philosophy of nature,—in the truths of history,—and in the experience of common life."[1]

No one today would apply this evaluation to the rule against hearsay developed in the common law tradition, and far more would agree with the description of Professors Morgan and Maguire approximately a century later that the exceptions appear like "an old-fashioned crazy quilt made of patches cut from a group of paintings by cubists, futurists and surrealists."[2] Indeed, a number of contemporary scholars seek the replacement of the pattern of rules with a radically different system.

The common law's insistence upon a high quality of evidence for judicial fact-finding that helped to produce the hearsay rule was sound. However, the rules as they developed appear not to have yielded a quality commensurate with the high price they have exacted. The chief criticisms are that the rules are too complex and that they fail to achieve their purpose of screening good evidence from bad.

First, with respect to the complexity of the rule against hearsay and its exceptions, the number of exceptions naturally depends upon the minuteness of the classification. The Federal Rules contain thirty exceptions and exclusions. Wigmore requires over a thousand pages to cover hearsay, and its treatment occupies one quarter of the original edition of the present work.

Most of the complication, of course, arises in connection with the exceptions, leading readily to the conclusion that a general rule so riddled with exceptions is "farcical." The conclusion may be somewhat exaggerated. While admittedly complicated, probably less than a dozen of the exceptions are encountered with any frequency in the trial of cases. Gaining mastery of these, plus an awareness of the others and a working knowledge of what is and is not hearsay, should not unduly tax the intellectual resources of the legal profession.

The second complaint that the rule against hearsay and its exceptions fail to screen reliable from unreliable hearsay on a realistic basis is more substantial. The trust-worthiness of hearsay statements ranges from the highest reliability to quite questionable value. Whether these almost infinitely varying, plastic situations can ever be completely and satisfactorily treated by a set of rules may well be doubted.

If the heart of the problem is that the exceptions are unacceptable in detail, the problem persists. The preceding chapters dealing with hearsay indicates that while some progress has been made in rationalizing the rules and improving their practical workability, they remain quite complex. If the basic difficulty is simply that no hearsay system based on classes of exceptions can truly succeed, a totally different approach would be required. As discussed briefly in § 327, although not likely to succeed in the short term, such proposals have been advanced in civil cases, but are quite unlikely to progress in criminal litigation because of the Confrontation Clause. Perhaps the most notable recent development has not been a broad revamping of the system of exceptions but rather the substantial flexibility introduced by the frequent admission of hearsay through ad hoc judicial action under the residual exception.

§ 326. The Path of Modern Hearsay Development

Wholesale efforts to reformulate the traditional common law hearsay pattern have been for the most part legislative in nature rather than judicial, and some of the more notable legislative efforts are discussed below.

Pursuant to a suggestion from Thayer, the Massachusetts Hearsay Statute of 1898 was enacted as follows: "A declaration of a deceased person shall not be inadmissible in evidence as hearsay if the Court finds that it was made in good faith before the commencement of the action and upon the personal knowledge of the declarant." After a quarter century of experience under the act, a questionnaire was addressed to the lawyers and judges of the state regarding its merits. The vast majority of those responding thought that its effects were

---

§ 325

1. Greenleaf, Evidence § 584 (1st ed. 1842).

2. Morgan & Maguire, Looking Backward and Forward at Evidence, 50 Harv.L.Rev. 909, 921 (1937).

positive. The American Bar Association in 1938 recommended a liberalized version of the act for adoption by the states.

The English Evidence Act of 1938 allowed the introduction of written statements, made on the personal knowledge of the maker or in the regular course of business, if the maker was called as a witness or was unavailable. Even though the maker was neither called nor unavailable, the judge might admit the statement if satisfied that undue delay or expense would otherwise be involved. Statements made by interested persons when proceedings were pending or instituted were excluded from the act. It applied only in civil cases.

These limitations were relaxed and new ones added in 1968. Under the act, hearsay statements, whether written or oral, were admissible to the extent that testimony of the declarant would have been admissible, regardless of whether he or she was called as a witness, though prior statements were not ordinarily admissible at the request of the proponent if the declarant was called. Notice was required of intent to offer a hearsay statement under the act, and the opposite party had the right to require production of declarant as a witness, if available. The picture was conceptually simplified by the Civil Evidence Act of 1995, which abolishes the hearsay rule as a basis for excluding evidence while retaining the notice requirement, some restrictions on prior statements, and the right of the opponent to call and cross-examine declarants. Like its predecessors, the new act applies only to civil cases. Efforts to reform in any substantial way the English law of evidence in criminal cases have not been successful.

The drafters of the Model Code of Evidence of the American Law Institute took a bold course about hearsay. They drafted a sweeping new exception to the hearsay rule that allowed admissibility "if the judge finds that the declarant (a) is unavailable as a witness, or (b) is present and subject to cross-examination."[1] This rule, however, was qualified by other rules which limited its applica-

tion to declarations by persons with personal knowledge, excluded hearsay upon hearsay, and empowered the trial judge to exclude such hearsay whenever its probative value was outweighed by the likelihood of waste of time, prejudice, confusion, or unfair surprise. In addition to this new rule, the traditional exceptions were generally retained. The liberalizing of the use of hearsay was a chief ground of opposition to the Model Code and no doubt substantially accounted for the failure of the code to be adopted in any jurisdiction.

Nevertheless, the controversy over the Model Code awakened a new interest in the improvement of evidence law. Accordingly, the Commissioners on Uniform State Laws, in cooperation with the American Law Institute and building on the foundation of the Model Code, drafted and adopted a more modestly reformative code, the Uniform Rules of Evidence. The American Bar Association approved this action.

Instead of admitting virtually all firsthand hearsay of an unavailable declarant, the original Uniform Rules, like the Model Code rule quoted above, substituted a hearsay exception for statements by unavailable declarants describing a matter recently perceived and made in good faith prior to the commencement of the action.[2] A similar provision is found in Rule 804(b)(5) of the Revised Uniform Rules, but Congress removed its counterpart from the Federal Rules. As to prior statements by witnesses present at the hearing, the original Uniform Rules adopted substantially the broad provisions of the Model Code rule quoted above, but the Revised Uniform Rules (1986) follow the much narrower congressional version of the Federal Rule of Evidence 801(d)(1). The original Uniform Rules, like the Model Code, retained and liberalized the other traditional exceptions.

The Advisory Committee on the Federal Rules of Evidence approached its task with awareness of the criticisms that had been leveled against the common law system of class exceptions to the hearsay rule. It also was

§ 326
1. Model Code of Evidence Rule 503 (1942).

2. See supra § 251.

aware that the Model Code's lack of acceptance was largely the result of having exceeded the profession's willingness to accept a fundamentally altered approach to hearsay that permitted broad admissibility of prior statements of unavailable declarants.

In its first draft circulated for comment, the committee endeavored to rationalize the hearsay exceptions in general terms, while at the same time maintaining continuity with the past. For these ends, two rules were included, one covering situations where it made no difference whether the declarant was available and the other applying only when the declarant was unavailable. The first of these rules opened with the following general provision:

> A statement is not excluded by the hearsay rule if its nature and the special circumstances under which it was made offer assurances of accuracy not likely to be enhanced by calling the declarant as a witness, even though he is available.

This general provision was followed by twenty-three illustrative applications derived from common law exceptions, which were not to be considered an exclusive listing. The second of the rules again opened with a general provision:

> A statement is not excluded by the hearsay rule if its nature and the special circumstances under which it was made offer strong assurances of accuracy and the declarant is unavailable as a witness.

It was also followed by a list, albeit a shorter one, of illustrative applications derived from the common law with again a caution that the enumeration not be considered exclusive.

While the response indicated a willingness to accept a substantial revision in the area of hearsay, the legal community opted for a larger measure of predictability than the proposal was thought to offer. As a result, the two general provisions quoted above were withdrawn, and the two rules were revised by converting the illustrations into exceptions in the common law tradition, with the addition of two residual exceptions to accommodate unforeseen situations that might arise. In this form, the rules, with some alterations, were enacted into law by the Congress as Rules 803 and 804. In addition, rules modeled on the Federal Rules are now in effect in forty-one states, with local changes of varying significance. The pattern of a general rule excluding hearsay, subject to numerous exceptions, has shown substantial resilience.

§ 327. The Future of Hearsay

Regardless of whether the hearsay rule was as a matter of history the child of the jury system,[1] clearly the concern for controlling the use of hearsay is more pronounced in jury cases than in nonjury cases. In part, this attitude may be a product of the close association between the right to a jury and the right of confrontation in criminal cases. The English developments in the direction of relaxing limitations on hearsay in civil cases[2] were apparently inspired by the virtual disappearance there of jury trials in such cases. Corresponding changes have not transpired with respect to criminal cases where the jury remains.

In the United States, the constitutional rights of confrontation and jury trial combine to make unlikely any formal wholesale opening of the gates to hearsay in criminal cases or radical changes in the traditional hearsay exceptions. One may, however, reasonably assume that the civil jury will continue to decline somewhat in importance. As noted in an earlier section,[3] courts often exhibit a more relaxed attitude in administering the exclusionary rules of evidence in nonjury cases, including the rule against hearsay. An even more relaxed attitude prevails in administrative proceedings.[4] Perhaps no more than an acceleration of this process is involved in the vigorous advocacy by some reformers to eliminate the hearsay rule entirely in nonjury civil cases.

§ 327

1. See supra § 244.

2. See supra § 326.

3. See supra § 60.

4. See infra §§ §352–353.

Two scholars have suggested that admissibility of hearsay in civil cases, jury or nonjury, should be made more flexible. Judge Weinstein argued that admissibility should be based upon the judge's ad hoc evaluation of its probative force accompanied by several procedural safeguards. They included: notice to the opponent of the intention to use hearsay, expanding the judge's ability to comment on the weight of such evidence, greater control by judges over juries, and greater control by appellate courts over trial courts.[5] Almost two decades later, Professor Park argued that in civil cases a residual exception should be added that would permit admission without any reliability screening. The exception would require notice to the adversary and would allow the adversary to exercise a rule of preference, which if exercised would require a showing that the declarant was unavailable or, if available, must be called to testify.[6] Despite some attractive features, neither proposal has approached acceptance.

More than fifty years ago, Professor McCormick wrote, much in the Benthamic tradition:

> Eventually, perhaps, Anglo–American court procedure may find itself gradually but increasingly freed from emphasis on jury trial with its contentious theory of proof. With responsibility for the ascertainment of facts vested in professional judges, the stress will be shifted from the crude technique of admitting or rejecting evidence to the more realistic problem of appraising its credibility. Psychologists meantime will have built upon their knowledge of the statistical reliability of witnesses in groups a technique of testing the veracity of individual witnesses and assessing the reliability of particular items of testimony. Judges and advocates will then become students and practitioners of an applied science of judicial proof.[7]

It becomes increasingly evident that this optimistic statement represents at best a very long-term view and is unlikely ever to be achieved.

Several scholars have argued that although complicated and fraught with substantial problems, the existing system and even its complexity have some benefits that suggest caution in making radical change. These reasons include: the likelihood that oral statements may be misreported, the potential effect of relaxing hearsay rules on the advantage that the prosecution and wealthy organizations enjoy in litigation due to superior facilities for generating evidence, a distrust of the ability and impartiality of trial judges, and certain other process concerns.[8]

Two general propositions appear almost unavoidably true. First, for the considerable future, a hearsay rule and set of specific exceptions strongly resembling the present system will continue. Second, changes will move in the direction of liberalizing admission of hearsay.

---

5. Weinstein, Probative Force of Hearsay, 46 Iowa L.Rev. 331 (1961).

6. Park, A Subject Matter Approach to Hearsay Reform, 86 Mich.L.Rev. 51 (1987).

7. McCormick, Evidence, 3 Encyclopedia of the Social Sciences 637, 645 (1931, reissue of 1937).

8. Lempert & Saltzburg, A Modern Approach to Evidence 519 (2d ed. 1982); Mueller, Post–Modern Hearsay Reform: The Importance of Complexity, 76 Minn.L.Rev. 367 (1992).

*

Title 11

JUDICIAL NOTICE

Chapter 35

JUDICIAL NOTICE

Table of Sections

§ 328. The Need for and the Effect of Judicial Notice

The traditional notion that trials are bifurcated proceedings involving both a judge and a panel of twelve jurors has obviously had a profound impact on the overall development of common law doctrine pertaining to evidence. The very existence of the jury, after all, helped create the demand for the rigorous guarantees of accuracy which typify the law of evidence, witness the insistence upon proof by witnesses having first-hand knowledge, the mistrust of hearsay, and the insistence upon original documents and their authentication by witnesses. Thus it is that the facts in dispute are commonly established by the jury after the carefully controlled introduction of formal evidence, which ordinarily consists of the testimony of witnesses. In light of the role of the jury, therefore, it is easy enough to conclude that, whereas questions concerning the tenor of the law to be applied to a case fall within the province of the judge, the determination of questions pertaining to propositions of fact is uniquely the function of the jury. The life of the law has never been quite so elementary, however, because judges on numerous occasions take charge of questions of fact and excuse the party having the burden of establishing a fact from the necessity of producing formal proof. These hybrid questions of fact, dealt with by judges as if they were questions pertaining to law, are the raw materials out of which the doctrine of judicial notice has been constructed.

A moment's reflection on the law-fact distinction is in order. The statement that it is necessary in a certain jurisdiction to have a testator's subscription attested by three witnesses if the document is going to be admitted to probate is an assertion that a certain state of affairs obtains. A speaker might actually preface the assertion with the words, "As a matter of fact * * *" Whether the statement is true or false presents, in the everyday vernacular, a question of fact. Persons engaged in social conversation might not agree on the accuracy of the statement, but agree to settle their difference by a straw poll of the other persons present. All of which would be of no moment, provided always no one present actually planned his or her estate on the basis of the result of the poll.

If this same conversation took the form of an argument between lawyers in a courtroom during an official proceeding wherein the answer was germane to the disposition of the matter at hand, very different considerations would come into play. The answer could not be seen to vary between cases in the same courtroom or between courtrooms across the jurisdiction. There must exist a standardized answer if the law *qua* system of dispute resolution is to maintain the necessary appearance of fairness and rationality. It is the apparatus of appellate review and one ultimately highest court in the jurisdiction which guarantees uniformity. Thus it is the case that, within the vernacular of the law, a question which can have only one right answer must be answered in a courtroom by a judge and is, therefore, a question of law.

The question who did what to whom when, where and in what state of mind implicates another set of considerations. The concrete human actions or inactions which precipitate lawsuits are water over the dam, history as it were. Reflection may suggest that history is actually a current event, because history is our present best judgment as to what happened in the past. Past events cannot be reconstituted; only a facsimile of them can be constructed in the mind's eye on the basis of the evidence presently available. In a courtroom the evidence available is a factor of the rules of evidence and the cleverness as well as industry of the opposing counsel.

If there is produced at trial enough evidence upon which seriously to deliberate about what actually happened in the past, and provided that in a civil case the evidence is not so overwhelming as to make deliberation unnecessary, there is no scientific litmus by which to assay the accuracy of the opposing versions of the affair. A verdict either way is possible. In the law's vernacular, we are met with a question of fact, which in Anglo–American tradition is meet for a jury to decide. But this compels the conclusion that a question of fact is one to which there are two right answers.

This model finds its roots in Lord Coke.[1] Ad questionem facti non respondent judices: ad questionem juris non respondent juratores. To questions of fact judges do not answer: to questions of law the jury do not answer. Implicit in this model, however, is the notion inherent in the adversarial system that a judge presides over a trial after the fashion of an umpire who governs the play according to known rules but who does not participate in it. Implied, too, are the notions that trials involve straightforward contract or tort disputes, that complaints are abruptly dismissed if they do not state a familiar cause of action and that the concise elements of a well pleaded common law cause of action make the issues of fact at trial, if it comes to that, few and simple. Finally, the model presupposes that the law itself is composed primarily of private law rules which by and large remain immutable over the life of any one generation.

If during a trial a proposition of fact were to be implicated, the truth of which brooked no dispute among reasonable persons, this proposition would not fit comfortably within the principle that either of two answers is appropriate to a question of fact. The application of common sense to the principles thus far rehearsed leads inexorably to the conclusion that the existence of one right answer signals a question of law. Thus, at least if requested to do so, a judge would have to treat this question of fact as one of law and instruct the jury that the proposition could simply be taken as established in its own right.

With what manner of questions pertaining to facts do judges concern themselves? Whether a well known street was in fact within a local business district as alleged by a litigant, in which case a certain speed limit obtained, may be dealt with by the judge during the trial of a negligence case. That is to say, the judge may instruct the jury that the street in question was within a business district, dispensing thereby with the need to introduce evidence to this effect. Then again, questions of fact arise about which reasonably intelligent people might not have in mind the information in

1. Coke's Commentary Upon Littleton 155b (1832 ed.).

question, but where they would agree that the facts are verifiable with certainty by consulting authoritative reference sources. At a time when Sunday contracts were taboo, for example, the question arose during the trial of a warranty action whether the relevant sales instrument, dated June 3, 1906, had been executed on a Sunday. In this instance the trial judge was reversed for leaving the question to the jury to deliberate upon as a question of fact. Experience reveals, therefore, that two categories of facts clearly fall within the perimeters of judicial notice, these being facts generally known with certainty by all the reasonably intelligent people in the community and facts capable of accurate and ready determination by resort to sources of indisputable accuracy.

In both of the examples enumerated thus far it should be carefully noted that the facts of which judicial notice was taken were "adjudicative" facts. They were facts about the particular event which gave rise to the lawsuit and, like all adjudicative facts, they helped explain who did what, when, where, how, and with what motive and intent. Further, either because they were facts so commonly known in the jurisdiction or so manifestly capable of accurate verification, they were facts reasonably informed people in the community would regard as propositions not reasonably subject to dispute.

Another species of facts figures prominently in discussions of judicial notice which, to employ the terminology coined by Professor K.C. Davis, are denominated "legislative" facts. Judicial notice of these facts occurs when a judge is faced with the task of creating law, by deciding upon the constitutional validity of a statute, or the interpretation of a statute, or the extension or restriction of a common law rule, upon grounds of policy, and the policy is thought to hinge upon social, economic, political or scientific facts. Illustrative of this phenomenon was Clinton v. Jones[2] in which the Court refused even on prudential grounds to grant to a sitting president automatic immunity from a civil suit arising from acts occurring before he took office, rejecting the argument that private litigation might interfere with the President's performance of his official duties. All but one of the justices agreed that it was highly unlikely that a civil suit could take up any substantial amount of presidential time. This premise rested upon a certain view of the facts of political life, but these facts were hardly indisputable. Indeed, the presidential deposition taken in the case brought on a maelstrom of legal and political controversy that came close to monopolizing the president's attention. Carefully note, however, that these facts were not part and parcel of the disputed event being litigated but bore instead upon the court's own thinking about the tenor of the law to be applied in deciding the dispute.

The generic caption "legislative facts" fails to highlight any distinction between the use of extra-record data by judges when they craft a rule of law, whether of the constitutional or private law variety, and when they resort to extra-record data to assay whether there exist circumstances which constitutionally either legitimate the exercise of legislative power or substantiate the rationality of the legislative product. Resort to a new subdivision like "law-making facts" might not, in its turn, bring home the reality that judges regularly resort to extra-record data not only when enunciating new substantive doctrine, but also employ them in deciding questions which pertain to everything from the alpha of civil jurisdiction to the omega of criminal sentencing.

Concern for legislative facts does signal the recognition both that judges do not "find" the law but rather make it, and that questions of public law have become a staple of the case law menu. A judge may no longer be quite the disinterested umpire in the steady state system suggested by the common law model, but more an active participant making work what has come to be seen as process of adapting law to a volatile socio-political environment. In a very real sense it may be that a judge used to a steady diet of private law cases and a judge dealing with disputes arising out of a multi-

2.   117 S.Ct. 1636 (1997).

plicity of administrative agency actions may actually live in different worlds. At the same time modern procedure and trial practice have served to create a complexity that would confound the serjeants of yesteryear.

The picture is further complicated by a tendency of any bright-line distinction between adjudicative and legislative facts to dissolve in practice. Assume, for example, a statute making it a crime to possess coca leaves or any salt, compound or derivative thereof. If believed, the testimony of witnesses, lay and expert, establishes that defendant possessed a quantity of cocaine hydrochloride and that the item is indeed a salt, compound or derivative of coca leaves. The last proposition is indisputable and subject to judicial notice. If this is an adjudicative fact, a federal judge would not feel free to instruct the jury that, if they were to find the defendant possessed this item, they must find the item was a proscribed one.[3] No such compunction would obtain if it were a legislative fact. Yet one judge might visualize the question in terms of, "What is it that defendant possessed?", which is part of the who, what, when and where litany signalling an adjudicative fact, while another judge might inquire, "What was it that the legislature intended to criminalize?", access door to the realm of legislative facts. All of which may warn the reader that the judicial notice of fact phenomenon has many of the characteristics of an universal solvent: it cannot be totally contained in any known vessel.

It is axiomatic, of course, that the judge decides whether a given set of facts constitutes an actionable wrong or a certain line of cross-examination is relevant. A judge, unless he is to be reversed on appeal, is bound to know the common and statutory law of his own jurisdiction. Commonly enough even this truism has been incorporated into the law of evidence by saying that judges must judicially notice the law of their own forum. This manner of speaking has served to interpolate into the field of judicial notice the procedural mechanisms by which the applicable law is fed into the judicial process. Foreign law, of course, was once more germane to the topic of judicial notice because that body of law was (for convenience) treated as fact, so much so that the law of a jurisdiction other than the forum had to be pleaded and proved just like any other question of fact, but a peculiar one which only the judge came to decide, which justified its inclusion within the topic of judicial notice. Indeed, lumped along with foreign law as a proper subject for treatment under the caption of judicial notice has been the forum's own administrative law and local municipal ordinances, together with a hotchpot of internal judicial administrative details concerning the courts themselves, such as their own personnel, records, organization and jurisdictional boundaries. The recognition appears to be growing, however, that the manner in which the law is insinuated into the judicial process is not so much a problem of evidence as it is a concern better handled within the context of the rules pertaining to procedure.

§ 329. Matters of Common Knowledge

The oldest and plainest ground for judicial notice is that the fact is so commonly known in the community as to make it unprofitable to require proof, and so certainly known as to make it indisputable among reasonable men. Though this basis for notice is sometimes loosely described as universal knowledge, manifestly this could not be taken literally[1] and the more reflective opinions speak in terms of the knowledge of "most men," or of "what well-informed persons generally know," or "the knowledge that every intelligent person has." Observe that these phrases tend progressively to widen the circle of facts within "common knowledge." Moreover, though usually facts of

---

3. Fed.R.Evid. 201(g).

§ 329

1. The late Dean F. McDermott of Suffolk Law School aptly exposed the absurdity of this approach by succinctly translating it into the rule that "Judicial notice may only be taken of those facts every damn fool knows." See,

however, Layne v. Tribune Co., 146 So. 234, 237 (Fla. 1933) ("What everybody knows the courts are assumed to know, and of such matters may take judicial cognizance."); In re Buszta's Estate, 186 N.Y.S.2d 192, 193 (Surr.1959) ("Generally speaking, a court may take judicial notice of facts which are universally known and recognized.").

"common knowledge" will be generally known throughout the country, it is sufficient as a basis for judicial notice that they be known in the local community where the trial court sits.

What a judge knows and what facts a judge may judicially notice are not identical data banks. A famous colloquy in the Year Books shows that a clear difference has long been taken between what judges may notice judicially and the facts that the particular judge happens personally to know.[2] It is not a distinction easy for a judge to follow in application, but the doctrine is accepted that actual private knowledge by the judge is no sufficient ground for taking judicial notice of a fact as a basis for a finding or a final judgment, though it may still be a ground, it is believed, for exercising certain discretionary powers, such as granting a motion for new trial to avoid an injustice, or in sentencing.

Similarly, what a jury member knows in common with every other human being and what facts are appropriately circumscribed by the doctrine of judicial notice are not the same thing. Traditionally those facts so generally known within the community as not to be reasonably subject to dispute have been included within the perimeters of judicial notice under the caption of common knowledge. At the same time, however, it is often loosely said that the jury may consider, as if proven, facts within the common knowledge of the community.

When considering the award to make in a condemnation case, a jury were properly concerned whether the value of the remaining fee was diminished by the installation of a natural gas pipeline in the easement which was the discrete subject of the taking. The jurors factored in an amount to compensate for the contingency that, the fee being a farm, deep chisel-style plowing might rupture the pipe and cause an explosion, the very notoriety of

which would put off future purchasers of the farm. This possibility was taken seriously by the jurors, themselves residents of a farming community and familiar with local practices. Even though there had not been introduced into evidence any matter pertaining to deep chisel plowing, a court was willing to sustain the award precisely because, given the fund of common knowledge shared by this rural jury, there was no need for formal evidence to establish the point.

Had the same case been transferred for trial to an urban venue, deep chisel plowing would not likely have ever been considered by a jury absent the introduction of evidence alerting them to the practice. It would be manifestly improper were a juror to investigate farming practices and to introduce the subject for the first time in the privacy of the jury room. Information of this kind should be supplied to the jury through the testimony of a witness, and of course a juror is generally viewed as incompetent to perform this role. This leaves open the possibility that a former rural resident might introduce the subject into an urban jury room, pooling with his compatriots his distinct share of the fund of common knowledge. If the fund the jurors can draw upon is knowledge common to the community as a whole, this datum would appear to be illicit specie in an urban venue.

A similar problem would arise were evidence introduced for and against the existence of a real threat posed by deep chisel plowing and one or more of the jurors shared their unique experience with the practice with the rest of the panel. Jurors do not think evidence; jurors think about the evidence, and to think at all requires a person to draw upon his or her experience. Still, it has been held improper to invite jurors with personal experience on farms to share it with their fellows in a case which turned on the question whether an in-

---

2. Anon., Y.B. 7 Hen. IV, f. 41, pl. 5 (1406), from which the following is an excerpt: "Tirwhit: Sir, let us put the case that a man kills another in your presence and sight, and another who is not guilty is indicted before you and is found guilty of the same death, you ought to respite the judgment against him, for you know the contrary, and report the matter to the King to pardon him. No more ought you to give judgment in this case * * * Gascoigne,

C.J. One time the King himself asked me about this very case which you have put, and asked me what was the law, and I told him just as you say, and he was well pleased that the law was so." See Wilson v. State, 677 S.W.2d 518 (Tex.Cr.App.1984) (judge may personally know a fact of which he cannot take judicial notice, but he may be required to take judicial notice of a fact he does not know).

sured horse had indeed been killed by a lightning bolt. It has been held appropriate, however, to invite jurors with personal experience in and about saw mills to share their insights in a personal injury case arising out of an accident at a saw mill.

The parameters of the jury fund of common data may be vague precisely because trial lawyers find themselves embarrassed to insist upon bright-line rules when they themselves regularly employ summations to expose jurors to non-evidence facts masquerading as rhetorical hypotheses. What with voir dire examinations and challenges being available to exclude from juries anyone privy to information in excess of the local common denominator, any eccentric scenarios which do occur may simply be chalked up to self-inflicted hardship upon the part of counsel. Even so, all of this assumes that by and large each venue's jurors share relatively homogenous cultural roots so that, in fact, there does exist a rough hewn common fund of knowledge in which they all share.

In an increasingly heterogeneous and highly mobile society, further fractured by class divisions, there may no longer exist a common fund of knowledge shared by the jurors resident in a particular venue. Out of academe there has come the suggestion that a common fund can be guaranteed by imposing a definition of that fund's parameters community to community. This judge-imposed construct would not only be the basis for an instruction confining deliberating jurors to this fund, but would serve as a benchmark during voir dire examinations and in determining relevancy. The efficacy of any instruction purporting to limit the data jurors use in their thinking about the outcome of a case may be questionable at best. In fact, the very notion of imposing rigorous limitations upon the materials which a jury may use is likely, if taken seriously, to provoke intense debate.

Thus it is very easy to confound into one common denominator facts to which the evidentiary discipline of judicial notice applies and the residual data the jury members bring along with them as rational human beings. Whereas in the typical vehicular accident case

the well-known character of a street can be dealt with informally as background information which helps everyone visualize the scene, the question becomes a formal one to be dealt with as part of the doctrine of judicial notice if the precise character of the street becomes an adjudicative fact in the case being tried. Again, while the meaning of words is normally left to the informal common sense of the jury, the precise meaning of a word in a contract case which may be outcome determinative should be dealt with formally as a problem of judicial notice.

The cases in which judicial notice is taken of indisputable facts commonly known in the community where the facts noticed are actually adjudicative ones appear to be relatively rare. In most instances, notwithstanding the invocation of the language of judicial notice, the facts either involve background information helpful in assaying the evidence relevant to the adjudicative facts or involve facts relevant to the process of formulating the tenor of the law to be applied to the resolution of the controversy. Indeed, there is a growing recognition that the common knowledge variety of fact plays only a very minor role on the judicial notice scene.

§ 330. Facts Capable of Certain Verification

The earlier and probably still the most familiar basis for judicial notice is "common knowledge," but a second and distinct principle has come to be recognized as an even more significant ground for the invocation of the doctrine. This extension of judicial notice was first disguised by a polite fiction so that when asked to notice a fact not generally known, but which obviously could easily be ascertained by consulting materials in common use, such as the day of the week on which January 1 fell ten years ago, the judges resorted to calendars but purported to be "refreshing memory" as to a matter of common knowledge. Eventually it was recognized that involved here was an important extension of judicial notice to the new field of facts "capable of accurate and ready demonstration," "capable of such instant and unquestionable demonstration, if desired, that no party would think of imposing a falsity on the tribunal in the face of an intelligent adversary," or "capable of immediate and accurate demonstration by resort to easily accessible sources of indisputable accuracy." It is under this caption, for example, that courts have taken judicial notice of the scientific principles which, while verifiable but not likely commonly known, justify the evidentiary use of radar, blood tests for intoxication and nonpaternity, handwriting and typewriter identification, and ballistics. Whether the person employing any of these devices was qualified to do so, whether the equipment was properly maintained and whether it was used correctly remain questions of fact.

Attempts to formulate inventories of verifiable facts of which courts will take judicial notice have begun to fall into disrepute because the principle involved can better be illustrated by way of example. Thus in State v. Damm[1] defendant was on trial for rape after one of his stepdaughters gave birth to a child. The defense sought a court order authorizing blood tests by which it was hoped to prove his innocence by way of negative results. Even if the tests produced a negative result, however, the testimony recounting the tests would be relevant to the question of guilt or innocence only if it was true that properly administered blood tests evidencing a negative result excluded the possibility of paternity. To leave this preliminary question pertaining to the then present state of scientific knowledge to the jury to decide as best they could on the basis of possibly conflicting testimony would appear absurd. There being only one right answer to the question whether the principle was accepted in the appropriate scientific circles, the question fell within the province of judicial notice. Even so, the trial judge in this particular case was held not to have erred in refusing the request because, given the time and place, the defense was not able to produce the data necessary to illustrate to him that the principle was an accepted one within the scientific community. Presumably, of course, an opposite result would obtain today.

Thus it is that while the various propositions of science are a suitable topic of judicial notice, the content of what will actually be noticed is subject to change as the tenets of science evolve. It is manifest, moreover, that the principle involved need not be commonly known in order to be judicially noticed; it suffices if the principle is accepted as a valid one in the appropriate scientific community. In determining the intellectual viability of the proposition, of course, the judge is free to consult any sources that he thinks are reliable, but the extent to which judges are willing to take the initiative in looking up the authoritative sources will usually be limited. By and large, therefore, it is the task of counsel to find and to present in argument and briefs such references, excerpts and explanations as will convince the judge that the fact is certain and demonstrable. Puzzling enough in this regard, it has been noted that "nowhere can there be found a definition of what constitutes competent or authoritative sources for purposes of verifying judicially noticed facts."[2] And, it should be noted that after a number of courts take judicial notice of a principle, subsequent courts begin to dispense with the production of these materials and to take judicial notice of the principle as a matter of law established by precedent.

Illustrative as they are, scientific principles hardly exhaust the verifiable facts of which courts take judicial notice. Historical facts fall within the doctrine, such as the dates upon which wars began and terminated. Geographical facts are involved, particularly with reference to the boundaries of the state in which the court is sitting and of the counties, districts and townships thereof, as well as the location of the capital of the state and the location and identity of the county seats. Whether common knowledge or not, courts notice the identity of the principal officers of the national government and the incumbents of principal state offices. Similarly, while obviously not necessarily a matter of common knowledge, judges take notice of the identity of

---

§ 330
1. 266 N.W. 667 (S.D.1936).

2. Comment, *The Presently Expanding Concept of Judicial Notice*, 13 Vill.L.Rev. 528, 545 (1968).

the officers of their courts, such as the other judges, the sheriffs, clerks, and attorneys; of the duration of terms and sessions, and of the rules of court.

It would seem obvious that the judge of a court would take notice of all of the records of the institution over which he presides, but the courts have been slow to give the principle of judicial notice its full reach of logic and expediency. It is settled, of course, that the courts, trial and appellate, take notice of their own respective records in the present litigation, both as to matters occurring in the immediate trial, and in previous trials or hearings. The principle seemingly is equally applicable to matters of record in the proceedings in other cases in the same court, and some decisions have recognized this, but many courts still adhere to the needless requirement of formal proof, rather than informal presentation, of recorded proceedings in other suits in the same court. Matters of record in other courts are usually denied notice even though it would appear manifest that these public documents are logically subject to judicial notice as readily verifiable facts.

In the increasingly important practice of judicial notice of scientific and technological facts, some of the possibilities of error are, first, that the courts may fail to employ the doctrine of judicial notice in this field to the full measure of its usefulness; second, that they may mistakenly accept as authoritative scientific theories that are outmoded or are not yet received by the specialists as completely verified; and third, that in taking judicial notice of accepted scientific facts, the courts, in particular cases may misconceive the conclusions or applications which are supposed to flow from them. Of these, it seems that the first has thus far been the most frequent shortcoming.

In determining relevancy an informal system of judicial notice has always obtained, as for example, when it is decided that burglar tools are admissible evidence on the premise that only burglars likely possess such items. Whether the results of negative blood tests

were admissible was again a question of relevancy, but the results were not admitted until it was established as incontrovertible fact that the principle behind the test itself was valid. It seemed at the time quite self-evident that juries could not pass upon the validity of the test principle because, a rule of science being implicated, there had to be only one right answer. Concomitantly, there might have been worry that juries might be overawed by scientific evidence and that the risk of prejudice ought not be run unless the principle met the stringent test of absolute truth. Whether the classic model ought still to be followed, however, is a question which has to be faced. In a technological era scientific truths are more readily recognized as theorems themselves subject to modification rather rapidly and juries are likely aware of the frailties inherent in technological equipment and analysis, the ordinary juror being owner of electronic gear soon obsolete and always in need of fine tuning during its short life. This suggests that judicial notice, with its premise that facts must be indisputably true, be abandoned as the avenue by which scientific tests be admitted into evidence. Alternatives to judicial notice for this purpose are currently under debate and are treated elsewhere.[3]

§ 331. Social and Economic Data Used in Judicial Law–Making: "Legislative" Facts

It is conventional wisdom today to observe that judges not only are charged to find what the law is, but must regularly make new law when deciding upon the constitutional validity of a statute, interpreting a statute, or extending or restricting a common law rule. The very nature of the judicial process necessitates that judges be guided, as legislators are, by considerations of expediency and public policy. They must, in the nature of things, act either upon knowledge already possessed or upon assumptions, or upon investigation of the pertinent general facts, social, economic, political, or scientific. An older tradition once prescribed that judges should rationalize their result solely in

---

3. See Ch. 20, supra.

terms of analogy to old doctrines, leaving the considerations of expediency unstated. Contemporary practice indicates that judges in their opinions should render explicit their policy judgments and the factual grounds therefor. These latter have been helpfully classed as "legislative facts," as contrasted with the "adjudicative facts" which are historical facts pertaining to the incidents which give rise to lawsuits.

Constitutional cases argued in terms of due process typically involve reliance upon legislative facts for their proper resolution. Whether a statute enacted pursuant to the police power is valid, after all, involves a twofold analysis. First, it must be determined that the enactment is designed to achieve an appropriate objective of the police power; that is, it must be designed to protect the public health, morals, safety, or general welfare. The second question is whether, in light of the data on hand, a legislature could reasonably have adopted the means they did to achieve the aim of their exercise of the police power. In Jay Burns Baking Co. v. Bryan,[1] for example, the question was whether, concerned about consumers being misled by confusing sizes of bread, the Nebraska legislature could decree not only that the bakers bake bread according to distinctively different weights but that they wrap their product in wax paper lest any post-oven expansion of some loaves undo these distinctions. A majority of the court held the enactment unconstitutional because, in their opinion, the wrapping requirement was unreasonable. Mr. Justice Brandeis, correctly anticipating the decline of substantive due process, dissented, pointing out that the only question was whether the measure was a reasonable legislative response in light of the facts available to the legislators themselves. Then, in a marvelous illustration of the Brandeis brief technique, he recited page after page of data illustrating how widespread was the problem of shortweight and how, in light of nationwide experience, the statute appeared to be a reasonable response to the environmental situation.

Given the bent to test due process according to the information available to the legislature, the truth-content of these data are not directly relevant. The question is whether sufficient data exist which could influence a reasonable legislature to act, not whether ultimately these data are true. This is not the same case as when a court proceeds to interpret a constitutional norm and, while they still rely upon data, the judges *qua* legislators themselves proceed to act as if the data were true. In Brown v. Board of Education,[2] for example, the Court faced the issue whether segregated schools, equal in facilities and faculty, could any longer be tolerated under the equal protection clause. The question was no longer whether a reasonable legislator could believe these schools could never be equal, but whether the *judges* believed that the very act of segregating branded certain children with a feeling of inferiority so deleterious that it would be impossible for them to obtain an equal education no matter how equal the facilities and teachers. Thus the intellectual legitimacy of this kind of decision turns upon the actual truth-content of the legislative facts taken into account by the judges who propound the decision. While not necessarily indisputably true, it would appear that these legislative facts must at least appear to be more likely than not true if the opinion is going to have the requisite intellectual legitimacy upon which the authority of judge-made rules is ultimately founded.

When it comes to the utilization of these lawmaking facts, three problems can beset constitutional law decisions. The first is that the forest can sometimes be lost sight of for the trees. That is to say, so much historical and sociological data are rehearsed that an opinion appears to be bottomed upon purely pragmatic considerations and not upon any compelling constitutional norm. The second is that an outpouring of learning appears inordinate to the requirements of the problem at hand. The third is that data can appear to be included as an exercise in fustian excess, often

§ 331

1. 264 U.S. 504 (1924).

2. 347 U.S. 483 (1954), supplemented 349 U.S. 294.

in a losing cause. The first would appear to be a problem of draftsmanship, hard cases perhaps making bad law, but the latter two appear less defensible.

When making new common law, judges must, like legislators, do the best they can in assaying the data available to them and make the best decision they can concerning which course wisdom dictates they follow. Should they, for example, continue to invoke the common law rule of *caveat emptor* in the field of real property, or should they invoke a notion of implied warranty in the instance of the sale of new houses? Should they require landlords of residential units to warrant their habitability and fitness for the use intended? While sociological, economic, political and moral doctrine may abound about questions like this, none of these data are likely indisputable.

Thus it is that, in practice, the legislative facts upon which judges rely when performing their lawmaking function are not indisputable. At the same time, cognizant of the fact that his decision as lawmaker can affect the public at large, in contradistinction to most rulings at trials which affect only the parties themselves, a judge is not likely to rely for his data only upon what opposing counsel tender him. Obviously enough, therefore, legislative facts tend to be the most elusive facts when it comes to propounding a codified system of judicial notice. This seems to be confirmed by the fact that the Federal Rules of Evidence make no effort to regulate this type of judicial notice.

There are, however, efforts being made to rationalize this subject-matter. If one were to examine social science materials looking for help in enunciating a rule of law, one would be searching for authority much in the same fashion as one would be if one were looking to unearth decisional precedential authority. This has suggested to Professors John Monahan and Laurens Walker that a foray into social science materials is more akin to an effort to answer a question of law than one of fact.[3]

Thus judges should not see themselves taking judicial notice of legislative facts but promulgating law. Social science materials would not be introduced into the system by expert testimony but by way of written briefs, and judges would have no hesitation at all carrying on their own independent researches. The very recognition that a question of law was involved would promote a more critical attitude toward these materials, because they would carry more *gravitas,* being law, than do the only arguably true episodic facts of the current approach. Soon enough a canon of precedential authority would come into being based upon a calculus of the precise court which relied on particular data and the peer review each decision received in the law reviews and other opinions. Thus these materials could be quickly accessed by lower courts by simple reference and citation.

§ 332. The Uses of Judicial Notice

Judges have been prone to emphasize the need for caution in applying the doctrine of judicial notice. The great writers of evidence, on the other hand, having perhaps a wider view of the needs of judicial administration, advocate a more extensive use of the doctrine. Thus Thayer suggests: "Courts may judicially notice much that they cannot be required to notice. That is well worth emphasizing; for it points to a great possible usefulness in this doctrine, in helping to shorten and simplify trials. * * * The failure to exercise it tends daily to smother trials with technicality and monstrously lengthens them out."[1] And Wigmore says, "The principle is an instrument of usefulness hitherto unimagined by judges."[2]

The simple litany that judicial notice encapsulates facts commonly known and facts readily verifiable is useful as a rule-of-thumb but not as a precise litmus test. The courts' willingness to resort to judicial notice is apparently influenced by a number of less specifically definable circumstances. A court is more

---

3. Monahan & Walker, *Social Authority: Obtaining, Evaluating, and Establishing Social Science in Law,* 134 U.Pa.L.Rev. 477 (1986).

§ 332
1. Thayer, A Preliminary Treatise on Evidence 309 (1898).
2. Wigmore, 9 Evidence at Trials At Common Law § 2583, p. 819 (Chadbourn rev. 1981).

willing to notice a general than a specific fact, as for example, the approximate time of the normal period of human gestation, but not the precise maximum and minimum limits. A court may be more willing to notice a fact if it is not an ultimate fact, that is, a fact which would be determinative of a case. Suppose, for example, that a plaintiff in a vehicular negligence action specifically alleged that the defendant was driving too fast in a business district and the testimony, if believed, would indicate that the automobile in question caused a long skid mark on the highway surface. The trial judge might be less willing to notice that the street in question was within the business district than he would to notice that any properly equipped automobile travelling at the maximum speed appropriate in such a district could be stopped within x feet of the braking point. In the first example, the trial judge would appear to be invading the province of the jury to determine the facts pertinent to what had happened, whereas in the second he would be merely establishing rather quickly a piece of data which would aid the jury during their deliberations on the ultimate issue of negligence.

Agreement is not to be had whether the perimeters of the doctrine of judicial notice enclose only facts which are indisputably true or encompass also facts more than likely true. If, on the one hand, the function of the jury is to resolve disputed questions of fact, an argument can be made that judges should not purport to make decisions about facts unless they are indisputable facts. If this argument is accepted, it follows that once a fact has been judicially noticed, evidence contradicting the truth of the fact is inadmissible because by its very nature, a fact capable of being judicially noticed is an indisputable fact which the jury must be instructed to accept as true. If, on the other hand, the function of judicial notice is to expedite the trial of cases, an argument can be made that judges should dispense with the need for time-consuming formal evidence when the fact in question is likely true. If this argument is accepted, it follows that evidence contradicting the judicially noticed fact is admissible and that the jury are ultimately free

to accept or reject the truth of the fact posited by judicial notice.

A facile resolution of this conflict suggests itself readily enough. That is, the controversy might be exposed as a misunderstanding caused by a failure to take into account the distinction between "adjudicative" and "legislative" facts. This would be true if the instances where judicial notice was restricted to indisputable facts involved only adjudicative facts whereas potentially disputable facts were only noticed within a legislative context. Whether the decided cases sustain this symmetry is itself a matter of dispute because authority exists which illustrates that some courts are not loathe judicially to notice a potentially disputable fact within what is at least arguably an adjudicative context.

The most recent efforts to deal with judicial notice have exhibited a trend away from extrapolating an all-inclusive definition of a doctrine in favor of promulgating modest guidelines which would regularize what are perceived to be the essential applications of judicial notice. One approach would restrict formalized judicial notice regulation to those situations in which only adjudicative facts are involved. Limiting judicial notice to adjudicative facts and then only to indisputable ones leaves unresolved the question whether a jury in a criminal case should be instructed that they must accept the inexorable truth of the noticed fact. In terms of logic and pure reason it would appear that a jury as a rational deliberative body must accept proper judicially noticed facts. But, viewed through the lens of democratic tradition as a protection against an overbearing sovereign, a criminal trial jury may be a body which ought to be free to return a result which as an exercise in logic flies in the face of reason.

Another approach would narrow the range of judicial notice by reducing the significance of the conflict between questions peculiarly the province of juries and questions of fact handled by judges. Judges have, for example, always dealt with preliminary questions of fact even in jury trials. Thus, while the admissibility of the results of blood tests raises a question of fact pertaining to the reliability of such tests, the judges deal with this question as a preliminary step in ruling on relevancy, a function that is itself peculiarly a judicial one. Indeed, if trials are examined functionally, it can be demonstrated that judges have always had to decide questions pertaining to facts without any apparent infringement of the jury's domain, whether this be in ruling on demurrers, during pretrial hearings, on motions for nonsuit or to set aside verdicts, or at sentencing. This may indicate, after all, that the scope of judicial notice varies according to the function the judge is performing when judicial notice is taken.

It may be the case that there is no easy rule-of-thumb technique adequate unto the day to serve as an easy capsulation of the judicial notice phenomenon. Protagonists of the indisputable-only definition of judicial notice concede that in criminal cases the jury must be left free in the ultimate analysis to determine the truth or falsity of any adjudicative fact. Protagonists of the disputability thesis might be expected to resolve the controversy by suggesting that, whereas in jury cases there is some merit in the notion that judicial notice should be restricted to indisputable facts in order not to infringe on the role of the jury, the disputable theory works quite efficiently within the context of the jury-waived cases, which probably means that it applies in most cases which come to trial. The fact of the matter is that this solution has not received as much notoriety as might be expected.

The very fact that the trend of these recent investigations has been calculated to resolve the problems associated with judicial notice by narrowing the dimensions of that concept has, however, raised a new problem which must be dealt with in the future. If judicial notice is restricted to instances where judges deal with facts in an adjudicative context, the instances where judges deal with legislative facts is left unregulated insofar as procedural guide-lines are concerned. The significance of this problem can be best illustrated within the context of the next section.

§ 333.　Procedural Incidents

An elementary sense of fairness might indicate that a judge before making a final rul-

ing that judicial notice will be taken should notify the parties of his intention to do so and afford them an opportunity to present information which might bear upon the propriety of noticing the fact, or upon the truth of the matter to be noticed. Although the original version of the Uniform Rules of Evidence required it, only a rare case insists that a judge must notify the parties before taking judicial notice of a fact on his own motion, and some authorities suggest that such a requirement is needless. It may very well be the case that a trial judge need only consider notifying the parties if on his own motion he intends to take judicial notice of a less than obviously true fact. In every other instance, after all, the request by one party asking the judge to take judicial notice will serve to apprise the opposing party of the question at hand. While there may, nevertheless, exist in practice a rough consensus with regard to procedural niceties when trial judges take judicial notice of adjudicative facts, this is not the end of the matter. The cases universally assume the nonexistence of any need for a structured adversary-style ancillary hearing with regard to legislative facts. Indeed, even with regard to adjudicative facts, the practices of appellate courts tend to support the argument that there exists no real felt need to formalize the practice of taking judicial notice.

Legislative facts, of course, have not fitted easily into any effort to propound a formalized set of rules applicable to judicial notice. These facts, after all, tend to be less than indisputable ones and hence beyond the pale of judicial notice. What then of the requirement that, before judicial notice is taken, the parties be afforded a reasonable opportunity to present information relative to the propriety of taking judicial notice and the tenor of the matter to be noticed? By and large the parties have this opportunity during arguments over motions as to the appropriate law to be applied to the controversy, by exchanging briefs, and by employing the technique exemplified by the Brandeis brief. It appears, therefore, that there exists no felt need to formalize the procedures pertaining to the opportunity to be heard with reference to legislative facts. Even so, there are cases where the legislative facts which form the basis of an appellate opinion first appear in the decision itself and counsel never have the opportunity to respond to them. Presumably current practice relies upon the sound discretion of judges to maintain discipline in this regard by presupposing a general insistence among the judges on a fundamental notion of elementary fairness. However ill-defined because rooted in a sense of due process rather than bottomed on a precise calculus of rules, this notion of fairness may prove to be the common denominator which will continue to link together judicial notice of legislative and adjudicative facts.

With regard to the treatment of adjudicative facts by appellate courts, the common starting point is the axiom that these tribunals can take judicial notice to the same extent as can trial courts. At the very least, this rule suggests the obvious fact that appellate courts can review the propriety of the judicial notice taken by the court below and can even take judicial notice on their own initiative of facts not noticed below. Nonetheless the recitation of these principles fails to portray the full flavor of the actual practice of appellate courts in taking judicial notice on their own initiative of what would appear to be adjudicative facts.

In this regard the case of Mills v. Denver Tramway Corp.,[1] may be instructive. Plaintiff had alighted from a trolley car, walked behind it and crossed the parallel set of tracks, where he was struck by a car going in the opposite direction. Plaintiff appeared to be manifestly guilty of contributory negligence, a sound enough conclusion plaintiff next attempted to overcome by invoking the doctrine of the last-clear-chance. That is, at the penultimate moment of the trial, plaintiff requested a jury instruction to the effect that, if the motorman had had a chance to sound the trolley bell, the harm might still have been avoided, in which case plaintiff was entitled to prevail. The trial judge refused the instruction because no evidence was ever introduced to indicate that the

trolley had a bell. The appellate tribunal reversed, giving plaintiff a new trial, reciting the fact that "streetcars have bells." If all trolley cars had bells, a fact the trial court could have taken judicial notice of had it ever been requested to do so, it would be quite appropriate for the appellate court to take notice of the very same fact. But was it an indisputable fact that *all* streetcars had bells? Arguably most did, in which case the appellate court was taking judicial notice, not of an indisputable fact, but only of a more-than-likely-true fact. More plausibly, the court reasoned that, in all likelihood, the trolley had a bell, in which instance plaintiff should have, as part of his case, proceeded to introduce evidence to substantiate a plausible claim on the last-clear-chance theory. Alternatively, had no bell existed, plaintiff should have made that omission the basis of his claim. In either event, a sense of justice cried out for a trial of the case with all the facts fully developed. If, however, this was the sense of justice which moved the appellate tribunal, their invocation of the statement that "all streetcars have bells," a disputable proposition, sheds no real light either on the question whether judicial notice extends to disputable adjudicative facts or whether the parties must be afforded a hearing before judicial notice is taken. Given the need for appellate courts on occasion to reverse results below on a factual basis, judicial notice serves as a convenient device by which to give the practice the appearance of legal propriety. This being true, it would appear that the chances of adequately formalizing judicial notice even of adjudicative facts at the appellate level may be a slim one indeed.

§ 334. Trends in the Development of Judicial Notice of Facts

It appears that, by and large, agreement has been reached on a rough outline of the perimeters of judicial notice as applied to adjudicative facts at the trial level.[1] A workable procedural format which would appear to guarantee fairness already exists in the event

§ 333

1.   155 F.2d 808 (10th Cir.1946).

§ 334

1.   See Fed.R.Evid. and Unif.R.Evid. 201.

that judicial notice is restricted to indisputable facts. The only question remaining is whether, in order to expedite the trial of cases, judges should be allowed to excuse the proponent of a fact likely true of the necessity of producing formal evidence thereof, leaving it to the jury to accept or reject the judicially noticed fact, and of course, allowing the opponent to introduce evidence contradicting it. Indeed, the present controversy might be put in a new light by limiting judicial notice to indisputable facts and then raising the question, whether, as part of the law associated with the burden of proof and presumptions, a judge can properly expedite trials by himself ruling that very likely true facts are presumptively true unless the jury care to find otherwise.

Whatever the ultimate doctrinal synthesis of judicial notice of adjudicative facts comes to be, a viable formulation of rules laying down a similarly rigid procedural etiquette with regard to legislative facts has not proved feasible. Given the current recognition that nonadjudicative facts are inextricably part and parcel of the law formulation process in a policy-oriented jurisprudence, there may be no need to formulate a distinctly judicial notice-captioned procedure with regard to nonadjudicative facts. These data are fed into the judicial process now whenever rules of law are brought to the attention of judges in motions, memoranda and briefs. Thus, whatever rules govern the submission of law in the litigation process have already preempted the nonadjudicative field and made unnecessary separate treatment thereof within the context of judicial notice.

There has been an increasing awareness, moreover, that quite apart from judicial notice, the trial process assumes that the participants bring with them a vast amount of everyday knowledge of facts in general. To think, after all, presupposes some data about which to think. In an automobile accident case, for example, both the judge and the jury constantly draw on their own experiences as drivers, as observers of traffic, and as live human beings, and these experiences are reduced in their minds to propositions of fact which, since they have survived themselves, are probably fairly accurate. This substratum of data the participants bring into the courthouse has, however, tended to confuse the judicial notice scene. On the one hand, this subliminal-like data is sometimes confused with the "common knowledge"-style of adjudicative facts with which formal judicial notice is concerned. On the other hand, judges constantly invoke references to these same everyday facts when they write opinions because, when formally articulated, it is impossible "to think" without reference to them. It may very well be the case that judges have tended, when extrapolating the obvious, to invoke the words, "I take judicial notice of" to explain the presence of these facts in their minds, thereby unnecessarily glutting the encyclopedias with trivia which are, when formally collected, highly misleading indices of the true scope of judicial notice as such.

Federal Rule of Evidence 201 only applies to adjudicative facts, which might suggest that legislative facts simply cannot be fitted into the concept of judicial notice. If they cannot, legislative facts would have to come into the judicial process in the form of "evidence." A problem would then arise if a trial court had to decide the question of law whether it was constitutional totally to exclude from a bifurcated jury in a capital case persons opposed to the death penalty. After hearing testimony and accepting documentary material, the court might conclude on the basis of available social science materials that either death disqualification produced conviction prone juries or it did not. The court might bottom its decision of the constitutional issue on this "finding of fact." If the social science materials were not clearly inclined to sustain only one conclusion, and the ruling were treated as a factual ruling, the ruling, whichever way it came out, could not be reversed because it would not be clearly erroneous. Law would come to turn on fact and be susceptible to two right answers. This is not going to happen. Legislative facts are not "evidence" in the normal sense of the word, and judicial notice doctrine still obtains as to them. The problem is one of refining that doctrine, and not confusing it with evidentiary proof of adjudicatory facts.

Arguably legislative facts might better be handled by treating them as one would a search for law amidst a canon of conflicting cases, ruling on the tenor of the applicable economic or social rule as if it were a question of law. But as we have seen, judges are constantly asserting facts to be true in many contexts and at many stages of the judicial process, "facts" which while they appeal to common sense and prudence as work-a-day truths, lack the dignity and permanence of something that could be called "law." Law requires more than cracker-barrel folk wisdom behind it to command respect and obedience. What is needed is a new concept, perhaps oriented around the study of thinking-about-facts techniques involved throughout the judicial process. Judge Robert E. Keeton has spearheaded just such an endeavor in the most appropriate context of a William B. Lockhart Lecture, taking as his cue the notion that facts are the premise of innumerable rulings.[2] Oddly enough, this trend if continued would represent a return to Thayer.[3]

§ 335. The Judge's Task as Law–Finder: Judicial Notice of Law

It would appear to be self-evident that it is peculiarly the function of the judge to find and interpret the law applicable to the issues in a trial and, in a jury case, to announce his findings of law to the jury for their guidance. The heavy-footed common law system of proof by witnesses and authenticated documents is too slow and cumbrous for the judge's task of finding what the applicable law is. Usually this law is familiar lore and if not the judge relies on the respective counsel to bring before him the statutes, reports, and source books, and these resources are read from informally in discussion or cited and quoted in trial and appellate briefs. Occasionally the judge will go beyond the cited authorities to make his own investigation. In the ordinary process of finding the applicable law, the normal method then is by informal investigation of any

sources satisfactory to the judge. Thus this process has been traditionally described in terms of the judge taking judicial notice of the law applicable to the case at hand. Indeed, when the source-material was not easily accessible to the judge, as in the case of "foreign law" or city ordinances, law has been treated as a peculiar species of fact, requiring formal proof. We shall see, however, that as these materials become more accessible, the tendency is toward permitting the judges to do what perhaps they should have done in the beginning, that is, to rely on the diligence of counsel to provide the necessary materials, and accordingly to take judicial notice of *all* law. This seems to be the goal toward which the practice is marching.

Domestic law. As to domestic law generally, the judge is not merely permitted to take judicial notice but required to do so, at least if requested, although in a particular case a party may be precluded on appeal from complaining of the judge's failure to notice a statute where his counsel has failed to call it to the judge's attention. This general rule that judicial notice will be taken of domestic law means that state trial courts will notice Federal law, which is controlling in every state, and has been held to mean that in a Federal trial court the laws of the states, not merely of the state where it is sitting, are domestic and will be noticed. Similarly all statewide or nationwide executive orders and proclamations, which are legally effective, will be noticed. Under this same principle, even the laws of antecedent governments will be noticed.

State and national administrative regulations having the force of law will also be noticed, at least if they are published so as to be readily available. When such documents are published in the Federal Register it is provided that their contents shall be judicially noticed. Private laws and municipal ordinances, however, are not commonly included within the doc-

---

2. Keeton, *Legislative Facts and Similar Things: Deciding Disputed Premise Facts*, 73 Minn.L.Rev. 1 (1988).

3. See, Thayer, A Preliminary Treatise on Evidence at the Common Law 278–279 (1898) ("Whereabout in the law does the doctrine of judicial notice belong? Wherever

the process of reasoning has a place, and that is everywhere. Not peculiarly in the law of evidence. * * * The subject of judicial notice, then, belongs to the general topic of legal or judicial reasoning.")

trine of judicial notice and these must be pleaded and proved. To the extent that these items become readily available in compilations, it may be expected that they will become subject to judicial notice; in the meantime, it would appear appropriate for judges to take judicial notice of both private laws and municipal ordinances if counsel furnish a certified copy thereof.

Under this hoary practice when a required pleading and proof of the foreign law has been overlooked, or has been unsuccessfully attempted, the resulting danger of injustice is somewhat mitigated by the presumption that the law of the sister state is the same as that of the forum, or more simply the practice of applying local law if the law of the other state is not invoked and proven. But this presumption-tool is too rough for the job in hand, particularly when the materials for ascertaining the laws of sister states are today almost as readily accessible as those for local law, and in any event counsel as officers of the court are available to find and present those materials to the judge in just the same informal and convenient fashion as if they were arguing a question of local law.

In 1936 the Conference of Commissioners on Uniform Laws drafted the Uniform Judicial Notice of Foreign Law Act which was adopted in substance by more than half the states. This legislation provides that every court within the adopting state shall take judicial notice of the common law and statutes of every other state. While the Act removes the necessity to prove the law of another state, most courts do not feel obliged by it to notice the law of another state on their own initiative. Indeed, in order to invoke the benefits of the Foreign Law Act a litigant must give reasonable notice in the pleadings or otherwise to the adverse party of his intention to do so, failing which the courts are apt to refuse to take judicial notice or admit evidence as to the sister-state law relied on, invoking once again the presumption that it is the same as the law of the forum.

The Uniform Judicial Notice of Foreign Law Act pertained to the law of sister states and did not address the issue of the law of other nations. It was supplanted in 1962 when the National Conference of Commissioners on Uniform Laws approved Article IV of the Uniform Interstate and International Procedure Act. Calculated to address judicial notice of true foreign law, the new Act implicates the law of sister states as well because it imposes the same discipline when the law of *any* extra-forum jurisdiction is invoked. Thus a party who intends to raise an issue of the law of a sister state should give notice of an intention to do so, either in the pleadings or by any other reasonable method of written notice. It is the court which determines the tenor of what actually will be noticed about the law of a sister state, and the court may go beyond the materials furnished it by the parties in arriving at its own determination. Article IV, however, has yet to win widespread adoption.

The law of foreign countries. At common law, foreign law was treated as a matter of fact: pleading and proof were required, and the jury decided what the foreign law was. As early as 1936 the Uniform Judicial Notice of Foreign Law Act reflected the idea that the tenor of the law of a foreign country was a question for the court and not for the jury. What is significant is the fact that this selfsame 1936 Act, adverted to in the preceding section, contained no provision for the judicial notice of the law of other nations. The parties were left not only to pleading but proving, albeit to a judge and not a jury, the law of other nations.

The longevity of the ancient notion that a party had "to prove" the law of another nation was likely rooted in the fact that the sources of extranational law were not easily accessible even in urban centers. A healthy pragmatism seems to have ameliorated the harshness of any rule demanding strict proof. Sworn to or certified copies of extranational statutes or decisions gave way to the use of copies thereof in a book printed by the authority of the foreign state or proved to be commonly recognized in its courts.

Even so, the very idea that a party was engaged in "proving" a point of extranational law fairly invited complications. The written text of any law suggests that its "black letter" be interpreted in light of any germane decisions, treatises or commentaries. This under common law proof must be accomplished by taking the testimony in person or by deposition of an expert in the foreign law. The adversary of course is free to take the testimony of other experts if he can find them on his side, and the cross-examination of conflicting experts is likely to accentuate the disagreements. This method of proof seems to maximize expense and delay and hardly seems best calculated to ensure a correct decision by our judges on questions of foreign law. It could be vastly improved by pre-trial conferences in which agreements as to undisputed aspects of the foreign law could be secured, and by the appointment by the court of one or more experts on foreign law as referees or as court-chosen experts to report their findings to the court.

Following the lead of several states which by statute have provided that the court must take judicial notice or permit the court to do so in its discretion, the practice obtaining in the federal courts has been codified to make the tenor of foreign law a question of law for the court. Thus it is 'that a party who intends to raise an issue of foreign-nation law must give notice of his intention to do so, either in his pleadings or by any other reasonable method of written notice. Once the issue of foreign law is raised, the court need not, in its effort to determine the tenor of that law, rely upon the testimony and other materials proffered by the litigant, but may engage in its own research and consider any relevant material thus found.

In turn the new Uniform Interstate and International Procedure Act's Article IV will, if generally enacted, unify state practice along the lines of the federal model. Thus again the invocation of extranational law would necessitate written notice, by way of the pleadings or any reasonable alternative, and the court, licensed to engage in its own researches, would ultimately fix the actual tenor of whatever was noticed. Concomitantly, recourse to the law of a sister state is included within the same process so that a single procedure will obtain whenever the law of a jurisdiction outside the forum becomes an issue.

The unwillingness of the courts to notice the laws of other countries creates difficulties where the party whose case or defense depends, under conflicts rules, upon foreign law and he fails to prove that law as a fact. There are several solutions. First, the court may decide the issue against him for failure of proof. This is often a harsh and arbitrary result. Second, the court may simply apply the law of the forum on the ground that no other law is before it, especially if the parties have tried the case as if local law were applicable. Third, the court may presume that the law of the other country is the same as that of the forum,[1] thus reaching the same result as under the second theory but raising intellectual difficulties because the presumption is so frequently contrary to fact. When the doctrine involved is one of common law, but the other nation is not a common law country, some courts will decline to apply the presumption. On the other hand, when the common law rule invoked is a part of the common fund of all civilized systems, such as the binding force of ordinary commercial agreements, the presumption is applied though the foreign country is not a common law country. Moreover, by what is probably the prevailing and more convenient view, if the question would be governed locally by a statute, a like statute in the foreign country may be presumed.

International and Maritime Law. The rules, principles and traditions of "international law," or "the law of nations," will be noticed in Federal and state courts. Maritime law is similarly subject to judicial notice but only insofar as these rules have become part of the general maritime law. Less widely recognized maritime rules of foreign countries are treated like foreign law generally and are required to be proved, unless they have been published here by government authority as the

---

§ 335

1. See generally, the illuminating discussion in Nussbaum, The Problem of Proving Foreign Law, 50 Yale L.J. 1018, 1035 et seq. (1941); Medina Fernandez v. Hartman,

260 F.2d 569 (9th Cir.1958) (absent a showing to the contrary it is a familiar principle that foreign law is presumed same as domestic); Leary v. Gledhill, 84 A.2d 725 (N.J.1951).

authentic foreign law, or they have been embodied in a widely adopted international convention. Peculiarly enough, the presumption of identity of foreign law with the local law, which would seem to be unusually convenient and realistic in the maritime field, has been narrowly restricted.

The future of judicial notice of law. When a judge presiding in the presence of a jury decides a question of fact, a sufficiently unique event occurs to merit special treatment because the jury is thought to perform the fact-finding role in common law countries. This appears to explain why judicial notice of facts has been a topic of evidence law ever since Thayer authored his pioneering treatise. There is nothing very remarkable about a judge ruling on the tenor of the law to be applied to the resolution of the controversy, however, because by definition this is the very function judges are supposed to perform. When the sources of law were dubious at best, the job of sorting out the applicable law was shifted to the jury, witness how foreign law and municipal ordinances were treated as questions of fact. When next judges began to rule on the tenor of this law, even though it was still "fact" to be developed by the parties, there may have been some justification for describing this process as judicial notice. As all law has become increasingly accessible and judges

have tended to assume the duty to rule on the tenor of all law, the notion that this process is part of judicial notice has become increasingly an anachronism. Evidence, after all, involves the proof of facts. How the law is fed into the judicial machine is more appropriately an aspect of the law pertaining to procedure. Thus it is that the electronic bleeps sounded by today's data processing equipment may be actually tolling the intellectual death knell of this discrete subject-matter hitherto dealt with as a subdivision of the law of evidence.

Old habits, however, are hard to break. An afternoon spent in the law library canvassing the scene at state level will quickly turn up a number of states wherein the Uniform Judicial Notice of Foreign Law Act still obtains, together with a hotchpot of discrete statutes detailing judicial notice of local statutes, some administrative regulations and some if not all municipal ordinances. These materials cry out for rationalization and it is little wonder than that several states, in the process of adopting the Federal Rules of Evidence have added a Rule 202 governing the judicial notice of law. Coming full circle there now exists a proposed revision of the Federal model that would add rules creating a coordinated regimen for inputting law into the judicial process through the judicial notice of law mechanism.

Chapter 36

THE BURDENS OF PROOF
AND PRESUMPTIONS

Table of Sections

§ 336. The Burdens of Proof: The Burden of Producing Evidence and the Burden of Persuasion

"Proof" is an ambiguous word. We sometimes use it to mean evidence, such as testimony or documents. Sometimes, when we say a thing is "proved" we mean that we are convinced by the data submitted that the alleged fact is true. Thus, "proof" is the end result of conviction or persuasion produced by the evidence. Naturally, the term "burden of proof" shares this ambivalence. The term encompasses two separate burdens of proof. One burden is that of producing evidence, satisfactory to the judge, of a particular fact in issue. The second is the burden of persuading the trier of fact that the alleged fact is true.

The burden of producing evidence on an issue means the liability to an adverse ruling (generally a finding or directed verdict) if evidence on the issue has not been produced. It is usually cast first upon the party who has pleaded the existence of the fact, but as we shall see, the burden may shift to the adversary when the pleader has discharged its initial duty.[1] The burden of producing evidence is a critical mechanism in a jury trial, as it empowers the judge to decide the case without jury consideration when a party fails to sustain the burden.

The burden of persuasion becomes a crucial factor only if the parties have sustained their burdens of producing evidence and only when all of the evidence has been introduced. It does not shift from party to party during the

§ 336

1. See § 338 infra.

course of the trial simply because it need not be allocated until it is time for a decision. When the time for a decision comes, the jury, if there is one, must be instructed how to decide the issue if their minds are left in doubt. The jury must be told that if the party having the burden of persuasion has failed to satisfy that burden, the issue is to be decided against that party. If there is no jury and the judge is in doubt, the issue must be decided against the party having the burden of persuasion.

What is the significance of the burden of persuasion? Clearly, the principal significance of the burden of persuasion is limited to those cases in which the trier of fact is actually in doubt. Possibly, even in those cases, juries disregard their instructions on this question and judges, trying cases without juries, pay only lip service to it, trusting that the appellate courts will not disturb their findings of fact. Yet, even if an empirical study were conclusively to demonstrate both a regular disregard for jury instructions and a propensity on the part of judges to decide issues of fact without regard to their express statements concerning the allocation of the burden of persuasion, rules allocating and describing that burden could not be discarded by a rational legal system. A risk of nonpersuasion naturally exists any time one person attempts to persuade another to act or not to act. If the other does not change her course of action or nonaction, the person desiring change has, of course, failed. If no burden of persuasion were acknowledged by the law, one possible result would be that the trier of fact would purport to reach no decision at all. The impact of nondecision would then fall by its own weight upon the party, usually the plaintiff, who sought a change in the status quo. Although this is generally where the law would place the burden anyhow, important policy considerations may dictate that the risk should fall on the opposing party.[2]

Another possibility would be that the trier of fact would itself assign a burden of persuasion, describing that burden as it saw fit by

substituting its own notions of policy for those now made available to it as a matter of law. Such a result would be most undesirable. Considerations of policy that are sufficient to suggest that in some instances the burden of persuasion be assigned to the party desiring a maintenance of the status quo are strong enough to dictate the need for a consistent rather than a case by case determination of the question. Other policy considerations, such as those that have led the law to require that the prosecution in a criminal case prove the defendant guilty beyond a reasonable doubt,[3] are sufficient to require that the jury be explicitly and clearly instructed as to the measure of the burden as well as its allocation. Although judges and juries may act contrary to the law despite the best attempts to persuade them to do otherwise, we can at least give them the benefit of thoughtful guidance on the questions of who should bear the burden of persuasion and what the nature of that burden should be. In jury trials, perhaps the problem has not been in the concept of a burden of persuasion, but rather in the confusing jury instructions that abound on this point of law. In nonjury trials, if judges are not in fact following rules of law allocating the burden, the fault may lie not in the concept but with thoughtless judicial and legislative allocations and descriptions of the burden.

§ 337. Allocating the Burdens of Proof

In most cases, the party who has the burden of pleading a fact will have the burdens of producing evidence and of persuading the jury of its existence as well. The pleadings therefore provide the common guide for apportioning the burdens of proof. For example, in a typical negligence case the plaintiff will have the burdens of (1) pleading the defendant's negligence (2) producing evidence of that negligence and (3) persuading the trier of fact of its existence. The defendant will usually have the same three burdens with regard to the contributory negligence of the plaintiff.

2. See § 337 infra.

3. See § 341 infra.

However, looking for the burden of pleading is not a foolproof guide to the allocation of the burdens of proof. The latter burdens do not invariably follow the pleadings. In a federal court, for example, a defendant may be required to plead contributory negligence as an affirmative defense and yet, where jurisdiction is based upon diversity of citizenship, the applicable substantive law may place the burdens of producing evidence and persuasion with regard to that issue on the plaintiff. More significantly, reference to which party has pleaded a fact is no help at all when the rationale behind the allocation is questioned or in a case of first impression where there are no established pleading rules.

The burdens of pleading and proof with regard to most facts have been and should be assigned to the plaintiff who generally seeks to change the present state of affairs and who therefore naturally should be expected to bear the risk of failure of proof or persuasion. The rules which assign certain facts material to the enforcibility of a claim to the defendant owe their development partly to traditional happen-so and partly to considerations of policy.

The determination of appropriate guidelines for the allocation of the burdens has been somewhat hindered by the judicial repetition of two doctrines, one erroneous and the other meaningless. Statements are found primarily in older cases to the effect that even though a party is required to plead a fact, it is not required to prove that fact if its averment is negative rather than affirmative in form. Such a rule would place an entirely undue emphasis on what is ordinarily purely a matter of choice of forms. Moreover, these statements were probably to be understood as properly applying only to the denial by a party of an opponent's previous pleading, and now one who has the burden of pleading a negative fact as part of its cause of action generally has the accompanying burdens of producing evidence and persuasion. The second misleading doctrine is that the party to whose case the element is essential has the burdens of proof. Such a rule simply restates the question.

The actual reasons for the allocation of the burdens may be no more complex than the

misleading statements just discussed. The policy of handicapping a disfavored contention probably accounts for the requirement that the defendant generally has all three burdens with regard to such matters as contributory negligence, statute of limitations, and truth in defamation. Convenience in following the natural order of storytelling may account for calling on the defendant to plead and prove those matters which arise after a cause of action has matured, such as payment, release, and accord and satisfaction.

A doctrine often repeated by the courts is that where the facts with regard to an issue lie peculiarly in the knowledge of a party, that party has the burden of proving the issue. Examples are the burdens commonly placed upon the defendant to prove payment, discharge in bankruptcy, and license. This consideration should not be overemphasized. Very often one must plead and prove matters as to which his adversary has superior access to the proof. Nearly all required allegations of the plaintiff in actions for tort or breach of contract relating to the defendant's acts or omissions describe matters peculiarly in the defendant's knowledge. Correspondingly, when the defendant is required to plead contributory negligence, it pleads facts specially known to the plaintiff.

Perhaps a more frequently significant consideration in the fixing of the burdens of proof is the judicial estimate of the probabilities of the situation. The risk of failure of proof may be placed upon the party who contends that the more unusual event has occurred. For example, where a business relationship exists, it is unlikely that services will be performed gratuitously. The burden of proving a gift is therefore placed upon the one who claims it. Where services are performed for a member of the family, a gift is much more likely and the burden of proof is placed on the party claiming the right to be paid.

In allocating the burdens, courts consistently attempt to distinguish between the constituent elements of a promise or of a statutory command, which must be proved by the party who relies on the contract or statute, and matters of exception, which must be proved by its adversary. Often the result of this approach is an arbitrary allocation of the burdens, as the statutory language may be due to a mere casual choice of form by the draftsman. However, the distinction may be a valid one in some instances, particularly when the exceptions to a statute or promise are numerous. If that is the case, fairness usually requires that the adversary give notice of the particular exception upon which it relies and therefore that it bear the burden of pleading. The burdens of proof will not always follow the burden of pleading in these cases. However, exceptions generally point to exceptional situations. If proof of the facts is inaccessible or not persuasive, it is usually fairer to act as if the exceptional situation did not exist and therefore to place the burden of proof and persuasion on the party claiming its existence.

As has been stated, the burdens of producing evidence and of persuasion with regard to any given issue are both generally allocated to the same party. Usually each is assigned but once in the course of the litigation and a safe prediction of that assignment can be made at the pleading stage. However, the initial allocation of the burden of producing evidence may not always be final. The shifting nature of that burden may cause both parties to have the burden with regard to the same issue at different points in the trial.[1] Similarly, although the burden of persuasion is assigned only once—when it is time for a decision—a prediction of the allocation of that burden, based upon the pleadings, may have to be revised when evidence is introduced at trial.[2] Policy considerations similar to those that govern the initial allocation of the burden of producing evidence and tentatively fix the burden of persuasion govern the ultimate assignment of those burdens as well.[3]

In summary, there is no key principle governing the apportionment of the burdens of proof. Their allocation, either initially or ultimately, will depend upon the weight that is given to any one or more of several factors,

including: (1) the natural tendency to place the burdens on the party desiring change, (2) special policy considerations such as those disfavoring certain defenses, (3) convenience, (4) fairness, and (5) the judicial estimate of the probabilities.

§ 338. Satisfying the Burden of Producing Evidence

Let us suppose that the plaintiff, claiming an estate in land for John Smith's life, had the burden of pleading, and has pleaded, that John Smith was alive at the time the action was brought. She seeks to fulfill the burden of producing evidence of this fact.

To do this she may offer *direct* evidence, e.g., of witness Jones, who saw Smith alive in the clerk's office when the complaint in the action was filed. From this the inference of the truth of the fact to be proved depends only upon the truthfulness of Jones. Or, she may offer *circumstantial* evidence, which requires a weighing of probabilities as to matters other than merely the truthfulness of the witness. For example, she may secure the testimony of Jones that Jones received a letter in the mail which was signed "John Smith" one month before the action was brought and that she recognized the signature as Smith's. Patently in this latter case, the tribunal may be satisfied that Jones is speaking the truth, and yet the tribunal may decline to infer the fact of Smith's being alive when the action began.

How strongly persuasive must the offered evidence be to satisfy the burden? A "scintilla" of evidence will not suffice. The evidence must be such that a reasonable person could draw from it the inference of the existence of the particular fact to be proved or, as put conversely by one federal court, "if there is substantial evidence opposed to the [motion for directed verdict], that is evidence of such quality and weight that reasonable and fairminded men in the exercise of impartial judg-

1. See § 338 infra.

2. See § 344 infra.

3. See § 343 infra.

ment might reach different conclusions, the [motion] should be denied."[1]

One problem that has troubled the courts is whether the test for the granting of a directed verdict should vary, depending upon the required measure of persuasion should the case go to the jury. For example in a criminal case where the prosecution must persuade the jury beyond a reasonable doubt,[2] should the test for a directed verdict be whether the evidence could satisfy reasonable people beyond a reasonable doubt? Some courts have said no, perhaps believing with Judge Learned Hand that, although the gravity of the consequences often makes judges more exacting in criminal cases, the line between proof that should satisfy reasonable men and the evidence that should satisfy reasonable men beyond a reasonable doubt is, in the long run, "too thin for day to day use."[3]

However, most courts have applied the stricter test. A clear trend toward universal adoption of the stricter test was effectively solidified into a constitutional dictate in Jackson v. Virginia,[4] where the Court held that a federal court reviewing a state court conviction on a *habeas corpus* petition must determine whether a rational factfinder could have found the petitioners guilty beyond a reasonable doubt. Arguably no trial judge should apply a lesser standard on a motion for a directed verdict.

Generally no difficulty occurs where the evidence is direct. Except in rare cases, it is sufficient, though given by one witness only, however negligible a human being she may be. But if the evidence is circumstantial, forensic disputes often arise as to its sufficiency to warrant a jury to draw the desired inference. In fact, in few areas of the law have so many words been spoken by the courts with so little conviction. One test frequently expounded in criminal cases is that where the prosecution relies upon circumstantial evidence, the evidence must be so conclusive as to exclude any

other reasonable inference inconsistent therewith. The test is accurate enough in criminal cases, but adds little at least to the stricter test for criminal cases discussed above. A similar formula is sometimes expounded in civil cases but seems misplaced in civil litigation. It leaves little for the jury and far exceeds what is needed to prevent verdicts based upon speculation and conjecture. Courts rejecting the formula in civil cases have stated that the burden of producing evidence is satisfied, even by circumstantial evidence, if "there be sufficient facts for the jury to say reasonably that the preponderance favors liability."[5]

Other tests and other phrasings of the tests discussed here are myriad, but irrespective of the test articulated, in the last analysis the judge's ruling must necessarily rest on her individual opinion, formed in the light of her own common sense and experience, as to the limits of reasonable inference from the facts proven. However, certain situations recur and give rise repeatedly to litigation, and a given judge, in a desire for consistency and the consequent saving of time and mental travail, will rule alike whenever the same situation is proved and its sufficiency to warrant a certain inference is questioned. Other judges follow suit and a standardized practice ripening into a rule of law results. Most of these rules are positive rather than negative. They announce that certain types of fact-groups are sufficient to enable the person who has the first duty to go forward with evidence to fulfill that burden, i.e., they enable the party to rest after proving them without being subject to the penalty of an adverse ruling.

Suppose the one who had the initial burden of offering evidence in support of the alleged fact, on pain of an adverse ruling, does produce evidence barely sufficient to satisfy that burden, so that the judge can just say, "A reasonable jury *could* infer that the fact is as alleged, from the circumstances proved." If the

§ 338

1. Boeing Co. v. Shipman, 411 F.2d 365, 374 (5th Cir.1969).

2. See § 341 infra.

3. United States v. Feinberg, 140 F.2d 592, 594 (2d Cir.1944).

4. 443 U.S. 307 (1979).

5. Smith v. Bell Telephone Co., 153 A.2d 477 (Pa. 1959).

proponent then rests, what is the situation? Has the duty of going forward shifted to the adversary? Not if we define that duty as the liability to a peremptory adverse ruling on failing to give evidence, for if at this juncture the original proponent rests and the adversary offers no proof, the proponent will not be entitled to the direction of a verdict in her favor on the issue, but rather the court will leave the issue to the decision of the jury. But it is frequently said that in this situation the duty of going forward has shifted to the adversary, and this is unobjectionable if we bear in mind that the penalty for silence is very different here from that which was applied to the original proponent. If she had remained silent at the outset she would irrevocably have lost the case on this issue, but the only penalty now applied to her adversary is the risk, if she remains silent, of the jury's finding against her, though it may find for her. Theoretically she may have this risk still, even after she has offered evidence in rebuttal. It is simpler to limit "duty of going forward" to the liability, on resting, to an adverse ruling, and to regard the stage just discussed (where the situation is that if both parties rest, the issue will be left to the jury) as one in which neither party has any duty of going forward.

In the situation just discussed, the party who first had the duty, i.e., the necessity, of giving proof, has produced evidence which requires the judge to permit the jury to infer, as it chooses, that the fact alleged is or is not true. It is a permitted, but not a compulsory, inference. Is it possible for the original proponent of evidence to carry her proof to the stage where if she rests, she will be entitled to a directed verdict, or its equivalent, on the issue? Undoubtedly, with a qualification to be noted, this is possible, and when it occurs there is a shifting to the adversary of the duty of going forward with the evidence, in the strictest sense. Such a ruling means that in the judge's view the proponent has not merely offered evidence from which reasonable people could draw the inference of the truth of the fact alleged, but evidence from which (in the absence of evidence from the adversary) rea-

sonable people could not help but draw this inference. Thus, as long ago as 1770, Lord Mansfield told the jury that upon the issue of whether defendant had published a libel, proof of a sale of the book in defendant's shop was, being unrebutted, "conclusive."[6]

In the case first supposed at the beginning of this section, if the plaintiff brought forward the *direct* evidence of Jones that Smith was alive when the complaint was filed, and there is no contrary evidence at all, or if she brings forward circumstantial evidence (that is, evidence that Smith was seen alive in perfect health 10 minutes before the complaint was filed) which is, in the absence of contrary circumstances, irresistibly convincing, the jury should not be left to refuse to draw the only rational inference.

If we do not permit the jury to draw an inference from insufficient data, as where the proponent has failed to sustain her initial duty of producing evidence, we should not permit the jury to act irrationally by rejecting compelling evidence. Here again the ruling, from repeated occurrence of similar facts, may become a standardized one. However, the statement that one who has the duty of going forward can go forward far enough not merely to escape an adverse peremptory ruling herself, but to subject her opponent to one if the latter declines to take up the gage by producing evidence, has the following qualification. Obviously if the testimony were conflicting as to the truth of the facts from which the inference of the fact in issue is desired to be drawn, and the judge believes the inference (conceding the truth of the premise) is irresistible to rational minds, he can only make a conditional peremptory ruling. He directs the jury, if you believe the evidence that fact A is so then you must find fact B, the fact in issue. In some jurisdictions, if the party seeking the ruling has the burden of persuasion on the issue, as assigned on the basis of the pleadings, she can only get a conditional ruling, though her witnesses are undisputed and unimpeached. But, in either event, if the inference is overwhelming, the jury is instructed not to cogitate over

6. Rex v. Almon, 5 Burr. 2686, 98 Eng.Rep. 411 (K.B. 1770).

that, but only over the truthfulness of those who testify to the basic data.

We have seen something of the mechanics of the process of "proceeding" or "going forward" with evidence, viewed from the point of view of the *first* party who is stimulated to produce proof under threat of a ruling foreclosing a finding in her favor. She may in respect to a particular issue pass through three states of judicial hospitality: (a) where if she stops she will be thrown out of court; (b) where if she stops and her adversary does nothing, her reception will be left to the jury; and (c) where if she stops and her adversary does nothing, her victory (so far as it depends on having the inference she desires drawn) is at once proclaimed. Whenever the first producer has presented evidence sufficient to get her to the third stage and the burden of producing evidence can truly be said to have shifted, her adversary may in turn pass through the same three stages. Her evidence again may be (a) insufficient to warrant a finding in her favor, (b) sufficient to warrant a finding, or (c) irresistible, if unrebutted.

§ 339. Satisfying the Burden of Persuasion: (a) The Measure of Persuasion in Civil Cases Generally

According to the customary formulas a party who has the burden of persuasion of a fact must prove it in criminal prosecutions "beyond a reasonable doubt,"[1] in certain exceptional controversies in civil cases, "by clear, strong and convincing evidence,"[2] but on the general run of issues in civil cases "by a preponderance of evidence." The "reasonable doubt" formula points to what we are really concerned with, the state of the jury's mind, whereas the other two divert attention to the evidence, which is a step removed, being the instrument by which the jury's mind is influenced. These latter phrases, consequently, are awkward vehicles for expressing the degree of the jury's belief.

What is the most acceptable meaning of the phrase, proof by a preponderance, or great-

er weight, of the evidence? Certainly the phrase does not mean simple volume of evidence or number of witnesses. One definition is that evidence preponderates when it is more convincing to the trier than the opposing evidence. This is a simple commonsense explanation which will be understood by jurors and could hardly be misleading in the ordinary case. It may be objected, however, that it is misleading in a situation where, though one side's evidence is more convincing than the other's, the jury is still left in doubt as to the truth of the matter. Compelling a decision in favor of a party who has introduced evidence that is simply better than that of his adversary would not be objectionable if we hypothesize jurors who bring none of their own experience to the trial and who thus view the evidence in a vacuum. Of course, no such case could exist. We expect and encourage jurors to use their own experience to help them reach a decision, particularly in judging the credibility of witnesses. That experience may tell them, for example, that although the plaintiff has introduced evidence and the defendant has offered nothing in opposition, it is still unlikely that the events occurred as contended by the plaintiff. Thus, it is entirely consistent for a court to hold that a party's evidence is sufficient to withstand a motion for directed verdict and yet to uphold a verdict for its adversary.

The most acceptable meaning to be given to the expression, proof by a preponderance, seems to be proof which leads the jury to find that the existence of the contested fact is more probable than its nonexistence. Thus the preponderance of evidence becomes the trier's belief in the preponderance of probability. Some courts have boldly accepted this view.

Other courts have been shocked at the suggestion that a verdict, a truth-finding, should be based on nothing stronger than an estimate of probabilities. They require that the trier must have an "actual belief" in, or be "convinced of" the truth of the fact by this "preponderance of evidence." Does this mean that they must believe that it is certainly true?

1. See § 341 infra.

2. See § 340 infra.

Hardly, since it is apparent that an investigation by fallible people based upon the testimony of other people, with all their defects of veracity, memory, and communication, cannot yield certainty. Does it mean a kind of mystical "hunch" that the fact must be true? This would hardly be a rational requirement. What it would most naturally be understood to mean by the jury (in the unlikely event that it should carry analysis so far) is that it must be persuaded that the truth of the fact is not merely more probable than not, but highly probable. This is more stringent than our tradition or the needs of justice warrant, and seems equivalent to the standard of "clear, strong and convincing proof," hitherto thought to be appropriate only in exceptional cases.[3]

Much of the time spent in the appellate courts over the metaphysics of "preponderance" has been wasted because of the courts' insistence upon the cabalistic word. This bemusement with word-magic is particularly apparent in the decisions dealing with the use of the word "satisfaction" or its derivatives in referring to the effect of the evidence on the jury's mind. Some courts, with more logic than realism, have condemned its use as equivalent to proof beyond a reasonable doubt unless qualified by the word "reasonable." Other courts have pragmatically, although perhaps reluctantly permitted its use, even without the qualification. Although certainly juries should be clearly and accurately instructed with regard to the question of the measure of persuasion in civil cases, it is hard to believe that variations in language such as those involved in the courts' difficulties with the use of the word "satisfaction" lead to any differences in jurors' attitudes. Thoughtfully drafted pattern jury instructions should prove helpful in reducing unnecessarily spent appellate court time on these questions. Where no pattern instruction is available, however, trial judges would be wise to search for the locally accepted phraseology and to adhere to it religiously.

§ 340. Satisfying the Burden of Persuasion: (b) Requirement of Clear and Convincing Proof

While we have seen that the traditional measure of persuasion in civil cases is by a preponderance of evidence,[1] there is a limited range of claims and contentions which the party is required to establish by a more exacting measure of persuasion. The formula varies from state to state, but among the phrases used are the following: "by clear and convincing evidence," "clear, convincing and satisfactory," "clear, cogent and convincing," and "clear, unequivocal, satisfactory and convincing." Some courts have used all of these phrases and then some to describe the applicable standard. The phrasing within most jurisdictions has not become as standardized as is the "preponderance" formula, but even here the courts sometimes are surprisingly intolerant of slight variations from the approved expression. No high degree of precision can be attained by these groups of adjectives. It has been persuasively suggested that they could be more simply and intelligibly translated to the jury if they were instructed that they must be persuaded that the truth of the contention is "highly probable." But as former Chief Justice Burger stated:

> We probably can assume no more than that the difference between a preponderance of the evidence and proof beyond a reasonable doubt probably is better understood than either of them in relation to the intermediate standard of clear and convincing evidence. Nonetheless, even if the particular standard-of-proof catchwords do not always make a great difference in a particular case, adopting a "standard of proof is more than an empty semantic exercise." * * * In cases involving individual rights, whether criminal or civil, "[t]he standard of proof [at a minimum] reflects the value society places on individual liberty."[2]

3. See § 340 infra.

§ 340

1. See § 339 supra.

2. Addington v. Texas, 441 U.S. 418, 425 (1979).

To this end, the United States Supreme Court has held that proof by a clear and convincing or similar standard is required, either by the United States Constitution or by the applicable federal statute, in a variety of cases involving deprivations of individual rights not rising to the level of criminal prosecution, including commitment to a mental hospital, termination of parental rights, denaturalization and deportation.

Not all instances of requirements of proof more than usually convincing concern cases involving individual liberty. Indeed, the requirement of proof of this magnitude for certain types of contentions seems to have had its origins in the standards prescribed for themselves by the chancellors in determining questions of fact in equity cases. However, it has now been extended to certain types of actions tried before juries, and the chancellors' cautionary maxims are now conveyed to the jury in the form of instructions on the burden of persuasion.

Among the classes of cases to which this special standard of persuasion commonly has been applied are: (1) charges of fraud and undue influence, (2) suits on oral contracts to make a will, and suits to establish the terms of a lost will, (3) suits for the specific performance of an oral contract, (4) proceedings to set aside, reform or modify written transactions, or official acts on grounds of fraud, mistake or incompleteness, and (5) miscellaneous types of claims and defenses, varying from state to state, where there is thought to be special danger of deception, or where the court considers that the particular type of claim should be disfavored on policy grounds.

The appellate court, under the classical equity practice, tried the facts *de novo,* upon the deposition testimony in the record, and thus it was called on to apply anew the standard of clear and convincing proof in its study of the evidence. But in the modern system there are usually restrictions upon appellate review of a judge's findings of fact, even in equity issues. Thus, in the federal courts under Rule 52(a) the trial court's findings will be

reversed only when "clearly erroneous." And in jury-tried cases the verdict will be reviewed only to the extent of determining whether there was evidence from which reasonable people could have found the verdict. Will the appellate court, then, today, if there was substantial evidence from which the judge or jury could have made the findings it did, consider the questions whether the evidence met the "clear and convincing" standard, in a case where it applies? The United States Supreme Court, in reviewing a summary judgment in a libel case where the plaintiff's burden was to prove actual malice by clear and convincing evidence, stated that the test on appeal should be "whether the evidence in the record could support a reasonable jury finding either that the plaintiff has shown actual malice by clear and convincing evidence or that the plaintiff has not."[3] However, in some jurisdictions it is for the trial court, not the appellate court, to draw a distinction between evidence which is clear and convincing and evidence which merely preponderates.

§ 341. Satisfying the Burden of Persuasion: (c) Proof Beyond a Reasonable Doubt

As we have seen with reference to civil cases, a lawsuit is essentially a search for probabilities. A margin of error must be anticipated in any such search. Mistakes will be made and in a civil case a mistaken judgment for the plaintiff is no worse than a mistaken judgment for the defendant. However, this is not the case in a criminal action. Society has judged that it is significantly worse for an innocent person to be found guilty of a crime than for a guilty person to go free. The consequences to the life, liberty, and good name of the accused from an erroneous conviction of a crime are usually more serious than the effects of an erroneous judgment in a civil case. Therefore, as stated by the Supreme Court in recognizing the inevitability of error even in criminal cases, "[w]here one party has at stake an interest of transcending value—as a criminal defendant his liberty—this margin of error is reduced as to him by the process of placing

3. Anderson v. Liberty Lobby, Inc., 477 U.S. 242, 255–256 (1986).

on the other party the burden * * * of persuading the factfinder at the conclusion of the trial of his guilt beyond a reasonable doubt."[1] In so doing, the courts may have increased the total number of mistaken decisions in criminal cases, but with the worthy goal of decreasing the number of one kind of mistake—conviction of the innocent.

The demand for a higher degree of persuasion in criminal cases was recurrently expressed from ancient times, but its crystallization into the formula "beyond a reasonable doubt" seems to have occurred as late as 1798. It is now accepted in common law jurisdictions as the measure of persuasion by which the prosecution must convince the trier of all the essential elements of guilt. In 1970, the Supreme Court explicitly held that the due process clause "protects the accused against conviction except upon proof beyond a reasonable doubt of every fact necessary to constitute the crime with which he is charged."[2]

A simple instruction that the jury will acquit if they have a reasonable doubt of the defendant's guilt of the crime charged in the indictment is ordinarily sufficient. Courts, however, frequently paint the lily by giving the jury a definition of "reasonable doubt." A famous early instance was the oft-echoed statement of Chief Justice Shaw in the trial of Prof. Webster for the murder of Dr. Parkman: "It is that state of the case, which, after the entire comparison and consideration of all the evidence, leaves the minds of jurors in that condition that they cannot say they feel an abiding conviction, to a moral certainty, of the truth of the charge."[3] It is an ancient maxim that all definitions are dangerous and this one has been caustically criticized as raising more questions than it answers. Other definitions, often more carefully balanced to warn against the overstressing of merely possible or imaginary doubts, have become customary in some jurisdictions. Reasonable doubt is a term in

common use almost as familiar to jurors as to lawyers. As one judge has said it needs a skillful definer to make it plainer by multiplication of words,[4] and as another has expressed it, the explanations themselves often need more explanation than the term explained.[5] If a definition of the term is not requested by the accused, it is not required. Whether if so requested it is the judge's duty to define the term, is a matter of dispute, but the wiser view seems to be that it lies in the court's discretion, which should ordinarily be exercised by declining to define, unless the jury itself asks for a fuller explanation.

There are certain excuses or justifications allowed to the defendant, which although provable for the most part under the plea of not guilty, are spoken of for some purposes as "affirmative defenses." Among these are self-defense, duress, insanity, intoxication and claims that the accused is within an exception or proviso in the statute defining the crime. Sometimes only the burden of producing evidence will be assigned to the defendant. Under certain circumstances the burden of persuasion with regard to some of these defenses may be allocated to the defendant and correspondingly, the prosecution may be relieved of proving the absence of the defense. The allocation and operation of the burdens of proof with regard to these defenses present difficult policy, as well as constitutional, problems. These problems will be discussed together with the special problems related to presumptions in criminal cases.[6]

Despite occasional statements to the contrary, the reasonable doubt standard generally has been held inapplicable in civil cases, regardless of the nature of the issue involved. For example, when a charge of crime is at issue in a civil action, the threatened consequences of sustaining the accusation, though often uncommonly harmful to purse or prestige, are not generally as serious as in a prose-

§ 341

1. Speiser v. Randall, 357 U.S. 513, 525–526 (1958).

2. In re Winship, 397 U.S. 358, 364 (1970).

3. Commonwealth v. Webster, 59 Mass. (5 Cush.) 295, 320 (1850).

4. Newman, J. in Hoffman v. State, 73 N.W. 51, 52 (Wis.1897).

5. Mitchell, J. in State v. Sauer, 38 N.W. 355 (Minn. 1888).

6. §§346–348 infra.

cution for the crime. Accordingly the modern American cases have come around to the view that in the interest of justice and simplicity a reasonable doubt measure of persuasion will not be imposed. Most courts have said that a preponderance of the evidence is sufficient, although some have increased the standard to "clear and convincing."

§ 342. Presumptions: In General

One ventures the assertion that "presumption" is the slipperiest member of the family of legal terms, except its first cousin, "burden of proof." One author has listed no less than eight senses in which the term has been used by the courts.[1] Agreement can probably be secured to this extent, however: a presumption is a standardized practice, under which certain facts are held to call for uniform treatment with respect to their effect as proof of other facts.

Returning for a moment to the discussion of satisfying the burden of producing evidence,[2] assume that a party having the burden of producing evidence of fact A, introduces proof of fact B. The judge, using ordinary reasoning, may determine that fact A might reasonably be inferred from fact B, and therefore that the party has satisfied its burden, or as sometimes put by the courts, has made out a "prima facie" case. The judge has not used a presumption in the sense of a standardized practice, but rather has simply relied upon a rational inference. However, in ruling on a motion for directed verdict the judge may go beyond her own mental processes and experience and find that prior decisions or existing statutes have established that proof of fact B is sufficient to permit the jury to infer the existence of fact A. The judge has thus used a standardized practice but has the court necessarily used a presumption? Although some courts have described such a standardized inference as a presumption, most legal scholars have disagreed. They have saved the term to

describe a significantly different sort of a rule, one that dictates not only that the establishment of fact B is sufficient to satisfy a party's burden of producing evidence with regard to fact A, but also at least compels the shifting of the burden of producing evidence on the question to the party's adversary. Under this view, if proof of fact B is introduced and a presumption exists to the effect that fact A can be inferred from fact B, the party denying the existence of fact A must then introduce proof of its nonexistence or risk having a verdict directed or a finding made against it. Further some authorities state that a true presumption should not only shift the burden of producing evidence, but also require that the party denying the existence of the presumed fact assume the burden of persuasion on the issue as well.[3]

Certainly the description of a presumption as a rule that, at a minimum, shifts the burden of producing evidence is to be preferred, at least in civil cases. Inferences that a trial judge decides may reasonably be drawn from the evidence need no other description, even though the judge relies upon precedent or a statute rather than personal experience in reaching a decision. In most instances, the application of any other label to an inference will only cause confusion. In criminal cases, however, there are rules that traditionally have been labeled presumptions, even though they do not operate to shift even the burden of producing evidence. The jury is permitted but not required to accept the existence of the presumed fact even in the absence of contrary evidence.[4] Recently, the Supreme Court has resurrected the term "permissive presumption" to describe these rules.[5] The term presumption will be used in this text in the preferred sense discussed above in referring to civil cases, but with the qualification suggested in referring to criminal cases.

There are rules of law that are often incorrectly called presumptions that should be

---

§ 342

1. Laughlin, In Support of the Thayer Theory of Presumptions, 52 Mich.L.Rev. 195, 196–207 (1953).

2. See § 338 supra.

3. See § 344 infra.

4. See § 346 infra.

5. County Court of Ulster County v. Allen, 442 U.S. 140 (1979).

specifically distinguished from presumptions at this point:

Conclusive presumptions. The term presumption as used above always denotes a rebuttable presumption, i.e., the party against whom the presumption operates can always introduce proof in contradiction. In the case of what is commonly called a conclusive or irrebuttable presumption, when fact B is proven, fact A must be taken as true, and the adversary is not allowed to dispute this at all. For example, if it is proven that a child is under seven years of age, the courts have stated that it is conclusively presumed that she could not have committed a felony. In so doing, the courts are not stating a presumption at all, but simply expressing the rule of law that someone under seven years old cannot legally be convicted of a felony.

Res ipsa loquitur. Briefly and perhaps oversimply stated, res ipsa loquitur is a rule that provides that a plaintiff may satisfy his burden of producing evidence of a defendant's negligence by proving that the plaintiff has been injured by a casualty of a sort that normally would not have occurred in the absence of the defendant's negligence. Although a few jurisdictions have given the doctrine the effect of a true presumption even to the extent of using it to assign the burden of persuasion, most courts agree that it simply describes an inference of negligence. Prosser called it a "simple matter of circumstantial evidence."[6] Most frequently, the inference called for by the doctrine is one that a court would properly have held to be reasonable even in the absence of a special rule. Where this is so, res ipsa loquitur certainly need be viewed no differently from any other inference. Moreover, even where the doctrine is artificial—where it is imposed for reasons of policy rather than logic—it nevertheless remains only an inference, permitting but not requiring, the jury to find negligence. The only difference is that where res ipsa loquitur is artificially imposed, there is better reason for informing the jury of the permissibility of the inference than there is in the case where the doctrine simply describes a

rational inference. Although theoretically a jury instruction of this kind might be viewed as violating a state rule prohibiting comment on the evidence, the courts have had little difficulty with the problem and have consistently approved and required, where requested, instructions that tell the jury that a finding of negligence is permissible. Obviously these instructions can and should be given without the use of the misnomer "presumption."

The presumption of innocence. Assignments of the burdens of proof prior to trial are not based on presumptions. Before trial no evidence has been introduced from which other facts are to be inferred. The assignment is made on the basis of a rule of substantive law providing that one party or the other ought to have one or both of the burdens with regard to an issue.[7] In some instances, however, these substantive rules are incorrectly referred to as presumptions. The most glaring example of this mislabeling is the "presumption of innocence" as the phrase is used in criminal cases. The phrase is probably better called the "assumption of innocence" in that it describes our assumption that, in the absence of contrary facts, it is to be assumed that any person's conduct upon a given occasion was lawful. In criminal cases, the "presumption of innocence" has been adopted by judges as a convenient introduction to the statement of the burdens upon the prosecution, first of producing evidence of the guilt of the accused and, second, of finally persuading the jury or judge of his guilt beyond a reasonable doubt. Most courts insist on the inclusion of the phrase in the charge to the jury, despite the fact that at that point it consists of nothing more than an amplification of the prosecution's burden of persuasion. Although the phrase is technically inaccurate and perhaps even misleading in the sense that it suggests that there is some inherent probability that the defendant is innocent, it is a basic component of a fair trial. Like the requirement of proof beyond a reasonable doubt, it at least indicates to the jury that if a mistake is to be

---

6.   Prosser, Torts, § 40 at 231 (4th ed. 1971).

7.   See § 337 supra.

made it should be made in favor of the accused, or as Wigmore stated, "the term does convey a special and perhaps useful hint * * * in that it cautions the jury to put away from their minds all the suspicion that arises from the arrest, the indictment, and the arraignment, and to reach their conclusion solely from the legal evidence adduced."[8]

§ 343. Reasons for the Creation of Presumptions: Illustrative Presumptions

A presumption shifts the burden of producing evidence, and may assign the burden of persuasion as well. Therefore naturally the reasons for creating particular presumptions are similar to the considerations which have already been discussed,[1] that bear upon the initial or tentative assignment of those burdens. Thus, just as the burdens of proof are sometimes allocated for reasons of fairness, some presumptions are created to correct an imbalance resulting from one party's superior access to the proof. An example of such a presumption is the rule that as between connecting carriers, the damage occurred on the line of the last carrier. Similarly, notions, usually implicit rather than expressed, of social and economic policy incline the courts to favor one contention by giving it the benefit of a presumption, and correspondingly to handicap the disfavored adversary. A classic instance is the presumption of ownership from possession, which tends to favor the prior possessor and to make for the stability of estates. A presumption may also be created to avoid an impasse, and reach some result, even though it is an arbitrary one. For example, presumptions dealing with the survivorship of persons who died in a common disaster are necessary in order that other rules of law may operate, even though there is actually no factual basis upon which to believe that one party or the other was likely to have died first. Generally, however, the most important consideration in the creation of presumptions is probability. Most presumptions have come into existence primarily because the judges have believed

that proof of fact B renders the inference of the existence of fact A so probable that it is sensible and timesaving to assume the truth of fact A until the adversary disproves it.

Obviously, most presumptions are based not on any one of these grounds alone, but have been created for a combination of reasons. Usually, for example, a presumption is based not only upon the judicial estimate of the probabilities but also upon the difficulties inherent in proving that the more probable event in fact occurred.[2] Moreover, as is the case with initial allocations of the burdens, the reasons for creation of presumptions are often tied closely to the pertinent substantive law. This is particularly true with regard to those presumptions which are created, at least in part, to further some social policy.

Although it would be inappropriate to attempt to list the hundreds of recognized presumptions, following is a brief discussion of a few illustrative presumptions and the reasons for their creation:

Official actions by public officers, including judicial proceedings, are presumed to have been regularly and legally performed. Reason: probability and the difficulty of proving that the officer conducted himself in a manner that was in all ways regular and legal.

A letter properly addressed, stamped and mailed is presumed to have been duly delivered to the addressee. Reason: probability and the difficulty of proving delivery in any other way.

When the plaintiff has been injured by the negligent operation of a vehicle, then upon proof of further facts he may have the benefit of presumptions in moving against the non-driving defendant. The plaintiff seeking to prove agency may secure the advantage of the presumption that the person driving the vehicle was doing so in the scope of his employment and in the course of the business of the defendant, merely by proving that the defendant was the owner. In a number of states the

---

8.   9 Wigmore, Evidence § 2511 at 407 (Chadbourn rev. 1981).

§ 343

1.   See § 337 supra.
2.   See § 337.

plaintiff must not only prove ownership to gain the benefit of the presumption of agency, but also that the driver is regularly employed by the defendant. If the plaintiff seeks to prove liability in a state having a statute making the owner liable for acts of one driving with the owner's consent, the plaintiff may secure the advantage of the presumption that the person driving was doing so with the owner's consent merely by showing ownership. In some states the plaintiff must not only prove ownership to gain the benefit of the presumption but also that a special relationship existed between the driver and the defendant. Reasons behind these presumptions: probability, fairness in the light of defendant's superior access to the evidence, and the social policy of promoting safety by widening the responsibility in borderline cases of owners for injuries caused by their vehicles.

When a bailor proves delivery of property to a bailee in good condition and return in a damaged state, or a failure to return after due demand, a presumption arises that the damage or loss was due to the negligence or fault of the bailee. Reason: fairness in the light of the superior access of the bailee to the evidence of the facts surrounding the loss; probability.

Proof that a person has disappeared from home and has been absent for at least seven years and that during this time those who would be expected to hear from the person have received no tidings and after diligent inquiry have been unable to find the person's whereabouts, raises a presumption that the person died at some time during the seven year period. The rule, though not very ancient, is already antiquated in that the seven year period is undoubtedly too long considering modern communications and transportation. Reasons: probability and the social policy of enforcing family security provisions such as life insurance, and of settling estates.

In the tracing of titles to land there is a useful presumption of identity of person from identity of name. Thus, when the same name appears in the chain of title first as grantee or heir and then as grantor, it will be presumed

that it was the same person in each case. Reasons: the convenience of enabling the court and the parties to rely upon the regularity of the apparent chain of title, until this is challenged by evidence contesting identity; the social policy of quieting claims based on the face of the record; and probability.

Proof that a child was born to a woman during the time when she was married creates the presumption that the offspring is the legitimate child of the husband. Despite the controversy over whether presumptions generally shift the burden of persuasion upon the opponent,[3] it is universally agreed that in the case of this presumption, the adversary contending for illegitimacy does have the burden. This burden, moreover, is usually measured not by the normal standard for civil cases of preponderance of the evidence, but rather by the requirement of clear, convincing, and satisfactory proof, as most courts say, or even by the criminal formula, beyond a reasonable doubt. In addition, as pointed out elsewhere in this work, the contender for illegitimacy is further handicapped by a rule rendering incompetent the testimony or declarations of the spouses offered to show nonaccess, when the purpose is to bastardize the child.[4] Reasons: social policy, to avoid the visitation upon the child of the sins of the parents caused by the social stigma of bastardy and the common law rules (now generally alleviated by statutes) as to the incapacities of the *filius nullius*, the child of no one; probability.

When violent death is shown to have occurred and the evidence is not controlling as to whether it was due to suicide or accident, there is a presumption against suicide. Reasons: the general probability in case of a death unexplained, which flows from the human revulsion against suicide, and, probably, a social policy which inclines in case of doubt toward the fruition rather than the frustration of plans for family protection through insurance.

§ 344. The Effect of Presumptions in Civil Cases

The trial judge must consider the effect of a presumption in a civil jury trial at two

---

3. See § 344, infra.

4. See § 67 supra.

stages: (1) when one party or the other moves for a directed verdict and (2) when the time comes to instruct the jury.

Sometimes the effect of a presumption, at either stage, is easy to discern; it follows naturally from the definition of the term. Thus, where a party proves the basic facts giving rise to a presumption, it will have satisfied its burden of producing evidence with regard to the presumed fact and therefore its adversary's motion for directed verdict will be denied. If its adversary fails to offer any evidence or offers evidence going only to the existence of the basic facts giving rise to the presumption and not to the presumed fact, the jury will be instructed that if they find the existence of the basic facts, they must also find the presumed fact. To illustrate, suppose plaintiff proves that a letter was mailed, that it was properly addressed, that it bore a return address, and that it was never returned. Such evidence is generally held to raise a presumption that the addressee received the letter.[1] Defendant's motion for a directed verdict, based upon nonreceipt of the letter, will be denied. Furthermore, if the defendant offers no proof on this question (or if she attempts only to show that the letter was not mailed and offers no proof that the letter was not in fact received) the jury will be instructed that if they find the existence of the facts as contended by plaintiff, they must find that the letter was received.

But the problem is far more difficult where the defendant does not rest and does not confine her proof to contradiction of the basic facts, but instead introduces proof tending to show the nonexistence of the presumed fact itself. For example, what is the effect of the presumption in the illustration given above, if the defendant takes the stand and testifies that she did not in fact receive the letter? If the plaintiff offers no additional proof, is the defendant now entitled to the directed verdict she was denied at the close of the plaintiff's case? If not, what effect, if any should the presumption have upon the judge's charge to the jury? The problem of the effect of a presumption when met by proof rebutting the presumed fact has literally plagued the courts and legal scholars. The balance of this section is devoted to that problem.

(A) The "Bursting Bubble" Theory and Deviations from It

The theory. The most widely followed theory of presumptions in American law has been that they are "like bats of the law flitting in the twilight, but disappearing in the sunshine of actual facts."[2] Put less poetically, under what has become known as the Thayer or "bursting bubble" theory, the only effect of a presumption is to shift the burden of producing evidence with regard to the presumed fact. If that evidence is produced by the adversary, the presumption is spent and disappears. In practical terms, the theory means that, although a presumption is available to permit the party relying upon it to survive a motion for directed verdict at the close of its own case, it has no other value in the trial. The view is derived from Thayer,[3] sanctioned by Wigmore,[4] adopted in the Model Code of Evidence,[5] and seemingly been made a part of the Federal Rules of Evidence.[6] It has been adopted, at least verbally, in countless modern decisions.

The theory is simple to state, and if religiously followed, not at all difficult to apply.

---

§ 344

1.　See § 343 supra.

2.　Lamm J. in Mackowik v. Kansas City, St. Josephs & Council Bluffs Railroad Co., 94 S.W. 256, 262 (Mo.1906), quoted in 9 Wigmore, Evidence § 2491 (Chadbourn rev. 1981).

3.　Thayer, Preliminary Treatise on Evidence, ch. 8, *passim*, and especially at 314, 336 (1898).

4.　9 Wigmore, Evidence § 2491(2) (Chadbourn rev. 1981).

5.　Model Code of Evidence Rule 704(2) (1942): " * * * when the basic fact * * * has been established * * * and

evidence has been introduced which would support a finding of the nonexistence of the presumed fact * * * the existence or nonexistence of the presumed fact is to be determined exactly as if no presumption had ever been applicable * * *," and Comment, "A presumption, to be an efficient legal tool must * * * (2) be so administered that the jury never hear the word presumption used since it carries unpredictable connotations to different minds * * *."

6.　Fed.R.Evid. 301.

The trial judge need only determine that the evidence introduced in rebuttal is sufficient to support a finding contrary to the presumed fact. If that determination is made, certainly there is no need to instruct the jury with regard to the presumption. The opponent of the presumption may still not be entitled to a directed verdict, but if its motion is denied, the ruling will have nothing to do with the existence of a presumption. As has been discussed, presumptions are frequently created in instances in which the basic facts raise a natural inference of the presumed fact. This natural inference may be sufficient to take the case to the jury, despite the existence of contrary evidence and despite the resultant destruction of the presumption. For example, in the case of the presumption of receipt of a letter, referred to above, the defendant may destroy the presumption by denying receipt. Nevertheless, a jury question is presented, not because of the presumption, but because of the natural inference flowing from the plaintiff's showing that she had mailed a properly addressed letter that was not returned. On the other hand, the basic facts may not present a natural inference of sufficient strength or breadth to take the case to the jury. In such an instance, the court may grant a directed verdict against the party who originally had the benefit of the presumption.

Deviations from the theory—in general. The "bursting bubble" theory has been criticized as giving to presumptions an effect that is too "slight and evanescent" when viewed in the light of the reasons for the creation of the rules.[7] Presumptions, as we have seen, have been created for policy reasons that are similar to and may be just as strong as those that govern the allocation of the burdens of proof prior to the introduction of evidence.[8] These policy considerations may persist despite the existence of proof rebutting the presumed fact. They may be completely frustrated by the Thayer rule when the basic facts of the presumption do not give rise to an inference that is naturally sufficient to take the case to the

jury. Similarly, even if the natural inference is sufficient to present a jury question, it may be so weak that the jury is unlikely to consider it in its decision unless specifically told to do so. If the policy behind certain presumptions is not to be thwarted, some instruction to the jury may be needed despite any theoretical prohibition against a charge of this kind.

These considerations have not gone unrecognized by the courts. Thus, courts, even though unwilling to reject the dogma entirely, often find ways to deviate from it in their treatment of at least some presumptions, generally those which are based upon particularly strong and visible policies. Perhaps the best example is the presumption of legitimacy arising from proof that a child was born during the course of a marriage. The strong policies behind the presumption are so apparent that the courts have universally agreed that the party contending that the child is illegitimate not only has the burden of producing evidence in support of the contention, but also has a heavy burden of persuasion on the issue as well.[9]

Another example of special treatment for certain presumptions is the effect given by some courts to the presumption of agency or of consent arising from ownership of an automobile.[10] The classic theory would dictate that the presumption is destroyed once the defendant or the driver testifies to facts sufficient to support a finding of nonagency or an absence of consent. Some courts have so held. However, other courts have recognized that the policies behind the presumption, i.e., the defendant's superior access to the evidence and the social policy of widening the responsibility for owners of motor vehicles, may persist despite the introduction of evidence on the question from the defendant, particularly when the evidence comes in the form of the party's own or her servant's testimony. These courts have been unwilling to rely solely upon the natural inferences that might arise from plaintiff's proof, and instead require more from the de-

---

7. Morgan & Maguire, Looking Backward and Forward at Evidence, 50 Harv.L.Rev. 909, 913 (1937).

8. See § 343 supra.

9. See § 343 supra.

10. See § 343 supra.

fendant, such as, that the rebuttal evidence be "uncontradicted, clear, convincing and unimpeached." Moreover, many courts also hold that the special policies behind the presumption require that the jury be informed of its existence.

Deviations from the theory—conflicting presumptions. Frequent deviations from the rigid dictates of the "bursting bubble" theory occur in the treatment of conflicting presumptions. A conflict between presumptions may arise as follows: W, asserting that she is the widow of H, claims her share of his property, and proves that on a certain day she and H were married. The adversary then proves that three or four years before W's marriage to H, W married another man. W's proof gives her the benefit of the presumption of the validity of a marriage. The adversary's proof gives rise to the general presumption of the continuance of a status or condition once proved to exist, and a specific presumption of the continuance of a marriage relationship. The presumed facts of the claimant's presumption and those of the adversary's are contradictory. How resolve the conflict? Thayer's solution would be to consider that the presumptions in this situation have disappeared and the facts upon which the respective presumptions were based shall simply be weighed as circumstances with all the other facts that may be relevant, giving no effect to the presumptions. Perhaps when the conflicting presumptions involved are based upon probability or upon procedural convenience, the solution is a fairly practical one.

The particular presumptions involved in the case given as an example, however, were not of that description. On the one hand, the presumption of the validity of a marriage is founded not only in probability, but in the strongest social policy favoring legitimacy and the stability of family inheritances and expectations. On the other hand, the presumptions of continuance of lives and marriage relationships are based chiefly on probability and trial convenience, and the probability, of course, varies in accordance with the length of time for which the continuance is to be presumed in the particular case. This special situation of the questioned validity of a second marriage

has been the principal area in which the problem of conflicting presumptions has arisen. Here, courts have not been willing to follow Thayer's suggestion of disregarding both rival presumptions and leaving the issue to the indifferent arbitrament of a weighing of circumstantial inferences. They have often preferred to formulate the issue in terms of a conflict of presumptions and to hold that the presumption of the validity of marriage is "stronger" and should prevail. The doctrine that the weightier presumption prevails should probably be available in any situation which involves conflicting presumptions, and where one of the presumptions is grounded in a predominant social policy.

Another and perhaps even better approach to the problem is to sidestep the conflict entirely and create a new presumption. Such a presumption has evolved in cases involving conflicting marriages. Under this rule, where a person has been shown to have been married successively to different spouses, there is a presumption that the earlier marriage was dissolved by death or divorce before the later one was contracted. While of course the presumption is rebuttable, as in the case of the presumption of legitimacy, many courts place a special burden of persuasion upon the party attacking the validity of the second marriage by declaring that the presumption can only be overcome by clear, cogent, and convincing evidence.

Deviations from the theory—instructions to the jury. Because of the strength of the natural inferences that generally arise from the basic facts of a presumption, judges are seldom faced with the prospect of directing a verdict against the party relying upon a presumption. Similarly, conflicting presumptions are relatively rare. However, far more frequently courts have justifiably held that the policies behind presumptions necessitate an instruction that in some way calls the existence of the rule to the attention of the jury despite the Thayerian proscription against the practice. The digests give abundant evidence of the widespread and unquestioning acceptance of the practice of informing the jury of the rule despite the fact that countervailing evidence has been adduced upon the disputed inference.

Given the frequency of the deviation, however, the manner in which the jury is to be informed has been a matter of considerable dispute and confusion. The baffling nature of the presumption as a tool for the art of thinking bewilders one who searches for a form of phrasing with which to present the notion to a jury. Most of the forms have been predictably bewildering. For example, judges have occasionally contented themselves with a statement in the instructions of the terms of the presumption, without more. This leaves the jury in the air, or implies too much. The jury, unless a further explanation is made, may suppose that the presumption is a conclusive one, especially if the judge uses the expression, "the law presumes."

Another solution, formerly more popular than now, is to instruct the jury that the presumption is "evidence," to be weighed and considered with the testimony in the case. This avoids the danger that the jury may infer that the presumption is conclusive, but it probably means little to the jury, and certainly runs counter to accepted theories of the nature of evidence.

More attractive theoretically is the suggestion that the judge instruct the jury that the presumption is to stand accepted, unless they find that the facts upon which the presumed inference rests are met by evidence of equal weight, or in other words, unless the contrary evidence leaves their minds in equipoise, in which event they should decide against the party having the burden of persuasion upon the issue. It is hard to phrase such an instruction without conveying the impression that the presumption itself is "evidence" which must be "met" or "balanced." The overriding objection, however, is the impression of futility that it conveys. It prescribes a difficult metaphysical task for the jury, and, in actual use, may mystify rather than help the average juror.

One possible solution, perhaps better than those already mentioned, would be for the trial judge simply to mention the basic facts of the

presumption and to point out the general probability of the circumstantial inference as one of the factors to be considered by the jury. By this technique, however, a true presumption would be converted into nothing more than a permissible inference. Moreover, the solution is simply not a feasible one in many jurisdictions without at least a new interpretation of another aspect of the law. The trial judge in most states must tread warily to avoid an expression of opinion on the facts. Although instructions on certain standardized inferences such as *res ipsa loquitur* are permitted,[11] the practice, wisely or not, may frown on any explanation of the allowable circumstantial inferences from particular facts as "invading the province of the jury."

Where the "bursting bubble" rule is discarded in favor of a rule which operates to fix the burden of persuasion, the problem of alerting the jury to the presumption should not exist. Under this theory, a presumption may ordinarily be given a significant effect without the necessity of mentioning the word "presumption" to the jury at all. There is no more need to tell the jury why one party or the other has the burden of persuasion where that burden is fixed by a presumption than there is where the burden is fixed on the basis of policies apparent from the pleadings. The jury may be told simply that, if it finds the existence of the basic facts, the opponent must prove the non-existence of the presumed fact by a preponderance of evidence, or, in some instances, by a greater standard. Even in those instances in which the presumption places the burden of persuasion on the same party who initially had the burden, there would seem to be no reason to mention the term. If the courts feel that the operation of the presumption warrants a higher standard of proof, the measure of persuasion can be increased as is now done in the case of the presumption of legitimacy. However, unless we are willing to increase the measure of persuasion, nothing can be gained by informing the jury of the coincidence. The word "presumption" would only tend to confuse the issue.

---

11. See § 342 supra.

(B) Attempts to Provide a Single Rule Governing the Effect of Presumptions

Perhaps, the greatest difficulty with the "bursting bubble" approach is that, in spite of its apparent simplicity, the conflicting desires of the courts to adopt it in theory and yet to avoid its overly-rigid dictates have turned it into a judicial nightmare of confusion and inconsistency. This state of affairs has caused legal scholars not only to search for a better rule, but for a single rule that would cover all presumptions.

Many writers came to the view that the better rule for all presumptions would provide that anything worthy of the name "presumption" has the effect of fixing the burden of persuasion on the party contesting the existence of the presumed fact. A principal technical objection to such a rule has been that it requires a "shift" in the burden of persuasion something that is, by definition of the burden, impossible. The argument seems misplaced, in that it assumes that the burden of persuasion is fixed at the commencement of the action. However, as we have seen,[12] the burden of persuasion need not finally be assigned until the case is ready to go to the jury. Thus, using a presumption to fix that burden would not cause it to shift, but merely cause it to be assigned on the basis of policy considerations arising from the evidence introduced at the trial rather than those thought to exist on the basis of the pleadings.[13] Certainly there is no reason why policy factors thought to be controlling at the pleading stage should outweigh factors bearing upon the same policies that arise from the evidence. Just the reverse should be true.

Certainly, some presumptions have been interpreted consistently as affecting the burden of persuasion without a great deal of discussion of a "shifting" burden of proof.[14] The real question is more fundamental: should this rule which is applicable to some presumptions be applicable universally? The answer to that query depends, not on theoretical distinctions between shifting as opposed to reassigning the burden of persuasion, but upon whether the policy behind the creation of all presumptions is always strong enough to affect the allocation of the burden of persuasion as well as the burden of producing evidence.

One of the leading proponents of the rule allocating the burden of persuasion as a universal rule was Professor Morgan. Although Professor Morgan served as a reporter for the Model Code of Evidence, he was unable to persuade the draftsmen of that code to incorporate into it a provision embracing this view of the effect of presumptions. The Model Code instead takes a rigid Thayerian position.[15] However, Morgan also was active in the drafting of the original Uniform Rules of Evidence where he had considerably more success in inducing an adoption of his theory. The original Uniform Rules provided that where the facts upon which the presumption is based have "probative value" the burden of persuasion is assigned to the adversary; where there is no such probative value, the presumption has only a Thayerian effect and dies when met by contrary proof.[16]

The Uniform Rules, although having much to commend them, presented problems. Obviously, they did not provide for a single rule. Different courts could give different answers to the question whether a particular presumption has probative value. The possibilities of inconsistency and confusion, although reduced by the rules, were still present. Further, the distinction made was a thin one that disregarded the existence of strong social policies behind some presumptions that lack probative value. Certainly if a presumption is not based on probability but rather is based solely upon social policy, there may be more, and not less, reason to preserve it in the face of contrary proof. A presumption based on a natural inference can stand on its own weight either

---

12. See § 336 supra.

13. The policies behind the allocation of the burden of persuasion are discussed generally in § 337 supra. The policies behind the creation of presumptions are discussed in § 343 supra.

14. See § 343, supra, concerning the presumption of legitimacy.

15. Model Code of Evidence Rule 704.

16. Original Unif.R.Evid. 14 (1953).

when met by a motion for a directed verdict or in the jury's deliberations. A presumption based on social policy may need an extra boost in order to insure that the policy is not overlooked. Morgan apparently recognized the weakness of the distinction made by the rule and seemed to have agreed to it only to allay fears that a provision giving to all presumptions the effect of fixing the burden of persuasion might be unconstitutional.

An approach almost directly opposite to the one taken in the Uniform Rules is taken in California's Code of Evidence, adopted in 1965. Under the California Code, presumptions based upon "public policy" operate to fix the burden of persuasion;[17] presumptions that are established "to implement no public policy other than to facilitate the determination of a particular action" are given a Thayerian effect.[18] The California approach is an improvement over the Uniform Rules but is still not completely satisfactory. The line between presumptions based on public policy and those which are not may not be easy to draw. Furthermore, although the California distinction is sounder than that made in the Uniform Rules, it is not completely convincing. The fact that the policy giving rise to a presumption is one that is concerned with the resolution of a particular dispute rather than the implementation of broader social goals, does not necessarily mean that the policy is satisfied by the shifting of the burden of producing evidence and that it should disappear when contrary proof is introduced. California asks the wrong question about the policies behind presumptions. The inquiry should not be directed to the breadth of the policy but rather to the question whether the policy considerations behind a certain presumption are sufficient to override the policies that tentatively fix the burdens of proof at the pleading stage.

The Federal Rules of Evidence, as adopted by the Supreme Court and submitted to the Congress, took the approach advocated by Morgan. The proposed Rule 301 provided that

"a presumption imposes on the party against whom it is directed, the burden of proving that the non-existence of the presumed fact is more probable than its existence." However, the draft did not survive congressional scrutiny and Rule 301, as enacted, has a distinct Thayerian flavor:

In all civil actions and proceedings not otherwise provided for by Act of Congress or by these rules, a presumption imposes on the party against whom it is directed, the burden of going forward with evidence to rebut or meet the presumption but does not shift to such party the burden of proof in the sense of the risk of non-persuasion, which remains throughout the trial upon the party of whom it was originally cast.[19]

Some legal scholars have argued that Federal Rule 301 does not preclude instructions which at least alert the jury to the strength of logic and policy underlying a presumption, even though evidence contrary to the existence of the presumed fact has been introduced. Furthermore, there has been willingness on the part of the federal courts to find that certain acts of Congress create presumptions of greater vitality than that provided by Rule 301 or even that certain presumptions in existence at the time of the adoption of Rule 301 are not subject to the procedure set forth in that rule. On the other hand, the rule has also served as a guideline for courts wishing to give a "bursting bubble" effect to a presumption, even where the court may not necessarily believe itself bound by the dictates of Rule 301.

The matter is further complicated by the fact that many of the states thus far adopting new evidence rules based upon the federal rules, have taken the approach of original Rule 301 and allocate the burden of persuasion based upon the presumption. Likewise, the Revised Uniform Rules of Evidence (1974), reject the "bursting bubble" and contain a Rule 301 almost identical to the rule submitted by the Supreme Court to the Congress.[20]

---

17. West's Ann.Cal.Evid.Code §§ 605–606.

18. Id. §§ 603–604.

19. Fed.R.Evid. 301.

20. Rev. Uniform Rule Evid. (1986) 301(a) provides:

In all actions and proceedings not otherwise provided for by statute or by these rules, a presumption imposes on the party against whom it is directed the burden of

(C) The Search for the Grail

Despite the best efforts of legal scholars, instead of having one rule to govern all presumptions in all proceedings, we are left in some ways in a more confusing state than that which existed prior to the adoption of the Federal Rules. Neither Morgan's view that all presumptions operate to assign the burden of persuasion nor the Thayerian concept of a disappearing presumption has yet to win the day.

The problem may be inherent in the nature of the concept of a "presumption." At least one author has argued that the concept is an artificial one, an attempt to do through a legal fiction what courts should be doing directly;[21] that the term "presumption" should be eliminated from legal usage and the functions which it serves replaced by direct allocations of the burdens of proof and by judicial comment accurately describing the logical implication of certain facts. In one sense, the suggestion is attractive. The courts should indeed be discussing the propriety of allocating the burdens of proof, rather than the conceptual technical application of a presumption. Yet, both the term and concept of a presumption, however misunderstood, are so engrained in the law that it is difficult to imagine their early demise. Furthermore, as the author recognizes, there are instances in which the evidence introduced at the trial may be such as to give rise to a rule of law which shifts or reassigns the burdens of proof. He calls this a "conditional imperative" and recognizes that in such a case the allocation of the burdens of proof cannot be made prior to trial. While the term "conditional imperative" may be just as good as "presumption," it is no better and the same set of problems which exist with regard to presumptions are just as likely to occur regardless of the label employed.

The answer may be that there is no single solution to the problem. The resistance of the courts and legislatures to a universal rule of presumptions is reflective of the fact that there are policies of varying strength behind different presumptions and therefore a hierarchy of desired results. In one instance, the policy may be such as only to give rise to a standardized inference, a rule of law which gets the plaintiff to the jury but does not compel a directed verdict in its favor. In another instance, the policy may be strong enough to compel a directed verdict in its favor, thus shifting the burden of producing evidence to the opposing party, but not strong enough to reassign the burden of persuasion. In still another instance, the policy may be strong enough to reassign the burden of persuasion.

Attempts to categorize presumptions according to policy considerations have been thoughtful and well-meaning. Unfortunately, they have fallen short of the mark, largely because of the inherent difficulty of the task. Each presumption is created for its own reasons—reasons which are inextricably intertwined with the pertinent substantive law. These substantive considerations have a considerable impact on the procedural effect desirable for a particular presumption. The diversity of the considerations simply defies usable categorization. The law and lawyers are accustomed to considering the dictates of the substantive law in determining the initial allocation of the burdens of proof. The task should not be thought too onerous in connection with the operation of presumptions which, after all, simply operate to reallocate those burdens during the course of the trial.

Rather than attempting to provide a single rule for all presumptions, a task which has thus far proved futile, the drafters of evidence codes might instead provide guidelines for the appropriate but various effects which a presumption may have on the burdens of proof. The courts and legislatures would then have the opportunity to select the appropriate effect to be given to a particular presumption. The term presumption seems likely to be with us forever; it also seems likely that different pre-

proving that the nonexistence of the presumed fact is more probable than its existence.

21. Allen, Presumptions, Inferences and Burden of Proof in Federal Civil Actions—An Anatomy of Unneces-sary Ambiguities and a Proposal for Reform, 76 Nw. U.L.Rev. 892 (1982); Allen, Presumptions in Civil Actions Reconsidered, 66 Iowa L.Rev. 843 (1981).

sumptions will continue to be viewed as having different procedural effects; we can only hope to insure that the concept which the term "presumption" represents is applied constructively and rationally.

§ 345. Constitutional Questions in Civil Cases

Serious questions under the United States Constitution are raised by the creation and use of presumptions in criminal cases. Those questions are discussed in subsequent sections.[1] Although there are constitutional considerations involved in the use of presumptions in civil cases, the problems are simply not of the same magnitude. In a criminal case, the scales are deliberately overbalanced in favor of the defendant through the requirement that the prosecution prove each element of the offense beyond a reasonable doubt.[2] Any rule that has even the appearance of lightening that burden is viewed with the most extreme caution. However, there is no need for this special protection for any one party to a civil action. The burdens of proof are fixed at the pleading stage, not for constitutional reasons, but for reasons of probability, social policy, and convenience.[3] There is no reason why the same policy considerations, as reflected in the operation of a presumption, should not be permitted further to effect an allocation of the burdens of proof during the course of the trial.

Nevertheless, the courts articulate a "rational connection" test in civil cases, which requires that such a connection exist between the basic facts and the presumed facts in order for the presumption to pass constitutional muster. Recent cases have applied the test, but upheld the presumption. Perhaps under certain circumstances a presumption could operate in such an arbitrary manner as to violate fundamental due process considerations, even in a civil case. But to impose a strictly applied "rational connection" limitation upon the cre-

ation of presumptions in civil cases would mean that only presumptions based on probability would be permissible. Such a limitation would ignore other, equally valid, reasons for the creation of the rules. Considerations which have been either explicitly rejected or severely limited in criminal cases, such as the comparative knowledge of the parties with regard to the facts and the power of the legislature to do away with a claim or a defense entirely, should remain significant in determining the validity of a civil presumption.

Perhaps the most difficult question with regard to civil presumptions is whether a presumption may operate to assign the burden of persuasion. The question arises from the contrast between two Supreme Court cases considering the validity of presumptions of negligence operating against railroads. In the first, Mobile, J. & K.C.R.R. v. Turnipseed,[4] decided in 1910, the Court considered a Mississippi statutory presumption of negligence operating against a railroad in an action for death of an employee in a derailment. The statute provided that proof of injury inflicted by the running of railroad cars would be "prima facie evidence of the want of reasonable skill and care" on the part of the railroad. Noting that the only effect of the statute was to impose on the railroad the duty of producing some evidence to the contrary, the court held that the rational connection between the fact proved and the fact presumed was sufficient to sustain the presumption.

However, in 1929, in Western & Atlantic R.R. v. Henderson,[5] the Court struck down a Georgia statute making railroads liable for damage done by trains, unless the railroad made it appear that reasonable care had been used, "the presumption in all cases being against the company." In Henderson the plaintiff alleged that her husband had been killed in a grade crossing collision. The jury was instructed that negligence was presumed from

---

§ 345

1. Sections 347–348 infra.

2. See § 341 supra with regard to the nature of the prosecution's burden; see § 347 infra with regard to the constitutional limits on the effect that a presumption may have upon that burden.

3. See § 337 supra.

4. 219 U.S. 35 (1910).

5. 279 U.S. 639 (1929).

the fact of injury and that the burden was therefore on the railroad to show that it exercised ordinary care. The Court held that the mere fact of a collision between a train and a vehicle at a crossing furnished no basis for any inference as to negligence and that therefore the presumption was invalid. *Turnipseed* was distinguished on the ground that the Mississippi presumption raised "merely a temporary inference of fact" while the Georgia statute created "an inference that is given effect of evidence to be weighed against opposing testimony and is to prevail unless such testimony is found by the jury to preponderate."[6]

Although perhaps a grade crossing collision differs from a derailment and therefore *Turnipseed* and *Henderson* can be distinguished on their facts, it is nevertheless fair to read *Henderson* as imposing constitutional limitations on the effect of at least some presumptions. However, as has been cogently pointed out, *Henderson* may simply no longer be valid law. The case assumed the necessity of a showing of negligence. But the concept of negligence has lost most of its sanctity since 1929. Although there is considerable doubt as to what the Court would have done in that year, there is little doubt today that a legislature would be permitted at least to relegate lack of negligence to the status of an affirmative defense. If negligence could be so reduced, a presumption which assigned the burden of persuasion could logically be treated no differently.

Since *Henderson*, the Court has, on at least one occasion, approved a state presumption that operated to fix the burden of persuasion on the party controverting the presumed fact. In that case, Dick v. New York Life Insurance Co.[7] the Court approved a North Dakota common law rule that imposed on the defendant insurance company, defending against the operation of an accidental death clause, the burden of persuading the jury that the death of the insured was due to suicide.

The questionable status of *Henderson* in light of recent developments in tort law, the holding of the Court in *Dick,* and the illogic of treating presumptions differently from other rules of law allocating the burden of persuasion, all make it extremely unlikely that there are now serious constitutional limits on the effect that may be given to presumptions in civil cases.

§ 346. Affirmative Defenses and Presumptions in Criminal Cases: (a) Terminology

As has been earlier pointed out, the courts and legislatures do not always use the term presumption in the sense either that the term is used in this text or by the same courts and legislatures on other occasions.[1] The use of loose terminology is perhaps even more prevalent in dealing with presumptions operating in criminal cases than in civil cases. The best example is one that has already been given. The "presumption of innocence" is not a presumption at all, but simply another way of stating the rule that the prosecution has the burden of proving the guilt of the accused beyond a reasonable doubt.[2]

Similarly, the courts and writers have struggled to define and distinguish presumptions and affirmative defenses. Certainly, these procedural devices have factors in common. Yet, as the devices are traditionally defined, there are some significant variations between them that have caused the courts to treat them differently.

1. Affirmative defenses. The term affirmative defense is traditionally used to describe the allocation of a burden, either of production or of persuasion, or both, to the defendant in a criminal case. The burden is fixed by statute or case law at the beginning of the case and does not depend upon the introduction of any evidence by the prosecution. For example, a crime may be statutorily defined as consisting of elements A and B. However, the accused may be exonerated or the offense reduced in

---

6. Id. at 643–644.

7. 359 U.S. 437 (1959).

§ 346

1. See § 342 supra.

2. See § 342 supra.

degree upon proof of C. C is an affirmative defense. In some instances, the defendant may simply have the burden of production of evidence with regard to C; in the event that burden is satisfied, the prosecution will then have the burden of persuading the jury of elements A, B, *and* C beyond a reasonable doubt. In other instances, the defendant will have both the burden of production and the burden of persuasion. Thus, the prosecution will have no burden with regard to C; the defendant must both introduce proof of C and persuade the jury of its existence. Usually, the measure of persuasion imposed on the defendant with regard to an affirmative defense is a preponderance of the evidence.

2. Presumptions. Presumptions have already been defined as a standardized practice under which certain facts are held to call for uniform treatment with respect to their effect as proof of other facts.[3] In civil cases, the term presumption is properly reserved for a rule that provides that upon proof of certain basic facts, at least the burden of producing evidence with regard to certain presumed facts shifts. As has been discussed, a presumption may in some instances operate to allocate the burden of persuasion as well.[4]

A somewhat different terminology has been used more or less consistently in criminal cases. The tendency in criminal cases has been to describe any standardized rule which permits the inference of one fact from another as a presumption, regardless of whether the rule operates to shift the burden of production. Thus, assume a crime with three elements, A, B and C. A rule of law provides that fact C may be inferred from proof of A and B. Such a rule is usually described as a presumption, whether or not any burden is actually shifted to the defendant. In most instances, no burden shifts; the presumption operates only to permit the prosecution to make out a prima facie case by proof of A and B alone. The jury will be instructed that it may, but is not required to, infer the existence of fact C from proof of facts A and B.

The United States Supreme Court has resurrected terminology used in the first edition of this text to describe the different effects of presumptions in criminal cases. In County Court of Ulster County v. Allen,[5] the court distinguished between mandatory and permissive presumptions. A mandatory presumption is one which operates to shift at least the burden of production. It tells the trier of fact that it must find the presumed fact upon proof of the basic fact, "at least unless the defendant has come forward with some evidence to rebut the presumed connection between the two facts."[6] The Court further sub-divided mandatory presumptions into two parts: presumptions that merely shift the burden of production to the defendant and presumptions that shift the burden of persuasion. A permissive presumption is one which allows, but does not require, the trier of fact to infer the presumed fact from proof of the basic facts. Under the *Allen* decision, these various kinds of presumptions differ not only procedurally, but also with regard to the tests for their constitutional permissibility as well.

§ 347. Affirmative Defenses and Presumptions in Criminal Cases: (b) Constitutionality

Recent years have brought some noteable developments with regard to the constitutionality of both affirmative defenses and presumptions.

1. Affirmative defenses. Historically, many states placed both the burden of production and the burden of persuasion on the accused with regard to several classical affirmative defenses, including insanity and self-defense. The allocation to the defendant of the burdens of proof with regard to insanity survived constitutional challenge in 1952. In Leland v. Oregon, the Supreme Court held that the defendant could be required to prove his insanity at the time of the alleged crime beyond a reasonable doubt. On the other hand, some limitations were imposed on the

---

3. Section 342 supra.

4. Section 344 supra.

5. 442 U.S. 140 (1979).

6. Id. at 157.

creation or effect of affirmative defenses. For example, one United States Court of Appeals held unconstitutional a state's allocation of the burden of persuasion to the accused with regard to alibi. The court reasoned that an alibi was a mere form of denial of participation in the criminal act, not a true affirmative defense.

Although perhaps foreshadowed by the treatment given the defense of alibi, the real revolution in thought with regard to affirmative defenses occurred in the mid–1970's with two pivotal Supreme Court decisions.

In Mullaney v. Wilbur,[1] the Court reversed a Maine murder conviction where the jury had been instructed, in accordance with longstanding state practice, that if the prosecution proved "that the homicide was both intentional and unlawful, malice aforethought was to be conclusively implied unless the defendant proved by a fair preponderance of the evidence that he acted in the heat of passion on sudden provocation," in which event the defendant would be guilty only of manslaughter. The placing of this burden on the defendant was said to violate the dictates of In re Winship[2] that the due process clause requires the prosecution to prove beyond a reasonable doubt every fact necessary to constitute the crime charged. Although recognizing that under Maine law murder and manslaughter were but degrees of the same crime, the Court noted that Winship applied to instances in which the issue is degree of criminal culpability as well as to cases of guilt or innocence.

The Mullaney case was surprising in view of the long history in some jurisdictions of placing the burden of reducing the degree of a homicide on the defendant. However, given the holding and rationale of Winship, it was not totally unexpected. It was certainly possible, and perhaps fair, to read the Mullaney case broadly so as to require the imposition of the burden of persuasion on the prosecution with regard to many, if not all, of the traditional affirmative defenses. Indeed, the opinion was

read by several state courts as constitutionally compelling the prosecution to bear the burden of persuasion with regard to various affirmative defenses. Only the existence of the Leland opinion, not expressly overruled in Mullaney, prevented one federal court from applying Mullaney to impose upon a state the burden of persuasion with regard to an insanity defense.

The first real indication that the holding in Mullaney had far more narrow limits came when the Court, in Rivera v. Delaware,[3] dismissed, as not presenting a substantial federal question, an appeal from a conviction in which the defendant had borne the burden of proving his insanity. The indication became a certainty when the Court decided Patterson v. New York.[4] In Patterson, the Court upheld a New York procedure under which an accused is guilty of murder in the second degree if he is found, beyond a reasonable doubt, to have intentionally killed another person. The crime may be reduced to manslaughter if the defendant proves by a preponderance of the evidence that he had acted under the influence of "extreme emotional disturbance." The Court held that the New York procedure did not violate due process noting, in the language of Winship, " 'every fact necessary to constitute the crime with which [Patterson was] charged had to be proved beyond a reasonable doubt.' "[5] Mullaney was distinguished as dealing with a situation in which the defendant was asked to disprove an essential element of the prosecution's case—malice aforethought. New York, unlike Maine, did not include malice aforethought in its definition of murder. By this omission, New York had avoided the defect found fatal in Mullaney, even though the defense involved in the Patterson case was but an expanded version of the "heat of passion on sudden provocation" involved in Mullaney.

The Court in Patterson decided the constitutionality of the allocation of the burden of proof by a formalistic analysis of state law: due process was not violated because the defendant

§ 347

1. 421 U.S. 684, 686 (1975).

2. 397 U.S. 358 (1970). See § 341 *supra*.

3. 429 U.S. 877 (1976).

4. 432 U.S. 197 (1977).

5. Id. at 206.

did not have the burden of proof on any fact that state law had identified as an element of the offense. Despite significant and persistent criticism, the durability of this approach was confirmed ten years later in Martin v. Ohio[6]. In *Martin,* Ohio had defined the crime of murder as purposely causing the death of another with prior calculation or design and placed the burden of proving self-defense on the defendant. The Court upheld the conviction because the defendant did not have the burden of proving any of the elements included by the state in its definition of the crime. The dictates of *Winship* were not violated so long as the instructions to the jury made it clear that State had the burden of proving all of the elements—including prior calculation and design—beyond a reasonable doubt, and that the self-defense evidence could also be considered in determining whether there was reasonable doubt about any element of the State's case.

The lower courts have, of course, followed the pattern of *Patterson* and *Martin,* holding invalid allocations of the burden of persuasion thought to involve nothing more than the rebuttal of an element of the offense and sanctioning allocations where the jury has been instructed that the affirmative defense is held to come into play only after the state has proven the elements of the crime beyond a reasonable doubt.

The analysis in *Patterson* and *Martin* deals only with the allocation of the burden of persuasion. As suggested by dicta in *Patterson,* the courts have had no trouble with an affirmative defense which simply requires the defendant to bear a burden of production. For example, even though a state includes absence of self-defense as an element of a crime so as to prohibit the allocation of the burden of persuasion to the accused, the accused may be required to introduce at least some evidence of self-defense in order for the issue to go the jury.

　2.　*Presumptions.*

Like affirmative defenses, the Supreme Court's analysis of the constitutionality of presumptions has evolved significantly in recent years. The 1979 decisions in County Court of Ulster County v. Allen[7] and Sandstrom v. Montana[8], constitute the watershed in the Court's analysis of the issue.

Prior to *Allen* and *Sandstrom,* the Court had set limitations on the creation and application of presumptions in criminal cases in a series of cases beginning with Tot v. United States.[9] In *Tot,* the Court invalidated a presumption contained in a federal firearms statute stating that possession of a firearm was presumptive evidence that the weapon was received in interstate commerce. The Court stated that "a statutory presumption cannot be sustained if there be no rational connection between the fact proved and the ultimate fact presumed, if the inference of the one from proof of the other is arbitrary because of lack of connection between the two in common experience."[10]

Tot was followed by two 1965 cases dealing with presumptions enacted to aid the government in prosecuting liquor cases. In United States v. Gainey,[11] the Court applied the rational connection test of *Tot* to uphold the validity of a statute which provided that presence at the site is sufficient to convict a defendant of the offense of carrying on the business of distilling without giving bond, "unless the defendant explains such presence to the satisfaction of the jury." However, in United States v. Romano,[12] the Court struck down as violative of *Tot* an identical presumption with regard to the companion offense of possession of an illegal still. The Court distinguished *Gainey,* noting that the crime of *carrying on* an illegal distilling business, involved in *Gainey,* was an extremely broad one. A person's unexplained presence at the still made it highly likely that he had something to do with its operation. However, no such natural inference existed with regard to the presumption of *pos-*

6.　480 U.S. 228 (1987).
7.　442 U.S. 140 (1979).
8.　442 U.S. 510 (1979).
9.　319 U.S. 463 (1943).

10.　Id. at 467.
11.　380 U.S. 63 (1965).
12.　382 U.S. 136 (1965).

session from unexplained presence involved in *Romano.*

Tot, Gainey and *Romano* left several questions unanswered. Most significantly, the "rational connection" test was vague. Was it a test of relevancy or a test of probative sufficiency? If it was a test of sufficiency, the existence of the presumed fact would have to be shown to be more likely than not to exist or perhaps even have to be shown to exist beyond a reasonable doubt.

The question was partially answered in 1969 and 1970 by two cases involving presumptions in narcotics prosecutions. In Leary v. United States,[13] the Court considered a presumption providing that possession of marihuana was sufficient evidence to authorize conviction of transporting and concealing the drug *with knowledge of its illegal importation* unless the defendant explained his possession to the satisfaction of the jury. The Court held that the presumption of knowledge was unconstitutional, stating:

"The upshot of *Tot, Gainey* and *Romano* is, we think, that a criminal statutory presumption must be regarded as 'irrational' or 'arbitrary,'" and hence unconstitutional, unless it can be said with substantial assurance that the presumed fact is more likely than not to flow from the proved fact on which it is made to depend * * *."[14]

In a footnote to this statement, the Court added that because of its finding that the presumption was unconstitutional under this standard, it would not reach the question "whether a criminal presumption which passes muster when so judged must also satisfy the criminal 'reasonable doubt' standard if proof of the crime charged or an essential element thereof depends upon its use."[15]

The next year, the Court dealt with two presumptions in Turner v. United States.[16] One was identical with the presumption struck down in *Leary,* except that the drugs involved in *Turner* were heroin and cocaine rather than

marihuana. The other provided that the absence of appropriate tax paid stamps from narcotic drugs found in the defendant's possession would be "prima facie evidence" that he purchased or distributed the drugs from other than the original stamped package. The Court extensively reviewed the legislative records with regard to the statutes and surveyed the records of other narcotics cases for evidence to support or rebut the inferences called for by the statutes. It concluded that the "overwhelming evidence" was that the heroin consumed in the United States is illegally imported and that Turner therefore must have known this fact. Based upon this conclusion, the Court upheld the presumptions of illegal importation and "stamped package" as to heroin. In contrast, the Court struck down the same presumptions with regard to cocaine, finding that it could not be "sufficiently sure either that the cocaine that Turner possessed came from abroad or that Turner must have known that it did," and that there was "a reasonable possibility" that Turner had in fact obtained the cocaine from a legally stamped package.

In *Turner,* the Court again found it unnecessary specifically to adopt a test that would require that the presumed fact be shown to exist beyond a reasonable doubt. However, the Court's frequent reference to that standard in *Turner,* coupled with its decision in In re Winship[17] recognizing that such a measure of proof is constitutionally required in criminal cases, seemed to make it likely that the reasonable doubt standard would be applied to test the validity of presumptions.

Not long after *Turner,* the Court applied the rationale of the cases involving statutory presumptions to a common law presumption. In Barnes v. United States,[18] the Court upheld a conviction for possession of stolen treasury checks in which the jury had been instructed in accordance with the traditional common law inference that the knowledge necessary for conviction may be drawn from the unexplained

13. 395 U.S. 6 (1969).

14. Id. at 36.

15. Id. at 36 n. 64.

16. 396 U.S. 398 (1970).

17. 397 U.S. 358 (1970). See § 341 supra.

18. 412 U.S. 837 (1973).

possession of recently stolen goods. The Court still refrained from adopting either a more-likely-than-not or a reasonable doubt standard in its review of the presumption, but held rather that the presumption in question satisfied both. The only question that seem to remain after *Barnes* whether the Court ultimately would require that all presumptions be tested by a reasonable doubt standard. Surprisingly, a whole new set of considerations arrived in 1979.

The New York prosecution in County Court of Ulster County v. Allen[19] was for illegal possession of, inter alia, handguns. Four persons, three adult males and a 16-year-old girl, were tried jointly. The evidence showed that two large-caliber handguns were seen in the front of the car in an open handbag belonging to the 16-year-old. A New York statute provided that, with certain exceptions, the presence of a firearm in an automobile was presumptive evidence of its illegal possession by all persons then occupying the vehicle. The jury was instructed with regard to the presumption but told that the presumption "need not be rebutted by affirmative proof or affirmative evidence but may be rebutted by any evidence or lack of evidence in the case."

The federal Court of Appeals affirmed the District Court's grant of habeas corpus, holding that the New York statute was unconstitutional on its face because it swept within its compass many individuals who would in fact have no connection with a weapon even though they were present in a vehicle in which the weapon was found.

The Supreme Court reversed, stating that the Court of Appeals had improperly viewed the statute on its face. The Court stated that the ultimate test of any device's constitutional validity is that it not undermine the factfinder's responsibility at trial, based on evidence adduced by the state, to find the ultimate facts beyond a reasonable doubt. Therefore, mandatory and permissive presumptions must be analyzed differently. It is appropriate to analyze mandatory presumptions on their face. Where

a mandatory presumption is used, the defendant may be convicted based upon the presumption alone as the result of the failure of the accused to introduce proof to the contrary. The Court reasoned that in such an instance the presumption would be unconstitutional unless the basic facts, standing alone, are sufficient to support the inference of guilt beyond a reasonable doubt. In the case of a permissive presumption the jury is told only that it may, but need not, find the defendant guilty based upon the basic facts. Thus, the validity of the presumption must be tested, not in the abstract, but rather in connection with all of the evidence in the case. The Court stated:

> "Because this permissive presumption leaves the trier of fact free to credit or reject the inference and does not shift the burden of proof, it affects the application of the 'beyond a reasonable doubt' standard only if, under the facts of the case, there is no rational way the trier could make the connection permitted by the inference. For only in that situation is there any risk that an explanation of the permissible inference to a jury, or its use by a jury, has caused the presumptively rational factfinder to make an erroneous factual determination."[20]

The Court found that the instruction in *Allen* created a permissive, not a mandatory, presumption. The Court considered all of the evidence in the case and found a rational basis for a finding of guilty beyond a reasonable doubt, noting that the jury could have reasonably rejected the suggestion advanced on appeal by the adult defendants that the handguns were solely in the possession of the 16-year-old.

In Sandstrom v. Montana,[21] the defendant was charged with deliberate homicide, which under Montana law would consist of purposely and knowingly causing the death of another. Defendant claimed that the degree of the offense should be reduced in that he suffered from a personality disorder aggravated by alcohol consumption. The jury was in-

---

19.   442 U.S. 140 (1979).

20.   Id. at 157.

21.   442 U.S. 510 (1979).

structed in accordance with Montana law that the "law presumes that a person intends the ordinary consequences of his voluntary acts." Defendant was convicted and his conviction was upheld by the Montana Supreme Court. The United States Supreme Court reversed, holding that the jury could have interpreted the instruction with regard to the presumption of intention of the ordinary consequences of voluntary acts as creating either a conclusive presumption or shifting the burden of persuasion with regard to the question of intent to the defendant. Citing *Mullaney* and *Patterson* as well as *Ulster,* the Court found that such a shift of the burden would be constitutionally impermissible. The fact that the jury could have interpreted the instruction either as permissive or as shifting only the burden of production did not matter so long as the instruction could also have been interpreted as imposing heavier burdens on the defendant.

Several years later, in Francis v. Franklin,[22] the Court held that an instruction in a Georgia homicide prosecution, stating that the "acts of a person of sound mind and discretion are presumed to be the product of a person's will, but the presumption may be rebutted," violated *Sandstrom*. The Court held that the instructions had created the kind of mandatory presumption prohibited by *Sandstrom,* even though Georgia had interpreted such language as amounting to no more than a permissive inference. The fact that the presumption was expressly made rebuttable was not controlling so long as the jury could have interpreted the instruction as shifting the burden of persuasion to the accused.

The upshot of all of these cases seems to be as follows: Presumptions in criminal cases will be divided into mandatory and permissive presumptions. A permissive presumption is one that will permit the jury to find the presumed facts, but neither compels the acceptance of such facts nor allocates a burden of persuasion to the defendant with regard to those facts. Regardless of how the state char-

acterizes the presumption, the courts will analyze the jury instructions to determine their possible effect on the jury. A permissive presumption will be constitutionally acceptable if, considering all of the evidence in the case, there is a rational connection between the basic facts proved by the prosecution and the ultimate fact presumed, and the latter is more likely than not to flow from the former. A mandatory presumption is one that shifts the burden of production or persuasion to the defendant. Although the Supreme Court has not specifically so held, dictum in *Allen* and the holdings of lower court decisions seem to make it clear that a presumption that clearly shifts nothing other than the burden of production will be scrutinized in the same way as a permissive presumption and pass constitutional muster if it meets a rational connection test. Could a presumption that shifts the burden of persuasion be created? The Court in *Allen* suggests the possibility that such a presumption could be constitutional if a rational juror could find the presumed fact beyond a reasonable doubt from the basic facts. Some authors have suggested that such a presumption may not constitutionally exist after *Allen* and *Sandstrom*. The courts have not had occasion to rule on the question. Certainly, the test suggested in *Allen* is a stiff one.

§ 348. Affirmative Defenses and Presumptions in Criminal Cases: (c) Special Problems

Not surprisingly, several questions remain from the active constitutional development in this area of the law.

1. The creation of affirmative defenses. The *Patterson*[1] case tied the question of the constitutionality of affirmative defenses directly to the formalistic notion that a true affirmative defense is one that does not simply go to negative an element of the offense. The question remains as to when something is an element of an offense. Many cases have looked only to the language of the statute although

---

22.   471 U.S. 307 (1985).

§ 348

1.   Patterson v. New York, 432 U.S. 197 (1977).

some have considered how the statute has been interpreted by the state courts.

Can the state create an affirmative defense simply by carefully excluding it from the elements of the offense? The answer to this question seems to be a qualified yes. In *Patterson*, the Court suggested that there were constitutional limitations on the creation of affirmative defenses. Those limits may depend upon whether the state may, under the U.S. Constitution, punish the activity without reference to the affirmative defense. For example, assume an offense which has consisted of the elements A, B, C, all of which had to be proved by the prosecution beyond a reasonable doubt. The legislature carefully amends the statute covering the offense so as to make the elements of the offense A and B only, but provides that the accused may be exonerated if the defense proves C by a preponderance of the evidence. Such a new statute would be constitutional if the state may, consistent with the Eighth Amendment and substantive due process, punish the individual to the extent provided by the statute based upon proof of A and B only.

Such an analysis has suggested another, less formalistic, approach to the treatment of affirmative defenses to some legal scholars. Under this approach, if the state can constitutionally exclude an element from an offense, it can require the defendant to bear the burden of persuasion with regard to that element. In other words, in the above example, if the state could exclude C from the definition of the crime, it could make the accused prove C, whether or not C is formally removed as an element of the offense. Other scholars have rejected an Eighth Amendment approach entirely and have proposed tests that would more severely limit the state's options in the creation of affirmative defenses.

As yet, no court has struck down an affirmative defense because the Eighth Amendment prohibited punishment based only upon the elements assigned to the definition of the offense. Indeed, the Eighth Amendment and related concepts of substantive due process

have not proved to be an effective check on legislative decisions with regard to punishment. Moreover, no court has used an alternative approach suggested in the law journals to limit the creation of affirmative defenses. Instead, the courts have relied upon the safer, formalistic notions of *Patterson*.

One possible approach to assessing the validity of affirmative defenses that is neither inconsistent with case law nor directly tied to the Eighth Amendment was suggested by Justice Powell in his dissent in *Patterson*. Powell suggested that the prosecution be required to prove beyond a reasonable doubt at least those factors which "in the Anglo–American legal tradition" had made a difference in punishment or stigma.[2] Although troublesome if taken to its logical extent, the notion that we should consider historical factors has merit. At the very least, it would be appropriate for a court in assessing the validity of the creation of an affirmative defense to take into account not only the statutory language and judicial statements of the elements of the offense, but also the nature of the burden traditionally borne by the state with regard to the same or analogous factors.

2. Affirmative defenses or presumptions? Despite the differences between affirmative defenses and presumptions as the terms are used by the courts and legal scholars, the impact of these procedural devices on the accused can be identical. Thus, in one state, the accused may have the burden of producing evidence that she acted in self-defense—an affirmative defense. In another jurisdiction, the law may provide that, once the state has proved that the defendant intentionally killed the deceased, there is a presumption of unlawfulness that requires the defendant to introduce evidence with regard to self-defense, although the ultimate burden of persuasion remains with the state. The defendant must introduce some evidence of self-defense in order for the jury to be instructed on the issue. The effect of this presumption is identical to that of the affirmative defense. Both devices used in this way have been held to be constitutional.

2. Patterson v. New York, supra note 1 at 226–227.

An affirmative defense that places the burden of persuasion on the defendant with regard to a factor that is not an element of the offense may be constitutional. Could the state accomplish the same allocation of the burden of persuasion in the form of a presumption, i.e., a rule that states that once the state has proven the elements of the offense, the defendant is presumed guilty unless he proves some other factor? Such a rule simply delays the allocation of the burden of persuasion until after the state has proved its case. It places no different burden on the accused than would an affirmative defense. However, as framed, the presumption would seem to run directly afoul of *Sandstrom*. The matter may simply be one of legislative drafting. The prudent legislature will choose the affirmative defense route rather than the presumption language. It is yet to be seen whether the courts will look to the designation of a procedural device as a presumption or as an affirmative defense or whether they will more realistically decide the constitutionality of the procedural device based upon its actual effect on the defendant.

3. *When is it Proper to Submit an Issue Involving A Presumed Fact to the Jury?* In deciding the question whether a case involving a presumed fact should be submitted to the jury, the trial judge must necessarily be guided by the dictates of Jackson v. Virginia:[3] a jury verdict will be upheld, even against collateral attack, only if the evidence was sufficient for a reasonable person to find the defendant guilty beyond a reasonable doubt. In the rare instance in which a mandatory presumption is involved, the problem is not difficult. *Allen* suggests that the presumption will be tested by the constitutional test of whether the presumed fact flows beyond a reasonable doubt from the basic facts. If the presumption meets that test, it is by definition sufficient to get to the jury, provided the other elements of the crime are supported by sufficient evidence. However, because of the rigid requirements for the validity of mandatory presumptions, virtually all presumptions will be permissive. Therefore, under the *Allen* case, the trial judge must look to the rational effect of the pre-

sumption in connection with all of the other evidence in the case. Perhaps the best statement of a test for the sufficiency of the evidence under these circumstances is contained in Revised Uniform Rule (1974) 303(b):

(b) Submission to the jury. The court is not authorized to direct the jury to find a presumed fact against the accused. If a presumed fact establishes guilt or is an element of the offense or negatives a defense, the court may submit the question of guilt or of the existence of the presumed fact to the jury, but only if a reasonable juror on the evidence as a whole, including the evidence of the basic facts, could find guilt or the presumed fact beyond a reasonable doubt. If the presumed fact has a lesser effect, the question of its existence may be submitted to the jury provided the basic facts are supported by substantial evidence or are otherwise established, unless the court determines that a reasonable juror on the evidence as a whole could not find the existence of the presumed fact.

Given the dictates of Jackson v. Virginia and County Court of Ulster County v. Allen, no other proposed formulation of the rule seems acceptable.

4. *Instructing the Jury on Presumptions.* The distinction made in the *Allen* case between permissive and mandatory presumptions, makes the exact language of instructions on presumptions critical. Unless a presumption is strong enough to meet the stringent test for mandatory presumptions, the trial judge must use caution in charging the jury so as to place no burden whatsoever on the defendant.

Again, the Revised Uniform Rules provide a suggested pattern for such an instruction. Uniform Rule 303(c) provides:

Instructing the Jury. Whenever the existence of a presumed fact is submitted to the jury, the court shall instruct the jury that it may regard the basic facts as sufficient evidence of the presumed fact but is not required to do so. In addition, if the presumed fact establishes guilt or is an

---

3.   443 U.S. 307 (1979), see § 338 supra.

element of the offense or negatives a defense, the court shall instruct the jury that its existence, on all the evidence, must be proved beyond a reasonable doubt.

This instruction seems to meet most of the problems raised in the *Allen* case, as well as those suggested by Sandstrom v. Montana. One additional problem has been suggested. In *Allen,* the court stated that the prosecution could not rest its case entirely on a presumption unless the facts proved were sufficient to support the inference of guilt beyond a reasonable doubt. Therefore, where the prosecution relies solely upon a presumption and not any other evidence, as in *Allen,* not only must the presumed fact flow beyond a reasonable doubt from the basic facts, but the jury must be able to find the basic facts beyond a reasonable doubt. At least two states have adopted the essence of the Revised Uniform Rule, but, in order to cover this situation, have added language which requires that the basic facts be proved beyond a reasonable doubt.[4]

§ 349. Choice of Law

The significance of the burdens of proof and of the effect of presumptions upon those burdens has already been discussed. Certainly the outcome of litigation may be altered depending upon which party has the burden of persuasion.[1] Where there is little evidence available on an issue, the burden of producing evidence may also control the outcome.[2] Recognizing the impact of these rules upon outcome, the federal courts, applying the doctrine of Erie Railroad Co. v. Tompkins,[3] have consistently held that where an issue is to be decided under state law, that law controls both the burdens of proof and presumptions with regard to that issue. Federal Rule of Evidence 302 limits the operation of this rule with respect to presumptions to cases in which the presumption operates "respecting a fact which is an element of a claim or defense as to which

state law supplies the rule of decision." "Tactical presumptions," those that operate as to a lesser aspect of the case, will be governed by the federal rule. While no reported case has specifically made the distinction contemplated in the rule, the reasoning is sound. Although tactical presumptions may in some instances influence the outcome of a case, their effect is no greater than that of a rule governing the admission or exclusion of a single item of evidence. As in the case of those rules, the desirability of providing a uniform procedure for federal trials through a fixed rule governing tactical presumptions outweighs any preference for increased certainty of identity of result in state and federal courts.

Of course *Erie* problems are not the only choice of law problems. The question remains, even for federal courts having resolved to apply state rather than federal law: what state's law is applicable? Unlike the federal courts applying the *Erie* rule, the state courts generally have not considered the impact of the burdens of proof and presumptions on the outcome of the lawsuit to be controlling. The general rule expressed is that both the burdens of proof and presumptions are "procedural" in the sense that the law of the forum governs rather than the law of the state whose substantive rules are otherwise applicable. However, as in the case of most general rules with regard to the subject matter of this chapter, instances in which an exception to this general rule has been held applicable are perhaps as numerous as instances in which the rule has been applied. The principal exception to the basic dogma has been variously phrased but its gist is that the forum will apply the rule of a foreign jurisdiction with respect to the burdens of proof or presumptions where that rule is inseparably connected to the substantive right created by the foreign state.

The general rule and its principal exception have proved difficult to apply. The pletho-

---

4. Hawaii Evidence Rule 306; Oregon Evidence Rule 309.

§ 349

1. See § 336 supra.

2. See § 338 supra. See also §§ 342 and 344 supra as to the operation of presumptions with regard to both the burden of producing evidence and the burden of persuasion.

3. 304 U.S. 64 (1938).

ra of conflicting decisions under the test amply illustrates the problems inherent in attempting to distinguish between rules that are inseparably connected with substantive law and those that are not. The distinction is indeed a hollow one. Regardless of the nature of the claim or defense, rules with respect to the burdens of proof always have the same potential effect upon the decision in the case. If insufficient evidence is available, the party having the burden of producing evidence will lose the decision. If the jury is in doubt, the party having the burden of persuasion will lose. As has been observed, cases in which the burden of proof is so closely interwoven with the substantive right as to make a separation of the two impossible constitute either all or none of the litigated cases.

A somewhat better approach to the problem is taken by the Second Restatement of Conflict of Laws which states that the forum will apply its own local law in determining which party has the burdens of proof "unless the primary purpose of the relevant rule of the otherwise applicable law is to affect decision of the issue rather than to regulate the conduct of the trial."[4] The rule sounds very much like

the test applied in *Erie* cases. However, the comments and illustrations to the applicable sections of the Restatement indicate that the Restatement is to be interpreted in much the same way as the more traditional statements just discussed; the assumption is that the rule is one concerned with "trial administration," not the decision of the issue. The assumption seems wrong. The burdens of proof are almost always allocated for the primary purpose of affecting the decision in the case where there is no evidence or where the jury is in doubt. To say that these rules merely govern the conduct of the trial, as in the case of rules concerning the admission and exclusion of evidence, gives far too much emphasis to form over substance.

A better approach to the choice of law problem would be to adopt the federal rule used in *Erie* cases as a rule of general application. Such a rule would provide that the law of the state or states supplying the substantive rules of law should govern questions concerning the burdens of proof as well as presumptions operating with regard to a fact constituting an element of a claim or defense.

---

4.   §§ 133, 134 (1971).

Appendix A

RESEARCHING THE LAW OF EVIDENCE ON WESTLAW®

Analysis

Section 1. Introduction

McCormick on Evidence provides a strong base for analyzing even the most complex problem involving the law of evidence. Whether your research requires examination of rules, statutes, case law, expert commentary or other materials, West books and Westlaw are excellent sources of information.

To keep you abreast of current developments, Westlaw provides frequently updated databases. With Westlaw, you have unparalleled legal research resources at your fingertips.

Additional Resources

If you have not previously used Westlaw or have questions not covered in this appendix, see the *Westlaw Reference Manual* or call the West Group

Reference Attorneys at 1–800–REF–ATTY (1–800–733–2889). The West Group Reference Attorneys are trained, licensed attorneys, available 24 hours a day to assist you with your Westlaw search questions.

Section 2. Westlaw Databases

Each database on Westlaw is assigned an abbreviation called an *identifier*, which you use to access the database. You can find identifiers for all databases in the online Westlaw Directory and in the printed *Westlaw Database Directory*. When you need to know more detailed information about a database, use Scope. Scope contains coverage information, lists of related databases and valuable search tips. To access Scope, click the Scope button while in the database.

The following chart lists Westlaw databases that contain information pertaining to evidence law. For a complete list of databases, see the online Westlaw Directory or the printed *Westlaw Database Directory*. Because new information is continually being added to Westlaw, you should also check the Welcome to Westlaw window and the Westlaw Directory for new database information.

Selected Westlaw Databases

Database	Identifier	Coverage
Federal Rules, Orders and Statutes		
Federal Rules	US–RULES	Current data
Federal Orders	US–ORDERS	Current data
Federal Rules of Practice & Procedure Advisory Committee Minutes	US–RULESCOMM	Varies by committee
United States Code Annotated®	USCA	Current data
United States Public Laws	US–PL	Current data
Congressional Bills	CQ–BILLTXT	Current Congress
Federal and State Case Law Combined		
Federal & State Case Law	ALLCASES	Begins with 1945
Federal & State Case Law–Before 1945	ALLCASES–OLD	1789–1944
Federal Case Law		
Federal Case Law	ALLFEDS	Begins with 1945
Federal Case Law–Before 1945	ALLFEDS–OLD	1789–1944
U.S. Supreme Court Cases	SCT	Begins with 1945
U.S. Supreme Court Cases–Before 1945	SCT–OLD	1790–1944
U.S. Courts of Appeals Cases	CTA	Begins with 1945
U.S. Courts of Appeals Cases–Before 1945	CTA–OLD	1891–1944
U.S. District Courts Cases	DCT	Begins with 1945
U.S. District Courts Cases–Before 1945	DCT–OLD	1789–1944
State Rules, Orders and Statutes		
State Court Rules	RULES–ALL	Varies by state
Individual State Court Rules	XX–RULES (where XX is a state's two-letter postal abbreviation)	Varies by state
State Court Orders	ORDERS–ALL	Varies by state

Individual State Court Orders	XX–ORDERS (where XX is a state's two-letter postal abbreviation)	Varies by state
State Statutes–Annotated	ST–ANN–ALL	Varies by state
Individual State Statutes–Annotated	XX–ST–ANN (where XX is a state's two-letter postal abbreviation)	Varies by state

State Case Law

State Case Law	ALLSTATES	Begins with 1945
State Case Law Before 1945	ALLSTATES–OLD	1821–1944
Individual State Case Law	XX–CS (where XX is a state's two-letter postal abbreviation)	Varies by state

Texts, Periodicals and Research Tools

Texts & Periodicals–All Law Reviews, Texts & Bar Journals	TP–ALL	Varies by publication
Bankruptcy Evidence Manual	BKRMANUAL	1997 edition
California Evidence	WITEVID	Third edition
Daubert Citator	DAUBERT	Begins with January 1994
Federal Rules Decisions® (Articles from West Reporter)	FEDRDTP	Begins with 1986 (vol. 108)
Handbook of Federal Evidence	FEDEVID	Fourth edition and 1999 pocket part
Reference Manual on Scientific Evidence	RMSCIEVID	Published in 1994
The Rutter Group™–California Practice Guide: Civil Trials and Evidence	TRG–CACIVEV	1998 edition
The Rutter Group–Practice Guide: Texas Civil Evidence	TRG–TXEV	1998 edition

News and Current Events

All News	ALLNEWS	Varies by source
American Journal of Trial Advocacy	AMJTA	Selected coverage begins with 1982 (vol. 6); full coverage begins with 1993 (vol. 17)
Legal Newspapers	LEGALNP	Varies by publication
National Law Journal, The	NLJ	Begins with October 1989
United States Law Week	BNA–USLW	Begins with January 1986
Westlaw Topical Highlights–Litigation	WTH–LTG	Current data

Section 3. Retrieving a Document with a Citation: Find and Hypertext Links

3.1 Find

Find is a Westlaw service that allows you to retrieve a document by entering its citation. Find allows you to retrieve documents from anywhere in Westlaw without accessing or changing databases. Find is available for many documents, including rules (state and federal), the *United States Code Annotated*®, state statutes, case law (state and federal), administrative materials, texts and periodicals.

To use Find, simply access the Find service and type the citation. The following list provides some examples:

To Find This Document	**Access Find and Type**
Fed. R. Evid. 612	**fre 612**
Colorado R. Evid. 612	**co st rev 612**

Frye v. United States, 293 F. 1013 (App. D.C. 1923)   **293 f 1013**
State v. Cary, 264 A.2d 209 (N.J. 1970)   **264 a2d 209**

For a complete list of publications that can be retrieved with Find and their abbreviations, consult the Publications list. Click the Publications button after accessing Find.

3.2 Hypertext Links

Use hypertext links to move from one location to another on Westlaw. For example, use hypertext links to go directly from the statute, case or law review article you are viewing to a cited statute, case or article; from a headnote to the corresponding text in the opinion; or from an entry in a statutes index database to the full text of the statute.

Section 4. Searching with Natural Language: WIN—Westlaw is Natural

Overview: With WIN, you can retrieve documents by simply describing your issue in plain English. If you are a relatively new Westlaw user, Natural Language searching can make it easier for you to retrieve cases that are on point. If you are an experienced Westlaw user, Natural Language gives you a valuable alternative search method.

When you enter a Natural Language description, Westlaw automatically identifies legal phrases, removes common words and generates variations of terms in your description. Westlaw then searches for the concepts in your description. Concepts may include significant terms, phrases, legal citations or topic and key numbers. Westlaw retrieves the 20 documents that most closely match your description, beginning with the document most likely to match.

4.1 Natural Language Search

Access a database, such as Federal Case Law (ALLFEDS). If the Terms and Connectors Query Editor is displayed, click the **Natural Language** tab. In the *Natural Language Description* text box, type a Natural Language description such as the following:

is testimony of a witness after hypnosis admissible

4.2 Next Command

Westlaw displays the 20 documents that most closely match your description, beginning with the document most likely to match. If you want to view additional documents, click your right mouse button and choose Go to Next 10 Documents from the pop-up menu.

4.3 Natural Language Browse Commands

Best Mode: To display the best portion (the portion that most closely matches your description) of each document in your search result, click the **Best** Section arrow at the bottom of the window.

Standard Browsing Commands: You can also browse your Natural Language search result using standard Westlaw browsing commands, such as citations list, Locate, page mode and term mode. When you browse your Natural Language search result in term mode, the five portions of each document that most closely match the concepts in your description are displayed.

Section 5.   Searching with Terms and Connectors

Overview: With Terms and Connectors searching, you enter a query, which consists of key terms from your issue and connectors specifying the relationship between these terms.

Terms and Connectors searching is useful when you want to retrieve a document for which you know specific details, such as the title or the fact situation. Terms and Connectors searching is also useful when you want to retrieve documents relating to a specific issue. If the Natural Language Description Editor is displayed when you access a database, click the **Terms and Connectors** tab.

5.1   Terms

Plurals and Possessives: Plurals are automatically retrieved when you enter the singular form of a term. This is true for both regular and irregular plurals (e.g., **child** retrieves *children*). If you enter the plural form of a term, you will not retrieve the singular form.

If you enter the nonpossessive form of a term, Westlaw automatically retrieves the possessive form as well. However, if you enter the possessive form, only the possessive form is retrieved.

Automatic Equivalencies: Some terms have alternative forms or equivalencies; for example, *5* and *five* are equivalent terms. Westlaw automatically retrieves equivalent terms. The *Westlaw Reference Manual* contains a list of equivalent terms.

Compound Words, Abbreviations and Acronyms: When a compound word is one of your search terms, use a hyphen to retrieve all forms of the word. For example, the term **cross-claim** retrieves *cross-claim, cross claim* and *crossclaim*.

When using an abbreviation or acronym as a search term, place a period after each of the letters to retrieve any of its forms. For example, the term **f.r.e.** retrieves *fre, f.r.e., f r e* and *f. r. e.* Note: The abbreviation does *not* retrieve *federal rule of evidence* or *Fed.R.Evid.*, so remember to add alternative terms to your query such as **"federal rule of evidence"** or **fed.r.evid**.

The Root Expander and the Universal Character: When you use the Terms and Connectors search method, placing the root expander (!) at the end of a root term generates all other terms with that root. For example, adding the ! to the root *admiss* in the query

admiss! /5 evidence

instructs Westlaw to retrieve such terms as *admission, admissive, admissible* and *admissibility*.

The universal character (*) stands for one character and can be inserted in the middle or at the end of a term. For example, the term withdr*w

will retrieve *withdraw* and *withdrew*. Adding two asterisks to the root *jur*

jur**

instructs Westlaw to retrieve all forms of the root with up to two additional characters. Terms such as *jury* or *juror* are retrieved by this query. However, terms with more than two letters following the root, such as *jurisdiction,* are not retrieved. Plurals are always retrieved, even if more than two letters follow the root.

Phrase Searching: To search for an exact phrase, place it within quotation marks. For example, to search for references to *judicial notice,* type **"judicial notice"**. When you are using the Terms and Connectors search method, you should use phrase searching only if you are certain that the terms in the phrase will not appear in any other order.

5.2 Alternative Terms

After selecting the terms for your query, consider which alternative terms are necessary. For example, if you are searching for the term *admissible*, you might also want to search for the term *inadmissible.* You should consider both synonyms and antonyms as alternative terms. You can also use the Westlaw thesaurus to add alternative terms to your query.

5.3 Connectors

After selecting terms and alternative terms for your query, use connectors to specify the relationship that should exist between search terms in your retrieved documents. The connectors are described below:

Use:	To retrieve documents with:	Example:
& (and)	both terms	**expert & opinion**
or (space)	either term or both terms	**relevan! irrelevan!**
/p	search terms in the same paragraph	**hearsay /p exception**
/s	search terms in the same sentence	**character /s witness**
+s	the first search term preceding the second within the same sentence	**burden +s prov*** proof**
/n	search terms within "n" terms of each other (where "n" is a number)	**refresh! /3 memory**
+n	the first search term preceding the second by "n" terms (where "n" is a number)	**excited +3 utterance**
" "	search terms appearing in the same order as in the quotation marks	**"past recollection recorded"**

Use:	To exclude documents with:	Example:
% (but not)	search terms following the % symbol	**d.n.a. "deoxyribonucleic acid" % criminal**

5.4 Field Restrictions

Overview: Documents in each Westlaw database consist of several segments, or fields. One field may contain the citation, another the title, another the synopsis and so forth. Not all databases contain the same fields. Also depending on the database, fields with the same name may contain different types of information.

To view a list of fields for a specific database and their contents, see Scope for that database. Note that in some databases not every field is available for every document.

To retrieve only those documents containing your search terms in a specific field, restrict your search to that field. To restrict your search to a specific field, type the field name or abbreviation followed by your search terms enclosed in parentheses. For example, to retrieve a case in the Federal & State Case Law database (ALLCASES) entitled *Daubert v. Merrell Dow Pharmaceuticals,* search for your terms in the title field (ti):

ti(daubert & "merrell dow")

The fields discussed below are available in Westlaw databases you might use for researching evidence issues.

Digest and Synopsis Fields: The digest (di) and synopsis (sy) fields, added to case law databases by West's attorney-editors, summarize the main points of a case. The synopsis field contains a brief description of a case. The digest field contains the topic and headnote fields and includes the complete hierarchy of concepts used by West's editors to classify the headnotes to specific West digest topics and key numbers. Restricting your search to the synopsis and digest fields limits your result to cases in which your terms are related to a major issue in the case.

Consider restricting your search to one or both of these fields if

- you are searching for common terms or terms with more than one meaning, and you need to narrow your search; or

- you cannot narrow your search by using a smaller database.

For example, to retrieve state cases that discuss nonverbal conduct as hearsay, access the State Case Law database (ALLSTATES) and type the following query:

sy,di(non-verbal /s conduct /p hearsay)

Headnote Field: The headnote field (he) is part of the digest field, but does not contain topic numbers, hierarchical classification information or key numbers. The headnote field contains a one-sentence summary for each point of law in a case and any supporting citations given by the author of the opinion. A headnote field restriction is useful when you are searching for specific statutory sections or rule numbers. For example, to retrieve headnotes from federal cases that cite Fed. R. Evid. 803(1), access the Federal Case Law database (ALLFEDS) and type the following query:

he(803(1))

Topic Field: The topic field (to) is also part of the digest field. It contains hierarchical classification information, including the West digest topic names and numbers and the key numbers. You should restrict search terms to the topic field in a case law database if

- a digest field search retrieves too many documents; or

- you want to retrieve cases with digest paragraphs classified under more than one topic.

For example, the topic Evidence has the topic number 157. To retrieve U.S. district courts cases that discuss the admissibility of hearsay evidence based on the excited utterance exception, access the U.S. District Courts Cases database (DCT) and type a query like the following:

to(157) /p "excited utterance"

To retrieve cases classified under more than one topic and key number, search for your terms in the topic field. For example, to search for cases discussing hearsay evidence, which may be classified to Criminal Law (110), Evidence (157) or Searches and Seizures (349), among other topics, type a query like the following:

to(hearsay)

For a complete list of West digest topics and their corresponding topic numbers, access the Key Number Service: click the **Key Number Service** button or choose **Key Number Service** from the Services menu.

Note Slips opinions, cases not reported by West and cases from topical services do not contain the digest, headnote and topic fields.

Prelim and Caption Fields: When searching in a database containing statutes, rules or regulations, restrict your search to the prelim (pr) and caption (ca) fields to retrieve documents in which your terms are important enough to appear in a section name or heading. For example, to retrieve federal rules regarding hearsay, access the Federal Rules database (US–RULES) and type the following:

pr,ca(hearsay)

5.5 Date Restrictions

You can use Westlaw to retrieve documents *decided* or *issued* before, after or on a specified date, as well as within a range of dates. The following sample queries contain date restrictions:

da(1999) & "dying declaration"

da(aft 1995) & "dying declaration"

da(10/23/1998) & "dying declaration"

You can also search for documents *added to a database* on or after a specified date, as well as within a range of dates. The following sample queries contain added-date restrictions:

ad(aft 1996) & "dying declaration"

ad(aft 2–1–1998 & bef 2–17–1998) & "dying declaration"

Section 6.   Searching with Topic and Key Numbers

To retrieve cases that address a specific point of law, use topic and key numbers as your search terms. If you have an on-point case, run a search using the topic and key number from the relevant headnote in an appropriate database to find other cases containing headnotes classified to that topic and key number. For example, to search for federal cases containing headnotes classified under topic 157 (Evidence) and key number 551 (Hypothetical Questions and Answers), access the Federal Case Law database (ALLFEDS) and enter the following query:

157k551

For a complete list of West digest topic and key numbers, access the Key Number Service: click the **Key Number Service** button or choose **Key Number Service** from the Services menu.

Note: Slip opinions, cases not reported by West and cases from topical services do not contain West topic and key numbers.

Section 7.   Verifying Your Research with Citator Services

Overview: A citator service is a tool that helps you ensure that your cases are good law; helps you retrieve cases, legislation or articles that cite a case, rule or statute; and helps you verify that the spelling and format of your citations are correct.

7.1   KeyCite

KeyCite is the citation research service from West Group.

KeyCite for cases covers case law on Westlaw, including unpublished opinions.

KeyCite for statutes covers the *United States Code Annotated* (USCA®), the *Code of Federal Regulations* (CFR) and statutes from all 50 states.

KeyCite Alert monitors the status of your case or statute and automatically sends you updates at the frequency you specify when their KeyCite information changes.

KeyCite provides the following:

- Direct appellate history of a case, including related references, which are opinions involving the same parties and facts but resolving different issues

- Negative indirect history of a case, which consists of cases outside the direct appellate line that may have a negative impact on its precedential value

- The title, parallel citations, court of decision, docket number and filing date of a case

- Citations to cases, administrative decisions and secondary sources on Westlaw that have cited a case

- Complete integration with the West Key Number System® so you can track legal issues discussed in a case

- Links to session laws amending or repealing a statute

- Statutory credits and historical notes

- Citations to pending legislation affecting a federal statute

- Citations to cases, administrative decisions and secondary sources that have cited a statute or federal regulation

7.2   Westlaw As a Citator

For citations not covered by KeyCite, including persuasive secondary authority such as restatements and treatises, use Westlaw as a citator to retrieve cases that cite your authority.

Using Westlaw as a citator, you can search for documents citing a specific statute, rule, regulation, agency decision or other authority. For example, to retrieve federal cases citing Fed.R.Evid. 801, access the Federal Case Law database (ALLFEDS) and type a query like the following:

f.r.e. fed.r.e! evid.r! f.r.ev! fed.ev! fed.rules evid! /5 801

Section 8.   Researching with Westlaw—Examples

8.1   Retrieving Law Review Articles

Recent law review articles are often a good place to begin researching a legal issue because law review articles serve 1) as an excellent introduction to a new topic or review for a stale one, providing terminology to help you formulate a query; 2) as a finding tool for pertinent primary authority, such as rules, statutes and cases; and 3) in some instances, as persuasive secondary authority.

Suppose you need to gain more background information on the factors that courts have considered in determining whether it is appropriate for lay witnesses to give opinion testimony.

Solution

- To retrieve law review articles relevant to your issue, access the Journals & Law Reviews database (JLR). Using the Natural Language search method, enter a description like the following:

opinion testimony by lay witnesses

- If you have a citation to an article in a specific publication, use Find to retrieve it. For more information on Find, see Section 3.1 of this appendix. For example, to retrieve the article found at 12 Touro L. Rev. 513, access Find and type

12 touro l rev 513

- If you know the title of an article but not which journal it appeared in, access the Journals & Law Reviews database (JLR) and search for key terms from the title in the title field. For example, to retrieve the article "The Movement from Frye to Daubert: Where Do the States Stand?" type the following Terms and Connectors query:

ti(movement & frye & daubert & states)

8.2 Retrieving Rules

Suppose you need to retrieve federal rules dealing with relevancy of character evidence.

Solution

- Access the Federal Rules database (US–RULES). Search for your terms in the prelim and caption fields using the Terms and Connectors search method:

pr,ca(relevan! & character)

- When you know the citation for a specific rule or statute, use Find to retrieve it. For example, to retrieve Fed. R. Evid. 410, access Find and type

fre 410

- To look at surrounding rules, use the Table of Contents service. Click a hypertext link in the prelim or caption field. You can also use Documents in Sequence to retrieve the rule following Fed. R. Evid. 410, even if that following section was not retrieved with your search or Find request. Click your right mouse button and choose Documents in Sequence from the pop-up menu.

- When you retrieve a rule on Westlaw, it will contain an Update message if a court order amending or repealing it is available online. To display the order, click the hypertext link in the Update message.

Because slip copy versions of laws are added to Westlaw before they contain full editorial enhancements, they are not retrieved with Update. To retrieve slip copy versions of laws, access the United States Public Laws database (US-PL), then type **ci(slip)** and descriptive terms, e.g., **ci(slip) & evidence.** Slip copy documents are replaced by the editorially enhanced versions within a few working days. Update also does not retrieve legislation or court orders that enact a new rule. To retrieve these materials, access US-PL or the Federal Orders database (US-ORDERS) and enter a query containing terms that describe the rule.

8.3   Retrieving Case Law

Suppose you need to retrieve New York case law dealing with the priest-penitent privilege.

Solution

- Access the New York Cases database (NY–CS). Type a Natural Language description such as the following:

waiver of priest-penitent privilege

- When you know the citation for a specific case, use Find to retrieve it. (For more information on Find, see Section 3.1 of this appendix.) For example, to retrieve *Darrow. v. Gunn*, 594 F.2d 767 (9th Cir. 1979), access Find and type

594 f2d 767

- If you find a topic and key number that is on point, run a search using that topic and key number to retrieve additional cases discussing that point of law. For example, to retrieve cases containing headnotes classified under topic 410 (Witnesses) and key number 215 (Confessions or other communications to clergyman or minister of religion), type the following query:

410k215

- To retrieve cases written by a particular judge, add a judge field (ju) restriction to your query. For example, to retrieve cases written by Justice White that contain headnotes classified under topic 157 (Evidence), type the following query:

ju(white) & to(157)

8.4   Using KeyCite

Suppose one of the cases you retrieve in your case law research is *Frye v. United States*, 293 F. 1013 (App. D.C. 1923). You want to determine whether this case is good law and to find other cases that have cited this case.

Solution

- Use KeyCite to retrieve direct history and negative indirect history for *Frye v. United States*. While viewing the case, click the KC button.

- Use KeyCite to display citing references for *Frye*. From the History display, click the Citations tab.

8.5   Following Recent Developments

As the evidence law specialist in your firm, you are expected to keep up with and summarize recent legal developments in this area of the law. How can you do this efficiently?

Solution

One of the easiest ways to stay abreast of recent developments in the area of evidence and litigation is by accessing the Westlaw Topical Highlights–Litigation database (WTH–LTG). The WTH–LTG database contains summaries of recent legal developments, including court decisions, legislation and changes in the area of litigation. Some summaries also contain suggested queries that combine the proven power of West's topic and key numbers and West's case headnotes to retrieve additional pertinent cases.

- When you access WTH–LTG you will automatically retrieve a list of documents added to the database in the last two weeks.

- To read a summary of a document, double-click its entry in the list.

- To view the full text of a document, access Find while viewing its summary.

- To search this database, choose New Query from the Research menu. At the Terms and Connectors Query Editor, type your query. For example, to retrieve references discussing a patient's treating physician testifying as an expert, type a query like the following:

treat! /5 doctor physician /p expert

Table of Cases

Table of Statutes and Rules

---

*

Index

0–314–23238–9